Routledge Library Editions

SOCIAL ECONOMICS

ECONOMICS

HISTORY OF ECONOMIC THOUGHT
In 23 Volumes

I	A Select Bibliography of Modern Economic Theory	*Batson*
II	Early British Economics	*Beer*
III	Nassau Senior	*Bowley*
IV	The Theory of Marginal Value	*Birck*
V	Ricardo and the Theory of Value Distribution and Growth	*Caravale & Tosato*
VI	Productive Labour and Effective Demand	*Coontz*
VII	London Essays in Economics	*Gregory & Dalton*
VIII	Capitalism and the Historians	*Hayek*
IX	The Origins of Scientific Economics	*Letwin*
X	The Individual in Society	*Macfie*
XI	Essays on Hayek	*Machlup*
XII	The Economics of Physiocracy	*Meek*
XIII	Karl Marx	*Mehring*
XIV	Marx's Critique of Political Economy I	*Oakley*
XV	Marx's Critique of Political Economy II	*Oakley*
XVI	J R McCulloch	*O'Brien*
XVII	A Key to Ricardo	*St Clair*
XVIII	Roads to Freedom	*Streissler*
XIX	Economics in the Twentieth Century	*Suranyi-Unger*
XX	Elements of Pure Economics	*Walras*
XXI	The Common Sense of Political Economy I	*Wicksteed*
XXII	The Common Sense of Political Economy II	*Wicksteed*
XXIII	Social Economics	*von Wieser*

SOCIAL ECONOMICS

FRIEDRICH VON WIESER

Routledge
Taylor & Francis Group
LONDON AND NEW YORK

First published in 1928

Reprinted in 2003 by
Routledge
2 Park Square, Milton Park, Abingdon, Oxon, OX14 4RN
or
270 Madison Avenue, New York, NY 10016

First issued in paperback 2010

Routledge is an imprint of the Taylor & Francis Group

British Library Cataloguing in Publication Data
A CIP catalogue record for this book
is available from the British Library

Social Economics
ISBN 978-0-415-31343-8 (hbk)
ISBN 978-0-415-60732-2 (pbk)
ISBN 978-0-415-31320-9 (set)

Miniset: History of Economic Thought

Series: Routledge Library Editions – Economics

SOCIAL ECONOMICS

By

FRIEDRICH von WIESER

Translated by

A. FORD HINRICHS

Assistant Professor of Economics, Brown University

With a Preface by

WESLEY CLAIR MITCHELL

Routledge
Taylor & Francis Group
LONDON AND NEW YORK

CONTENTS

FOREWORD

Friedrich von Wieser's *Social Economics* holds a place in the literature of the Austrian School such as John Stuart Mill's *Political Economy* holds in the literature of classical theory. It sums up, systematises, and extends the doctrines developed by the founder of the school, the author, and his fellow workers. Like Mill's great book, it is distinguished by admirable exposition—elegant in proportions, mature in expression, authoritative in source. And it promises to become like Mill's book the point of departure from which a generation of younger men set out in their efforts to increase knowledge.

Yet in certain respects a comparison with Mill does less than justice to Wieser. *Social Economics* is the first systematic treatise upon economic theory at large produced by the Austrian School, whereas several attempts to cover the field of classical theory had been made before Mill wrote. Wieser's economic work is also more original than Mill's. His own early writings rank higher among the constructive contributions which he weaves into a balanced exposition than do Mill's *Essays upon some Unsettled Questions of Political Economy.* More than that, in deepening and broadening his earlier discussions, Wieser reveals again the thoroughness, vigor, and originality for which he has always been notable. Mill wrote his *Principles* at high speed to round out his social philosophy. Even in later editions he did not incorporate all the changes which he admitted were desirable in the classical doctrines. Wieser, on the contrary, brought his full power to bear upon his treatise. It is the fruition of a lifetime's reflection as well as the crowning achievement of a famous school.

In his *Gymnasium* days, von Wieser had been fascinated by Homer, Virgil, the Niebelungenlied, and by history which followed epic traditions. He dreamed of becoming an historian. But he came from one of the aristocratic Viennese families whose sons commonly enter the public service, and the path to public service was the law. While following this path at the University, he chanced upon Herbert Spencer's early writings on sociology, and was fired with a new ambition. Spencer's logic convinced him for the time that the "great-man theory" of history is an illusion; it is the culture of a people which produces the hero. Therefore, to understand history one must understand society first. The aspect of social relations most open to understanding is the economic aspect. And the central problem of economic life is the problem of value. So the young jurist concentrated upon the economic courses of the law curriculum, and began to ponder the problem which he was later to illuminate.

Carl Menger had published his *Grundsätze der Volkswirtschaftslehre* in 1871, and been appointed to a professorship at Vienna in 1873. Von Wieser did not attend Menger's lectures, but he found in Menger's book the clues he needed. After taking a law degree in 1875, he and his friend Eugen von Böhm-Bawerk spent two years at the Universities of Heidelberg, Leipzig and Jena. While at Heidelberg in the spring of 1876, the two Austrians presented reports to Karl Knies' seminar. One report dealt with "The Relation of Cost to Value," the other report with the theory of interest. At the next opportunity, Wieser showed his manuscript to Menger, and was encouraged to seek a university career.

On returning to Vienna from his German studies, the young economist received an appointment in the Tax Administration. In 1883 he became *Privatdozent* at the University. Next year he published the book expected from aspirants to an academic chair, *Ursprung und Hauptgesetze des wirtschaftlichen Werthes,* and was soon made professor in the German University of Prague. In this first book, von Wieser analyzed a valuation made apart from others by a single person, but a person who represents the population of a modern nation. In his second book, *Der natürliche Werth,* he attempted "to exhaust the entire sphere of the phenomena of value without any exception." The analytic power here revealed ranked the writer with Menger and Böhm-Bawerk as one of the three masters of the Austrian school. When Professor William Smart was introducing the Austrian theory to English-speaking economists, he chose Wieser's *Natural Value* for translation in preference to Menger's *Grundsätze.*

So far von Wieser had concentrated his scientific effort upon one central problem. After the publication of *Der natürliche Werth* in 1889, he turned to questions of money, public finance, politics, and sociology. In 1903 he left his chair in Prague to become professor of economics in Vienna. He also served for a while as Minister of Commerce. During the twenty-five years following 1889, his publications dealt mainly with detailed problems; but all this time he was quietly developing and maturing his thoughts upon economic theory at large, and upon his still earlier problem of the relations between society and its leaders. Always critical of his own work, he seldom offered it to the public except under pressure. But what he had already accomplished made it sure that pressure would be applied by those who felt concern for the development of social science. When the new *Grundriss der Sozialökonomik* was planned, Max Weber, who had a leading share in the direction, made it a condition of his own participation that von Wieser should provide the chief section upon economic theory. Reluctantly Wieser consented. He spent some three years in perfecting further the system on which he had been working so long, and it appeared in 1914 under the title *Theorie der gesellschaftlichen Wirtschaft.*

Under ordinary circumstances, the publication of a systematic treatise upon economics by Friedrich von Wieser would have aroused the liveliest interest in all countries where economics is cultivated. But the war years and the early years of peace passed before many economists realized what an important addition had been made to their science on the eve of the catastrophe which bent men's minds on destruction. When a second edition of the volume containing Wieser's treatise came out in 1924, the work was probably new to most of its readers. The present translation into English is therefore less belated in effect than it seems in years. The influence upon economic theory exercised by von Wieser's formulation lies more in the future than in the past. Among the active agents of this influence may be readers who make their first acquaintance with von Wieser through Dr. Hinrichs.

In the United States, and perhaps in other countries, there seems to be current an impression that the Austrian school of economic theory has done its work—an impression which may arise from the fact that this group of investigators won a recognized place in the history of economic doctrines when Menger was in his prime and when Wieser and Böhm-Bawerk were young. Most of the present generation of active workers in economics studied the Austrian theory in college, much as they studied classical political economy. But von Wieser does not present his treatise as a completed system. This is a further respect in which the comparison with John Stuart Mill fails. When the second edition was called for, it is true that the author declined to make any changes in his text. He had turned once more to the conflict between his youthful conceptions of epic history and Spencer's argument that heroes are by-products of culture—a problem of which his solution appeared last spring in *Das Gesetz der Macht.* As for his exposition of economic theory, he hoped others would find what is to be added, what is to be changed.

That *Social Economics* incites its readers to independent thought is, of course, its great merit. A scientific worker owes most to solutions which set new problems. It has been characteristic of von Wieser as a teacher that he has shown students how to work rather than what to believe. The same trait is characteristic of him as a writer. A number of the ablest of his students have become disciples, and we may expect that they will make vigorous efforts to carry further the leading principles of the Austrian School. But perhaps his students who have cultivated a different type of theory have profited by Wieser's teaching not less than the men who can be called disciples. The translation of his exposition into English should enlarge both of these interlinked groups—the men who work upon Austrian lines and the men who find the Austrian experiments a help toward trying something different. To whichever group a reader inclines he will owe a debt of gratitude to Friedrich von Wieser. Hours devoted to the study of *Social Economics* are hours of contact with a living force in the world of thought.

* * *

Since the foregoing words were written, von Wieser has died. His heart failed on July 23, 1926, a fortnight after his seventy-fifth birthday, while he was recuperating from pneumonia at his summer home near Salzburg. A pupil and friend, Fr. Friedrich A. von Hayek, has published a sketch of his career in the *Jahrbücher für Nationalökonomie und Statistik*. How widely he was esteemed will soon be revealed by two memorial volumes, to which economists of many lands are making contributions. There is no need to alter what I wrote a year ago: though Wieser himself has gone, his work remains "a living force in the world of thought."

WESLEY C. MITCHELL.

New York City,
May 1st, 1927.

TRANSLATOR'S PREFACE

The presentation of Friedrich Freiherr von Wieser's SOCIAL ECONOMICS to a larger group of English readers requires no apology. In his foreward to this translation Professor Mitchell has briefly summarized the position which this work holds in the development of economic theory. That it is the only systematic treatise of the Austrian school is ample justification for its presentation. While any further word with reference to the general place of this treatise in economic literature is uncalled for, I take this opportunity to pay tribute to certain features of the work and to forewarn the reader of certain qualities for which he may not be prepared.

The work has a logical sequence that is admirable, Von Wieser starts with an idealized simple economy and ends with a presentation of the protectionist plea in a world economy. (The method and development are described in Sections 1 and 2.) Thruout the course of the argument no concept is introduced that later proves extraneous. At no time does he find it necessary to develop a point that could have been elaborated earlier. He develops a point and puts it by, later returns to it and carries it forward. But there is no confusion; the thought never becomes snarled.

The table of contents gives some clue to his logical method. The book progresses with an accelerating tempo. The groundwork is laboriously laid in the simple economy. It is further elaborated in the first two parts of Book II on the social economy. At about this time his method of reaching back for earlier conclusions becomes conspicuous. More and more frequently he makes passing reference to a conclusion worked out in an earlier section. His presentation becomes briefer and briefer, until he reaches the end with a suddenness that is startling to one who has grown used to the meticulous development and qualification in the earlier sections.

In addition von Wieser manifests a clearness of observation and appreciation of the limitations of idealized thought that make the book a valuable contribution to economic theory. He frequently points out that the classical writers drew conclusions from idealized premises and then erroneously applied them without modification to actual life. In his own work he clearly shows the dangers of applying idealized conclusions without restriction. He explains his method at length in the early sections of the book, which I shall not anticipate. The reader may take issue with conclusions based upon preliminary idealization and a later approximation of actual conditions; he may indeed not believe in the validity of deductive reasoning on economic problems. But it may never be said of von Wieser that he has not himself clearly stated the limitations of his theory. It would be a great injustice to quote from the theory of the simple economy without examining the later restrictions which he imposes on the applicability of the conclusion to reality.

In this connection one should clearly distinguish between the small type at the end of many sections and the ordinary footnote. The main text follows to a conclusion. Then comes an addendum: at times a critique of general theory, again a critical analysis of the applicability of his own thought, sometimes a mere footnote. It is quite evident that in selecting the change of type von Wieser distinguished the relative importance of the two. The translator hazards the advice, however, that many of the best passages are found in these sections where the author throws aside the logical drive of his main argument and rests by the wayside. It is here that I have most enjoyed the keenness—but more important, the honesty and realism—of his thought.

A translation has certain obvious disadvantages. There is first the difficulty of a precise rendition of words that may usually be perfectly understood by any reader of the original. A *Rechtsubjekt* is given in the text as the "legal owner" without doing violence to the sense of the text, although I know of no justification for such a translation except that it avoided either a two-line explanation of a non-essential or a rather shocking Germanism. *Kapitalwidmung* is actually a dedication of capital. It is more than saving. But in the course of repetition "a will to dedicate capital" has seemed to me to justify the slight inaccuracy of "a will to save." A few words are quite difficult in their shaded meanings for one not born to German. *Wirtschaft* has several related meanings that can only be nicely selected by the original author. May I further beg the occasional sympathy of the reader in rendering words that are adapted to an unusual sense in the original—the rendition of two of which causes a kind critic in Austria to complain, with the addition, *"die Stelle ist auch in Deutschen reichlich unklar"?*

In the second place certain words are either coined or adapted for the entire presentation that carry a usual English connotation other than that desired in this book. Specific has no meaning in English that even suggests the sense developed in Section 15. At times this is confusing. A reference to "specific goods" may be conceived to be more particularization, an order to stop thinking of goods as an abstraction and to think instead of cows or wheat. Actually the author intends thruout to contrast "specific character" with cost-character. To minimize the confusion as far as possible I have never used this word in any other sense than that established in Section 15. Another word, acquisitive, may give occasional pause. "Natural" is almost always used in opposition to monetary, not to signify something which exists in nature. "Historical" is often used to imply nothing more than an actual condition.

Even more serious are subtler obstacles to translation. Von Wieser's language and thinking are both German. In German even the most involved sentence may have character. In the face of such passages the translator's duty lies in a compromise between offensive transliteration and the danger of a subtle change of meaning as dependent and qualifying phrases are reordered. It is unnecessary to add that I have done my best to hold the original meaning.

Finally there is danger in the translation of a word with shades of meaning in a passage that involves the prejudices. By study of the context and of other passages, and by consultation I have sought never to put into von Wieser's mouth a phrase that would better suit my temper than his convictions. My duty has been that of a translater who, though he has no responsibility for the ideas set forth and in fact disagrees with them in part, must be completely faithful in their presentation.

Aside from these matters the book has certain characteristics of which American economists should be aware. One section of the book, Section 70, can only be read against the background of German corporation law. A few other passages are colored by national institutions. In contrast with this natural limitation are a few archaic illustrations. Von Wieser is describing truths that know no national boundaries, that recognize time only in changing external manifestation. The illustration of these truths may therefore be drawn without particular reference to time. Nonetheless the pre-war illustrations are occasionally startling. The Franco-Prussian War is "the last war." He disregards "our latest acquisition, Bosnia-Herzegovinia." Von Wieser himself explains in his preface that he did not feel it essential to revise his references in the 1924 edition and why.

Parenthetically one may remark that this lack of "window-dressing" is in one sense admirable. For one who believes with von Wieser that in the near future all essentials of the simple economy, all true fundamentals of economic theory, may be established, there is no reason to revise all the illustrations in the book except to make them intelligible to a class whose social experience dates back only to 1923. It is the clearest admission of the limitations of the theory. There is no attempt to hide abstraction in statistical table revised for the latest census.

The work of translation has been made possible by the cooperation of others. Mr. W. F. G. Geisse of Great Barrington, Mass., prepared a first draft that enabled me to give especial attention to the economic terminology and the English rendition of the whole. Dr. Friedrich A. von Hayek, a pupil and close friend of von Wieser, has read the proofs and submitted many suggestions. Finally the loyal help and cheerful good humor of my wife pulled this translation thru long evenings of drudgery that inevitably occur as part of such work.

Brown University, A. F. Hinrichs
May, 1927.

AUTHOR'S PREFACE

The *Theory of the Social Economy*, which I published shortly before the outbreak of the World War, brings together the results of the studies with which I have been concerned since the beginning of my economic thought. Like other writers of the Austrian school, I began with the theory of value. Gradually, I passed through the entire circle of phenomena in social economy, state economy and world economy. To all of these I attempted to apply the same method which the Austrian school developed for the theory of value and price. My aim was to show that the entire social economy is built up with a view to management and value. To be sure, only a part of the organization may be explained in purely social terms. Another part must be explained in terms of those who possess power in the nation and in the world. But the meaning of power also has a social basis. No power has ever been sufficiently great to proceed entirely without consideration of the general meaning of management and value. Powerful persons are merely in a position, in building up the economic organization, to carry through their personal interests rather than the general interest. Thus they are able, at those points which they regard as critical, to replace the social mind by their own. By this means the social consciousness is falsified and made to appear contradictory. It seemed to me that the highest task of theory was to show in what relations this consciousness and power were in harmony and in opposition in the creation of the social, state and world economy. A theory which succeeded in showing this would enable one to see clearly the direction in which the interference of counter-force and, above all, of enlightened statesmanship was needed, in order that the economic organization might become truly social. Such a theory will also indicate for the modern state the theoretical groundwork for a suitable internal and external political economy. In particular, it will point the way to needed reforms. Reaching forward, it will also serve a more purely social state of the future, which the proletarian thinkers interpret as socialistic, but the final form of which we cannot yet see accurately. It will serve this state in that it will establish those most general elements of management and value which have always existed and will always exist and which, therefore, cannot be absent in any economic order. Thus this theory may clearly indicate to the state of the future what it must take over from the present order.

Even when I published *The Theory of the Social Economy,* I was aware that I was in a position only incompletely to reach my far distant goal. In the ten years which have since passed, the deficiencies of my work have become even more apparent to me. But owing to the pressure of other events, I have been unable to find leisure to express my thoughts more pertinently. As the publisher advised me that a new edition of the book had become necessary, I was forced to explain to him that I was not in a position to undertake revision. We therefore agreed to publish the second edition as an unchanged reprint of the first. I have merely increased the references to the literature. In the text itself few corrections were made. The reader is therefore not to be surprised if he finds references, for example, to pre-war monetary conditions or the economic condition of Austria-Hungary as it existed before the war. It may also be remarked that I believe such mention of pre-war conditions has greater illustrative value than mention of the opaque and transitory condition in which the world finds itself today. But all this is incidental, for in the main I think I can establish that the same goal of theory that I set up in the first edition exists for any theory of the social economy after the World War and revolution.

Never has there been as deep and pressing a need of economic theory as in the present. At the time when the representatives of the classical school were thinking out their principles of economy, practical interest was confined to the question of the degree of freedom which the state should give to private economy as such. The socialistic thinkers fought the laissez-faire attitude of private management. One who gave no great weight to their objections set himself scientifically apart from them. One did not dream that the day would come, was indeed near, when the proletariat should be strong enough to give pertinence to its demands by force. In the wake of the World War this day suddenly arrived. In Russia the experiment in socialism was carried through in the most extreme form of bolshevism. Almost everywhere in Europe the proletariat has come forward with such strength that it must be considered and a counter-reform of the economic order proposed. It will not be long before the same thing will come to pass in the United States. The flourishing America of today can better satisfy its workers than aging Europe. In the rapid progress of its development it may allow greater benefits to the entrepreneurs who lead the way. But as soon as the movement begins to ebb the workers will be as eager to undermine the power of the entrepreneur as they are today in Europe.

The final distinction between possessors and proletariat will not be successful without the aid of theory. Both classes have sought scientifically to strengthen that position which their own interests have led them to take, and both have thus made errors with serious consequences. The proletarian thinkers have fastened on untenably impractical dogmas. The *bourgeois* thinkers on the one hand have developed their own case, but on the other they have left too many loopholes in the explanation. Endless sacrifices would be required were there no other means than that of trial and error to clear up the order. Of course, it is necessary that there be such attempts. Power will also make its influence felt. In time, however, theory will be called upon. This time will come so soon as one begins seriously to suffer from the errors of practice and so soon as it is realized that raw power can work evil but cannot heal it. But when this happens, theory must have unified its thought sufficiently so that men may find the necessary help in it when once their thoughts advance to a point at which they may subject their wishes to the insistent commands of reality.

The classical theory and the socialistic theory deduced from it have not come to an agreement. The classical theory pushed into the relations of the social economy only so far as seemed necessary to give grounds to the demand that labor be freed from governmental constraint. The socialistic theory eagerly took over the unfinished classical theory, as the strongest support for the demands of the workers seemed to be here. The openly unsatisfactory nature of the classical-socialist theory that comes into insoluble conflicts with actual conditions led many economic scholars, particularly in Germany, to discard it entirely. The scholars devoted themselves to the great practical task that was constantly and forcefully raised by the stormy modern development, and remained satisfied to raise the scientific foundation which is required from the historical development of the national economy. Just as the last scientific generation in Germany turned in this manner from the theory to the problems of socio-economic politics, this appears now to be happening in the United States. In England, the home of classical theory and the country in which this theory best fitted the conditions of life, the connection between theory and practical politics was best maintained. But even here the merchant class lacked the strongest support of a convincing theoretical foundation. The proletarian class alone found this support which might be deduced with forceful logic so soon as one had passed over the unreal fictions of the classical labor-theory. There is no doubt that the increased scientific self-confidence of the proletarian thinkers, which the masses shared, has been a powerful aid in increasing the feeling of power by the masses. They thought that they had infallible evidence that they were in the right at all points.

In the meantime, in all countries that led in scientific thought, serious thinkers had begun to attack the fundamental economic problems from a new point of view without immediately considering the practical application of their ideas. Men writing in German, English and French, who were later followed by Hollanders and Italians, found themselves together on a new path, in that they derived the meaning of economy and of the closely connected value from the care for the utility of goods, and in that they clearly laid down the law by which men measure utility in the economy. Just as the discoveries of physics, which were the result of purely scientific inquiry, opened the way to numerous technical applications, so the new truths of economic theory, because they are pure truths, may be called upon to give a firm foundation to the ends and means of the social order. The experience of management and value, extending over many thousand years, cannot be meaningless; it cannot be a single great error. It is a necessary result of the nature of man and the economic environment. Modern theory has succeeded in pointing out these experiences. The contradictions which the classical-socialistic theory could not solve, have been removed by the theory of marginal utility. This theory gives us the key to the understanding of economic computation as it is applied in practice. But at the same time that it enables us to understand, the sense of the economy may be perverted from a social point of view when the mighty utilize their superiority for themselves. The powerful person may extend his margin of the use of goods to include the superfluous and vain uses, while he presses the weak down to the bare needs of existence or even below this level. One sees that it is foreign to modern theory to defend the degenerations of power. On the contrary, it is quite apparent that the modern theory in its fundamentals is nothing less than a theory of possession, and that it gives the most effective weapons to the socialistic critic. To be sure, it takes from socialism the theoretical foundation on which it has stood until now, but in so doing it does not weaken the position of socialism but rather increases its critical power. In the place of a doctrine that appears logically forceful but is actually foreign to experience, is given a foundation of laws that are rooted in the experience of thousands of years and that will hold in all future time. These laws will become invalid only if the most unlikely condition arises and the want which calls forth anxiety for the utility of goods disappears before a free superfluity of goods.

Revolution has brought forth no new fundamental economic thought. The bolshevistic experiment seeks to give reality to socialistic doctrines whose thought had stiffened to dogma. Whether the experiment has succeeded or not is still in dispute. Therefore the experiment at least at present does not have conclusive force. He who would form a judgment of its significance must first see clearly the sense and absurdities of the practical economy. The highest duty of theory could not be performed by the classical theory and even the more deeply penetrating theory of today has not completed its work. To complete this work is the task of the present.

The firmness with which I oppose the classical theory must not be interpreted to mean that I lightly appraise its significance. On the contrary, I recognize it as one of the most brilliant and practically significant efforts of the scientific mind. In spite of all attacks it has not yet lost its influence on theory and practice. Being complete in itself, it has withstood every attack that does not rest on a similarly closed system. Every new economic theory must first be measured by the classical theory. No matter how great an advance may be made, it will only deserve to be considered as a continuation of the work begun by the great classical masters. In this case, however, the continuation entails at many important points also a retracing of steps. At certain difficult cross-roads we must follow a different direction from that taken by the classicists. But in spite of this, their fame remains undisturbed as the first to have been on the ground and even to have showed, by their mistakes, the way to those who followed.

Because of the dominating significance which attaches to the classicists, it has seemed required of me to compare the modern theory with their propositions at all decisive points in order to place the opposition in the clearest light. I have, however, satisfied myself to refer to the classical doctrine in its most general thoughts without entering into details and following the changes which the fundamental ideas received at the hands of each author.

I have not had space to concern myself with the literature of derived ideas. The sum of the expositions which I have to present to the reader is of itself so heavy, that I had to avoid increasing it by an arrangement of the literature. I could do this all the more easily because in the *Fundamentals of Social Economics,* of which *The Theory of the Social Economy* is a part, a specific section by Schumpeter has already been seen on *Epochs of the History of Dogma and Method.* I commend this excellent presentation to the reader.

F. VON WIESER

INTRODUCTION

§ 1. The Method of the Following Study

The "Psychological School"—The instruments of the isolating and idealizing hypothesis and of decreasing abstraction—Language and its concepts—The task of modern economic theory.

The remarks on method which follow do not aspire to the dignity of a methodology. All I desire is sufficiently to acquaint the reader with the method of my investigation so that without distrust or misunderstanding he may accept my starting point seemingly so remote from actuality. From this point the enquiry may proceed to its completion in the economy of society, of the state and of the world at large. For further enlightenment I refer to my earlier works: *Ueber Ursprung and Hauptgesetze des Wirtschaftlichen Wertes*, 1884, (I. *Die wissenschaftliche Bedeutung der Sprachbegriffe* and, *Wesen under Hauptinhalt der theoretischen Nationalokönomie* (Zeitschr. F.G.V. 1911).

This investigation uses the method recently designated as the "psychological." The name is applied because the theory takes its point of departure from within, from the mind of the economic man. I myself once spoke of economic theory in this sense as applied psychology. The designation, however, is not a fortunate one. It may lead to the misunderstanding that the "psychological" economic theory starts from scientific psychology. This is by no means the case. It has still less to do with physiology, as an even more serious misunderstanding has tried to make it appear. The observations concerning the inner life of man, which our "psychological" theory of economics develops, have been made by it independently. They are entirely independent of the result which scientific psychology might reach with regard to the psychical elements, the analysis of which are within its province. Physiology is even more markedly outside of economic theory. One should especially emphasize the fact that Gossen's law of satiable wants, the foundation of the modern theory of value, has nothing to do with Weber's law. Economic theory would be benefited, had scientific psychology advanced further beyond its beginnings; but our discipline does not seek and could not find direct aid from this source. The tasks of the two branches of knowledge are entirely distinct.

It is the problem of economic theory to exhaust scientifically the content of everyday economic experience and to interpret it. All persons are familiar with a narrow, practical sphere. From these limited views theory deduces a broader interpretation which enables us to understand the meanings of the economy even in those wide social relations that far transcend the experience of the individual. In doing this it cannot be expected that theory should follow the sequence of ideas in the individual consciousness beyond the point at which the promptings to action are explained. It should, on the contrary, avoid any more penetrating psychological analysis. Our theory finds in the consciousness of every economically active human being a wealth of experiences which are common property of all. These are experiences which every scientist shares with the layman, without resort to special scientific instruments. They are experiences concerning facts of the outer world, as for example, the presence of goods of various sorts; experiences concerning the source and current of the economic activity of mankind. Can we conceive of economic theory refusing to draw from a fountain-head so inexhaustible in its riches, so dependable in its purity! It will be the natural method of its investigations, to follow the guidance offered by our recollection of the course and significance of the economy which is practically familiar to all of us. No theorist will be able to ignore his practical consciousness of economic relations. Were he even to regard with suspicion the results to which it leads, he could never silence the psychical consonances of his economic experiences. He can never obliterate his intimate knowledge of himself and his economic surroundings. There never has been a theoretical school of economics which, ignoring these psychical consonances, has accomplished its aim unaided by them. The "psychological" school is distinguishable from its earlier confrères solely by the fact that it has transformed a naïve procedure into conscious method. Let this method be abandoned today, and but little time will elapse ere logical precision will demand that we elevate once again this psychical aid from an unacknowledged coöperator to a carefully planned method.

The sphere of economic theory has the same limits as this common experience. The task of the theorist ends at the boundary of common experience; it ends where science feels constrained to collect its observations by historical or statistical investigation or by whatever other means may be adjudged reliable. All information of this sort the elaborator of a theory must turn over to other workers in the field of scientific economics, men who by their method are qualified to utilize the results theoretically obtained. The theorist, nevertheless, will not have to dispense entirely with the consideration of the historical growth. There are numerous historical economic processes which, having filled decades and centuries, persist to this very day, while common experience discloses their interconnection. Instances of this kind are the evolution of the division of labor, the amassing of capital, the increase of the rent derived from land, additions to the store of money and the displacement of barter by the use of money. It is within the province of the theorist to deduce the law which regulates processes such as these, a law discoverable only in the general relationship of economic facts. But it is the historian's task to collect historical proofs and to assign their share of importance to the historical events.

The method of economic theory is empirical. It is supported by observation and has but one aim, which is to describe actuality. Nevertheless, economic theory does not attempt to describe the actual in its entirety, as purely empirical sciences are wont to do. They strive to remain true to nature in every minute detail. But the economist is like an historian unfolding an individual historical course of events or a statistician summarizing a series of cases. He endeavors to place before us the typical phenomenon, the typical development, and to eliminate whatever may be subordinate, accidental or individual.

Isolation and idealization are his instruments, just as without demur they have always been the instruments of man pursuing other truly empirical sciences, for example, the exact physical sciences. Like the naturalist performing an experiment, the theoretical economist is bound to isolate, when making observations. It is even more necessary for him to do so because reflectively he will have to perfect his observation by the memory image of his experience. It is thus perfected with all the greater difficulty and requires consequently all the greater scientific caution in its process. Complex experiences cannot possibly be interpreted as wholes. They must be isolated and separated into their elements in order that their effects may be known. The elements, moreover, must ideally be protected from all disturbing influences, in order that the pure effect may be recognized. When these disturbing factors are themselves introduced into the thought, they in turn must be stripped of everything accidental in order to study their typical progress. Side by side with the isolating assumptions which embrace less than the entire truth, the theoretical economist then proceeds to form numerous idealizing assumptions which embrace more than the truth. In these he raises the empirical fact reflectively to the highest degree of perfection conceivable. But the most perfect state is at the same time the most simple and the most readily understood. Thus the theorist assumes the existence of a model man, a man such as actually has never existed, nor can ever exist. One of the best known instances of isolating assumption is Thünen's "State in Isolation." The name only imperfectly indicates the idea. This state is isolated not only against its surroundings. More important still it is conceived of as idealized in itself. Thünen assumes that within its boundaries the conditions of agriculture are uniformly distributed about the central point of a single market—an arrangement which actually is never met with and can never be expected to be found.

This example establishes, moreover, the fact that the "psychological" school is not the first to introduce the idealizing assumption. This instrument of thought was used by the economists of all schools in Thünen's day and since. Before Thünen the classical school resorted to it, as indeed investigators generally have resorted to it ever since the earliest rise of scientific thought among mankind. Mathematics and mathematical physics could never approach their problems without the idealizing assumption. The geometrical point, the line, the plane, the regular solid, all these are idealized forms employed with the utmost success in spite of the fact that everybody is aware that they lack actuality and can never attain it. They are bodiless constructions of purely ideal forms. Without their aid the irregular forms of actual experience would defy computation. Whenever the economic theorist idealizes, his object is this only: he endeavors like the mathematician to simplify experience, in order more perfectly to understand his problem. This alone prompts him to idealize.

No more than the geometrical point or the line, are his idealizing assumptions hypotheses. Hypotheses are assumptions concerning the unknown. The idealizing assumptions, here discussed, are conscious transformations of the known. The naturalist makes use of the hypothesis in order to explore fields where observation fails. But economic theory may not exceed those limits within which observation may be practiced. It is held strictly to the confines which, according to the testimony of common experience, the economic sense traverses in witnessing the formation of the economy. If we may use as an analogy one of the most effective means of artistic expression, we would say that the idealizing assumption is a stylicism designed to accentuate essential features.

The theorist starts from the most abstract isolating and idealizing assumptions. In these he seizes the unalloyed elements of actuality, without disclosing the fulness of its image. However, if he would accomplish his task he must not stop with these extreme abstractions. Should he do so, he would fail to convey an understanding of reality. Step by step by a system of decreasing abstraction, he must render his assumptions more concrete and more multiform. The means at his disposal do not allow him to show the full picture. Some details can result only from historical proof, statistical compilation or the insights vouchsafed to a statesman in uninterrupted contact with national life. The economist cannot draw upon those details. They may be inserted only when theory enlists the continuous labors of other scientific methods, of practical politics even. These other sciences will give the further realism that a stylistic theory must eschew. To this extent the final theorems of theory are not empirical, they are too general in their formulation. But they are not conceived unempirically; they are formulated only as looking to their empirical complements. True economic theory shuns speculation in a vacuum. From its very beginning it looks towards a union with the methods of purely empirical science for whose efforts it prepares the ground. It does not conflict with these methods; it remains in touch with them and complements their aims.

The reproach that the classical school has indulged in speculation is not altogether unjustified. This reproach, however, applies only to the manner in which use has been made of the idealizing method; it does not apply to the method itself. The most striking mistake, the mistake of the classical school which has met with the most heated opposition, is that its exponents stopped at abstractions too remote from actuality, and hence unequal to the task of making it fully intelligible. Historical interpretation and practical politics have on this account lost sympathy with its trend.

Over and above this, a more important and theoretically more disastrous error must be laid to their door. They have not appreciated correctly the very elements of economic life. Their fundamental assumptions are not rooted in adequate observation. When they stopped with abstractions that are separated by the breadth of the universe from actual conditions, they did so because, in the first place, they never idealized correctly. They constructed an economic body politic, calculated to accentuate emphatically the demand for freedom. In harmony with their times this was their first concern. This demand they set out to vindicate. Right or wrong, they meant to prove that freedom was the ultimate good. On this assumption they formulated their doctrine of economic life. If we would be just, however, we shall have to admit that even with the half-truths which they discovered, burdened though they were with prejudices of this sort, the men of the classical school have accomplished a splendid scientific feat. Their theory reached the goal of their period, the goal of increased political liberty, a goal justly insisted upon. A theory equally successful in preparing the scientific basis for the tendencies of our own day, in as able a manner as the classical economists prepared for their own period, might confidently be said to have accomplished a noble and far reaching task.

Much of the store of common experience that is shared by the economic community is deposited in the national language, especially in the basic designations relating to economics and the law of economic relations. A naturalist may discover a wealth of new substances or relations, long inaccessible to naïve observation. For these he must needs find names. But economic theory, like other practical sciences, has for its subject the content of common experience, long familiar and already named. Therefore it does not seek to invent a general terminology. It is bound to preserve existing terms, to interpret the meaning of those already current and by means of the light that is shed on widely accepted concepts by the primitive roots to penetrate to the core of their meaning. The most important part of the task of economic theory, as regards terminology, is to establish the limitations of terms current in the market and in law, to purge them of confusing vulgar meanings and to restore them to their rich, inherent splendor. New names which it may find itself called upon to add to its vocabulary will have to be selected in accordance with the radical fund of the language. Were the theorist to essay the creation of an entirely new terminology, he would deprive himself of one of his most effective instruments. He would destroy the association of ideas, that is already established for the reader by familiar terms. A discussion in novel terms would come like a discussion of strange and unheard of things, not like one of familiar occurrences, as by right it should come. Thus the author would deprive himself of one of the most effective means of enquiry, forgetful of the fact that the creative popular spirit has, in the concepts of language, laid down guiding traces of ideas which, understandingly used, penetrate to the depths of every most essential relation assignable to the economic impulse. In these concepts scientific acumen discovers the traces leading to the phenomena. Anterior to all scientific observation, these present a first image of things. This image may sometimes be confusing in its movements but fundamentally it must be true.

The theoretical economist need never deplore a lack of the instruments which are employed in the exact natural sciences. Whatever advantages they may otherwise enjoy and great as are their achievements, they are none the less strangers to their object, nature. They may never scan the innermost recesses of nature. Let their instruments be infinitely refined, still they must be content to describe a succession of happenings, abandoning the hope of showing how the effect springs from its cause. The group of practical sciences, of which economic theory is one, can accomplish more. The object of investigation is man in a condition of activity. Hence our mind ratifies every accurate description of the processes of his consciousness by the affirmative declaration that such is the case, and by the compelling feeling that it must be so necessarily. In this way the description becomes an exposition, although it may always be true that the final "why" is never brought forward, as no explanation is at any time forthcoming of stimuli which subconsciously affect consciousness. For all actions which are accompanied by a consciousness of necessity, economic theory need never strive to establish a law in a long series of inductions. In these cases we, each of us, hear the law pronounced by an unmistakable inner voice. What unequalled advantage to the naturalist, could he, too, appeal to the voices of nature for their confirmation of the laws prevailing in the organic and inorganic world! Where the natural sciences can only offer proof, the theory of economics can persuade; it can enlist the unqualified inner consent of readers.

In this way the appearance of the classical theory exerted an influence on the governments of all countries and on the people, which stands unparalleled in the history of science. Public opinion has only deserted its standards when, pitted against the rising capitalistic power, the doctrine of freedom lost prestige. If, in our day, socialism has won over the assent of the multitudes, it has to ascribe most of its strength to the theoretical force of its doctrines, doctrines derived from assumptions idealized pessimistically, just as the assumptions of the classicists were idealized optimistically. Are those, who do not follow either the classical or the socialist theory, to renounce altogether the powerful aid of theory? Just as the classical period experienced the need of a theory of freedom, our own period feels the needs of a modern theory. This should interpret the practical tendencies of the present age according to their true meaning. It should be equally remote from optimism and pessimism. It should appraise both the lights and the shadows. It should discern the community of interests, but no less should it recognize power, the conflict of motives and the economic evil. It should furnish a sound theoretical basis for freedom and also for restrictions on freedom.

§ 2. The Division of the Subject Matter

The author's attitude towards the mathematical method.

There are four parts of the following study. The first starts with the most idealized assumptions. The later ones proceed by decreasing abstraction to conditions of reality.

The theory of the "simple economy" in the first book begins with the idealizing assumption that the subject is a single person. However, we do not have in mind here the meagre economy of an isolated Crusoe. The imagined conditions of production have a breadth that is only realized in the activities of an entire nation. At the same time millions of persons are regarded as a massed unit. In the same way one contrasts humanity and nature or thinks of a people directing its great forces to some common goal.

Up to a certain point the theory of the simple economy coincides with the presentation current in German economic texts under the heading "Fundamental Concepts." The theory is not confined, however, to mere concepts of speech. Great as is the aid which it finds in these, it is concerned with phenomena themselves. This gives it an entirely different approach to its subject matter. It seeks the elementary laws of economic activity, especially those laws concerning value which provide the standard of economic comparison. In this connection our exposition follows the lead of the doctrine of marginal utility as set forth by the Austrian school. The individual in the simple economy is assumed to be an ideal economic subject. In full possession of his powers he obeys economic principles and is liable neither to error, passion or weakness. The presentation is that of pure theory. The conditions of wealth and the state of the technical arts are considered, but we maintain independence from time and place. As mankind is treated as a unit and is contrasted with nature, there can be no more consideration of conflicting interests or of economic justice than there would be in the economy of a Crusoe.

All problems that are presented in the theory of the simple economy are capable of ultimate solution. The task may be difficult, but the assumptions can always be so definitely formulated as to overcome all obstacles. Why should the theorist be forbidden to follow the same path that common sense leads the businessman to traverse daily? As there is no opposition of interests and no problem involving the justice of relationships, the most extreme individualists and socialists will be able to agree with our results without abandoning their points of view. Despite attendant difficulties, there is no doubt that in the near future the theory of the simple economy will be scientifically settled. It will lead the way for a doctrine destined to be common property of all future economic schools. This justifies severing this theory from the entire remaining content of economic doctrine. The latter will, at all times, be the subject of sharper dispute, as unavoidably it becomes involved in the conflict of interests.

The second section, the theory of exchange, presupposes a social economy, unhampered by interference on the part of the state. The theory of the simple economy having shown in what manner a single subject manages and calculates his economic affairs, we now show how the numerous juridical subjects, who meet in the course of exchange as they seek their economic advantage, determine prices and thus erect the structure of a social economy. Private property is presupposed. To this extent the subject matter of the second section is the same as that on which the attention of the classical school was centered. But in the first place we shall be more fully prepared to treat it, inasmuch as the theory of the simple economy forms a preface, that was almost entirely lacking to the classicists. Moreover we shall enrich the material employed. The classicists confine themselves in the main to cases of well regulated, balanced competition. True enough, they mention various instances of disturbance by superior power, especially by monopolies; but they look upon all these as exceptions, unworthy of consideration in establishing an exhaustive theory. At the present day monopoly and other inequalities of power make themselves felt more sharply than during the classical period.

It is thus that the social economy of which we are about to treat, acquires novel and typical features. Over and above the idealized current of the economic process which becomes active in the sense of the utmost economic efficiency, a complete economic theory is now bound to describe, as well as the principal types, the displacements brought about by the occurrence of power, especially of the capitalistic power. The current, as progressing in the conflict with power, is of far greater practical interest to us today than that of normal, unimpeded action. If our theory is to smooth the way of political progress, it must shed light on these problems that are the most important ones we face today. A modern theory in its assumptions will, therefore, have to consider the inequality of possessions as well as the inequality of personal aptitudes due to natural talents and education. It must modify the idealizing assumption of the model householder in so far at least as to place in his stead the types of the principal classes of society in all their most important gradations. There can be no doubt but what common experience is altogether adequate to this end also and that the theorist employing the aids at his command, can cope with the situation. In still another direction a modern theory will have to advance beyond the confines mapped out by the classical theory. So long as the assumption of a well regulated, balanced competition is brought prominently forward, the conclusion is justified that self-interest is being forced into subserviency to the general welfare. One may take it for granted that the power of competition will direct selfseeking efforts towards that goal and may acquiesce in a theory of the economic society, which merely analyses it into a sum of individuals. This is no longer true, once attention has been drawn to the full extent of the conflict waged between power and weakness. Thereafter it will be possible to acknowledge social unity only if more effective unifying forces than self-interest are observed, forces that are strong enough to bend even the most powerful. In order to be convincing, therefore, a modern economic theory requires for its completion a more profound theory of society. This also may be adequately treated by the method of social theory that invokes common experience. The knowledge of self and of others which everyone possesses, embraces all the material required by such a theory of society as we contemplate.

Our third section introduces the theory of state economy. Today there is not an economic school bent upon excluding the state from the social economy. Scarcely anyone will longer gainsay the statement that the state is an indispensable factor in this field. But if the cooperation of the state is needed in order that the well regulated current of the economic process be secured, economic theory, on its part, will have to be described in its most general features the influence which it exerts. In doing this, it does not trespass upon the territory of political science and the theory of finance. The problems of economic administration and the administration of the state are not its problems. For a task of this sort the means at its disposal are inadequate. Its endeavor must be to respect the limits ascribable to the general forms of governmental influence in economics. In common experience are to be found whatever facts are demanded for such an investigation. The theory of state economy sets out from the original idealizing assumption of a model householder guiding the private concerns of the household; in decreasing abstraction it proceeds to the concrete assumption, approximating actuality, that private households are under the ægis of a central power, the state. This power, directed to the tasks of public economy, complies with the interests of society and with the economic principle, as far as social means permit. The theory thus takes for granted an ideal state. It is well aware that the law deduced by it for a state of this sort, does not find concrete application in a single instance. It does so in precisely the sense in which it has laid down the ideal law of the simple private economy. By these means it is led to understand the general forms governing the economic action of the state. It can then leave to other methods and to practical political wisdom the enterprise of suggesting trend and standard in individual instances.

The final section treats of world economy. The problems falling under this head have always been treated since Political Economy first took its rise, and they have always been counted among the most important of all economic problems. The classicists, also, turned their attention to them, and the free-trade doctrine at which they arrived in connection with the commerce of the world, numbers among their most significant achievements. Nevertheless they here make one of their most disastrous errors. In strict application of their fundamental individualistic views, the classicists have transferred the theorems discovered by them with regard to national division of labor, to an international division of labor. But actually the course of affairs in national commerce is conditioned very differently from that in the commerce of the world; the individuals in the one place and in the other are actuated by different socio-historical powers. A modern theory must never ignore the economy of the world, when formulating its doctrines. For its deduction as well common experience affords ample material.

In our exposition we shall but infrequently resort to the mathematical expression of propositions. Only occasionally formulæ of the lower branch of that science will be used; those of the higher branches, however, will be invariably avoided. With by far the greater number of readers they are not conducive to ready understanding, and they offer no advantage that could outweigh the objection on this score. There can be no doubt that the mathematical method is properly applicable in economic theory; but the field of its usefulness is to be found in those portions of the material in which the most abstract, idealizing assumptions are admissible; namely, the theory of value and the theory of price, in so far as these doctrines are presented with the assumption of a static economy, showing neither progress nor retrogression. As regards an economy in process of development, even the doctrines of value and price can no longer be presented in strictly mathematical form. An investigation confining itself to this narrowest group of theoretical problems, a group open to extreme idealization, may resort to mathematical expression as the most exact instrument for formulating results. But an investigation passing by decreasing abstraction to the remaining problems of theory will find itself compelled to discard, in its further advance, the mathematical formula. None of the great truths of economic theory, none of their important moral and political applications, has been justified by mathematical means. The justification could not have been thus established. The classical school retained its dominion thru several generations without resorting to mathematical proofs. Similarly the socialist school has won over armies of votaries without appeal to mathematics. A modern theory, too, should be able to present convincingly the theoretical bases of domestic and foreign economic policies and of taxation without the aid of mathematical formulæ. The theory of the economic organization impresses the reader by opening the understanding to the meaning of economic action. By the constraint of numerical expression it would abjure the force of vital imagery.

Even in that narrowest field, embracing the doctrines of price and of value under the most extreme idealization, the fundamental truths may be expressed without the aid of mathematical symbols. In fact the true problem does not consist here in assigning to the relation of the discovered magnitudes the most exact numerical expression possible. It consists in the search of an explanation as to the right by which the life-values of the economy can be appraised in numerical money values. It is imperative that we first explain the meaning of the computation in money. To solve this problem, pecuniary computation must be deduced from the significance of the economy. If we succeed in presenting convincingly the meaning of the economy and, concurrently, the significance of the method of economic computation, we shall have accomplished far more toward understanding quantitative economic relations than the most far-reaching employment of the mathematical method could ever achieve.

BOOK I

THE THEORY OF THE SIMPLE ECONOMY

Gossen, *Entwickelung der Gesetze des menschlichen Verkehrs*, 1854, new ed. 1889; Jevons, *Theory of Pol. Econ.*, 1871, 3. ed. 1888; Menger, *Grundsätze der Volkswirtschaftslehre*, 1871, 2. ed. 1923; L. Walras, *Eléments d'écon. pol. pure*, 1874, 4. ed. 1900; Gide, *Principes d'écon. pol.*, 1884, 19. ed. 1917; also, *Cours d'écon. pol.*, 5. ed. 1921; Wieser, *Ursprung und Hauptgesetze des wirtsch. Wertes*, 1884 also, *Der natürliche Wert*, 1889 (English edition 1893); Pierson, *Leerbock der Staathuishondkunde*, 1884–1890; Böhm-Bawerk, *Grundzüge der Theorie des wirtsch. Güterwertes*, J. f. N., N. F. Bd. 13 (1886); also, *Kapital und Kapitalzins*, 2. Bd. 1889, 4. ed. 1921; Pantaleoni, *Principii di economia pura*, 2. ed. 1894; Marshall, *Principles of Economics* 1890, 8. ed. 1922; Patten, *Theory of Dynamic Econ.* 1892; Philippovich, *Grundrisz der Pol. Oekon.* I, 1894, 15. ed. 1920; Wagner, *Grundlegung;* also, *Theor. Sozialökonomik* I. 1907; Sulzer, *Die wirtschaftl. Grundgesetze*, 1895; Dietzel, *Theoretische Sozialökonomik*, 1895, 2. ed. 1923; Pareto, *Cours d'Econ. pol.*, 1896; also, *Manuel d'Econ. pol.*, 1909; Carver, *Distribution of wealth*, 1904; also, *Principles of National Economy*, 1921; Fetter, *The Principles of Econ.*, 1904, 2. ed. 1912; also, *Econ. Principles*, 1915; Flux, *Econ. Principles*, 1904, 2. ed. 1923; Seager, *Principles of Econ.*, 1904, 3. ed. 1923; Seligman, *Principles of Econ.*, 1905, 9. ed. 1921; Clark, *Distribution of wealth*, 1908, last edition 1923; Graziani, *Institutioni d'Economia Politica*, 1908; Schumpeter, *Wesen und Hauptinhalt der theoret. Nationalökonomie*, 1908; Davenport, *Value and Distribution*, 1909; Wicksteed, *Common Sense in Pol. Econ.*, 1910; Oppenheimer, *Theorie der reinen und pol. Oekonomie*, 1911, 5. ed. 1923 and 1924; Schullern-Schrattenhofen, *Grundzüge der Volkswirtschaftslehre*, 1911; Taussig, *Principles of Econ.*, 1911, 3. ed. 1922; Wicksell, *Vorlesungen über theoretische Nationalökonomie*, 1915; Liefmann, *Grundsätze der Volkswirtschaftslehre*, 1917 bis 1919 (s. hiezu die Kritik von Amonn, Archiv Bd. 46, Heft 2 und Bd. 47, Heft 2); Cassel, *Theoretische Sozialökonomik*, 1918, 3. ed. 1923; Gelesnoff, *Grundzüge der Volkswirtschaftslehre;* Spann, *Fundament der Volkswirtschaftslehre*, 1918, 3. ed. 1923; Oswalt, *Vorträge über wirtschaftliche Grundbegriffe*, 1905, 4. ed. 1922; Verrijn Stuart, *De Grondslagen der Volkshuishouding*, 1920; Stolzmann, *Grundzüge einer Philosophie der Volkswirtschaft*, 1920; Ansiaux, *Traité d'Economie politique*, 1920; M. Weber, *Wirtschaft und Gesellschaft*, Grundr. d. Sozialök., Bd. III, 1921; Truchy, *Cours d'économie politique*, 1921; Taylor, *Principles of Economics*, 8. ed. 1921; Ely, *Outlines of Economics*, 4. ed. 1923; Birck, *The Theory of Marginal Value*, 1922; Loria, *I fondamenti scientifici della riforma economica*, 1922; Lederer, *Grundzüge der ökon. Theorie*, 1922.

The bibliography above, as we stated in our preface, is confined to a selection of modern literature. In Book I the dominant line of theoretical thought follows that which was introduced by Gossen and is spoken of today as marginal utility. Only systematic treatises on the subject matter of Book I are included above; important monographs will be cited in appropriate places.

For all of the earlier literature we refer to Schumpeter's history of dogma, already mentioned. We have only to indicate the relative positions of the advocates of marginal utility and the older theorists. Thruout economic literature two fundamental, contrasting views are found. One, adopted by the classical school, sees the fundamental form of value in value-in-exchange. The other stresses value-in-use. In the first group of theories the labor-theory is distinguished by its energy. This theory has gained further importance because in it the socialistic theory takes its rise. In the text when we refer to the classical theory, we have reference to the labor-theory.

Marginal utility has been associated with the concept of value-in-use because of its invocation of use. But the doctrine is more closely related to the labor-theory. Except for certain minor advances there has been little progress in the explanation of the concept of value along the line of value-in-use. This is especially true of the explanation of the formation of price and income. There would be almost no gap in the theory of price or income if everything that the German text-book says in its section on "fundamental concepts" of value-in-use were omitted. This is not true of the discussion of the labor-theory. Although this doctrine starts from false premises and must be inconclusive, it has approached the important economic problems and has established relationships that must be noted by all later theories. The analysis of marginal utility has taken over the problems touched upon by the labor-theory. It has even accepted a number of the latter's conclusions. But it endeavors to pass from the half truths of the labor-theory to the foundation of use and to furnish a general explanation that is not dependent on the form of exchange. The final analysis should be an exhaustive elementary theory of value and the economic process, that would be no less valid for the socialistically ordered economy than for the exchange economy. Lewis is of the opinion that the theory of marginal utility has deepened the psychological aspects of value-in-use, but that it has contributed nothing to our understanding of the economic mass-process and especially of prices. If this be correct, the marginal analysis has failed of its purpose.

§ 3. Purpose and Power in the Economy

Purposeful desire and the motor stimuli—The simple process of natural economy.

There is a double root to every purposeful action. The most apparent of these is the desire of achievement. The other is more hidden; it is the outgrowth of the power that must be exerted to achieve success. There is a double stimulus: purposeful desire that our efforts attain their object, and an active motor stimulus that is massed under tension and strives to be discharged. Fundamentally the desire and this force are intimately associated, but on the surface of consciousness they appear distinct. Frequently a considerable effort is necessary to unite them. In this union volition is born. The latter is impulse controlled by purpose. On occasion these impulses with their stimuli may mislead us, but they are nevertheless the most important vital values at our disposal. Weak individuals who lack them are not affected by examples of successful striving by their stronger brethren.

Socially the motor stimuli are discharged at the expense of enormous friction during great popular movements and spiritual outflow. Only a strong people can apply the powers of the multitude to social ends with the utmost efficiency and without appreciable waste. When this can be done, a nation is at the apex of its historical development. Such unity of effort can be achieved only after centuries of preparatory attempts, errors, struggles and wasted effort.

This is true of all action. It also characterizes the economic activity of the individual and, still more, of society. No economic progress is possible unless a force becomes kinetic. This power must seek its goal. The force itself exists while it is still unconscious of its aims. It has been truly said that the mere desire of gain would not urge men into the regions of eternal ice or into uninhabited space. Before they do this, an inner impulse must move them to exert their full powers at all risk. Even the routine process of the economy must be actuated by the joy of work; otherwise in the humdrum of daily life energy will be deadened.

The same is true of social economic activity. The motivating forces must be cultivated—trained, disciplined and grouped—amid a ceaseless conflict of interests and powers. The values that must be sacrificed often exceed the gains that are actually realized. The social economy is not soberly utilitarian activity dominated by common sense. One holding this point of view can never fully comprehend the social economy. The human economy, in search of a happy equilibrium that is in the highest sense utilitarian, is after all always set in motion by the calling forth and developing of social economic forces. At times in this process it is precipitated into revolutions of worldwide importance.

In the theory of the simple economy we shall examine only the effects of economic purposes on economic processes. We shall not consider the conditions that accompany the formation of the socio-economic powers except to remark the condition of fatigue that attends the expenditure of personal energy.

The simple economy, as described in our introduction, is the economy of a single subject. Here one does not find the contrasts that are manifest in the social formation of forces. But we do not have in mind the scant economy of an isolated householder. Rather we envisage an economy that has the breadth of a national economy with all its wealth, technical knowledge and problems of economic calculus. But this broad economy is guided by a single mind. It answers its purpose in an unimpeachable manner because a systematic and penetrating mind guides it. This director foresees ends, weighs them without error or passion and maintains a discipline which ensures that all directions are executed with the utmost precision and skill and without loss of energy. We shall further assume that all requisite individual forces are placed at the disposal of this social management as cheerfully as though enlisted in their individual interest. It is not relevant whether this assumption, which we neither affirm or deny, is compatible with human nature. The concept of a model economic people is only an idealizing assumption. It is embraced only to enable us to fasten our attention exclusively on the effects that emanate from economic purposes.

In the money economy of today there is a flow of goods and services that issues from every individual household participating in exchange. This flow is intended with the aid of money exchanged to induce a counter-movement of other goods and services that shall supply the needs of the individual household. The great social circulation is composed of a number of minor circulatory movements, each participating household being a nucleus.

In the simple economy as we conceive it, no matter how extensive it may be, the economic process of periodical production and utilization of goods goes on as a process of natural economy. Only one movement of goods need be considered, the flow from sources of production to the final consumer. Therefore the economic process is simple in this sense as well, and the significance of economic action at once becomes more apparent than it can be in the labyrinth of intersecting movements in the exchange economy. We must leave to later discussion the question, whether or not the significance of economic activity is thwarted in the economy of exchange. This question cannot be answered until the significance of this activity is itself understood.

We deduce the theory of the simple economy by the assumption of the greatest usefulness of economic action. This is a rationalistically utilitarian point of view. We take this position in order to determine the maximum influence of purpose on national economy. But we expressly protest that this does not imply that we are either rationalist or utilitarian. We expect to show later by a process of decreasing abstraction what diminution of this maximum is required by typical conditions. More than one of the expositions of the classical school suggest pure rationalistic and utilitarian doctrine to the reader. But in every instance it is impossible to say in how far the authors intended to unfold a complete picture of economic life and in how far, to simplify the presentation, they resorted to idealization. It is possible that they themselves did not discriminate nicely in this respect.

§ 4. Human Needs

Demand—The narrower concept of economic need—Utility—Foresight. Solicitude for others. Common need. Social need.

Cuhel, *Zur Lehre von den Bedürfnissen*, 1907; Kraus, *Das Bedurfnis*, 1894; Tiburtius, *Der Begriff des Bedürfnisses*, 1914; Oppenheimer, *System der Soziologie*, vol. III, 5th ed., 1923; A. Voigt, *Begriff der Dringlichkeit*, Z. f. Stw., vol. 55; Mayer, art. *Bedürfnis*, in Hdw. d. Stw., 4th ed.

The economic organization is directed to meeting the human needs. The household requires a certain quantity of goods and services to satisfy its needs. This quantity is called the demand. As we shall later show, the economy is not concerned with the direct satisfaction of needs. Rather, its aim is to cover the demand. This explains why the term, need, occurs infrequently in the speech of economic life while the term, demand, is used daily.

Current speech regards the concept of need in its most general form. It embraces a multitude of meanings that can never be the basis of economic demand. Thus economic theory must fashion a narrower concept. It must discriminate the specific need, which leads to demand, from all other needs. This refinement requires no more exact analysis of the psychological nature of human needs.

This is the province of scientific psychology. Economic theory has only to explain needs in their economic sense. Briefly, they may be called economic needs. And even this explanation is sufficient if it distinguishes them from the most closely related phenomena.

Cuhel (*a.a.o.s.* 61) describes a need in this economic sense. It is the desire to use, i. e., a desire directed to the employment of the means of satisfaction. Schumpeter appropriately identifies its nature by referring to it as a "felt want." Thus, for example, economic theory should not be expected to analyze the physiological requirement of warmth. Its interest is directed rather to the need of fuel, of clothing and of shelter. Again it is not concerned with the nature of hunger, as such. Its attention is focused on the need of nourishment which demands the absorption of food of a definite kind. Economic theory is even less concerned with that vague impulse which is conscious of wanting something without being aware of its object. This impulse is the original, primitive phenomenon. The economy, however, takes its rise in the desire which is plainly aware of its object and strives toward it. The problem of economic theory starts only at this point.

Needs may be classified on the basis of their physiological effects as needs of preservation or of amelioration. The former are directed to the maintenance of an existing state of well being. Thus one seeks by means of clothing to prevent the loss of heat already stored in the body. The latter group pertains to new or higher conditions of life such as a starving man, for example, would experience when he receives nourishment. But such a distinction is both immaterial and inadmissible to economic theory. It enters too deeply into the nature of desire. Both economic theory and practice are concerned only with the outward manifestation of the instrument of satisfaction. Even the preservative needs are important only as they create a desire to use some object. Therefore theory will have to distinguish, precisely as does practice, as many kinds of need as there are principal classes of the means of satisfaction.

In economic theory the concept of use is closely related to that of need. But it employs this term also in a way which diverges from ordinary usage. The term is expanded to signify every condition of the satisfaction of needs. Every act, by which needs are satisfied, is an act of use. Food becomes useful as it is consumed. But a work of art also possesses utility. The satisfaction of needs, without exception, may be compared as to relative importance. So also the utility of all things may be compared as to relative amount.

The broader concept of need, as embodied in daily speech, includes all cases where a motor stimulus is felt, one of those previously mentioned stimuli which accompany the exertion of force. For example, one says of an industrious man that he feels the need of working. One refers to the need of talking in the case of a loquacious man. The need of freedom with its enormous power is also to be grouped among motor needs. In this instance the man desires to give vent to his forces by his own impulses, unhindered by the inhibitions of others and unconcerned with their commands. This desire has its source deep in the nature of the motor stimuli themselves.

The motor need is satisfied in the expenditure of energy. In extreme cases it is exhausted by fatigue. The economic need reaches a condition of satiety when a sufficient quantity of instruments of its satisfaction has been absorbed.

There are several respects in which the usages of scientific and daily speech differ. The latter is often terse and restricted. Thus it refers to a need only as a strongly felt desire. But scientific terminology may not allow this limitation. It is as much concerned with the most easily suppressed wishes as with the strongest desires. Even the most easily spared articles of luxury should be regarded as objects of human need.

Furthermore, no economic distinction may be allowed between true and false needs, permitted and forbidden, or moral and immoral. These may be easily distinguished where one views them from the effect of their satisfaction. But this theory is concerned only with the impulses which such needs give economic action.

In the case of future needs a precise distinction must be made by the scientist. Occasionally in every day speech the foreseeing of such a need is regarded as an actual need. Food is stored away and fields are tilled to meet a need for food tomorrow or during the ensuing year. Both these acts spring from the expectation of future need. But the need itself is plainly distinguishable from the anticipation. They belong in two separate psychological categories. The immediate need of food is the product of a physiological sensation of hunger which is accompanied by a desire to eat. But foreseeing the need of food is merely a state of mental unrest that is produced by the idea of a hunger which will be felt in the future. This idea is accompanied by a desire to make sure of food for future use.

In this latter case the emotional excitement is frequently obscured so effectively that we are hardly aware of it. This is especially true whenever a regular provision for the future has become habitual. Habit abridges motivation and renders its detail operation nearly subconscious. Provision for the future is thus apt to figure as a desire but without emotional foundation. It is sustained merely by considerations of utility. Only when the regular course of events is disturbed does the emotional agitation become sufficiently intense to be appreciable. In extreme cases it may amount to actual despair.

Ordinary speech allows the term, need, to be applied whenever a desire exists which is founded on a felt want. Therefore we not infrequently have people speak of a need of the provision for future nourishment. But the effect of the satisfaction of these two "needs" is very different. The end of a present need of food is in consumption. The "need of the provision of food" induces other acts. It urges a man to secure ample stores to provide means of satisfaction. It impels him to acquire goods and to control other individuals who are likely to render helpful services. It leads to a consideration of the more remote stages of production, of all that goes to cover the demand. If we may say so, the prevision of the need of food is far more voracious than hunger.

We owe much to this foresight which endeavors to provide for the demand of the future. Indeed it is the primary agent which makes the adequate satisfaction of our needs possible. Wealth could never be acquired without it. Except for it we should inevitably be submerged by unknown future dangers in the form of enemy hosts and convulsions of nature. But the foresight may also become a heavy burden. It frequently hangs over the rich like a cloud and shadows the serenity of their days. From this shadow the unpretentious poor are free. If one calls needs insatiable, the indictment is directed in no small measure against the demands of an excessive foresight.

Solicitude for the needs of others and the anticipation of future needs differ in their moral aspects. But psychologically they are to be grouped together. They are alike a state of emotional unrest. However, in the first case we break the egoistic shackles imposed by self-seeking demands. Thru our sympathies we become aware of the wants of others. This solicitude may be directed either to the immediate satisfaction of the needs of others or, by way of precaution, to the supply of outside demands. There is a group of persons who are scarcely aware of their wants. For example, little children and the sick often do not feel them. Thru a care for the needs of such people, these needs are drawn into that group of objects towards which economic action is directed. The will to provide for the stranger supplements the scarcely conscious need. It arouses the dormant need and gives it a strength that makes it comparable to a fully developed need in the sense of economic doctrine. However, in this case one will must be supplemented by another. This may make itself felt by various disturbances.

Even the impulse to provide for the needs of others is not infrequently spoken of as a need: "it is a necessity of his nature to provide for others as though he were providing for himself." This can only mean that the stimulus experienced is as strong as that aroused by an egoistic need. Here, again, we have reached a point where scientific terminology must distinguish sharply in order to avoid the most serious misunderstandings. Self-seeking and sympathy may be separated only if the coarser, original stimulus of the need is distinguishable from the more refined, derivative one of the care for others. What has just been said of foresight applies here as well: solicitude has a different emotional basis and pursues other ends than do the needs.

On the other hand the narrower meaning embraces the common or collective need. This is a need which everyone, conscious of being a member of a community, experiences precisely as he does his own most intimate, personal need.

The name, "social need," may be applied to this group. However, it is better reserved for the need which the individual experiences in regard to his position in society. Such are the desires of recognition, rank or distinction, of appreciation in whatever form, even though it be only as to external observances. This social need is among the strongest felt by humanity. It rests upon a sound basis, even though it is occasionally censured by moralists. In its absurd excesses, it of course deserves the ridicule which it receives. But the position which a man occupies in society is among the important values of life. The development of the individual is largely dependent upon it. In so far as personality is of importance to society, social welfare must acknowledge a similar dependence.

In a certain sense, however, every need is to be regarded as social. The appraisal of even the purely individual need, which is the result of the most intimate desire, is influenced by society. In most instances one measures his personal demand by the standard of his times and environment. The individual judgment is influenced by the social decision. This process is frequently carried to excess in order to avoid social disapprobation. A man may plunge into excessive disbursements to maintain outer show. These he endeavors to retrieve by curtailing his most intimate requirements. He feels that he must act thus for fear of losing caste and of being relegated to a lower social level.

A further transition carries one from the desire to emulate to the keener effort of excelling his peers in outward show, in social distinction, in power. The result is a peculiar confusion of the personal and the common need. The ruler and the ruling classes see in themselves the embodiment of the pretentious of the commonwealth. They even inflate the standards under the influence of a personal craving: exaggerate them to an importance which the mass of the community do not feel except as a burden.

However, all these are manifestations which cannot be perceived in the model, social state. Nevertheless, they deserve notice in a systematic exposition.

§ 5. Gossen's Law of the Satiety of Needs

The connection between inherent values and the quantity of the means of satisfaction.

No sound need is insatiable. The quantity of goods required to satisfy it completely is even smaller than might be expected. Consider, for example, the desire for knowledge. The mental receptivity of the masses is ordinarily very limited. Only a small minority aspires to better things. The great intellects whose aspirations are unbounded are few indeed. Even a Faustian intellect is satisfied by the known truth and is insatiable only in the sense that it searches in ever new directions and kindles new needs.

There are degenerate needs that demand new sensual pleasures and constant change of refinement. Such needs are creative in augmenting methods of enjoyment. But wherever man is influenced only by his own being, human nature prescribes narrow limits which cannot be permanently exceeded. Desires are only inflated to immeasurable proportions when the social degenerations of vanity and love of fame are brought to bear.

We may accustom ourselves to measure that which we wish to obtain for ourselves as an excess over what others can achieve. When this standard is once established, demands are necessarily infinite. They are not related to man's inner nature but to the outer world. This statement is particularly true of the desire for power. This expands enormously as soon as it takes its standard from the desire to exceed the development of power in neighboring communities or in the entire world. It is a mistake, however, to suppose that only the personal ambition of the men in power is unbounded. The thirst of an entire people for power may be boundless when driven by the passions of competition and actual warfare.

Considering all cases, one must regard the emotions which lead to insatiable desires as exceptional. They do not change the general statement that applies to the remaining needs or to most men. We may lay it down as the rule that the receptivity of the individual need is strictly limited, although human needs may be insatiable in discovering new directions of desire.

The temporal extent in needs must also be considered. There are transitory needs and permanent ones. The former are generally induced by accidental circumstances. Needs may accompany only certain phases of a man's development or they may cling to him thruout his life. Permanent needs may also be classified as periodic and continuous. The former are satisfied for a given space of time and then arise anew. In the latter group are those which allow of interference and those whose satisfaction may be suspended over longer or shorter periods of time. It is not of particular interest to us to investigate the different varieties of these types.

By far the greater number of needs—one may well say nearly all—are divisible: i. e., one satisfies them by a series of distinct acts. Bohm-Bäwerk has called attention to the existence of indivisible needs. He instances the case of the myopic patient who obtains complete satisfaction by the use of eye-glasses. But in what follows we shall speak of divisible needs, unless other reference is expressly indicated. Of this divisible group a few are so urgent that they must be satiated in order to sustain life. Man is asphyxiated where there is not enough air to breathe. In most cases, however, the gratification may be suspended before satiety is reached. Such an act may result in a serious hazard to health or to mental and physical development. In other cases no perceptible disadvantage follows. Some of the stimuli are dangerous to man and should not be fully satisfied. One need hardly say that there are some desires which should be absolutely suppressed.

The gradual satisfaction of divisible needs takes place subject to a law. The recognition of this law has had the greatest influence on the progress of economic theory. We may call it the law of satiety. The process may be followed most plainly in the case of a need of food. Let us assume a man who is weak from lack of food. A portion of food just adequate to save him from collapse is set before him. His desire for this nourishment is measured only by the intensity with which he would cling to life. He consumes a second, identical portion and feels his strength returning. His craving in this case was great but of a less intensity than in the first instance. The same remark applies to a third ration. We may assume that he now feels completely recovered. After this a fourth, perhaps a fifth portion may be desired and consumed with a feeling of physical comfort and complete satiety. There will be a still further decrease of the intensity of his desire in each case. With comparative rapidity a condition of satiety is reached. If food continues to be taken, the system will be surfeited. The body is no longer receptive. It refuses additional nourishment. Desire turns into loathing and revulsion. There is no healthy need of which the same observation might not be made.

Continuous physical needs are also subject to the same law. A given weight of fuel raises the room-temperature slightly. It is intensely desired. Every succeeding equivalent unit is less urgently wanted. Finally the need is satisfied. Then comes a reversal of feeling as additional heat is generated. It ends in discomfort and an attempted protection against the heat. We may remind the reader of Menger's instructive example. He deals with the need of shelter and shows that the desire for each additional room is successively less. Finally additional space becomes a burden. Sound mental needs are not excepted from this law. These are also subject to a decreasing intensity as satiety is approached. Here, as elsewhere, the series closes in surfeit. There are few people who would wish to re-read a book immediately after the first reading, or who would wish repetition of the same piece of music. Continued repetition would be painful to everyone.

The applicability of the law is more difficult to estimate in the case of degenerative social needs and cravings for power. Unusually large outlays are often required for even the first partial satisfaction. Moreover, they are generally continuous and intolerant of interruption. In addition there are many which excite a stimulus to outdo the first feat. This calls for a constant increase of the outlay. All this gives the appearance of insatiability. But insatiability in this sense and the law of satiety, as we interpret it, are not contradictory. We may, however, entirely disregard the case of degenerate needs. They have no significance in the theory of the simple economy. The latter describes only the regular course of the economic process.

One important exception must be noted. Individuals and society require time to correctly appraise a new desire. Innovations first meet with resistance and are underestimated. When the masses later become interested, the appreciation is unreasonably high. Then, it would seem, there may come a set-back of public estimation. Finally, a sound mean is determined. New developments of this sort present an interesting problem to the social psychologist and historian. They need not be considered by an economic theory which is bent upon ascertaining the true current of the economic process. The latter presupposes the existence of customary needs that no longer overwhelm man. It is only for needs of this sort that the law of satiety is formulated.

In general terms the law is to be formulated as follows:—In the case of every divisible need the first unit of satisfying goods is desired with the greatest intensity. The use of further units is less intensely desired. Finally, satiety is reached. Beyond this point desire is transformed into aversion. The size of the unit is conditioned by the nature of the need and the agent of satisfaction. Also one must decide whether the utilization of additional units is conceived of as taking place over a period of time or as an aggregate at one time.

One can hardly sufficiently appreciate the great significance of the law of satiety to the theory of economic value and price and, consequently, to economic theory in general. Our theory first found a solid foundation in this law. Before it was discovered, theory had regarded the particular value of each need as homogeneous. For example, the need of food with all its demands was treated as a unit mass. It was a need of existence. Thru the law of satiety this general need has been analyzed. It may be resolved into various degrees of decreasing intensity. It passes from the extreme necessity of preservation to the zero-point of satiety. Since the degree of gratification that may be obtained depends on the quantity of the means at our disposal, we see plainly the connection between the intensity of need-values and quantities stored up for use. Once this connection is known, a bond is established between the quantities of goods and ascertained degrees of value.

Bernouilli was the first to employ an observation of this sort in economic theory. However, he limited his deductions to the narrow field of the theory of probabilities. Bentham explained the law of satiety with his usual penetration; but, although he was one of the leading thinkers of England and his works were most widely read, his exposition made so little impression that it was speedily forgotten. Only in recent times has it again enlisted attention. Bentham, it must be remembered, did not draw from the law of satiety those deductions with reference to the theory of economic value which constitute its scientific significance. He stopped at the traditional theory of value as it had been set up independently of the law of satiety. His exposition is psychological. He did nothing with it for economic theory.

The connection with the law of value was not recognized until Gossen. His formulation of the law of value is not entirely precise. His exposition of the law of satiety, in the main masterly, may still call for certain changes. None the less he must receive credit for discovering the law of satiety. Theory pays a debt of honor by naming the law after its founder. For some time his leadership also was obscure. The law had to be rediscovered by later investigators. However, this does not detract from Gossen's merits. Jevons, Menger and Walras each made the discovery independently. They turned the law to account in their theories of value. The following exposition is a sequel to the formulation which they gave the law. The certificate of its validity is better because a series of investigators, in substantial agreement, have settled upon it.

§ 6. The Degrees of Human Needs

The tensional span and receptivity of needs—Vital needs and those of mere enjoyment; composite needs—Measuring the intensity of needs—Value of the need as an inherent value—Economic theory and valuation.

A scale of satisfactions is obtained if all variations of the intensity of the need are noted as increased quantities of a particular commodity are used. This scale commences at the highest point for the first unit employed. If the record is complete, the lowest intensity is reached with the last unit just before complete satiation. The scale may indeed be continued beyond this point by annexing a negative section. On this one might record the growing aversion as over-satiety increased. We shall call the highest degree on our scale of needs the point of maximum tension. The disappearance of stress is marked by that intensity which accompanies the final desire as complete satiety is reached.

In our daily life we are accustomed to refer to indispensable and dispensable needs, to urgent and less imperative needs. This distinction is based on the magnitude of the particular need at the point of its greatest intensity. In the case of those referred to as indispensable to existence, self-preservation depends upon their satisfaction. The point of maximum tension is accompanied by the greatest desire of which human nature is ever capable. It is not surprising that this point has been clearly recognized. Ordinary speech has found an expression by which such needs may be differentiated from the great mass. The point of maximum intensity for those latter is frequently of a much lower order. Their satisfaction may often be neglected without harmful effect to our natures. In some of the cases, most men do not even seek gratification.

However, it is a matter of importance to the practical economy—and, consequently, to theory—to know the relative intensity as the tension is reduced. On this condition depends the prospect of the complete satiation of a particular need. In the case of the physical needs of existence, tension disappears rather high on the general scale. For example, water is essential to life. But the needs of the body are satisfied after a relatively small quantity has been absorbed. The connoisseur of wine, the habitual drinker and the drunkard have a longer range of desires of a lesser intensity. The same remark may be made of the need of food. The primary need concerns itself merely with consuming that food which is indispensable to self-preservation. Tension is relaxed at a high point. The stimuli due merely to gastronomy are of a different order. The disappearance of stress in the case of dispensable needs of luxuries, on the other hand, is often found at a low point in the general scale. For some of them this point has never been discovered. Wholly degenerate needs, moreover, may be insatiable.

In order to measure the spread between the points of maximum tension and disappearance, one must construct an ideal, general, graduated scale of desire. The degrees on this scale must extend from the highest to the lowest appreciable desire of which experience shows human nature to be capable. Every individual scale of needs may be compared with this universal one.

The magnitude of this tensional space is to be distinguished from receptivity. The latter is indicated by the quantity of goods required to satisfy a need to the point where tension disappears. There is a wide range in the intensity of the need of drinking water. The minimum is relatively high. The maximum tension, however, is much higher. Between the two points are a vast number of degrees. The receptivity of this need, on the other hand, is narrowly limited when compared with that of the habitual drinker of alcoholic beverages.

The arrangement or form of the scale will depend on the divisibility of the good yielding satisfaction. The quantity of water required to quench thirst is most minutely partible. If we may be allowed the expression, the satisfaction takes place in a constant flow. We may fitly speak of such needs as flowing needs. From these must be distinguished those whose unit of gratification is larger. These we may call "stepped" needs. The need of shelter is an example. The unit is a single room. The desire for the first shelter is separated from that for a second unit, and this from that for a third by a comparatively large interval. Within this spread the scale of needs is not important in the case of shelter.

As regards the form of the scale, two important groups of needs should be distinguished. The first of these includes the simple, healthful, vital needs; the second, those which are merely pleasurable. There are all manner of transitional forms which link the two extremes. These we are not required to consider here. The first group includes all those needs which must be satisfied in order to ensure the sound continuance of life. As a subdivision of this group those needs appear which are essential to preservation. These must be gratified to preserve life and to banish actual distress. But the sound needs of life are not thus narrowly limited. For their complete satisfaction they demand that human nature be catered to in such a manner as to result in strength and vitality. Even this gratification still confines us to the needs of existence. This restraint, however, does not oppress us. Rather, it is felt as an impulse to progress still to be achieved. In the satisfaction of these primary needs the motor stimuli are strongly excited. The true joy of living is induced thru the immediate connection of the pleasure of satisfaction and the even greater delight of the expenditure of force. The gratification of the second major group, the merely pleasurable needs, does not lead to an increased excitement of the motor stimuli. When overdone it leads to their deadening and ultimately to a dulling of the capacity of enjoyment itself. Their most lamentable outgrowths are the degenerative needs of luxurious desire.

Under simple conditions of life both classes of need are not infrequently directed to the same variety of goods. They may be distinguished only in the quantities demanded. The healthy need of food, for example, is satisfied with a quantity that appeases hunger and gives strength. The pleasurable need demands more, possibly to the point of gluttony.

Where the art of living has been more highly developed, the two groups of needs are also distinguishable in the types of goods to which they are directed. Thus, the healthful need of food is satisfied by more simple means of nourishment. The pleasurable need seeks intensified delights at the table. To the mere agents of appeasing hunger it adds others which serve only to afford enjoyment. It may go even further and result in a search for pleasure which finds satisfaction only in a general refinement of foods. The epicure appeases his craving for food by consuming the most skilfully prepared viands. He quenches his thirst by means of carefully selected vintages. Even in satisfying the needs of self-preservation he is in search of additional stimuli of enjoyment. The needs of existence and enjoyment coalesce to form a composite need. The progress of this composite is ultimately destructive of the sound basis from which the simple, vital need arises. As in this case, the needs of all other classes may be made to blend and form composite needs.

No other human impulses are so strong as those arising from vital needs. That of self-preservation is constantly active in every individual who is adapted to his environment. Moreover, an impulse of self-development operates in the strongest individuals and races. This awakens new needs. The latter give the motive for a broadening of the economy. Were it not for these original impulses which are constituents of our nature, nothing would endure and progress would be barred.

Their very power, however, also becomes the source of endless evil. Those who face the miseries of life are thrown into a conflict which threatens to exhaust their powers of production in order to satisfy the needs of existence. Our impulses always tend to overstep the boundaries of the permissible and the wholesome. Thus those who are placed above want may yield to the temptations to excess, so impairing the capacity for enjoyment. Gross excess is the vice of barbarism. True cultivation inculcates moderation in our simple needs, but it tends to increase our composite needs. These are harmful. They forestall the laudable sentiment of frugal contentment. They incite one to exhausting, excessive acquisitive efforts. But still more important, they lead to degeneration either directly or by the tempting, circuitous path of over-refinement. The demand for the greatest possible measure of satisfaction exacts the constant increase of the means of gratification. The requisite is accumulated wealth whose acquisition governs the majority of men. For most men it becomes axiomatic that the more one is able to enjoy and the greater wealth one possesses, the happier he should be. This axiom was accepted uncritically by the early economic theory. Only in its later development has it come to appreciate the inevitably resultant evil arising from an uncontrolled striving after ever more riches.

In our theory of the simple economy we presuppose an idealized, model condition. This is conceived of as perfect also in that the permissible boundaries of desire are nowhere exceeded. It is assumed that thruout the entire structure human activity is directed to wholesome, vital needs and to permissible needs of enjoyment. In every instance no excess of effort should be needed to satisfy them. Over-satiety should never be approached. Subject to this assumption, the demands for an increase of satisfactions, greater productivity and more extensive possessions are wholly justified.

Our scales of needs measure the significance of needs: i. e., the value which attaches to their satisfaction and the consequent condition of well-being. These scales appraise the need-value according to the relative intensity of the desire. The criterion of this intensity is the action which is induced by the force of the value. Of two values, that one is the stronger which most influences our practical decision. Such a decision is made in every instance where only one of two needs can be satisfied. The greater value is chosen even though the temptings of passion must be overcome. For this value which we desire with the greater intensity is by no means the one which we would "rather" have. Generally, the most keenly desired are all those values which tend to preserve life. Those which embellish it are usually placed lower on the scale. One strives first to satisfy those needs which are accompanied by the maximum pain. Some may be suppressed without causing pain. Of these one is far less acutely conscious. But it is precisely these latter which increase the joys of existence.

Need-values are of a primary order; they have individual value.[1] Economic theory is as little concerned in their analysis, as in the analysis of the need itself. The proper appraisal and classification of the values of life is the task of philosophy, ethics and religion. It is the practical art of living and knowledge of life. The forms of this valuation should be described by a psychological doctrine of value. But so far as economic theory is concerned these vital values are accepted as so many facts. It does not enter the endless discussion of their appraisal and revaluation. It does not even concern itself with the problem whether they are or are not subject to scientific determination and measurement.

The economic value which engages the attention of economic theory is not an inherent value. It is a secondary magnitude. As we shall show later, it is derived from the transfer of the primary values of the satisfaction of needs to the economic means of gratification. This transfer is independent of the source of the primary value. Its laws must be capable of exact scientific determination. If economic theory enters the discussion of valuations, it is in danger of losing its exact, scientific character. It is sure to maintain its strict, theoretical rigor so long as it describes only the transfer of primary value to economic means of satisfaction. It may then go further and show the influence of this transferred, secondary value on economic transactions.

The conclusions which theory reaches in this manner, cannot be shaken by any revised appraisal of the social values of life. The results are compatible with any system of primary valuation. The economic principle of maximum utility, in the form in which it is to be presented by economic theory, is not inseparable from hedonistic philosophical views. There is no doubt that it may be harmonized with ascetic views. It merely states that goods must be employed so as to function in most perfect agreement with, or furtherance of the aims of our existence. It postulates more than is implicit in any act of utilization. It makes no attempt to determine what are the ends of existence and how they should be chosen. Neglecting all such philosophical ends, the economic principle of the greatest utility shows what rules of economic action result from

[1] Eigenwert.

the fact that, in this action, we use means over which we have complete power in purposive employment.

Economic theory explains the laws of economic valuation and trade in a manner which differs conspicuously from that in which the natural sciences explain the laws of nature. The latter show a necessary connection of cause and effect, a compulsion.[1] Economic theory presents a sequence arising under economic pressure, a desideratum.[2] Economic valuation is that demanded by economic duty. Economic action is that demanded by economic necessity. For example, the formula of the law of value is not expressed by saying: "One's will is controlled by a superior power. Therefore one must appraise every good according to the greatest utility obtainable from it." The formulation is rather: "Being a competent economic manager, one must appraise goods in such and such a manner."

The theorist may easily seem to transgress the boundaries of his problem. He describes a theoretical obligation, a valuation which is demanded. In so doing, he may appear to establish a controlling force over the person of a man. The position of pharmacology is analogous. The latter discovers that certain remedies cater to the desire of the patient to regain health, that certain other agents induce death which he would escape. In the establishment of such relations as these, pharmacology is a descriptive science. With like purpose economic theory demonstrates that a certain process of valuation and action results in the greatest gain, that another process does not.

Nevertheless it must be admitted that economic theory may not hold to this point of view at all times. No assurance can be given that it will not swerve from such purely descriptive character. This description of economic action is intended to lay down certain fundamental truths for the guidance of the science and art of politics. The latter in turn should lay down rules or at least offer advice as to the method by which existing conditions can be improved or by which further evil can be prevented.

If the theory is to accomplish this purpose, it must aim to find a solution of such problems. From this point, politics may advance directly to further conclusions without a break in the thought. Our theory and politics are so intimately related that the student will never be able to guarantee that his valuations of political aims have not influenced his theoretical opinions. All of us are too deeply interested in human problems to meet them thruout with that serene indifference, which the scientist preserves as he approaches the processes of the external world.

However, the theory of the simple economy is saved from the temptation to adopt partisan views by virtue of its narrower problem. All economically active men are regarded as one. This mass is contrasted with the world of goods. Thus the theory adopts the point of view of the naturalist. There may be here no egoistic application of the principle of the greatest utility against the interests of fellow men. The theory establishes its one incontestable position in reference to the world of goods which offer to man the means of well-being. The ideal point of view of the theory is a further advantage. This assumes a model state of affairs in which passion and weakness never mislead in the evaluation. The proposition that the higher yield is always the more advantageous may be granted under these conditions. It is part of the assump-

[1] Ein Mussen.

[2] Ein Sollen.

tion that this greater yield is not to be used to satisfy degenerate needs and, further, that it has not been acquired thru the exploitation of the worker.

In both these respects the theory of exchange differs. On the one hand, partisan interests are rampant. For example, the theorists representing the wealthy class and those representing the workers will have difficulty in agreeing upon the importance to the social economy of the directing entrepreneur. They will not easily overcome the impression which their practical valuations exert on this theoretical view. Such appraisals, however, are formed under the influence of a partisan point of view. On the other hand by a process of decreasing abstraction the assumptions must be extended to include the general types of economic error which are experienced. It will not be true in every instance to say that the greater yield is more important than the lesser. Consideration must be given to the effects of excessive labor and undue pleasure upon the motor stimuli and the human capacity of enjoyment.

§ 7. The Appraisal of Future Needs

Equating present and future needs—The rule of the preservation of economic reserves and the conservation of working force—Under-estimation of the value of future needs as typical of the weak economy.

A number of psychologists and economists maintain that, as human nature is constituted, future needs are appraised at a lower valuation than present ones. It is said that one habitually discounts the full inherent value which the future need will attain when it becomes actual. The deduction is greater, the more distant the day at which the need is expected to materialize. It is never certain that an anticipated need will become actual. The duration of human life is always uncertain. But the most important factor is that admittedly, as human nature is constituted, vital, present desires have greater power over us than the mere fanciful ideas of a desire which, we assume, may be felt one of these days.

Starting from this basis, Böhm-Bawerk developed [1] his famous theory of the interest on capital. The latter is not to be discussed in this place. At present we limit ourselves to a consideration of the manner in which a model social economy would value future needs. Is there not an economic under-estimation of future needs, if they are regularly appraised at a lower value than present ones? or, on the other hand, are they not over-assessed, if one anticipates without discount the entire future continuity of social life? Would not such

1 See, *Positive Theory of Capital:* Excursus XI. We shall not follow him here into the field of psychological construction. In § 4 we have described the manifestation of need so as to distinguish it from the phenomena most nearly akin to it. We would also remind the reader in this connection of our remarks concerning "prevision."

foresight with its endless burdens inevitably oppress men beyond endurance, if they were unable in some manner to free themselves for the demands of the present and the immediate future?

John Stuart Mill in his treatise on political economy tells us of Indians in the Jesuit community of Paraguay. They were sent out to plow the fields but they killed the oxen harnessed to the plows. When they had eaten their fill, they left the meat to rot where it lay. They felt no concern for its preservation.

A primitive people, so little appreciating the need of tomorrow as compared with that of today, is altogether incapable of economic progress. Civilized peoples could never have reached the present stage of advancement, if they had lacked the desire and power to maintain for future times the particular capacities for the satisfaction of needs, which they had attained. Efficient economy requires that the future satisfaction and need shall not be deemed less important than the vividly experienced desire of the moment. It is essential that every strong person or people shall maintain a sense of enduring values. They may not be impaired by passing solicitation.

After all, the actual requirements of production are such that we need not burden ourselves excessively on their account with the cares of the future. The conditions to which we are here subject, are quite different from those which obtain in the household. In our housekeeping there is a given, determinate stock of goods which is measured by our income. This must meet our needs until additional income accrues. Accordingly the stock has to be apportioned to the needs of months, weeks and days. But in production the problem is an entirely different one. The needs recur periodically. At the same time the human capacity for work is regenerated. Thus period after period secures that additional income which may be applied to the satisfaction of needs.

True economy, therefore, in the absence of disturbing influences, may assign the cares of the future to the future and its income. There is a necessity of considering an economic policy beyond the current period only when special risks are foreseen, when more rapid economic progress is aspired to, or when other changes in accustomed incomes and expenditures are planned or expected. Even as regards such extraordinary incomes and expenditures, however, it is never advisable to over-emphasize future events too largely. Here, too, the re-establishment of the equilibrium may largely be left to itself. Regular incomes and expenditures need never be adjusted for other than the current period. Depending upon the period on which the computation is based, the next year or month or week no longer occupies one's attention. The more remote future does not vanish gradually in perspective as one endeavors to provide for the morrow. All one tries to do is to appraise clearly the nearest period. To this one adjusts his economic care.

When it comes to more distant contingencies, it is enough that working powers and economic capital be maintained unimpaired. To a certain point man's working efficiency is protected from excessive strain by his very nature. Fatigue hoists the danger signal. That part of the capital stock which depends upon the inexhaustible forces of the soil is also, by its nature, permanent and unassailable. To be sure, in other respects the stock is constantly being consumed and must be reproduced again and again.

Economic foresight is thus confronted with numerous problems that are not easily resolved. All of them, however, are included within the rule that the capital stock must be preserved. Those men who follow this precept and at the same time husband their working efficiency, also comply as a matter of course with the rule which enjoins that for all future times an identical state of well-being shall be preserved. One provides for the future roughly. He does not burden his imagination with ideas of the individual cases of future needs.

It is of course true that the man does not thus overcome for all time the temptations of immediate desires. The man has not lived who has not succumbed to the latter on one occasion or another. The frivolous and the improvident surrender to them with unbroken regularity. Perhaps even the average man might not be able to resist, if, like Robinson Crusoe, he were to find himself entirely isolated.

But human beings never are so entirely isolated. They live in society. In social communion they receive those psychological restraints which sustain them. Each man feels his steps controlled by his family, his associates and his surroundings. Others do not feel the temptations which he feels. They do not appreciate the excuses by which he endeavors to exculpate his uneconomic surrender. It is the urgency of the desires which he pleads in extenuation of the fault. His critics see the error into which he has fallen. They condemn him without mercy. So far as may be in their power, they seek to interfere by prohibitions, penalties or other measures which they hope may hold him to the performance of his economic duty. The rules of economic life are creations of society, just as are the laws of property. The individual forces called into play to carry these laws into effect have also been socially trained.

Here is one of the situations in which the purely individualistic theory misses fire in confining man to his own self and his most personal aims and resources. The preservation of the capital stock is not the sole concern of the temporary owner. It is of interest also to the family, the children, the brothers and sisters or more distant relatives who may be claimants in case of the owner's death. Thus in the older systems of jurisprudence the disposition of the family estate required the consent of the family. Today this consent is dispensed with in most cases. The explanation of this change may be the greater maturity of our economic judgment. It is thus allowable, without risks to the property in most cases, to vest in the incumbent the power of disposition. In former times the church and local authorities vied with each other in promulgating laws regulating undue consumption. Today sumptuary laws and all related laws of the past have fallen into disuse. The power of social custom is now sufficient in most cases to hold within bounds all such luxury as is calculated to endanger future well-being. Large groups of people today are conscious of a sentiment which induces a reasonable limitation of personal expenditure. They feel that one's substance is to be preserved, lest one incur the reproach of managing his affairs negligently. As a further restraint on parents there is added the care of children. Their future is to be provided for. A smaller number of productively employed persons feel a solicitude for the future of the poor and needy. This solicitude may even embrace the great concerns of the nation and humanity at large. Altruism carries the day against egotism. It secures to human foresight beneficial results beyond the length of the individual's life. In many cases the insecurity of man's life may contribute a large share of his solicitude for the future well-being of his children. It is not to be forgotten that even parental love is controlled by social forces which keep it alive and intensify it.

One may thus safely say that it is a sound maxim among all peoples of normal development to appraise alike the present and the future. It is generally observed by most individuals of such a people. Everywhere and at all times careless managers and spendthrifts are to be seen side by side with individuals who are anxiously making excessive provision for the future. The latter begrudge to the present those enjoyments which might readily be permitted. Beyond this group are to be found the most extreme aberrations of avarice. The greater number of mankind, however, steer a middle course between these two extremes. Thus when economic theory lays down the rule that present and future should be kept equally in mind, it is not describing an unrealized ideal. Rather, it realistically portrays the normal, sound type. It is a fitting application of our theoretical method that this balanced condition is idealized only in disregarding individual disturbances, which can probably never be entirely avoided in actual life.

None the less the undervaluation of future needs is sufficiently wide-spread to demand theoretical consideration. This condition is the source of the improvident loan negotiated by the spendthrift. Far more important than this group are those who suffer under the pressure of circumstances. The management of their affairs is influenced by these errors. Loans negotiated by individuals and even by the state in distress are liable to such undervaluation of the future. So also is the supply of labor and its wages among the poorest strata of the population. Those who have subsistence only for the day will always consume what they have. They will justifiably relegate to the future the needs of the morrow. Undervaluation of future needs is a widespread characteristic of the weak economy. The theory of the simple economy treats only of the idealized, strong type. However, the theory of exchange considers gradations of power. It would not complete its analysis if it did not give an appropriate amount of attention to the weak economy. In the appropriate place, therefore, we shall return to a consideration of the latter type.

§ 8. Commodities

Utility—Latent commodities and commodity-elements—Complementary qualities—Natural commodities and those of civilization—Material goods and personal services.

Böhm-Bawerk, *Rechte und Verhältnisse vom Standpunkte der volksw. Güterlehre*, 1881; Wieser, article, *Gut*, in Hdw. d. Stw. (and also further literature in the same source); Ammon, *Objekt and Grundbegriffe der Theoretischen Nationalökonomie*, 1911; Weyermann, *Nationalökonomische Begriffentwicklung des Vermögens und Volksvermögens, zugleich Beitnag zur volkswirtschaftlichen Güterlehre*, Jahrb. f. N., 1911.

The means of satisfying man's needs are found partly in nature. In part he derives them from his own forces. Some of the natural factors exercise tremendous power in their furtherance of economic ends. These are not subject to human interference. The sun is an example. But some of these factors are part of man's natural environment and may readily be controlled by him. They are thus fitted to be materials of economic activity and are especially conspicuous in the human economy. We speak of them as commodities.

Commodities are thus to be defined as useful objects subject to man's power of disposition. The theoretical concept of utility is as broad as the idea of use. It embraces every quality that is calculated to bring about the satisfaction of need, or that merely prepares it effectively. The fruit of the soil, which we consume, is useful; the soil which produces it is also useful. A work of art has utility; it satisfies the need which craves beauty. But those things are not considered as commodities, whose usefulness man has not yet discovered and which have consequently not yet been subjected to his power. One may call them latent commodities. An enormous advance in the possession of goods may be made within the shortest space of time merely by an increased knowledge of nature which enlarges our familiarity with its stores.

Akin to latent commodities, are those goods whose utility is known but of which man has so far never been able to avail himself effectively because he lacks the power or apparatus to do so. To understand this condition fully, it is necessary to comprehend clearly one point: no commodity possesses utility of its own nature. Menger has accurately stated that all goods are fundamentally complementary. Their effectiveness can only be assured thru the use of other goods. Thus, food will preserve life only if thirst can be quenched with water or some other beverage. The complementary relationship of the means of production is even more intimate. Materials without tools or without workers, workers without materials and tools can accomplish nothing. They are useless. If one, none the less, says that they are useful, he can only mean that he expects the missing element to be added. Some goods we know to possess useful qualities, but they cannot be usefully employed at present as the complementary agents are lacking. They may be called commodity elements. Where the means of mining and transporting coal do not exist, it is a commodity element. Even the existence of these elements in such unusable form is of considerable economic importance, for they may attain their full estate as commodities without other adaptation than the addition of the complementary goods. The soil of the desert will always remain sterile. But the fallow virgin soil of a newly settled country will yield enormous crops, as soon as the population has increased sufficiently to cultivate it.

Few goods are offered by nature ready for man's immediate use. She is more generous of those agents which enable him thru his labor to fashion satisfying commodities. Such agents also go ultimately to the gratification of needs. They too are commodities; productive goods they are called. Primitive man was able to apply his labors effectively to only a small number and variety of such goods. Their acquisition was so uncertain that only an insignificant number of human beings could be maintained—and these in only a primitive and precarious fashion. Step by step human ingenuity devised new varieties of these useful commodities. Goods of civilization have been added to those of nature. They were newly contrived. The materials in them rendered much more efficient service to our satisfactions. With less inconvenience they were directed to a far more extended series of needs. They added subsidiary uses to their principal one.

The result may be seen in the services of many classes of goods. Food does more than nourish the body in a rude and primitive way. Clothing is more than a bodily protection against cold. Houses give more than shelter. Each of these goods in its own fashion satisfies the demand of sanitation, of decency, of our sense of beauty, comfort, convenience and social consideration. The crude, natural good yields a simple satisfaction. This is often attended by many disadvantages and hazards. The commodity of civilization yields, if one may so express it, a refined, complexly composite satisfaction. In times of degeneration this is carried to extremes of exquisite pleasure.

Man's progress in the production of pleasurable goods has become possible only because of the increasing supply of commodities of civilization which have made growing demands upon his inventive spirit and his energy. The present enormous accumulations of capital are to be regarded as an outgrowth of civilization. These alone have given man access to the gifts of nature. The latter can be fully utilized only by means of such capital because nature is more lavish in her offerings of commodity-elements than of finished goods ready for use. Thus agriculture and cattle-raising utilize products of the soil most of which are lost to the hunter. He can use what the earth brings forth only in so far as it has served to nourish the game which he kills. The most sudden increase in man's possession of goods has occurred when the complementary capital goods of civilization have been added to the commodity elements found in the soil. It was only in the course of this process that the natural wealth of the soil, of which one likes to speak, became true wealth. Measured in terms of potential accomplishment, a country which lacks capital is a country of poverty.

We regard the useful objects of external nature merely as things. Some exception is made in the case of animals. We feel somewhat differently disposed towards them as their exhibitions of life remind us of our own vital feelings. But the other objects are nothing more to us than mere means of satisfaction.

Such objects are essentially distinguishable from personal services. These may also be employed as agents to the satisfaction of our needs. They may be used directly as personal or social services, or they may be employed indirectly as productive services in the manufacture of material goods. We are not only at liberty but are bound to make use of such services as means to our economy. No scheme of economic organization would be complete without them. Nevertheless, a fully developed moral sentiment will always distinguish between personal services and inanimate, useful things. Over and above the characteristic of utility, a second and essential one may be discerned in personal services. Expediency alone should not be allowed to determine this use. They must never become mere agents of gratification, for their employment is at the same time a personal experience. They live. They embrace vital aims. When goods are drawn into the sphere of the economy, they are entirely absorbed by it. Thus their destiny is determined forever. But personal service should never be thus entirely spent. It should always retain an independent, living significance.

The inherent value of the satisfaction is reflected in the goods which yield it. Personal services also have a value that is derived from their useful effects. But beside this they carry an independent, vital value which must never be allowed to die. Such services should be cherished and allowed to bear fruit. Commodities, as things, are controlled by the owners. But the worker should never be subjected to the employer to a degree that destroys the former's right of self-determination. The economic importance of labor is so great that it is perfectly true that those in power have always had designs on it. The history of mankind is replete with accounts of the struggles to obtain first the personal freedom of the worker and later the freedom of labor itself: as yet, these struggles have nowhere been ended.

In the theory of the simple economy actual conditions are idealized. It assumes the perfect relationship in which labor is legally and actually free.

The technical ability of men and their willingness to work—the latter fact is not to be overlooked—have been remarkably increased in the course of the development of our civilization. One may be bold enough to be confident of further progress. Like the historical liberation of latent commodities and commodity elements, the release of the latent productive energies of the race is a social process which has taken place in continuous waves. Great periods of discovery and invention, of technical progress and advances in organization are interrupted by others in which the development is slower. A static period may intervene. There may even be retrogression. In the course of all great changes crises occur. This is true even when the change represents an improvement of conditions. Human beings fail to observe proper proportions. Thru feverish activity they strive to reach the allowable upper limit and often overstep it. The theory of the simple economy disregards all these phenomena of change. It assumes a given, habitual state of economic efficiency. This is a static condition which has reached an equilibrium.

§ 9. Building up the Simple Economy

Free goods and economic goods—Consumption and management—The economic principle—Production and the technical arts—Productive stages and stems—The relationship of production.

The traditional division of economics into Production and Consumption is not theoretically serviceable. Economic theory has much to say of production and has said it often. Of consumption it says nothing, or just enough to veil its silence. Consumption, in the broadest sense of the term, is the destruction of commodities, particularly that which arises in the utilization of goods. In a narrower sense in contrast with production, consumption means that using up of commodities which takes place as needs are satisfied. There is also a further meaning of the term: the satisfaction of needs brought about by consumption, or merely the satisfaction itself.

But economic theory has never been interested in the physical process of consuming commodities. It will never treat of this. It is equally indifferent to the manner in which the satisfaction of needs, as such, may be made most complete. Economic theory regards it as the task of the moralist, physician or artist to teach which enjoyments are morally permissible, healthful or artistically valuable. Commodities are the agents of material pleasures, but it is no function of economic theory to show how these goods may be most delicately prepared. Those who are adepts in the practical art of living are the proper instructors in such matters. Consumption as such, the satisfaction of needs as such, is not an economic act at all.

It is precisely under those conditions in which goods are most abundant that their consumption has no economic importance. Assume, for example, that nature were to supply man with goods ready for use in the plenty of an ideal paradise. There would be no economy at all. The existence of the present extended economic organization is contingent upon the fact that there are few commodities that are available without stint, few of the so-called free goods. Within the narrow confines of urban life there is hardly one which is free to all except the air. In some localities beyond the urban centers water is accessible in natural plenty. So is arable land in sparsely settled countries. If all other goods which men apply to their needs were accessible under equally favorable conditions, they would no more regard consumption as an economic act than they do breathing and drinking where air and water exist in superfluity. To have economic consumption, the mere act of using up a good must be joined to another element which gives the act an economic character and marks the commodities as economic goods.

There is a conflict of opinion in economic theory as to the precise "something" by virtue of which commodities become economic goods. The connection is clear only in the case of what may be called "rarity-commodities." These form an exceedingly small group. Their supply cannot be augmented, certainly not appreciably so. In this class one finds works of art of unusual merit, particularly those which are legacies of old art-periods. However, most economic goods are obtained by systematic production and are turned out in quantities. These masses are large absolutely. Even in relation to human needs they are not small. Articles of food or all the various widely used necessities and utensils of the household serve as illustration.

There are two opinions as to what constitutes the distinguishing characteristic of this principal group of economic goods. One holds that in the case of these commodities also, man is subject to the pressure of a not wholly adequate supply, although there is no scarcity in the true sense of the word. The other maintains that in this instance man incurs the inconvenience of labor in order to produce such quantities as are needed. The first opinion is founded on economic quantitative relationships and might fitly be called the quantitative theory. However, the utilitarian theory is an even more apt name, because, as we shall later show, it deduces the origin of economic relationships and of value from utility which is a function of quantity. The second statement is the labor theory.

The contrast of these two opinions pervades the entire theory of economics. The spirit of the economy is a radically different one, according as the origin of the organization is traced back to one source or the other. Our study has not advanced sufficiently to allow this difference to be explained in detail at this point. We may not yet even define more accurately the economic quantitative relationship which the utilitarian theory presupposes. For the present we shall have to confine ourselves to setting up the quantitative relationship in a general manner. From this foundation we may ascertain the economic element of consumption.

He who does not command sufficient goods to consume without any restraint, must husband his resources. In a twofold sense he is obliged to be saving. First, he must not leave unused any part of the means at his disposal nor of their useful content. He must realize from them the largest degree of utility which can be obtained without harm. In the second place he is forced to accept the even more momentous task of choosing between alternative uses. His choice must be a use which satisfies a need of maximum intensity. Invariably the more important uses are to be selected, the less important ones passed over. It would be an error if he were to apply his means to the less important satisfactions while compelled to deny himself the more important ones.

Choice is guided by the rules of morality, a sense of beauty, considerations of hygiene or good taste. In most cases there are added the admonitions of economic prudence. Not until these are applied is there economic consumption. Consumption becomes an economic act when it is accompanied and controlled by a consideration of the available means. To consume means to partake of. Where goods are free, one may partake of them without restraint. There is no need of economizing. But where they are available in limited amounts and the maximum total satisfaction is to be derived from their use, one is held by economic foresight to the rule of sparing enjoyment, to the curtailment of those present pleasures which desire would lead one to seek.

Economics may better be divided as Economic Management and Production than as Consumption and Production.

Economic management is charged with the economic direction of consumption. As has been pointed out, this involves securing the most important satisfactions with the means available and barring the less important ones. Economic management is also charged with the duty of preventing the loss of economic goods thru deterioration or in any other manner. Therefore such goods must be suitably stored and protected. The personal services which are required for this management, must also be administered economically. The same principle applies in public management to public services.

It is the task of production to furnish the "household" with those goods which are lacking at any time. Free goods are never objects of production. Under some circumstances, however, they may be used as means of production which are all the more effective if they can be obtained in free abundance. Human labor is an indispensable factor of production, as the latter always consists in applying labor to certain material factors in order to obtain new commodities. Human labor, however, can never itself be an object of production. When man trains his power of labor, he does not produce in the strictest sense. He may be largely guided in such efforts by considerations of economic expediency. But labor is not merely a commonplace means to an end. It is part of life. Each act of learning is a significant personal experience.

In both economic management and production the aim of the economic principle is the same. This is the attainment of the maximum utility which may be realized under given, narrowly limited conditions. The producer must make an economic selection of his products. He must carefully consider his economic, productive agents. From a quantitative point of view, they must be protected from loss and deterioration. Furthermore, full advantage must be taken of their useful content, in so far as considerations of permanence will allow. In the case of the worker, consideration of his personal life may indicate somewhat narrower limits of exploitation.

The art or knowledge of the most effective methods of exploiting the useful content of productive goods is called technology. In its highest development this becomes a technical science. The control of the technical process is among the economic duties of the producer. But one should distinguish in production between the technical and the economic characteristics. Up to a certain point there is the same contrast here as exists between economics and consumption.

There are technical arts in which there is no economic calculation. The artist, for example, does not ask the price of canvas and paint. Regardless of these he pursues his work, looking only to the æsthetic effect. So also the man of wealth may perform experiments without counting the expense, if the enjoyment of research is all he seeks. Inventive genius is moved in the first instance by non-economic forces. Faced with a difficult technical task, the inventor is subject to a tension that finds release in experimentation. He gives only secondary consideration to the question: will the new technical achievement possess commensurate utility. Thus his technically penetrating mind will often gladly deceive him by arbitrary assumptions and unfounded expectations concerning economic difficulties. In all these cases which have been considered, the technical achievement is due in large part to the motor stimulus which seeks discharge. If all production were relieved of consideration of the amount of the productive means required; if it were all to become merely a happy exercise of power and audacity such as is found in play, in sport, in art or in science, the technical process of the production of commodities would be as little an economic act as is the process of their pleasurable consumption.

But as a matter of fact the controlling motive of production and also of the technical arts is to be found in purposive, economic desire. In by far the greater number of cases the technical plan and the controlling calculation of the available economic goods are interwoven from the start. One of the triumphs of the technical arts is the subjugation of want thru the attainment of the maximum, realizable efficiency. Technology is engaged for the most part in economic creation. Thus each step must be weighed in economic terms. The technician errs not only economically but technically when his calculations are confined to his immediate ends. The problem which he faces is not completely solved; he does not gain his end by the simplest means. Hence it follows that he does not achieve those maximum results which are his goal. His calculations must be well considered in every aspect. Profits and losses must be accurately entered as they arise at various times or in various phases of his operations.

The technical arts have made an almost endless variety of goods accessible. But economic theory needs to insert in its outline of production only a few indispensable details of these advances.

The first essential is the arrangement of the stages of production. We may keep Menger's apt designation of orders. The most important group to meet our needs are those goods which are supplied to the household for daily use or enjoyment. This includes food, clothing, shelter and furniture. From the point of view of the satisfaction of our needs this group may be considered as the first order. From the technical standpoint such goods fall in the last stage as ultimate products. In this sense they are spoken of in the market simply as products. All other commodities, the production goods which are required for creative purposes, may be classed together as goods of higher or more remote orders. Machinery, raw materials and land will serve for illustration.

Most of this group are themselves obtained by production. They are produced productive commodities. When one contrasts them with the materials from which they were created, they are products. In contrast with the goods which they serve to produce they are productive commodities. Thus it is that the group of goods of the higher order must be divided into subclassifications. A genealogy of production may be arranged in second, third or even higher orders. In tracing this history one starts from the ultimate product and falls back upon those goods which might be regarded by the consumer as partly fabricated. From these one passes to the goods which served to form them. Ultimately one reaches the raw materials and the primary forms. The final, most remote order consists of those goods which, like land, are provided by nature without the assistance of man.

This stratification of production is not complete if it concerns itself only with the material organization of the fabricating process in its narrow sense. One must include all other stages which are essential to the process. Thus the transportation of goods from the place of manufacture to the place of use must be included. The development of the means of transportation increases the series. The provision of the modern highways of transportation is an enormous process. It calls in itself for a large number of stages. Furthermore, productive labor is complementary to the material goods. These services must be included in the series of orders. The farmer's labor in cultivating the soil, for example, should occupy the same stage as the soil itself, as the plow which he uses or the seed which he plants.

But productive efforts are always to be regarded as of the highest, most remote order. They are not themselves produced. Their source is, therefore, not to be particularly mentioned in the genealogy.

Economic theory must also observe the productive stems. As we shall use this term, it is intended to convey the picture of all the dependent commodities and their relationship to the generating, productive element. It embraces all such goods down to the ultimate products. In this sense there is a coal-stem which starts with coal and embraces all products in whose manufacture coal is consumed. So also there is an iron-stem and another of unskilled labor.

There is a horizontal relationship as well as this vertical one. To describe this we shall use the shorter term, productive relationship.[1] Every product is thus related to every other commodity that has some stem-element in common with it. Thus there is a horizontal relationship between all products of the stem of coal, of iron or of unskilled labor.

The technology of modern production is exceedingly complex. It has given this productive relationship an extraordinary extent. Modern production combines in each of its numerous stages a variety of productive elements into organic and inorganic compounds. In this way every product has numerous stem-elements and thru these it derives a great number of collatorally related branches. A product of iron is presumably also one of coal, unskilled labor and an entire series of other productive elements. It is simultaneously related to many stems. In as many directions as there are stems, there are productively related goods.

Let us imagine a complete genealogy of production. It will show both the vertical and horizontal relationship of all productive goods and all products. One may trace in such a chart the functional organization of production: i. e., the course which production follows. But the chart shows more than this. It shows also the paths followed by the productive calculation in forecasting the plan of production. The practical labor of production starts in the remotest order to end with ultimate products. The calculations of the producer, on the other hand, move backward from the ultimate products. From these he traces the course to the necessary productive elements. From these in turn the full extent of the productive relationship may be traced in order to strike a proper balance.

In practice such a calculation would almost inevitably be erroneous. In each individual case the paths to be traversed are too diverse. The individual producer includes in his calculation the ready-made results of the market. These are formed on the basis of calculations of all other subjects of the economic process. In a social model-state this entire calculation would have to be bound together as one. Our idealizing method allows the assumption that this enormous task is being faultlessly performed.

Economic theory is not forced to trace finer distinctions in this genealogy than to differentiate three elements: personal labor, the cultural formation of capital, and land, the gift of nature. Furthermore it should separate "cost-productive-means" (see § 15) from other productive goods. Starting with these assump-

[1] *Produksions verwandschaft:* Production-relationship is a better translation but is so lacking in euphony that productive relationship, relationship of production and (as a verb) productively related have been used synonymously thruout.

tions, one may interpret all the basic relations and may solve all the fundamental problems of the simple economy. But this simplicity makes it all the more necessary to give a careful explanation of the fundamental theory of labor, of capital, of land and also of the important concept of the "cost-productive-means." Before passing to these considerations, however, we must end our discussion of the structure of the simple economy by showing the unity which is implicit in the manner by which it is built up.

§ 10. The Unity of the Economy

In reference to establishing an "economic statics"—The maintenance of an "economic equilibrium" or an "economic level"—General, narrower and broader margins of use—Marginal needs—The economic principle and marginal use.

Unless there be a natural economic residue, it is obvious that every individual economy based exclusively on exchange must form a unit. In the last analysis its current receipts are summed up in a single figure of money-income. This gives a definite expression to the inner unity. The expenses of the household are to be met from this income in such a manner as to proportion each item of expenditure to the general economic situation. There is unity in point of time as well; for each period there is to be a fair balance of receipts and expenditures.

The natural, simple economy is entirely detached from exchange. It therefore lacks the connecting medium, money. Nevertheless the unity persists. Such unity is given by the domestic, economic production which foreshadows the magnitude of the entire economy. This production is unified in the labor of the producer. All the products belong to the one stem of this labor and are thus bound together. The producer seeks the most economical exploitation of his forces. This purpose connects all resulting products. Any change in the conditions affecting a single group of products must influence others thru the common factor of labor; for it follows that, as more or less effort is applied in one direction, less or more of it is available in others.

Modern economic production is social. It is also externally unified by the medium of money and the market. But is there also an internal unity? This social production may be analyzed into thousands and millions of individual establishments. Thus owners are legally independent of one another. Each man is guided by his own individual interest. The unifying purpose, that is obvious in the household, is lacking. If we were to assume in the theory of the simple economy that we are describing a social process directed by a single intelligence, it might almost appear that we had idealized conditions beyond allowable limits. One might raise the question, may one simplify where multifariousness is of the essence?

However, despite its extreme differentiation and manifold contrasts, the economic process of today is actually a whole. It is not a unit in the true sense of the term; and yet it functions with an all-embracing homogeneity which may be idealized and represented as unity. This condition is founded in production. All productive stems are related to one another. The products of the stem of unskilled labor are more than the products of labor. A similar statement may be made for those of the soil. Both groups belong to other stems as well and are productively related to their products. Some products have all stems in common, fully related products one might call them. A table and a chest made by a carpenter of the same kind of wood and other materials thruout are examples. Others are only partially related; they have only certain stems or some one stem in common. But it would scarcely be possible to name one product which has no such connection with any one of the many other goods in use. There may be specific instances of products which have no stem in common. But in such instances one finds some third commodity which establishes an indirect relationship between the first two because they both have some stem in common with it. The intimate affiilation of productive groups, all of which ultimately coalesce into one all-embracing productive body, is fittingly described by their accepted designation, branches of production.

Owing to this general unity, every considerable change in supply [1] or demand that occurs within one stem will communicate its effect to all the others as well. All productive branches of which unskilled labor is a constituent will be affected, if the number of such workers is diminished. The influence, however, will be broader than this. Indirectly, most or all other branches will be concerned. Materials and other goods to which labor may be applied, will be set free in the branches which are directly affected. This release will modify conditions wherever the same materials are habitually used. If the primary impulse be sufficiently strong, its effect may be communicated to the most remote branches of production. A far reaching adjust-

[1] Trans. note: Wieser is using *Vorrat* thruout Part I. It clearly stresses physical volume. Later he uses *Angebot* to introduce the concept of quantity at a price. In the English, "supply and demand" often loses some of its physical significance. The translator tried to use "stock" for *Vorrat*. It is still retained occasionally. However, Wieser has used so many terms that are not common in English, that it seemed wise to drop any unnecessary deviation from common usage.

ment will be made. The entire plan of production will require careful revision to reëstablish the realization of the greatest possible total utility. Such movements will be greatest in those branches most nearly related to the first one affected. The disturbance must extend in all directions, however, if the initial impulse is sufficiently strong.

A number of mathematical economists have perceived this unity and have been led to try to exalt economic theory into an economic statics.[1] This would conceive the economic organization as a unitary system moved by some inner law. It strives always to maintain an inner equilibrium. Wherever this is disturbed, the organization endeavors to reëstablish it by compensating movements. In this sense, too, one hears of levels of economic action, of housekeeping and of production.

This static conception is useful to economic theory: it stresses most forcibly the unity of political economy. However, it threatens to introduce the methods of mathematical physics, which are not suited to the subject-matter of economics. There is a further and even more serious risk that by the use of this method heterogeneous, though associated, ideas might creep in. In its most extreme form, this statics would treat theory like a physical science of economic goods; it would nearly eliminate the active impulse of the economic sense of mankind. But even when it does not go to these lengths, it simplifies its assumptions concerning man in his activities and concerning goods and needs in such a manner as to allow the deduction of a condition of perfect equilibrium. In so doing, however, it contradicts the facts of experience. No adjustment is ever effected[2] which tends to establish a condition of strict equilibrium, a perfect level. This approach to economic theory, however, is barred by two additional facts, even if one disregard the disturbances which arise in human volition.

The first of these is found in connection with a study of goods. It is the diversity of natural wealth in terms of commodities. In southern countries the grapevine flourishes, but wood and coal may be more scarce. The population of such a country may well cultivate the vine more assiduously and enjoy its product more freely than some

[1] See Furlan, article *Economic Equilibrium*, in Hdw. d. Stw. for an excellent summary.

[2] Trans. note: The translator has frequently taken the liberty of omitting the adjective, "economic," which appears in the German text. If one be meticulous, it is probably necessary to reassure the reader constantly that the statements made apply only to economic activity. To avoid endless repetition, the translator has taken it for granted that the reader assumes that the statements apply only to economic life. This particular statement should read "ever effected in economic life."

northern people. They may also fail to protect themselves in their houses so thoroughly from the rigors of winter months. But one is scarcely entitled to censure them for a neglect to adjust the satisfaction of their needs economically; their conduct is regulated by the circumstances. They adjust themselves to prevailing conditions; they enjoy abundance where they find it and suffer privations where the means of satisfaction are but sparingly offered by nature. In the face of such diversities in the accessibility of goods it would be a most uneconomic utilization of commodities if a strict adjustment were made. Where there is pronounced scarcity of one item, the margin of satisfaction will have to be closely drawn. It will come relatively high as measured on the general scale of desire. In the case of exceptional abundance the margin will be more extended, in contrast with the bulk of goods whose utilization is more narrowly confined by their productive relationships.

Rather than to economic equilibrium, theory should turn its attention to margins of use. We shall endeavor to distinguish a general margin from a narrower and a wider one which may be observed where commodities are either scarce or abundant. In the household this is the margin of domestic use; in production it is the productive limit. In both these instances the same three types of margin are to be distinguished.

The second obstacle to the static approach deals with the scale of needs. Even if one were to assume that goods were evenly distributed in all localities, it would never be permissible to reach the same point of satiety for all needs. The graduations of such scales are not exactly commensurate. On any general scale of desires the tension induced by the simple needs of life is completely relaxed at a much higher point than is the case with mere pleasurable needs. For those who have ample means to gratify the latter generously, the satisfaction of the former ceases at a point much higher than the general margin of use. All those needs whose point of relaxation is at or below the general margin of use we shall call marginal needs. In so doing, as might be expected, we presuppose the point of their highest tension to be above this limit. They thus admit of economic satisfaction. In the case of graduated needs, the upper grades may fall above the margin of use, while the lower ones may be excluded from economic satisfaction.

The doctrine of an economic statics does not recognize any of these facts. It disregards both the values of a condition of scarcity and of superabundance. It looks upon all needs as marginal needs in a constant state of flux. This simplification is a great aid in the understanding of certain fundamental economic relationships; but it obstructs the solution of other problems which, as we shall see later, are of no inconsiderable importance and, as much as others, demand theoretical explanation.

With this statement we may proceed to a more accurate formulation of the economic principle of the greatest possible utility than we have so far been able to offer. This demands that the use of economic goods shall be as extensive as is consistent with their actual occurrence and with the relative intensities of the dependent needs. The general margin of utilization is to be established so that it shall include the greatest possible number of degrees of utility. Complete satiety is to be obtained for all more narrowly bounded needs. But, furthermore, the narrower margins of use of scarcity values, as well as those of abundance, are to be indicated so as to allow for the most extensive gratification possible. The maximum total satisfaction is the decisive factor in every individual instance. Each economic means of satisfaction is to be disposed of in such a manner as will add the greatest utility to the otherwise assured total. No use is to be countenanced so long as some alternative disposition would result in a more beneficial effect.

§ 11. The Theory of Products

The assumption that products may be augmented at will—The economic quantitative relation of products—Marginal products, products of narrower and wider margins of use, products of relatively abundant occurrence.

We have now reached a point at which we may pass from the description of productive relationships and the unity of production to the economic quantitative relation of products. This will be described in its various forms.

The classical doctrine interprets the fundamental economic relations of products in terms of the labor theory. Ricardo, who is taken in this connection as in many others to represent this school, admits the factor of scarcity in the case of a few types of product which can be produced only in limited quantities; for example choice wines, the grapes for which only develop well in certain localities. In the case of most goods which are obtained in the regular course of production, however, he asserts that there are no definite, ascertainable, quantitative limits. It is only necessary that "we stand ready to apply the labor which may be required." To this day the German textbook speaks of "goods augmented ad lib." Most industrial products are classed among these. Agricultural products are not of this type as their production is limited by specific conditions of the soil.

Ricardo and the German text-book here confuse the technical and economic possibilities of increase. This occurs because they adhere to the view-point of the simple economy. For this reason they fail to grasp the facts of the general relationship of products and the unity of production, which are conspicuous only when the economy is seen as a social whole. Of course it is technically possible to produce clothes, shoes or many other manufactures in quantities so great as to over-supply the existing need. However, any such increase is economically precluded. It conflicts with the principle of the greatest utility. Clothes and shoes may be produced in excess of the need only by simultaneously decreasing the manufacture of other productively related goods. This means that things which are not suited for use and are therefore useless, are turned out at the expense of others which could be used and would consequently affect an increase in available utilities. One may not assume that clothes or shoes can be made in unlimited quantities without compelling a retrenchment in related lines. If such an assumption were made, it would lead logically to the statement that mass-production may be indefinitely expanded where there are no specific, restraining conditions and "we stand ready to apply the required labor." This is utopian. It contradicts all experience. The latter shows beyond a shadow of doubt that the total stock which may be produced is always less than are total needs.

It is a matter of common observation that households which command large or even moderate incomes are abundantly supplied in point of many needs. Complete satiety is often effected. Such families have accumulated stores that assure such gratification in the event of all but the most extraordinary disturbances. Even in the case of lower income groups, where actual poverty is not present, the most urgent needs are usually fully satisfied. In these cases there are sufficient quantities of coarse food to allay hunger and to preserve strength and health; enough clothes and shoes to afford protection from cold; an adequate supply of all the other necessaries of life to keep things going, though it may at times be scantily. It is not a utopian dream to assume that such a condition obtains in times of peace in countries of fertile soil. Here, in the familiar saying of Henry IV, every peasant has his pullet in the pot.

And yet in all these cases where the supply is adequate to allow complete satiety, the quantities involved are held in economic proportions. One and all are husbanded under the pressure of economic foresight. None of them should be used thoughtlessly or without weighing consequences. Were this not done, one of two things would occur: either the particular needs involved would not be fully satisfied, or, if the losses were to be recovered by subsequent acquisition, a shortage would result in productively related goods. If any appreciable portion of these goods were to perish unused, the total obtainable utility would always be reduced.

This economic proportionality is not confined to cases of distress, poverty or insufficient means. It extends to all cases where an assured superfluity does not prevail. It applies to all products which cover needs with high margins of use as well as to all those which, measured by the general margin, satisfy marginal needs.—The latter group of goods we shall call marginal products.—But there is a quantitative proportion even in the case of those abundantly supplied goods whose margins of use are low; even these may not be obtained at pleasure. They are still well within the universal bond which holds productively related goods. In the case of this group the community is more favorably situated only in so far as nature more generously rewards the means employed than she does in regard to the mass of products. These goods may be obtained with relative ease, but there is no absolute excess of supply.

Where the entire scheme of production is correctly planned, all products without exception preserve quantitative economic proportionality. An excess of supply at any point could only occur when, thru error or some disturbance, more had been produced or become available than human needs call for. Great improvements in productive methods have been made but they have never been able to change this condition. These industrial advances have made it possible to increase production during prosperous times more rapidly than population grows. The quantitative relationship of goods is thus improved not only for the rich but for broad strata of the population. But so far mankind has not even approximated a condition in which an indefinite production of goods could be ensured by the mere will to labor.

The theory of products must be sustained by a theory relating to the agents of production. All the mistakes into which the theory of value and price have fallen, have had their origin in some error or lapse of thought in regard to the elementary relations of the economy. The more circumspect and mature the preparatory investigations of the fundamental relations of productive agents, the more precise and clear will be the consequent theory of value and price. We begin with the theory of labor.

§ 12. THE THEORY OF LABOR

Labor theory and the theory of labor—The onus of labor and the economic principle—The economic quantitative relation of labor.

J. Shields Nicholson, *Principles of Political Economy,* 2nd. ed. 1902; Patten, *Theory of Prosperity,* 1902; Whitaker, *Labor Theory of Value,* 1904; Salz, *Arbeitswert und Arbeitsleid,* Z. f. V. vol. XX.

The contrast of the theory of utility and the labor theory runs thruout economics. It becomes sharpest in the doctrine of labor. The labor theory traces the source of economics and the measure of value back to labor exclusively. In its exposition, the theory of labor is the core. The significance of the labor theory was vastly increased when the socialists discovered the scientific foundation of their system in the classical presentation. The theory of utility gives a far less unique position to the doctrine of labor which stands side by side with theories of capital and of land.

Labor is the dominant force in production. It selects the ends. As a court of last appeal it determines the standards of production. It directs the natural forces involved in the productive process. Capital and land are at all times merely the tools of the worker. He is the producer. By worker is meant, of course, not only the wage worker but everyone who actively furthers the process of production in any manner. All products are exclusively those of the worker and in this sense are wholly labor products.

Is this statement true, however, in any sense? Are not the products at all times also those of the soil which contributes in bringing them forth? Is it possible that the popular term, "fruits of the soil," is entirely absurd? Furthermore, are they not also all products of capital, which lends its aid? Must we not recognize land and capital by the side of labor as active factors in production?

Carried to its logical conclusion, the labor theory returns the answer that all production is due to labor alone. Land and capital cannot be accepted as factors of production. The account of costs has only those of labor to consider. The entire system of the labor theory has been rigidly constructed to establish the proposition that all costs of production are to be shown to be ultimately the outcome of labor. Capital is to be eliminated from this reckoning by showing that it is only a special manifestation of labor—it is true that Ricardo here actually makes a reservation in favor of the interest on capital. The reservation shatters his entire artificial system.—Land is to be eliminated by the theory of ground-rent. Ricardo has made this a part of his system in order to show that land is never an element in the account of costs nor in the calculation of prices. We shall not be able to examine these assertions until we come to the theory of capital and the theory of land. We shall be able to dispose of them finally only with the doctrine of productive attribution.

The scope of our immediate inquiry is narrower. We shall disregard the significance of land and capital and try to determine what feature confers an economic character upon labor as such. To this end our assumptions are so formulated as to bring labor under consideration as a single economic factor. We make the idealizing assumption that all the material aids at labor's command are furnished in such superfluity that they need not be husbanded. Imagine a Crusoe lording it over more land than he can possibly cultivate by his individual efforts. Let him be providentially endowed with tools and other capital goods in such abundance that he can never be embarrassed by a shortage of such commodities. Let us assume that he has to take account of nothing but the efforts of his two hands. Let us then ask in what way he will have to make an economic disposition of his labor power.

The explanation offered by the labor theory is surprising from the beginning. When examining land and capital it constantly emphasizes the superior creative power of labor. But as soon as labor is examined in isolation, this falls wholly into abeyance. It is not the creative power and the joy of accomplishment which is dwelt upon, but the toil and danger, the burden of labor, the encroachments on "peace of mind, freedom and happiness" which work, according to Adam Smith, inflicts on the laborer.

Truly, this condemnation of the burden of labor is well founded. Any labor whatever, when continued under compulsion without rest, results in fatigue. The latter grows until the motor stimulus is no longer felt at all and a feeling of aversion appears. In the end even the strongest effort of will cannot overcome this revulsion. If the over-exertion continues beyond this point, it brings in its train serious injury to bodily health and vigor.

The burden of labor has given human intelligence as well founded a motive for economic management as that which results from the usefulness of commodities. If labor were to be performed in every instance with the joyful alacrity which accompanies the overflow of individual energy, productive labor would have no more economic character than exists in the case of the consumption of part of an inexhaustible supply. Fully as much as the pressure of the economic quantitative relation is essential to the explanation of the economy by the theory of utility, the pressure of fatigue resulting from exertion is necessary to the labor theory. In production economic activity is no more a liberated enjoyment of active effort, than it is in consumption an unrestrained enjoyment of means of satisfaction. In either connection there is care and a solicitude for future needs.

Human happiness demands that the burden of labor be reduced to a minimum. Thus the labor theory gives a convincing explanation of all those acts which the theory of utility explains by resort to the economic quantitative relation. This is true not only of labor itself but of the products of labor. If men would reduce the burden of labor to a minimum, they must conserve the working power and consequently also the products of that labor. All of them are called upon to make an economic selection of products, the objects of their efforts, and to preserve and use in the most careful manner those goods which have been acquired thru their work. Everyone is familiar thru his general experience with the manner of motivation in all its ramifications.

The labor theory thus appealed to facts amply evidenced in daily life. This accounts for the promptness of the scientific recognition of the labor theory. It afforded a convincing explanation of a series of the simpler economic relationships long before the theory of utility had been sufficiently elaborated to be consistent with the most conspicuous experiences of economic life. Indeed they were the keenest minds who turned in the early days of our science to the labor theory. It was in this direction that the greater probability of success then lay. It was only when it became apparent that despite the most strenuous efforts no complete explanation could be expected from this quarter that investigators felt compelled to renew their attempts by means of the theory of utility.

To estimate correctly the influence which considerations of the burden of labor or of utility may exert in a given case, it is necessary to recognize one fact clearly. In any particular instance only one influence or the other is decisive. They never act jointly. Let us illustrate by the simplest possible example the fundamental idea of the labor theory.

Let us assume that by years of application an author has completed a large and important work in manuscript. He will of course wish to preserve this document to the best of his ability. In this wish he will be prompted either by the "motive of labor" or by the "motive of utility." In no case will he be moved by both. Considerations of utility would govern him, if he felt that the manuscript could never be duplicated if it were lost. He would fear that the loss might deprive him of the fruits of his labors; in terms of the theory of utility, he would lose certain utilities. But in case he felt that he had the power to replace the manuscript if the need arose, the loss would not be irreparable. However, it would necessarily involve rewriting that which was once finished. In this act there would be no renewal of his earlier creative enthusiasm. All that he would experience is the repetition of an onerous task which he might well wish to avoid. Speaking generally, the creative labor involved in any particular instance either can or cannot be repeated. In the first case the interest in the conservation of the product is due to a desire to avoid the renewed burden of labor. Where the effort cannot be repeated, one economizes to avoid loss thru the destruction of utility. Both motives cannot govern for it is obvious that labor cannot be repeatable and non-repeatable at one and the same time.

Speaking from an economic point of view, work may be duplicated where the means of labor are present in superabundance. It cannot be repeated where this quantity is of economic proportions. The labor-motive, then, applies in cases where labor is to be had in abundance. Considerations of utility control when it is economically limited.[1]

Utility gives little concern, where labor is abundant. The utility which is derived through work may always be obtained, if one is willing to incur the required effort. But for all that utility does not cease to be considered. It is this consideration which excites the desire and induces work. But under the condition here assumed it does not excite economic foresight. One is confident that he can procure whatever he may want. Furthermore, economic foresight would never be aroused, if labor were performed without travail and risks. All of the requirements of the economic principle are satisfied when the particular benefit is derived with the minimum, necessary burden of labor. Naturally, such utilities as are less than this burden must be abjured.

On the other hand where the total quantity of labor is limited, the amount of the benefit which may be derived from its expenditure is also limited. For the sake of these utilities alone one must economize. The degree of foresight which will be exercised is contingent upon the resulting benefit. Expenditures of effort are graded according to the utility which will result from the outlay. The burden of labor

[1] Trans. note: The translation should read "remains within economic quantitative proportions." This term which Wieser uses frequently is clumsy in English. There is no simple, exact synonym. The translator will occasionally sacrifice perfect precision to gain ease. Where there can be any doubt as to the context, he will return to the longer phrase.

does not cease to receive active consideration; but under the assumed conditions it does not excite economic foresight. The latter has already been awakened by attention to the dependent benefits. Neither does it intensify this foresight, for the burden which is accepted is never greater than the anticipated benefit. In most cases it is much less. Considerations of this burden are purely personal and accompany productive labor. Much of the happiness of human life depends on the manner in which this burden is borne. However, it only indirectly influences economic foresight as the supply of labor would be greater and there would be less pressure from the quantitative proportion if labor could be performed without fatigue.

We must now examine the economic proportionality of labor itself. The ultimate solution of our problem lies at the bottom of this analysis.

The history of human economy begins with an excess not only by natural forces, which lie fallow in uncultivated soil, but also of human forces, which are dormant for want of economic employment. In the earliest periods the forceful peoples found an outlet for the desire for action in wars and the excitement and hardship of the chase. Effeminate peoples perished in idleness. Both groups had labor-power greater than could be economically employed. Yet both lived a precarious existence of privations and hardships.

Then came a change. The workers were slowly trained in skill in the arts. Little by little the complementary capital wealth grew. With these two conditions the opportunity of employment and the demand for labor increased. Finally the existing quantities of labor became less than the potential demand.

The increasing scarcity of labor is not indicative of decay. It is rather a sign of increasing wealth. In the transitional periods adolescent society is happiest. It is in these that educative and economic ease originate. The overflowing volume of national vigor has not yet been exhausted by the burden of productive labor. During later periods this condition changes. When the population becomes enormous, the requirements for the preservation of life become more and more difficult for the multitude, notwithstanding all industrial progress. The burden of labor becomes more and more oppressive.

In all highly developed economies labor is proportionately so unfavorably situated that the utmost efforts are demanded of the workers. All experience indicates that in no such nation can the productive efforts of the workers be so increased that such acts may be repeated. The quantities of labor are on the whole as little "augmentable at will'' as the products are. Where production has miscarried, those acts will be repeated which are indispensable to the replacement of urgently needed goods. Thus the work of agricultural cultivation will be begun anew when an unfavorable winter destroys the seed. But such repetition is only possible by curtailing the amount of labor that would otherwise have been applied in some other direction.

By virtue of the bonds of productional relationships the economic process is a unit. If labor once becomes interwoven with the economic quantitative proportion, any particular change in its application will be felt in every other section of the process. There are everywhere workers seeking employment who are unable to find it. There are idlers in plenty and productive spheres not fully operative. None the less it is certain that even an organization which succeeded in placing all laborers at work would not result in a large enough influx of labor to offset the loss that would result from an adequate relief of unduly burdened workers. There is an urgent cry in our times for a reduction of this load which presses upon the masses. This would seem to furnish ample proof not only of the fact that labor has become interwoven with the general economic quantitative proportion but also that the relationship of available labor to demand has become most inauspicious.

The advocates of the labor theory like to select their illustrations from the scenes of the early beginnings of an economic organization. They picture the rude conditions of tribes who live as hunters, fishers or in other primitive fashion. This choice is not purely accidental for it is only in these early historical periods that labor has that quantitative proportion which is an essential presupposition to a convincing presentation of the labor theory. The reader can follow the argument when he is told that the economic consideration of a tribe of hunters concerns itself with the quantity of labor necessary to kill the game: that, for example, a beaver is regarded as twice the value of a deer, if on the average it takes twice the time to kill a beaver. The reader understands this because the modern man also is not unfamiliar with the motive of work. To be sure, labor which is economically employed no longer furnishes an opportunity to understand this problem; but even today there are plenty of activities which function under such conditions as revive the labor-motive. Those tasks with which a man busies himself in his leisure hours, when he is free from the preoccupation of his business, are often of this sort. To many extra-economic activities the strict concept of available supply and demand cannot be applied simply because they are non-economic. The labor-motive is applicable in these cases now as heretofore. Because of the experiences which all of us have under these conditions, we become familiar with this motive and learn to measure our cares by time-duration and other conditions which obtain while we are subjected to the burden of labor. The labor theory gains its convincing effect by an appeal to such non-economic phenomena as these. By this means it lays bare to our understanding the economic relations of a bygone age. In the economic conditions of today it no longer finds support.

Strictly the labor theory is valid only for services performed under stress. It does not embrace work which is cheerfully rendered as a result of the creative impulse, that stimulus which makes the genius. The theory has no place for labor in the highest sense of greatest efficiency and merit. Even in the case of that work to which it does apply, the mere measure of the burden sustained is not sufficient; the useful effect of the activity is frequently greatly in excess of the inconvenience suffered.

On the other hand a theory, which derives the economic standard of labor from a measure of the useful effect, embraces all types of work. It includes the highest as well as the lowest kinds, those services most gladly rendered as well as those most oppressively felt, as long as they fulfill their economic end. This theory gives to each variety the position which it should hold. It recognizes labor as the force which has relieved the pressure of the economic quantitative relation and which has won the advance from the precarious margins of early times to the proud condition of modern abundance. It thus does ample justice to the economic effect and creative force of labor.

§ 13. The Theory of Capital

The contrast of capital and land—The complete process of production—The service of direct production and capital reproduction—Materials, tools—The concept of capital, capital goods and fractional capitals—The service of capital in the progressive economy—Improvements in and increases of capital—Capital and labor.

Menger, *Zur Theorie des Kapitals*, J. f. N., N. F., vol. XVII; Landry, *L'intérêt du capital*, 1904; Irving Fisher, *Nature of capital and income*, 1906; Spiethoff, *Lehre vom Kapital*, E. d. K.; Böhm-Bawerk, *Einige strittige Fragen der Kapitalstheorie*, 1900; and, *Zur neuesten Literatur über Kapital und Kapitalzins*, J. f. V., vol. XV and XVI (in this connection see Clark's *Entgegung* and Böhm-Bawerk's *Replik*, vol. XVI); Jacoby, *Streit um den Kapitalsbegriff*, 1908; Fetter, *Economic Principles*, 1915.

All references in the theory of the simple economy to the nature of capital must be such as will meet the approval not only of the supporters of the existing order but also of the most radical apostles of socialistic views. To accomplish this, it is necessary to eliminate from the current, practical concept every reference to the pecuniary form of capital and to private property. Every suggestion of capitalistic power and exploitation of workers must be banished. The concept must therefore refer exclusively to natural economic capital, the indispensable aid to all effective production. Thus when we use the term, capital, in the theory of the simple economy, reference is made to this narrower, natural form.

The producer is accustomed to the use of money as a medium of exchange. He is not familiar with the concept of natural capital. In his speech, as in the accounting of his business, he adheres at first to the monetary form of capital. And yet the natural form is by no means unknown to him. On the contrary it is the core and substance of his idea, where money represents the economic transactions. He is fully conscious of the manner in which the natural form is transcribed into pecuniary terms. Therefore we shall find that all the facts necessary to describe natural capital are available in daily experience and in practical concepts of capital.

Natural capital consists of capital goods. The relation of the two is essential to an understanding of the latter. Therefore we shall not be in a position to define accurately the nature of such a commodity, until we shall have formed a definite notion of the nature of capital itself. Our inquiry will start with a determination of the occurrence of capital. Then we shall endeavor to formulate the concept. Finally we shall return to the exact meaning of the term, capital commodity.

In their occurrence capital goods are essentially distinguished from land and other natural goods which are offered to man in the earth and above it, in the water or in the atmosphere. The inventory of the farmer is made up of animate and inanimate objects. That of the industrialist comprises raw materials and manufactured articles, tools, implements and machinery. These are all the work of man and are fashioned as the result of historical development. Capital goods are the products of civilization. To this extent they are correctly designated by the traditional term, produced means of production.

It is quite correct to regard the soil also as a cultural product, as it is fashioned step by step by the human hand. Cultivation of the soil is an accurate description of the manifold labors of leveling, draining and clearing and of the never-ending detail of annually repeated planting. These do more than affect the surface conditions. They become an integral part of the soil itself and transform its nature. Nevertheless it is obvious that one may not properly speak of the soil as a produced means of production. Cultivated soil is the somewhat changed, natural commodity. But in its substance it is always too homogeneous and pristine to be considered the result of human labor.

On the other hand dwellings, buildings for agricultural and industrial use and industrial improvements of all kinds show the characteristics of produced means of production. So also does every capital commodity, which is attached to the soil in the course of economic pursuits, provided it does not coalesce with the soil so completely as to lose its identity but rather maintains the latter in such a manner as to require economic care. All goods of the latter sort are in their nature essentially detached from the soil. They resemble ore taken from the ground or fruit when it has been gathered. They are clearly distinguishable as products of human industry.

As products, all capital goods are under the pressure of economic quantitative proportionality. Thus it is possible to increase the supply of this or that particular commodity beyond existing needs, but one is bound by the economic principle to observe in each case the limits imposed by the given, total wealth. However, just as the quantitative relation is not necessarily one of want, scarcity and rigid restraint, so in the case of capital wealth also this is not to be expected. The enormous accumulations of capital during the past century do not nullify the economic nature of this wealth. So long as the utopian assumption is not realized and capital wealth does not guarantee unlimited affluence, such goods will have to be treated as economic commodities.

Capital goods are produced by man. Therefore they are perishable. They cannot perform their productive services as constantly as can the enormous natural forces and stores. The latter are practically inexhaustible and even in cultivated soil retain an almost undiminished effect. We do not mean to say that perishable constituents may not be held by the soil also. Much of that elemental content, which provides the fertility of the soil, may be destroyed. Ore is nowhere so plentiful that mining operations may not exhaust it. However, after all spoils have been allowed for, there still remains in the ground an inexhaustible substance of natural matter which human agencies and even the most powerful natural forces cannot destroy. Confining the theoretical concept of land to this substance, we may appropriately contrast the economic characteristics of the soil and of capital goods by describing the former as inconsumable, the latter as consumable.

The periods of time, over which capital goods are consumed in the course of this productive service, differ greatly. Those which make up liquid capital disappear during a single act of utilization. The effective service of coal, for example, cannot be delivered except as it is burned. This group also includes such raw material as is transformed in the course of manufacture into a differently constituted commodity. Thereafter such material is dropped from the raw-material inventory of the business, just as the burned coal was dropped, in order to reappear on another page of the account in its new form. Goods constituting the permanent or fixed capital are more durable. Tools and machinery are examples. Under some circumstances they admit of repeated use for many years; but even the least destructible of them is subject to appreciable deterioration in comparatively short periods of use. In the course of this service they are ultimately, within a practically calculable period, completely destroyed. Such destruction should be allowed for in every painstaking economic account.

Every one of the individual capital goods is consumed as it is employed; but in its totality capital is inconsumable. While constantly undergoing changes in its constituent components, it is constantly being renewed. This statement brings out the essential truth of the theory of capital. It focuses our theoretical interest. So far the exposition has been merely introductory to this axiom. None requires more careful consideration than the latter.

It is not necessary to demonstrate the fact that capital, as a whole, is not consumed. This is universally acknowledged. It is confirmed by daily experience in all cases in which human enterprise extends to a sufficient number of capital goods so that the total effect of this capital may be appreciated. This has been so at all times. It is a condition which will continue so long as the existence of capital is not so extraordinarily altered as to tear asunder the interconnection of the whole economy. Should the present economic order be displaced by a socialistic one, the newly established economic community would take into consideration the inconsumability of natural capital in precisely the same manner in which the man of affairs does so today. In fact the phenomenon would be ever more clearly apparent than it is at present, for the capital would not be broken up into many individual holdings but would be concentrated under one embracing control.

From time immemorial every-day economic experience has taught that men can find or make consumable goods through whose utility they may satisfy their needs. In like manner it establishes the fact that the race is able to produce production goods, which aid in forming other products, and also to reproduce those goods which have been used up in productive service. In agricultural pursuits there is an interweaving of capital and the vital organic processes of plant and animal. It is in the flow of this life-process that capital is repeatedly renewed. The capital consumed in industry is always being replenished from agricultural or mineral raw materials. These types of primary production themselves receive the means of maintaining the current from industry. Furthermore history demonstrates not only that capital is renewed but also that there is an expansibility of capital wealth to which no definite limit may be assigned at present.

While it is unnecessary to make further efforts to prove the inconsumability of capital, there is considerable difficulty involved in an accurate and consistent theoretical expression of all its details. To accomplish this purpose, we shall have to distinguish more nicely the services rendered by capital. In the first place, capital aids in the production of new consumption goods; secondly, it furthers the reproduction of consumed capital commodities. In both cases one must distinguish two types of capital goods; raw material and the tool are the outstanding respective illustrations. Thus we shall designate goods of the first group as material commodities or materials, and those of the second as work goods or tools.[1]

"Materials" are exclusively liquid capital. The latter term is highly significant in suggesting the productive service performed. The productive movement terminates in the household. Toward this goal the materials are carried in the current of production from one stage of development to the next, like the waters of a river flowing from one level to another towards the estuary. Raw materials are supplied by primary production. In each successive productive stage they receive their useful composition and form as other materials are integrated with them or their outer shape is changed. Even after they are in the form of ultimate products, further manipulation and change will probably be necessary to make them ready for household use. They will have to be transported from the place of manufacture to that of use. In those cases where they have been massed in wholesale quantities to facilitate productive service, they must be separated into smaller units which are adapted to the convenience of the household. The goods may also require ripening in storage as is the case with wine.

In the exchange economy those activities, which succeed formative production, are distinguished from, and no longer mentioned as production properly speaking. These activities belong for the most part to commerce, the mediator between production and consumption. In the simple economy such a distinction is uncalled for. The formative process, which gives the ultimate form, and the succeeding activities, which enhance its readiness for consumption, perform one and the same service from the economic point of view. Each fulfills its task

[1] Trans. Note: *Stoffgüter* and *Werkgüter* are probably better rendered by the longer terms. Particularly *Werkgüter* is inaccurate in the shorter term, "tools." "Material commodities," however, is also unfortunate in English as it suggests a contrast with services. In this section the shorter terms are used to Anglicize the text. Later in the book, where the terms are used only occasionally, the translator reverts to the more awkward phrases.

and carries the materials one stage nearer to consumption. The "material commodity"[1] does not become a consumption good or one of the nearest order until the very moment at which it is turned over to the household ready for use. Until then it remains a capital commodity, one of a more remote order. As such its relation to the consumption good is that of a productive commodity to a product.

It is the function of the tools to maintain the flow of the materials from level to level. "Tools" are for the greater part standing or fixed capital goods. They include not only tools but machinery and the manifold implements of production, industrial buildings, and other improvements, means of transportation and store-houses. It is only in exceptional cases that the "materials" of liquid capital are used jointly with these tools. Coal or firewood are examples of materials whose complementary use allows a realization of the forces of the tools.

Again the term, fixed capital, suggests aptly the use to which these tools are put. They have a constant position in the order of commodities. From this station they serve to bring about the changes in the materials which are required to advance these goods to the next stage. They are not bodily incorporated in the material. Therefore they do not move with the flow of the liquid capital. Nevertheless they are to be regarded as productive commodities in relation to the products of all succeeding stages down to the final product which is ready for consumption. It is partly due to their influence that the movement is communicated to succeeding stages and that the series terminates with the ultimate products which are ready for use.

The organization, which is essential to the reproduction of capital in a fully developed economy, is exceedingly far reaching. It requires its own raw materials,[2] such as ore, timber and lumber. Its own liquid capital is maintained. This is evolved from these raw materials thru a long series of manufacturing and transportation processes until the goods are at last ready for their productive service. This division of the economy has its own enormous capital in tools and auxiliary materials. These goods, which have been manufactured, are

[1] Trans. note: In several places the translator has used quotation marks to call attention to one of Wieser's phrases where the term might have been mistaken in rapid reading. This is never done if there can be any suggestion from the context that Wieser is quoting.

[2] Trans. note: A clause is omitted in which a new name is suggested for this group: *"die wir als Werkstoffe bezeichnen können."* Such word building, in which *Werkstoffe* are contrasted with *Werkgüter* but are a special case of *Stoffgüter*, does not lend itself to intelligible English.

turned over to the predetermined stage in one of the two sections of the productive process: *(translator's note.) i. e., to the service of capital reproduction or the manufacture of consumption goods.* Many of these commodities are carried back to the remotest stage of the reproduction process. For example, the finished elevator may be sent back to the very mine from which the ore was supplied that is embodied in the contrivance. All tools and auxiliary materials of this reproduction process are also related to the ultimate, consumable goods as productive commodities. In the genealogy that is traced back from the ultimate products these tools should be placed among the progenitors. Accounts should be so drawn as to show the proportion of their participation in the final result.

The two functions of reproduction and immediate production obey, like the entire productive activity, the law of the unity of the economy. The demands of "economic statics" would not be fulfilled if the preparation of such materials and tools were not brought into equilibrium. A productive scheme, which looked only to the preparation of raw materials, would be as foolish and self-contradictory as another planning only the production of machines. From the highest to the lowest stage in planned production, there should be proper proportionality. The quantities of raw materials obtained must be calculated to supply materials to all succeeding stages as fully as the given circumstances allow. There should be no obstruction in the transition from one stage to another because of which some materials, already obtained, would have to remain unused. The quantity of tools and auxiliary materials, set aside for each stage, should be such that it is always fully employed. At the same time this quantity must be adequate to ensure an adequate, constant flow of materials without avoidable interruptions. If these conditions are fulfilled, there should also be the greatest possible temporal regularity of productive services. In some cases, however, natural conditions may be such that tasks pile up at certain times, while at others men and capital goods are under-employed or idle. Especially in agriculture the total duration of the productive process and of its individual phases from seed to harvest is so strictly controlled by nature as to permit of but little adjustment of operations.

Wherever unified planning controls the two important sections of production, capital will have to gain its ends in a manner similar to inconsumable lands. Its substance must be maintained undiminished by the process of uninterrupted change involved in consumption and replacement. Man culls the fruits of the land year after year.

So also he should be able to secure periodic uses of consumption goods from the productive process.

We shall later resume in detail the discussion of the employment of capital. At present we must formulate the concept of capital which is to be deduced from the facts presented.

Capital in terms of the simple economy, i. e., natural capital, is to be defined as the aggregate of all capital goods which are systematically used in the complete process of production. We feel bound to repeat expressly that the latter process includes not only such capital goods as are assigned to the immediate service of production but also those that are used in capital reproduction.

A simple economy, which was unable to reproduce its capital, would be most grievously disappointed in its expectations. It would soon be recognized that certain commodities, which had been considered capital, actually were not such, since they were consumed in use and not replaced. If the stores of coal in the earth and now subject to human control were to be used up and if they could not be replaced by the discovery of new deposits or by the adaptation of new elementary forces, human economy would suffer the most deplorable calamity of its experience. Man would then have consumed his coal-capital. This could only result in bankrupting the enormous mass of capital and labor to which coal is a necessary complement. More accurately speaking, man would discover that this complementary wealth, which had been considered capital and which constituted perhaps the largest part of capital wealth, was indeed not capital at all. Instead it was a complementarily associated sum of produced production goods, capable of being converted into a definite, limited quantity of products. But since it was incapable of reproduction, the economy would not be able continuously to obtain consumption goods beyond the aggregate of this sum.

From this concept of capital may also be derived that of the capital commodity which we seek. The latter is an individual commodity of the total capital of the simple economy. It is a produced productive agent, systematically employed in the process of production.

We must needs add an important qualification. The commodity must be integrated in the continuity of the entire process. One which has been torn out of this continuity is no longer a capital commodity. Let us assume that a hunter and trapper, searching the northern snowfields for spoils of the chase, loses touch with his ship and his companions. He saves only his gun and a small store of ammunition.

He will make an entirely different use of these than that originally planned. He knows that when his last bullet is spent he can no longer maintain life. Those few bullets which are left must be so used as to afford the greatest possible number of means of self-preservation. The gun ceases to be a capital commodity in his eyes; he uses it only as a productive means by which to secure a certain limited quantity of goods by which to satisfy his personal needs. As the last shot is fired, the gun's usefulness ends and it ceases to be a commodity at all. On the other hand, when handled by a hunter who remains in touch with a social economy, the gun in connection with the ammunition serves as the means of its own reproduction. The hunter uses it to kill game in amounts over and above those required by his personal needs. He turns his bag in at a trading post and from this station he again replenishes his ammunition. The gun, whenever it becomes useless by deterioration, is similarly replaced.

A number of capital goods, complementarily united and systematically used in their appropriate relation to the total capital of the community, is fractional capital. The stock of capital goods of every independent industrial plant and of every department of such a plant is fractional capital. One can go still further in the subdivision of the varieties of capital and distinguish working-capital from capital improvements. Both of these are fractional capitals; the former is the sum of the liquid capital goods in a plant or its departments; the latter is the sum of the fixed capital commodities. In practice such fractional capital is regarded simply as capital and is invariably so designated. The concept of the total economic capital of society is so large that it cannot be grasped within the limits of individual vision. Practical life, therefore, is not familiar with anything but the notion of fractional capital. This is called capital without qualification.

Theory must see beyond fractional capital. The latter does not possess the essential marks which are demanded even in the practical idea of capital. It is not simultaneously a means of production and reproduction. The undiminished fractional capital cannot be reproduced from itself. It is even more impossible to detach an enduring benefit from it alone. All these effects are only generated in the economic continuity of all fractional capitals. Theory, therefore, must transcend the practical concept and establish a scientific one which brings together in one unity all the various fractional capitals.

So far our exposition has presupposed a static economy which shows neither progress nor retrogression. For an advancing economy the presentation must be modified.

In a progressing social economy capital is not only constantly re-created; it is augmented as well. New capital is earned and added to the original total; replacement is supplemented by the creation of new capital. The most effective gain would be realized were this increase at the same time an improvement, an elaboration of numerous and superior forms of capital goods. In an advancing economy both the increase and replacement of capital are accompanied by improvements. In place of the deteriorated older forms, more modern and serviceable ones make their appearance; capital reproduction becomes the renewal of capital.

The increase of capital, like capital generally, is to be regulated in the use to which the product is to be put so as to conform to the law of economic unity. Such increase should not be confined to any one stage of the process of production, although it may be advisable to begin at a single stage. The beginning may therefore be made by building more efficient machinery. In such a case, however, it will be necessary to provide auxiliary materials by the time the machines are ready for operation. It is only thru a larger supply of materials that it is possible to utilize the increased capacity made available by the machines. Large increases of wealth result in increased capital in all branches of production. The introduction of machinery in one branch of industry produces capital and labor for related branches of industry as well as for agriculture and the economic process generally.

In a static economy capital is used only to bring forth consumption goods. In a progressive society it is also used to bring about an increase of productive commodities. Where this increase involves an improvement of capital as well, the latter in an advanced period of the economic life will be of a materially different composition from that at the start. As a matter of history, human labor was at first but scantily assisted by capital; a small number of simple auxiliaries had to suffice in obtaining the desired articles for consumption. At first such goods could only be obtained somewhat after the manner in which hunters and fishers seize wild life. The earliest capital wealth consisted of the total stores of game and fish and the rude implements and weapons required. The reproduction of the implements was performed in the greater part thru labor which was aided by only the most meagre supply of the simplest tools. The controlling capital goods were to be found in the collected stores which secured to the hunter or fisher the leisure which he required for the reproduction of his appliances. It represented enormous progress where greater quantities and varieties of auxiliary materials were added to the capital possession with the advent of the industrial arts. Not until much later were "tools" more elaborately developed.

The farther the development progresses, the more of such capital is allied to the labor of the human hand. The activity of the worker is being confined more and more to the direction of an apparatus which forms the product without intermediary or which generates also the motive power. The dimensions of this machine become larger. It grows more durable. Its composition becomes more complex and its performances more stupendous. Vast investments of capital in the form of an extensive plant are added to the tools which a single worker wields. To keep this plant running an army of coöperating workers is employed under the direction of leaders or a staff of leaders.

It is of especial importance to the theory of capital to remember that capital in its simultaneous increase and improvement is applied to more and more remote stages of production. Agriculture first cultivates the most accessible fields. It passes to more and more distant ones at later periods as the settlement of new countries or the discovery of new continents opens new opportunities. So industry goes farther and farther abroad with its raw materials and establishments. It seeks first the richest deposits, the most efficient forces. Just as agriculture penetrates deeper and deeper strata of the soil, so production at all times explores more and more inaccessible stages. The advances of natural science make latent commodities available. By the aid of complementary wealth and an improved technology new commodity-elements may be used. In many instances nature is more lavish of her concealed and inaccessible treasures than she is of those which lie open and at hand. The greatest advances of production are made by the penetration of new realms and the extension of industry.

In order that these advances may be more effectively exploited, every stage in this progression must be supplied with capital. Thus each advance in production is parallelled by an expansion of capital stages. An intermediate series of processes is developed which give access to the region in which the gifts of nature are offered in greater abundance. Thus the period of time required by the production process becomes longer. This extension is accompanied by a similar one of the period during which capital is employed, unless indeed the progress of the technical arts should reduce the duration of production periods just as it elsewhere reduces the cost of production. As production becomes more highly developed, it extends through a greater number of stages. It operates with the aid of many more capital goods and much more labor. It therefore demands proportionately greater expenditures than primitive and simple production which is adjusted to a rapid discharge of finished goods. The advanced methods, however, tap more abundant natural resources and the total yield is therefore greater.

There can be no doubt that advances in production cannot continue indefinitely. At one point or another a limit will be reached. Both the ancient world and the Middle Ages exhausted their capacity for progress. The present era of progressive scientific technology will also reach a point at which further progress is barred. Some distant age may then possibly start from new fundamentals of knowledge and once more advance towards the ultimate goal, until mankind shall arrive at the point where further efforts are unavailing. For the present and the calculable future, however, our knowledge of nature opens possibilities which may secure an increasing reward to the application of productive labor and of an enlarged and improved capital equipment. This prediction presupposes that civilized peoples will not improvidently exhaust their natural capital resources of coal and ore but will succeed in providing ample compensations for the enormous consumption to which mineral deposits are being subjected.

The labor theory, more than any other, is forced to reconcile its statements with existing capital resources. A theory, which explains all economy from the standpoint of labor, finds a serious drawback in the important service rendered by capital. An attempt must be made to eliminate the latter. As we know, the labor theory fails to solve its problem when it comes to the fully developed economic organization. It would make a similar failure in the case of primitive economy, if it were not able to express all capital in terms of labor. By two methods it has sought to eliminate the factor of capital. It has advanced the doctrine that all capital in its effect may be reduced to labor. Furthermore it has contended that, as regards its origin also, capital is the outgrowth of labor.

The first of these assertions starts from the fact that human labor is partially replaced by capital. A large share of the effort, which rested on workers personally, is assumed by capital. There are many cases in which a practical decision must be reached as to whether a given result may be more effectively achieved thru the application of capital or of labor. However, the two factors are not interchangeable at all points where one or the other is used. Capital can never render the directing service of labor. No more can labor, substituting merely its own efforts, dispense with raw materials. Only the services of directed labor and "tools" compete to a certain extent; for the rest each of the two factors has its own particular function in production which it alone can assume.

The second point is of far greater significance. It starts from the fact that capital is an historical product, the outgrowth of human effort. Does this mean that it is the result of human labor and nothing more? Partizans of the labor theory are untiring in devising vivid illustrations, meant to exemplify this idea. They speak of capital as the "embodiment of labor," "labor performed in advance," "gelatinous labor," "labor in the pluperfect" and the like. One of the advocates of this theory explains in a most attractive manner the historical process by which he contends mankind, little by little, amassed the capital wealth of today. A stone of peculiar formation, a piece of wood of unusual consistency and shape or a lump of meadow-ore may have furnished the first tools by which prehistoric men seconded their labors. Such objects made possible the construction of other more suitable tools. By the aid of the latter even more appropriate ones were perfected, until finally the progressive development made available the perfected machinery and all other tools of the modern technic. The effective use of these tools had drawn into their service masses of raw materials and other material commodities.

If one were prepared to accept this historical account as substantially correct, he would indeed be justified in tracing the origin of capital back to the efforts of labor. The first simple tools were man's original indebtedness to happy accident. However, they need scarcely be considered; the contributing natural forces, as we know, are not appraised economically. If it were practicable to repeat this historical development and to create capital goods, as they are needed, by the mere concert of labor and free nature, one might be compelled to say that capital may be resolved into labor not merely because of historical analysis but also because of the practical conditions of the economy.

Where do we find this presupposition confirmed? How could the capital commodities be produced as they are needed by every advanced productive process, particularly by those of today, if they were not at hand a large inventory of capital goods handed down from earlier periods? Capital, though due to human effort, though historically it may be the product of labor, has become an independent factor of production in the practical economic organization. Labor and free nature alone are no longer sufficient to create it. It is a productive factor *sui generis;* practice and therefore also economic theory have to take into consideration its unique nature.

There is still an uninterrupted flow of literature on the theory of capital. In this connection we refer to the monumental work of Böhm-Bawerk, *Capital and The Interest on Capital,* already mentioned in our introductory summary. The first part of this work, "History and critique of the theories of interest on capital" (4th ed. 1921), contains a history of the dogma which may be called a classic and which stands unequalled in economic science. In the second part, "Positive theory of capital" (4th ed. I, 1921; II, 1921), we are most interested in this connection in the equally painstaking and lucid exposition of the controversy regarding the concept of capital.

The fact that new definitions of the concept of capital are constantly being proposed may only be explained by the assumption that the traditional definitions have failed to be entirely satisfactory. The chief reason for the search for those elements, which are operative in our daily thinking but are not yet significantly expressed in theory, is the remoteness of the scientific formulation of the concept from that of daily life. We shall return to and conclude this consideration, when we reach the discussion of the money form of capital. At present we would only emphasize the fact that the relation which we have established between the capital commodity or fractional capital and total capital is meant to facilitate the transition to the idea of every-day speech. This relationship entirely resolves the conspicuous contrast between the total, which is a permanent fund, and the good which is consumed. Because of this relationship it is seen that the individual commodity, considered as a part of the whole capital, must necessarily receive the standard of its use from the entire productive plant. The latter is constantly held to the task of replacing again and again all those portions which are consumed in use.

We are not so far in accord with Böhm-Bawerk's expositions of the function of capital in production. We see capital as an independent factor of production. Böhm-Bawerk recognizes only labor and nature as such factors. He looks upon capital as an intermediate product of these two. He makes an extensive examination of round-about production. (See in the 3rd edition especially the incisive investigations on this subject.) He contrasts a scheme of production, which is devoid of capital and is directed immediately to obtaining consumption goods, to "capitalistic" production. The latter works in a more round-about fashion. It mingles labor with more remote and primitive antecedents of the desired commodities, until finally after several or possibly many intermediate steps the means of satisfaction are ready for use. These expositions coincide essentially with our own views, which deduce the productivity of capital from the fact that the latter affords to man the possibility of resorting to the more remote stages for the natural treasures there deposited. We would not use the term, round-about, to describe this use of capital. The term suggests the idea that the selected paths of production have been needlessly protracted: a meaning which it is not intended to convey. From an economic point of view the productive process falls back upon more distant stages only in so far as conditions can there be seized which promise increased yield with the maturity of skill and of the available means.

§ 14. The Theory of Land

Classes of land and soil forces—The law of diminishing returns from land—The possibility of increase of land and of capital.

Diehl, *Erläuterungen zu Ricardos Grundsätzen der Volkeswirtschaft*, 1905; Oppenheimer, *Ricardos Grundrententheorie*, 1909; Esslen, *Das Gesetz des abnehmenden Bodenertrages* 1905; Waterstradt, *Das Gesetz vom abnehmenden Bodenertag*, Thünen-Archiv, vol. I; Ballod, *Die Productivität der Landwirtschaft*,

Schr. d. V. f. S., vol. 132; Weisz, article, *Abnehmender Ertrag*, Hdw. d. Stw., 4th ed.

The theory of interest must be preceded by a theory of capital. So also that of rent must follow one of land that sheds light on the fundamental economic relations of land.

The latter are far more easily understood than are those of capital and of labor. At any rate the relations of the great mass of favored parcels of land and soil qualities are very prominent; if one may use the simile, they tower like mountain peaks above the general level of the economy indicated by the relationships of capital and of labor. No matter how little one may realize the conditions which determine the general level, everyone observes the relative elevation. It is this which accounts for the fact that the classical school, although unable to give a satisfactory theory of capital or of labor, nevertheless laid down an entire series of important truths regarding the theory of land. It is because of this fact that the teachings of Ricardo are significant. It is for this reason that his work has survived to our day in preference to any other part of the classical theory and continues to receive an enduring recognition as authoritative doctrine. However, it goes without saying that also Ricardo's thought requires careful verification. The latter will ultimately put his doctrines in an entirely new light.

Like Ricardo, we shall give our attention mainly to agricultural land. Whenever we speak simply of land, it is this variety which is referred to. The peculiar conditions of urban property can be most conveniently discussed in connection with urban rent. We cannot examine this yet in our theory of the simple economy.

At first glance the quantitative relations of land seem to be entirely different from those of the other two factors of production. The economic proportionality of capital holds from the moment of its first appearance through every succeeding period. Man produces it with the limited means at his disposal. There have been both improvements and increases of capital. It is this fact which explains how it has been possible in the course of historical development to increase capital wealth more rapidly than population has grown. Land, however, exists in the beginning and during long ages that follow in quantities which greatly exceed every conceivable need of mankind. It is adjusted only slowly to the economic quantitative relation as the demand for it increases. To this extent land is akin to labor; for the latter has also been gradually adjusted to quantitative proportionality. But while the working forces of mankind increase as rapidly as the number of human hands and the skill of the workers, the amount of land available on the earth can hardly be increased in practice. It would therefore appear that at the apex of historical development the quantitative relations of the soil will become an insurmountable barrier to the further increase of the human race and advance of civilization.

The picture of these contrasts changes on closer examination. Agricultural land is not a homogeneous mass. It is not all equally suited to a particular use. Even within these variations of kind there are different degrees of fertility. We shall therefore have to grade this soil for types of use and for fertility. The latter task is of far the greater theoretical importance. The richer the soil, the greater the yield which is returned for a given expenditure of capital and labor. There are, however, not only gradations of fertility; there are also differences of accessibility to the markets as measured in the cost of transportation. The latter reduces the net yield quite as much as do the immediate costs of production.

Ricardo has correctly appreciated the starting point for the theory of land. He neglected differentials of market distance, but the division of the soil into classes gave him the skeleton on which to build his doctrine. He also approaches the problem judiciously, in so far as he endeavors to show things in their historical genesis. In this way one gains a much clearer view of the interconnections of the process than when one is confronted with the completed phenomenon. In this respect we shall follow his example. Such a procedure does no violence to our method, for it is not necessary to desert the paths of daily experience. We disregard all chance variations that occur historically. In our idealizing process it is only necessary to assume a gradual, continuous growth of population. The experiences of daily life are wholly adequate to be a guide to the interpretation of the consequences of such an occurrence; this increase and its consequences are as obvious to our generation as they were in the past.

The first condition which we must assume is one in which the number of persons living on the land is so small that not even all the most fertile and best located acres have to be cultivated. Under such an assumption lands of this class are still to be regarded as free goods. The supply is greater than the demand for them. Strictly speaking, one may not even regard inferior grades of land as commodities. It is true that they possess natural fertility. However, the complementary means of labor and capital are lacking to make use of such soils. The entire available supply of these two factors is turned to the cultivation of the best class, for it is here alone that they are sufficiently rewarded. This statement disregards the fact that these lands may be used in hunting or in some nonagricultural employment. The inferior lands are only commodity elements. Together with the latent commodities of the undiscovered land they constitute the reserves for the future.

It is only little by little that the population increase necessitates bringing the remaining tracts of the best land under cultivation. At the end of this process such land enters the economic quantitative relation and becomes an economic commodity. Thereafter lands of the second class enter the sphere of the economy. They are recognized as commodities. They are cultivated at first as free goods and later, as soon as all tracts have been absorbed, as economic goods. The development of succeeding grades takes precisely the same course.

In the case of every newly comprehended class these two phases must be recognized: the first, the free condition; the second, that of economic proportionality. It is possible that in the individual case the transition may be so rapid that the two periods cannot be distinguished. Notwithstanding this practical fact, the theory of land must take into consideration all phases which must be passed thru and must also set down the formulæ for the course of each. In countries with an old civilization the fertile lands have all long been cultivated and carried into the quantitative relation. Even most of the lands of the Western Hemisphere have been made productive. But even today there are unexhausted reserves of virgin, free land.

From this historical reflection the theorist is led to the important conclusion that from the point of view of the practical economy land also may be increased. Moreover, the increase is not yet ended. The geographer may regard the quantity of land as unchangeable, for the portions, which are added or lost in historical periods by natural forces, are negligible when compared with the whole. But the economist has a different angle of vision. Only the lands known to man need be considered by him. Even within the boundaries of this discovered territory, he need take notice only of the economically available land. It is only of this latter portion that practical economy takes account and economic theory must so define its concepts as to have them interpret practice.

There are two different processes by which the expansion of agricultural land takes place. In part it results from discoveries, conquests, migrations and settlements or from improved means of transportation. The latter method may have such vast consequences and may be accompanied by such great increases of yield, as to place the social conditions and economic relationships on an entirely new foundation. Under different circumstances the expansion takes place by the increase of population and a consequent increase of the available means of capital and labor. When the latter process occurs, it is usually accomplished under the law of diminishing returns. The best adapted land is always selected and cultivated before others. The later expansion consequently can avail itself only of lands which yield a more scanty return to both capital and labor, unless indeed new land of greater fertility is opened up by grading or drainage or unless agricultural methods are improved and bring about other uses and different subdivisions of the land.

In the course of historical development there has been an actual increase of the cultivated area and also of the number of qualities of the soil which it has been found possible to utilize on different parcels of land. In large part this has been due to the progress of agricultural methods. It became possible especially when man learned to replace the exhaustible elements and could thus turn to full account the inexhaustible reserves. But even without any improvement of agricultural technique men have been forced by the pressure of needs resulting from an increased population to apply more capital and labor to the land, wherever it was in any way possible to command these factors. Experience has shown that this process still utilizes some of the reserve soil-content. In order to carry out any agricultural enterprise to the best advantage, some minimum expenditure of labor and capital is necessary. The extensive systems demand less; the intensive ones more. However, within broad limits either type admits of an increased application and rewards this expenditure with larger yields.

These gains, however, are subject to the law of diminishing returns. The simplest theoretical expression of this relation is obtained, if the forces of the soil are conceived of as grouped in strata. The latter are related to one another in the same manner as are the classes of agricultural land. The extension of cultivation to include the less favored strata takes place in the same manner in which resort to less favored areas takes place. Every increment, which is added to the minimum necessary expenditure, is applied to less productive forces which respond with a less remunerative return.

Our inquiry has shown that historically, both the quantity and qualities of the soil are capable of increase and improvement. But it has further shown that in the regular course of events the increased yield is obtained under the law of diminishing returns. This statement must be modified to allow for changes due to progress. Usually, however, this law will not permit the increase to be for the better; it knows only increases for the worse. Even the latter is denied to a people which is chained down within its national boundaries, which has already brought all agricultural land under cultivation and whose civilization is so unprogressive that it cannot raise new capital to increase production. There have been long periods of this sort in history. Under the pressure of such conditions agricultural progress languished. There are conditions in which the soil may be robbed of its destructible elements and may completely lose its productivity.

So far this has not been the case with ambitious nations. They have always succeeded by advances of all sorts in opening up new reserves of virgin soil and of soil-qualities. Thus the operation of the law of diminishing returns has been set aside for a certain period. The possibilities of progress do not seem to be at an end. Should the attempts to produce artificial fertilizer from the nitrogen of the atmosphere be successful, we would find ourselves on the threshold of new and extraordinary prospects for agricultural progress. Even bolder fancies foresee the day when man's food will be gained directly from atmospheric nitrogen. At one bound this would shake free the trammels of the soil. The technique of food production would be revolutionized. The whole process of provisioning mankind would be capitalistically industrialized.

It is not for theoretical enquiry to judge in how far technical possibilities of this sort may be realized. We have to content ourselves with a reference to the second half of the nineteenth century. In this period civilized nations increased their capital wealth in a degree that was without precedent. But the advance in the control of the soil was of scarcely less significant proportions. The law of diminishing agricultural returns did not show its ominous influence for many decades. An increase of population has been possible such as the world never before knew. It is only in the most recent times that the advances in the settlement of the soil have lagged behind population increase and that the pressure of the agricultural law seems again to be felt. In contrast with these facts the improvement and augmentation of capital continues. Even without further progress of the industrial technique it is destined to continue while mass-production can find scope for extension and while it yields increasing returns.

The fact that capital is assembled by human agency, while the soil is a gift of nature, makes itself felt with all its advantages and disadvantages thruout our entire economic development. Man does not control the soil quite to the extent to which he controls capital which he made to serve his purposes. He finds himself in his economy constantly depending on the gradations of the natural supply. He can no more completely abolish distance and the diversities of fertility, peculiar to the soil, than he can equalize all elevations of the ground. As regards land, therefore, the gradations of soil-classes[1] must remain important even to the most highly developed economy. As a rule progress is only possible according to the law of diminishing returns: i. e., by falling back from the better upon the inferior classes of land. On the other hand there still remain, beside the better grades which have already entered the economic quantitative relation, the inferior classes of the natural wealth, which are provided in free abundance.

In the case of capital, progress is accomplished by entirely different means. Only to the most limited extent is an effort made to utilize more effectively the still hidden, unused, reserve forces in existing capital goods. The more advantageous way is left open, and will probably remain so for a long time, of obtaining a larger yield thru the simultaneous improvement and increase of the capital commodities. But for all this, there is probably no chance of our ever raising capital, the narrowly bounded creation of human effort, beyond its economic proportionality and thus of securing the abundance of a free good.

Ricardo saw clearly most of the important facts of the theory of land. More especially he did not fail to note the juxtaposition of indigence and affluence. But he was absorbed in the labor theory and did not succeed in giving the appropriate theoretical expression to the facts of his observation. He did not know the concept of the economic quantitative relation. Thus, where an absolute excess of free reserves of soil does not exist, he goes too far and speaks of a monopoly of the soil arising from scarcity. It is true that the best classes of those soils which are devoted to the cultivation of the least widely scattered varieties of products, for example vinelands, approach the relation of scarcity; but in the other medium and lower grades and in those devoted to the most widespread types of cultivation land exists, like capital and labor, in absolutely and relatively great quantities. Ricardo does not recognize that capital and labor also occupy a position in the economic quantitative relation. Thus he accentuates too sharply the contrast of land to the two factors, capital and labor. In his presentation ground-rent has the malicious appearance of depredation and the future of agricultural life is clouded by far too somber shadows.

The relations between Ricardo's theories of land and price are of especial importance. Thruout, he sees capital and labor alone as the elements in the computation of costs. He never considers land in this connection. Hence the curious contradiction that he, who speaks of the monopoly of the soil, always presupposes in his theoretical deductions the superfluity of the qualities of the soil. The consequence is that his theory of price is as incomplete as his theory of land. In both instances he disregards cases where the most important soil-classes have come into the economic quantitative relation.

It is true that land, even when the latter condition has come to pass, as a rule occupies a very different position in the computation of costs fróm that of capital and labor. For the most part it is not an immediate element in the computation at all. This circumstance, however, cannot be explained from the theory of the soil as such. It arises from the opposition of "cost-productive-means" and "specific productive means," variously related to the contrast of

[1] Trans. note: In this discussion soil-classes includes both groups which Wieser has discussed—inferior lands and inferior qualities in a given tract.

land to capital and labor but not coincident with it thruout. For this relation an explicit exposition is imperative and to this we shall now proceed.

§ 15. Cost Productive Means and Specific Productive Means

Cost Products and Specific Products

Special scarcity products or products of superabundance—Marginal cost products and products of narrower marginal use—Cost, the predominating characteristic of capital and labor—The predominantly specific character of land and capital investments.

What we know in everyday life as costs of production are those pecuniary outlays which the entrepreneur must make in order to realize the gains of his venture. Obviously, however, the expression of costs in the form of money covers a natural form of cost which we must be able to present without a remainder in a non-monetary, simple economy. For example, one may speak of the economic costs of cultivating land in a sense which is altogether independent of pecuniary expression and which will demand consideration as much in some future socialized state as it does today. The natural costs in this case consist of the two natural measures: the services of labor and the capital goods required. Nevertheless, there are certain capital commodities and services which do not possess the characteristic of cost, just as there are certain uses of land in which the latter has a cost character. Thus the work of the entrepreneur lacks this characteristic, while the plot of formerly agricultural land on which one erects an urban dwelling must surely be set down among the costs of building. One and the same productive good may be placed among the costs in contrast with certain productive agents but not in contrast with others.

We shall call cost-productive-means—or briefly cost-means—those productive agents which have to be placed among costs. The others we shall call specific productive means. Let us first determine with precision the phenomena to which these two terms are to be applied. As this is done, the significance of the distinction will be most effectively brought out.

Cost-means constitute the bulk of all productive wealth. Their available quantity determines substantially the yield which may be realized and the general extent and the general intensity of production: i.e., the general margin of production. Cost-means are never rigidly confined to one special type of production. They are distributed over the entire productive process in such a manner as to make possible the highest possible total yield. Only such productive agents, therefore, as possess variegated qualities of usefulness can figure as cost-means. Furthermore these goods must be available in large enough quantities so that their usefulness may find an outlet in many directions. Each of them belongs to numerous productive stems. With even more connecting strands they form the large network of the production-relationship. Through them the individual branches of production are bound together. Productive and economic unity depends upon them. If all productive agents were cost-means, the yield of the individual branches of production would be almost completely equalized.

The remaining productive goods have certain specific qualities which distinguish them from cost-means. Consequently, those branches of production where their influence is decisive are distinguishable in their yield from the principal mass in which each branch is balanced against the others. The most conspicuous of this specific group are those which are remarkable for the pronounced scarcity of their occurrence. A spring of mineral water which has specific remedial virtue is an illustration. But even objects which occur more abundantly are to be regarded as specific productive means, provided they may be applied to only one use or a limited number of uses. Thus cinchona-bark is important only in the manufacture of quinine. It would retain its specific character, even though it were obtainable in large quantities.

As in the case of the soil, even objects of frequent occurrence and somewhat far reaching usefulness may rank as specific productive means. Even when the settlement of new countries is begun, when land is still so abundant that only the best tracts are cultivated, land does not have the character of a cost-commodity. At the same time, although capital wealth is strictly limited, the agricultural capital goods are to be classed as cost-commodities. After all the service of fertile land is permanently confined to agricultural production, while capital is important from the very beginning for all branches of production. The universality of its use is its distinguishing characteristic even during the early period of inadequate supply. Fertile land, therefore, determines the extent only of agricultural production. Capital, in contrast, gives the general measure of the extent of all production. So long as land may be had in superabundance, agriculture may be carried beyond the general productive margin set by available quantities of labor and capital. Later, when land, in contrast with needs, is more scarce, it depresses agricultural production below the general level. In either case it gives to agricultural products a specific margin of use. This will be different from the general margin and will deviate in the direction of abundance or scarcity.

In the manufacture of some products, therefore, both specific and cost-means must be applied. These thus acquire a specific character and may be referred to as specific products. Where the specific productive means required for such products are peculiarly plentiful, the latter should also be. The quantity of the products will be scanty, when the supply of the means is meagre. We shall call the former specific frequency-products, the latter specific scarcity-products. Furs have a specific character when the animals which furnish the skins are being killed in great numbers, as well as when they have commenced to be rare. Under the first condition the hunters, who bring in the skins and use them as well, will be liberally supplied far beyond the general margin of their households. Under the second conditions furs will have become expensive. Only the wealthiest families will be able to purchase them. Even these families, unless they are extremely rich, will be able to acquire skins only in an amount that is within the margin of the general domestic economy.

Those products, whose creation requires only cost-productive-means, may be called pure cost-products or, more simply, cost-products. The latter are provided in a much more equalized supply than specific products. But even for this type the general margin of use cannot be exactly maintained. In an earlier connection (§ 10) we saw that the diversity of the points of relaxation is an obstacle in the way of complete equalization. This condition can be attained only in the case of the marginal products which serve fluid marginal needs. Special limits apply to cost products which have a narrower marginal use, for example, the graded needs; but these products do not for this reason lose their cost character. They may always be distinguished from specific products by the fact that it is only the latter which are governed by special conditions of production that preclude adherence to the general margin of use. The cost-products are adjusted to the general level of production, while specific products characteristically stand out either above or below these general limits.

In my earlier investigations I have not made use of the idea of specific productive means and products. I have made shift with the too narrow concept of "monopoly commodities," emphasizing their specific character. (See, *Natural Value*, § 30.) Neither have I used the idea of cost-means. In this connection I confined myself to "cost-commodities." I hope that the terms selected for the broader notions are not found objectionable from considerations of the proprieties of our speech.

If one adheres to the definitions laid down, it follows that labor and capital goods must almost always be regarded as cost-productive-means, and that land is usually to be classed with specific productive means.

Human labor can be applied to a great variety of uses. When all its accomplishments are considered, it has universal applicability. No product can be turned out without labor, which is the connecting element between all goods. In the early periods of economic activity the primitive, crude use of human strength naturally sharply limited its applicability. But in such an age the labor of each individual might have been called a universal agent. As nearly as one could tell, each person was qualified to perform all the simple tasks which were then called for. The development of the manual arts has resulted in innumerable subdivisions. Today unskilled labor has somewhat retained the ancient universality; it finds application almost everywhere, though only as an auxiliary. As such, however, it has uniformity, the typical characteristic of the original labor. There is no trace of qualitative individualization in such labor. The gradations are only in the quantitative performance of individuals or groups of workers. There are differences in the services rendered by the strong and weak, the experienced and inexperienced, the industrious and indolent. These differences, however, may be reduced offhand to a common measure.

The case of skilled labor, which is trained in a particular trade, is different. The training requires considerable time and not inconsiderable expense. As a result there is no easy transition from one group to another. There is no longer an unrestricted communication between groups. Personal preference, the outgrowth of habit, frequently makes the flow still more limited. Nevertheless, even for skilled trades a certain equalization takes place in manning the different groups. The experienced mechanic cannot easily change his trade, but the apprentice is less hampered in his decisions. He is readier to turn from the over-manned trade and to adopt one which is less congested.

However, in the theory of the simple economy we may disregard unhesitatingly all difficulties of this sort. In our idealization we may assume a condition of complete equalization which gives the maximum effect to the cost-character of labor. We may do this not merely for the skilled employments of the regular mechanic but for others requiring even higher qualifications. It is merely necessary that more persons be trained to them. A properly specific character is likely to be shown only in connection with rare technical feats which demand exceptional talents and a pronounced inner impulse. This is the case with the highest performances in art, science or other social fields.

Capital goods are produced productive commodities. It is this fact which confers a cost character upon them in almost every case. Their production is adjusted to the greatest possible equalization. Only those goods have a specific character whose production is conditioned by natural circumstances and is controlled but little, if at all, by human intervention. The more complete such control is, the more pronounced is the cost character of the capital good. "Tools" are destined to aid human labor by raising its productivity or by replacing labor. They are the "means of labor" in the narrower sense. They have been variously affected by the diversity of human labor. They frequently possess a more marked cost character than do raw materials. But this character is peculiar to all of the latter whose production is controlled in any equalizing manner. Coal is the most indispensable auxiliary material of machines. It has the same manifold applicability as machinery. So also has iron and wood. The different machines, tools and other workshop commodities are precisely adapted in their finished state to a special use; they are thus individualized. But when these goods are systematically produced in the regular course of the productive process—a necessary assumption to the theory of the simple economy—they are distributed over the entire process in an equalizing manner. Thus they gain the character of cost means.

It is only for exceedingly large investments of capital that another assumption is required. Commodities of this sort represent an extraordinary investment of capital. In the simple economy these goods will be available only in isolated cases. Older, but still workable plants are not likely to be immediately scrapped, as soon as technical progress has made possible larger and more efficient ones. In our day of technical transitions large investments of capital possess a specific character. They are not as widely scattered as are the cost-productive-means properly speaking.

Land is not the creation of man but a gift of nature. Therefore its productive effect is less equalized. The immobility of land results in the fact that the location, at which the effect will take place, has been fixed for every tract. This fact alone precludes complete equalization. In the case of gold it is invariably found as the pure element, but each individual mine is subject to peculiar conditions of productivity, exhaustibility and geographical location. Of course not all varieties of capital goods have the same uniform quality as gold. In general every species embraces obvious differences of quality. Nor is every gold mine, every vineyard and every acre of arable land an isolated type. Within the various classes of land groupings may be made according to productivity. But as a rule the differences of quality are less pronounced in the case of capital goods than in that of land. Capital goods are consequently more uniform, more nearly of a type, than land. As the three productive factors act jointly, therefore, labor and capital usually are the typical cost-means and land is the typical specific productive means. To be sure, in any particular instance the question will always be which of the productive agents involved is the more widely used and the more generally available.

If we examine Ricardo's theory of rent again, we shall see that he correctly recognized in the special case of land and the cost of its cultivation the marks of the specific position and computation of costs. The significance of the contrast, however, is not exhausted in the theory of ground rent; it extends to all fields of the computation of value and the determination of prices. The grouping of the productive agents into land on the one hand and labor and capital on the other is most intimately related to the division into specific and cost-means. The two classifications, however, do not coincide completely.

The division of the productive agents according to their specific or cost character, in connection with the similar classification of products, gives an exhaustive, objective foundation for all the principal problems of economic accounting. To these problems we shall now turn our attention.

§ 16. Marginal Utility in the Isolated Household and the Fundamental Law of the Economic Computation of Utility

Komorzynski, *Bestimmung der natürl. Höhe der Güterpreise*, Z. f. Stw. 1869; and, *Der Wert in der isol. Wirtschaft*, 1889; Böhm-Bawerk, *Grundzüge der The-*

orie des w. Güterwertes, J. f. N., N. F.; vol. XIII; and, *Der letzte Maszstab des Güterwertes*, Z. f. V., vol. VII; Sax, *Die neuesten Fortschritte der nat. ök. Theorie*, 1888; Dietzel, *Die klassische Werttheorie und die Theorie vom, Grenznutzen*, J. f. N., N. F., vol. XX and 3 F. vol. I (in this connection see *Entgegnungen*, by Böhm-Bawerk, vol. XXI, or 3 F., vol. III; and also by Zuckerkandl, vol. XX); Smart, *Introduction to the Theory of Value*, 1891; Wicksell, *Ueber Wert, Kapital und Rente*, 1893; Ricca-Salerno, *La Teoria del Valore*, 1894; Ehrenfels, *System der Werttheorie*, 1897; Cassel, *Grundriss einer elementaren Preislehre*, Z. f. Stw., vol. 55 or 57; Berardi, *Utilità limite costo di riproduzione*, 1901; Furlan, *Cenni su una generalizzazione del concetto d'ofelimità*, *Giornale degli Economisti*, 1908; Urban, *Valuation, its Nature, its Laws*, 1909; Mayer, *Untersuchungen zu dem Grundsetze der wirthschaftlichen Wertrechnung*, Z. f. Volkstw., N. F., vols. I and II; Moeller, *Die sozialökonomische Katagorie des Wertes*, 1922; Keilhau, *Die Wertungslehre* 1923; Meinung, *Zur Grundlegung der allgemeinen Werttheorie*, 2nd ed. 1923.

We now pass from the theory of economic organization to that of value. The latter will occupy our attention to the end of this section. The most important, recent contributions to the theory of value are contained in the bibliography at the head of this section. This list supplements that one of systematic works which was inserted earlier. As we have stated before, the entire classical theory and a large part of the modern theory of value has been deduced from the phenomenon of value-in-exchange. Our method contrasts with these and follows the example of the Austrian school in the deduction of the most general features of these laws. To achieve this, the following exposition is intended to show that the laws of value are fundamentally those of the computation of utility. These latter laws must be obeyed in every economic system, so long as the pressure of economic proportions compels mankind carefully to consider utility.

Karl Marx maintains[1] that value in exchange "makes social hieroglyphs of all the products of labor." In his presentation value-in-exchange is a "fetish," a "mystical characteristic" of goods, a "perceptible sense-transcending thing.[2] He expresses the opinion that this "mystery of the form of goods," this "mysticism of the universe of wares," would necessarily disappear in the economy of a Crusoe, in which there is neither exchange nor value in exchange, and also in a communistic economy of the sort an "association of free men" would establish. "All relations between Crusoe and the objects which constituted his self-created wealth" were "simple and transparent." Similarly in the economy of an association of free men or, to use our phrase, in the simple economy of a people "the social relations of men to their work and the products of their work would be transparently simple in production as well as in distribution."

[1] *Capital*, chap. § 4. "The fetish character of merchandise and its secret."
[2] "Sinnlich übersinnliches" Ding.

Karl Marx errs in these statements. The economy of a Crusoe or of the free, socialistic state of the future does not become transparently simple through the elimination of exchange and value-in-exchange. In both cases appears the problem which gives rise to the peculiar difficulties of the theory of value. This relates to the economic computation of utility. The classical theory and older theories in general failed to see that such a problem existed. It is only here and there that one finds isolated remarks and observations which suggest that the question might be raised. In general there has been a perfect accord with the ideas just quoted from Marx. It has been supposed that the execution of the law of the economic principle, by which the maximum utility is sought, will be found to be "transparently simple." Consequently it was regarded as a waste of words to lay down rules covering the practical computation of utility. Endless pains, however, were taken to discover the laws of value and of price.

The theorists completely overlooked the fact that laws of the computation of utility are actually observed, that these constitute the immediate basis of laws of value and price and that the latter cannot possibly be explained except by familiarity with the former. Every reckoning according to value-in-exchange is fundamentally a computation of utility. It can only be understood as such. Once the latter laws are explained, the interpretation of the former will no longer offer excessive difficulties. The ordinary exchange of goods will have no mysterious elements when the secrets of the economy of a Crusoe, of an individual economy, are explained.

The laws of the computation of utility, which are followed by every person, are obscure. It is only with difficulty that their theory may be comprehended. The controlling factors are deeply hidden in human desires. People live in an already fully organized economic environment. Everyone therefore finds his motivation in actual conditions. He learns through daily experience to follow such impulses. The fact that he has actually behaved in a rational manner does not necessarily qualify him to give a theoretical explanation of his trading. In order to succeed in this difficult task he must accurately recall in full detail the scene within which he moved, confident of his success. He must live over the activities induced by his desires and yet he may not experience the desires. This process renders him liable to make the most bewildering mistakes. It is one thing to act understandingly; it is another to appraise oneself and one's surroundings as an outsider. We have in this contrast the difficulty—if you would have it so, the secret—of all economic theory. We need expect to find no other secret or mysticism inherent in the wares as such.

The penetration of the secret which is peculiar to the laws of the computation of utility, requires that the methodological aids of idealization and isolation be most completely invoked. Let us therefore assume an isolated household. The latter will be simplified by idealization to admit only the consideration of utility. All influences, which might be exerted by labor, by production generally or by exchange, will be barred. In this assumed household all consumption goods used are available as though there were no question as to how they were obtained: i. e., the relations incident to their acquisition have no influence in the management of the economy.

By way of illustration let us consider the conduct of sailors on the high seas. We shall assume that owing to some accident their supply of drinking water is beginning to run short. In this connection their most important duty is well-considered selection of the uses which are still permissible. Several uses which were allowable when water was more plentiful must be abandoned. Heretofore some water may have been used for animals aboard the vessel and for kitchen and laundry purposes. Henceforth it must only be used to quench the thirst of human beings. Daily rations are assigned for each legitimate remaining use. The amount in each case is carefully determined by an organization of the demand. The process of assignment is guided by the one controlling idea of safeguarding the greatest possible utility. If one assumes that the same scale of needs covers all permitted uses, the rations must be assigned in such a manner as to curtail gratification in each instance at precisely the same margin of satiety. Where, on the other hand, the scales are of unequal gradations, the act of satisfaction naturally ceases at different limits; but no allowance can properly be given for a satisfaction of lower intensity while one of higher intensity may still be obtained through some other use. Those needs which fall below the permissible margin of utilization must be rigidly excluded.

In modern theory the term, "margin of utility" is used to designate the degree of utility at which satisfaction is arrested. This margin is measured by the lowest of the most important uses that can be gratified by the available stores. The utmost utilization of the supply and the most careful scrutiny of the needs is presupposed. The margin indicates the lowest partial use at which a unit of an existing supply may still be economically employed. All less important uses are forbidden; their adoption would result in loss. All greater or equal uses are permitted. More than this, such employments should be made; otherwise the full utility which can be obtained will not be realized.

The margin of utility is also significant for those units of the supply which are utilized above the margin. Let us assume that ten tons of water have been stored on the vessel. One of these is kept in readiness in one of the boats against an extreme emergency. The crew will save themselves by means of this boat if the vessel sinks. This ton of water has been reserved for the most urgent need. However, so long as the ship is not in danger only the marginal utility is dependent upon this ton. At present it may be replaced by another. Let us assume that by some accident this ton is destroyed. Another will be placed in the same boat to be ready in case of need. The loss sustained by the crew through the loss of the particular ton of water is confined to the marginal utility of the water. The case would be the same should any other of the ten tons be lost. So long as each of these is considered singly, and the remaining stores last, only the marginal utility is dependent upon the particular ton in question. The original assignment contemplates various useful effects according to the special disposition which shall be made of the concrete units of the store. However, no matter what the difference in useful effect, only the marginal utility is dependent on the single unit where the latter alone is affected.

The assumption of accidental loss to which we resorted just now in our illustration, is best calculated to explain the distinction between the affected utility and the dependent or conditioned utility. But we must not stop at this. The regular plan of the household is not laid down with a view to this assumption. It must be remembered that the accidental loss is a disarrangement of all calculations. The expectation is that all uses shall take place in accordance with the established dispositions. If the theoretical argument is to be conducted in accordance with practical economy, we must assume that all events take the regular systematic course of the forecast. We have to disregard altogether the accidental loss; it may never be assumed. We must always bear in mind the ends to which the economic purpose of the household is directed. Furthermore, the actual environment with all the conditions which have influenced the plan of management, must be constantly remembered. Above all else we must clearly understand the relation between management and consumption. A theory which fails to distinguish between these two will never be able to interpret correctly the meaning of the economy or of its rules of computation. In a former connection (§ 9) we explained in some detail that it is the economic duty of the householder in the use of the means at his disposal to husband these in the face of the temptations to consumption which are the outgrowth of present desire. Through these means the highest total benefit must be permanently secured. An economic scheme which enforces the performance of this duty permits, under any circumstances, only those uses which do not fall below the margin of utility. To accomplish this purpose the plan will always compute all units of the consumable supply according to the measure given by the margin of utility. This will be done not only for those units which are meant to secure the marginal utility but also for the others through which even the highest satisfactions are to be obtained.

This is the rule which is actually adhered to by the domestic consumer. The truth of this statement may be seen most clearly in observing the computation by the consumer in the case of goods bought for household use. The appraisals which have controlled the choice are unmistakably standardized in the numerical expression of the prices allowed. The example is daily repeated in innumerable instances that consumers measure all their purchases according to the margin of utility. Each unit of a given store is computed and paid for at the same amount and for each of them the computation and payment is not higher than the marginal utility. It would be altogether uneconomic to pay a higher price for any one unit; such a purchase had better not be made at all. It is not only the experienced business man who reckons in this fashion; everyone does so. The housewife of the proletarian does so when she buys in advance the week's bread for her family. She would never dream of appraising one loaf higher than another nor of paying more for any loaf than the benefit which accrues to her through its acquisition. Her purchases of food are destined to preserve the life of her family. The magnitude of this service may hardly be measured. And yet she does not compute the value of the food according to this great service which it is expected to render, but rather each unit is measured according to the greatly inferior standard of the marginal utility.

It seems paradoxical to say that without exception all the units of a particular supply are computed at the marginal utility. It is also true that most theorists who have otherwise adopted the doctrine of marginal utility, do not agree with it in this respect. The objection is raised that alternative and cumulative computation are not distinguished in this statement. The possibilities open to the commander of a company of soldiers are analogous to those available to the householder. The former may pick any one of his men to act as file-leader, but he can never simultaneously make file-leaders of all the soldiers. So also the householder may alternatively select any single unit of his supply for the marginal use, but this employment can never simultaneously be filled by all of the pieces. But how can a theory which accords only alternative validity to the law of marginal utility explain the purchases of the laborer's wife? In her buying she appraises every loaf of bread at the same value. In so doing she follows the example of every purchaser in the open market; she does what he does and will do now and at all times. A theory of marginal utility which restricts itself in this way does not pass in its explanation beyond the case of the accidental loss. It describes nothing essential to the regular course of the economy and renounces at the start every attempt to explain the elementary facts in the formation of prices. Anyone who is not prepared to admit that the marginal utility is cumulatively valid for all units deprives the theory of marginal utility of its most important application.

The paradox is easily explained. The statement that all units of a store of goods are to be computed cumulatively according to the marginal utility ceases to appear paradoxical when we interpret it as economically active men would. The theorist may not be permitted to inject a meaning which is not confirmed in practical life. The housewife buying the bread needed by her family is aware in her own way that she is fully performing her economic duty when she appraises all the necessary loaves at equal values. There is nothing absurd in her conduct. The theorist is at fault if the formula which he establishes for her actions makes these appear inconsistent. He has failed to devise the proper expression for their rational significance. The highest possible utility is also included when the computation at the marginal utility embraces all units. The marginal utility must be observed cumulatively for all units in order that the economic margin of use shall be reached at all points. This could not be ensured if the application were made only to the last remaining units of our stores, the "file-leaders" of the supply. In any event, there is an apparent paradox only for those persons who fail to keep in mind the nature of the service rendered in consumption by the computation of utility. To repeat, its task is not in the least to find motives for consumption as such. Desire gives the direct motivation. The purpose of the computation is merely to exercise a painstaking supervision of consumption, which shall repudiate all desires which fall below the admissible margin of use. It guards the margin of use at all points by preserving unimpaired the marginal utility.

The application of an appraisal by marginal utility is limited to physically divisible stores: i. e., to such as consist of homogeneous portions of matter that admit of separate disposition. However, it does not apply to masses or other entities which form inseparable units either because of the natural qualities of the goods or the intentions of those who may dispose of them. A dike may serve as illustration. It efficiently protects an island from the incursions of the sea only while its entire length is unbroken. Another case in point is afforded by the monopolistic vendor who refuses to sell his stores except as a whole. The purchaser is thus faced with the alternative of buying everything or nothing. In all cases where aggregates are treated as units, the dependent utility is the total utility which may be realized from the aggregate. The dike must be preserved intact, if the safety and total utility of all the stores and economic goods, which benefit the islanders, is not to be jeopardized. A tidal wave, which should break through the dike and destroy the stores of goods, would surely wipe out the entire utility that was to be obtained from the harvested supply. This total utility embraces a series of values, which reach from those highest ones inherent in the preservation of life to the marginal utility of the existing store. The latter, however, is an inconsiderable magnitude in comparison with the former. The crops themselves fall in a different category so long as the economy follows an undisturbed course. They are regarded as a divisible store. The more finely divisible they are, the more carefully the plan for their utilization is laid down. The plan will provide for dispositions down to the smallest quantities.

It goes without saying that these remarks do not imply that the available quantities do not influence the scheme of the economy. A plentiful harvest and a failure of crops lead to different plans of management. Similarly under ordinary conditions the partial quantity in the framework of the whole will always be the object of regular dispositions. The stores are regarded as sums capable of separation into parts. The latter are to be disposed of by numerous contemporaneous or successive acts. But at all times such dispositions are to be made in proportions which are well balanced with reference to each other. Similar considerations govern the detailed utilization of the available masses of personal services. This is also done in accordance with the standards presented by the general circumstances. Personal services also are susceptible to subdivision. Whatever statements may be made concerning divisible stores apply to services, saving, very naturally those restrictions which are to be made in view of their personal character. In what follows, whenever we speak of stores, the term always includes the available quantities of personal services unless special exception is expressly taken.

We shall make no mention in the theory of the simple economy of the relations governing masses and other economic wholes. They are scarcely of importance in the regular course of the private economic process. Later, in the theory of the social economy, when we discuss monopoly, and still more in the theory of the state economy, we shall have to turn our attention to those problems. We shall be able to show that valuation in the economy of the state is distinguished in numerous cases from private valuation in that the former regards the total utility while the latter takes for its standard the marginal utility. In the following examination of the economic computation of utility, we assume throughout the typical relations of the private economy, dealing with stores which admit of separation into parts. The rules which we deduce are the rules of the typical private partial computation.

This being presupposed, the fundamental law of the economic computation of utility may be stated to be that all units (fractional quantities, pieces) of a stock should be reckoned uniformly at the marginal utility. We shall refer to this law as the law of marginal utility, or, more briefly, as the marginal law.

From the latter, it follows that every divisible stock should be economically valued as a multiple of the marginal utility. The multiple corresponds to the number of units (fractional quantities, pieces). When a stock consists of ten units, each with the marginal utility *n*, the sum of the units is to be computed as *10 n*. This is not a new law, but only a different formulation of the marginal law. It is important because in it we have to key to the understanding of practical economic computations as it is generally practiced. We shall consider it more fully in our final exposition of economic calculation.

The marginal law establishes the basis for all other rules of the economic computation of utility. In the isolated household, two of these require special attention whenever changes occur in the quantities of the stock,[1] or as the case may be, of the demand. We shall designate these as the law of supply and the law of demand.

First then, let us consider the law of supply. Where needs remain the same and the supply increases the computed marginal utility must be lowered. We may assume in the illustration already employed that a hitherto unopened compartment of the ship, discloses an additional number of tons of drinking

[1] Trans. note: Throughout this section "stock" may be replaced by "supply," "need" by "demand"; in some places the change has been made. Since later what is clearly, "supply" is rendered by "Angebot" and is evidently distinguished from "Vorrat" as used in this section, it has seemed wise to use "stock" to convey an idea of physical volume.

water. In such a case it would probably be permissible to increase the daily consumption of this water by uses which until then were forbidden. Where needs remain the same and the stock decreases, as let us say, by the loss of a number of tons, the computed marginal utility must necessarily rise. Employments which up to that event were allowable must afterwards be excluded.

As against these instances, take the case where the computed marginal utility remains unaffected: where the reduction of supply comes about only in the course of the regular use of the commodity as satisfaction is obtained for the expected needs. Needs and supply are reduced coincidently. To return to the example of the ship: the stock is ten tons; the journey is to occupy ten days. The daily consumption will be one ton of water. On the first day one of the ten tons will be computed at exactly the same rate as will obtain on the second day for one of the remaining nine tons, or, as on the last day, for the final ton. When the ship reaches port and takes in new stores in the same proportions, the marginal utility will be unchanged as before. A household experiencing month after month the same income and the same needs will, in the regular course of events, have to deal with the same marginal utility. On the first day of the month it draws its income and anticipates the needs of the entire month. The marginal utility which is computed at that time will not differ from that of the last day when what remains of the income is expended to defray the needs of the last day. These cases are no exception to the law of supply. The latter takes cognizance merely of changes of stocks when the needs remain the same. It maintains that when this latter condition is fulfilled, the computed marginal utility changes in the opposite direction to the variation of the supply.

The law of stock corresponds to the law with which the market has been familiar, that prices vary in the opposite direction to changes in the supply. The law of stock forms the theoretical basis for the explanation of the law of supply. On the other hand, the former finds its confirmation in the latter, which is demonstrated by experience. But for this very reason we may ask if the marginal law does not find empirical confirmation. The law of stock is derived from the marginal law. Then, if the latter law is established, is not the general theory of marginal utility also confirmed? We must insist on these contentions all the more, since it is precisely in the explanation of these market experiences that the older formulations of the theory of marginal utility failed to satisfy. In its earliest forms the theory started from the total utility realized or else from the usefulness. Therefore, it was unable to explain the market phenomenon involved in the fact that the more abundant the harvest, the lower the degree of the computed utility; the scantier the harvest, the higher the utility.

In the theory of marginal utility the object of economic computation is the unit in the frame-work of the supply. The marginal utility is the significant magnitude of utility by which the unit is measured. All difficulties disappear for this theory. The computed marginal utility of the unit of grain is bound to be lowered when the harvest is more plentiful; it must rise when the harvest is scanty. There are occasionally cases in which, as stocks increase, not only the marginal utility of the unit is lowered but also the product of the marginal utility and the number of units is decreased. It may happen, for example, that this product is less in the case of an abundant harvest than in the case of a meagre one. One of the most earnest advocates of the older theory said that such instances were a *crux vera* for the theory. But it is now possible to offer a consistent explanation of these cases also. The situation in such an event is just this: because of the course followed by the scale of needs the marginal utility of the unit decreases more rapidly than the number of units increases.

The explanation of the law of demand offers no further difficulties. This law deals with variations of the computed marginal utility which are caused by variations of the demand while the supply remains the same. These changes invariably take place in correspondence with the variations of demand. The computed marginal utility rises and falls with the magnitude of the needs. The latter term is not used here to describe the sum of the needs, or that quantity of means of satisfaction which is needed to cover completely all requirements. A narrower meaning of the term is used. This is the so-called "effective demand," and embraces those needs which could be covered in any event by the stores provided. Only variations within the limit of effective demand exert an influence upon the degree of the computed marginal utility. Variations of those impulses which urge inadmissible satisfactions are immaterial. In the illustration already used, we may assume that the supply of water on the ship has fallen so low that only a small quantity may be allowed to the crew for drinking purposes. All other uses are barred. In this case it will be a matter of entire indifference to the computation of utility what changes take place in regard to the need of prohibited employments.

In a much quoted passage in the *Wealth of Nations*, Adam Smith explains that value-in-use and value-in-exchange are to be carefully distinguished. Things possessing the greatest value-in-use often have little or no value-in-exchange, and vice versa. Nothing is more useful than water; but nevertheless it has scarcely any purchasing power. On the other hand a diamond is nearly devoid of use-value, and yet, as a rule, a large quantity of other commodities can be obtained for it. These considerations determined Adam Smith to abandon the theory of utility in favor of the labor theory.[1]

However, would he not have made a different choice had he been familiar with the fundamental law of the economic computation of utility? Smith assumes that water is a free commodity. In such a case the utility of water is not to be computed economically. Free goods are available in such abundance that no one need stint himself for economic reasons in making use of them. Economic foresight sets no limit to their employment. They possess no marginal utility for the obvious reason that every fractional use which may be demanded can be filled. The available stocks of diamonds are small. Diamonds are rare in the true sense of the term. It is therefore in full agreement with the law of the economic computation of utility that a comparatively high marginal utility is accorded to them. This may be higher than the one computed in the case of food stuffs, for example, where these are available in large quantities. It must be admitted that the entire difference which may usually be pointed out between the prices of diamonds and of foodstuffs, is not explained by these remarks. Other conditions of the market must also be considered, which for the present we are not able to discuss. Still, even here, we may assure the reader that it does not appear to be a hopeless problem to explain the phenomenon of the high price of diamonds from

[1] See Book I, Chap. IV. Smith, to be sure, does not consistently adhere to the labor theory.

the theory of utility. However this may be, the fundamental law of the economic computation of utility is essential to theory. This law holds for the simple economy of the individual. Without its aid no theory will be able to explain the factors which go to make up the price of diamonds or any other prices. There is no exception to the statement that all prices are the outgrowth of personal computations of utility on the part of the demanders.

§ 17. Marginal Utility in Idealized Production

The marginal utility of products and productive means—The cumulative computation of marginal utility in production.

We wish to formulate our assumptions so as to simplify our statements as far as possible with regard to idealized conditions of production. We assume, then, that we have at our disposal the personal services necessary to production. This supply of labor seeks an outlet for its creative energy. It is fresh. It will not be necessary to conserve human effort either because of its quantity or from considerations of the effects of the burden of labor. We shall further assume that iron is the only productive agent to be used. There are 1000 units of this material that will be used to produce ten different kinds of product. Each of the latter requires the same amount of iron: one unit of iron will produce one unit of any product. The final assumption which we make is that the same scale describes each of the ten needs which are served by different products. The question to be answered is: by what plan will production be organized in this case so as to realize the maximum utility?

Under these assumptions it would be a mistake to devote the 1000 units of iron to any one product. It would even be a mistake to provide a larger proportion for one product than for another. One may assume that the increment of utility due to the hundredth product is 10. It follows from Gossen's law that the added utility due to the use of more iron to produce an additional unit must be less than 10. Since this particular use of the iron means that only 99 units of some other product can be manufactured, the gross loss of utility must be more than 10. By the same reasoning, the further one carries the practice of favoring one product at the expense of the other the greater is the utility sacrificed and the less the utility gained. The total utility therefore declines. This will be a maximum when the 1000 units of iron are equally distributed to all products: i. e., when the production of each of the ten fractional quantities is adjusted to 100 units. In other words the most favorable scheme of production will be established through a calculation involving the marginal utility. Each type of production will be stopped as soon as the marginal utility, 10, has been reached.

This accounting is fundamental and controls the scheme of production. However it would be incomplete if it were confined to a consideration of the various products. It must also be extended to embrace the masses of productive supplies. The productive stock is kept on hand in order to be transformed into products which are to yield a utility increment. However, every such transfer diminishes the quantity of the productive stock and thus results in a loss of utility. Both the utility increment yielded by the products and the loss of utility due to the disposition of the productive agent must be considered by economic foresight. If the expression may be permitted, the controlling economic account is kept by double entry: it sets down the increment of utility against products and the loss of utility against the productive means. Both computations are made according to the marginal utility. In our example, one unit of iron has a marginal utility of 10. No technical transformation of the iron could therefore be permitted unless the resulting product yielded the marginal utility, 10. It is not sufficient that the producer is aware that iron, being likely to aid in turning out useful products, is itself useful. He should also know the exact measure of the utility which is assured to him by his stock of iron, according to prevailing circumstances. Then, just as he infers the usefulness of iron from that of its products, he will deduce the amount at which the utility of iron is to be computed from the amount by which the usefulness of its products is measured. Both the iron and its products must therefore be computed according to the marginal law. In general, a series of productive means are expected to yield a series of products. The anticipated marginal utility of the latter is imputed beforehand to the former series. The marginal law states that all units of a stock are to be computed cumulatively according to the marginal utility. This cumulative computation must therefore apply to both products and productive means. The total available supply of iron is thus to be reckoned as 1000×10, or 10,000. The stock set aside according to schedule for each fractional mass of products is figured as 100×10, or 1000. The sum of these ten masses is therefore also reckoned at 10,000. The cumulative computation in the economy does not even have the semblance of a paradox in production. It is obvious that this method of appraising the masses insures adherence to the most advantageous productive scheme, and that, moreover, it is the simplest process of estimation that could be devised under any circumstances.

To simplify the factors, we assumed but one series of productive means in our illustration. As a matter of fact there is always a large number of such series in a developed industry. There are as many series as there are productive stems. The marginal law holds for each of these. However, in the discussions that follow, we shall continue to simplify and shall speak collectively of the marginal utility of only one series of productive agents. We shall contrast this with the marginal utility of the products. Only in so far as it may become necessary to follow up the computation within the system of the productive classes do we propose further to analyze productive utility.

As for the other idealizing assumptions, we shall dismiss them one by one and resort to others which more nearly duplicate the actual facts of production. Hitherto we have assumed only a single mass of productive cost-means. We shall broaden the assumption to show the joint action of land, capital and labor. Furthermore, we shall differentiate specific- and cost-productive-means. So far we have considered only cost products. We shall now speak of specific products also. In place of the simplest quantitative relation between productive means and products we shall grade the cost-norms. Instead of uniformly graded scales of needs we shall take account of scales which are variously graduated. Finally, the element of time is to be introduced to replace the time-neglecting course of production which has been discussed. We shall have to distinguish permanent productive goods from those which deteriorate while in use. In these connections we shall have to speak of the law of costs, productive imputation, computation of net yield, rent and capitalization. The doctrine of the computation of utility will thus broaden and deepen into the theory of economic computation.

§ 18. The Law of the Cost of Production in the Simple Economy

The usual and the scientific concepts of costs of production—The two series of individual utility and cost utility—The law of the cost of production and the basic law of the computation of utility—Inter-connected costs of production —Quality products.

The business man contrasts profits and costs. As he looks at the use to which wares will be put, he regards them as goods meant to bring in profits. As he considers their source, he thinks of them as products whose manufacture involves cost. The comparison of profits and costs runs through the whole of the accounts of production. The business man's constant endeavor is to obtain the largest profit at the lowest cost. He will never incur greater outlays than he anticipates can be recovered through the resulting utilities. However his practical experience never aids him to solve the problem of the manner in which the two magnitudes which he is constantly comparing are, in the last resort, fit objects of comparison.

Theory received its notion of costs from practical life, a classic illustration of the relations obtaining between economic practice and theory. The concepts inherent in the customary language of the market are the beginnings of all economic theory. This fact gives a potent influence to market parlance. This is not of itself an evil; rather it is of incalculable advantage to scientific reflection. It provides direct guidance to the deeply buried treasures of daily experience. A wealth of experience has been brought together in the generally current ideas of profits and costs. The influence of ordinary speech becomes a menace to theory only when its concepts are accepted uncritically and when scientific inquiry stops short there. The business man is a keen observer, but his field of vision is often narrowly bounded. He is apt to consider only that side of the economy which lies within the range of his practical interests. On the other hand the theorist must grasp the unity of all the phenomena of the economy.

The concepts of profits and costs are also ultimately in close contact. Their full significance is only realized when their intimate connection is understood. But looking closely at the matter, is not this significance at least suggested in the current idea of costs? The language of every civilized people is rich in meanings which may be felt although they are not expressed in detail. This is the case with the term "costs." As one uses it he receives a suggestion of the idea which forms the link between costs and profits. Anyone gifted with a keen feeling for living speech may uncover the connection by following the associations aroused by the word. Thus "costs" furnishes a classic example of the greatest service performed by the language of living men to scientific thought. It points to the avenue by which we may enter the wordless wisdom of our deepest experiences.

Whenever the business man speaks of incurring costs, he has in mind the quantity of productive means required to achieve a certain end; but the associated idea of a sacrifice which his efforts demand is also aroused. In what does this sacrifice consist? What, for example, is the cost to the producer of devoting certain quantities of iron from his supply to the manufacture of some specific product? The sacrifice consists in the exclusion or limitation of possibilities by which other products might have been turned out, had the material not been devoted to one particular product. Our definition in an earlier connection made clear that cost-productive-means are productive agents which are widely scattered and have manifold uses. As such they promise a profitable yield in many directions. But the realization of one of these necessarily involves a loss of all the others. It is this sacrifice that is predicated in the concept of costs: the costs of production or the quantities of cost-productive-means required for a given product and thus withheld from other uses.

It is thus shown in what respects costs and profits may be compared. The yield is the individual utility [1] of the particular product. In costs one includes the more remote gains which are promised by the available cost-productive-means in the utility of all other goods which may be produced. Thus we have, if we may say so, a cost-utility, an iron-utility, and a labor-utility. The business man, comparing the profits of one product with its cost, compares in truth two masses of utility. He contrasts the particular amount of utility peculiar to a single type of product and the general mass of utility of all products of the same stem. Costs of production and yield are not actually in thorough-going contrast. The yield is the utility of the individual products. The costs of production determine the general yield in the series of productive means. Whenever economic production functions with a minimum of costs it results in the maximum utility.

In the idealized example of the stock of iron, the productive marginal utility of the cost-means, the cost-utility, coincides exactly with the individual marginal utility of all of its products. The marginal utility of iron and also of every product is equal to 10. Consequently, whenever production is carried on according to the original scheme, the outlay in costs is exactly counterbalanced by the realized utility. Actually the two series do not by any means always completely coincide. There are many deviations which arise partly from temporary disturbances and partly from permanent conditions of production. For the present we shall confine our attention to the latter.

We here recall the results of earlier stages of our investigation. We ascertained (§ 10) that production can never be carried to an exact state of equilibrium; that even the preparation of pure cost-products

[1] Trans. note: *Eigennutzen.* This may perhaps best be rendered as above. The translator first used "inherent utility." This was discarded because it already has a definite meaning—or lack of meaning—in economic theory. Wieser does not mean to maintain that there is inherent utility in this rejected sense. As the phrase recurs frequently it is possible that in one or two passages the word "inherent" is left. If so it should be read as synonymous with individual—particular—utility.

can never be brought entirely to one "level" as the diversity of the scales of needs forms an insurmountable obstacle. We then spoke of a "general margin of use," indicated for every economy by its available means. We added that the individual cost-products can only be made to approach the general limit of use in so far as the gradations of the individual scales of needs permit. From this point of our inquiry, let us now proceed further.

The illustration of the iron-supply and the products of iron, of which we have just made use, will again serve our ends; but we shall have to supplement it for the present purpose. We had assumed ten varieties of product, the marginal utilities of which were equally represented by 10. In addition to these, let us now bring forward another group of products, the scale of needs of which is not to influence the marginal utility of 10. Let us further assume that, over and above the original 1000 units of iron, 200 more are available. These are destined for the erection of two iron bridges to connect sections of a city separated by a river. Each of the bridges will require an outlay of 100 units of iron. Let the utility resulting from the erection of the first bridge be so large as to exceed considerably the outlay of 1000, ascertained by multiplying the required iron-units by the marginal utility. We will assume it to be 2000 or 3000. This is equivalent to 20 or 30 for each unit of iron. A second bridge, also, is to yield a utility in excess of the outlay of costs. We will assume this to be 1500, or 15 for each unit. A third bridge, however, would yield only 500, or 5 for the unit of iron. It would follow that a third bridge must not be built. Its yield of utilities would not compensate for the costs to be incurred. Assuming these figures, the general margin of use of the iron-unit is 10. It is determined by those types of production which can be extended exactly to the marginal utility, 10. Designating these as marginal productive processes and their products as marginal products, we may define the "general margin of use" as the limit, determined by the marginal utility of marginal products. The striking economic characteristic of the product, "bridge," is that it is not a marginal product. We shall speak of all products of this sort as products of a narrower margin of utility, and of the production processes as those of the narrower margin of utility. For marginal products, the marginal utility and utility-cost coincide; for the particular product "bridge" they do not. Here the individual marginal utility is higher than the utility-cost.

By what standard, then, is a product of narrower marginal utility to be computed, economically? Should it be by that of the higher individual marginal utility, or according to that of the lower utility-cost? This is the crucial point. Conditions surely might be conceived in which the individual marginal utility would supply the standard. If one of the bridges is carried away when the ice breaks up, the loss sustained until the bridge is reconstructed, is to be computed according to the full measure of its marginal utility of 1500. This measures the damage during the entire period. If the second bridge also should be destroyed, the damage sustained should be computed according to the still higher standard of utility of 2000 or 3000 that is dependent on its preservation. In case of war, victory and even the safety of the country may depend on the possession of the two means of crossing. Under these conditions, sacrifices will possibly be made for their defence, far exceeding the standard which would have formed the basis of an appraisal in time of peace. Thus, in the press of battle one may offer "a kingdom for a horse," although in the ordinary routine of economic work, the utility of a horse is not appraised at an extraordinary figure.

The routine economic computation, however, is neither concerned with an estimation of the damage resulting from an unforeseen loss nor with an appraisal induced by the unusual vicissitudes of war. Economic computation is effected solely for the purpose of establishing a scheme of production of use in the economy. The resulting numerical values are only such as these ends require. Further possibilities, beyond the sphere of the economic current of affairs, are disregarded. For these purposes it is quite adequate to confine attention to the standard of the utility-costs. Thus, in our example, the two bridges are appraised as structures, each of which calls for an outlay of 100 units of iron whose marginal utility is 10. This figure is an accurate measure of the utility which is significant in the regular course of the economy. This proposition we now expect to demonstrate.

In order that our illustration may be more in keeping with the multiform variety of actual conditions, we shall abandon one of the idealized assumptions. We shall no longer assume that the same simple cost-rate and the same regular scale of needs applies to the ten species of products other than the bridges. The great variety of iron-products which modern industry turns out are of the most diverse sizes. They demand very different quantities of iron, from the finest wire to enormous blocks. The scales of needs to be served are as variously graded. Our illustration was devised so as to show only for the bridges a divergence of the inherent marginal utility and the cost-utility. For all other iron-products these were assumed to coincide. But probably the reverse is a better description of actual conditions. Only for comparatively few kinds of products do the two series coincide; for the greater number they diverge. In other words, the number of production-processes of the narrower margin of utility is probably greater than that of the marginal production-processes.

However that may be, the iron-products of the narrower margin of utility, as explained in our illustration for the bridge, will have to be appraised not at the individual higher marginal utility, but only at the lower cost-utility. Could this be otherwise? The fundamental law of utility-computation, the marginal law, demands like computation for all like units. As it is valid for the stocks of commodities of the first order in the household, this law is valid for the stocks of commodities of higher orders in production; all units of iron in the crude state are to be computed alike. No matter what the finished products into which they are to be turned, they will have to be estimated, unit by unit, according to the productive marginal utility, the measure of which is determined by the marginal utility of the marginal products. But could the iron, turned into finished products, be estimated differently, when used according to plan? Entering every iron-product fashioned according to schedule in the account of the economy as the product of the number of iron units and the marginal utility of the iron-unit, we obtain an arithmetic expression that corresponds exactly to the correct scheme of production and is all the more advantageous, inasmuch as the arithmetic expression is extremely simplified. Even in planning the scheme of production we need not endeavor to carry out in all cases with punctilious accuracy the rather difficult appraisal of the individual utility. It answers every purpose for example to ascertain that the usefulness of both a first and second bridge is larger than the utility cost. The exact numerical expression of the general margin of utility will have to be accurately calculated. But if it is once established that the individual utility equals at least the utility cost, the remaining calculations may confidently be completed by the numerical expression of the utility cost. That this manner of computation is correct, can be shown by practical results. It extends to the entire output of human economic activity, to every employment of materials, wherever these are economically permitted; it bars all those that are economically barred.

If we now also abandon the idealizing assumption that merely the raw material, iron, need be computed economically, and broaden the assumption so as to include the entire array of cost-productive means as objects of economic computation, efforts of labor as well as cost-commodities, we shall reach the same result even under this greatly extended assumption. Cost-products are always to be regarded as compounds of the cost-elements required for turning them out in the regular course of economy. Just as, technically considered, they are allotropic modifications of their component elements, they will have to be accepted as such arithmetically.[1]

This is the Production Cost Law of the simple economy. We must perfect it by an explanation in order to introduce the factor of duration of time in production which our ideal outline has hitherto neglected. In order that our inquiry be complete in all respects, we must still answer the question as to how the productive yields should be redistributed to the cost-means which have worked together in earning them. As to both these problems, we shall have to defer the supplementary investigation just as we shall have to introduce the law of computation for specific products later on.

The law of the cost of production of the simple economy is observed by every individual producer, even in a fully developed social economy. Every producer in his accounts computes the cost-products which he turns out as compounds of the productive elements required to get them ready. The formulations in which the market traditionally predicates the law of costs, as well as the older, theoretical interpretations, do not by any means completely reproduce the computation which the producers actually follow. They stress cost-quantities, quantities of required cost-units, but they find no expression for the manner in which the cost-units themselves are to be estimated. Our formula gives complete expression to the cost-law in that it also points out the standard by which the cost-units are to be computed. The productive marginal utility of the cost-unit is the standard; it is deduced from the marginal utility of the marginal products. This complete expression gives the cost-law its correct meaning. It is not a new law; it merely transfers the fundamental law of the computation of utility to the widely ramified conditions of the relationship of production. It traces products back to the productive stem-elements, and it computes the latter at the beneficial yield which they promise in the case of their most profitable employment. There is a much smaller number of stem-elements than of variations by which they may be compounded and therefore of kinds of products. Thus the calculation according to costs results in a much

[1] v. Wieser, *The Source of Value*, p. 152.

more simple expression than the calculation according to the individual utility of the products. As we have already shown, the calculation according to the marginal utility is much more simple than the calculation according to total utility; the computation according to costs is another step towards simplification of the economic account.

We are accustomed to speak of joint costs of production or, as the case may be, joint products. Waste products and by-products offer the most familiar illustration. Both are obtained in the course of the manufacture of a principal product: waste-products, without requiring an additional expenditure of any kind; by-products on the other hand, still necessitating a moderate, though possibly small, productive outlay. The peculiarity of either class of goods is that the supply is built up without any immediate regard to needs. As many waste-products are accumulated to be disposed of as the increase of the principal product brings in its train. When it comes to by-products, their special costs will naturally have to be charged to their account. This account is to be arranged so as to exhibit how principal costs and subsidiary costs are balanced by the yield in principal products and by-products. The subsidiary costs will never be the more significant.

In a broader sense, all those products are to be classified as joint products which are obtained under one system of operations. For all these, certain general expenses are joint expenses: certain plant costs and costs of operation which are to be distinguished from special costs, as they arise separately for individual products. There are various transitions between general expenses and special expenses. The general expenses are joint costs and have to be apportioned among all products of the output or its subdivisions, as the case may be. The apportionment is to be made with the aim of realizing the greatest total benefit that can possibly be secured. Let this general proposition suffice for the present; all details will be taken up later on in connection with the doctrine of prices.

There are numerous quality-products which are obtained by employing specific productive means of special quality. Possibly, however, the superior quality is due only to intensified additions of cost-means, for example, by using a greater number of hours of labor. Quality-products of the latter kind are cost-products; they are compositions of the same kind of cost-elements as the cruder products, but the required expenditure for cost-elements is greater per unit. An economy of more limited means will have to content itself with the cruder products which satisfy the principal need less fully and are subject to many inconvenient and injurious counter-effects. An advanced economy, having at its command more abundant stores of materials as well as a larger supply of labor, increases its satisfactions not only by making more but also better products.

For both types of progress the law of satiety holds. The added productive elements, in the one case as in the other, are employed with decreasing utility. In both cases they serve a decreasing need. Over-satiety may finally result, on the one hand, by increasing the acts of satisfaction to exceed healthful limits; on the other, by an over-refinement that leads to degeneration. This observation is important inasmuch as it traces the quality of products to cost-quantities, and thus broadens the field within which the cost-law has validity and simplifies the economic account.

§ 19. Changes of Costs and the Computation of Utility

Temporary disturbances of production—Decreasing costs—Technical progress and the law of supply—Increasing costs—Diminishing returns from land and increasing industrial returns—The law of the cost of reproduction—The law of maximum costs.

Under all conditions changes of cost bring about changes of price. It is this fact which is largely responsible for the opinion that prices are chiefly responsible for costs, an opinion that is widely held in business circles and has thus been communicated to theorists. As a matter of fact this is not an immediate relationship. Costs, and consequently their changes, can only affect prices in so far as these factors influence the computation of utility. Therefore the effect on prices of changes in costs can only be understood when one comprehends their influence on the computation of utility.

Changes of costs are due to a variety of causes. In part they are the result of changes in the actual conditions of supply and demand; in part of changes occurring in the technique of production. Not infrequently both of these are contributing factors. First, as regards the changes of demand and supply, there are minor fluctuations which frequently occur but never exert a very appreciable influence. But at times there are also more extensive changes which occur so rapidly that production cannot be immediately adjusted to them. Such changes disturb production, demoralize the relationship of one branch to another, and may possibly for some time sever such connections entirely. Under these conditions, utility-cost may be partially or completely displaced; the individual utility gains independent prominence. For example, when war suddenly breaks out, the need of fire-arms unexpectedly becomes pressing. If part of the store of weapons is seized by the enemy, the interconnections of the production relationship will be practically destroyed. For the time being, those weapons which are ready for use will no longer be regarded as products: i. e., as compounds of their elements. They will be considered as commodities of a given kind which are to be appraised at their higher, individual utility. However, it will be observed that in such a case an extreme tension is set up between the utility-cost of iron and of the other productive elements on the one hand, and the individual utility of weapons on the other. This tension gives a strong impetus to extend production and once more to increase stocks. Costs will be incurred which had never been allowable in other circumstances, until finally the disturbance will be overcome and an equilibrium re-established between the results of the two methods of computation. An opposite type of disturbance may also occur, due to the sudden falling-off of needs or the unexpected inflation of available stocks. In cases of this sort, the individual utility of existing products will drop below the margin of costs. It is likely that an effort will be made to restore an equilibrium between the two computations by stimulating consumption. When durable products are involved, a considerable falling-off of demand will of necessity lead not only to a temporary retardation of production, but to its permanent cessation. For example, in a city whose population has greatly decreased, new dwellings are not likely to be built so long as those already erected are habitable. These older habitable houses will no longer be appraised as compounds of their cost-elements, but rather according to the lower standard of their marginal utility which fails to compensate for the costs of construction.

The changes in the technique of production are of two kinds. On the one hand there is the progress of the technical arts which lowers the rates of cost. On the other hand, production may be carried on under less favorable conditions at higher rates, as may happen where an increase of population necessarily leads to increased needs.

It is easy to trace the effect of limited technical progress which lowers the cost only for minor groups of products. The number of cost-units by which the affected products must be computed will be reduced. Simultaneously, savings will be made in cost-means. At the same time production may perhaps be extended, thus increasing the need of cost-means. As the one or the other effect predominates, certain movements are started to restore an equilibrium with reference to other products. Such displacements in one segment of the productive process will always be insignificant and will scarcely exert an appreciable influence on the computation of the utility of related products. It is otherwise with technical progress of general significance. The employment of steam power in the factory economy has lowered the rates of cost for a long series of products. Railroads have had an even wider influence which has extended to all products in inland transportation where rivers and canals were not accessible. Should the airship become the vehicle of transportation in the future and surpass the railroad in efficiency and cheapness as the latter surpassed the turnpike, it would have a momentous effect in an equally extensive sphere. Such far-reaching technical progress has manifold influences on the computation of utility. It directly lowers the costs of many products. According to the law of supply, it depresses the marginal utility of the cost-unit, for an increased quantity of products can now be manufactured. In this way technical advances also affect products whose costs are not lowered. These may likewise be produced in larger quantities owing to the depression in the margin of use. Finally, by the law of costs these improvements affect even products of a narrower marginal utility whose costs are not lowered and which are not produced in increased quantities.

A general advance in prices is accompanied by the same broad effects in an inverse order. Not only the cost rates of the directly affected products, but the appraisal of the cost-units is increased. Furthermore the general margin of use is raised for other productive processes as well. This may even extend to all economic production. For example, let us assume that no cheaper source of power has been discovered to take the place of steam, that the best coal mines have been exhausted, and that producers have been forced to resort to inferior deposits which may be worked only at greater cost. Such an occurrence will seriously curtail the efficiency and extent of the world's productivity and the possibility of supplying its needs. It will find expression not merely in a far-reaching increase of the most important costs but also in an enhanced computation of all cost-units. It will consequently result in an extensive shrinkage of the economic margin of use of the world.

The influence of the changes of costs on the computation of utility extends also to stocks of products which are retained from a period when the old rates were valid. When technical improvements are made, a certain lapse of time will of course always be required until the new methods can be completely applied. But even if one grants this, where the accumulated earlier stocks were very large the reduction of costs may have a certain anticipatory effect. In using the stocks, the new line of marginal utility is prepared for or approximated. When the transitional period is passed and the qualities of the old products and the new are the same, probably no distinction will be made. All products are appraised alike at the new reduced rate of cost; or, as one may also put it, the determining consideration in the case of the older products is not their original cost but rather the cost of their replacement or reproduction. This law of the costs of reproduction will probably not require further demonstration. It goes no further than to say that the controlling factor at all times is the lowest expenditure which is required by industrial conditions.

Diversities in cost rates appear not only in consequence of changes in cost, but also, technical conditions remaining the same, as the result of the different external conditions to which establishments are subject. Such diversity need not be considered in connection with the computation of utility. The best adapted classes of land yield their produce at lower cost than the medium and inferior ones. However, no matter on what land the crop is produced, so long as it is of uniform quality, it is invariably appraised at the same rate. The highest of all these rates of cost is the controlling one, where the outlay for cultivation is still economically required in order to meet the outlay for the demand. In this sense one may speak of a law of highest costs. When, on the other hand, in consequence of negligence, want of skill, want of knowledge, or indolence, excessive costs have been incurred, these are not decisive in the computation. They are not "required," they do not correspond to the highest attainable degree of exploitation, or, in the familiar expression of Marx, to the social average degree of skill and intensity.

All the propositions which have now been deduced with respect to changes of costs are already familiar in their effect on price. It must be borne in mind that they come into play as regards not only the price but also the computation of utility. Concretely they affect the price by means of the computation of utility.

Like all other products, capital goods are also subject to the law of the costs of reproduction: i. e., they are to be appraised at the smallest expenditure which the technique and actual conditions of the period require. A fully developed technology beyond doubt requires capital goods for the production of other capital commodities. The attempt of the labor theory to explain capital as a mere product of labor (see closing remarks of section 13) is inconsistent, therefore, with the law of the costs of reproduction. Historically extinct methods of production exert as little influence in the appraisal of capital as of any other product. A theory which falls back on such methods completely abandons the current trend of economic thought.

The law of diminishing returns from land is an illustration of a widely felt increase in cost that occurs frequently in practice. It is possible that the general advance of all prices which is now so universally complained of in all countries of the world is to be traced to the fact that this law, after prolonged suspension, has again become effective. It may be that the food requirements for the enormously increased population of our period are becoming such as can no longer be met by resort to new lands. Even were this law not the universal rule in agriculture, and if all outlays on the soil were rewarded by equal yields, the production of food-stuffs for an increasing population would still require an increase in the absolute costs. Such an increase would only be possible without corresponding retrenchments, where the capital of the people is growing proportionately.

The law of diminishing returns from land becomes more burdensome as it increases the relative per capita costs. Only in countries where the growth of capital proceeds at least in equal proportions with the increase in population, can the onerous effects of the law be overcome.

The effects of the operation of the law on the appraisal of agricultural and industrial products may be most clearly shown by a numerical illustration. For the sake of simplicity let us select our facts so as to confine all agricultural production to the one product, wheat. We shall assume that up to the period contemplated by our example, an addition of ten cost units was required in order to reap one hundred pounds of wheat. For the future, to feed the larger population, eleven units will be required. Let us start with the most unfavorable combination of circumstances: the increase of capital is not sufficiently large to supply the entire additional outlay, and wheat is a marginal product. Hitherto wheat has had a marginal utility of ten, which has exactly corresponded with the required outlay. The expenditure of eleven units will not be permissible until the marginal utility of wheat has risen to eleven. In other words, where conditions are of the sort assumed, an increase of production is only allowable where there is at the same time a corresponding reduction of the quantity of wheat per capita, and where therefore, food consumption per capita has decreased. At the same time, all other marginal production will have to be curtailed proportionately. The standard of living of the middle classes will therefore also be lowered as regards the use of a number of industrial products.

If wheat is not a marginal product but is one with a narrower margin of use, the conditions are more favorable. Let us say that the marginal utility is twelve. In this case, the increased outlay of eleven will be allowable without of necessity reducing per capita food consumption. The outlays required for increased cultivation will be withdrawn from marginal industrial production to which they would otherwise have been directed. The fact that the productive marginal utility must now be appraised at a higher figure will be felt only in the curtailed supply of these industrial products.

Finally, let us assume the most favorable circumstances: the universal increase of wealth is large enough to provide the additional outlay for cultivation even without curtailing marginal industrial production. The law of diminishing returns from land will not result in an increase of the appraisal of the cost units. Its effect will be confined simply to an alteration of the proportions in which agricultural and industrial products are valued. The former will thenceforth be subject to a higher comparative computation, since their costs are rising, while those of the latter are falling. The alteration of this relationship will be all the greater, the more extensively the progress of industry allows it to function with increasing yields.

§ 20. The Problem of Attribution of Yields

The complementary quality of productive means—The creative force of labor and the "product of labor"—Apportionment of yield and distribution of income —The relation of juridical and economic attribution to the causal nexus— The variability of productive inter-relations—Menger's attempted solution— Final statement of the problem.

The factors of production are complementary. Neither capital, land nor labor, unsupported by other forces, produces a yield. That which the soil brings forth without cultivation as the spontaneous gift of nature, is uncertain and extremely scanty. The "fruits of the soil" which are not "products of labor" disappear in contrast with the returns drawn forth by the hand of man. But even so, the mere garnering of the fruits, whenever it is continuously performed, involves labor. This is clear in the case of hunting and fishing. It is especially true that mining is a laborious acquisition of the products of the earth. In order to fashion the simplest products, labor requires raw materials. When the results of labor are to be increased, it must be reinforced by tools. In an advanced economy there are numerous stages of technical manipulation and transportation for every product, that extend from the recovery of the raw material to its delivery into the hands of the consumer. Every product thus absorbs the effects of almost innumerable means of production. When one speaks theoretically of the three productive factors, land, capital and labor, one gives a collective designation to the three comprehensive groups into which the thousands and thousands of productive means may be divided.

In order to direct production systematically, the producer must be able to judge in any given case the extent to which the yield is the result of any one of the many jointly active productive means that have been used. He must be able to apportion the joint product among the coöperating factors. Practical production is constantly engaged in this task. There is no doubt that it can perform the task with any degree of accuracy that may suit its purpose. Great industries with a world market have precise methods that facilitate such calculation. It is not necessary that such large scale endeavor be involved in order to ascertain what every laborer, machine and new plant brings in. Ever since there has been such a thing as an economy, the problem of the attribution of yields has been presented and has been solved in an appropriate manner. We cannot conceive of its being absent in the economy of a Crusoe. There are traces of a consciousness of this problem in the development of the most primitive races of hunters and fishes. If the future ever witnesses the rise of a socialistic economy, the problem will be equally present. The solution will have to proceed along the same line of trial and error which has characterized the method of a Crusoe or of an early race of hunters and fishers.

In § 12 we have already seen that the three factors of production are by no means coördinate. Labor is the directing force. It commands the complementary material factors which are merely its tools. The latter are dead instruments, while labor, conscious of its ends, is creative and is the living force. In this sense one may say that labor alone is the producer. One may confidently add that land and capital are merely the conditioning prerequisites to production by labor. In this sense one may also adopt the familiar statement that every product is fundamentally a labor-product.

It would be a serious blunder, however, to assume that in the practical economy the entire productive yield should be ascribed to labor alone. In practice, cognizance will always be taken of the fact that the amount of the yield is dependent on the extent to which the creative worker is aided by material instruments. The worker himself distinguishes the more and the less effective aids. Whenever he thus feels that a greater or smaller proportion of the yield is dependent on such instruments, only a remainder of the total product may be allotted to the reward of his labor.[1]

[1] In those industries in Germany in which relatively the most capital is used the pecuniary, per-capita yield is about 4000 Marks. [Trans. note: These are of course pre-war references.] In others where relatively less capital is used the yield is roughly 2000 Marks. It is obviously inconclusive to explain the difference in yield of 2000 Marks as the mere product of the labor employed in the industries using a large amount of capital. Even in the second group of industries the entire yield is not to be set down as the product of labor. Only a portion of the yield may be attributed directly to labor. The residue, disregarding the share of the entrepreneur, must be attributed to the capital employed. No entrepreneur could make any other calculation without incurring serious loss. Even the model social state will have to adhere to this rule.

The labor-theory itself does not conclude that the full amount of the yield of labor is to be attributed to the share of the labor immediately employed. It partitions the yield. That portion, which the entrepreneur reserves as the share of capital, it imputes to the indirectly employed labor: i. e., such labor as is represented in the capital which, in the terms of the labor-theory, is itself a product of labor. Economic practice refutes this proposition. (See § 13.)

Even should a socialistic labor-party at some distant day succeed in enforcing its demand that the social income be distributed only among actively employed workers, the problem of apportioning yields would still retain its importance. The distribution of income and the attribution of yield are two entirely distinct problems. Essentially the socialist demands that land and capital, as necessary instruments to labor, be not held as private property but be under the control of the socially organized working community. The shares of the income which are realized by land and capital are not to be distributed to private appropriators, least of all as personal income to non-workers. But in the socialistic economy as well as any other it is essential to systematic, economic conduct that these shares be accurately ascertained.

On the other hand, although we may admit that land as well as capital has contributed its share of the yield, this does not supply an argument against the essential demand of socialism. It is not legitimate to conclude from this fact that land and capital should be private property and should form the basis of private incomes. The problem of the attribution of yield is a problem of the inner organization of the economy. It has a place in every economic code and is therefore consistent with all of them. It is a problem of the simple economy. As such, it should be above the wranglings of party animosity.

Once the true nature of the problem is admitted, however, it is evident that the socialist party loses one of its most effective arguments. If it is conceded that land and capital have no share in the yield, one must also concede that all incomes received by land-owners and capitalists go to them at the expense of the workers who created the yield. So long as such conditions obtain, there can be no name other than exploitation to describe these incomes. To this extent, then, the partisans of private property have strong reason to wish to demonstrate that land and capital are also entitled to share in the yield. The theoretical defence of private property in productive means would be untenable and should have no prospect of success, if it were found to be true that all earnings are produced by labor,

For practical purposes capital is not purely a product of labor. It is impossible to eliminate the factor, capital, from the field of practical economy. The theory is correct in the assertion that from the share of the yield which is imputed in the first instance to capital a certain amount must be attributed to the labor which was used in the production of the capital. However, there will always remain a residual which cannot be traced back to labor but must be credited to capital as such.

and that the problem of the apportionment of yield, non-existent in the simple economy, had only been raised by the greed of the wealthy classes.

The economic theory of business enterprise[1] has nevertheless given little attention to the problem. This may be explained by the fact that the great proponents of business economy, the classicists, advocated the labor theory. Being economists of business enterprise they have not carried the labor theory to its logical consequences. This task was reserved to the socialist investigators who found their most useful weapon ready at hand in the classical labor theory. However, they were so deeply impressed by the labor theory that they were unable to make proper approach to the problem of the attribution of yield. Only in Ricardo's theory of rent is an especially obvious instance of attribution discussed. When on superior soil with the same labors of cultivation a better crop has been raised than on inferior land, one may readily see that the credit for this excess belongs not to labor but to the condition of the land. Consequently it will always be spoken of as the excess product of that land. In this case the sequence of fact did not escape the acumen of Ricardo. However, he did not penetrate to an understanding of the full extent and significance of the problem of attribution.

Until most recently those economists of business enterprise who advocated not the labor theory but the theory of utility, have had little success in approaching the problem. They had scarcely reached a scientific comprehension of the elementary ideas of the theory of utility. The problem of attribution was set aside with a solemn declaration of its insolubility. And truly, taking the problem as it was stated, it had no solution. These writers attempted to point out for each of the productive means employed, the physical share to be ascribed to it in the formation of the product. This method of stating the problem might have been all very well if the art of production consisted merely in an external combination of materials, as flour, salt and spices are put together to make bread. Even with the simplest assumption, it is impossible to do justice to the labor forces which mix the ingredients. How could one expect to account for all the many formative forces which alter materials without adding new elements to their substance, or which transport finished goods from one place to another?

A correct statement of the problem must be made in accordance with economic practice. The problem of the partitioning of yield is not practically dependent on the discovery of physical causality but

[1] die bürgerliche Oekonomie.

on economic imputation. Juridical science, within the sphere of its subject matter, has long exploited the idea of attribution and its causal nexus. This legal doctrine furnishes a model which economic theory need only have followed in order to state its problem.

The judge cannot condemn anyone who has not in some way or other contributed to the criminal result: i. e., is not connected with the criminal event by causal nexus. This connection is by no means sufficient to establish the degree in which one is responsible for the crime. Only such persons may be condemned as are of sound mind and have acted with that degree of criminality which creates penal responsibility in the case before the court. The judge must exercise care that no link is missing in the chain of facts which establish the causal nexus. However, he need enter no more deeply into the connection of events than the proceedings require. He will be satisfied, for example, if a medical expert testifies that the poison used was capable of causing death. The question by what bodily changes death was caused, so important to the scientific pharmacologist, will not concern him at all. As soon as the judge has established the causal nexus and the presumption of sanity, he is bound to attribute the entire result to the accused. This is true even though he may know very well that the accused could never have accomplished it alone without instruments and without the peculiar contributing circumstances. The criminal may have made use of a third person now innocently implicated in the causal nexus. It is possible that the unsuspecting victim of the crime was himself induced to follow a course of conduct which accomplished his ruin, and therefore formed part of the causal nexus. These connections may have been widespread. Many causes and individuals may have operated. However, the judge pronounces the perpetrator alone as the responsible agent to whom the result must be attributed.

A decree of this sort is not in the least illogical. It does not purport to be a proposition concerning the causal nexus. It does not say that the perpetrator alone did commit, or could have committed, the deed without the aid of tools or the other persons of whom he made use. It says that among the many contributing factors the perpetrator is the only responsible agent. He is the only one whom the judge can punish in order to carry out the intention of the law and to satisfy the end of punishment.

It may be that in this instance the decree of the judge is necessarily different from that of the philanthropist, the moralist or the statesman of broad views. The judge is controlled by ends which are pointed out in the law and by the purpose of punishment. These other critics pursue different ends. They may acquit the accused of all culpability, laying the deed at the door of entirely different individuals or social classes that the law does not reach. It is even possible that they hold the state itself, the maker of the law, responsible. Each man starts from the same facts and follows the identical causal nexus. Each of these observers logically reaches a different attribution, for each has particular ends in mind. The problem of attribution is necessarily that of selecting from among the multitude of agents and causes those particular ones which are determining, and therefore practically decisive as regards the end in view.

No branch of human activity including economic production could accomplish its ends without resorting to the process of attribution. The attention of economic inquiry should not be confined to the causal nexus. The analysis should neither endeavor to penetrate the series of causation more deeply than is demanded by practical interest, nor should it stop at the threshold of the intricacies of this causation. In the case of production the problem is to throw sufficient light upon the causal nexus to move from it to the practical problem of attribution. Numerous causes are contributing factors. Productive imputation will select only those which come into the sphere of influence of the practical economy. It disregards all those causes which were effective during an earlier but terminated period of production. It disregards all those peculiar to other fields of human life as, for example, to politics or to general social conditions, important as these may be in their reaction on the general social organization. It does not consider those elements of nature which may not be dominated by man, as sunlight and the sun; or even those elements which are subject to human control but may be used in superabundance as free goods. It confines itself altogether to existing economic commodities and services.

The attribution of the entire productive effect to these goods is not illogical nor does it falsify the facts. The method merely confines itself, as attribution always does, to those causes which are of practical importance for the purpose in hand. The farmer does not feel called upon to determine what general causes brought forth his crops. It is only important that he know which of the causes were practically and economically significant. He is fully justified, therefore, if he does not attribute any share in the fruits of his land to the free air above his field, although the air is undoubtedly an active and even indispensable factor of the thriving condition of his crops. With good reason he attributes the entire yield to the economic productive means which could never have produced the result by themselves. In practice these are the only important causes among the many which stand in a causal nexus to the yield. They are the only ones which he as a producer is interested in controlling. When the producer begins to partition the yield among these various significant factors, he must consider the causal nexus and attribution separately. He will not speculate too deeply concerning the former. He will center his attention on the important relationships, and once more will turn to attribution. It would be a hopeless task for the farmer, in the illustration used above of the better grade of land, to attempt to determine by physical analysis of the crop the effects of the soil, the labor, the seed, the manure, the plow and all the other tools. His purpose is sufficiently served by a determination of the fact that equal outlays return larger yields from the better grades of soil. He will probably attribute this entire excess of yield to the qualities of the superior soil, although he well knows that this addition to his crop is not merely a fruit of the soil, but is fully as much the result of labor, seed and other capital goods which he used. Under such circumstances, the practical cause of the larger harvest is the superior soil, and hence the farmer's reasoning leads him to act correctly. Any other course would be mistaken. The owner would lose in the sale of his land if he disregarded the larger yield of the best soil and placed the price as low as that which he would fix for the poorest.

The partitioning of yields is an act of attribution. As such it is neither more nor less than a computation of utility. Until now we have examined the latter act subject to the simplifying assumption that every good renders its service in isolation. In the theory of attribution we must examine the laws of the computation of utility for the more complicated case of productive goods whose services are rendered jointly.

It is easy to deduce the law of attribution in the case of the larger yield from the good soil. But how is the yield of poorer grades to be imputed to land, capital and labor? In general, in what manner is a typical yield to be apportioned to the jointly active productive means?

One of Menger's great achievements is that he stated the problem of the apportionment of yields so as to make its solution more probable also in the general case. He has shown that productive means are complementary. However, the proportions in which they are used are not rigid. Were land, capital and labor always associated in the same proportion, it would be impossible to determine the share of each with practical certainty. No further statement could be confidently made than that the three productive factors, when combined in typical proportions lead, as total cause, to a certain result. However, the effect to be ascribed to each partial cause could not be determined. It would even be improper to speak of a partial cause. The case would be exactly that of the familiar illustration of the shears, which Mill uses in his *Logic* when he endeavors to explain the concept of cause. Provided they must always be combined in the same proportions, land, capital and labor would act in conjunction like the two cutting edges of the shears, as a single indivisible cause. But this assumption does not give a true picture of actual life. Far from it, experience shows that the three factors are combined in endless variety in production. Each of the productive means has most diverse uses with the complementary productive means. It must therefore be possible to determine from the differing yields of these variations, the particular effect for which one factor is responsible as a partial cause.

It is true that Menger has not succeeded in finally disposing of the problem of attribution. He failed even to state the problem correctly, for he never grasped the full significance of the concepts either of attribution or of the computation of utility. He proceeds as follows: experience demonstrates that when a single productive unit ceases to function, all other elements of a productive combination are not necessarily thrown out of action. It may happen that they continue to work together and produce a reduced yield. It may be that the lost unit is replaced by another. Such a substitution leaves a gap at some other point in the productive process. It may also be that it is considered more advantageous to break up entirely the combination originally planned and to apply the units thus saved to other productive combinations. The yield of the latter will be increased, although the increase may not fully compensate for the yield of the abandoned combination. If ten units of each of ten different elements are combined to give a yield of 100, the entire yield does not depend on any one unit.—Such a supposition would make the solution impossible.—Every single unit has only a determinate, partial yield dependent on it. This condition seems to offer a basis for the apportionment of yield.

On closer examination, however, we conclude that the desired result cannot be achieved in this manner. This is most clearly recognized in the fact that entirely different results are arrived at according to the element selected for elimination and the number of the eliminated units. We also find on further reflection that Menger's method always leaves an unapportioned residue. The plan of production must be adjusted to the most remunerative variation. Therefore any alteration must give a smaller yield. The difference may indeed be trifling as between the most profitable and the next best combination. It must, however, be finite or the first combination would not have been chosen. At all events the difference must never be wholly neglected theoretically.

Menger's controlling idea is that practical economic accounting starts from the probability of accidental loss. Actually the computation of utility is never connected with this assumption. If it were to start from this assumption, the marginal law and the cumulative attribution of marginal utility might be charged with an internal contradiction. It always rests on the assumption that the most beneficial result is expected and actually will be realized. In any event, nothing is decided in reference to the computation of utility by variations of inferior yields which are not part of a determinate scheme. Neither has the difference between the yield of the originally planned combination and that of the next most profitable combination any significance in the computation of utility. When the most favorable combination as planned promises a yield of 100, it is entirely immaterial whether the next obtainable yield be 99, 98, 50 or 1. Attribution must start invariably from 100. No deduction may be allowed from this amount in the rate at which the jointly active productive means are calculated. These must be computed at the marginal yield which they promise when most fully utilized. This law is not invalidated by the necessity of an apportionment of the yield. The problem of the attribution of yields is to be so stated that no residue is left unapportioned.

§ 21. Common and Specific Attribution of Yields

Marginal cost products—Cost-products of narrower marginal utility—Specific products—Specific yield—Degrees of intensity and specific attribution in the case of land and of specific capital goods.

Schumpeter, *Bemerkungen über das Zurechnungsproblem* Z. f. V., vol. XVIII; Broda, *Die Lösungen des Zurechnungsproblems*, ibid., vol. XX; Aftalion, *Les trois notions de la productivité*, Revue d'Econ. pol., 1911; Mohrmann, *Dogmengeschichte der Zurechnungslehre*, 1914; Hefendehl, *Das Problem der ökon. Zurechnung*, 1922; Landauer, *Grundprobleme der funktionellen Verteilung des wirtschaftlichen Wertes*, 1923; and, *Der Meinungsstreit zwischen Böhm-Bawerk und Wieser über die Grundsätze der Zurechnungslehre*, Archiv. vol. 46.

In the problem of attribution as stated in the above terms the only satisfactory solution must be in accord with the following conditions. In the first place, the entire yield which was anticipated in the productive plan must be accounted for without any remainder, when it is referred to those goods which were used in its production. Secondly, each of the productive goods must be credited according to the degree to which it contributed as a practical cause in obtaining the yield. These two conditions may be condensed into one statement: the entire yield realized as expected under the scheme of operations must be attributed without a remainder in the measure of the productive contribution. The latter is the absolute amount of the increased yield due to the contribution of an individual productive means. It may also be represented as a part of the total yield. This is simpler. When an agricultural undertaking has produced a certain number of bushels of wheat the imputation must show the part to be attributed to the soil, to capital goods and to labor.

This share is differently computed for cost products and specific products. In the case of pure cost products, the yield is obtained only from cost-productive-means. In the case of specific products it is also to be reckoned for specific-productive-means. The first type of attribution we shall call common, the second specific attribution. The formula of common attribution is the only difficult one to obtain. The application of this formula to specific products is simple. Again in the case of common attribution, the difficulty is confined to marginal products. It is easy to apply the method to products of a narrow marginal utility.

Let us assume that a table is a marginal product of the two productive means, wood and labor. The marginal utility of the table is n; 20 l hours of labor and 10 w of wood are required. So long as these are our only data, the attribution of yields cannot be carried out. There are two unknown quantities l and w and only one equation. Let us assume that a chest is another marginal product of the same two goods. If it happens that the expenditure is the same in this case, i. e., l and 10 w are required, then the marginal utility n is probably correct. We would be no nearer the solution of our problem, for there would be no new equation, but only a repetition of the first one. However, if marginal products of these goods are found in which the ratio of the two quantities varies, or for which new equations may be formed by combining the two productive means with other cost-means, the case will be different. There is no doubt that such equations may be found. There are many more variations of the cost-elements, labor, wood, coal, iron and others, than there are types of cost element. The problem of attribution is solved if this is so. A definite magnitude may be computed for l and w. Thus we shall be able to ascertain the amount to which 20 l and 10 w participate in the yield. Just as we are able to make these theoretical calculations, the producer has a basis on which he may find the solution of his particular problem through trial and error.

Once the amount is determined by which cost-elements participate in the utility of marginal cost-products, the cost law determines the rate of computation for these elements in the case of products of narrower marginal utility as well. As we know, whenever the regularity of production is undisturbed, these elements are to be calculated alike for all products.

This same value applies to the cost-elements in the case of specific products as well. The utility-cost thus ascertained is to be deducted from the inherent marginal utility of the specific products. The residual yield is to be imputed to the contributing specific factor. This residual we shall call the specific yield. It closely approaches the net yield, but as we shall show later the two do not completely coincide. When there are several jointly active specific factors, they are first compared as to the degree in which they possess specific character. The yield attributable to the most specific factor is a residual found by first determining the yield due to those of less specific character and then subtracting this amount. This latter amount is determined as in the case of cost-means. The less specific its character, the more numerous are the possible combinations of a given factor. Therefore there are always equations by which its utility in other connections may be determined.

By far the most conspicuous example of attribution is the specific variety. For this reason it was the first to be observed by theory, just as it engages the closest attention in practical life. Ricardo's theory of rent is a theory of specific attribution for agricultural land. In his time land was the most striking specific good. His theory is necessarily defective, because he had no general theory of attribution nor even a theory of the computation of utility for agricultural products. Nevertheless he recognizes clearly the fundamental concept of specific attribution. He deducts from the gross crop an amount which covers the expenses of production and puts down the remainder as the yield of the soil.

In practice, attention is first directed to those cases of specific attribution in which the imputed yield is largest. Scarcity-commodities furnish cases of this sort: the best agricultural land, and centrally located, urban land particularly. Analogous cases may be found in the manifold monopolistic relations of the market, but we do not deal with these in the theory of the simple economy.

In these cases the absolute amount of the specific yield, that is the result of specific attribution, is large. What universally attracts even more especial attention is that these absolute amounts are still further increased as the productive yield is increased. This increase is often so large as to take an ever greater share of the total increment. For this reason the customary statement of specific attribution in the market emphasizes the fact that the entire excess of yield over and above costs is to be attributed to land or to the otherwise favored factor.

This statement disregards another aspect of specific attribution. In contrast to the specific scarcity-product is the specific product which occurs in superabundance. Favorable as attribution generally is in the case of the former, it is unfavorable in the case of the latter. So long as the population is small and land is therefore relatively abundant, only the residual is attributed to it as its share of the yield.

Specific scarcity leads to increased intensity of production. The latter in turn influences the numerical expression of attribution. Before we may explain this inter-relation, we must explain the meaning of intensive production as such.

The contrast of intensive and extensive production exists only for specific products. Technical improvements and the increasing abundance of the means of production lead in the case of cost-products to the production in greater numbers of more elaborately combined and more costly manufactures. The crude furnishings and decorations of dwellings give way with progress of the arts and increasing wealth to more numerous, more tasteful, more costly and substantial belongings, in the creation of which considerably more material and labor are consumed. However, one speaks of intensity of production only where specific productive means are being used as well as numerous cost-means.

Intensive production develops when once needs have grown so considerable that certain important groups of specific means, especially land, become relatively scarce. At the same time there must be an increased productive wealth which permits the use of larger masses of cost-means to overcome the obstacle to the production of goods entailing the use of specific scarcity-goods. So long as the specific goods are relatively abundant, production remains extensive and the costs incurred are proportionately small: i. e., the quantity of cost-means to be used with the specific unit is negligible. The peculiarity of intensive production is that the quantities are large and constantly growing.

In any given case the most desirable degree of intensity may be determined mathematically. In every case the cost-means must return the general marginal yield. The added utility of the yield must at least equal the added costs before an increase in the degree of intensity by further expenditures may be permitted. If this condition obtains, a further outlay is not only permissible but is obligatory, inasmuch as the yield of the total production is thus increased. As a consequence, the amount attributed to the specific factor may possibly be lower because the residual yield, attributable to the specific factor, may be decreased. In a coördinated economy this fact would deserve no consideration, for in such an economy the decisive factor is the general welfare.

With these explanations let us show by the classic illustration of land the relations existing between degree of intensity and specific attribution.

Where there is a real scarcity of land, the amount of the outlays is absolutely small. Production has to be stopped at a point at which additional outlays would still bring good returns. The differential between the utility-cost and the marginal utility of the products is still great. On the other hand, in view of the fact that the marginal utility of the products is large, a small part of the yield is adequate to cover costs. Therefore a proportionately large part is attributed to the specific factor, land, and the unit of area is consequently appraised at a high value.

Conditions are somewhat similar where relative scarcity obtains. In this case, however, there is a relaxation in the restraints on the absolute amount of the expenditures. Where there is relative scarcity of good vineyards, there will still be relatively intensive cultivation of the grape-vine. It may be less intensive than in the best localities. None the less an effort will be made to obtain the greatest possible benefit that inheres in the differential between the utility-cost and the inherent utility.

The more widely distributed the superior soil is, the lower the marginal utility of the crops will be because of their larger quantity. The costs which may be incurred per unit of area will be smaller. A larger proportion of the total crop will be required to cover the costs and a smaller excess may be attributed to the land.

The excess will be still smaller if land is relatively so abundant that people may enjoy the fruits of the soil in a degree that approximates the general margin of use. Even under these conditions there will always be a surplus above that which is needed to meet costs, for the cost-means in combination with the soil will be made to yield more than they could have yielded alone.

If land is so abundant that crops are harvested in greater amounts than are in accord with the general margin of use, agriculture will be conducted altogether extensively. It is assumed that the quantitative relation of the crops is merely more favorable than the general quantitative relation of cost-products, not that the harvest has lost its economic character. The admissible costs per unit of area will be very small. The marginal utility of the crop will be very low and a comparatively large amount of the yield is necessary to balance the utility of the cost-unit. The residual product to be attributed to the land will be small. Moreover, as the marginal utility of the product is low, the residual will be appraised at a low rate. Still there must always be a remainder so long as land is not available in super-abundance.

The entire yield is needed to defray costs only when land is a free good. The application of cost-means will be only most extensive as the marginal utility of the crop is extremely low. There may be certain parcels of land preëminently favored by location or fertility that remain in the economic quantitative relation by the side of the free land. The surplus yield of such parcels is to be attributed to them. If they were more intensively cultivated, their yield would be increased. For such land the outlays bring larger returns.

What has just been illustrated by reference to land holds for all specific goods. Where specific capital goods are concerned, a new condition is involved; they are themselves specific products. Specific attribution must not stop with the capital commodity; it must go back from these to the specific productive means to which the specific character of the capital is due. If these means are themselves capital goods, specific attribution must continue still farther back until a factor is reached which is not itself a product, as in the case of diamond mines. In the economic theory of exchange we shall have to bring this idea to bear also on performances of labor and on market conditions which by legal provisions or for other reasons have a specific character. In the case of capital investments whose specific character inheres merely in their size, the specific attribution acts as an incentive to further increase of investments until they lose specific character and become mere cost-products. This impulse will overcome, in the course of time, the hindrances which oppose the extension and increase of such investments.

The Austrian school has, it is true, taken up the term used in my treatise, *The Origin of Value*, as well as the idea of attribution developed in *Natural Value*. It has not done so, however, without energetically controverting the suggested formula of a solution. (See especially the incisive criticism of Böhm-Bawerk in Excursus VII of the fourth edition of his *Positive Theory.*) It will be impossible to attempt here to refute his objections in detail. They demand extensive argument. However, I am confident that I shall be able to maintain my positions which are now embodied in more circumspect phrase and supported by more precise demonstration. The manner in which I now distinguish common and specific attribution itself reduces the contrast of our views. My present formula of specific attribution closely approaches the solution of Böhm-Bawerk. However this may be, I adhere to the opinion that specific attribution alone is inadequate; it must be supplemented by common attribution.

§ 22. The Economic Computation of Utility

The value of needs as incomputable magnitudes of intensity—Marginal utility, the arithmetic unit of the economy—The computation of costs, units of cost, units of utility—The computation of utility for specific products—The computation of utility in case of disturbances and changes in the economy—The "antinomy" of the computation of utility.

The primary values of needs cannot be computed or reduced to a common standard in multiples of which they may be represented. They have no objective numerical magnitude but have only degrees of intensity. The latter may be compared, but only in relative terms: i. e., greater, less or equal. These degrees of intensity do not have a relationship to some unit in terms of which they may be numerically expressed as multiples or fractions. In the comparison of these intensities there is only a feeling that there is a greater spread between one pair of magnitudes than between another. This feeling gains more definite expression only in so far as the observer's perception of the distance traversed in passing from one intensity to another involves a greater or less number of intermediate degrees. Thus, for example, one is not able to say how much greater the stimulus of an extreme sensation of hunger is than that of a simple æsthetic pleasure. However, one may estimate the divergence by reviving the experiences and finding a more definite expression of the spread in a comparison of each with a series of stimuli all of which are less intense than hunger and more intense than the æsthetic pleasure.

The human economy, however, is able to appraise its services with precision even in the midst of a universe of need-values. The fundamental law of the computation of utility states the fact that a divisible stock of goods is to be considered economically as a sum of units each of which is computed by the marginal utility. The units of mass are at the same time units of utility; when mass is computed, there is a simultaneous computation of utility. A mass [1] of 200 when compared with one of 100 is to be appraised at twice the latter. Practical decisions which rest on such an estimate, which is not only approximate but exact, are well advised. It goes without saying that this estimate does not answer the question: how do the satisfactions derived from the 200 units compare with those afforded by the 100? However, it is not within the province of the economic computation of utility to measure these satisfactions. This computation merely points out the

[1] *Trans. note:* Wieser uses *Teilmasse*, partial or fractional mass. Where no confusion can arise the translator drops the qualifying word which is not customary in English economic texts.

limits to which satisfactions may proceed. If one computes the quantities at his disposal within this limit, he will be dealing with true magnitudes and will still be fulfilling the task of economic control.

One of the doctrines of a modern school of philosophy is the economy of thought. There is scarcely any other illustration of this doctrine so apt as this method of computation. As men bring to bear just that measure of foresight which corresponds to the marginal utility, they proceed according to the principle of least exertion. An economic selection of need-values is most accurately made by determining the limit to which the satisfaction of needs may be pushed. Through this delimitation all values are included that are economically required, all improper ones are excluded; "what lies above is good, what lies below is bad."[1] What a saving from the temptations of interest this represents. We make sure of existence, health, strength and comfort. We need be careful only to conform to the margin of comfort to which circumstances permit us to advance. How greatly this also simplifies the appraisal of the economic means used in securing the need-values. The entire "surplus-value" of need-values is ignored, as it is beyond the marginal utility. It is not necessary in every case to gage the intangible magnitude of the individual values. The marginal value is strictly adhered to. All adopted values are reduced to this common measure which has the extraordinary advantage of subjecting them to an objective, arithmetic computation.

The law of marginal utility is valid for all divisible stocks of goods. It derives its full significance from the laws of cost and of attribution. Because of the laws of cost we recognize all cost-products as combinations of their productive elements. In so doing the law reduces all cost-products—even those which are not produced to stock but only piece-meal—to the divisible productive supply of goods. In a static economy each cost-product is a multiple of the units of cost of which it is composed. This multiple is a function of the required rate of cost. The units of cost for their part, however, are arithmetically comparable because they may be reduced through the law of attribution to the common unit of utility of the marginal products.

In this way, for purposes of practical economic accounting or more especially for computations of cost, the masses of different cost-productive-means and cost-products at the disposal of a people become one great stock of goods. The magnitude of this supply may be expressed in any units of cost: in units of labor or indirectly through these in units of utility. When each cost-productive-means and cost-

[1] *Ursprung des Wertes*, p. 131.

product is set down as the sum of the units of utility which it contains, one obtains the arithmetic foundation for a plan of production and management. This plan may be closely drawn, for it determines the limits of productive activity as well as of consumption. The dedication to a particular type of use of even the smallest part of the total supply is included. Criticism falls before the success of such an account; the figures are not, as some may think, a more or less inaccurate approximation of a comprehensive expression of value, but are an arithmetically correct statement of the units of mass which are at the same time units of utility.

The greatest difficulties are found in explanations involving specific products, for their marginal utility may be either greater or less than the general margin of use. Let us assume that marginal cost-products have a utility of *n*. In this case specific products of absolute or relative scarcity have a marginal utility of more than *n* for each unit; the marginal utility of those of relative abundance is less than *n*. The spread between these two utilities cannot be directly measured in numerical terms; these are primary need-values and defy computation.

In practice, however, a way has been found to obtain numerical expression for these cases as well. This method attains its objective accurately. Its success demonstrates it to be strictly according to mathematical rule. In practice the numerical values are obtained from the quantities of the products in the various utility-series involved. Let us assume, for example, that sable furs are goods of relative scarcity, that ordinary country wine is one of relative abundance and that wheat-bread is produced in such quantities that its consumption takes place, like that of a pure cost-product, exactly at the general margin of use. Under such circumstances it is impossible to find a direct numerical expression for the relation of the primary values involved in owning a sable coat, satisfying a craving for wine and allaying the hunger which is appeased by bread. However, one may determine exactly the quantity of bread or units of wheat whose utility is equivalent to that of the sable coat or of a gallon of wine. For degrees of intensity, as for other things, the condition of equality may be determined. This process gives the correct numerical expression from the reduction of specific products and productive means to the general arithmetic unit of the economy. Again the serviceability of the figures confirms their accuracy; by such calculations the plan of production and management may be laid out to suit conditions. More especially they will demonstrate the extent to which cost-means are to be applied to specific production. When 100 gallons of country wine equal 50 units of utility of the general account of the economy and also equal one sable coat, the standard is established according to which cost-units may be expended for a sable coat or a gallon of wine.

When production is disturbed, the connection between productively related goods and stems is more or less impeded. It may even be completely broken down. In such a case, cost-products become, if not absolutely isolated goods, specific products of relative scarcity or abundance. During the continuation of the disturbance such goods are subject to the same type of arithmetic computation that permanently characterizes specific products.

Changes in cost which are confined to rates of cost influence the computation of utility only in so far as thereafter the products affected are computed with a greater or less number of units of cost. Changes, which are so extensive that the marginal cost utility is itself raised or lowered, affect primary values and displace the unit of the account. As a rule changes of this sort take place gradually. Single products, then more, and finally all cost-products fall away from the former general margin of use. Practical accounting finds an exact expression for all changes of this sort, for the relation in such a case is no different than that established on principle in the case of specific products. At all times one may calculate the quantity of goods which under the new conditions of utility is equal to the unit of the former series.

When an economic period has become a matter of history, the situation is changed. In times of transition people invariably have a consciousness of the primary need-values. These feelings they wish to preserve. They cling especially to the conspicuous magnitudes of value, the standards by which all others are compared as they arise. In the case of a dead era this means of transition to the present is lacking, just as it is lacking when we compare the economies of different countries. As a result, numerical data of the economy lose their practical meaning because the consciousness of the unit to which they have reference is not preserved.

Even the loss to the national wealth and income, which is occasioned by an unusually great catastrophe, is scarcely susceptible to numerical expression. At all events the expression will be imperfect when the sum of the quantities of destroyed units of utility is accepted as a multiple of the arithmetic unit which is used in calculations during normal periods. The economic account presupposes a divisible stock of goods; but the quantity of commodities lost in an elementary catastrophe is experienced as a whole.

The construction of the account arises from the practical tasks of the economy. When it is separated from these, it loses its meaning. The figures lose their exact value; at best they are approximations. A numerical expression which indicates that social resources have doubled between two periods does not actually furnish a standard to measure the proportionate change in the satisfaction of social needs. This proportion can never be expressed numerically; an exposition of this change must abandon arithmetic and resort to a detailed description of human existence.

Even in the practical economy there are exceptional instances in which computations according to the marginal utility will fail. These are the cases which have frequently been observed to illustate the paradoxical nature of value-in-exchange. In commerce there are examples of vendors who seek through the destruction of part of their stocks to augment the yield of their sales. In the same way a monopoly may restrict output in order to raise the net yield. In such instances the increase in the price of the unit of goods more than compensates for the decrease in the number of units. The total yield is greater where the quantities sold are smaller. A vendor who is able to determine the amount of the stock of goods is able to further his own advantage by injuring the social interest.

The assumptions of the simple economy are so framed as to demand the domination of the general interest. A paradox that arises in the opposition between personal power and social interest is therefore excluded. Yet even in the simple economy there are such glaring cases of this sort that the semblance of paradox is apt to arise. This mystery is most easily solved if we presuppose the extreme case in which a method of production makes possible an increase of stocks to the point of superabundance. Let us assume, for example, that by driving an artesian well or opening up a copious mountain spring it is possible to provide a town with pure water in superabundant quantities. If the principle of marginal utility were strictly adhered to, such an enterprise would never be started; a superabundant stock of free goods has a marginal utility of zero. But will such a consideration deter the public from incurring expenses for such an enterprise? Surely not. The undertaking guarantees the greatest possible benefit. The public will realize this benefit irrespective of the fact that the utility which results can not be computed. It will be seen that the computation according to marginal utility does not simplify matters in this case, as it usually does in others. Rather it leads one astray. Hence the more complicated computation of total benefit will be resorted to.

This is precisely the state of affairs where we examine all other cases of apparent paradox. Whenever the increase of the supply, computed at the marginal utility, leads to a lower numerical expression, the reckoning by marginal utility ceases to simplify and the plan of production must be drafted on the basis of total utility.

Marginal utility may be used as a basis for calculations where the larger stock still gives a larger product. It is inapplicable when the product is smaller. Cases of the first kind are altogether too general; the latter are exceptional. Human economy has so far approached superabundance too rarely to attain or even approximate complete satiety. Whenever satiety is approximated it is generally because of some chance event, an over-abundant harvest or a succession of such crops. In the industrial branches of production, which are more thoroughly controlled by technical art than agriculture, it is possible to bring costs and yields into closer adjustment. Constant technical advances allow greatly increased yields in these fields, but needs on the other hand are multiplied by the continued increase of population. Therefore we have to content ourselves with achieving a gradual amelioration in the average conditions of material well-being. This explains why there is scarcely ever any practical doubt that the computation according to marginal utility is confirmed in the success of the method. It has become a habit of thought among business men to such an extent that they look upon it positively as the unassailable method of economic computation. They stare in astonishment if its use in exceptional cases miscarries.

§ 23. Net-Yield and the Productivity of Capital

Yield—Gross-yield, costs of renewal, net-yield—Attribution for renewal of capital and the net-earnings—General percentage of accretion—Physical and arithmetical productivity of capital.

In the simple economy we call the yield that quantity of goods which results from productive exchange. It must be in a form more nearly ready for consumption than the productive agents used in the process. It is distinguished from those additions to wealth which take place merely by entering into possession, as when we find things or take new land for pioneer cultivation. It likewise differs from increases in the appraisal of utility which may occur in the case of old possessions; and finally from improvements on old possessions by means of valuable additions. Contrasted with all these different additions of utility, the yield is conspicuous by the permanent or repetitive nature of the act through which it is acquired, and consequently offers the means for that continued satisfaction of needs which is demanded by human nature. It must be conceded that even with such productive exchanges as take place only once, we must speak of a yield. The gains from a single hunting or fishing excursion are a yield. The mine that will be exhausted as it is worked produces a yield. But, as a rule, production is meant to be of some duration, and when we speak of a yield pure and simple we assume that it can be obtained recurrently over a considerable period of time. In the process of reckoning this yield this factor is taken into consideration; the account is periodically closed according to intervals of time which correspond to the periods of exchange.

The yield may be referred to the whole of economic production, to single branches of it, or to a single sub-division of a branch. More especially it may be referred to the individual factors which are jointly active in production. In this latter sense we speak of the yield of land, of capital and of labor, meaning the amount to be attributed to the individual productive factors owing to their productive contribution.

In deducing the rules of attribution, we have disregarded the relationships arising from the duration of production. In this direction we have now to supplement our exposition. We shall be chiefly concerned with the attribution of the yield of capital. There is little more to say about the attributions of yield for land and labor.

In the simple economy the yields of land and labor appear as net yields, i. e., they may be permanently received without requiring that a portion be retained towards the renewal of its sources. In the case of land this relation is established because the theoretical concept of land has been confined from the beginning to the unconsumable, inexhaustible qualities of the soil. The consumable quality of the soil possesses, as regards its use, the character of capital. Whatever part of this quality is consumed by production demands renewal like any consumption of capital. The renewal of the force of labor is, in the case of a vigorous people, adequately procured by births and the training of labor. The losses because of sickness, accident, age and death are compensated for, if not exceeded by, births. In order to preserve health and vigor, the individual laborer must naturally care for the reëstablishment of his personal efficiency; but this process may by no means be brought into the same category with capital renewal. Labor is not a product in the sense of economic science and the expenditures which the laborer incurs in order to preserve health and vigor are not productive expenditures. The food and other means of subsistence which he consumes are not productive commodities, they are consumption goods. Or to be more exact, they are productive goods only so long as they are kept stored in quantities at the end of the manufacturing process, and change to consumption goods as soon as they are placed at the disposal of the laborer for consumption. This ends the introductory production-process, and the new one does not begin until the laborer starts a new series of performances. The intermediate period of consumption does not by any means initiate a new production-process; it is a concern of the household and of personal life.

In contrast with labor, capital, as we know, is not only a productive means but is itself a product. We know, too, that in the former capacity it is consumed, and that as a product it must therefore be constantly renewed so that the capital sum may remain unchanged and permanently capable of further production. We also know that capital, while serving directly as a means of production, must at the same time reproduce itself. Consumable productive means employed solely in the service of direct production are not employed as capital. Let us assume that a tribe of nomads, having made one attempt at agriculture, tilling and planting, decided to reap the one crop and wander on. In this case the seed has been used, not as capital but as a simple productive means. The entire crop has been consumed. No portion of it has been preserved to replace the seed consumed in planting and to become seed for a new harvest. In employing the entire yield as a net yield and consuming it, we gain the advantage of meeting immediate needs. But, on the other hand, we lose the greater utility of having our capital become a source of permanent yields. An economy aspiring to enduring service must distinguish between gross-yields and net-yields. It must lay aside sufficient reserves to entirely renew its capital, treating only the residue as net-yield. To consider the present and the future as of equal importance is one of the requirements of economic management. The satisfaction of future needs must not be jeopardized by conditions of production inferior to those of the present. Thus the complete renewal of capital is a demand of a rational economy. If an increasing population must be provided for, provision should be made to enlarge the net-yield absolutely in order to maintain the per capita supply at the same level. An efficient people wanting to advance economically will go even further in its demands; it will enlarge the capital reservation sufficiently to increase the individual provisioning.

The expenditures required from the gross-yield to renew the capital consumed are called costs. They do not coincide with the costs of production, hence we shall speak of them by the differentiating name of "renewal-costs." They form only a part of the costs of production which include other very important elements. But they go beyond the costs of production in so far as they concern the specific capital as well. Net yield may be defined as the residue left after deducting renewal-costs from the gross-yield. In a static economy, by which we mean one which perpetuates itself but does not progress, the bulk of the gross-yield may be divided into two groups: those goods for capital renewal, and those which constitute the net-yield. The latter consists exclusively of consumption goods devoted to the current use of the household. The former are capital goods. In a progressive economy two classes may be distinguished in the net-yield itself: consumption goods, and capital goods destined to increase capital. Therefore in such an economy the gross-yield is divided into three classes.[1] Those goods intended for the renewal and increase of capital are both obtained by reservations from the gross-yield. The former is reproductive saving; the latter is progressive saving. The formation of both masses may be called capital formation. However, it is customary to use this term in a narrower sense; i. e., it refers to the new accumulations that constitute the increase of wealth.

It goes without saying that the division of the gross-yield is already

[1] Trans. note: "We will call them for brevity's sake renewal-mass, consumption-mass and augmentation-mass." The sentence is omitted from the text because the brevity of the German compound does not seem desirable in the English translation.

provided for in the plan of production. In forming this plan we may decide what means are to be devoted to reproducing or augmenting the capital stock, and what to the service of immediate production. After production is finished and products have received their permanent shape, it is usually too late to change the application of these means. Cases like the one of the seed, already discussed, which is available both for the immediate preparation of bread and for a new planting, are exceptions. Ordinarily the natural consumption good cannot be used for production as well, and vice versa. In its completed shape, its use is already determined. A machine can only be used as a machine. It is no longer available for consumption. Consumption goods are available only as such and are useless for anything else. However, the latter may be turned over for consumption more or less slowly. The more rapidly they are dispatched, the sooner will the new production-process have to be set on foot; the more slowly they pass into employment, the longer will be the period over which the current production-process may extend.

The renewal of capital is a matter of universal interest to every economic body. It is necessary both for the safety of capital and the welfare of the laborer. The model social state will have to insist on it, as does the capitalistic entrepreneur. The axiom that costs of renewal must be deducted from gross-earnings in order to find net earnings, is sure to find the united assent of all parties. However, the account as it is kept by the capitalistic entrepreneur shows the peculiarity of placing the renewal-mass exclusively to the debit of capital and of attributing to capital a share in the net earnings as well. Is this method of attribution in harmony with the laws of computation of the simple economy? Will the model social state have to adopt similar methods of computation? According to the theorist's reply to this question, he will take his stand on the subject of interest on capital, a problem on which opinions diverge more widely than on any other in our theory.

We answer it here altogether in the sense of the capitalistic entrepreneur. A share of the net-earnings has to be attributed to capital, i. e., with orderly economic management the share of the gross earning attributed to capital must be sufficiently large to completely provide for capital-renewal and to leave a surplus over and above this. This rule is deduced with logical rigidity from the meaning of attribution. It would be inconsistent if capital, playing its part in securing the net earnings, were not to receive its share in the attributions of these earnings. Only if capital goods were free, would they not be entitled to the attribution. But capital goods, in the regular course of events, are never free. They invariably exist in the economic quantitative proportion. Every individual capital good and every appreciable portion of capital must therefore be recognized as an important contributing cause in securing a portion of the net earnings. If capital did not even contribute enough toward the product to justify its own renewal, it would surely not tempt one to incur further expense for its preservation. A producer, appraising its services at so low a figure, would surely be wise to imitate the example of the nomad tribe who devoured their seed when their agricultural venture did not suit them. A producer of this sort should no longer treat capital goods as capital goods. He should look upon them merely as productive goods, employed once and not again for productive exchange, their entire proceeds being used up as net earnings. Every economic management in renewing its capital recognizes the truth that capital is not to be regarded as a simple productive means but as an indispensable tool for gaining net earnings, and that it must accordingly be granted a share in the net earnings.

The simple productive good, which is susceptible of productive transformation but is used up in the process, also acts productively. The result of the transformation is attributed to it. Capital is productive in a higher sense: it may be continuously transformed. As a result of this process a share of the gross earnings is attributed to it which exceeds capital renewal and leaves residual net earnings. When we speak in the following pages of productivity, we mean invariably this higher productivity of capital by which, despite its consumability, it attains the enduring quality of the non-consumable land and produces a yield like that of land.

The productivity of economic capital is primarily physical. The gaps torn in its broad expanse by the use to which it is put are physically filled up by renewal. Thus the complete body of capital by which social economy initiated production is finally replaced. A physical net yield is also available.

This productivity may be shown arithmetically as well. Numerical expression may be given to the mass of utility units at which the capital was to be computed when it was introduced into production. In like manner the number of utility units may be shown for the attributed volumes of goods that comprise the gross yield, the replacement fund and the net yield. From these figures the ratio of net yield to capital may be reckoned. The coefficient thus obtained we will call the general percentage of increment. It is the numerical expression for the degree of the calculable productivity of capital.

Every part of the social economic capital participates in the productivity of the whole. It will answer every purpose if we illustrate the process in a stationary economy where the entire net yield consists of consumption goods. The same principle that holds in this simple case will also obtain for the complex conditions of the progressive economy which receives its net yield both in consumption goods and capital goods. Let us simplify our assumption as much as possible and presuppose the exclusive use of cost capital. For the present we shall neglect the specific capital to which we shall later return when we discuss the details of the appraisal of capital.

The physical productivity of capital goods can never be directly observed. The gross yield which is attributed to it for its productive contribution always consists of goods of the next lower order. These are not suited to the physical replacement of the goods of higher order which have been consumed. Thus the yield attributed to capital goods of the second order is in terms of goods of the first order, i. e., consumption goods; to capital goods of the third order, goods of the second; to capital goods of the tenth, those of the ninth. To illustrate this, let us remind the reader that in the manufacture of sugar a certain quantity of coal is consumed, and that a particular amount of the consumption good, sugar, is attributed as the gross yield to this coal-capital. The gross yield attributed to the mine hoist used in the mine where the coal is obtained is expressed in terms of coal. Physically, neither the coal consumed nor the deterioration of the machinery can be replaced directly out of the attributed mass of sugar or of coal.

When the process has been systematically conducted, however, the number of units of utility of the attributed mass of sugar must equal the number of utility units of the coal consumed, plus the general percentage of increment. A similar relationship must exist between the deterioration of the machinery and the coal attributed to the machine. If these relationships do not hold, the processes have not been conducted systematically. Hereafter they will have to be extended or curtailed sufficiently to bring the account into conformity with the general trend of production. If this result cannot be achieved, then the use in question must be abandoned.

In a model social economy, the responsible manager of each section who acts in harmony with the general scheme of production must be able to demonstrate arithmetically the same transformations which the entrepreneur now effects by means of exchange, in order to defray from the gross yield the renewal of capital and to obtain a net yield which shall furnish him with the means of obtaining consumption goods which are needed in the household. It is true that in a model social economy the responsible director of operations will not receive the proceeds as his own personal income; they will inure to the social group. In no event will the natural values be transformed into money. None the less, they will have to be computed with the utmost accuracy. The manager of a sugar refinery in the model social state will be responsible for an adequate gross yield so that he may credit the coal account with an amount to cover the consumption of coal debited, and may return a net yield out of which consumption goods may be assigned. In a similar manner, in the case of the coal mine the account will have to close with a credit against which consumption goods may be issued from the net yield.

These rules apply with equal force to all capital goods which are used in the service of reproduction. It makes no difference how remote the order may be. Capital reproduction for its own sake would be absurd. There must be a suitable net yield. Otherwise all efforts devoted to it would be vacuous, mere labors of Sisyphus. The capital goods used in reproduction must be recognized as significant causes in the acquisition of corresponding quotas of the consumption goods which constitute the net yield. In the final accounting, the share attributed to all capital goods collectively must be sufficiently large to exhaust the entire renewal mass and, moreover, to divide without remainder the entire net yield when taken in connection with the amounts attributed to land and labor.

§ 24. Capital Computation

Interest and the interest rate—Computation of capital-substance—Interest and cost-computation—Discount and capitalization—Rent, interest on capital, rent of land.

Because of the arithmetically calculable productivity of cost-capital its net yield may be expressed as a ratio of the original capital. When the productive scheme is followed, this ratio in the case of each aggregation of capital or of each capital commodity coincides with the general percentage of increment. The net yield of the cost-capital is called interest on capital or simply interest. The economic ratio of net yield to capital, the general percentage of increment as we have called it, is the rate of interest.

There are other relationships which may be expressed numerically and which start from interest. The appraisal of capital is derived from its interest. The exact economic control over the use and period of use of capital is based on interest.

This accurate appraisal of capital is essential to every individual enterprise today. It will be equally indispensable in the model social state.

The problem of capital appraisal is far more complicated than that of evaluating the simple consumable productive commodity. In the case of the latter the yield is consumed as a whole. The yield therefore offers a uniform base for the evaluation of the productive commodity. In the case of capital goods the gross yield is divisible into a renewal fund and the net yield. These two portions serve different purposes. As the purposes differ, they must be held apart in the appraisal.

In practice there are two methods of appraising capital. The results coincide although the starting points of the computations are distinct. One method starts with the net yield. This is multiplied or capitalized according to the prevailing rate of interest. This method is employed in the case of specific capital and also of land. The other is used for cost-capital; in it the amount of the capital substance is determined by deducting the net yield from the gross yield. This second procedure is the fundamental method; that of capitalization is derived from it. Capitalization alone would be unintelligible were it not for the second method, that of discount.

At first in our explanation we shall assume the simplest conditions and speak only of circulating capital. The case of the capital stock of coal used in a sugar-refinery, which we have just discussed, may serve as an illustration. We shall assume that the gross yield of sugar attributed to the coal amounts to 105 units. We shall further assume that the cost of the coal is equivalent to 100 units and that the general percentage of increment of the economy is 5. Under these assumptions the gross yield of 105 units is apportioned so that 100 units go to replacement and 5 units are treated as net yield. The capital substance is therefore set down as 100, a figure indicated stock by cost and yield. The attributed gross yield might be less than 105 units so that less than 100 units would remain after deducting the general percentage of increment. It might be more than 105 units with the opposite result. Either of the latter two conditions would indicate that coal production, the refining of sugar or both were out of line with the general process of production. It would then be necessary either through expansion or retrenchment to bring about a closer adjustment to the general level.

We indicated in our deduction of the law of the appraisal of productive means that the utility-yield of the products is the basis of evaluation. Is it not contradictory if we figure the yield in our illustration at 105 and the capital at only 100? How may we justify the separation of the yield into two parts, the net yield and the replacement fund, of which only the latter is added to capital?

We account for this condition as follows: when deducing the former law, we took for granted the case of the simple productive means. With such goods the yield is destined solely for consumption and is to be attributed in full to the productive agent. Now we are dealing with capital. In the latter case the account must allow for the fact that the gross yield is composed of two constituents which serve distinct economic ends. Were the gross yield to be accounted for as a whole it would have to be credited in its entirety either to renewal or net yield.

Both such acts are inconsistent with the deliberately planned ends of production. In the first case the gross yield is entirely charged off to renewal; no net yield could remain. But a consumable product is the end of production. In the second case there would be no renewal of capital. We should have to content ourselves with treating coal as a simple productive means whose productive power is spent in a single process. Such a procedure would make it impossible to secure capital yields in the future. It would even end the power to draw yields from labor or land, both factors which are dependent on the complementary aid of capital.

Net yield has been defined as the remainder of the gross yield after the replacement fund has been deducted. Do we not now involve ourselves in a contradiction when by an inverse operation we deduct the percentage of increment from the gross yield in order to find the renewal mass? Is this not arguing in a circle?

This question also may be answered. The renewal mass is not an unknown magnitude. Irrespective of the fact that it is fixed by unnumerical coincidence of cost and yield, it is even physically perceptible. As soon as the gap in capital, occasioned by the act of production, has been covered by physical replacement, the net yield is shown as a physical excess which may be separated from the capital substance. The determination of the net yield establishes the general percentage of increment which brings the physical excess, at all points where capital is used, into equal proportions with the capital substance. It is not a violation of the rules of logic to appeal in the theoretical explanation of any particular case to the general percentage of increment. There is a mutual relation: in general the rate of interest is established by the productivity of cost-capital in all employments; on the other hand in each particular case a net yield is demanded which coincides with the generally obtainable rate of interest.

The rate of interest is nothing more nor less than an expression of the marginal productivity of capital. It indicates the utility cost which might be obtained by other uses of cost-capital. The practical business-man, therefore, obeys the law of marginal utility when he demands the established rate of interest from his capital. Every use of cost-capital is uneconomic which does not give net earnings adequate to cover the established rate of interest. It ties up capital in a manner that is less beneficial than conformity with the general marginal utility demands. The converse is also true; moreover such use is not only permissible but obligatory. If capital is not employed according to this rule, the maximum utility is not attained. Consequently interest on cost-capital, like capital itself, is one of the productive elements in the formation of cost-products. When men figure interest as one of the costs, they attain the maximum utility as regards the quantity of capital to be used and the period of its employment. They calculate in accord with the spirit of economic accounting. The model social state could scarcely permit itself to figure in any other manner.

The coal-capital just examined was studied under the simplifying assumption of a static economy. Furthermore, in the illustration, coal was liquid capital of the second order. In the case of fixed capital and higher orders or of progressive and retrogressive economics the accounting is more complicated but the fundamental idea is the same. In every individual case a net yield is insisted upon which accords with the general rate of interest, the amount of the capital used and the period of its employment. The gross yield is always to be separated into net yield and replacement fund. The latter figure coincides with capital costs in the regular, undisturbed course of affairs. It gives the measure for capital appraisal. The renewal of liquid capital, which is completely consumed in a single process, always takes place at one time. The renewal of fixed capital which withstands repeated employment has to take place gradually. The amortization is adjusted to the length of time required for wear and tear to complete its work. The details of the computation do not concern us. They do not in any way affect the principle of the method of capital appraisal.

The computation of interest and discount are correlated. Assume that the productive use of 100 units of capital will yield 105 units at the end of a year. Then 105 units, which are an anticipated income due in one year, cannot be entered on the books today as 105. Instead they will be set down at 100, for their economic effect is completely counterbalanced by 100 present units. The 5 units to be added are placed to the account of anticipated interest. They must be deducted when the present capital value is determined. A deduction to be made from a future receipt of goods because of the expected interest is called discount. It is made according to the standard of the established rate of interest. The discount is therefore larger as the productivity of capital increases, smaller as it decreases. During periods which exceed the ordinary duration of capital-transformation, interest has to be compounded.

Discount is not confined to cost-capital. Whenever the present value of goods to be received at a future date is determined, a deduction from the future value must be made. This is especially true of such receipts as are expected in the future from land and specific capital. From discount we derive the practical capitalization of land and specific capital. Let us first take up the more simple case of land in order to then pass on to the more complicated conditions of specific capital.

In the capitalization of land the anticipation of an endless series of net yields is presupposed. Capitalization gives finite expression to the infinite series by multiplying the annual yield by 100 and dividing by the rate of interest. When the rate of interest is 5 per cent, for example, the annual yield is multiplied by 20. This formula of capitalization equals with mathematical accuracy the discounted value of a perpetual annuity. The later the date that the yearly increment is due, the smaller is its present value. The result is that the yields in the more distant years no longer count in the present, and a finite expression is obtained for the infinite annual series.

The result of the capitalization of land points the fact that the value of land is equivalent to that of a cost-capital producing an identical yield. There is no other way in which to give numerical expression to this value. The method of discount used in ascertaining the value of cost-capital cannot be used directly for land. In the case of the latter there is no gross yield that may be split into a replacement fund and net yield. There is only an indivisible net yield. Nevertheless an adequate appraisal is indispensable in the case of land; occasions constantly arise in which property is to be disposed of, and a numerical expression must be available. What figure is better suited to this purpose than that determined by capitalization at the established rate of interest? Granted equal security and the same future conditions, why should it be assumed that a different ratio expresses the relationship between the substance of land and capital and their respective net yields? The disposition of the property involves the disposition of the future yields; the substances should therefore be so computed as to maintain an equal ratio to their yields. This rule is followed in practice, as the same rate of capitalization is adopted if other conditions are equal.

Fundamentally the procedure is the same in the case of specific capital. It is merely somewhat more complicated. The yield of specific capital may be divided into two parts: one is the same in character as the yield of cost-capital, the other partakes of the qualities of the yield of land. Let us take as an illustration an investment of capital that consists exclusively of cost-capital goods. However, because of its unusual magnitude this investment has a specific character so long as no one succeeds in establishing another like industry of the same dimensions. From the yield of this plant the gross earnings are first to be distinguished and attributed to the cost-capital. This gross figure is composed of that of the replacement fund and the net yield. The latter is the product of the capital substance and the established rate of interest. Owing to the increased productivity of the specific capital, there may remain an excess yield which we have called the specific yield and which is a net yield. This excess is capitalized. The sum of this capitalized value and the amount of the cost-capital is the estimate of the total capital of the establishment.

The methods of discount and capitalization established the economic account and extend it to cover anticipated yields. The appraisal of expectations is accomplished by the same simplification, economy of thought and mental relief which we have already discussed in the fundamental law of the computation of utility. The law of marginal utility disregards the entire surplus utility which is included above the margin. Just so the method of capitalization and discount eliminates all the infinite prospective yield by the deduction of discount. This infinite series is a surplus from the point of view of the present. It may be disregarded because practically the yields are included by the finite expression of present value. In the never ceasing flow of time the present is engulfed in the past and the future becomes the present. The figures of future transactions now diminish in perspective. But as time passes they gradually assume the full proportions of present values and a new set of figures, hitherto so remote as not to engage men's foresight, comes into view. The greater the productivity of capital, the lower are the present values by which future receipts are anticipated. The shorter also is the period of years for which we have to calculate, for we must allow for more rapidly unfolding productive effects. Conversely when the productivity of capital declines, the series of years is prolonged and future yields are anticipated in the present by greater values.

We should, however, always aim in our appraisal at a complete equalization of present and future needs. Discount is not resorted to because the future need-value as such is appraised at a lower figure. It is used because, owing to the productivity of capital, a lower estimate in the economic account of today is accorded to goods which will satisfy identical future need-values.

The net yield of land and of specific capital is not known as interest but as rent: ground-rent and capital-rent. In the exchange economy the name, "rente,"[1] is employed for all incomes by permanent title not directly based on labor. For example, we speak of life-annuities, alimony and old age or accident annuities. The differentiation of rent and interest corresponds to an exceedingly important material distinction. In the case of interest the computation starts from the capital. Interest is predicated as a certain quota of capital, the ratio being determined by the marginal productivity of cost-capital. In the case of annuities the computation proceeds in the inverse direction: given the amount of the annuity, its present capital value is a multiple determined by capitalization at the established rate of interest. As the rate of interest rises, the capital value of a fixed annuity drops, and vice versa. Physically there has been no change in the capital substance or its yield. Interest is an element of computation of cost; rent, the result of specific attribution, is a surplus over costs of production. Only in exceptional cases, in which one specific productive means is contrasted with another of even more specific character, is rent also added to costs. Finally, inasmuch as interest is attributable to costs while rent is a specific surplus over costs, the law of the movement of interest and rent must needs be different. The rate of interest varies directly with the marginal productivity of cost-capital. Rent has an opposite behavior; it must be higher, the lower the interest costs which are to be deducted, and vice versa.

These contrasts are suggested in the traditional names of interest and rent. However, it required a prolonged period of critical in-

[1] Trans. note: In English the continental term, "rente," is seldom used. It is never compounded as it has been in the German text. In the latter there is perfect continuity from this sentence to the next in which the author speaks of *Leibrente*, *Alimentationsrente*, etc. In the translation the sentence defining "rente" is unrelated to the following one unless one bears in mind that a life-annuity is a "life-rente," etc.

vestigation for theory to discover explanations for these oppositions which are disposed of with such unerring certainty in the practical use of the terms. Current speech has shaped the two terms and enriched their meaning. In so doing it has given invaluable aid to theoretical enquiry. How often theory has departed from the obvious path of explanation to which the meaning of the traditional terms pointed in the clearest manner! We may well doubt that the true solution of the problem would ever have come to light had it been left to the unaided and independent efforts of the technical investigator. It is probable that the entire structure of the practical economic account would have defied scientific exposition. The structure is admirable both in the simplicity of its fundamental idea and in the wealth and ramifications of its application. The creative expressionism of practical life invested this structure with traditional names that became instrumental in disclosing its meaning.

For the literature of interest on capital, as for that on the theory of capital, we refer to Böhm-Bawerk's *Capital and Interest* (Part I. History and Critique). The leading ideas of Böhm-Bawerk's personal theory of interest and their influence on the present position of theoretical investigation are adequately treated in Schumpeter's exposition (*Epochen der Dogmengeschichte und Methodengeschichte.*) Our view is fundamentally opposed to that of Böhm-Bawerk in the matter of the appraisal of future needs (§ 7). Böhm-Bawerk also has raised fundamental objections to our views concerning the attribution of capital yield which were already developed, although in less detail, in *Natural Value.* We cannot consider these now in all their details. The essential positions have been under review, especially where the computation of yield for capital goods is contrasted with that for simple and consumable productive means.

Under the assumption of the simple economy only a portion of the phenomenon of interest may be examined: i. e., the so-called natural interest of productive capital as drawn by the owner of capital when he is himself the entrepreneur. Contractual interest on loans and especially consumptive interest are absent. These forms we shall not have to discuss until we reach the theory of exchange.

§ 25. Economic Value

The significance of the economy—Primary need-value and the derivative value of goods—The narrower concept of economic partial value—"Values"—Value in use and value in exchange.

The theory of the simple economy has shown us clearly the significance of human economy when the influence of power is eliminated. The economy arises whenever the means for the satisfaction of needs exist in economic proportions. Its object is to secure the highest utility that is possible under the pressure of this proportionality. From this practical end, applied reason has deduced all the manifold and complex rules of appraisal: the marginal law, the laws of supply, of demand, of costs, of common and specific attribution, and of capital appraisal. In each method there has been the presupposition that value is rigidly subjected to arithmetical processes, that the estimate of partial masses may be based on the multiplication of mass and the value of the unit. By trial and error, through thousands of years of experience, practical wisdom has formed the rules of computation which it adopts. An admirable structure has resulted, rich, yet rigidly self-contained. It is easy to see why the inquiring theoretical mind could not readily grasp its full significance.

As the economic computation of utility has been explained, one sees in it an achievement of the human mind. Thus the accountant who is employed by others and who is unaffected by any active interests of his own, attends to his functions and calculates faithfully the relations involved between goods and the labors performed upon them. Whenever ownership is real, that is, when gains and losses are personal, it is so because the owner infuses the vital feelings of personal interest into his computation of utility. The significance of the latter process expands and it becomes an estimate of living values. The laws to which we submit are none other than the laws of the computation of utility. Thus in acquainting ourselves with these laws we have fulfilled the mission of the theory of value as regards the simple economy. There remains but the task of completing our exposition by a formal definition of the concept of economic value.

We define it as the value which is assigned to units or groups of commodities and of labors employed in economic transactions. In economic valuation we associate the primary need-values with the ideas of those goods and labors which in economy are recognized as their practically important causes. The primary need-values are felt in personal experience. We transfer from them derivative, secondary values to the material goods of the economy. The existence of these goods is really a matter of indifference to us when they are considered merely as things. At the same time we recognize that our life is dependent upon them and that the abundance of primary values which may meet our need is dependent upon the abundance of these goods. A similar interest attaches also to labor, over and above the interest which inheres in it as a personal experience. Labor is seized upon as a material means to an economic end.

The laws of economic value are those which we obey in economic transactions when we attach our interests to goods and labors.

Economic value is a material value; back of it lies an egoistic[1] love of external things. The name is well adapted to emphasize this essential feature which arises in economic pursuits. Predicating value as an attribute of the means of satisfaction emphasizes the close association between the experience of an estimate of value and the simultaneous concept of the means of satisfaction. Inasmuch as the deduced experience of value is designated by the same name as the primary one, no doubt is left of the subjective origin of the term.

In the market one speaks not only of value but also of "values." Material goods or any other objects of exchange which are valuable are spoken of as "values." We too shall employ the term in this transformed meaning to speak collectively of all objects having economic value. We shall particularly embrace within this term all economic goods and services for which a different collective name is not already available. Such a name is distinctly needed in order that qualities may be assigned to these objects which they jointly possess as vehicles of economic value.

All rules of the computation of utility value which we have deduced in the theory of the simple economy are observed in the computation of exchange value as it is universally practiced. Whenever we disregard the stress of economic power we shall find that the utility value of the simple economy is precisely the same economic value which functions in the transactions of economic exchange. To this extent, then, every economy in computing according to value in exchange complies with the original aims of economy. If there should ever be an economic order which was able wholly to eliminate the influence of power, it could not dispense with utility value and the rules of its computation. If it should do so it would be disqualified for the performance of economic duties. Civilized peoples possess treasures of economic culture in the practical rules for the computation of utility value. They could not possibly dispense with the aid of these rules.

Utility and labor are the respective central themes of the utility theory and the labor theory. Both arrive at a subjective interpretation of value. In the latter theory the primary force is a desire to avoid the pain of labor. From this is deduced a value, an interest in the products of labor whose possession is the means of avoiding the pain of labor. The subjective nature of value is even clearer in this case than when utility is seen as the central motive. The utility theory runs the danger of being inveigled into considering not only the use and usefulness of goods, which are its proper concern, but of regarding value as a natural or indispensable quality of goods as such. Strenuous efforts have been

[1] Interessierte.

necessary to correct the errors which are apt to accompany this objective treatment. It is Menger's fundamental definition to which all succeeding achievements of economic theory trace their origin. It was he who formulated the subjective interpretation of value. He defines the value of goods as "the importance attached to concrete goods or quantities of goods because of a conscious dependence upon them for the satisfaction of our needs."

Our own definition is broader than that of Menger in so far as it includes not only goods but labors. Otherwise it is narrower, resting only on economic value proper. Menger defines the value of things generally. We define a partial value that is correlated with economic transactions. Continuous efforts are required to use the available partial quantities according to the plan of the economy. The distinction is so important that we must explain it in more detail.

In the regular course of economic processes we deal with sums of commodity- and labor-units. The instances are rare in which some elementary catastrophe involves the existence or non-existence of large aggregates of goods. Practical conditions may also call for off-hand decisions in which details and particulars cannot enter but which involve such aggregate masses. More frequently governments find themselves in positions where fundamental decisions are called for as to measures of public economic policy. However, the quantitative relations most familiar to men engaged in economic pursuits are those which call for the appraisal of partial utility. Value which is thus economically associated with the idea of commodities and labors is the arithmetic partial value of the units. They have this value in mind and refer to it alone when they speak economically of value, pure and simple.

The estimates of value that are expressed when large aggregate masses of goods are considered in bulk are undoubtedly also expressions of egoistic material preference. They are subject to the law of dependent utility. However, the quantities involved often differ greatly from those for which partial values are practically computed. These quantities are not connected with the ideas of goods and labors. Usually we do not regard these computations as estimates of value at all. We contrast them as expressions of general interests with the narrower economic value. Where, for example, we estimate the value of a railroad, we customarily adopt only the pecuniary value of the yield to give expression to the partial value. All those other interests, military, political, economic, which inhere in the railroad are separately distinguished from the purely commercial value. This happens when we say that the construction of a railroad cannot be justified by its commercial value but is necessary for other reasons.

In the computation of partial values the interconnections of the productive process become most prominent: the relation of costs to profit, of yield to productive means. They present the most important task to economic calculation. Therefore they are most strongly associated with the concept of goods. The relation to need, though always suggested, is less prominent in this presentation. For this reason in the regular course of production the estimates of value are compared not directly with the relation to need but with units of cost or yield. The relation of the last two to need, however, are never wholly lost to view. When Menger defines the value of goods as the significance which commodities gain because of the satisfactions of needs which we feel to be dependent upon them, he passes somewhat beyond practical consciousness. In the latter the subjective origin of value is not as clearly prominent, as the definition might lead us to assume. Our definition is more in accord with practice. It makes economic value somewhat more distinctly objective. It does not exclude the relation to the primary need-value but emphasizes it only slightly. The "significance of economy" of which we speak points in the first instance to the external relations of the economy.

BOOK II

THEORY OF THE SOCIAL ECONOMY

PART I

THEORY OF ECONOMIC SOCIETY

Schäffle, *Ges. System;* and, *Bau und Leben*—Wagner, *Grundlegungen*—Schmoller, *Grundrisz* I—Menger, *Untersuchungen*—Philippovich, *Grundrisz*—Wieser, *Recht und Macht*, 1910.—Loria, *Die wirtschaftlichen Grundlagen der herrschenden Gesellschaftsordnung*, 1895—Kistiakowski, *Gesellschaft und Einzelwesen*, 1899—Span, *Wirtschaft und Gesellschaft*, 1906; and, *Gesellschaftslehre*, 2nd ed. 1923—Oppenheimer, *System der Soziologie*, I. 1922, III. 5th ed. 1923—Simmel, *Grundfragen der Soziologie*, 1917—Tönnies, *Gemeinschaft und Gesellschaft*, 1919—Böhm-Bawerk, *Macht oder ökon. Gesetz?*, Z. f. Volksw. vol. XXVI—Stammler, *Wirtschaft und Recht*, 3rd ed. 1919—Giddings, *Studies in the Theory of Human Society*, 1922—M. Weber, *Wirtschaft und Gesellschaft*, 1921 (*Grundrisz der Soz.—Oek.*, vol. III).

§ 26. The Economic Process and the Theory of Society

Economic contracts—The social processes of economic production, acquisition and exchange—The problems of economic unity and of power—Classical individualism.

So far we have considered the national economy in an idealized manner as that of a unified people. Actually only a relatively small part of the process is carried forward under unified direction, i. e., that part in which the state enters with its economic leadership. The largest part by far is carried out independently by the private economies. These are numbered by the million in all the great nations. In the present legal order these economies are independent. If they wish to bind themselves together, it can be done only by contract.

There are three forms of binding compensatory contracts: the social contract, the exchange contract and a contract of insurance. In the social contract a larger or smaller number of persons pledge themselves to unite values, goods or services, for some given purpose, especially acquisition. The contract of exchange as a rule is concluded by only two parties; by means of it the many-sided surrenders of goods, services or money are reconciled. The contract of insurance at times most resembles the social contract, at other times that of exchange. Its purpose is to distribute the effects of loss over many private economies. It has attained great importance in developed economies. But it has to do only with the security of the economic body, not with its creation. We shall give no more attention to this form of agreement than we do uncompensated contracts; fundamentally we are concerned only with the erection of the social economic organism. Next we may disregard also the social contract. One should expect that it be adopted to the integration of the social economy. Nevertheless in its effect it is overshadowed by the exchange contract which, although it is made as a rule only between two parties, has manifested itself the coördinating instrument that binds the individual economies into the national economy.[1] The social contract is used in its fullest form only in a relatively small number of cases. We shall therefore make full reference only to those institutions that are created by its agency. Our main task is to describe the institutions of exchange and erection of the national economic body that is brought about by these.

The private economies that are embraced in the national economic body retain in their domestic management rather the spirit of the simple economy. They associate themselves with the social body in only a few respects. These associated activities are for the purpose of attending to the fulfillment of consumption by means of common economic leadership. But in their external affairs these economies are bound fast to the economic body in which they have a most important function to perform. In a fully developed money economy, in which individual self-sufficiency disappears, all households must finally turn to the market for a satisfaction of their needs. From them arise the consumer's demand, which in turn give rise to a producer's demand. In further sequence, everyone who maintains a self-supporting household is faced with the necessity of securing a monetary income. To do so, he must engage in acquisitive activity. He may do this as a large entrepreneur, a master-craftsman, a landlord or as some other type of independent producer. He may as a worker, a lessor, a creditor or in some other manner introduce goods or services into the process of preparing values. Thus every private economy is doubly interwoven in the social economic process: on the one hand the demand for natural values emanates from the household; on the other, the individual pursues an acquisitive course that gives him

[1] Trans. note: In this section *Volkswirtschaft* is rendered as national economy, *gesellschaftlichen Wirtschaft* as social economy. The latter phrase almost never reappears in later sections of Wieser. Later, therefore, *Volkswirtschaft* is rendered as social economy or, simply, economy, unless the reference is clearly to the national economy.

products or other values. So long as a private economy wishes to maintain itself, it must sustain the circulation induced by these two movements with their manifold conditioning and with a counter-movement of money.

There are millions of minor circulatory movements that bind the private economies to the social body. These all unite in the great circulation of the national economy. In the latter, the total supply and demand are offset against each other. This process is spoken of as the distribution of goods. It is better spoken of as a process of transposition or exchange. In the strictest sense one could refer to a distribution of goods only on the assumption that the aggregate production had been conducted in common and that the resulting products were then apportioned for the satisfaction of the needs of individuals in some such manner as is contemplated for a socialist state. There is no division of goods in this sense in the established order. Products and other natural values are not produced by common effort; they are prepared by separate acquisitive organizations that are socially related. The process that follows their production is nothing more than one of exchange in which each individual economy surrenders the values which it has prepared for those that it requires.

Nevertheless, the legally independent acquisitive enterprises are instruments of a great social productive and acquisitive process following a division of labor. This social productive and acquisitive process and, with it, the inseparable process of exchange together comprise the social economy.

The theory of the simple economy is an essential prerequisite to the description of this social economic process that is encumbent upon the following study. The collective private economies that are associated in the national economy are in themselves simple economies. Without a theory of the simple economy we would be unable to understand the law that they follow within the social body. Nevertheless, the preface thus afforded is incomplete. We must add to it a still further prelude. For the theory of the simple economy only explains the condition of the isolated and idealized individual economy that follows its laws of motion without restraint. But in the social economy these individual units meet from all directions. Indeed, they clash with great force. We must, therefore, ascertain whether their conjunction does not alter their law of motion and whether in particular the amount of power does not exercise a decisive control. Under some conditions it will be noted the individual movements are so well coördinated that the spirit of the economy is fulfilled for all particpants and therefore for the entire social economy. This is true in the case of institutions, such as money, that serve the common interests of all. Where this is the case, we must ask by what power the individuals, each of whom independently follows his own law, are held to a common purpose and enabled to work to a single end. Under other conditions the personal interests cross and in the resulting conflict the stronger wins. In this victory still greater power arises that is capable of dominating entire classes of society. In these instances we must inquire if there is not also a law for the economic movements of power. It is especially necessary to ascertain whether the social significance of the economy is destroyed. The question becomes still more important as we notice that power is not always introduced into the economy from without but frequently develops from within. As soon as this fact is established one must inquire whether the exchange economy of the people is not perhaps erected on a foundation that leads to absurdity.

All these questions relate to general social theory. They involve the unity of society and the source and operation of power. The national economic process is a social one. It must, therefore, present the same problems that arise in all social intercourse. If there were a complete theory of society, we might resort to it for an explanation of the fundamental types of social activity that concern us. But sociology is still in the making. If we wish such explanation as seems to be needed, we must offer it ourselves and describe the fundamental types of social activity as fully as an explanation of the economic process requires. Naturally, this must be brief. Therefore, without any attempt at demonstration, we shall set forth in brief sentences those sociological phenomena with which we must introduce a description of the economic process. If these concepts prove to be useful in the explanation of the economic process this is in itself the best proof that could be adduced for them.

The extraordinary interest of private persons and governments in the success of economic endeavor led scientific thinkers to inquire into the social relations of the national economy at an earlier date than was the case in any other field of social intercourse. Furthermore, the fact that economic value is a commensurable quantity in which the motives that lead to economic intercourse are clearly expressed made possible more rapid and more certain progress in explaining these relations than in other sociological fields. This explains the fact that economic theory has been an advance guard of sociology. From the start, the economist has had to rely upon himself in dealing with sociological problems. Economics is only one phase of social science, but it has developed more rapidly than the main body of the theory of society. Therefore it has been placed in a position of being able to render greater service to the latter than it could receive from it. The scientific greatness of the classical masters manifested itself in the force with which they attacked the sociological problems of economic theory. In their doctrines they laid certain of the foundations for later social science.

The classicists dealt especially with the first problem that we set forth above,—the problem of the unity of economic society. Their healthy optimistic thinking left them in no doubt of the parallelism of individual and social economic interest. They maintained that every individual best recognizes his own advantage and that he is led to protect it more effectively by his own egoism than would be possible by any other method. But as one must always serve others in exchange in order to profit oneself, in competitive exchange it must follow that the strongest personal forces which are used in the national economy are introduced for the service of society. From this simple premise the classical masters deduced the law of price and explained the erection of the acquisitive economy. Of the principles that they established, that of the division of labor is outstanding. It offers a deep insight into the erection of the national economic body. It is the most important and at all events the best established contribution of the classicists to social science.

The classical theory of economic society is called individualistic. It is; but one must add that the individualism of the founders of the classical theory was by no means so far-reaching as their critics have maintained. They always conceived of the economy as restrained by law and morality. They demanded freedom of action for the individual only on the assumption that the state and other social organizations that set standards are responsible for the protection of law and morality. They never maintained that the state itself is an individualistic creation. Therefore, the responsibility is not theirs if an extreme school has carried individualism to anarchy and the breakdown of the state. Just as the classical masters conceived of the individual, so when they dealt with freedom of action they conceived of personal egoism as controlled by law and morality. Moreover, they clearly recognized that certain dangers inhered in personal egoism and that certain precautions must be taken against them. The belief in personal liberty grew out of the historical setting in which they lived. Their error lay in the fact that they gave somewhat too much room for the play of personal freedom. The methodological instrument of idealization was carried by them to a point at which it became idealized observation. As a consequence they overestimated man's capacity for freedom. If they also failed to formulate theoretically the necessary restrictions on freedom, it was because they regarded such restrictions only as important exceptions, whereas freedom should be the general rule. If they are not completely individualistic in their theory, the fact remains that from a practical point of view they carried their individualism too far.

The full application of this individualism was first made by their disciples, their Epigones. These accepted the rule of freedom word for word without noting any of its accompanying restrictions as set forth by the masters. The disciples were the first to develop the doctrine of the harmony of all interests. In their doctrinaire presentation they committed the serious blunder of maintaining a dogma of unrestricted freedom, although the conditions of life had so changed in the meantime that unlimited freedom must have worked social ill.

It follows from this that the classicists must have left open the second problem mentioned above,—that of power. Only incidentally did one or the other of them note that the product which originally belonged to the worker was later reduced by those in power who would reap where they had not sown. There is an emphatic passage in Smith that is particularly quoted. Nevertheless Adam Smith, as well as Ricardo and the later leading theorists, neglected to draw any particular theoretical conclusions from their observation. They all accepted the existing conditions of power. Their Epigones accepted the conclusion that the prevailing inequality was necessary. As conditions stood in the classical period—particularly as they were idealized—it was possible to dispose of the problem of power in the economy far more easily than was later the case. One might at that time rest content with the statement that the general interest of society would be furthered if the higher service of the talented and proficient were rewarded by a larger income, while the unskilful, the lazy and the poor workman were left behind. That the individualistic dogma failed to take into account the fact of power, first became apparent when capitalistic development reduced great strata of the population to the direst straits. An economic theory that should suffice for our times is inconceivable without a social theory that is consistent with the fact of power.

Modern economic policy has departed from the theory of freedom represented by the individualist school. A detailed discussion of this transition forms no part of our theoretical presentation, but belongs rather to a study of the periods that comprise the history of dogma and method and of the economic and sociopolitical concepts. It is no more a part of our task to determine whether or not modern economic policy has set the correct limits to the freedom of individual action. Our duty is rather, in this as in all other connections, to determine the theoretical basis in which such marginal determinations may be fixed. What valid substitute may we offer for the individualistic theory of society? In its naïve formulation it has become inadequate. But one cannot get away from its fundamental concept, that the individual is the subject of social intercourse. The individuals who comprise society are the sole possessors of all consciousness and of all will. The "organic" explanation, which seeks to make society as such, without reference to individuals, the subject of social activity, has patently proved a failure. One must hold himself aloof from the excesses of the individualistic exposition, but the explanation must still run in terms of the individual. It is in the individual that one must look for those tendencies that make the social structure,—that dove-tail (if we may use that expression) in such manner as to give the firm cohesion of social unity and at the same time provide the foundation for the erection of social power.

§ 27. The Basic Forms of Social Action

The social existence of man—Natural controls,[1] compulsion and domination—Leaders and masses—Anonymous leadership and power—Classes and social stratification.

In the following section is briefly presented a view of the basic types of social intercourse. From this we shall proceed to a description of economic activity.

[1] Trans. note: The author here writes Freiheitsmächte, for which I know no English equivalent. He means, as is explained in the text, those forces, natural

Man is too weak to assure his preservation and to develop his life if he stands as an isolated individual. The impulse to self-preservation and to further development,—the egoistic interest that grows from an appreciation of weakness,—leads to social organization. In part, men are thus led by conscious deliberation. But fundamentally, a social impulse is operative; man is by nature a social being. When first he appears in history he was also associated in social groups, hordes or clans that possessed a social power over their members. In the course of historical development, the social organizations became even more inclusive. They spread by the power of success. Those tribes that are victorious in war and prosperous in peaceful endeavor, expand, while the others lag behind.

There are two types of social force: natural controls and compulsion. Natural controls are recognized by the individual as aids to the assertion and development of his being. He feels them as increasing his individual power. He hardly recognizes that he is ruled by them. The deeper their dominion is bedded in man himself, the less conscious is he of their control, and the more readily does he fulfil their commands. And precisely when he is most completely dominated by them,—when his innermost being assents to them,—then for the first time does he believe himself to be quite free. True freedom does not consist in total lack of control. It consists rather in a relation of the individual to society.

Compulsion, on the other hand, is recognized as a restriction on the individual life. Its powers are most keenly appreciated when they arise from the armed force which has subdued the vanquished to the will of the victor. But as we shall show later, these forces also develop within the ordinary intercourse of a society. The victorious people may themselves be subject to a prince. Domination is oppressive compulsion.

Between the natural controls and compulsion,—between the latter and domination,—there are imperceptible gradations, extraordinarily difficult to distinguish, whether subjectively by those who are controlled or objectively by those who observe from without. There may be cases where a power is still regarded by its victim as a natural control, although it already operates by compulsion, in that it restricts the development of his life. The weak man still feels himself to be supported by that which a stronger man, eager for independence, feels as restraint. It is one of the evil effects of slavery, that the slave loses all sense of oppression.

or social, to which the freest man submits, whether willingly or unconsciously. To express this idea, I have coined the phrase "natural controls."

The strongest social forces develop where unified common activity is necessary; for example, in resisting foreign attack. Such activity on the part of large masses demands leadership. The mass as such, the unorganized multitude, is incapable of action. In order to act, it must place itself under the direction and control of leaders. Originally, foreign leaders were called to leadership, i. e., those who were qualified by their outstanding fitness. Later, when historical powers of leadership had arisen, these forces control the selection of leaders. New leaders can establish themselves only by overcoming the opposition of the old. The success that attaches to fortunate leadership elevates the position of the leader and eventually transforms mere personal superiority into true personal power. In the course of our studies we shall show how this may develop historically to become domination.

As the major part of economic activity does not require a unified direction, so the power of economic leadership never attained the same strength as military, political, and religious leadership. It is only in the era of capitalism that large enterprises gave a basis on which to erect great power of economic leadership.

Even in those cases of social intercourse where a legal right of self-determination is preserved to the individual and in which unified leadership plays no part, leadership and the accompanying power of leadership do develop. Even in their personal affairs, the mass of individuals are too weak to rely upon themselves alone. They could not thus maintain life and develop further. Even the strongest man is not strong enough for this if he relies only upon his individual power. Everything that man has accomplished whether in spiritual or physical evolution, has been attained only through social relations in that the best leadership has furnished the example, the advice, and the knowledge; and that others were induced to follow them because of the success which these leaders have attained. The decisions which the common man regards as his own are induced by the power of his education and by the widespread practice of others who have been placed in like circumstances. The play that is possible to freedom of action, which exists legally, is narrowly restricted by morality, the state of the technical arts and other conditions. The mass retains its independence for the most part only in the selection of leaders or laws which shall be followed or in the precision with which the existing pattern is followed. Nonetheless, the mass plays a decisive rôle in the development of social powers. By its very weight it decides how far the examples offered by the leaders shall be realized. It determines what shall and shall not be, and the leaders themselves in the final analysis subject themselves to popular opinion.

In private life the leaders are often not conspicuous. They may be known only to a small circle or may relieve each other in rapid succession, as now one, now the other has the happy thought that sets a standard for those about him. This type of leadership we shall call anonymous in contrast to personal leadership in which the personality of the leader stands out strongly and is widely known. Anonymous leadership operates on a small scale. It operates only to preserve a given cultural level or very slowly to advance beyond an existing level. Great advances to new practices require great leaders who occupy the centre of the stage, although that which they seek to bring about may be a matter for which the soil has been prepared for a long time. Corresponding to anonymous leadership, there are anonymous powers that inure to the entire society or to a particular social group. Anonymous powers are felt by the mass of men to be natural controls that approximate compulsion only insofar as occasionally men submit unwillingly to social considerations that restrict individual movement.

The fate of society is dependent on the relationship of leadership and the masses. The contrast between them is necessary; it must be more or less intense, if action is to result, but it must not be too great. Leadership is impossible without some inequality. Absolute equality would restrain all social progress. But too great a power conferred on the leaders may also restrain progress, indeed, it may lead to the oppression of the masses. An especially gifted man or one favored by external conditions possesses a certain superiority; but this alone cannot be referred to as power. It is only when this superiority is so great as to give its possessor a marked advantage that it gives him power. As examples we may cite the superior purchasing power of rich consumers or the greater competitive ability of particularly favored producers. One speaks of social power, when the superiority places a large number of other people at a disadvantage and particularly when it is not individual possessors of power who are involved but social groups that are opposed. This social power is most marked when these groups are legally superior and subordinate.

The groups that are thus distinguished are called classes. It is customary to contrast a superior ruling class with a subordinate class. In regard to economic conditions, it is customary to speak of the ruling class is propertied; of the ruled, as a propertyless or proletarian class. But a correct analysis must distinguish at least three classes of which one is a clearly distinguished middle class. There are gradual transitions from this to the higher and the lower classes. Property alone is not necessarily a criterion of superiority. No less decisive for the domination of large groups are conditions for historical growth. There are large groups that belong to the propertied class, but who attain a position that enables them to gain large incomes only because of their higher education. It may be that they possess no acquisitive wealth.

We shall speak of this relationship of social domination and subordination, whether it is established legally or by actual superiority, as stratification. We shall speak of dominant and subordinate strata. As such, not only are the classes themselves significant but also the individual gradations within each class. Various similar social groups are divided by their callings or in some other manner. This horizontal division of society is to be distinguished from the vertical one which we have been discussing. The division of labor described by the classical school is a horizontal division of economic society. An economic theory that studies the problem of power may not overlook the fact of stratification.

§ 28. The Individual in Economic Society

The social training as economic education—The social nature of needs and impulses—The associative economic principle—The social egoism of the individual.

In his economic conduct also the individual is determined by social forces. Law and morals, of which the classicists made mention, are not the only forces. A man is also influenced in all those relations where law and morals leave him free. He is a creature of his period and his environment—of his nation, his class and his profession. That which appears as individual in him is a particular form of the typical manner of life. The latter he receives through the education that flows from historical powers that operate through his circle. That his knowledge and skill are the result of his education in the school, the family and life requires no further discussion. But some further elaboration is necessary to show that this social education penetrates to the very heart of his individual being. Needs, impulses and egoism itself are dominated by social powers.

The social nature of needs is the most easily recognized. Educative social forces determine not only the so-called social needs, but also the personal ones that are usually contrasted with the former. It is even true that the bare physical need has a social cover; not even the measure of the physiological minimum of existence is determined entirely individually. Such strata of the people as have been oppressed for a long period have been educated to an almost inconceivable poverty with a decided narrowing of the impulse to improve themselves economically. This is the "damnable absence of need" of the worker of which Lassalle complains. Fundamentally every man requires that which the standard of living of his circle forces him to demand. Only a few are strong enough to be more independent. He who rises to a higher class ordinarily accepts the standard of living of that class. If, perhaps, for his own person he maintains the simpler habits of the class to which he has been educated, still he does not feel that his children should be forced to accept any other standards than the needs of the class to which they will belong. Even man's senses are socially educated. Sight is not merely a physiological impression on the retina but it is at the same time an appreciation of the significance of the image. This is determined by a comparison of things earlier apprehended that are called up in memory images. In every period, men see from a different artistic and technical point of view because their interests differ and that which they see therefore has a different significance. Indeed these changes may direct their attention to entirely different details.

Also the impulses to activity are not purely personal. For the average man they are entirely dependent upon the practice of his time and environment for their direction and their strength. In one period it may be a warlike spirit, in another, an acquisitive one that stimulates the mass of men under the given conditions and their historical education. Will is schooled impulse; even more than the impulse itself, will is socially developed. Every nation has a certain average degree of energy of will. This is determined not only by race, but also in every period by the historically transmitted culture. The will to economy is of one order for the mass of the Russians, and another for the mass of Englishmen or Anglo-Americans; it differs as between the propertied class and the proletariat.

The goals of economy are derived from the needs; its powers come from the impulses and will. Therefore the direction and standard of economic endeavor cannot be determined entirely personally. The injunction to achieve the highest utility with the lowest cost is interpreted by everyone in the light of his social environment. The spirit of his times leads him. For the mass of average men the economic principle that they follow is simply to "be as economical as your associates": i. e., fulfill the law of lowest costs and highest utility as far as is customary in the circle to which you belong and in which you would maintain yourself. The current individualist concept of the economic principle is a theoretical idealization. Methodologically it is well adapted,—indeed it is essential, to a deduction of the elements of economics. From this idealization one must make a transition, by decreasing abstraction, to the social concept that is actually current, if one would understand the concrete phenomena of life. Economic leaders raise themselves above the mass of their associates, but they themselves cannot get away entirely from the social concept of the economic principle. They also are unable to attain complete individual freedom. They cannot neglect entirely the force of the examples set by their associates.

Through long experience, the plan of domestic management and acquisition in all of its most general phases has been socially tested and determined for every income-class and for every type of calling. Every newly-established individual economy finds a pattern already set. It is not necessary that a man make a personal choice of tasks to determine the direction of productive uses on the standard of the allowable margin of use. All these things have been done by his fellows. There are few economies which do not hold strictly to the social example. Most men confine themselves quite closely within the boundaries laid down for them, and anxiously avoid the blame or criticism of their fellows. Personal energy expresses itself for the most part in the degree to which one approximates the prevailing rule, or in the independence with which one fits the rule to the particular conditions in individual instances. He who lacks independence will be led astray by the associative principle whenever his conditions depart from the rule. Therefore it happens so often that those at the lower margin of an income-class are seduced into living beyond their means because they believe that they must conform to the practice of their associates. When an entire class lives beyond its means, this usually occurs because for historical reasons they have been educated to maintain themselves on a level with or above some richer class.

Even the consciousness of self,—the inner assurance of each man that he is a being apart from all others,—is influenced by social forces, and thus takes a direction that is not merely personal. There are innumerable breaches in consciousness through which social influences enter, impelling it to courses prescribed by society. We do not wish to lay stress at this point on the fact that the outlook of men who have been educated in a similar culture is made uniform. But we note that the socially educated individual in his efforts to serve himself, fits himself perfectly [1] with the social organism. His Ego is not satisfied unless it finds itself in all important respects at one with society. If one is truly socially educated, his Ego departs from him and finds its end in society; it ceases to be purely personal and becomes social egoism; it wishes to conform in all respects to law and custom and in general to the social forces of the economy; it demands only so much for itself as social precept indicates that it may and should demand. This statement holds true not only of those cases in which a man clearly feels himself bound by social conscience but also where he believes himself to be entirely independent. In most matters a man accepts the social code of the industrial or social group of which he is a member; it is only in certain major relationships, that are uniform for the whole of society, that a universally accepted rule obtains.

By reason of the social egoism a man is ready to fit into a social order which includes both submission and domination. The feeling of fellowship makes easier the submission of the masses to the historically maintained power or domination of a class of leaders—one submits more readily when others are seen also to submit. In a class of servitors, content with its lot, there arises a class-spirit which regards submission as a point of honor and creates the good will of the faithful servant. In one not content with its fate, there arises the spirit of class-conflict with a feeling of solidarity. It becomes a point of honor to stand faithfully by one's fellows and to dedicate and sacrifice individual welfare for the welfare of the class. A slavish class that has been pressed to the ground and has become callous to its state loses the power to maintain a strong egoism. Its egoism is limited to the most proximate personal needs. It degenerates to a short-sighted and impotent self-seeking. Each individual thinks only of himself. The mass is really nothing more than a loose multitude without ties; it is not a people, but a mob. On the other hand, the class of leaders, accustomed to command, unites its members in the demands made upon their underlings and in the sternness of attitude that they must maintain in order to carry their demands into effect. The class resents, as a weakness and as an insult to its honor, the failure of one of its members to use to the full his lordly right of domination. At its apex this class-egoism of the leaders becomes a social egoism. It recognizes its social task. It incites to high service, and feels ennobled by the knowledge that its own advantage marches with the advance of society. Enlightened absolutism, that accomplished such great things in economic education and did so with

[1] In einem überaus hohen Grade.

benevolence, spirit and boldness, may well serve as an example. But the egoism of a dominating class of leaders all too easily degenerates when it no longer meets an opposition that restrains it. It changes to a short-sighted, self-seeking of dominion.

As in all other activity, so in the negotiation of economic contracts, the average man is governed by the social power of the associative principle. In his individual dealings he uses the type of contract that has been generally developed. As a rule he adds nothing more to this form than a specification of the particular persons and values involved. For example, in contracts of exchange he is satisfied to establish the contracting parties and the kind and the amount of the consideration; for the rest, it is understood that the given case follows the requirements that typically prevail in the market. If one looks more closely, one finds that as a rule even in the selection of persons and the specification of consideration he is governed by class and social powers; and his legal freedom of contract as matter of fact shrinks into an extremely limited freedom of choice. If one points to private contract as the unifying medium of the national economy, and if one seeks to faithfully reproduce actual conditions, one must add that the private contracts are themselves governed by class and social powers.

§ 29. Social Institutions

The origin of money—The individualistic significance of social institutions, Menger's Theory—Historical power.

The economy is full of social institutions which serve the entire economy and are so harmonious in structure as to suggest that they are the creation of an organized social will. Actually they can only have originated in the coöperation of periodically independent persons. Such a social institution is illustrated by money, by the economic market, by the division of labor in acquisition, and finally by the national economy itself, which is the greatest of these institutions, and includes all the others.

Economic inquiry has long been concerned with the origin of such social institutions. The earlier, naïve explanation that regarded them as institutions of the State, or as dependent on a social contract, now has few adherents. Money, for example, existed before the state and, as world-money, is today more extensive than the state. How could any general contractual agreement be reached as to institutions whose being is still hidden in the mists of the future, and is only conceived in an incomplete manner by a few far-seeing persons, while the great mass can never clearly appreciate the nature of such an institution until it has actually attained its full form and is generally operative? Also the mere contract into which one freely enters, and from which one may freely withdraw, could never establish the binding, compelling power that characterizes all true social institutions.

Much more satisfactory is the explanation based on gradual historical evolution, which takes into account the powerful factor of time. As the constantly repeated impact of falling water cuts a deep course in the hardest rock by the power that is in each separate drop of water, or as the cretaceous animalculæ in the course of ages may tower into mountains, so the service of individual forces working together and working in successive generations, through centuries and millennia, toward the same end, may slowly build great economic structures. Thus one may understand the evolution of the acquisitive process with its division of labor that has now spread to tremendous proportions and diversity. Step by step one occupational group after another abandoned the closed natural domestic economy for the money economy, but each of these groups in itself developed further and was subdivided. To understand this process, however, one must first perceive the readiness of the individual to range himself in the social order. One must see him as a social being who develops through social education.

For complicated social institutions the historical explanation requires further refinement. We shall show this by the classic illustration of money, whose unknown origin has provoked almost as much interest among men as the origin of the state or of speech. But we must also show that the more subtle explanation at which one finally arrives, necessarily involves a reduction of the individualistic stress. The long series of writers who sought to explain money as an individualistic institution, ends with Menger's penetrating investigation. He uses the phenomenon of money as a paradigm by which he assumes to show that all social institutions of the economy are nothing more than "unintended social results of individual-teleological factors."[1]

The factual presentation of the origin of money that he gives in this connection is in itself conclusive. But from these same facts we are forced to a different conclusion as to the significance of historical social institutions.

Without following Menger's presentation word for word, we shall next reproduce its essentials.

The advantage of exchange can be availed to the greater extent, the greater the number of persons who take part in it. In this fact originated the desire to split up an act of natural barter into a number of exchanges. Here and there, under certain conditions it oc-

[1] Untersuchungen, pp. 171–187.

curred to some bright men that they would be in a position to increase the advantage of their exchanges, if, instead of arranging for the barter with some one contracting party, they should introduce a third into the trade. Let us assume that a hunter wishes to exchange game against wine. It may happen that he will have better results if he does not deliver the game directly to the possessor of the wine. The latter may himself be a hunter, and therefore have no use for the game. He may do better to offer it to a farmer who is prepared to offer grain in exchange, which the hunter knows that the man with the wine requires. To accomplish this purpose the natural exchange must be divided into two acts in which one deals with two different contracting parties. The first act is the surrender of a particular good for an intermediate exchange good that one does not wish to retain. The second act is to exchange the intermediate good for that commodity which he originally desired. Little by little, this process, as it justifies itself by success and is improved, is employed by more and more persons. They are able, by comparing expenses, to determine which goods are best fitted to be used as media of exchange. Those goods that are particularly acceptable in exchange may be taken by a shrewd trader even though in the particular case he has not decided for what good he will further exchange them; for he may expect that they will be willingly taken by any one. It will finally come about that certain goods, whose successful use shows them to be particularly fitted to serve as media of exchange, will be universally used, because everybody may be convinced that there is no one who will refuse to accept them. At this point a universal medium of exchange has arisen; money has developed.

If we grasp the operative motives in general by whose introduction Menger has elaborated the explanation of the development of money, we find that they are two that are already thoroughly familiar from our presentation of the fundamentals of social activity. On the one hand, we see that the participating persons are divided into the two groups of the leaders and the masses. On the other hand we see that success is the driving force that moves the masses to copy the example of the leaders. The type of leadership that Menger invokes is what we called anonymous leadership. Menger's explanation would be entirely satisfactory if he had appreciated as fully the part that the masses play in the development of money as he did that taken by the leaders. The function of the masses consists in the case of money as in all other social activity in that their imitation establishes the universal practice which gives to a rule its binding force and social power. It is in the nature of money that an obligation to accept it is felt that protects the payer against the shifty refusal of payment. This obligation arises from the mass habit of accepting money. It is in keeping with Menger's individualistic point of view that he should not fully appreciate the part played by the masses in the creation of money. He sees in money as in all social institutions of the economy nothing more than unintended social results of individual-teleological tendencies. Therefore it is impossible for him to say the last word in the explanation of money, and to concede that money represents something more and stronger than the will of participating individuals. A money for which a mass habit of acceptance has once been established is no longer the mere result of the individual aims of leaders whom the masses follow. Neither in the beginning nor later did the leaders have in mind a social institution. Their wishes were confined to much smaller, more proximate goals. For their personal purposes they wanted a well-adapted or better-adapted medium of exchange that they could use as they desired. None of them dreamed nor could have dreamed of a universal medium of exchange with a binding power that could compel them like all others to make use of it. The tremendous influence of the mass practice which grew up extended the final result far beyond their expectations. None of them would recognize in the final form of money an exact embodiment of their purpose. The final form of money is not a mere resultant; because of the universal social resonance that it awoke it represents a tremendous strengthening of their endeavors. It needs no special discussion to establish the fact that it passed far over the goal of the imitating mass. Indeed, the mass never acts with a clear consciousness of aim. It is not teleological. Rather it follows the path of success opened by the leaders without measuring its operation. In following this course they give it the weight of their mass and release a power which produces results far beyond those set by the masses or desired by the leaders. Only a part of the force that builds social institutions is directed by purpose; the final decisive mass-influence operates beyond the purpose.

In the presence of social institutions we must drop the rationalistic utilitarian assumption to which we might hold in the theory of the simple economy.

The fundamental error of individualism appears in dealing with social institutions. It views individuals as though by nature they were entirely independent and carry through their activity entirely by their own will. Men always act with diverse emotions. They act under the control of the more or less felt influence of the natural controls or compulsion that give them the power or force them to decision. From the influence of these powers not even the strongest leaders can entirely free themselves. From the coöperation of unnumbered persons, each independent in his sphere and each of whom is in contact with few others, harmonious institutions with a universally binding force arise. This could not be explained if the participating individuals were not disposed by nature to adjust themselves to each other and to fit themselves into the general situation.

The further evolution of social institutions occurs in the same manner as their origin. The older institution creates a historical force because of its binding power. This may be broken only by new leaders whose success sets the masses in motion. Until the general power to adopt new practices is found, the old institution remains valid in so far as its services are required. This is true even if the institution itself is incomplete or because of changed conditions is unable to render its service as fully as earlier. The much-quoted phrase "the good is the enemy of the better" holds especially for social institutions and their historical power. The individual is helpless against the historical force of old institutions. He must take them as he finds them. But when we say that the individual is helpless one should not merely understand that this or that individual is helpless. Rather, we have in mind all the individual members of society in so far as they do not cease to be isolated and incapable of action because they do not find the way to raise themselves to social action by leadership and mass following.

In every nation there are historically determined classes of leaders from which the personal leaders emerge. In the world there are historically determined leading nations. The leading classes and nations have a reversion in dominion in so far as society does not find in itself the power to oppose decisive obstacles through new leadership and mass following.

At this point we close our sociological introduction. Later we shall concern ourselves with the problem of domination. At present so far as may be possible we shall neglect the influence of power in order to show to what extent the economic acquisitive and exchange process develops in the spirit of the economy.

PART II

THE INSTITUTIONS OF EXCHANGE

Beside those works already mentioned in § 3 and § 16, should be added: Auspitz and Lieber, *Unters. über die Theorie des Preises*, 1888; Zuckerkandl, *Theorie des Preises*, 1889; and art. *Preis* in Hdw. d. Stw.; Lexis, *Volkswirtschsl.*, 2nd ed. 1913; Fisher, *Mathematical Investigations in the Theory of Value and Prices*, in Transactions of the Conn. Acad., vol. IX, 1892; Osorio, *Théorie mathématique de l'échange*, 1913; Zawadski, *Les mathématiques appliquées à l' economio politique*, 1918; Engländer, *Fragen des Preises*, J. f. G. V., vol. 43: and, *Gleichförmigkeit von Preis und Nutzen*, *ibid.*, vol. 44; and, *Bestimmungsgründe des Preises*, 1921; Spann, *Theorie der Preisverschiebung*, Z. f. Volksw., vol. XXII; Diblee, *The Laws of Supply and Demand*, 1922; Ely, *Monopolies and Trusts*, 1900; Weisz, art. *Monopol.* Hdw. d. Stw.; Jenks-Clark, *The Trust Problem*, 1922; Davenport, *The Economics of Enterprise*, 1913; Liefmann, *Kartelle und Trusts*, 4th ed. 1920; Cournot, *Recherches sur les principes mathématiques de la theorie des richesses*, 1838; Schäffle, *Die nationalökon. Theorie der ausschliessenden Absatzverhältnisse*, 1867; Edgeworth, *La teoria pura del monopolio*, Giornale degli Economisti, 1897; Forchheimer, *Theoretisches zum umvollständigen Monopol*, J. f. G. V., 32 Jahrg.; Payen, *Les Monopols*, 1920 (in Encyclopédie Scientifique); Clark, *The Control of Trusts*, 1912; Aarum, *Okonomiske sammcuslutninger med monopolistic stendens*, 1921.

§ 30. Exchange

Foundations and limits of natural exchange—The exchange of the weak economy—Exchange by the use of money—The chain of paired exchanges—Money.

Exchange has been defined as the surrender of the superfluous for the necessary. The definition is too narrow; it applies only to the extreme, most conspicuous case. Nevertheless, it comes close to the matter of which we treat, and forms an excellent starting-point whence to deduce the exact law of natural exchange. Each of the two parties entering into a natural exchange desires to secure for himself superior value. Each surrenders something to which he attaches less utility-value than he does to the good or service which he obtains in exchange. He may even attach no utility-value at all to that which he offers if it is actually "superfluous" to him. Thus it must happen that the two parties estimate the two objects of exchange in a directly opposite manner so that both may be able simultaneously to receive better value by the same transaction. As we recognize this fundamental fact, we recognize the limits of exchange. There is an end to exchange, whenever one of the contracting parties ceases to find an advantage in the continuance of the arrangement, no matter how much the other may desire to go on with that which offers him an increase in values. This limit must ultimately be reached since, according to the law of supply, continued decrease of units increases the value of those which remain, while the continued addition of units lessens the value for all the supply collected. As soon as the marginal utility of all the units to be surrendered equals or exceeds that of those received, no further gain in value can be realized and continued dealings would become economically futile.

When thus formulating the law of exchange, we do not by any means say that the association of exchange must be advantageous for all its members. We do not at all mean to contend that there is a complete harmony of interests. The law of exchange holds only in case it is economically completed; it does not, therefore, apply where there is external compulsion, fraud or error. In order that the law should hold, it must also be assumed that the contracting parties have full economic strength. Exchange by the man of small means is typically to be distinguished from the exchange of the nabob. The economic position of the poor man is characterized by an estimation of the needs of the future below the estimates of present needs. He will thus in exchange, also, be all too ready to content himself with an advantage of present value without taking into consideration that to obtain it he contracts for future performances that may involve altogether disproportionate, if not ruinous losses of value. The most obvious illustration is the usurious loan, where a present payment of money is exchanged for a future one, and an unscrupulous, wealthy creditor deals with a debtor who is poor because of careless habits, thriftlessness or misfortune. A similar illustration is presented by the contract of labor. Here the mercenary employer engages workers without the means of resistance, to render exhausting services at starvation-wages. We shall later discuss these two cases at length. Here we only refer to them in passing, to show how the law of exchange is only too frequently not carried out according to its full import in the transactions of the poor. It is carried out equitably only when the lasting effects of the exchange have been correctly appraised at their economic value.

In its beginnings, exchange is fortuitous. Neighbors accommodate each other by exchanging things which one of them needs urgently, while the other can spare them for the time being. Later on, exchanges are also made from land to land of commodities which nature produces bountifully in one locality, while in another they are wholly lacking. Little by little, men learn to adjust their acquisition to exchange; production is directed more and more to the preparation of values through whose sale increases of value may be obtained. The body of the old natural economy, consisting in the main of a juxtaposition of independent rural households, is transformed ever more and more into the economic community based on division of labor and exchange and employing a well established medium of exchange, money.

In order that this transformation may be accomplished, the early form of natural exchange must pass into the fully developed form of exchange by the use of money. In natural exchange both parties to the transaction give and acquire natural performances, meaning economic material commodities or the use of such, as well as personal services. In other words, each of the two parties surrenders and acquires natural values, material or personal. Where the exchange is effected by the use of money, the transaction is bifurcated. Men are satisfied in the first act of the enterprise to surrender the natural value of which they desire to dispose, in exchange for a counter-performance which they receive vicariously in money, the permanent possession of which they do not expect to retain. The next, or second step is to lay out the money in the purchase of the natural value which was the object whose ultimate acquisition and use in the household or in the economy of acquisitive trade was desired. In the first step, one receives in the form of money the advantage in value, which he wishes to secure; in the second only, does one realize it. In this process the parties change position, as they exchange; every vendor, becomes vendee; every vendee becomes vendor. Uninterruptedly thus, exchanging parties, link after link, join to form a never-ending chain; every pair of them is connected with the preceding and succeeding pair by one of the contracting parties.

The enormous advantage offered by money in the community of exchange is explained solely from the fact that it dissolves the entire turnover into links of such individual transactions of one exchanging couple each. The effect of it is, that men, in their acquisitions, are never tied down to the one contracting party with whom they have just dealt. They are altogether unfettered and can with complete mobility turn to any other man who may have the stock required. Every individual may confine himself in a division of labor to the production of one single species of values; and yet, his means being sufficient, he can procure whatever he wants, because he may, in turn, deal with all the individuals who produce the values he desires. The entire sum of opportunities of exchange offered by a large community may be exhausted without more than two persons at any one time having to deal with one another simultaneously. The exchanging parties go in pairs. Their intercourse may thus extend all over the world. Exchange may unite millions of human beings, of whom each will have to know his immediate predecessors and successors only. A society, having at its command only the form of natural exchange, would at all times, in order to exhaust all opportunities of exchange, be compelled to summon to a general council all its members, and thus get to the end of the matter. A proceeding so cumbersome could not be successfully carried out even in the small village—much less in a large city, a populous nation, or in the world as a whole.

Money is one of the most perfect instruments which the human mind has devised and perfected. In the simplicity of conception, in the variety of its applications and effects, it may be most aptly compared to the letters of the alphabet. These reduce the representation of spoken sounds to an exceedingly small number of simple symbols. By the combination of the latter the entire cultural wealth of a highly developed language may be expressed in images of sound waves. It is taken for granted that an instrument of such perfection as money could not in all its fullness have suddenly become an historical fact. The selection of the precious metals among civilized peoples and their habitual acceptance by the masses represents a social growth of thousands of years. How the gradual rise and development of an historical institution such as this must be conceived, has already occupied our attention. The succeeding pages of our exposition will have to deal exclusively with the actual phenomenon of money, as we find it.

As a matter of course, the organization of the social-economic whole, with its division of labor, does not set out from monetization. The impelling forces must issue from the economic body itself, and the development of the monetary form is merely a concomitant. The division of labor presupposes a highly developed technical art and the entire wealth of instruments of labor, which it requires and which it collects only very gradually, rising step by step to greater achievement. We see at once that a tribe of hunters, for example, can never rise to a very pronounced division of labor; all its members have to follow the same occupation, hunting, in order to subsist. If there is to be a fine division of labor, the work to be performed must be of a sort which can technically be differentiated and separated. The technical art of the Middle Ages was barely sufficiently developed to result in division of labor in the larger cities; but, to this day, modern technical art is not sufficiently developed entirely to dissolve the rustic remnants of the self-contained household through a division of labor of the national economy.

The method of pecuniary exchange, employed at first to exchange natural values one against the other, is later on used also to acquire or surrender capital-funds or the use of such in consideration of the payment of money. Anyone desiring to exchange money-capital against some other form or against natural values will likewise make use of money as the medium of exchange. He, too, will divide the entire transaction into the two acts of sale and acquisition. The idea of exchange under the institution of money is consequently very broad; it includes not only the contract of sale of chattels and real estate, the lease of real property and the wage contract, but also loans and the related agreements as to credits, the contract of sale of obligations, securities and international exchange.

The law of monetary exchange has to be formulated somewhat differently from the expression laid down in the opening of our exposition concerning natural exchange. In every instance monetary exchange is only half of the natural exchange; consequently, only by this half can it meet with the conditions of the law of natural exchange: a second, subsidiary exchange of money will always be required to complete the transaction. We expect to lay down the more accurate formulation of the law of exchange, applying to economic monetary exchange, as we formulate the law of price. For the present, we shall be satisfied to have shown that the gain of value, which it is intended to secure by exchange, is obtained in the form of money by the first act of pecuniary exchange and is realized in the form of natural values by the second or supplementary act.

§ 31. The Market

The parties of the market—Supply and demand—Quotations of the market—The market-position of monopoly and competition; monopoloid positions in the market—Wares.

As trade by exchange develops, markets come to be established where the parties habitually meet, who supply and who demand commodities. The parties supplying the market consist of those individuals who wish to surrender natural objects or money-funds in exchange for money; the bidders are those who wish to acquire natural values or money-funds in exchange for money. The parties of the market always or nearly always conclude their agreements in pairs: one vendor on each occasion enters a legal agreement with one demander. Each individual contracting party, however, is constantly under the influence of all the individuals of his own group and the opposing group. In this way the legal freedom of contracts does not lose its significance; it asserts itself in the market just as individual freedom asserts itself under the aegis of social power. The market is a social institution, where the freedom of exchange operates as a freedom of choice; it grants liberty in the selection of the individuals to be dealt with, in the selection of the objects of exchange in which men deal and, up to a certain point, it grants liberty also in regard to the determination of the price to be agreed upon. The parties always retain the right to decide whether or not they will deal at the terms of the market. The market-price itself is not arrived at by any individual exchanging pair; it is the result of the entire condition of the market, and can only be settled by pressure and counter-pressure of all the parties constituting the market.

Language, as ordinarily employed, means by the term, market, on the one hand the furnishings of the market—the market-square, the market-buildings, the entire institution of the market; but on the other hand it means also the sum of parties dealing in the market and the district represented by those who deal there. Theory does not concern itself with the equipment of the market; it looks upon the market as a social institution and understands by the term a regular communion between the parties who represent supply and demand for any given district. In the theory of the social economy, the entire economic organism constitutes one market, within which, however, local partial markets are to be distinguished.

The magnitude of the supply and of the demand depends on the prices obtaining. The supply in the markets is greater, the higher the prospective price; while the lower the price, the greater is the demand to be expected. This rule applies, at any rate, up to certain price limits, which the market only exceeds in exceptional cases. In all these cases, again, it is obvious that the quantities of goods supplied and demanded are not greater or less in definite proportions to the prices quoted. It by no means follows that, prices being doubled, the supply of the products must be doubled as well or the demand reduced by one half. There can be no doubt but that the increase of the demand is determined, wholly or in part, by the gradations of the scale of needs involved in each individual case. The numerical expressions must follow a different law, for example, for necessities of life and for objects which gratify merely luxurious habits. When it comes to the supply, costs of production undoubtedly have their influence in determining prices. Thus, for example, as regards agricultural products obeying the law of diminishing returns of the soil, the fluctuations of prices would occur according to a different standard from that applicable in the cost of industrial products. Ascertaining for every condition of prices the quantities of values offered and demanded, we obtain series peculiarly constituted for each type of commodity in exchange. We will call these series, market-indices; and we shall speak of supply-indices and of demand-indices.

The market-indices are of the utmost importance in the establishment of prices. The effect of supply and demand on prices is exerted according to the standard of the market-indices; and the deduction of the establishment of prices from the market-indices may be said to be the problem of the theory of prices. The mathematical method has approached this problem by representing the market-indices in curves of supply and demand. For a long series of cases an exact expression is thus obtained, which could never be arrived at by any other method. We shall not employ the mathematical method in the theory of prices any more than we used it in the theory of the simple economy. Rather we shall direct our efforts to a description of the market-indices, sufficient to enable us to understand the whys and wherefores of the decisions of parties as to price.

Theoretically, we have to distinguish in the universal economic market as many varieties of partial markets as there are varieties of market-indices. One set of market-indices prevails in the produce-market, others in the labor-market and in the market of agricultural or urban real estate. The most disparate from all others are the indices of the money-market, which is itself again subdivided into loan-market and stock-market. Each subdivision has radically distinct indices. In the markets where speculation enters, the indices of bona fide supply and demand appear side by side with speculative indices. The former are occasionally crowded out. The true supply appears from the existing stocks, the actual demand arises in the existing need; the offers thus constitute the portions of the stock brought to the market, the demand, the portions of the need influencing the market. With speculation, on the other hand, multitudes of bids and offers are created, which do not arise from existing amounts of stocks or needs.

Both parties of the market, that of the supply as well as that of the demand, may have a monopolistic or competitive position. A monopoly is the exclusive control of supply or of demand by a single subject, as well as by a single will. This subject may be a single, physical or juridical person or a plurality or multiplicity of such persons, who as in a kartell, a trust, ring, syndicate or coalition are united by contract. As regards its origin, a monopoly may be a natural monopoly, taking its rise in some unique natural occurrence, say a spring of mineral or medicinal waters. It may be an accidental monopoly, like a factory producing certain manufactures which have not attracted competitive enterprise. The monopoly may also be created by law, like the tax-monopolies of the state or like private monopolies in the nature of a privilege, such as a patent, a copyright or franchise of any kind whatever. There are also actual monopolies created by agreements not recognized by law.

Competition is a condition in which a number of persons in rivalry with one another pursue identical aims of supply and demand. By deflection of its meaning, the term may also be made to stand for this rivalry in trade itself.

The monopolistic position secures to the parties a far greater influence in the establishment of prices than the competitive position. Theory, therefore, will have to distinguish sharply between the two categories. In every-day practice as well as in scientific use, the term, monopoly, is frequently used inaccurately or improperly. Men often speak of a monopoly, meaning the superiority attaching to great power in the market, although this power may not by any means exclusively control either supply or demand. In this sense they speak, for example, of the monopoly of capital or of a monopoly of the most advantageously situated realty in the centre of the city. Advantageous positions in the market, approximating monopolies but not altogether amounting to such, we shall call monopoloid positions in the market. We shall examine later on what cases belong in this category.

In all important markets of products, the commodities stand out in strong contrast to money. The wares exchanged in natural transfer from producer to producer, in an exchange which was primarily fortuitous, did not have their origin in an expectation of exchange; they were produced by the intending user for his own needs. Some chance event brought it about that the two parties to the transfer of possession found mutual advantage in exchanging as they did. Here both performances are in natural values. Their functions in the exchange are exactly alike; on one side as well as on the other, the good is also a payment. In the developed markets of products it is otherwise; there performances and counterperformances are differentiated. Just as the function of payment is accomplished exclusively by money, so the natural commodity or service, for which payment is surrendered, has changed its character. It has been prepared in the course of prolonged processes. Producers and dealers with a division of labor have arranged for whatever is involved in its production.

The nature of merchandize is indicated in this description. Wares, or merchandize, are products which are prepared by producer or dealer under a division of labor and in due course are destined to be disposed of; they are products in the way of transmission to the ultimate purchaser, who does not expect to hand them on to others, but to use them in his trade or in his household. Differing from money, which is constantly being handed out anew and which maintains its character in the hands of every successive holder, wares, or merchandize, divest themselves of their character as soon as they reach the ultimate user. Owing to the fact that producers and dealers have to look forward to sales, the wares acquire a peculiar supply price, which is lacking in the case of the original natural exchange. The division of labor once regarded as complete, wares as such have no utility-value for their owner; he has to dispose of them, whenever he would make them yield value at all. In the case of wares which are continuously to be offered in the market, producers and dealers must, moreover, expect to recover completely the costs of production which they plan to incur. These costs should include at the least a moderate entrepreneur's reward, and will form an item in the supply price. This part, too, of the index of supply is most intimately connected with the production of commodities. Personal production not adjusted to exchanges need not, in case of an occasional exchange, insist on refund of costs. It is otherwise in the case of wares wholly depending on exchange; here a refund of costs must invariably be insisted on.

Wage-labor, up to a certain point, partakes of the character of wares. Owing to the division of labor and the economic stratification, the supplier of labor is dependent on the disposal of his labor just as much as producer and dealer are dependent on the disposal of their wares. Even more strongly than the latter, the laborers—their personal condition being what it is—are under all circumstances dependent on this disposal. Frequently, therefore, labor is spoken of as an article of trade; and the socialistic writers do so speak of it with particular emphasis, to make it clear that "labor-ware" [1] is completely subject to the merciless law of price of every market. The classical theory of wages, whose disciple socialistic theory has here become most unreservedly,

[1] Trans. note: die "Ware Arbeit" might perhaps be more familiarly rendered as "labor as a commodity." Since Weiser evidently wants to distinguish "Waren," as merchantable products, from "Güter" which need merely possess utility, I use the more labored phrase.

goes so far even as to transfer to labor, also, the supply price of the costs of production. The means of subsistence, indispensable or customary for the worker and his family, are then described as "costs of production of human labor." It is maintained that these costs influence the price of labor in the same way in which costs of production influence the price of products.

We shall not now inquire what relations actually exist between the costs of preservation of the laborer and his wages, but without further investigation we shall be able to lay down the rule, that these costs of subsistence are not strictly an example of costs of production. Labor is not a product; it is not the result of a process comparable in any way to that of producing merchandise. In some respects its supply-index may closely approach that of the merchantable product. However, there is no doubt that it has unique qualities of its own, which distinguish it from the latter and require separate consideration. To speak at the start of labor as merchandise can only befog the true state of affairs. The phrase, "labor-ware," has been devised as an indictment of the existing economic order; it will consequently have to be examined as such; but, entering upon its descriptive problem, theory will have to decline to consider it thus.

In the money-markets, the bonds or stocks offered for sale are also spoken of as wares. As a matter of fact, the securities offered to the public by the underwriting[1] banks are like merchantable products, being carried for purposes of exchange from entrepreneur to purchaser. The banks, like producers, must see to it that they negotiate the sales, if they would carry on their business successfully. Then too, the securities which are kept on hand for the purpose of sale by brokers and others, or which speculators accumulate in order to sell them, partake somewhat of the character of merchantable products. In this respect the two are much alike. However, securities after all do not possess in full the typical qualities of wares. Bonds are not products; more especially they have not the supply-index of the costs of production. It is also to be remarked that once a commodity is used in the household or in trade, indeed as a rule even before it has been actually used there, it may only be sold by the buyer at a low or very low price. On the other hand, securities are readily salable by everyone and in fact return often to the channel of exchange in the market. Neither have stocks and bonds the demand-index of products: it is only circuitously that they supply a personal need, to which products cater directly or at any rate more immediately. Bonds, indeed, supply the "need of investment," which is not a need in the true sense of the word at all, but merely a desire to provide for future needs by the ownership of invested values which will yield a return in money. We see, thus, that there is good reason for the stock-market or the money-market generally to be distinguished from the produce-market. Especially in theory the separation will have to be strictly insisted upon; the different market-indices for both groups of objects of exchange call for particular investigation of the formation of prices.

In the realty-market, it is not customary to speak of wares or merchandise. The indices of supply and demand are here too conspicuously different from those of commodity-products. In the rules to be laid down for the determination of prices, they are more nearly akin to the market-indices of investment-capital.

We shall only speak of wares in connection with commodity-products. By

[1] *Emissionsbanken.*

the market of wares, consequently, we mean the market of products, where producers and dealers are the offering or supplying parties.

§ 32. The Problem of the General Doctrine of Prices

Price—Doctrine of prices and of income—Our assumptions for the general doctrine of prices—Closed and open markets.

In the developed money-economy, where exchange is effected exclusively in consideration of a money-payment, price is defined as the amount of money given for an economic service by way of recompense for the exchange. Here the economic performance may consist in material or personal natural-values, or in any form whatever of money-capital. We can easily understand why the theory of prices has been considered from the very beginning as one of the most important problems of economic theory. The level of prices furnishes the key to the distribution of the natural values comprising the social income to the individual households which constitute the demand. Inversely, it also gives the key to the distribution of the money-income of the economy to the supplying individual economies. Over and above this it explains the circulation of the national wealth and, finally, furnishes the foundation for the calculation of values in the economic process. The theory of prices prepares us for the understanding of the economic distribution of goods, distribution of incomes and computation of value, and no economic theory, therefore, can fail to encounter the problem.

In its beginnings, theory did not do full justice to the importance of the theory of prices. Even to-day, many theorists confine its functions within too narrow limits. It was formerly, and is frequently still the practice to look upon the price of products or of wares as the only one which concerned the theory of prices. This approach leaves the discussion of ground-rents, of contractual interest on capital and of wages to the investigations, not of the theory of price but of the theory of income. There are good reasons to connect these subjects with the theory of the formation of income or the structure of acquisitive economy. Only by such reference can the particular market-indices be developed, which hold for land, and the use of the soil, capital and labor. But one must not overlook the fact that ground-rent, interest and wages are not merely forms of income, but are special forms of price as well. The laws of rent, interest and wages are not independent laws; they are particular forms of a general law, known as the fundamental law of the formation of prices. We, too, shall treat of the rent of land, of interest and wages in connection with the study of income and acquisition. In so doing, however, we shall bear in mind that this is supplementing the doctrine of prices by a special exposition for the great branches of income. In contrast with these special studies the doctrine of prices which is to be first laid down, may be designated as a general theory of price.

The task of deducing the fundamental law of the formation of prices and the law of price for products in the case of competition, monopoly and the typical monopoloid market conditions are assigned to the general theory of price. We shall confine our investigations at first to the markets of the natural exchange-values. Later we shall return to the market of moneyed capital.

In dealing with the problem of the general theory of prices, we shall have to bring the idealizing assumptions, to which we resorted in the theory of the simple economy, somewhat closer to actuality. This will be done by the process of decreasing abstraction. We shall, however, do so only in so far as there is absolute necessity. The power of wealth is one of the decisive factors of the market. The stratification of wealth, as it exists in the social community, will therefore have its place in our assumptions. We shall, however, assume this stratification as given, and we shall not inquire further as to its origin. We shall disregard in the theory of prices those social stratifications which arise from differences of personal aptitude and education. With the exception of the single case of usury, which we expect to neglect hereafter, we shall throughout assume model-economies, using the term to describe a social egoism which submits voluntarily to the dictates of law and morality. For the rest, let us state that, unless the contrary be expressly posited, we deal only with a normal course of affairs, free from errors or disturbances. The occurrence of market-panics or crises is not to be considered in these investigations except in passing; speculation we shall not have to mention until we reach the section concerning the economy of acquisition.

We shall first follow the process of the formation of prices under the assumption of a closed market: i. e., a market in which the entire supply and the entire demand are brought together as on the exchange. Only later shall we consider the course of affairs in an open or disjointed market. The latter is a market where the supply, demand, or both are locally dispersed; i. e., are distributed among enterprises or streets within a certain town, or among certain separated localities, within one national economy. The social economy is a disjointed or open market. The economic formation of prices would, therefore, be only incompletely described, were our exposition to stop with the assumption of a closed market.

§ 33. The Fundamental Law of Price-Formation

Price-formation by custom—The elementary market-index for consumption-values—Marginal supply series, effective and non-effective demand, the law of the marginal supply—The universal price, the equitable price—Personal and social egoism in the price-competition—The lower margin of prices.

The assertion is sometimes made that prices are by no means invariably the result of the economic facts of the market but that prices occur which rest upon custom only. The statement is not correct. The power of custom is never sufficient to perpetuate prices which are inconsistent with economic market conditions. At any rate, the proposition would not hold good, unless we assumed that sacrifices were being made to maintain such prices. On the other hand, it may be said of any price whatever, that up to a certain point it rests upon custom. For the market always connects the prices of to-day with the prices of yesterday; it requires the aid of the traditional prices, in order to regulate its dealings. If it were possible that all dealers in the market should simultaneously lose the whole of their experience of existing prices, all dealings would be thrown into confusion from which the market could not recover without incurring considerable losses. Every unexpected change of market-conditions, even for a small number of values, is accompanied by serious disturbances. It is difficult to see how the continuously interconnected prices of thousands and thousands of values could be reëstablished from the very bottom in an economic chaos that had been deprived of price. However, market-conditions invariably change only in the most gradual way. For many values, the conditions remain constant during a long period of time. The earlier prices, then, continue to remain in force for these persistent values without opposition; and as this condition lasts, it may well seem that the prices are adhered to merely by force of custom. As a matter of fact, however, their validity continues because, in the very beginning, they were regularly established and the facts which contributed in their formation, continue to exist without change.

Just as the market works out new prices from old ones, theory also at first contented itself to lay down a mere law of changes of prices. It was a signal progress when prices of products began to be explained from cost-prices. Such an explanation, however, is only partial. A complete explanation must start from a condition without any prices whatever; it will have to avail itself, moreover, of the aids of isolation and idealization, in order to bring within the boundaries of its assumptions the entire wealth of market-facts, which may not be otherwise comprehended. With such an end in view, we will start from the most simple market-index possible and deduce from it the law of price for a stock of wares in the competitive market.

We ascertain this simplest market-index by conceiving a stock of consumption-commodities in isolation. It is the primary end of exchange, to meet the needs of consumption even in the most highly developed exchange-economy. The fundamental law of price must, therefore, be deducible from the occurrence of consumption-values.

To isolate this case from all other facts, we assume a stock of consumption goods ready for sale and for whose preparation no costs may be ascribed. In other words, we assume a supply, the cost of which is equal to zero. We thus completely disregard the factor of costs in the supply-index which we assume. We further assume that the entire stock of goods, ready for sale, is intended for trade. The vendors are not able to use even the smallest part of it for their own consumption. Therefore the utility-value of these wares from the point of view of the vendors is also to be set down at zero and may be neglected in ascertaining the supply-price. We also disregard the possible choice that is open to a monopolist to carry over an unsold portion of the stock. We disregard the possibility that all or part of the supply may be preserved for a later market or carried to a different one. Therefore as regards time and locality, we assume a narrowly bounded, closed market in which the only effective motive of supply is the desire to sell at the highest price. The sale is to be effected subject to the condition that the entire existing supply be disposed of immediately. It should, however, be expressly remarked that this last assumption is not equivalent to requiring that the entire stock be sold in bulk, in one unbroken quantity. As in our earlier investigation, we assume here, too, not an indivisible total-stock, but a divisible supply which may be sold piece by piece, by units of weight or in any other units whatever. The vendors will not be in a position to impose on the purchaser the condition, that he must buy the whole or leave the whole. It is left to the discretion of every buyer to name the quantities which he wishes to acquire; such is the rule of the frėe market, and under this rule we are bound to deduce the law of price. For the present we need not inquire by what standard the vendors are to appraise the sums of money which they receive. It will be sufficient to assume that a sale is effected at the highest possible price, that the highest price is the most acceptable to the vendor and that those purchasers are preferred, who offer more money than others.

The important factor in the supply-index, as here described, is the quantity of the stock offered. The price which the vendors are able to obtain for the quantities offered, depends for the rest exclusively on the demand-index. Had the purchasers little to offer, the vendors would have to be satisfied with little. The values which they offer are not of value to the sellers themselves. Only by the instrumentality of the demand do the goods become values at all. To express the situation metaphorically, it is first the demand which inscribes value-figures on these goods.

The effective motive in the demand-index of consumers is the desire of securing the greatest benefit from the sums of money which have to be expended. In a stationary economy, which is here taken for granted, the sums of money which have to be expended to defray the expenses of the household are taken from the income. Every consumer endeavors to turn his money-income into the highest possible consumption-values. Therefore in every case he strives to purchase at the lowest price. But on the other hand, he must always allow for the competition of all the other consumers who, under some circumstances, will compel him to increase his offer to the highest permissible limit.

To ascertain the margin for the highest offer which a man may be justified in making in a particular instance is an exceedingly complicated problem. Every individual offer is influenced by the expenditure which has to be incurred to meet other needs; all prices which the consumer agrees to pay in order to acquire consumption-values are interconnected by the unity of the economy. In order to simplify the inquiry, we shall, for the present, still disregard these complications which arise from the integration of the economy. Under these conditions the highest offer which the consumer expects to make in the individual case will be indicated by the amount of money-income which he controls; aside from this, it will depend on the amount of the marginal utility to be secured by the purchase of the consumption-goods. This utility is conditioned by the state of his need, the degree to which it has been satisfied and the extent to which he has provided goods to meet it; every consumer appraises this marginal utility according to the rules of computation of the simple economy. If we assume that the need of all consumers is entirely unsatisfied and unprovided for, the highest offers will be made by those persons whose needs are most intense and who at the same time have the largest purchasing power. Last in order will appear the individuals whose needs are least intense and who command the smallest means. Those with relatively large incomes will be able to offer the same price for the satisfaction of less important needs as those who husband their smaller means offer to provide at least for the urgent needs.

The following illustration, wholly schematic in details, provides the simplest possible numerical expression for the demand-index of consumers. The consumer with strongest need and greatest ability to pay, K_1, may enter a maximum offer of 100 money-units, where he does not wish to acquire more than one unit of the stock; where he wishes to secure two units, he may figure for each of the two units a marginal utility and, therefore, a maximum offer of 90; when buying three, a maximum offer of 80 for each. The intending purchaser next in order, K_2, may figure for a single unit a maximum offer of 90; when acquiring two or three, he may appraise each unit respectively at 80 and 70. K_3, for the case assumed, may figure 80, 70 and 60; K_4, 70, 60, 50. Starting from these figures, what shall we say that the prices must be? Let us first think in terms of what would occur at an auction-sale. At first the would-be purchasers will scarcely be inclined to give prices, equaling the highest offers that their calculations allow. They will endeavor to make their acquisition with the lowest bid which market-conditions permit; only gradually will they raise their bids to the upper limit as they become convinced that their end cannot be reached otherwise.

If only one unit of the wares has been brought to supply the market, K_1 will be successful in the competition and will obtain the merchandise. However, in order that this may happen, he will have to enter a bid that will exclude his most dangerous competitor, K_2: i. e., an offer higher than 90. The price consequently will move between 90 and 100; or more accurately, the price must be higher than 90 but cannot exceed 100. Let us assume the stock which the supply offers to consist of three pieces, all to be sold. In this event as high a price cannot be realized. K_2 may in no event pay more than 90. Even K_1, if he is to buy more than one of the three pieces, will not be willing to pay over 90, because this would exceed the marginal utility which he has computed. He would be wiser to give up buying the second piece, than to pay more for it than its marginal utility to him. The price, therefore, must not exceed 90. However, it must be over 80, for it must be held above that figure by K_1 and K_2 who both are interested in shutting out their most dangerous competitor, K_3. At this price, then, K_1 will purchase two pieces, K_2 one piece. If there are six units, all of which must be sold, K_2 will purchase three pieces, K_2, two pieces, K_3, one piece; the price will be above 70 without, however, exceeding 80. For every quantity offered, there is a latitude given to price-formation. This is strictly circumscribed by the order of the demand-series, for only at a price within these limits is the demand able to absorb that quantity. At what point within the margins indicated the price will rest, depends on circumstances. Economic theory as such has not the means to distinguish between these circumstances, and consequently from the standpoint of the theory they must be called accidental. Only one exceedingly important condition will have to be mentioned: for all simultaneous exchanges in a closed market within the latitude of price-formation the price must be the same. No vendor will be satisfied with a price, when the man beside him is able to obtain a higher one. No purchaser will pay a higher price, while some one at his elbow pays less. In the closed market, the law of equality of prices applies: or the same wares at the same time, there is only one price.

Expressed in general terms, the fundamental law of the price of commodities is the following: for all units of the supply of wares destined to be sold, the price is regularly fixed between the maximum offer of the lowest demand-series that must be still admitted to trade in order that the entire quantity offered may be sold, and the highest offer of the next succeeding demand-series, which must be over-bid in order that the higher series may be protected against their competitors. The demand-series, admitted to acquisition, form the effective demand; those excluded, the ineffective demand. These terms, however, must not be interpreted in the sense that effective demand, by itself, determines the price; for the uppermost series of the ineffective demand also plays an important part in the formation of the price. The two important series in the effective and ineffective demand may be spoken of as the last admitted and the first excluded demand-series, more briefly as the marginal-offer-series, or marginal series of the demand. By the aid of this term, the law may be formulated in its most concise expression: for all units of mass, a single price will be set between the marginal series of the demand. The traditional formula of the market, also to be found in earlier theory, that supply and demand determine the price, is not incorrect; it is merely inaccurate, if—as was the meaning originally—by supply and demand nothing more is meant than the quantities supplied and demanded. By contrasting the two opposing quantities alone, the law of price could never be deduced; the exchange of the quantities is rigidly delimited only when the quantities, at least on the side of the demand, become vehicles of values. The decisive relations of value must thus be understood in connection with them, whenever supply and demand are to be made determining causes of price.

The limits within which the formation of prices takes place, are frequently far apart in the case of scarcity-commodities. A comparatively small number of wealthy individuals constitute the effective demand for costly antiques. The outcome of the price-war between these parties for an ardently desired work of art can hardly be anticipated. The prices here realized, vary in amount from sale to sale by considerable sums, as fashion or the whim of the moment may sway connoisseurs one way or the other, or as means may be available to gratify expensive tastes of this sort. The prices which are realized are amateur-prices, and may be called fortuitous prices, in so far as there is wide room for the play of chance between the maximum offers, irrespective of the variations of circumstances which are decidedly subject to chance but by which collectors determine these bids. However, it is incorrect to say, as did Ricardo, that prices of this sort are not subject to any law whatever. They are, strictly speaking, subject to the same law which applies to wares generally; the receptivity of the market decides their fate also, as it is limited by the order of the demand-series. The major distinction is that the latitude of movement is great.

For the bulk of the commodities which are not luxuries the demand-series are generally close together. At the same time, the economic bases for the computation of bids are not readily displaced. When, finally, we come to the goods that result from mass production, goods offered in large quantities for the use of multitudes of consumers, the series are so closely packed, the figures of offers so permanently fixed by steady requirements of subsistence and relations of income among the people at large, that they shade one into the other imperceptibly and are subject to only very gradual fluctuations. The series of demand are here formed not by individual persons, but by classes of the people whose stratifications are shaded into one another. These series are interwoven into a net-work of narrowest meshes, leaving to the formation of prices a scarcely perceptible latitude of movement. For the bulk of commodities, the law of price may be condensed into the statement that the price follows the marginal offer of the effective demand, i. e., the lowest offer compelling acceptance, in order that the entire stock may presently be disposed of without an unsold remainder.

The elementary law of price deduced for wares is as valid for all other consumption-values meant to be sold like merchandize, as it is for consumption-wares themselves. It holds especially as regards the price paid as wages for the services of domestic servants and as salary, remuneration or honorarium for superior personal services; it is valid for rent of urban dwellings. As the effect of the law extends thru consumption-values to all natural productive means without exception, and from these again to the investment and money-market, it may rightly be called the fundamental law of price.

The price, ascertained according to the fundamental law, holds uniformly for all individuals or persons desiring to exchange in the market; it is the universal and, thus, the common price. It is, however, the common price in a still broader sense: it is the resultant of general economic conditions. The most strictly individualistic school regards every departure from the common price as uneconomic, even when made with benevolent intent to ease difficulties for some weaker opposing party.

Where the general conditions are considered socially satisfactory and morally and legally correct, the general price is found also to be the just, or equitable, price. No one does injury to the other in demanding the just and the common price; one and all, they can subsist under it. The general interest is well taken care of if, man by man, they adhere to it. The individual, coöperating in the establishment in the market of this price by looking out for his individual interest, protects at the same time the social interest; he fulfills a personal and a social duty; he contributes his share to the establishment of the market-series —an establishment required, if we would observe the economic margin in the distribution of the commodities which is to be accomplished in the market. In this way the struggle of price-competition will be purged of objectionable elements and will cease to be a struggle at all at the height of social progress, but will become a coöperative endeavor of supply and demand to socially appraise stocks and needs. The frequently ruthless conditions of actual life will still continue to make it a struggle, a struggle, however, not fought out man to man, but group to group and class to class, in which the members of each class and group are personally satisfied with the advantage attainable by the groups and classes collectively.

The common and equitable price attains its true significance in the disjointed market. In the closed market on the Exchange where the total supply and the total demand of the wholesale trade come together, or at a public auction where all interested parties of the market meet, the correct common price is ascertained by means of the practical assertion of the personal desires of each participant in the market, provided only that in other respects the rules and regulations of the market are preserved. At an auction, for example, the gradual overbidding of each other by the parties desiring to buy, will lead exactly to the ascertainment of the marginal bid. The more extensive trade of social economy, however, is cared for in the dissociated competition of the open markets, where the individual participants of the market are but loosely, if at all, in touch with one another. Were every individual here to follow his personal egoism only, then the struggle for the best price would break up into any number of single combats, where the stronger would too often find opportunities of mercilessly exploiting the weaker. Competition in regard to prices would become a personal conflict, a conflict of unbridled, personal egoism; a social law of prices would never assert itself. Thanks, however, to the way in which mankind has been trained historically to social egoism, the establishment of prices in the disjointed market does after all, as a rule, take place in the spirit of the price-law. The exploitation of the individual case is not countenanced; men endeavor to ascertain the just, the common price; the multitude of individuals falls voluntarily into line, following the call of those "natural controls" which, step by step, have taken the lead in human affairs. Experience has gradually driven home its lesson, that the common price will best work out for the benefit of all concerned. But, in addition, historical powers of various kinds have lent their compelling influence to secure this common price; moreover, the social nature of mankind is sufficiently receptive to recognize this price as just and to maintain it even where it is not directly demanded by the pressure of the competition.

Man is not fully educated to social egoism in any social economy today. This we must admit. In the smaller markets of earlier days, this altruistic education commenced; but after the good work had been accomplished with respect to these, larger and larger markets were added to the existing ones. These added new and more seductive temptations to personal egoism against which the morality of the average mortal proved insufficient. Now, since in the most advanced national economies the largest gains may be realized, it is there that the fiercest commercial struggles may be witnessed. It is in these that the greatest temptation is presented to grasp powers unthought of before and to use or abuse them at pleasure. Were we to attempt to confine ourselves in our assumptions to model-economies, entering the competition of prices subject to socially controlled egoism, we would find ourselves unable to explain these occurrences. They can only be explained when by decreasing abstraction one finally comes to replace the assumption of social egoism by that of an unbridled personal egoism.

To deduce the law of price, we assumed that the consumption wares to be sold have no utility-value for the vendor personally. If now we modify this assumption and assign a position in the supply-index to the utility-value for the vendor, we shall find a lower limit established for the price, below which it must not be allowed to fall. The vendor will have to test the price offered to him by the utility-value, of which direct personal use would always assure him. He will not be satisfied with anything less than a money-price whose use in exchange still promises a gain over and above the utility-value. For this lower limit the same motive of gain of value asserts itself in money-exchange, which we have already disclosed for natural exchange; otherwise the fundamental law of price as deduced remains unaffected. In the case of industrial products this lower limit does not find its way into practical affairs. The industrial vendor, with scarcely an exception, has no intention of retaining part of his products for individual use; his personal conditions being what they are, he could frequently find no personal use for the products of his trade, no matter how much he might wish to do so. In any event, the quantity which he might wish to retain would always be so small as to be practically negligible. The lower limit is important even at this day for agricultural products, wherever agriculture has adhered to the old, natural-economic basis of production for personal use. In the determination also of the lower limit the intensity of the need is not alone decisive. Wealth is also to be considered. A small land-owner raising Tokay wine is not so situated as to retain for his own use any quantity whatever of this precious vintage. The margin of this man's domestic economy is so narrowly drawn, that it will permit no such use. There would be a loss of value, compared with that which the economic use of the money-price promises to yield. Similarly, a wealthy manufacturer turning out cheap, crude mass-products will retain none of these for his own use. For his individual consumption he demands luxurious commodities.

§ 34. The Stratification of Prices

Mass-values—Medium-values—Luxury-values—The stratified marginal utility.

The law of price leads us to a most important deduction for the mutual relation of commodity-prices. This relation is determined not only by the marginal utility; it is also determined by the force of the demand of the marginal series. The consequence of this may be that the difference in price is one entirely unequal to that in the marginal utility. It might even happen that the commodity of lower marginal utility obtains a much higher price.

There are mass-commodities of the most general use which are brought to the market in such large quantities, that the purchasers of more ample means do not feel called to exert their purchasing ability to the utmost in order to fully cover their needs. Bread, for example, is brought to the market in such large quantities that the consumption-needs of all strata of people can be supplied. The wealthier purchasers are able even to provide for their requirements to the point of complete satiety. Only the buyers of the most restricted incomes are compelled to retrench according to their circumstances. The marginal series for all such goods are formed by the strata of lowest purchasing power. The magnitude of such prices is determined by these buyers. The wealthy buyer enjoys his larger means in such a manner that he is able to provide himself abundantly with many consumption goods for which he pays according to the standard of the poor. Should a higher price be charged to him for the same wares than to any other user, he will immediately feel that he has been imposed upon. He demands for himself the same price, the common price, that is demanded of any other purchaser. It is quite true to remark, that this man's wealth would not avail him, were he to be held to pay for all his wants according to his enhanced personal standard. Were the recipient of an income of 10,000 or 100,000 Crowns or Marks obliged to pay a tenfold or hundredfold price for whatever he buys, he would be no better off than the recipient of an income of 1000 Marks or Crowns, by whose standards the common price has been established. Pecuniary wealth is actual wealth only when it enables its owner to extend his enjoyments, as does natural wealth, beyond those of individuals of smaller means.

Contrasted with mass-commodities, we find the specific luxury-commodities. These are commodities of the most infrequent occurrence that are not urgent necessities but are called for by needs of considerable refinement or over-refinement with some earnestness of demand. Degenerate wealth is on the look-out for possessions suitable to gratify the desire of ostentation, because they are scarce, because they attract attention, because they differentiate their possessor from the multitudes who go without them. It matters not that, in all other respects, these commodities possess no qualities which would gratify refined sensibilities or artistic tastes. For articles of luxury, prices are offered according to a standard induced by the purchasing ability of members of the higher and highest income-strata who are bent on excluding the competition of all other rivals. Ever since the rise of American multimillionaires into a social stratum of their own, the prices of pictures by the old masters for which these men compete have been forced to figures, which the European nabob may not approach. If the rich buy salt and bread at a lower price than their individual average ability would allow, they are none the less forced to pay prices for diamonds which are above their average standard.

Midway between mass-commodities and the specific articles of luxury, we find certain intermediate goods, for which the marginal series are provided by the middle classes, while nothing or almost nothing can be taken up by the lower classes. For these intermediate goods, therefore, prices must needs be formed in keeping with the purchasing power of the middle classes.

As in the case of commodities, we may observe this cleavage in the case of all natural values generally. In all natural markets that still exist besides the markets of products, mass-values are clearly distinguishable in their prices from values of comfort [1] and luxury. The prices, for example, that are paid for urban dwellings according to location, are perceptibly graded according to the ability of their inmates to pay.

One may best describe this phenomenon as the stratification of prices. The greater the number of strata of income and wealth found in any economy and the more disparate the highest and the lowest strata in financial ability, the more conspicuous will be the stratification of prices. Had all the citizens of a state approximately the same incomes and assets, then the discrepancy of price between bread and diamonds—to revive the illustration of our earlier discussion—would not be nearly as great as it is in fact. If economists have strained their ingenuity for an undue length of time in the solution of this old illustration of the school room, the blame for the blunder is to be placed on the conviction that prices must necessarily be the expression of an economic or social appraisal. Such futile efforts can never explain why society should attach so much more value to diamonds than it does to bread. To tell the truth, the price of diamonds is anything but an expression of the uniform social appreciation of diamonds; it is merely the expression of the appreciation of that definite stratum, peculiarly able to pay, which form the marginal series of demand for diamonds. The offers, by which the great mass of the population would be able to express its appraisal of diamonds, are so low in comparison to the prevailing market-prices, that they open no prospects of corresponding purchases. The mass of the population does not even attempt to introduce a demand; it does not even turn aside to inquire, what might be the bids which it could possibly bring forward.

Price is a social institution, not simply because its magnitude is the result of a universal appraisal of value by society; it is so as the result of a social contest for the possession of the offered supply—a contest between individuals of varying appreciation and varying

[1] Trans. note: *Mittelwerten* has been stretched in translation because the recent discussion of standards of subsistence and of comfort for wage-earners seem to give a meaning to "values of comfort" that would not be conveyed by "middle-values."

powers of demand. The maximum offer of the marginal stratum is decisive. Therefore price does not take its standard from the marginal utility as such, but from a stratified marginal utility. This is a standard that frequently differs widely from that of a rational social appraisal of dependent need-values.

In the theory of the simple economy, the assumption is directed to the utmost possible equalization of the margin of use. In our social economy where the stratified marginal utility is decisive, the satisfaction of needs is exceedingly disproportionate. Nevertheless, while public opinion considers private property itself, and its existing distribution, as just, this condition is not felt as an injustice. The stratified, common price will be considered a just price, while things remain as they are. Only when the existing distribution of wealth or even private property is felt to be a social injustice, will this opinion call for review. Where unheard of prices are paid for luxuries, useless or extravagant in the extreme, public conscience is outraged and declares these to be immoral.

§ 35. The Demand-Index of Consumption and the Unity of the Household

The household's margin of expenditure, marginal expenditures and expenditures of the narrower marginal utility—Relation between price and quantity demanded.

We have deduced the general law of price by the illustration of a stock of goods, detached from the interconnections of the economy, and observed in isolation. As we recall the fact that all consumption-values to be acquired for the household are related in the unity of the economy, the formulation of the general law of price, as we have laid it down, requires an additional particularization.

We can start from results already obtained in the theory of the simple economy. We came to the conclusion that the unity of the economy has for its effect the inevitable maintenance or observation of a general economic margin of use which is exceeded in the case of products of specific frequency, but is not attained by the specific scarcity-products and by the cost-products of narrower marginal utility. These results we now have to apply consistently for the individual households which in economic exchange supply themselves no longer by home-production but by purchases in the market. The conditions remain fundamentally the same; only general margin of domestic use presents itself in the particular shape of the general margin of expenditure. Every household, with the means at its command and the state of its needs, faces a general limit of expenditures. As regards specific frequency-values, this limit may be exceeded because men may provide themselves with these to the point of satiety, which lies below the general expenditure-limit. We shall designate expenditures of this sort, as expenditures of the wider marginal utility. In cases of cost-value of narrower marginal utility and of specific scarcity-values, the expenditures must be stopped at a point of higher utility; we shall speak of these expenditures as expenditures of the narrower marginal utility. The bulk of expenditures which may be extended to the general margin, we shall call marginal expenditures. In households in which the income barely allows a minimum of subsistence, expenditures outside of those for the needs of existence cannot be incurred; outlays for subsistence are the marginal expenditures of such very modest economies. In households which can make "ends meet," the income is ample to satisfy fully these primary needs and to cover furthermore the entire subsistence considered suitable to the social position. In this case, the mere needs of existence no longer determine marginal expenditures. The same rule applies with further increases of income to all needs which the lower income was already ample to satisfy. The increase of income is applied to expenditures in other directions: for increased comfort, education and fashionable requirements. Where expenditures are increased for the more simple wants, this will be done by advancing from the coarser to the more refined means of satisfaction, such as serve the preservation of life with greater convenience and with corresponding increase of enjoyable stimulation. This explains the familiar fact that expenses for food and shelter form a larger proportion of the total in the case of smaller incomes than in case of medium and high incomes. On a par with the needs of physical existence, the mass of human beings appraises certain other needs, the satisfaction of which does not contribute to the preservation of life. But owing to the particular pleasurable stimulation which they afford, they are demanded with an insistence closely equaling that of the needs of existence. Of this sort is the craving for alcoholic beverages or for tobacco. The expenditures for wine, brandy, beer and all manner of smoking-tobacco are considered altogether indispensable by many human beings. Even consumers whose slender means force them to be satisfied with purchasing coarse qualities, strive—exactly as in the case of the needs of existence—to obtain full satiety; even cases of over-satiety, of immoderate and harmful enjoyment are not rare. Where these needs are fully satisfied, the expenditure for them with increasing income is not susceptible of increase as regards quantities consumed. If the expenditure is increased, as is generally the case with the stimulus which these means of satisfaction exert, the increase is effected by a resort to finer qualities at higher prices. The increases of income must be very considerable if these expenditures, too, are to disappear from the series of marginal expenditures and to advance into the class of expenditures of the narrower marginal utility.

The index of demand for such consumption-values of the narrower utility-limit is not developed according to the simple scheme that was used in the deduction of the general law of price. The demand for these goods is constant within wide limits, or at least it is subject to insignificant changes. It may, therefore, happen that with a decrease in prices the demand-series do not expand, that with rising prices they do not contract. To explain this situation more fully, we shall have to observe that advances of prices which consume a larger quota of the total income, must lower the buying power of the household, raise the general margin of use and necessitate retrenchment of all marginal expenditures. In so far as the expenditures for the urgent consumption-values are themselves marginal expenditures, these, too, will have to be curtailed. Where this is impossible, as consumption has already been reduced to a minimum of existence and cannot be cut further, the attempt will have to be made to shift the effect to the future either by resort to credit or by disposal of those portions of the available possessions which are least necessary. However, in so far as the expenditures for the urgent consumption-values are not part of the marginal expenditures but are expenditures of narrower marginal utility, it will be possible to maintain them in their accustomed extent. The retrenchment which must be effected will fall upon those goods more easily dispensed with, the actual marginal expenditures, unless indeed in these cases also it should be preferred to carry over the effect to a future day by reliance on credit and the sale of property. A progressive economy has, in addition to these makeshifts, the opportunity of reducing its savings, thus likewise relieving the present at the expense of the future. In one or the other of these ways, the total demand-index of consumption must, indeed, in its present or future shape be affected by changes of prices. In this broader sense, therefore, the old statement of every-day experience may be maintained, that the demand drops off whenever prices rise; it rises whenever prices fall.

At what point within the existing limits of movement the price for consumption-values of narrower marginal utility will be set, is not now to be discussed; we shall return to this problem when treating of cost-price and monopoly-price.

§ 36. The Fundamental Law of the Change of Price

The law of supply, the law of demand—Excessive supply and unsatisfied demand—The organization of the market.

The fundamental law of the formation of prices includes the fundamental law of the change of prices. We mean by change of prices, the transformation of prices induced by changed conditions of the market. This transformation will have to obey the identical law which controls the formation of prices itself. Price is bound to change whenever the decisive marginal bid changes. The conditions of supply and demand may give rise to the change, as the quantities offered or demanded in the market increase or decrease with accompanying fluctuations of prices. Whenever the change is due to the supply, the law of supply begins to operate. This corresponds to the law of stock in the simple economy, which states that the prices must vary in the opposite direction to the change in the supply. This law, however, does not mean that the prices will also have to change in the same degree as the supply. Where the demand initiates the change of price, the law of demand becomes operative, which corresponds to the law of the needs in the simple economy. In this case prices are bound to change in the same direction—meaning, again, direction only, not degree—in which the demand has moved. Changes in the demand may, again, be caused not only by changes in needs, but also by changes in the stratification of incomes. (This is an important distinction, when contrasted with the law of needs.) Probably the latter occurs more frequently. The changes of needs are often themselves consequences of altered abilities of demand. It must be pointed out in this connection, that the effective demand of an entire population may increase or decrease in the aggregate, or the conditions of the individual social strata may become relatively displaced, new income-strata coming into being or old ones disappearing. Many changes of prices have their cause in such displacements of social strata, which establish different stratified marginal utilities for numerous values.

The influence of fluctuations of price is different in the case of mass values, "middle" values and luxury values, just as it differs for values of narrower marginal utility and marginal values. Mass values are the most stable, for they are affected by the families who form the broad base of the pyramid of stratified incomes. At the base the intervals between the groups are smallest and the groups themselves are largest. Since the upper income-strata embrace the fewest persons and their membership is subject to the most severe fluctuations, the costly scarcity-values are less stable, for the demand comes from the uppermost layers. The supply need be but little diminished, in order to break through the narrow layer of purchasers of the maximum purchasing ability and to encounter, perhaps in the very next stratum, rapidly decreasing purchasing powers. It is for reasons such as these that luxury-values are especially sensitive to crises which unsettle purchasing power and, on the other hand, that they are the most expressive index of increases of economic prosperity. Such prices may be rapidly and enormously inflated, where newly-won riches craves all manner of enjoyment and endeavors to grasp whatever tempts the vanity of the parvenu.

As we have already said, the market invariably sets out from traditional prices. While the conditions of supply and demand remain unchanged, the traditional price precisely reflects the marginal offer, and distinguishes effective and ineffective demand; by it the market is maintained in balance. Those individuals who are unable to pay the current price, stay out of the market. The admitted, effective demand knows the quantities of values of any one kind; its means will enable it to purchase at the going price. These parties have laid out their plans of management with these facts in view; they feel assured that the supply will be sufficient to provide their wants to the accustomed extent, and thus they confine their acquisitions to the most immediate needs. On the side of the supply, men also feel confident that throughout the entire period of turn-over they will succeed in making the expected sales, and that they will enter the next trading-period without carrying over a greater stock of unsold wares than a provident management must always have at its disposal. Under circumstances like these, and while supply and demand remain in equilibrium, the trade of the market will continue to be transacted in due routine; no impulse will be given, which would bring about any change in price. No sooner, however, do changes take place in the proportions of supply and demand than, in a market which continues to maintain traditional prices, part of the supply becomes excessive or part of the demand, hitherto taken care of, remains unsatisfied. In consequence, a pressure is exerted which must lead to a change in price. This mechanism of excessive supply and unsatisfied demand will remain active until the appropriate price is settled, at which supply and demand again coincide.

Let us assume that the demand increases; i. e., that at the established price a greater quantity is being demanded than hitherto. For example, at a price of 10, 100 units are still offered. Hitherto at this price 100 units were demanded but now 120 are. Should the price remain unchanged at 10, an unsatisfied demand for 20 pieces would remain. At the existing price these would be as effectively demanded as the other 100. Such a result cannot settle the market. The interests of the excluded effective demand and, fully as much, those of the supply forbid it. As soon as it is known in the market that the quantity demanded has increased, the demanders will begin to outbid one another. Suppliers will hold back deliveries, until the weakest series of the demand are eliminated and a narrower selection of the effective demand has been completed, at whose marginal offer the quantities demanded and quantities supplied balance. The same course of events will take place whenever the supply drops off.

Let us reverse conditions: the demand drops off or the supply increases; for example, at a price of 10, 100 units are still supplied but only 80 demanded, or now as before, 100 pieces are demanded but 120 supplied. Were the old price maintained, a part of the supply must remain in excess. This remainder also was meant to be disposed of, but found no purchasers. This surplus might be an unsold balance of wares, for which buyers are wanted; unrented dwellings for which tenants are sought; a number of personal servants, seeking employment. In so far as the sellers do not possess other outlets for the surplus—an eventuality which we do not wish to consider in this connection—they will have to lower the hitherto existing price. New series of less forceful demand, hitherto excluded, will be admitted, until with the establishment of a new price, the market once more recovers its equilibrium and actual supply and effective demand coincide.

We find in the markets an habitual endeavor to discount changed conditions, without awaiting the automatic regulation of price by the mechanism of excessive supply and unsatisfied demand. A price which is still maintained after the condition of the market has changed, is uneconomic; it is opposed to the interest of those sellers who sold prematurely at too low a price; it is harmful to the interest of that part of the demand which has bought prematurely at too high a price, or which, having decided too late to outbid others, is no longer able to buy. It may be noted that such a condition results in corresponding gains to the opposite party; but gains of this sort are accidental and are obtained by chance prices. These profits are not as important as the protection of permanent interests. The latter may best be preserved, the plan of consumption and production in the individual economies may be kept on the most business-like basis and violation of the admissible economic boundaries may be most carefully avoided, where the greatest possible constancy of prices permits men to form estimates of operations for entire trade-periods of the production-process or for entire periods of the domestic management; i. e., when such prices hold good in this way or, better still, are the same from period to period. A vendor who profits by every transient, urgent need of the demand, in order to extort exceptional prices, offends against the social spirit which should animate even the conflict of economic interests. His dealings are more nearly those of the usurer than the merchant. The trustworthy business-man endeavors irrespective of all chance occurrences of individual demand, to maintain constant prices based on the general market-conditions and holding, as far as possible, for considerable periods of time.

From endeavors such as these, there is gradually developed in the various markets a sort of free organization which, subsequently, may become the basis for a formally developed market-organization. As between producers—among whom in theory we class dealers as well—and consumers, the first take the lead inside of this free organization. They are destined to do so by their permanent business interest and by their superior market-experience. They originate the supply and for this reason may decide what quantities are to be offered to current consumption, and what quantities are to be reserved for future contingencies. This fact enables these men to exercise the most effective influence on market-conditions. It is within their province to conduct the market by establishing prices on a basis which can be permanently maintained. While changes of supply and demand occur within moderate limits, their experience of the market enables these parties to perform these functions. Little by little, gradual displacements may transform the entire system of prices and large numbers of newly arising values may become embedded in the network of the old, without the market being necessarily appreciably disturbed in any way.

§ 37. The Formation of Prices in the Disorganized Market

Panic prices, Scare-prices, Cast-away prices—Formation of prices in an open market—Usury-prices.

Whenever violent changes arise in the conditions of supply and demand, especially when they are unexpected, the free organization of the market fails to function. Then the decisive marginal offer must be ascertained by the pressure of the excessive supply and the unsatisfied demand. It may possibly not be found until after all sorts of variations which shoot beyond the mark. Whenever the disturbances are excessive, the organization of the market may be so deranged that the mechanism of the excessive supply and the unsatisfied demand breaks down and the decisive marginal offer may not be ascertained for some time. A market of this sort, we shall call a disorganized market.

In the disorganized market, the marginal law loses its efficacy; the latitude of price-formation is greatly broadened. Chance-prices, above or below the position of the marginal offer, arise within these widened limits. To follow the course of events, we will assume the case which shows most clearly what happens in these circumstances; we will assume the case of a violent disturbance of the market, generally known as a panic. A panic of demand arises when consumers—conditions are the same where the demand is by entrepreneurs—for any reason whatsoever fear that the supply of wares will fall short of covering the entire urgent demand. The panic will be especially acute, when existence-values are involved. The terrified consumers will grab for the nearest stocks of the wares that offer; the price is no longer bargained for by a uniform system. Every man takes care of himself as opportunity offers; buyers of more abundant means make use of their power, without waiting to see whether or not they might buy at the marginal offer of less wealthy competitors. Even the less wealthy purchasers manage to increase their bids by concentrating their means as much as possible on the endangered existence-values. In this way extremity-prices may be conceded far beyond a point which is justified by the true state of things. The panic of supply may be witnessed when, in one way or another, an apprehension has been created that for one or the other group of wares, or even for an entire series of groups of wares, a sudden and catastrophic drop of prices is to be expected. The panic is intensified when the supply, as a matter of commercial self-preservation, is compelled to force sales. Stocks, which under different circumstances would have been held over for later disposition, are quickly thrown on the market in short order, just to unload them in any event. Possibly, on the other hand, the demand is induced to hold back by the identical conditions, and thus to increase the supply. As the proportions of supply and demand have become more unfavorable, the marginal offer will almost certainly be depressed, but the terrified vendors do not wait to see the marginal offer determined. Just as in the case of the panic of demand, the law of the single price is overthrown. Prices vary in rapid succession. Every seller strives to make sure of the nearest purchaser, and his ambition is satisfied if he can sell at all, even at ruinous prices. In the case of wares which have no inherent value-in-use for the suppliers, no lower limit can be set for such a catastrophic drop in prices. The market, in the grasp of a panic, not infrequently loses every vestige of sound judgment; under the influence of senseless rumors, the impossible may seem to become an accomplished fact. Once a few of the alarmists have set the example of selling at mad prices, the entire market may follow in their train, with never a man left to stand off the stampede.

Every scattered market, no longer unified by the sentiment of social egoism, is a disorganized market, where the law of the unity of price is ignored or, to say the least, encroached upon. In such markets the ranks of market-frequenters are disrupted; local or temporal partial markets differentiate from the principal market, individual groups of persons or even single individuals detach themselves from it, then and there. Market-experts or persons otherwise favorably situated still take advantage of the common price; others must content themselves with aberrant prices which often are, more or less, prices of chance. The supply is able to exploit, by advances in prices, the necessities of the demand, increased locally, temporally or owing to personal interests. Conversely the demand is able to exploit the necessities of the supply by depressing prices, where the latter is compelled to sell. A hackman, alone on the spot, need not observe the marginal offer, which would be established if the market were complete. He is in a position to charge his passenger a higher price for a very urgent trip. The upper limit will be determined by the personal appraisal of the intending passenger. In a case of this sort, the hackman is by no means a monopolist; he does not control the entire market. He controls only this single passenger, who has been cut off from the entire market. The fare prescribed by law in a case of this sort, simply keeps the individual price in line with the common price.

Usury, as practiced to-day, is a phenomenon of the disjointed market. The demand for capital on the part of persons of insecure financial standing is not admitted to the general capital-market, even if, on account of the greater risk to be incurred, this demand should offer to pay a certain premium on the transaction. Lenders in the general capital-market want to ensure safety in extending loans. Loans to unsafe debtors, i. e., such loans as are accompanied by risks, must be negotiated with money-lenders who make such loans as a specialty. Insecure loans, therefore, constitute a partial market by themselves, which is almost completely separated from the general market. In itself, too, this partial market is again disjointed; it is scattered to such an extent, that it may scarcely be spoken of as a market at all, for competition is scarcely effective among usurious creditors. The debtor, when he first embarks in the usurious transaction, is anxious to keep the matter secret. In this way, he is cut off from the general market, is isolated; but later on, once enmeshed in his obligations, he will be further isolated by the dependence in which he remains to his creditor, until it has become possible for him to discharge his debt. In the typical cases of usury, repayment is difficult; for in all these cases, the debtor is economically weak, in consequence either of having an economic standard below the average, or of personal distress so oppressive that even the average standard is not sufficient to avert it. The single, weak debtor on one side; the single, merciless creditor of large means on the other: this is the pure form of usury. The creditor may press his demands to the utmost limit at which the debtor appraises his service. He may advance this upper limit higher and higher, the more ruinous he render the position of the debtor, who ultimately struggles for the preservation of the great values of his economic existence and his honor. Indeed, when it comes to the helpless debtor, the creditor is not bound by the latter's appraisal. He has him completely in his power, and can dictate his conditions. If he does not proceed to extremities at once, it is due more than anything to the fact that, after all, he wishes to preserve a certain appearance of consideration. If help does not come from outside, either from other persons or other sources of means which relieve the debtor and enable him to effect the discharge of his onerous obligations, usurious transactions of this sort must end in the ruin of the debtor. As they pass beyond the standard of the common price, the performances which the creditor may enforce, also pass beyond the common form of the price. The creditor need not be satisfied to raise the rate of interest. He may exploit the debtor by the most varied transactions and practices, while he retains him in his power owing to the entanglements of the indebtedness. In this way usury may, especially, become a usury of wages. The exploitation of the wage-laborer reaches its most dangerous stage when the laborer, in virtue of a debt with its attendant entanglements, becomes permanently dependent on the employer.

Usury of earlier times started from other premises. The supply of capital was small; the demand for loans, as a matter of necessity or distress, was large; even the ordinary rate of interest was exceedingly high, and the interest on loans negotiated under stress was exorbitant. It is not to be wondered at, if the usury-laws of those days were prompted by the idea that it was immoral to take any interest for money loaned. The transitions from those earlier times to our own has gone thru many stages of development, presenting to legislation in the course of events a variety of difficult problems. To-day a large, well organized capital-market exists. It may with perfect propriety be left to self-direction because a common and just price is always being established automatically in the course of its operations. The task of usury-legislation has therefore been greatly simplified. It would be a fruitful undertaking to trace the theory of usury under all the changing conditions of the market; however, we have to confine ourselves to the exposition of modern conditions.

So, too, extortion in corn, bread and food-stuffs generally, occurred in earlier days under market-conditions which in the civilized communities of the present day are conditions of the past. It should be recalled in this connection that the state and the city of the past had to confront different and more difficult problems than any presented to-day. The monopolistic and monopoloid control of the market was more easily established in the narrower conditions of the past. With the pressure of the constantly returning failures of harvests and years of famine it was particularly obnoxious. The monopolistic or monopoloid control of to-day, attempted on the exchanges by pools, arises under different conditions and leads to different effects which are not discussed in this connection.

§ 38. The Price of Products

1. THE SUPPLY-INDEX OF COSTS

Costs of acquisition of the entrepreneur—Producer's costs—Money-form and natural form of costs of production.

There are markets for two sorts of products: markets for final products ready for use and for intermediate products which are those of higher orders, demanded that by their aid final products of immediate ultimate usefulness may be obtained. For the immediately useful, final products, the demand is created by the consumers; for the intermediate products, by the producers.—"Producers" is again used in the widest sense, which includes trade with all its auxiliary employments.—The producers' demand for intermediate products originates in the expectation that a demand by consumers will completely relieve the market of the ultimate products which are to be obtained by the use to the intermediate goods. The standard of producers' demand, therefore. is to be found in the prices at which they expect to dispose of the ultimate products. From the prices thus expected for ultimate products, the producers by the aid of the rules of attribution, compute the indices of demand for the intermediate products. On the basis of these indices the prices for producers' goods are calculated. We may confine ourselves to deducing the law of price for the decisive market of the ultimate products. As to the price-formation for intermediate products we shall later, especially when discussing demand-monopoly, add a few remarks. In the following pages, when we employ the term, products, we mean to refer —unless otherwise expressly indicated—to the immediately useful ultimate products.

We find, in the market of the ultimate products, the same demand-index of consumption with which we had to deal in deducing the fundamental law of price-formation. There is thus nothing further of interest to add with reference to demand. On the other hand, the supply-index is now fundamentally changed. Whereas we formerly worked with the simplifying assumption of a fixed supply, we are now face to face with a variable supply, ever changing with the conditions of production and the prospects of the market. The producers determine the size of the supply to be brought into the market by a calculation of which costs are the foundation. This supply-index of the costs will next have to occupy our attention. In approaching this problem we shall not at first distinguish the conditions of monopoly, competition and the intermediate monopoloid position. These positions of the supply in the market have their influence on price. But, for the present, it is not this effect which we desire to probe. We wish now to examine the computation of costs, which the supplying entrepreneur completes for himself, and we wish to determine the concept of costs, which he employs in doing so. In this respect the market position has no influence whatever: the monopolist's calculation is not essentially different from that of any other entrepreneur. It should be observed, however, that not only the producing entrepreneur and the merchant figure in this way; everybody does it, who incurs costs of any sort for the sake of acquisition. The banker does so, no less than the contracting builder who erects houses for his own account or for the account of others, than the owner of houses who lets dwellings to tenants, or than the physician and the lawyer. What we have to say as to costs of production, properly speaking, applies to all these other cases of acquisition.

The multiform nature of the phenomenon of costs is also shown in the computations of entrepreneurs. These men compute on the basis of two different classes of costs. In conformity with their computations we shall have to distinguish two concepts of costs.

In a broader sense, the producer or other entrepreneur includes in the term, costs, the entire outlay of money to be taken into consideration in calculating his assets or his profit or loss. This is his point of view when he seeks to determine the actual effect on his wealth of the costs he has incurred. All capital expenditures, especially all those for acquiring the necessary specific productive means, are charged to the capital account. The builder, for example, sets down the purchase-price which he actually paid for the lot. In the profit and loss account, besides all individual expenses of production, should be entered the entire outlay for taxes and other like expenses, the cost of compulsory insurance of workers and the like, and furthermore the entire loss of receipts in money with which the producer should debit production. From this last point of view, therefore, interest on the entire capital employed should be reckoned at the existing rate of interest; for the producer would have realized the customary interest in any other legitimate employment, and he would be the loser, did he not fully recover it in the production now carried on. The same consideration will lead the producer to charge to costs also the entire average wages of management, which he has a right to expect in other similar enterprises; for again he would consider himself the loser, if some particular activity did not yield him this income, or did not yield it fully. Costs of this character are most suitably designated as acquisition-costs of the entrepreneur. They include the entire money investment which the entrepreneur has actually "put up" or, as the case may be, must regard as invested, in order to earn the gains.

If we compare acquisition-costs with costs of production as defined in the theory of the simple economy, we are confronted by some striking contrasts. We find, in the first place, that among the elements of cost there are included taxes, all the performances akin to taxes, and also average wages of management. The inclusion of taxes and performances in the nature of taxes requires no further comment. As regards the wages of management, we shall have to defer more explicit consideration until the next section, where the theory of such income is to be discussed. For the present suffice it to say that, in its motives, the inclusion of the average wages of management is closely akin to the inclusion of interest at the customary rates. Several further contrasts, which we also find, are less obvious and demand explanation. We itemized the costs of the simple economy as natural expenditures, but in the costs of acquisition the commercial money-investment is put down; we formerly charged the socially indispensable costs, but in the costs of acquisition all costs actually incurred are charged; we finally charged only cost-productive-means, but in the costs of acquisition expenses also are charged for procuring specific productive means.

We find the explanation of these contradictions in the narrower concept of costs, which has to guide producing entrepreneurs in establishing the plan of production and in calculating, in connection with this plan, the prices which they will have to demand for the products in order to come out without losses. These costs, then, are the costs spoken of in commercial phrase as "producers' costs" of the entrepreneur. In the computation of producers' costs, the entrepreneur has to be guided thruout by the rules of the simple economy, for every individual enterprise is in itself a simple economy. Along with all other rules of the computation of utility, the rules of cost-computation have to be complied with. As we enter upon the consideration of the individual points just touched upon, we shall see that this in fact is the case.

A practical computation of producers' costs, intended to serve as an accurate basis for the plan of production and the calculation of prices, must set out from the natural cost-expenditure. It is true that the entrepreneur estimates not only acquisition-costs, but producers' costs as well in terms of money; but he cannot safely stop at the mere pecuniary expression. A producer, determined to effect savings in costs, could never consider merely the amount of money expended for procuring the productive means. He would have to endeavor to make savings in the natural quantities used, whether employed in production or laid out for plant. The producers have to check off accurately in terms of natural quantities, the outlay in materials and services of labor contained in each individual product—the special-costs, as men are accustomed to call them. For the general costs a more simple method of estimate is sufficient; they need not be specially computed in natural quantities for each product. Every requirement will be satisfied, if an appropriate quota for overhead is added to each monetary unit of the special costs.

An accurate computation of producers' costs is not likely to stop at the actual costs; it will insist on determining the necessary costs. Producers, pressed hard by the competition, are by this fact alone impelled to operate with the lowest possible outlay of money that is necessary under the existing social conditions, if they would not be driven from the field by their competitors. But even the monopolist has this same impulse, for every unnecessary cost-expenditure means a loss, to suppress which an effort must be made. The profits will be largest where costs are reduced to the unavoidable minimum. Whatever, over and above this imperative standard, has been used up by neglect or want of skill, should not appear in the accounts as cost; it is to be regarded a loss which might have been avoided by proper methods, and therefore should not be confused with the necessary costs.

Finally, a producers' cost computation which would furnish an accurate foundation for the plan of production and the calculation of the prices of products, will have to distinguish between cost-productive means and specific productive means. The latter should not enter into the account. The prices for the cost-productive-means, for the generally used materials and services, the individual entrepreneur finds in the market as accomplished facts; to these he must accommodate himself. He should never start a type of production for which his computations show that the price to be realized for the products is insufficient to cover such price-expenditures with an added quota for overhead. He will not continue permanently an undertaking in which computation shows results of this sort. He will increase the limits of his production, add to its degree of intensity and bring more products into the market, when these costs drop; he will curtail his supply when they rise.

Specific productive means are differently dealt with. In every individual case, the entrepreneur has to determine by specific attribution, what price he may allow himself to pay for these. For example, if he purchases land, he will have to ascertain whether a surplus will be left from the sale of its products, after deducting costs of cultivation and management. According to the amount of this surplus, he will estimate the price which he can afford to pay for the estate. The costs of cultivation and management which he counts on here, are costs in the narrower meaning, the producers' costs; the surplus is the "specific" return. The purchase-price which the buyer pays for the land has its significance for the cost-account in the broader sense of acquisition-costs; it will have to be considered, in order to ascertain how large the profit or loss was as compared with a former distribution of assets or as compared with a former annual yield. The purchaser loses, when he pays too high a price; he gains, when he pays a lower price. The extent and intensity of cultivation are not governed by the purchase-price actually paid, any more than the management of an industrial enterprise is by the price which someone pays for the stock of the concern. The extent of the enterprise is not broadened, simply because the price for land or for stock rises; it will not be contracted simply because the price drops. Just as the price of specific productive means has nothing whatever to do with the extent of their operations, it does not enter either into the producers' costs computation; it is, conversely, as a result of the producers' cost computation that the surplus is ascertained, which the yield returns beyond producers' costs.

In this sense every producer, in his producers' costs computation, is guided by the value-cost-law. He appraises cost-products as combinations of their cost-elements, in that he places a money-value on the required natural cost-means plus overhead. The first of these values is derived from the quantities required and the existing prices. Thus the supply-index of the production-costs is determined. The cost-price, thus computed, establishes the lower limit of the supply price. Below this producers will not sell; nor will they permanently be satisfied with a lower price. As to this conclusion all producers are agreed, no matter what their position in the market may be. We will later on endeavor to answer the question whether, under favorable conditions of the market, they will not insist on a still higher price. We shall observe that the monopolistic position has in this respect a decided advantage in the market over that of competing supply.

In the case of specific products manufacturers consider producers' costs in their calculations in so far, that they determine by reference to them the degree of intensity with which they apply cost-means; they will always apply cost-means only in so far as the money-expenditure required yields a corresponding money-surplus. On the other hand, the cost-expenditure, as such, never establishes the lower limit of their supply price. Producers will always go far enough in their demands to obtain, over and above the covering of costs, the largest possible monetary return for the contributing specific factors.

The price of the cost-means, also, is deduced from the yield. In so far they are governed by the same conditions as the specific productive means. The demand for all productive means, without exception, proceeds from a consideration of the probable physical yield and the anticipated prices of the products on the market. The quantities of cost-means, however, are so large, and their employment is so various, that the demand of each individual producer always coalesces with an extensive demand of other producers. It is thus largely deprived of its effect, although it is surely a codeterminant of price. The individual producer always has the impression that he does not contribute in determining the price of cost-means. He regards this price as an established fact. With the specific productive means, quantities are smaller and methods of employment are much less numerous. Here, too, every producer thru his demand comes in contact with others, often many others. Yet a general survey is much more easily obtained, and every producer recognizes that the price is a variable quantity which changes with the expected yield and is dependent on the price of the products. While, therefore, in his computation he figures the cost-means at the given price, he applies to the specific means the rule of specific attribution and attributes to them the excess or the remainder after covering producers' costs.

§ 39. The Price of Products

2. THE COMPETITIVE PRICE

The law of cost-price—Competition of the strong and the weak—Super-competition, disorganized competition—Personal and social effect of competition.

A vendor, not under the pressure of competition, may under certain circumstances find it to his advantage to withdraw part of his stock of wares from the market and to allow them to perish, unused. This is likely to happen, whenever their experience of the market leads vendors to infer that, owing to the consequent shrinkage of the supply, prices must rise sufficiently to enable them to obtain for the rest of their stocks a larger gross return [1] than they could have obtained by the sale of the undiminished stocks. Competitive sellers can never afford to do this. Each of them knows that his competitors alone would reap the advantage of his withholding wares; for these competitors would surely take advantage of the higher price, in order to throw as many of their wares as possible into the market. Prices would drop, and the business-man who had withheld his wares, would be left to lugubrious reflections. He would be compelled to dispose at disadvantageous prices of the portion which he retained for sale. This consideration will prevail upon the entire supply to seek its advantage in the quantities sold. Each man will bend his efforts on selling whatever can be sold.

The same reflection must apply to the progress of production. Competing producers feel constantly induced to exploit all personal and material means at their disposal to the limit, in order to increase production and to place upon the market the largest quantities of wares, appraised at the highest figures by the demand. They are induced to subserve the advantage of the purchasers with the same degree of care and skill, which the latter would bring to bear in their own, individual interest. Indeed we are safe in saying, that by the pressure of competition they are brought to use a higher degree of care and skill, than buyers would employ in their own behalf. In his own isolated household the peasant is more likely to persist in antiquated methods, no matter how much the art of the cultivation of the soil progress in the world beyond his barn. Possibly, the effort of re-learning, the uncertainties of innovations may deter this man; but even he, unwilling to move another inch for his own sake, will feel compelled to adopt technical advances in the service of the market

[1] Trans. *note*: *Gesamterlös*. I presume that Wieser has in mind a condition of constant cost when he says that attention is centered on total yield.

demand, when to do otherwise would mean that he might be left behind by his competitors, and deprived of the advantage of his sales. Those who have ability will strive to advance beyond the general ruck and will ever be eager to gain headway against their rivals, to wrest from them in the commercial conflict increasing sales. Competition exacts from producers all their power and care, the best that their talents and training allow them to give.

The net result will decide in what quantities the wares will be offered in the market by the competing producers. But quantities determine price; for according to the fundamental law of the formation of prices, the price is determined by the marginal bid, which reflects the receptivity of the market to the quantities supplied.

For the cost-products, the law of price takes the special form of the law of cost-price. Under the pressure of the competition, all producers are held to conform in price to the law of cost-value which in their producers' cost computation they used for themselves. In its details, the process of price-formation is a somewhat different one, according as the cost-products belong to the group for which marginal expenses are incurred or to groups of narrower expenditures.

In the case of cost-products which, for all purchasers, appear in the group of marginal expenditures, the cost-law is upheld. By the pressure of competition, manufacturers are compelled actually to produce the entire quantity of wares, which market conditions allow. Producers will not stop manufacturing, until the marginal bid, determined by the receptivity of the demand, coincides with the cost-price. Not until this condition of prices has been reached, will an equilibrium have been established in which the cost-elements in all their productive combinations are paid for at the same price. Not until this occurs, not while any products are being turned out whose sale price leaves higher remuneration for the cost-elements, will the pressure of competition cease to urge on an increase in the manufacture of these products.

In the case of cost-products which fall in groups of narrower expenditure for some or all purchasers, the cost-price is maintained without sufficiently increasing the quantities produced to bring them for all purchasers into the group of marginal expenditures. In this way cost-products of fine quality, too, which are exclusively demanded by the wealthier strata of the population, become subject to the cost-law. Competition will never permit any vendor to profit by the higher appraisal of the wealthy and to demand higher prices of these people. Even where quantities can no longer be augmented, sellers will mutually undersell one another, until cost-prices have been reached. Where this price prevails, the entire effective demand has been satisfied. Even though all admitted buyers because of their higher appraisal were in a position to pay a higher price, a condition has been reached at which the market is in equilibrium.

The effect of the price-cost-law in the economic exchange of the people is not quite the same as that of the value-cost-law in the simple economy of a unified society. In the latter, the line of utility cost coincides with that of the marginal utility of the products. By a compensated beneficial utilization of cost-means, an equalization of marginal utility is effected in the entire field of productionally related cost-products: i. e., this occurs in so far as this equalization is at all possible with the existing arrangement of the need-scales. In the economy of exchange, however, the wealthier strata will always be able to provide themselves more abundantly, perhaps to full satiety, with cost-products, while the poorer ones will have to retrench. In this sense the law of cost-price does not operate to reach the highest, universal satisfaction of needs.

In all other respects it operates, however, in the spirit of the social economic principle. By virtue of the price-cost-law, the productive values, in spite of the individual and independent character of management, are unified and concentrated, and their apportionment to the individual branches of production takes place as by a social plan. The spirit of a social economy is complied with, although there is not a unitary social management. The personal interest is expressed thru the mechanism of excess-supply and unsatisfied demand. The quest of gain by the producers and the pressure of competition, are in themselves sufficient to result in a social effect. The fact, also, that the strata best able to pay do not give their full, personal price but pay a socially conditioned cost-price, is a socially significant result insofar as it shows that the supply is not privileged to exploit independently the strength of the demand, but has to conform to the margin established by the general condition of the market.

The prices of specific products are not subject to the cost-law. The owners of diamond-mines, for example, will not submit to diamond prices which merely cover costs, leaving no residue for the yearly exploitation of the mines. Despite mutual competition, they are not likely to depress the increased marginal offer, which the wealthier strata allow on the basis of their higher appraisal of the demanded precious stones—and thus by underbidding each other, come down to "rock bottom" costs. This lowest price could, after all, be reached by other ways, than the circuitous one of specific production. But the mine-owners will fully exploit the opportunity of specific production, in order to realize for the specific factor the highest price-utilization which is obtainable in view of the quantity of specific products that can be produced.

It goes without saying that the law of cost-price, like the law of cost-value, is valid only for an undisturbed market in equilibrium. By changes of the supply, of the demand and of the cost-rates, this law is frequently temporarily suspended. But there are movements of equalization constantly at work, if we assume the absence of friction, which in time will reëstablish its validity. Whenever the supply has been increased unexpectedly or the demand has been unexpectedly cut down, or when the rate of costs has for some reason or other increased, the entrepreneurs will not cover costs by prices. They will consequently reduce the supply until the market-price again meets the cost-price. In the converse case, when the supply suddenly drops off or the demand is unexpectedly increased, or when technical improvements or some other cause has depressed the cost-rates, the entrepreneurs will obtain prices which exceed costs; then under the pressure of the competition, the supply will continue to be increased until the market-price has again fallen to the cost-price. Otherwise, the tendencies of prices to change because of the increase of population and the progress of the technical arts, are the same in the exchange economy as in the simple economy which we have explained. We can, in this respect, refer to our former expositions.

Competition has a more proximate and a more remote influence on the price of products. The more direct influence consists in the adaptations of price to cost, which take place in the market; the more remote is accomplished in the production-process, as the personal performances of the competitors are pushed to their utmost attainable limit and the costs are depressed to the lowest realizable standard. An investigation of this second, more remote effect has its place, properly, in the doctrine of acquisition; but we cannot altogether pass it over in the theory of price. We must, at least, throw sufficient light upon it to correct the exaggerations of the classical formulation, which have been carried into the doctrine of competitive price.

Also our exposition has given undue weight to the apparent effects of competition on the progress of production. This is because our discussion has rested upon the idealizing assumptions which, so far, we have adhered to in our work. To come back to every-day standards, we must now, by decreasing abstraction, familiarize ourselves with typical conditions of reality. We shall have to consider more especially the social powers which largely rule the destinies of man. The exaggerations in the classical doctrine are due to the fact that its authors carried the idealizing approach into actual observations. They were possibly not even conscious of this and accepted the results of such idealized observation for unimpeachable truth. The personal performances are only intensified, or the costs reduced as much as the prevailing compulsory powers permit. Under different conditions, however, under rules abolishing the sway of the compulsory powers, men might possibly succeed in accomplishing a higher, a much higher performance.

The doctrine of competition presupposes the model type of the strong individual. It reckons on an enhancement of individual forces; it therefore deals with individuals who have an excess of power, individuals sufficiently free externally and of their inner nature, to direct their active forces under all circumstances to the end of the greatest utility. The entrepreneur on a large scale, the master-workman or the landowner, all possess the freedom of action which is here required, in a much higher degree than the state-employee, who is tied down by rules and regulations; more especially in a higher degree, than the subordinate state-employee or the wage-laborer. Among the latter class of people, monotonous employment paralyzes the vital and active forces, rather than stimulates them; or a system of wages, opening no prospect whatever of advancement in life, may wholly deaden the stimulus of competition. The external freedom of action must be accompanied by a liberty of the mind and soul. Without this there can never be the force to make decisions which ripen into action affecting not merely material acquisitions but inner acquisitions, which shape the destiny and purpose of human life. This inner freedom is absent in all those who require the compulsion of external command to exert their best efforts. It is lacking also in all those who find their progress arrested by their ineptitudes. These last-named unfortunates are in all respects inaccessible to the stimulus of competition; unless, in rare instances, they react to it by efforts which consume the last remnants of their abortive powers. How many men are without the power to make whatever movements of adaptation may be required, when their accustomed opportunities of acquisition have been thwarted by excessive supply, or otherwise encroached upon. With the majority of men, force of habit is more powerful than the desire of acquisition; so long as they are able, they stick to the accustomed place in life, rather than exert the effort required to gain new vantage-points. The competition of the weak is aroused, not so much by the desire of advancement, as by the apprehension of defeat; driven by an over-excited fear, such competition easily loses all restraint and becomes disorganized super-competition. The modern labor market exhibits the phenomenon of the disorganized super-competition of the enfeebled more strongly than the produce markets. We reserve the detailed discussion of this subject to our theory of the wages of labor.

Even the strongest individual can only answer for his own performance. But productive success is dependent, not only on the individual's personal performance, but on the amalgamation of this performance with the sum of foreign elements: the performances of foremen, underlings and others in the production-process, the actions of competitors, the attitude of the demand in the face of the total supply. Although the force of competition may impel one to improve his own performance to the point of perfection, he will still be the loser in the conflict for success, unless he has correctly foreseen the measures resolved on by various other persons, unless he has properly estimated the conditions of the demand and divined economic changes that still lie in the future. The more active, the more aggressive, the development of a national economy, the more difficult it will be for the individual to adapt himself to a new state of affairs. Under the static conditions of agricultural enterprise, unaffected by the operations of foreign countries, while the home-market offers regular, increasing demands, we find difficulties of these sorts fairly well excluded. The effects of competition may be exhausted in that every man feels pressed merely to do his best in the zealous performance of his duties.

Modern industry experiences the spur of competition in very different connections: new methods, new products, new territories, new points of departure, are constantly being offered for the dealer to choose from. Since he who is first on the spot is apt to fare best, since the most forceful may possibly succeed in dominating the crowd, the friendly rivalry becomes a deadly contest, ending at times in ruin and desolation. As affairs gain headway, the dangers of competition are increased; opportunities are carefully watched, and quickly crowded by the numbers of those who profit by them; favorable conjunctions of conditions cannot but tempt to excessive production and, in connection with it, to over-competition.

This excessive competition of the rich has sometimes more serious consequences for both the market and production than the competition of the poor. The undulations arising from its disturbances are felt in much wider circles. They carry many dependent individuals and foreign economies into the collapse of the crises which occur as the penalties of economic extravagance. Only after enormous fluctuations and losses of values can quiet be restored by the mechanism of the excessive supply and unsatisfied demand. How many unjustified expenditures a nervously eager or apprehensive competition imposes on the economy of a people, even though things stop short of the extremes of overproduction and crises!

Even in the narrow markets of European towns as they existed in the Middle Ages, tradesmen saw themselves compelled to unite in gilds, in order to protect themselves from the evil temptations of overproduction and overcompetition and to secure the continuance of a well-ordered market. Some mutual understanding of this sort is even more necessary in the wide markets of modern economy. The classical masters announced their theory at the time of the transition from the medieval traditional restrictions to the modern freedom of activity and movement; they already felt the influence of the signal successes which accompanied the keen understanding of the principles of competition in the novel avenues of commerce. The high esteem in which they held competition, had its rise in the effects of the progress which was actually accomplished during the stirring events of the times. Nevertheless, they still frequently measured conditions and events by the old standards which had been handed down by men, living in the more quiet environment of the petty trader or peasant. They had no correct idea of the dangers which accompany competition on an enormous scale. Their later followers, looking at the new world around them, should have known better; but in their pedantry they clung to the dogma, careless of the breadth and depth of the cleft which separated them from actuality.

The victor in the conflict of competition is such not merely by virtue of his personal efficiency. He is so by the aid of the wealth of external means, more especially the pecuniary means, which he disposes. In the smaller or moderate sized business-ventures, capital is of less importance. Individuality, when contrasted with capital, becomes strikingly prominent. Even in large enterprises, capital is not the only factor which decides the issue. The most forceful personalities first find in large undertaking an outlet for their full powers. However this may be, the greater number of the gifts are no longer able to stand up against the power of vast aggregations of capital. On a smaller scale they were able to produce good results, but in the century of mammoth enterprises they no longer avail.

Since the passing of the classical period, conditions have greatly changed in this respect as well. Huge combinations of capital have made enormous progress; they have ousted entire strata of individual owners and made armies of workmen dependent on their will. The victory which they have won in this march of conquest over weaker competitors does not have the same social significance as that which pertained to victory in the competitive conflict under the conditions of the earlier years. Formerly one was justified in saying that the conflict of competition performed a service of personal selection. This selection worked in the interest of society, when it elevated the efficient worker and lowered the indolent, the unskilful or otherwise incapable one. In the case of those producers who succumbed through no fault of their own, simply because changes of external conditions deprived them of their accustomed means of livelihood, the aid of the equalizing movement could then safely be relied upon to enable them to turn to other employments, where their abilities would reëstablish their chances of success. Now, however, the revolutions of trade, brought about by the irresistible advances of mammoth capital, are mass phenomena. In the face of these changes the equalizing movement fails almost completely. The displaced multitudes cannot easily, certainly not quickly, find employment under approximately equal conditions; meanwhile these workers are handed over to abject misery, and more lamentable still their best powers may be scrapped forever.

With all these exceptions, competition none the less exercises so great an effect as, even under modern conditions, to entitle it to be classed among the most important social economic forces. In the strata of laborers and subordinate employees it is more limited. It asserts itself there only for a smaller number of ambitious individuals; but among the independent owners it affects all. Within each of these groups, it performs even to-day the functions of personal selection; peasant against peasant, master-mechanic against master-mechanic, large entrepreneur against large entrepreneur, each is weighed and measured, approved or condemned in the fierce struggle of competitive conflict.

In no other of the great fields of human activity, where men strive for supremacy through rival efforts, do they find broader scope for self-assertion. In every other quarter, as far as the multitudes are concerned, rivalry with others excites only the titillations of a sense of honor. Men do not wish to be last; they wish to measure up to the average performance, in order to stand well in the eyes of their fellows. Only a few individuals with special aspirations wish to rise above this level; urged on by ambition and the love of ostentation, they would be in the van or possibly would be first in order thus to enjoy the enhanced respect accorded to the leader or to win for themselves the moral and material power which are the attributes of leadership.

In economic competition, however, even with the man of the people, it is not merely the desire for honor which is kindled. Material success as such attracts a large share of the aspirations of individuals. As the conflict grows more heated, the end of material prosperity becomes the object—not infrequently the more cherished object—of human desires; honor is left to fight its own battles. The common man does not wish merely to imitate, the leader by instinct does not wish merely to walk in the foremost ranks; the one, by his imitation, would assure his acquisitions; the other, by his leadership, would increase his material gains. Frequently enough, we all know, the struggle is one for material existence. Although it is true, that competition only exalts the achievement which may be personally controlled and which the individual builds up in the economic process of production, yet so far reaching a personal operation is a social fact of the utmost importance. As regards the personal achievement of the leaders, this, in every sphere, becomes the model which others imitate; thus leaders, exalting themselves, exalt the type of their group. In judging the existing individualistic economic order it is necessary to consider the manner in which competition selects successive leaders and educates the masses through the agency of these leaders. No economic order, without suffering very great disadvantages, may dispense with the use, in one way or another, of the supreme power of competition towards social success.

§ 40. The Price of Products

3. THE MONOPOLY OF SUPPLY

Restricting the supply—The classification of demand—The monopolistic computation of costs, especially in the case of joint costs—The monopoly of the market—The monopoly of production—Unified industries.

Pure monopolies are very unusual. Possibly only the unified industries of states or of self-governing bodies possess that exclusiveness which satisfies the concept of a pure monopoly. Private monopolies, on the other hand, are usually so situated as to lose the character more or less of the ideal monopoly and to transform it into the monopoloid type. We would not, however, for the present, anticipate the investigation of the monopoloid type. We would only remark that in the following pages we have selected copyrights or patents, kartels or railroads as illustrations, by which to explain the formation of monopolistic prices, leaving it to later enquiry to ascertain whether or not in all these institutions the monopoly character has not been encroached upon by certain other characteristics.

The monopoly of supply will have to be distinguished from the monopoly of demand. We shall first take up the supply-monopoly, by far the most frequent type and the only one, as a rule, known as monopoly pure and simple.

The monopoly of supply, precisely like the competitive supply, conforms to the fundamental law of the formation of prices. It does not enjoy any special advantage in this respect, for the supply-monopolist has anything but the power to dictate prices according to his discretion. He, no more than others, can overcome the weight of the decisive marginal bid. However, his controlling position in the market certainly gives him a number of opportunities to influence the market, so that the marginal-offer occurs at a higher figure.

The most conspicuous advantage which he enjoys, is the power to restrict the quantities of his supply. Experience will soon teach him at what level he should maintain the quantity of supply, in order to obtain the greatest total price by the most advantageous combination of quantity and of price. For the present we will disregard the factor of costs which must naturally be carried into the combination. In so far as the monopolist allows himself to be guided solely by the inherent law of monopoly, he will decide in favor of the combination most advantageous to him, with little regard to the fact that the demand may fare better or worse. It is by no means impossible that the monopolist's advantage coincide with that of the demand; his total gains may be highest, when he sells the greatest quantity. Possibly this may be the rule. But it may also be, that with smaller sales he may have larger profits. In the history of commerce we find numerous examples of a monopolistic policy which went the length of destroying stocks, already transferred to the market, in order to secure larger gains. The gradations of the scales of needs in combination with the stratifications of effective purchasing power determine whether more is to be gained on the part of the monopolist by the factor of quantity or by the factor of price. Where the need-scales or the stratification of the purchasing-power are laid out in abrupt gradations, an increase of the quantity beyond the point of abrupt change will materially injure the price-conditions. The monopolist will, therefore, prefer to confine himself to the smaller sales. Where need-scales and purchasing power change very gradually, larger sales will be more advantageous to him.

The result will be the same, when the monopolist, rather than decide on quantities and then wait for the price-determination of the market, does things the other way and decides on the prices to be attained, awaiting on his part the market's action in respect of the quantities to be taken up. For very good reasons, the second method is the one generally determined upon, the calculations being more transparent. His experience of the market will soon teach the monopolist on what quantities of sales he may count with a certain definitely settled price.

The monopolist has the further advantage of being able—up to a certain point—to split up the market. In this way, he frees himself from the law of the single price, which confines competition for the entire quantity sold to the marginal offer of the least effective purchaser. The monopolist divides the entire unified market into partial markets, graded according to ability to pay. He uses the quantities sold in the markets of the better paying purchasers in such a manner as to secure the higher prices that the larger marginal bid allows. Such a procedure may be designated as classification of the demand. By way of illustration, we may mention the case of the publisher who makes use of his exclusive copyright to first publish a small edition at high prices for bibliophiles and for all those purchasers whose demand, for one reason or another, is more than ordinarily active. This publisher, later on, after the group of those most eager and best able to buy has been exhausted, gets out an enlarged edition, meant for the general public and sold at reduced prices. In the case of newly introduced patented articles, the same procedure is frequently resorted to. In all instances of this sort, the demand is temporally split up by strata of decreasing marginal bids who buy one after the other. But under some circumstances the monopolist may also succeed in dividing the market into partial markets, existing side by side. This enables him to benefit similarly by the marginal offers of the various strata but to reach them simultaneously. The publisher might, for example, issue a costly edition de luxe in a limited number of copies, and beside it, a cheap popular edition in large numbers of copies. When the administration of the tobacco-monopoly catalogues the various grades of tobacco which they offer to the people, it accomplishes a classification of the demand similar to the one here described. It subdivides the demand, according to strata of marginal offers expected, by adjusting the qualities offered, according to the individual classes of smokers, and by so grading the prices as to get the most from every purchasing class according to their means. The classification of the demand is a most effective tool of monopolistic policy. In another connection, we shall still have to deal with an additional variety of the classification of the demand, that is much used.

The monopolist is not bound by the law of the single price. Neither, therefore, is he bound by the law of cost-price, in which the single price of the cost-means asserts itself. It is combinations of these latter prices which are paid for in the products. In his internal calculation he obeys, like any other entrepreneur, the law of cost value; he appraises the cost-products as combinations of their productive elements. However, he enjoys the advantage of not being bound by this fact to reach the same conclusions as regards quantity of production and price, as competitors would reach. He can arrange matters so as to differentiate his cost-products from the unified market of productive-means, and to sell them as specific products at a price exceeding the cost-price and leaving him a greater profit than the average wages of management. In the case of those cost-products for which marginal expenditures are incurred, the monopolist accomplishes his purpose by reducing quantities. He will not push production to the limit of expenditure, or else the marginal offer would stand at the cost-price, leaving no surplus gain. With specific scarcity products, the monopolist, wishing to get back more than the costs of acquisition, will reduce production still further than already made necessary by the scarcity involved. On the other hand, in the case of cost-products which come within the narrower expenditure-zones, he need not retrench either production or consumption. He may produce quite the same quantity which would be produced in free competition, and may still realize a price above producer's costs, as he utilizes the differential between cost-price and the higher appraisal of the demand. Thus, for example, large gains may be realized from monopoly of salt without appreciably reducing the consumption of salt among the population. Articles, which fall in the zone of marginal expenditures for large parts of the population and therefore with every increase of prices show considerable falling off of sales, are thus not desirable as state-monopolies; they do not allow of a large monopoly profit, or they only allow it subject to marked curtailment of consumption, which is felt as anti-social.

The freedom enjoyed by the monopolist as regards the law of costs, gives him an additional advantage in the treatment of joint costs of production. We shall endeavor to explain the rather complicated conditions by an illustration, selecting for this purpose the process known as "dumping" often practiced by kartels. A kartel, enjoying in its own country a rather generous protective duty and thus enabled to uphold high monopoly-prices, is in the position to sell abroad very cheaply, to underbid competition there and to effect large sales. The high monopoly-profits of its home-trade make this possible. As against foreign competition, the combination has the advantage that at home it is not tied down by the law of cost-price. In the domestic market, therefore, it can obtain prices which cover not only the special expenses for the products sold at home but also the entire general or overhead expenses, leaving profits over and above these items. For the products sold abroad, the combination may therefore be satisfied with prices computed without overhead but which, nevertheless, still leave a profit and add to the total gain. The producers with which the combination competes in the foreign markets, cannot make such prices—assuming that they do not operate thru a monopolistic organization but are subject to the full pressure of the competition—because in order to get out whole, they have to recover on each unit a proportionate share of the general expenses, which is part of the producers' costs. In view of the unity of his management of production, the monopolist is able to build a more flexible price-structure than competition makes possible; with him one price supports the other. In this way in each instance he demands the highest price which can possibly be obtained. He makes his calculation of prices serve the classification of demand. He utilizes the latter more effectively by increasing his sales and controlling an extended, classified market.

Whenever "dumping" takes place, the anti-social effect of the monopoly becomes most pronounced at home; the home-market is grievously over-charged and its consumption may be curtailed. However, it should not be overlooked that the foreign country is being offered a lower price and, in connection with it, larger quantities for consumption, than free competition would be able to bring forward. Only because the kartel is in a position to offer these advantages, can it succeed in making a conquest of the foreign market. Looking at the matter more closely, we shall recognize in the monopolistic method of combining cost-account and market-classification, the application of the rule to the conditions of commercial intercourse which, in the theory of the simple economy, we have deduced for the treatment of the joint costs. Just as, in this way, the simple economy succeeds in realizing the highest possible total-gain, so the monopolist reaches the same results. He is guided in this matter by his "instinct" of acquisition, because by the highest possible gain he expects to arrive at the best possible utilization of price; but to attain this end, he is after all induced to use a method which enhances the utilization of the social productive forces beyond what free competition by itself could achieve.

There are circumstances, when the utilization of the price, which may be accomplished by the method here described, is in fact demanded socially. We find the most significant illustration in railroad tariffs and in the traffic-rates of former days on the great inland canals which were the forerunners of the railroads. The separation or gradation into passenger-classes in European day-coaches is a classification of the demand, established for the purpose of exploiting the greater price-paying ability of those passengers whose social position obliges them to avail themselves of the expensive carriages. The classification of freight rates amounts to the same thing; its object is to thrive on the higher ability to pay of individuals who disclose their financial means by purchasing wares of higher specific prices. The lower rates for mass-wares of lower specific value are made possible by partially relieving these goods in the computation of costs, bringing in only the special-costs. This system, also, of establishing tariffs for exploiting the demand may be misused in an anti-social enhancement of profit, but under some circumstances there may be no other means of securing the profitableness of large enterprises which is required in order to attract investment. It is a system which realizes the highest obtainable prices. The construction of railroads and the opening up of inland-canals would never have been possible in their full extent, had not the administrations of these institutions adhered to the rule, "charge what the traffic will bear."

So far we have only considered those effects which are peculiar to a monopoly of the market. The present trend to enterprises of vast dimensions attracts attention more and more to the effects of an exclusive control or monopoly of the process of production. The primary meaning of the term, monopoly, indicates the position occupied by the sole vendor. A derivative use of the term to describe the position of the sole producer is certainly allowable. Exclusive control of the process of production is especially advantageous wherever large-scale industry is distinguished by increasing returns. Competitive enterprise tends to the individual small plant in most industries. Thus in these cases, while his attention is focussed on his personal advantage, the monopolist serves the best interest of society as well by a better utilization of productive forces. He produces more goods than competitive enterprise would and sells them for a lower price. The latter statement follows from the marginal law. However, he may not sell as many goods at as low a price as he would sell, were he to renounce monopoly profits. Ample capital will be available to expand production, for the increased yield that is anticipated attracts large aggregates of capital which prefer to turn to the largest enterprises.

The tendency to expansion becomes most effective in what might be properly called single-unit enterprises, where the entire mechanism of administration is one unit. The Postal Service furnishes an excellent illustration of what we mean. Were the unified net-work of the Postal Service of any modern state to be divided into a number of locally distinct and independent enterprises, the result would be an unnecessary increase of labor and increased expenses of transfer and accounting. In the face of single-unit administration, the principle of competition becomes utterly abortive. The parallel net-work of another postal organization, beside the one already functioning, would be economically absurd; enormous amounts of money for plant and management would have to be expended to no purpose whatever. It will be far more advantageous to enlarge the facilities already existing and to increase the working force, trained in their duties by years of experience. For the single-unit methods of business, monopoly is the unavoidable form. We shall not now endeavor to ascertain by what means the state might interfere to remedy abuses, where the private monopolist employs inequitably the great power placed in his hands by single-unit economic enterprises. It would surely turn out to be a mistake, were the attempt made to find remedies by admitting free competition.

The opposition between the interests of the entrepreneur and the social economy is completely eliminated in the case of a state or any other public monopoly. The entrepreneur interest of public corporations coincides with the general social interest; the administrative monopoly is not directed to monopoly-gains and the monopoly-profits realized by the state in taxes, inures to the benefit of public receipts. Whether, indeed, the state and the other public corporations are suited to the successful conduct of production is a different question altogether, but it is one which we cannot take up in this connection.

The classical doctrine looks upon monopoly as anti-social, as accompanied by temptations to handicap production, and as tolerating prices which exceed costs and therefore unduly burden the demand. It is further insisted that the monopolist feels his wealth to be secure and lacks the incentive to progress which is established by vigorous competition and stirs the most vital forces of a people. It is finally added that the monopolist may possibly not command adequate capital; while competition, just as it sets in motion all personal resources, also brings forward those of a material kind to whatever extent they may be available in society. However, all this argument is logical only if we assume that the process of production is amicably disposed towards competition. In no event do the conclusions fit the conditions of the single-unit enterprises. They cannot even be applied to large-scale undertakings without considerable restrictions. The classicists were influenced in their judgment by the conditions of their times. In their day smaller and medium sized enterprises predominated; the tendency to large and very large dimensions and its full significance could not yet be discerned. Having denied the state's calling, as well as that of public corporations generally, to the conduct of economic enterprises, they likewise failed to observe the important form of the public single-unit enterprise. Moreover, they persistently examined only the pure forms of monopoly and of competition. The modern trend to production on a large scale has called into being numerous novel, intermediate, monopoloid forms, which to-day are far more important than either of the pure forms. The classical formula, unconditional approval of the social competition and absolute repudiation of the anti-social monopoly, can no longer do justice to the institutions of to-day.

§ 41. The Price of Products

4. THE DEMAND-MONOPOLY

Socialist doctrine maintains that capital exercises a monopoly of demand in the labor market. Were the contention well founded, the monopoly would be one of extreme importance. The proofs, however, which can be adduced as to cases of demand-monopoly, are of far less importance. Without precluding later examination of the socialist contention, we may avail ourselves of the theoretical proofs offered in its behalf as ready auxiliaries in formulating a general theory of the monopoly of demand.

We shall have to think of the demand-monopolist as an entrepreneur, who is the sole would-be purchaser of certain productive means. As regards the competing supply he is not bound by the fundamental law of price. The upper limit of the price allowed by him is established by his appraisal. This appraisal, according to every rule of attribution, the monopolist effects as to the desired productive-means on the basis of the expected price of his products. He need not, however, offer the whole of this price; he may depress it until he reaches a lower limit fixed by the conditions of the supply. At this limit he encounters a resistance which he is unable to overcome. In case of the wages of labor, this limit might be established by the lowest standard of subsistence—a problem which we do not now wish to approach; in other cases it is established by the value-in-use, possessed by the wares for the suppliers; in the case of cost-products it is fixed by the costs of production.

In its application to products, then, these explanations do not promise great possibilities of success to the demand-monopoly, at least, not in so far as cost-products are concerned. If the monopolist is compelled to pay costs-prices to producers, it is plain that they receive the very price which they have a right to expect if there is full competition of the demand. Wherein, then, consists the superior advantage of the monopoly?

In order to answer this question, and do justice to the circumstances, we shall first have to introduce some explanatory remarks. The demand-monopoly is at all times accompanied by a monopoly of supply. Thus, for example, the state in its tobacco-monopoly combines the two institutions. The administration of the monopoly does not admit, in the home-market, other purchasers of raw tobacco; it combines with a monopoly of the supply of tobacco-products, which affects the consumers, a demand-monopoly, affecting the domestic tobacco growers. A further illustration is found in the actual demand-monopoly of a sugar-combine by virtue of its monopoly of supply. In this case, no other concern can make use of the sugar beets, and hence no other concern is likely to demand them. It seems impossible to imagine a combination of circumstances, where a demand-monopoly does not also amount to a monopoly of supply; for the producer, controlling the demand for certain elements of production, controls, as a natural consequence, also the productive utilization of these elements.

In the case of cost-products, the demand-monopolist, as such, actually has no particular advantage over free competition because, as has just been shown, he cannot depress the price below cost. On the other hand, he need not relinquish to those who supply his raw material, any portion of the monopoly profit that accrues to him from the implied monopoly of supply. Those who sell to him have no share in the gains which he realizes thru the sale of his cost-products at specific-product prices. The cost-products, sold by these parties to the monopolist, do not also acquire the characteristics of specific products; their prices continue to be cost-prices. In the general run of cases, at any rate, these would be the results.

There may be circumstances, to be sure, when the demand-monopolist will have to consent to allow to his predecessors certain advances in price, in order to make sure of obtaining the quantities required for extensive production, and also the qualities of which he is in need. A manufacturer of beet-sugar, for example, could not count with absolute certainty on receiving from the competition of beet-farmers the full quality and quantity of sugar-beets which he requires. The beets cannot be transported long distances; consequently the manufacturer's demand is met by a small group of individuals. To ensure a full supply for all his needs, he will have to offer larger inducements by increased prices. To this extent, he will be willing to relinquish a certain portion of his monopoly-gains to his predecessors; these will fare somewhat better, than they could otherwise expect. The arrangement is to the advantage, also, of the monopolist; for he makes sure of the full benefit of his supply-monopoly.

An even stronger effect is produced by the monopoly of demand in the case of specific products. The demand-monopolists is in a position to buy specific products at cost-product prices, getting paid for them, when he sells, at specific prices. Should a diamond-combine possess either the right or the exclusive power to sell diamonds to the public at large, obtaining their diamonds from the mines, it would never need to pay the diamond-mine owners at the specific diamond-prices; they would soon offer prices, but little exceeding their costs. The demand-monopoly here interposes a restraining influence in the process of specific attribution, and prevents benefits from accruing to predecessors of the monopolist, the primary producers or others, from the specific advances paid by the consumers. In the state tobacco-monopoly this effect is particularly conspicuous. Here, the monopoly-gain would be materially reduced, had not the state made sure of the supply of domestic tobacco under monopolistic conditions. Were foreign countries permitted to compete for domestic plants, it would force up the price of the finer qualities, the price of such plants as thrive only in particular soils and possess specific character. By virtue of its monopoly of demand the state is able to procure the products of the better classes of soil as well, at prices which do not reimburse the tobacco-planter for more than the costs. A monopolistic counterorganization of the supply would be required, in order to preserve the balance of forces and to secure for the precursors in the productive process an equitable share in the specific prices.

§ 42. The Price of Products

5. the monopoloid institutions

The favored specific market positions—The monopoly of administration—Tax-monopoly—Private monopolies regulated by the state (patents, unit-industries regulated by the state)—The conflict of competition in the large scale enterprise—Kartels—Trusts.

Numerous intermediary forms occur in great variety between competition and monopoly. In their details they are of such diverse arrangement that, with the instruments at its command, theory could never expect to explain their entire array. It is, however, competent to discuss those types which have solidified sufficiently to become familiar to every-day experience. To describe these types is one of its problems. We shall go as far in our description, as is demanded by the doctrine of prices. It will be our object to exhibit in each type, the share attributable to the element of competition or, as the case may be, of monopoly.

The popular idea of a monopoly, current alike in theory and in practical life, embraces in fact every favored market position. We have already referred to the fact that the favored portion of large aggregates of capital over against the body of laborers is frequently designated as a monopoly. Similarly, all more favored specific supply-positions are customarily designated as monopolies. Ricardo, for example, speaks of a monopoly of agricultural soil; and to-day we hear of a monopoly of desirable urban locations, and even of a general monopoly of urban land.

Both expressions are improper. Monopoly is a favored position in the market; but not all favored positions in the market are monopolies. The owners of the superior classes of soil do not realize a monopoly-gain. Their gains are realized in the conflict of competition, according to the law of the highest costs. They have neither the monopolistic power to curtail production, nor the desire to do so. Their interest impels them, rather, to as intensive an economic management as possible, in order to achieve the maximum increase of the yield. As we shall later on see, urban ground-rent is no more endowed with a monopolistic character. The price of urban rents of realty is a competitive price: if urban speculators form monopolistic rings and seek their advantage, possibly, in restricting all building-operations, this is a matter by itself. This is precisely the case, when it comes to industrial "rents," benefiting an industrial enterprise which competes with others, and thus enjoys advantages in the conditions of production. To not one of these rents does the theory of monopoly apply. The theory of specific attribution is all that is required for these, and it may be applied to the special facts of the classes of soil, urban locations and industrial conditions.

The monopoloid institutions which we shall have to examine, are of a different sort. They have in fact traits of monopoly; they confer monopolistic power. But at the same time they are subject, in other directions, to the pressure of competition or are otherwise restricted. They are, as we have said, intermediate forms, lying midway between monopoly and competition. Neither the theory of pure monopoly nor the theory of pure competition, least of all the theory of attribution, will do them entire justice. As an intermediate form of this sort, we mention first the so-called imperfect monopoly, comprehending not the total, but only a considerable portion of supply and demand. But there are also true mixtures of the elements of monopoly and competition. Frequently they take rise in simple external coincidence. For example, a kartel may produce simultaneously for the home-market, which it controls monopolistically, and for the foreign market, where it is subject to competition. A railroad may possess a monopoly for certain sections of its route, which are not served by any other road, while for other points it is under competition. Again, a factory besides monopolized, patented articles may produce others under competition. Mixtures of this sort may, as we have seen from the practice of "dumping," have great practical and even theoretical importance, but it will be best to distinguish them from the monopoloid institutions proper. In the case of the latter, monopoly and competition do not simply coincide externally, but one and the same institution unites both forms intrinsically. Thus a new problem arises for theory, a problem for which no solution can be offered by the theory of the pure forms.

Among monopoloid forms are to be mentioned all the public monopolies which are carried on by the state and the municipal corporations. State monopolies as well as tax-monopolies are monopoloid. The state, it is true, exercises in the tax-monopoly the highest monopoly power, in order to secure the highest monopoly-gain; the prices which the state dictates, are monopoly-prices. But the power here exerted is not to be used oppressively; it is subjected to the considerations of just taxation, not to mention the fact that it is exercised for the benefit of public revenue. In the administrative monopoly, the interest of administration is supreme. Where the state reserves the monopoly for certain administrative institutions, it does so with the intention to combine the full production-monopoly with the market-monopoly, in order to carry out the principle of the single-unit management, which permits the greatest social achievement with the smallest outlay. But the state does not set up monopoly-prices; it does not seek monopoly-gains. The state would simply cover costs, and may possibly exact not even this; the state may take something less than costs, in the interest of the administration, if such proceeding should seem required. We find, in the postal service, this type of monopoloid institution very clearly illustrated.

Among monopoloid forms are further to be mentioned the private monopolies, recognized by statute for the sake of the advantages accruing through them to the general, public interest, and which are at the same time restricted by law so as to prevent the abuse of monopoly power. There are two types of these monopolies. One is shown in the patent-right of the inventor; akin to this is the author's copyright and a few other forms. The other type appears in the private single-unit enterprise, regulated by the state. The patent-right is granted to the inventor, in order to bring his technical leadership, his talents and genius into the service of society. By ceding to him the monopolistic utilization of his innovation, the community endeavors to encourage him in introducing inventions. At the same time, however, his monopoly is of limited duration, in order that (ultimately) society may succeed to the unlimited enjoyment of the invention. His invention is the successful outgrowth of a rivalry with others who were experimenting in the same direction as he. Social currents have carried him to his goal. Therefore, after a suitable period of grace, his achievement is once more thrown into the arena of free competition. The original grant is made on one condition, that the invention be put into actual use. The regulated private single-unit enterprise, as shown most plainly in the privileged bank of issue or the state-controlled private railroad, takes the place of the administration-monopoly, wherever good reasons exist for preferring private to public management. It still secures for society the advantage of single-unit operation. The type is closely akin to the administration-monopoly; provided only that, beside the general interest, the acquisitive interest of the private enterprise be protected, a proviso which, when it comes to details, may lead to all manner of straits. Let us point out, for example, the state-guarantee for private railroads and the remaining rules of the concessional right, or the state's share in the profits of private banks of issue. The development of private monopolies, recognized by the state, has surely not reached its end. New types may arise, or the old ones may be transformed. The possibility is not excluded that kartels or trusts, to-day not yet recognized legally or possibly even opposed by law, may perhaps at a future day, when their interests have been brought more nearly into keeping with the interests of society, be legally confirmed and at the same time restrictively regulated. It may then be that one or the other point of view of the two types, here described, will be transferred to these institutions also.

There are, finally, still to be mentioned those monopoloid forms which, owing to their actual power, maintain themselves, although legal recognition has been denied to them. Of these monopoloid institutions, only kartels and trusts are to be discussed in the theory of the price of products. Rings or pools exert their influence pre-eminently by the power of large capital; the large exchanges are the spheres of their activity. There, they do not always deal with products, but very frequently with securities. Even when they are interested in products, they do not influence production itself. They are exclusively monopolies of the market, and it seems best to discuss them in connection with speculation on the exchanges. Of trade unions we shall have to treat in the theory of the wages of labor. In that connection, too, the preliminary problem will have to be discussed, whether or not the coalitions are in any sense monopoloid institutions.

Kartels and trusts are the creations of large scale enterprise. The smaller and medium sized establishments are too numerous in the economic markets of the world to be combined effectively by contracts. The very large enterprises on the other hand, owing to their comparatively small numbers, enjoy, beside their other advantages, the further and very important one of being able to organize themselves by contract. At the start, organization was employed only in order to regulate mutual competition, to obviate the injuries of over-competition; only subsequently has there been organization for the purpose of effecting monopoly-earnings. The advantages of organization are so great that the combinations can dispense with the recognition of governments, so long as they are firmly enough knit together by the interest of their members. The state, should it wish to oppose them, would even have to employ drastic powers in order to do so effectively. The large-scale enterprises are all the more in need of organization, inasmuch as the competitive conflict is a greater menace to them than to the small and medium-sized enterprises. The large number of these latter types has, in the mutual conflict of competition, no further end to serve but to keep the struggle alive. Only a small number of conspicuously active, efficient business-men possess the impulse to expand. Here, however, their restricted means set a limit to their ambitions, and their development can never endanger the existence of the host of others. Should a single one of a thousand plants double or treble its business, the rest of them will scarcely be appreciably affected in their output. On the other hand, should one of a hundred or of ten industries double or treble its business, the effect for all the others will be, not merely noticeable but injurious and possibly disastrous. No sooner has an industry of large dimensions abundant capital at its disposal, than it finds itself in a position still further to achieve its aims by the conflict of competition. Possibly it may endeavor entirely to oust its competitors and to seize their plants. The conflict of competition is an aggressive one. Should the fear once arise among these enterprises that war is to be waged in this fashion, they will, one and all, immediately have to come to the attack. A general, fierce conflict will flare up, from which there will be no escape but the destruction of the weakest by the strongest or else a universal understanding and contractual compromise. Events of this sort have given rise to kartels and trusts and determined their nature, oscillating between competitive conflict and monopolistic unification.

Of the two monopolistic institutions which we shall now have to discuss, the kartel is the less fully developed. So long as its ends remain confined simply to the prevention of over-competition and to the protection of the cost-price, there is here in fact no monopoloid institution to be described. A combine, thus restricted, is a mere form by which to make sure of the regulation of competition. But when once the power of the kartel in preventing the underselling of the sound competitive price has been experienced, it is easy to take the next step and attempt to sell above it. The fully developed combine works out this principle, so as to create an effective market-monopoly that is complete in every respect. All the business concerns of the market offering the same product, or at least by far the greater number of such enterprises, are induced to join in a common method of market procedure. The kartel thus is enabled to determine the price like a monopolist. On the other hand, even the fully developed combine does not expect to create a production-monopoly; it restrains its members in the independent management of their industries just in so far as is necessary to ensure the effect of the market-monopoly, by agreeing upon the quantities which each establishment is to be allowed to produce. Possibly in connection with this agreement, there will be a division of productive labor, calculated to reduce costs of production. In the main, however, each associate is left to the independent conduct of his affairs. In this way, a considerable latitude is left open to the functioning of competition. Here we again find an explanation of the fact that the kartel is never agreed upon, except for relatively short periods of time. The owners of works which are capable of higher development, hope to secure a more favorable quota on the renewal of the agreement; or they may possibly retire altogether from the deal, unless more favorable concessions are made to them. Under some circumstances the germ of competition, which still lies within the kartel, may again be aroused to full strength. The dissolution of the combine may follow. In such a period of active, technical and organizing progress and of the increase of capital as the present, the impulse of competition will remain active even outside of the kartell. The latter will never be able to prevent the formation of new enterprises sufficiently strong to carry on the conflict of competition, at least up to the time when they will have forced an entrance into the combine on favorable terms. In these periods of great capitalistic-technical advance, also the effect of competition on the personal selection of the leaders remains active in the sphere, narrow though it be, whence the large enterprises of capitalistic origin derive their leaders. In periods, such as these, the combine must be looked upon as a monopoloid institution, where competition asserts itself with its most effective forces by the side of the monopoly. During periods of the quiescence of technical art, of organization and of augmentation of capital, the combine may contribute its share in the deadening of the last remnants of every incentive to progress. Just as the corporate monopoly, during the period of the decadence of the mechanical trades, became odiously apparent so the kartell, during similar periods, may strive exclusively to use or abuse its monopoly of the market, while not a trace remains of the socially beneficial use, which was to have been expected of the measure when independence of management was accorded to its members.

The trust is, in itself, much more firmly unified than the combine. The trust develops under economic conditions when the tendency of production to large scale operation is especially effective, and when the unification of large enterprises is accompanied by such advantages of production, that independent management no longer remains lucrative. Without depriving its members altogether of their legal independence, it unites their enterprises, actually, into a single-unit-enterprise. The management of all the united plants is directed by one central supervising body; and the lay-out of the works, also, is unitarily arranged; the most effective, broadly designed, technical methods are universally employed; works, producing at too great disadvantage, are closed. The desire for unification goes so far as to attempt to unite all stages of the production-process from the obtaining of raw materials to the distribution to consumers, in all cases where returns may be increased by such combination. The steel-trust will find its advantage in making sure of the mines of ore and coal; the oil trust will cut out intermediaries, in order to increase profits, to sell directly to retailers and to consumers. Railroads and steamship-companies will be drawn in, so as to make sure of the traffic-lines. In this concentration of forces the mammoth-bank especially must not be missed. The latter turns in the money-funds by which plants and management are to be expanded; by which competitors, predecessors and successors are to be bought out or overwhelmed in the conflict of competition; and thru which the structure of the giant-enterprise is crowned by security issues, realizing the increased gains in their cash-value. Enterprises of this sort may be referred to as total-enterprises; [1] they take advantage of all opportunities of gain, which offer in any direction whatever Their last aim must be to expand until all the essential means of the production-process are securely under their control, as regards quantities required, as well as prices to be paid. At the height of its power, it would seem, the trust would tolerate neither predecessors nor successors in the production-process, receiving other than cost-prices for their pains; all specific gains would have to be reserved to the trust exclusively; and wherever danger might exist of predecessors or successors organizing monopolistically on their part, the trust itself would have to gain possession of the means of the production-process. The steel-trust, itself owner of its ore- and coal-mines, is in this way more effectively protected, than it would be by a demand-monopoly, because the latter could always be met by a supply-monopoly of the ore- and coal-mines. The advantage, accruing to the trust from its total-enterprise, is so great that under some circumstances, it may renounce the monopolization of production and market. While a steel kartel would have to combine all or nearly all steel-works, in order to obtain power by a market-monopoly, a steel-trust may well leave a very large number of works outside its combination, and still realize its profit. A trust is enabled by its unitary organization to employ the most effective production-methods and to work thruout at the least outlay of costs. At a price, which barely covers the costs of competing enterprises, it earns an industrial rent, leaving a profit which could never be exceeded by an effective monopoly. A trust of this sort does not enforce monopoly-prices; neither does it require them; the competitive price, determined according to the law of highest costs, is favorable enough for the trust. A trust of this sort will exert extreme pressure on competing enterprises; by the magnitude of its supply and the lowness of its costs, it will crush the competitors who work under the most unfavorable conditions, but who had hitherto still been admitted in their supply. The trust cannot set the price quite so high, as it might have done monopolistically, even though the price is determined by the law of highest costs. None the less, the market-price will still leave a considerable surplus over and above trust costs. In a case of this sort, there is no monopoly, possibly not even a monopoloid institution, unless we should wish to suggest by the term the enormous dimensions of trust-industries, which far exceed the conditions of ordinary competition, and in their further development lead quite possibly to a monopoly. Certain partial markets, however, it must be remembered, may be controlled by a trust of this sort, monopolistically or monopoloidically. Once a trust has reached

[1] Trans. note: "Gesamtunternehmungen"—The ordinary English term is vertical trust or combination.

such an extent that, like a kartel, it embraces the great majority, or even all, of the plants, it has become a distinctly monopoloid institution of the highest power, or, in fact, a true monopoly. To judge it properly and estimate its effect, we shall have to inquire, how nearly it approaches the characteristics of the single-unit enterprise, in its completeness. A trust which despite the unitary organization of its productive service, has not yet become a full single-unit-enterprise, operates like an enlarged kartel; it operates like it, in the first place, by the control of the market. But it increases its gains by the advantages of production, which it offers. At the same time, the trust is subject, like the kartel, to the intermittent influences of the competition, and as to the duration of its existence dependent on conditions of trade. The individual enterprise of which the trust is composed, are qualified by the remnants of legal independence which they have retained, to re-assume their independence in fact, if the interest of competition should be revived. A trust, conducting a true single-unit enterprise, on the other hand, unites to the monopoly of the market a production-monopoly; and governmental rules would be required to subdue its power and reduce it to the lower level of a monopoloid institution.

How far the development of trusts has progressed towards the single-unit enterprise, must remain matter of empirical enquiry; by the instruments of theoretical enquiry, the problem cannot be approached. From facts which have become familiar to popular experience and hence do not call for specific investigation, it can only be concluded that in the United States, where the trusts originated, the development rests on peculiar conditions which are not relevant for European states and which in course of time may not be relevant in the United States either. The uninterrupted influx of immigration creates a vast increase of the demand, for the satisfaction of which, enormous new plants have constantly to be built. These establishments, are from the very beginning, planned for the most effective technical utilization. Without suffering the impediments of antiquated plants, the entrepreneurs are, moreover, in the fortunate position of drawing on industrial, virgin treasures of the soil, and to exploit any number of productive conditions which have not yet been specifically prejudged as to their merits; the extraordinary specific enhancements of value offered within the scope of these establishments, planned as they are for maximum requirements, fall into the laps of the bold organizers of the trust. It may well be doubted, whether the great units of organization, which are the order of the day, will permanently maintain themselves, after once industry will have been compelled to utilize to better advantage the scattered local values, and to look more carefully after the minor advantages in individual cases. In our day, when the trusts are still in the process of growth and development, the force of their leaders is greatly to their advantage; but, even here, a doubt may be permitted, whether later on other conditions may not develop. Today at any rate, it must be insisted on that the effect of the personal selection of leaders, usually ascribed to competition, is most strikingly illustrated by the trusts. The trusts are creations of men of extraordinary abilities in practical business pursuits, men who possess the insights, the knowledge, the energies, required to plan and organize the giant enterprises of modern commerce and industry. The rise of these great leaders is, to be sure, coincident with the downfall of others, more numerous perhaps, for the ranks of independent entrepreneurs are greatly cut down by the trusts. We must, however, not ignore the fact that the organizers, heading these great enterprises, are compelled to surround themselves, for their achievements, with a staff of collaborators, who are required for the enormous tasks of keeping things going. It must, furthermore not be overlooked especially, that among the most essential gifts of leaders is the one of properly estimating the abilities of fellow-workers. The selection of subordinates, by the organizers and general managers of these great industrial enterprises, is more effective than any that could be brought about by other means.

§ 43. Personal (Subjective) Value-in-Exchange

Price levels—Value-in-exchange and value-in-use—Personal exchange—Value of money—Value of yield in exchange—Acquisition value—Exchange value and the law of exchange.

The formation of price relates all prices which exist in the market at any one time. In the widest sense of the term they may be referred to as related prices. The relationship is established through demand and supply. In the case of supply the prices of all products and all productive means, both material and personal, are harmonized by the unity of production. The individual productive processes are related through all orders by the connections through the productive stems. In the case of cost products the relationship is clearly expressed in the law of cost. According to the latter, the prices of products are established as combinations of their productive elements or vice versa. But also the prices of specific products and specific productive means are firmly knit together by the law of specific attribution as regards all other prices. From the side of the demand, the relationship is established by the fact that every household is itself a unit, and that all households enter into competition in the market and are subject to the law of the single price. In the estimates of every income group, the quantities and prices of different articles are appraised against each other. These estimates of the groups result in a stratification of prices which are mutually conditioning. Thus every new price is fitted into the framework of old prices both on the part of the supply and the demand.

The sum of all prices prevailing in the market is shown in the general price level. No single individual has the practical opportunity of inspecting the whole of the general condition of prices. Only a narrow section of the general situation falls under the personal observation of an individual in the course of his acquisitive activity or of his consumption. The judgment, "this is cheap, this is dear," is founded primarily on the personal experience of the individual. He compares present prices with other prices which he has known elsewhere or at other times. This judgment does not acquire general significance until it is concurred in by all social groups or the greater number of these.

A new evaluation is suggested by this appraisal of the level of prices. It is one which has not yet occupied our attention in the theory of the simple economy. It is the value which is referred to economically as value-in-exchange. Exchange value is an institution arising out of economic exchange; in it we find the value which is attributed to objects because of the exchange relations which they bear to the economic process. Two forms of value-in-exchange are to be distinguished; they are usually called subjective and objective exchange-value. We will do well to adopt neither of these terms. They merely obscure the true state of affairs. We shall speak of the first as personal exchange-value, that which arises in the private economy; and of the second as social economic exchange-value.

Let us first examine the former. It is the fundamental one. The latter is deduced from it.

Personal exchange-value is itself deduced from the utility-value of the simple economy. It is an indirect utility-value derived from the fact that in exchange one object is received or surrendered for another, the utility of which is then set up as the measure of value. Thus, for example, goods whose utility the vendor himself cannot enjoy have a mediate utility-value through those goods which he expects to procure through their agency in exchange. Utility-value may be distinguished from exchange-value; the former is experienced without reference to exchange and is spoken of as value in use. All utility-value of the simple economy is use-value. It is customary, however, to reserve this term for consumption goods which are evaluated directly by their individual utility; it is not usually employed for the indirect forms of utility-value in the simple economy, for yield-value or cost-value.

The law of personal exchange-value may best be explained by the illustration of money. Everybody appraises money according to its value-in-exchange—in so far, at any rate, as the intention is to employ it as money, without regard to the qualities of the metal of which it may be composed and which may be made available for other uses by melting the coins. In order to determine the personal exchange-value of money a man resorts to the general price level which obtains in the market of which he has knowledge. On the basis of this level the plan of domestic economy is organized in such a way as to expand the margin of expenditures as far as his available money allows. The use-values of those goods which constitute the marginal expenditures of an individual economy, give to that particular economy a measure of the personal exchange value of money. More briefly, the margin of use of the household determines the personal value-in-exchange of the unit of money. The total needs to be provided for by the individual household and its total supply of money find expression in the marginal utility of the household. This stock of money is, as a rule, determined by the owner's income, at least in so far as no part of it is reserved for other than domestic use. In exceptional cases, of course, the fund is also enlarged by resort to credit or even by an encroachment upon permanent possessions. Finally, certain needs may be satisfied directly by natural utilization of property, as is the case with the owner of a dwelling house which he occupies as a residence.

In the personal exchange value of money, the law of marginal utility is extensively employed. While the marginal utility of a stock of wares is found upon the scale of the special need which the particular goods satisfy, the marginal utility of money is ascertained from the sum total of the needs to be provided for in the economy. When these needs increase, the personal appraisal of money according to the law of needs is also increased and the marginal zone of permissible expenditures is narrowed. When the income is increased, then, according to the law of supply, the personal value of money is lowered. The higher the income, the more slowly the value of money will be lowered as the income increases. In a household advancing from the first to the second thousand of income, from the level of a minimum of existence to succeeding levels, the personal value of money drops amazingly; the scales of basic needs pass with comparative rapidity from the point of highest tension to that of relaxation. A brief inspection of the management of the household in this case at once shows the observer the particular plane on which it stands. From the ninth to the tenth thousand, the decrease of the money-value, although perceptible, is already less marked. The investigator must be keen in order to discern the income level. From the forty-ninth to the fiftieth, or from the ninety-ninth to the hundredth thousand the decrease of money value becomes less and less noticeable; the marginal zones become broader and broader, and it becomes increasingly difficult for the observer to distinguish grades of satisfied desires.

The personal exchange-value of money is the basis for the personal exchange value that is attached to natural values in the single economy. The producer or the laborer appraises his performance according to the monetary return or wage which he expects, and these, in turn, according to the marginal value which he sets on the unit of money. Consumers also, in certain cases, are in a position where the value of their goods is an exchange value. The most striking example is the case of so-called consumer's rent where the wealthier purchaser buys commodities in the market at a price determined by the poorer marginal purchaser. If a buyer of this sort loses the commodities purchased, he doesn't lose the anticipated utility; his loss is confined to the costs of acquisition, the purchase price, which he must expend again. Consequently he does not evaluate the object by the value-in-use which is determined by its particular individual utility but by its acquisition- or exchange-value which is determined by the costs of acquisition. A similar condition exists in all cases where commodities falling in the narrower zone of expenditure can be replaced by curtailing marginal outlays. The value here estimated by the owner is simplified according to the law of costs and balances with the amount of the pecuniary sacrifice needed for reacquisition.

The exchange-yield-value is a peculiar mixed form of value. It is the value of the yield ascertained by capitalizing the pecuniary return realized by the sale of the products of a factory, the crops of land or the rent of a dwelling. All these are here appraised in anticipation of their sale, according to their value-in-exchange. The intention is not, however, to sell the factory, the land or the dwelling. They are therefore valued, as in the economy of natural exchange, on the basis of the capitalization of their yields. The exchange-yield-value is one of the bases for the computation of the exchange-value of the factory, land or dwelling in case it is desirable to dispose of them; but the two values are likely to be exceedingly disparate.

The nature of personal exchange-value is like that of value-in-use from which it is deduced. Both are true utility-values and subject to the law of marginal utility. At all times it is a matter of circumstance which of the two forms governs in the individual case. Money performing its unique function only in exchange, is always appraised according to its exchange value. Natural values within the inner sphere of the economy in which they are to perform their service are always appraised according to value-in-use, except in those cases of which we have just spoken where acquisition-value is used. These goods are likewise appraised according to value-in-use whenever they are purchased in the market for use in the household. As soon as conditions change so that it is desirable for the housekeeper to sell these natural values, value-in-use ceases to apply and value-in-exchange controls. Thus, for example, an impoverished nobleman will be compelled to dispose of precious family portraits at their value-in-exchange which he has hitherto been in a position to ignore. The producer appraises products intended for sale at their value-in-exchange. Only where it is his practice to retain part of the products for use in his own household will he have to compare value-in-use and value-in-exchange in order to determine accurately the margin of sale and natural use. The peasant-farmer, for example, should never sell any part of his crops which yields a greater utility when it is consumed at home than could be obtained by using its sales-price for the acquisition of other values.

During the period of natural economy, value-in-use was the current economic value in most cases; only an insignificant part of the products was prepared with a view to realizing exchange-values. However, the development, which led to production with division of labor under the ægis of monetary exchange, has gradually received its impetus from the fact that in an ever increasing number of households and for a growing quantity and variety of products value-in-exchange manifested itself as the true economic value. All this great economic change proceeded under conditions where the personal exchange-value remained supreme. Each of the thousands and millions of participating individual economies looked at all times to value-in-exchange to ascertain to what extent it had better adapt itself to the body of the economy with its division of labor. The entire structure of social economic production may be traced back to the individual actions induced by this value-in-exchange. In all production and other acquisitional pursuits, which are definitely accommodated to monetary exchange, value-in-use has become practically obsolete; incomes and expenditures are computed exclusively in exchange-value.

Personal value-in-exchange is deduced from prices. At the same time it reacts on prices and exchange generally. It is an indispensable adjunct of the market. Were value-in-use the only instrument in exchange available for a comparison of values, a monetary economy would scarcely be possible. Money would possess no value at all aside from its material value which is of little importance in exchange. It would simply be an order to hand out one or more of the thousands of imaginable things which men, for purposes of acquisition or domestic use, have to obtain from the market. But no one of these choices would stand out prominently in men's interest; an endless effort would be required to keep them all in mind at all times and not to succumb to the constantly recurring temptation to seize the first that might offer, not as the result of intelligent choice but simply because it was ready to hand.

Money, as we all know it, is more than such a mere order for the future delivery of values. It is saturated with exchangeable value and becomes, therefore, itself a living value. Indeed one might be tempted to say that it is a concentration of values and reflects at once all the values of the market for whose acquisition it offers the means. We do not merely feel that money has value; we feel even the numerical magnitude of its value. A sum of 10 Marks, 100 Crowns, 1000 Francs, is a definite symbol of economic power to the German, Austrian or Frenchman. When the entrepreneur arranges his orders or the housewife plans her purchases, the value of the money which they are about to expend is a constant monitor which advises prudence and a consideration of the limits which are dictated by economic principles under existing conditions.

Every economic value is an appraisal of needs still to be experienced. This anticipation of needs which are to arise combines the ideas of the means and ends to be served. The latter are kept in view during the entire time which separates procuring the means from the attainment of the ends. Exchange-value is the form which involves the longest period. It still maintains the interest of an individual economy in all its widely scattered relations with an economic whole, even where value-in-use does not. Value-in-exchange anticipates the increment in use value for the sake of which the exchange is undertaken. It associates the expected value with the money income which is available for the household; with the wares from the sale of which this income is to be derived; and also with the sums of money from the gross produce, which are again used for acquisition in order to finish new wares and obtain new prospects of gross yield and net income.

When the gain in value-in-use is finally obtained, for the sake of which exchange has been resorted to, it no longer comes as an unexpected increment. A man sees in it the realization of the antecedent value-in-exchange. He would be disappointed and would consider himself a loser if the exchange-value did not result in an accretion in value-in-use. The formula for the law of natural exchange with whose deduction we opened our investigation of the institution of economic exchange therefore requires further explanation along this line. So also does our exposition of the fundamental law of the formation of prices. In order to arrive at a radical theoretical explanation we deduced this law by assuming an economic condition without prices. As a matter of fact, however, prices are always made by starting with those already established. The formation of prices thus is always aided by appraisals of exchange-values which are founded upon previous market experience. In a quiet market, producers refuse every sale whose proceeds fail to bring the accustomed personal exchange-value of the wares, and consumers make no acquisitions whose use-value is not equivalent to the customary exchange-value of the amount involved in the price. In such a market, the exchange-value invariably determines the price, or, conversely, price is a realization of exchange-value. Price-formation by custom, therefore, is in truth the formation of prices by exchange-value. In a disturbed market where prices have to be formed anew the appraisal of exchange-value as indicated by the old prices also serves; it confines the functions of the market to the determination of the changes which are necessary in existing appraisals.

§ 44. Economic (Objective) Value-in-Exchange

What is the so-called objective or social economic value-in-exchange? We shall postpone answering this question as regards the extraordinarily complicated case of money until we enter upon the continuous exposition of the value relations of money; as regards wares and other natural values our answer can be couched in few words.

When the market price for certain wares is 100, all sellers without exception set the exchange value at 100, for they will all agree that the anticipated price measures the exchange-value. So far there is nothing personal about their appraisal. The personal characteristic is first introduced when each vendor appraises the price against the background of his particular circumstances. This statement throws light upon the facts which create a social economic exchange-value. The latter, by the universal confirmation of all parties interested, is the first step in their appraisal of exchange value. It precedes the personal evaluation of money. This first step is not a mere prediction concerning the price; it is a true appraisal. When we say that certain wares have an exchange-value of 100, we do not merely state its market price; we wish to indicate the position which it occupies in the market by virtue of the fact that its price is 100.

All the effects which originate in the simple economy from utility-value take their rise in the social economic process from the exchange-value which is here discussed. The costs which may be incurred in production are controlled by it. It forms the foundation of the attribution of yields to the actively employed productive agents. Amounts of income are stated in this value. It is subject to discount and capitalization. It fills the accounts of production and acquisition from beginning to end. It may properly be spoken of as social economic exchange value, as the general social value, for it is the basis of the social economic process. All individuals taking part in the latter make exclusive use of this price in all matters related to this process.

In daily intercourse economic exchange value has completely overshadowed both personal exchange-value and utility-value. It is this to which men refer when they speak of value pure and simple. When one asks what certain goods are worth, he expects and is given the figure for their market value. It is easy to understand that this value, uniformly the same for all persons interested, should obscure in common parlance all personal valuations. There is a social accord in regard to this value and its numerical expression which is clear and unequivocal. Compared with it, all other expressions of value are matters of sentiment, having standards which are personally experienced but are not readily susceptible to accurate interpretation.

Theory at first received its concept of value, like all of its fundamental ideas, from the interpretation and speech of daily intercourse. As in the other cases, so here the meaning of the term was taken as that of its most popular use. No attempt was made to enter into the more deeply hidden motives which condition personal action but are only suggested in the popular phrase. In this way theory obtained its contrasting concepts of "objective" and "subjective" exchange-value.

To tell the truth, there is no "objective" exchange-value. In one sense possibly the term may be justified: in other connections also we speak of that which is subjective, but at the same time common to many, as objective, in contrast to that of which the single individual is the subject. But not even in this sense is the term wholly justified, for objective exchange-value is not quite universal. It never holds for those persons who do not wish to take part in the exchange because the price, as it stands, is either too high or too low for their personal valuation. "Objective" exchange-value is the uniform result of the valuation of all those who take part in the exchange at the indicated price. These are the parties who in the case under consideration start the economic process.

The classical school gave no further attention to the "subjective," the personal exchange-value. It was assumed that the effects of this value were exhausted within the private economies and that these did not concern the doctrine of the social economy. Only the objective exchange-value was considered worthy of scientific investigation. Only to this form was economic importance attributed. Thus we find here one of the great truths of which but half the significance was grasped by the classical school—a result which barred the progress of these men toward the full truth. The effect of "objective" exchange-value is truly economic, but its roots are bedded in the subjective estimates of individuals, grouped to determine the result. The individualistic school reduced everything in the social economy to individual effort and fully recognized the concert of individual action in economic endeavor; yet it failed to realize one truth, that economic action is the confluence of individual valuations. This is the fundamental reason that the classical doctrine of value and of price could never finally solve its problem. The theory of value and of price must penetrate to the personal sources in order to complete its task.

§ 45. The Conclusions of the General Theory of Price

Price-margin and price-law—The law of price and the law of value.

Before we proceed, it may be well to summarize the results of our investigations of the formation of price which lead in many directions.

The process of the formation of prices is much more diverse than that of the appraisal of values in the model simple economy, because of the introduction of many new factors. In the former case money is used. Many legally independent individuals participate. These persons exercise varying degrees of power which are conditioned by the stratification of income, social class and market position. But whatever new elements we have had to introduce into our investigation have not brought with them any new forces. Even the new element, money, is merely an instrument to effect the exchange movement of natural values. When the social resultants of prices are analyzed into their component parts we arrive at the personal valuations of the interested parties. Each such valuation obeys the law of the simple economy. The diversity of power is evidenced only in the strength with which this personal interest may be displayed. If we neglect for the present truly usurious price, the personal valuations of the parties to the supply and the demand erect impassable barriers to the formation of prices above and below certain limits. Precisely as in the case of the simple economy, all objective facts which influence price, quantities as well as costs, must act through the agency of these personal valuations in order that the transaction have true significance, order and standard.

The share of each individual in the formation of the resultant prices is often infinitesimal and might almost be eliminated. But is this exceptional where average human beings coöperate in performing social functions? At all times the individual is lost in the multitude although the latter actually is effective only through the individuals of which it is composed. The individual feels bound by the objective facts, cost or prevailing prices; he helps in binding the ties and thus contributes in drawing the knots more tightly.

In the beginning of economic intercourse, the valuations of the exchanging parties leave a broad margin for the formation of price. The law of value establishes firm limits for prices; but price as yet has no well established law of its own. A rigid law of price has two prerequisites: the crystallization of a matured trade and a series of demands that are at least sufficiently homogeneous so that the decisive marginal bid for any particular quantity may be definitely ascertained, at least in the zone of marginal expenditures. However, it should be remembered that this law holds good only under a well regulated competition which assigns to everyone his proper position. A disjointed economic market is firmly adjusted only when the social interest of the community is established and forces all individuals, irrespective of direct competitive compulsion, to reach decisions which conform to all the existing social conditions.

The law of price is derived from the law of value of the simple economy. The important feature of each of these laws is not identical with that of the other. In the simple economy, the marginal utility is socially ascertained and determines value; whenever the economy is regulated by this value, the sum of the partial utilities thus secured must be the greatest possible. But price is also an outgrowth of power. On the part of the demand, because of the greater financial strength of the wealthy the decisive price is subject to the law of stratification and takes its standard from the stratified marginal utility. On the side of the supply, financial power as well as personal efficiency decides the competitive conflict. Victory in this contest, therefore, does not merely indicate a social selection of the fittest.

The cost-price of competition is not yet the common price. It does not correspond to the lowest social costs that might be realized, because it does not correspond to the highest attainable social yield, nor to the greatest massing of common force. Under modern conditions in the field of large-scale industry, competitive conflict leads to unifying mergers. In all fields of large enterprise today, there are institutions which are usually called monopolistic. They should, however, more properly be called monopoloid, because the elements of monopoly which one finds in them are interspersed with those of competition. The enormous productive forces of such enterprises depress the cost factors of price and thus far inure to the social benefit. But the accompanying excess of power and the compelling force of capital in "big business" relieve the men in power from the necessity of rigid conformity of price to costs. It enables them to obtain a resultant price which decreases the general utility and yields excessive profits to them personally.

A new form of value, value-in-exchange, issues from prices and establishes the standard for the economy of private enterprise. As personal exchange-value it gauges the movements which connect individual private economies with the social economy. It thus supplements value-in-use, which harmonizes the inner affairs of the individual economy. As economic exchange-value it measures the movement of the social economic process. In both forms exchange value carries out the law of price. Its effect, therefore, like that of price should lie between utility and power.

§ 46. Credit

The individual credit-transactions—The advantage of exchange for the creditor and debtor—The nature of credit—The distinction between property and assets.

For the doctrine of credit and money, the following are still to be mentioned: Knies, *Geld und Kredit*, 2nd ed. 1885; Wagner, art. *Kredit und Bankwesen*, Schönberg; and, *Theor. Socialökonomik*, II, 1909; Jevons, *Mechanism of Exchange*, 13th ed. 1902; Walras, *Théorie de la Monnaie*, 1886; Hertzka, *Wesen des Geldes*, 1887; Menger, art. *Geld*, Hdw. d. Stw.; Wicksel, *Geldzins und Güterpreise*, 1898; and, *Vorlesungen über Nationalökonomie*, vol. II, 1922; Wieser, *Der Geldwert und seine geschichtlichen Veränderungen*, Z. f. V., XIII; and, *Der Geldwert und seine Veränderungen*, Schr. d. V. f. S., vol. 132; Laughlin, *Principles of Money*, 1903; Walsh, *The Fundamental Problem in Monetary Science*, 1903; Helfferich, *Geld*, 6th ed. 1923; Komorzynski, *Die nat. ök. Lehre vom Kredit*, 1903; *Simmel, Philosophie des Geldes*, 3rd ed. 1920; Knapp, *Staatliche Theorie des Geldes*, 3rd ed. 1921; Spiethoff, *Quantitätstheorie*, 1905; and, *Lehre vom Kapital*, e. d. VI; Altmann, *Zur deutschen Geldlehre*, E. d. VI; Fisher, *Rate of Interest*, 1907; Fisher-Brown, *Purchasing Power of Money*, 3rd ed. 1913 (German by Ida Stecker, 2nd ed. 1922); Bendixon, *Wesen des Geldes*, 2nd ed. 1918; and, *Geld und Kapital*, 3rd ed. 1922; Mises, *Theorie des Geldes und der Umlaufsmittel*, 1912; Hildebrand, *Wesen des Geldes*, 1914; Anderson, *The Value of Money*, 1917; Engliš, *Die wirtschl. Theorie des Geldes*, Archiv, vol. 47; Liefmann, *Geld und Gold*, 1916; Guyot-Raffalovich, *Inflation et Déflation*, 1921; Doring, *Die Geldtheorien seit Knapp*, 1922; Moll, *Logik des Geldes*, 2nd ed. 1922; Heyn, *Probleme des Geldwesens, zum Inflationsproblem*, Weltwirtschl, Archiv, 1917; also, *Ueber Geldschöpfung und Inflation*, 1921; Soda, *Geld und Wert*, 1909; K. Elster, *Die Seele des Geldes*, 1920; and, *Zur Analyse des Geldproblems*, Jahrbuch f. N., vol. 54; Kaulla, *Die Grundlagen des Geldwertes*, 1920; Stephinger, *Wert und Geld*, 1918; Diehl, *Fragen des Geldwesens*, 2nd ed. 1921; Schlesinger, *Theorie der Geld-und Kreditwirtschaft*, 1914; Lexis, art. *Papiergeld*, Hdw. d. Stw.; Altmann, art. *Quantitätstheorie*, Hdw. d. Stw.; Palyl, *Die Streit um die staatl. Theorie des Geldes*, 1922; Schumpeter, *Das Sozialproduct und die Rechenpfennige*, Archiv, vol. 44; Cassel, *Das Geldproblem der Welt*, vol. I, 1921, vol. II, 1922; Keynes, *Traktat der Währungspolitik*, 1924; Hahn, *Volkwirtschl. Theorie des Bankkredites*, 1920; Bortkiewicz, *Das Wesen, die Grenzen und die Wirkungen des Bankkredites*, Weltwirtschl. Archiv, vol. XVII; Beckerath, *Kapitalmarkt und Geldmarkt*, 1916; Hilferding, *Das Finanzkapital*, Marxstudien, vol. III, 2nd ed. 1920; Fisher, *Senses of "Capital,"* Economic Journal, vol. VII; Marshall, *Money, Credit and Commerce*, 1923; Hawtrey, *Currency and Credit*, 2nd ed. 1923.

Money and credit, as the significant elements of the exchange-economy, are frequently associated with each other in daily speech. It is true enough that even in the natural economy in transactions between neighbors and even in wider circles business is occasionally transacted on a credit basis. However, it is not until money capital is created in the monetary economy and forms an easily transferable instrument, that the credit economy develops. The development is within the money economy; credit transactions are an institution of exchange.

The fundamental credit transaction is the loan. From this have radiated a series of kindred transactions, borrowing, lending, irregular [1] deposits, annuity purchases and others which we need not discuss here. The receiver of the sum lent incurs the obligations of a debtor. Usually he is bound to repay the principal after a definite time and in all cases he must pay interest.—The loan without interest cannot be discussed here.—This interest is the price paid for the loan of the principal. The sum of money thus received the borrower treats as his own. Thus he gains control of a corresponding portion of the money

[1] irreguläre Depositum.

economy. At the same time, however, the sum lent remains part of the assets of the creditor. Both before and after the loan he owns its equivalent value.

In an economy without credit, an owner's property and assets coincide almost completely. He may put down all his possessions at their full value as his wealth; if we neglect the unimportant exception which would have to be made in the case of easements and obsolete services for the period of grace, he must pay the price agreed upon. As a rule he will at this time have completed the economic process which started with the purchase of natural values.

There remains another important case of composite credit transaction: the assignment of a demand or, as the case may be, the discount of commercial paper. The assignee pays out a sum of money which becomes the property of another. In return he requires a right of demand. In these respects he is in the position of a creditor who makes a loan. The assignor or endorser of a bill who receives the amount of money as his property is not a debtor. At least he does not incur an initial liability, although he does guarantee the paper. The principal debtor is to be found in a third person who is not a party to the contract at all but is already obligated. The advantage to the assignor lies in the fact that he receives payment of his demand against the third party before it is due and may therefore renew his economic activity at an earlier date than would otherwise be possible.

A credit transaction is always an exchange and obeys the same law as the surrender of natural values for money. The relationship is less obvious in the case of the composite credit transactions; it is perfectly apparent in the case of the simple type of the loan. Supply and demand are contrasted in the loan market just as they are in the market dealing in natural values. The supply seeks and the demand offers a money price for a certain performance. It is a matter of indifference to the theoretical interpretation that the performance does not consist of natural values.

There are certain analogies between this performance and that of the lessor who surrenders to the lessee the use of an estate. However, we must not overlook the fact that the debtor cannot "use" the money as such throughout the period of the contract. In order that it give him any economic service at all, he must pay it out. Furthermore it is not accurate to say that the creditor surrenders to the debtor the "disposition" of the sum loaned. This expression is open to misinterpretation: the performance of the creditor is not confined to the surrender of money to be used on only one occasion. He is bound by the terms of the contract over the full period of the loan. The debtor, by receiving the initial right of disposition, is enabled for the entire period to continue an economic process which, in the absence of the loan, he could not have begun or continued. In the case of commercial credits this process is one of acquisition. The merchant turns the money into wares and these again into money; the manufacturer or primary producer executes not only the market transfers demanded by his business but also transformations thru natural production in many complementary combinations. The debtor who resorts to a consumption loan is enabled to maintain his domestic plant which may be necessary to his own life, that of his family or their social position.

The more accurate theoretical interpretation of the advantage in value obtained from loans by commercial or domestic borrowers we shall have to reserve for the theory of interest on capital. For the present it is clear that debtors may reasonably anticipate an exchange advantage from loans. This accomplishes our immediate purpose. Creditors who wish to secure such a benefit by lending money at a specified rate of interest rather than by using it themselves in the economic process, may lack the ability to engage in business as independent entrepreneurs; they may have neither the desire nor inducement to do so. Again, they may be entrepreneurs who do not wish to enlarge their plants by further investment but who desire even less to consume their savings in the household. Therefore on the part of both demand and supply there are sound premises for a mutually advantageous exchange, provided it is well considered on both sides and is the result of true freedom of choice. However, the necessity and inexperience of the borrower, as well as his improvidence and extravagance, may turn this exchange transaction into an instrument of serious and lasting injury. This menace is greater only in the case of the sale of labor.

It is customary to contrast credit and cash transactions. The opposition is usually defined by saying that in the case of the latter performance and counter-performance take place together, while with the former the counter-service succeeds the service by a considerable interval of time. However, this statement does not clearly explain the nature of the credit method of doing business. If the repayment of the principal is regarded as the counter-performance, the perpetual state debt which gives to the creditor no right to demand repayment cannot be regarded as a credit transaction. On the other hand if the periodic payment of interest is considered as the counter-performance, these payments appear to be unduly small returns in contrast with the initial service of paying over the principal. This temporal interpretation also does not sufficiently distinguish credit transactions from leases and contracts of labor in which the service and counter-service do not coincide in point of time.

One would therefore be forced to classify leases and contracts of labor with credit transactions; indeed the interpretation handed down in the German text book does just this. Here the objection arises that by their practical nature these contracts are separated by a wide chasm from credit transactions. The text-book itself departs from its concept of these transactions as soon as it embarks on the discussion of the policy, organization, laws and effects of credit. At no point in this discussion is there further reference to the other type of dealings. The analysis always turns exclusively upon the loan and the other leading forms of receiving and granting credit which we have discussed.

The essence of credit lies in the fact that for an adequate consideration the control of property is surrendered while its ownership is reserved. For a specified or unlimited period the creditor enables the borrower to engage in economic activity with means which remain the property of the creditor while the debtor becomes the ostensible owner. This is the creditor's performance. The counter-performance, or price, is the interest suitably adjusted to the length of the agreement. Repayment of the principal is not the counter-service, any more than is the return of leased property to the lessor. In many respects contracts of lease and credit are analogous; but, even aside from the fact that the tenant for a term of years is not the full owner, it must be remembered that the extent and importance of tenancy are less significant than those of credit.

Credit has always been of considerable economic importance. With the modern accumulations of capital, its importance has become enormous. In individual cases, the period agreed upon is often short. But because of the fact that new transactions are being constantly undertaken credit has a decisive influence upon the economic organization of property and ownership. There are many individuals who derive more or less important additions to their other income from the interest on capital which they have accumulated by saving. Side by side with these, the tremendous power of wealthy capitalists and great banks has come to the fore. Most businesses, though they differ widely in size and purpose, employ outside capital as well as their own. As they thus insure increased earnings for themselves, they likewise augment the national income. The rise of efficient entrepreneurs and the selection of financial leaders are greatly encouraged by the institution of credit. Credit is used in numerous economies to make an adjustment of the present and future. In the management of the commonwealth, this is most marked. We all know that the advantages of credit are not to be obtained without risk to the weaker economic organizations, without dangerous opportunities for the abuse of credit and without threatening ruin in the wake of panics and crises. Modern development has plunged large classes of the people into the servitude which arises out of excessive indebtedness. Not the least important cause of the burden of taxation which bears so heavily upon the weaker economies is the monstrous size of the public debt.[1]

[1] Trans. note. It must be borne in mind throughout this book that little change has been made in the text since the first edition which was written before the war. This statement would be even more strongly phrased if Wieser had been considering more particularly the post-war conditions.

§ 47. The Means of Payment by Credit

The effect of credit in increasing money: commercial paper, unsecured notes, transfers by check—Cash reserve, secondary reserves, commercial coverage—Economizing the use of money through credit: balancing the account.

Taking certain things for granted, men have become accustomed to accept money demands arising out of credit transactions as payment in lieu of money. This occurs on a large scale in highly developed commercial intercourse. Thus in addition to the fundamental significance of credit which it has attained in distinguishing ownership and wealth it has acquired a further and scarcely less important one. It has increased to an extraordinary extent the media of circulation of the social economy and in this connection has signally elaborated the methods and institutions of payment.

There are three forms of substitutes where the evidences of credit transactions pass for money: commercial paper or the bill of exchange, bank-notes and checks. The last two as credit instruments are not covered by cash to the face value. It is unnecessary for our present purpose to elaborate the details of their various established forms. It will be sufficient to describe the type so far as to explain the service which they constantly render in the financial adjustments of the community.

Commercial paper, as contrasted with other demand drafts that share with the latter the rigors of legal proceedings and the right to issue executions, is distinguished in offering an additional security in the personality of the debtors. The business man making an advance has, as a general rule, a sufficient insight into their earning capacity to estimate correctly their right to credit. The short period for which the commercial bill is generally drawn gives a fair presumption that the responsibility of the drawee is not likely to become less up to the day of maturity. But these are not the only advantages to be considered. Commercial paper is more than a bill of exchange drawn against a merchant; it grows out of a business transaction. Thus in addition to its legal guarantee it carries an internal commercial guarantee.

If, for example, a bill representing merchandise is drawn on a business man who buys a quantity of goods on credit, the time which the bill is to run is fixed so as to enable the purchaser to sell the wares and collect the proceeds. The proceeds furnish the fund out of which the bill may be paid—the commercial protection. The high value which attaches to this internal coverage which a commercial change receives by the mercantile transaction described, is shown by the fact that a good demand may be discounted as it stands on the books. This may happen even though no bill has been drawn against it so as to bring it under the rules of bills of exchange. This discounting of open-book accounts has increased greatly of late. To be sure, only a draft accompanied by all papers may be used as a means of payment. In the business circles in which a bill of exchange is issued it is regarded as so certain that a good commercial bill will be honored when due, and the due-date is so near that the money demand which it represents is looked on itself as money. As the phase runs the bill "is money," and in these circles it is used by way of payment when actual cash payment is not desirable or convenient.

The larger the number of hands through which the bill has passed, the better its currency becomes. The increased number of endorsements increases the security which it offers as it widens the commercial circle in which the bill is recognized. Nevertheless, this circle is very small when it is compared with the whole of the national economy. As the period for which it is drawn is short, the time during which it may remain in circulation is exceedingly limited. The bill, when taken up, ceases to function and new dealings in merchandise are required to create new bills of exchange which may again be put in circulation.

More important still is another condition to the use of bills of exchange. The draft or acceptance which is to function as payment, does not, in fact, serve as payment in full. Should payment not be made when the paper is due, the final holder may fall back on his predecessors. Each man thus resorted to may again have recourse to those before him. Not until the bill has been actually honored and paid, does the payment, which was supposed to have been made at its original delivery, become final. Until then, the payment is considered conditional. A bill of exchange is thus only a provisional means of payment, not a conclusive and final one such as is afforded by money itself.

"Unprotected" banknotes are notes for which no metallic equivalent of their face-value is held under government authority: i. e., such notes as the bank of issue, which we shall typify by the central bank for the entire national economy, places in circulation without always holding metallic or cash reserves in readiness for their full redemption.

Notes which are issued only within the amount of the metallic reserve have no theoretical interest for us in this connection. For large payments they are more convenient than metallic money which is coined in smaller units. They may be more conveniently and inexpensively safeguarded, counted and shipped. They are therefore a practical substitute for coined money which they represent. But this substitute substance, if one may so call it, does not in any way increase the total amount of money in the country. It circulates in lieu of the coins. The latter may at any time again take its place, for the notes must be redeemed in lawful money at sight on the demand of any holder.

On the other hand notes issued without cover of metallic coin are a peculiar means of payment by credit. They are added to the actual stock of metallic money and increase this "cash" effectually. This supplementary money, as it might be called, is of the utmost importance to the financial condition of a country. We shall have to discuss this money now at some length but we must warn our readers that externally this supplementary money cannot be distinguished from the substitute substance discussed in the last paragraph.

It is the essential basis of the legal status of the two types of issue that they are indistinguishably connected. Each confers on the holder the right to demand redemption. Of no individual note can it be confidently said "this is substitute money" or "this is supplementary money." In practice every note passes at its face value. However, as it may be safely assumed that all the notes issued will never be simultaneously presented for redemption, it is deemed sufficient to keep on hand a fund only in such proportion to the total circulation as experience has shown to be necessary. Over and above this fund, the bank of issue holds a secondary reserve to supplement its cash, i. e., the so-called "bankable reserve." This fund consists of those demands from its approved credit transactions, from loans arising in the business of the bank of issue or, more simply, "the Bank." This type of reserve consists of well-rated commercial drafts at short sight which the bank has discounted. The ingenious combination of these two reserves enables every bank to make good the promise of redemption given to the holders of the notes. In the first place it may use its cash reserve to redeem the notes presented. Then at the shortest notice, by cashing its demand represented by negotiable paper and kindred investments, it may obtain funds to redeem the rest of the notes also in so far as the notes themselves are not presented in repayment of the loans. Thus all notes issued by a well-managed bank, the supplementary as well as the substitute circulating media, can be used to obtain their face value in money and are accepted in all transactions as money.

In the case of money the mass habit of acceptance has become historical. This is quickly transferred to the notes of a central bank even without any legal enactments which enforce their acceptance or establish compulsory rates of exchange. It is unlikely that anyone would refuse to receive such notes in payment for in so doing he would be regarded as indulging in unbusinesslike chicanery. If the bank fails to observe the rules of protecting its notes, there will in the long run be a reaction which impairs confidence in the bank's notes even with the general public. But so long as the bank conducts its business with due regularity, the public and the entire business community receive and pay out the notes without so much as a thought of the cash reserve or the secondary reserve; or frequently without even having heard of these.

When the mass habit of acceptance once attaches to a note, it ceases from a practical point of view to be a mere demand for the payment of money. It becomes money, and practically, therefore, the country's total fund of effective money is augmented by the amount of the supplementary money.

This statement requires a restrictive explanation. This increase of the country's capital is not permanent. Notes which are paid out in discounting loans are subject to a law which has been called after its discoverer "Fullerton's law." When the credit granted by the bank expires the bank either receives back its note, or, if repayment is made in cash, an amount of cash which covers the note remaining in circulation. The notes which the bank issues in discounting commercial paper are no longer lived than the draft or acceptance itself. If they continue to circulate they are at any rate no longer uncovered notes. They come into existence when the draft is discounted; they die when the draft is honored. The payment of a draft gives to the bank a fund to cover the bank's note. During periods of slackening business activity when few drafts are offered for discount the supplementary fund decreases and vice versa.

The notes take the place of the draft which is deposited by the bank's cashier. Fundamentally, therefore, they are nothing more nor less than transformations of the draft which fit it to perform the functions of money. Drafts or acceptances are in amounts of uneven denomination; the notes of the bank are in round and convenient sums. Commercial paper is timed; notes are payable to the bearer on demand. The former appreciates in value, the nearer the time for its presentation and payment; the latter, as is the case with money, are not affected by the lapse of time. The former circulates only in its own narrowly restricted sphere; the notes of a central bank whose solvency is universally recognized are adapted to circulate throughout the entire national economy. Finally commercial paper is a means of only provisional payment. Notes are a means of final and conclusive payment just as is money. Should the commercial paper in place of which the notes were given, not be honored, the bank will fall back exclusively on the drawers and indorsers. The bank notes are in no wise affected and no one who has made payments by their instrumentality accepts any secondary liability. Why should he? The note is not, like the draft or acceptance, an individual promise to pay;[1] it is as representative as the money of the realm. It is national currency[2] as it should be in order to qualify as ultimate service for money through the mass-habit of use.

In most of its characteristics the "uncovered" bank check is the opposite of the unprotected note. Before explaining the check in detail we shall have to discuss a term which is not now in general use in precisely this form. The Austrian postal savings bank in its organization typifies the centralized clearing house arrangement. By the English method the parties draw in the first place on their bankers and these subsequently balance demands and counter demands in the clearing house. This method is substantially the same as the former, but its explanation is more difficult and does not give as clear a view of the relations which it is our object to disclose theoretically.

The centralized clearing bank accepts deposits of money. The creditors of account dispose of those funds by transfer checks. Payments are effected by debiting the account of the payer and crediting that of the payee. The arrangement amounts to the old exchange or giro trade on the greatly enlarged scale of a bank which operates over the entire national economy. As little theoretical interest attaches to that part of the deposit which is covered by cash on hand as does to notes covered by cash reserves. There are certain practical advantages in paying by check, but the country's media of exchange are not enlarged by drafts against cash on hand. But at this point the clearing bank avails itself of the experience of the bank of issue. Knowing that it is unnecessary to hold in readiness the entire coverage, it uses a certain portion of the funds entrusted to it for suitable investments which produce interest and enable it to allow a moderate interest to the depositors. This is an additional inducement towards increasing deposits. To the entire extent of these investments, the depositors renounce claims against a cash reserve and accept the secondary reserve in its place.

Therefore just as we distinguish between the covered and uncovered notes we shall have to distinguish between the credits which are pro-

[1] ein Einzelpapier.

[2] ein Massenpapier.

tected by metallic reserve and those which are covered only by the bank's investments. This distinction is without significance so far as transfers are concerned. Just as the notes of a well-managed bank of issue are accepted in daily exchange, whether they are covered by metallic money or approved security, and just as they form a homogeneous mass enjoying equal rights and used with equal effect without regard to the manner of security; so the credits of a well-managed clearing bank are looked upon as a homogeneous mass to be disposed of by transfer with identical effect without regard to the manner in which they are secured. But since the funds deposited are returned to economic circulation to the entire extent of the unsecured credits, it follows that to this extent the funds do double service and the media of exchange of the country are increased just as they are by "unsecured notes."

In many respects the clearing bank facilitates payments more effectively than the bank of issue. It is an improvement on earlier methods that the transfer takes place in the bank's accounts rather than by counting out and shipping funds. It is a further improvement that the balances, by the transfer of which payments are effected, at the same time yield a moderate rate of interest to creditors. In this way the method of clearing resumes a characteristic of the bill of exchange which was altogether lost in the case of the note, the representative of the bill of exchange. On the other hand, people must agree that their balances cannot be withdrawn at will, but their withdrawals are subject to certain short notice. This, too, is an improvement. While in the case of a bank note, the holder has a right to insist that it is payable on demand, payment by check has advanced beyond this stage. Depositors in the bank pay by money demands which cannot be withdrawn immediately but only after a trifling delay. Once the bank's patrons feel confident that payments are immediately effected by a transfer on the accounts, it is a matter of little importance that the withdrawal of funds is restricted by short notices. In this respect also the check revives a quality of the bill of exchange which is used by way of payment but subject to a certain number of days of grace. However, owing to the superior guarantee which the check receives in the combination of cash reserve and approved security, it surpasses the bill of exchange in effecting definitive or conclusive payment.

The amount of the unsecured balances, to the extent of which money does double work, fluctuates as elastically with the monetary requirements of trade as does the amount of unsecured notes. In periods with large financial requirements, the bank will increase its loans.

As the requirements drop off, there takes place a return flow of bank funds which is quite analogous to that described by the law of the return of bank notes.

The clearing method has developed much more rapidly than that of the use of notes. It has profited by the experiences of the latter and from the start has been in a much higher degree a matter of forethought and conscious purposeful organization. The charter and by-laws of the clearing bank regulate the legal effects of every event in all its details; the parties submit voluntarily to the established regulations and state legislation has little need of interference. Much depends on the extent to which the public makes use of the institution of banking. It is one thing when only large business houses lend their support. It is quite another when smaller concerns and, outside of the business world, the public, properly speaking, participate. The checking system is not well adapted to the needs of workers, small traders, petty officials and the like. These classes have the disposal of only small sums; they receive their incomes at short intervals and consume them as soon as they come in; they reserve no funds. However the system is well suited to the middle classes in easy circumstances. Not only in England but in many other countries it has found ready adherents among these classes.

The use of payment by check is fairly wide-spread as compared with the sphere of the use of notes as it was rigidly regarded by the older schools. Originally the note was intended only for the larger commercial transactions. It was not even thought desirable that the notes should find their way into the tills of petty traders and they were therefore issued only in higher denominations. Transfers by check, on the contrary, are made among the customers of the bank down to the smallest amounts, and are just as careful in effecting domestic payments as business transfers. Where the checking system has once taken root, its sphere of usefulness is wide enough to give rise to a mass habit. The strength of this habit is such as to place the individual under the spell of a universal practice. In the last instance it is this which creates for the check the quality by virtue of which it operates with the public at large as definite payment. It is the possibility of accomplishing this feat on so large a scale which gives the checking system the firm position in the public estimation which it now enjoys. The methods of the clearing bank by which guarantee of payment is established are after all a secondary consideration. It is true that under present conditions the guarantees cannot be dispensed with; the entire checking system would be shaken to its foundation if the security of the reserves were to be found insufficient. Confidence in the bank would be lost and balances would be withdrawn in large proportions. The checking system would be at an end. But while the credit of the bank is maintained, all these considerations have little weight; the public is guided first of all by the fact that these transfers have universal currency.

What in England and continental Europe is known as the Lombard business, in the course of which loans are granted on securities listed on the stock exchange, is looked upon, like the business of discount, as lending on approved security. When prudently managed, it actually offers a real secondary reserve, as the sums loaned may be withdrawn on the shortest possible notice. But it lacks that guarantee which arises from the connection with a business transaction, notes are placed in circulation without the support of new natural values to balance the face value of the obligation. For good reason therefore the Lombard business is confined to a narrower field. If it is transacted on too large a scale it must inevitably interfere with the smooth working of the institution of money.

Over and above the important result of adding materially to the ready money in any country, the institution of credit affects the methods of payment in still another way by minimizing the specific acts of payment. However, under present conditions this proves to be of far less importance. Between merchants with a regular and lasting business connection which leads to obligations of payment on either side, actual payment may be simplified by mutual credits and debits and a periodic settlement. Such adjustments minimize not only the acts of payment but also the means on both sides. Means of payment need only be held in readiness for the balances which are not otherwise cancelled. On the whole if we disregard settlements on the Exchange, the method of balancing accounts has not gone much beyond the limits of commercial business intercourse. Clearing house settlements on the English system which reach enormous dimensions are not considered in this connection; they merely supplement the checking system and are wholly unnecessary with a centralized organization. We have already discussed their effect in our exposition of the checking system.

Finally the institution of credit also admits of arrangements by which the trans-shipments of paper or metallic money can be done away with. Costs of transportation are thus saved and other considerable advantages secured without essentially influencing the structure of the economic community comprised of those who pay and are paid. It is therefore not necessary for us to discuss this feature at the present time. In the theory of the world economy, we shall have to discuss a function of credit of greater importance.

Precisely as money itself has been evolved, so the method of payment by credit has been developed largely by the tendency to experiment which is constantly manifested in the practical affairs of life. The task of theory is in the first place directed to a summary explanation of the significance of those things which have been worked out in detail by human ingenuity and skill. Theory has contributed to the practical shaping of results mainly by criticism which it is able to offer because of the breadth of its knowledge. In this spirit it dictates the necessary safeguards whenever the aggressive impulses of practical life tend to pass the limits of prudence. Theory is a conservative rather than a progressive element. With scarcely an exception theoretical criticism has been too cautious; so far developments have gone beyond the limits indicated by the rigid discipline of the schools. There can be no doubt that in the future also the practical quest will point out and attain methods which are still proscribed though they are destined to lead to the creation of media of payment bolder and more extensive than any we now dare fancy.

§ 48. The National Economic Community of Payment

Payment—Price-payments and payments by assignment—Original and derived income—The equation of supply and demand—Natural and monetary forms—Personal balances of wares and of payments.

The economic concept of payment is presupposed in the phrase, means of payment by credit. In attempting to define this concept, so important to an understanding of the institution of money, we shall assume an undeveloped economic condition where there are no credit media and the only means of payment is ready cash. At first we shall also assume for the sake of simplicity that we are dealing with a static economy which obtains the same social income year in and year out through a frictionless, undisturbed process of production and acquisition and which distributes this income to its members by similarly frictionless sales. We shall first examine the effects on the institution of money resulting from change, friction and disturbances in production, acquisition and the market. We shall then pass to changes in the value of money.

Payments in money may be made irrespective of exchange as well as a result of an exchange. Those made under the latter condition may be classified as payments made for natural values and those for money or capital. In our analysis we must begin with payments made for natural values. It is through these that all other payments receive their significance. If money were not able to buy natural values, it would be absurd to lend money and collect taxes.

The exchange of natural values for money is a necessary consequence of the division of labor in the economic process which has brought in its train the money economy. While the domestic production of the old natural economy resulted in a natural yield from which the household was immediately supplied, production in a monetized economy gives a natural yield to every individual of which he may be able to use little or none in his household. These products and the other natural values turned out in the process of acquisition must first be sold in the market to yield a money income. This, finally, must be changed into the natural income which leads to the satisfaction of needs in the household.

Acquisition is considered complete as soon as a money income has been obtained from the sale of the finished natural values. Turning the money income into natural income offers no further acquisitional difficulties; the essential problem here is to observe correctly the margin of use of the household. It thus happens that this purchase, although it also requires a certain market experience, is looked upon as a problem of the household where the ultimate preparation of the commodities for consumption is presumed to take place.

In disposing of his products for money, the producer effects a transition from the narrow field of his particular process—a limitation imposed by the division of labor—to the entire wealth of values in the market. He surrenders the natural form of a specially conditioned product for which the market possesses only a limited capacity of acceptance. In return he receives money, the general medium of exchange, which enjoys a mass-habit of acceptance and by which he is left to a greater or less degree master of the market. He may now come forward in the market with his demand. It is this shift from a restricted to a general command of the market that is significant in the concept of payment. In this sense payment is a monetary performance in exchange.

The process of production in the money economy leads to continuous sales not merely of consumption goods that are ready for use and are being transferred to the household, but also of material and personal productive means that are used in production and must be replaced. In the case of these sales also a concrete natural service is surrendered in exchange for the universal medium of exchange, money. Payment is made in money.

Once the position of money as a means of payment is established in the market of natural values, the development of the money economy leads to other types of payment in order fully to profit by the power money confers in the natural market. Loans and credits in the money and investment markets are examples. The payment of money gives to the borrower, according to the amount of the loan, a general market control. By the payment of interest and the repayment of the principal sum, he returns this control to the creditor. Credit transactions are made in the general means of payment, money. Therefore anyone may become a creditor who receives payments of money through any method of acquisition. Anyone who has to make money payments may become a debtor. Similarly anyone may fulfil his credit obligations who has received payments of money from some source.

The payments of public taxes are also made in money. In a natural economy circumstances require the payment of natural taxes. The state therefore is confined in its expenditures to the primitive natural values offered by the domestic production of its subjects. A tax paid in money gives to the state a control of the entire domestic and foreign market in proportion to the amount of the tax. On the other hand the performance of the tax bears less oppressively on both burghers and peasants as soon as their acquisitional activity is adjusted to yield money incomes. The same is true of the payment of fines and damages in money: it is most effective for the collecting party and least burdensome in the age of the money economy for the person paying.

Those payments which are made without involving any return from the beneficiary: liberal gifts of every description, donations, alms and foundations are most effectively made in money. There may be special reasons that make a natural performance desirable; it is possible that the particular natural form which is ultimately desired may be represented in the fund from which the donation is made. But if the gift is executed in the universal medium of payment, it allows the beneficiary the most unrestrained selection of natural values. The same remarks apply to properties to be placed in social enterprises. Finally in the insurance business the payment of premiums and the recovery of damages call for a transfer of money; indeed wherever the money economy prevails, such transfers cannot be differently conceived.

Payments are classified into two great groups: price payments and payments by assignment.

Price payments are the monetary consideration for natural values in the market. Strictly speaking, the term includes the payment of interest by a debtor, as interest is also a price; but we shall not consider it as a price payment, for it does not embrace the particular characteristic of price payment which involves the sale of natural values. Price payments are the auxiliary movements by which in the economic process of sale the principal movement of natural values is maintained. The title, which qualifies men to receive payments of price, is the fact that they have surrendered natural values which have been introduced to the economic process of the nation for exchange.

We shall call payments by assignment all those which are made under any title outside the market of natural values. In part they are payments in consequence of contracts: loans and other credit arrangements, contracts of partnership or other association, insurance agreements and those of gift. These contracts again are made either for a consideration or gratis. Some of these payments are founded on legal obligations as in the payment of fines, damages or taxes. The primary purpose of a payment by assignment is to transfer the control over the market of natural values, which the possession of money confers, from the existing owner to another. In the further course of transactions the purpose is so extended as to transfer also the power to make payments by assignment, be they with or without consideration, by contract or imposed by law. The creditor transfers his power of payment to the debtor; the latter returns it to the creditor. The taxpayer transfers his power to the community, the donor to his beneficiary, the member of an association to the society and the insured to the insurer. In some cases there is a return from insurer to insured. It is not an easy matter to find one collective name to describe all these payments originating in so many different titles. The name, payment by assignment, may be the most suitable that could be agreed upon. We think then of the party paying as the assignor who surrenders a certain general market control, considered as money, to an assignee. An especially important group of such payments are those discharging a debt which the party bound by contract or law makes in performance of his obligation. We shall later see that the state bases its control of money-matters mainly on the sovereignty which as legislator and judge of last resort, it exercises concerning the regulation of the payment of debts.

The income, acquired by participation in the process of production and acquisition, is spoken of as original income. In our science the term is used in several other meanings, but it is this meaning in which it is probably most aptly accepted. The original income is made up of the price-payments which men receive for the surrender of natural values, formed by their economic activity; we mean by the transformation of a natural form into the money-form. Original income is acquired by the farmer, the mine-owner, the manufacturer and every other industrial producer, the merchant, the freighter, the landlord, the physician, the lawyer, the priest, the military officer and the official of the state. Such income is acquired not only by the independent, individual entrepreneur. Every other person, performing some part in the process of acquisition and production, also receives it: the partner in any business-enterprise, the stockholder, and fully as much the wage-laborer or the owner of realty, leasing his real-estate.

In contrast with the original income we find the derived income, earned directly in money-form. Derived income is received by the creditor, the banker, the mendicant who lives on alms or the charity of the public, the beneficiary of an annuity. The income also of the state and of other commonwealths received in taxes and dues of all kinds is derived income. It is paid out of the money-income of the citizens whose income is correspondingly decreased without the compensating exchange of any natural value, although the community attends to the task of procuring out of this income the natural values, employed in the administration of government.

So long as the assumption of an undisturbed static economy is maintained, the principal movement of natural values must always balance with the auxiliary movement of price-payments. More accurately, the sum of natural values offered by the participants in the processes of production and acquisition must be equal to the sum of the money values at the disposal of buyers. Put most briefly: there invariably exists an equilibrium of supply and demand. In a static economy, functioning without progress or retrogression, there must more especially be an equilibrium between money income and natural income, i. e., between the money income and those natural values which are being consumed in the households. This proposition we shall now have to prove.

Let us first assume that all income is original income. In this case we may feel assured that, whoever has brought a natural value into the mechanism of production and acquisition and received a price-payment in return, may, in a static economy, count on finding a natural counter-value of corresponding magnitude offered in the market. The purchaser received the natural value by paying a price. But in order to obtain the money with which to pay, he must himself have placed a similar natural value in the economy. In the process of exchange, there are a series of successively linked pairs. In order to obtain the monetary commodity, each successor in this chain—those both near and remote from the pair under consideration here—had to bring forward a natural value. Somewhere, this chain of exchanges finally breaks as certain persons have not yet brought their wares into the economy. They wait for the successor on whose demand they will bring forward their goods. In a static economy, the farmer, selling grain, will find somewhere in the market, the industrial products which he is seeking, offered by producers, who are in quest of his demand, in order to obtain by sale the means of payment which they themselves are in need of, in order to push their own demands. When, finally, the last excessive supply and the last uncared-for demand have met and effected an exchange, the ring is closed in the series constituting trade. In the static economy, the demand—as far as the supply is concerned—does not come unexpectedly; supply and demand, by long continued relations in the market, have adjusted themselves to each other. The demand is expected in advance, and it thus exercises an effect equivalent to an order. The natural values, of which the demand is in quest, have been prepared by the supply in quantity and quality as desired, enabling the parties to effect the exchanges of the market in easy routine and without friction.

In a static economy, the equation of supply and demand is by no means interfered with by the influence of assignment payments or of derived income. By such payments only the individuals are changed, who make up the demand; persons with derived income take the places of those with original income. A producer may waive the right to receive from the market for his own consumption the natural values to the receipt of which he has become entitled by the products turned in. He may prefer to loan the price realized to a debtor. In this case, the debtor will exercise the demand, and his demand will operate as an order, as soon as the market has become accustomed to it. The reverse is true when the debtor proceeds to the payment of interest and repayment of principal. He can do this only through natural values which he prepares or which, in more complicated cases, a new creditor, some other provider of funds or his predecessor in the production process has turned in for him. Whenever the state collects monetary taxes, which are paid from original or derived income, the citizens, in paying, make over to the tax-collecting government their expectations or opportunities of obtaining market-supplies. In the more complicated cases, the transfers of market-certificates, accomplished by assignment payments, are very numerous. Thus, for example, the mechanic in debt may pay to the creditor-bank, the bank to the depositor, the depositor to the state, the state to its creditors, and from these the series may be similarly continued. But numerous as the shifts may be, the equation of supply and demand will always have to continue to exist in the market of natural values, where the economy is a static one; neither the quantity of natural values supplied, nor the amount of the sums of money giving title to demands, undergo any change whatever.

We can summarize the result of our investigation in the phrase that the closed enonomy is, for the entire people, a community of payments. By a universal habit of thought, we picture economic organization as a community of production and acquisition; but we shall have to think of it as well as a community of payments, a community settling the mutual claims which arise in the process of sale. With the aid of the universal means of payment, money, the necessary service is performed in a surprisingly simple manner and without the need of a superior management. As long as every individual, in making price- and assignment-payments, looks strictly to his own interest, the orderly settlement of affairs is assured. Every individual is a member of the community of acquisition who is ready to turn in a natural value, and who thus disposes of the natural form; he also is a part of the payment-community who disposes of the money-form. Sales are made as members of the two communities come together in exchange, two by two. In the exchange they change rôles, the supplying predecessor acquires in place of the natural form, the money-form; the demanding successor in place of the money-form, the natural form. This interchange of natural form and money-form in connection with the equation of supply and demand is sufficient to discharge in due routine the service of the community of payments. No one can achieve the control of the money-form, who has not himself or through another turned in a corresponding quantity of natural values; no one can aspire to the control of the natural form, who has not surrendered a corresponding quantity of values in the money-form. It is his personal loss, when one of the contracting parties errs and surrenders a greater value in the one form than he receives in the other. The equation of values in the total, however, is not affected by this error, for what he overpaid becomes the gain of the other party to the contract. Anyone who does not wish to employ the authority, conferred by the possession of the money-form, personally to withdraw natural values, will probably perform one or the other act of assignment-payment; he will lend out money, give it away or fulfil his public or private obligations to pay, and thus surrender his position in the community of payment to one or the other assignee.

The free-trade school has—as far as international commerce is concerned—maintained that, in the long run, wares can only be paid for in wares. As we shall see later on, the position does not hold good for the foreign trade of an individual country; it does hold good in a closed economy or in the whole of the commerce of the world. But we shall have to change somewhat the mode of formulation; rather than of wares, we shall have to speak of natural values, generally; and we shall have to substitute a more appropriate phrase for the term "paid," for in every instance payment can only be made in money. The true meaning of the statement is that the money-values, available for the demand of natural values, are ultimately derived from the sale of natural values which the supply has carried into the economic process. Thus formulated, the proposition coincides with the equation of supply and demand.

The equation of supply and demand does not hold good for a single section of a closed economy any more than it does for the commerce of a single nation with foreign countries. The sum of the products which the farmers of a closed state sell, does not necessarily coincide with the sum of products and other natural values, which they acquire for production and for domestic use. It will, even with entirely undisturbed economic processes, coincide with the latter only on the assumption that the original income of the farmers has not been reduced by the payment either of interest on indebtedness, of taxes or any other assignment-payments. An agricultural enterprise, heavily indebted and burdened by taxation, will withdraw from the economy a much smaller quantity of products, than it has itself raised and carried into the social fund. On the other hand, the group of capitalistic investors, who live entirely from derived income, will be able in its domestic economy to supply itself abundantly with means of enjoyment of every description, without itself producing natural values of any kind. These men find their natural needs supplied by the values brought to the market by their debtors to cover their payments of indebtedness. It may be the capitalists do not take out the very natural values brought into the general market by their personal debtors. None the less at some place in this market corresponding values must be found prepared.

What we have now explained as to individual sections of the national economy, applies equally to every individual economy. The natural values, coming and going in an individual economy, need not by any means be equally balanced. The personal balance of natural values or, as the case may be, the personal balance of wares, may be a credit or a debit balance. It will be a credit balance when more natural values, or wares, are sent out; a debit balance, when more come in. When thus interpreted, the personal balance of wares of the farmer, largely in debt, will be a credit balance; the personal balance of wares of the capitalist, a debit balance. These are ways of speaking which do not correspond to the personal relations; and still we adopt them, because since the days of the Mercantilists, they have been habitually used in our science for national and universal economic relations. We shall have to discuss them further in our theory of the economy of the world.

As we speak of a personal balance of wares, we may speak of a personal balance of payments. This is the balance of moneys received and paid out in the individual economy or of the payments which, during the economic period, should come in and go out. In a properly conducted individual economy, the personal balance of payments can never permanently be either a credit or a debit balance. Those who receive larger payments than they are willing to expend in the conduct of acquisition or in the domestic economy, will pay out money for some kind of investment; they will purchase securities of some kind, bonds, stocks or real estate; they will make a liquid deposit in banks; or they will turn part of the funds over to other individuals by liberal acts. The banks, on their part, will not permit funds to lie idle, which have been deposited with them; they will again place them in circulation by means of their loan-and credit-transactions. The hoarding of large sums of unused money, forming a treasure or thesaurus, as was the former practice, will find no advocates under modern conditions. No one will for any length of time so shape his personal balance of payments, as to carry a credit balance in the sense of taking in more money than, in one way or the other, he pays out. On the other hand, however, no properly conducted economy will so fashion its behavior as to produce a debit balance by becoming bound to expenditures greater than anticipated receipts. To cover expenses which unexpectedly disturb the equilibrium, and which cannot be met from regular receipts, extraordinary measures will have to be resorted to, by availing oneself of credit, proceeding to sales or omitting other intended expenditures. Rather than speak of credit and debit balances, we should speak of the favorable or unfavorable formation of the balance of payments. The favorable formation is one where payments come in after a manner which always supplies sufficient funds to meet expenses; the unfavorable are those where difficulties arise because payments become due before the funds required to meet them have been realized. Even in an household of small income, the balance of payments may be favorable, where affairs are well managed and certain reserve-funds kept in readiness; while in an economy of large income it may be unfavorable temporarily or even habitually, where things are ill managed and large obligations are assumed, which go beyond the available cash-resources.

It is difficult to grasp correctly the relation of money-form and natural form. The practical point of view for obvious reasons sees first of all the money-form; it looks not upon the whole, but upon things as presented by the private interest of the individual whose access to the wealth of the market is secured by the money-form. The scientific mode of thought, on the other hand, insists logically upon the importance of the natural form. Here, all individual aspects have to be united into a total representation, exhibiting the natural values as the nucleus of national wealth. However this may be, science has not, after all, won its insights without itself becoming ensnared in errors of exaggeration; and it has on occasion announced its axiom as though the natural form were the key to all verity, and the money-form were of no import whatever. Socialistic criticism went to even greater lengths. It thought to have found in the money-form and in the necessity of transforming the natural form—the community-form as Marx called it—into the money-form, which in an eternal circulation is retransformed into the natural form, the source of all exploitation. The correct view is probably the view which holds that, as long as there is an economy of exchange, the social institution of the money-form cannot be dispensed with; its service in the process of sale may assuredly still be elaborated by more perfected arrangements, but in no way may be replaced.

§ 49. The Developed Form of Money

The money-form and credit—Natural, monetary and credit economies—Definitions of money.

The economic community that arises through exchange did not stop with the original form of monetary payment. The introduction of credit and more especially the adoption of media of payment by credit has greatly extended the scope of the money form.

In the first place credit operates by deferring payment in ready money and substituting book accounts. When sales are made on credit, the vendor surrenders his position in the acquisitive community to the purchaser. The latter gains possession of the wares; the former cannot reënter the market until he has been paid. If we eliminate the possibility that the vendor may protect himself by taking a mortgage or bond, the transaction is wholly at his risk. If the purchaser fails to make the promised payment, the seller loses his position in the economic community. So long as the account remains open the transaction is incomplete; there is as yet no money income because the vendor is in possession not of money but of a demand for money. For the latter no habit of general acceptance has been established. Such credits are therefore always confined to a narrow circle in which the personal and business relations of the parties are such that the creditor can scarcely decline to accept the risk of the transaction.

In those cases where debits and credits are balanced on the books the use of money is dispensed with and as a means of payment money is economized. It is still used as an instrument of computation. The prices and interest are computed in money and the balance in terms of money is carried forward to a new account.

The development of demands for money, which may be used in wider spheres as means of payment by credit, is more important than open book accounts. As typical forms we have become acquainted with commercial paper, drafts, bank notes and checks. Neither of the last two is secured by a full cash reserve. These have all been amply described and we need only summarize their relation to the form of money. A draft is a provisional means of payment used in restricted business circles mainly to effect price-payments. It has grown out of the needs of commerce that receives its numerical value from the size of the commercial transaction covering it. It is an accessory means of payment which supplements money. It does not, however, actually become money but always remains a demand for money.

The "unprotected" note is a transformation of the draft. It is made to serve more perfectly as money; it is a means of definitive payment, supported by the general habit of acceptance. Suitable for larger payments in all fields of the national economy, it is issued or withdrawn in amounts equivalent to the commercial transaction which it covers. But even the note is only an accessory means of payment; it augments money but never completely displaces it. To be sure, in the mass habit of acceptance the note has individuality; one might say that it has a "call" to independence. It has a double basis: on the one hand it is a demand for money which presupposes money; on the other hand, through the general habit of acceptance, it has become fundamentally independent of money and stands "on its own." In a closed economy, which needed to give no attention to payments in foreign trade, it is not only possible but probable that the note would have achieved this independence in practice.

On the whole the same statement is true of checks. In all civilized countries the sphere in which checks serve as money has become so large that we may properly speak of a mass habit of using checks which might be strong enough to establish the check independently of metallic money. We are not concerned here with possible developments; our object is merely to describe actual conditions. At present the note and check are only accessory media of payment. They supplement metallic money to the extent of the needs of commerce: i. e., according to the commercial values which secure them.

With these limitations notes and checks do service as money in their own fields with precisely the effect of money. The recipient of a note or check becomes a member of a limited but still extensive community of payment. To an amount equalling his receipts he commands the money form and is able to make payments with full effect. The transaction closes with the receipt of the note or check; a monetary income is received by the man who is paid and who gains a position in the acquisitive community that formerly was the payer's.

The process is most clearly seen in the manner in which payments are effected on the central clearing bank. The bank unites its depositors into a community of payment. It enters on its books the values of which its patrons dispose in monetary terms. Payment is made by transferring a claim to the payee according to the amount of the credit. But does not the simple act of payment in ready money accomplish the same thing? A coin is a material token of value whose temporary possessor is enabled to pay. The note is a transitional form between the original—one may almost say the primitive or naturalistic—coined form and the refined money-form of the bank-book. It resembles the coined in that it must be physically transferred; but the trained eye of the modern observer sees these notes as precursors of the bank-book. They are merely the loose leaves of an unbound bank-book; their use prepares the way for the coming development.

The credit economy is frequently explained as being in the same manner a development of the money economy as the latter is of the natural economy. This is a mistake. The transition from the natural to the monetary economy is by far the greater. There is a fundamental difference between the active agents in the two, and hence in the effects of economic activity. In the natural economy the individual household must rely upon itself and its forces. The process of production is carried on within the limits fixed by the scanty natural resources of a household. There are no intermediaries between production and consumption. In the money economy all workers separate production and other acquisitive activities from consumption by two intervening acts: a transfer of the natural form to the money form and of this back into the former. This external opposition has the greatest material consequences. Through these two transfers the way is opened to the development, first, or the division of labor which releases an enormous social productive force, and second, of the community of payments which distributes the socially prepared values. Not until the rise of a monetary economy did the great, far-reaching national economy originate.

The establishment of the credit system did not introduce a fundamentally new set of conditions; it is not even desirable to speak of a special credit economy. What men refer to as the credit economy is merely an extension of the money-economy; it might be called the credit-and-money-economy. By means of loans and credits in their various forms individuals other than those owning property are given control of the property. In particular the group of entrepreneurs is renewed. By means of payment by credit the form of money is expanded; developing natural values offer a commercial security and themselves furnish the means of payment which facilitate their sale. Thus the avenues of production are enlarged. These are great results but they rest on a monetary economy within which they function.

According to these explanations any general means of payment, in exchange or outside of it, is money. A means of payment gains universality historically as soon as a mass habit of use has attached to it. Specie is independent money, money at its best, that on its own account may find universal employment. Bank notes and checks are accessory to this true money. A commercial draft has no general acceptability; it forms the transition to demands of various kinds for money which are accepted as payment by special agreement in each particular case.

The term, general means of exchange, that appears in many definitions is too narrow. It does not include payments by assignment and fails to emphasize sufficiently the effect of price-payments. The much used designation, circulating medium, does not properly limit the concept, for a commercial draft also becomes a circulating medium as soon as it is frequently endorsed.

Formerly the explanation was frequently inserted in the definition of money that is "the means of preserving values for the future." Even today this statement, which is a last remnant of the mercantilistic theory of money, is made. But the wealth of the future would be ill conserved if there were not also enduring natural values and sources of value. The durability of money is assuredly an important consideration, for future economic organizations will need means of payment; but it is hardly necessary to add that in all future periods the natural forms of wealth will be developed by the side of the monetary ones. Finally, it should be mentioned that for anticipated and also for unexpected future payments a cash reserve should be established that is proportioned to one's means. The continuing organization of credit accumulates the reserves of individual economies in the banks and thus effects a considerable saving in the monetary material.

In many definitions, money, having been declared a medium of exchange, is also set up as a standard of price. This addendum is superfluous. Money could never be a practical instrument of paying prices, if it were not qualified to measure them.

With far more propriety money has been described as a measure of value. But the idea which it is desired to convey, may be more suitably expressed in another way. What the phrase is intended to indicate is that money is used to symbolize values in other transactions than those of exchange. This happens when a later exchange is foreseen, as for example when an official appraisal precedes a sale at public auction. The same thing happens where no sale at all is expected to follow, as for example where the exchange-value of the yield is determined. At the end of this section we expect to take up again the applications and significance of computation in money; provisionally let us say that money is indeed the general instrument of appraisal in the processes of private economy.

Money is affected more radically by paper money than by the means of payment by credit. Paper money does not supplement but ousts specie. Externally it is of the same form as the bank note, but essentially it is in no way kindred to the bank note or other forms of credit media. Its origin is not in credit but in the edict of the state, establishing a nominal value. When we come to discuss the nominal value of money, we shall also go into details as to paper money.

§ 50. The Economic [Objective] Exchange Value of Money, or The Value of Money

The Concept—The law of its formation, its historical conditioning and continuity.

Theory is not likely to unravel the problem of the value of money in a satisfactory manner until it has grasped the concept of the money form and of the expanded form of money. The older theory was bound to fail when approaching this problem, if for no other reason than that it never succeeded in defining these concepts and hence could never determine the "quantity" of money which determines its value. In the older theory this quantity was the material stock of money. Actually it should be represented by the entire sum of the income of the economy which is available under the expanded form of money. A wealthy man who disburses his large income by checks drawn on his bank is unlikely to appraise the value of money by the standard which would be set merely by the sum of cash which he happens to carry at any particular time. As regards the personal exchange value of money, this is so apparent that any further discussion may scarcely be expected. But the conditions governing the value of money in the national economy are different and a more careful analysis is required in order to shed light upon the concept of this value and the law which governs it under the amplified form of money. In practical life it is the social economic exchange value of money which men have in mind when they say that money is worth more in one place than another or that it is worth more now than it formerly was. In this connection also, the prevailing scientific interpretation follows the procedure of daily experience. It accepts the value of money as it is objectively determined and refers to it as the objective exchange value. The same statements which we have ascertained to be true in connection with the objective determination of natural values hold good also in respect to money. The value of money is not an objective value; it is the general cross-section of the subjective or personal valuations of money; it is the value as to which all persons are agreed. We define this value as the significance which all parties concerned attach to money in the economic process under the general price level.

More is predicated in the value of money than the mere fact of a general level of prices. Not only is it stated that the goods which are being sold in the market are held at particular prices; it is implied that because of the general price level, money has a certain significance for everybody in the economic process. This significance of the value of money is more clearly experienced when economic changes affect its purchasing power than under conditions of perfect stability. The statement that money has risen or fallen in value does not merely inform us that the general price level has gone up or down, and that things are cheaper or dearer; it gives us to understand that simultaneously with the general change of prices, money has taken on a different value for everybody. In this statement it is predicated that the relation of the unit of money to that of utility has changed; that in order to cover the same marginal use, more or less money has to be expended. When more units of money have to be surrendered to secure the same degree of utility, the value of money has declined, and vice versa. When a general rise of prices has the effect that the provisioning of all households has to be curtailed, or when falling prices enable it to be expanded, the exchange value of all commodities has risen or fallen, while that of money need not be affected at all.

Accordingly we may define the value of money more accurately as the significance attaching to a unit of money because of its relation to a unit of utility. All factors which contribute to the determination of the general price level influence the value of money. But there are other circumstances which determine the ratio in which units of money are equated to the price level of a unit of utility. These should also be considered. In the final analysis, the general price level is always determined by the sums of the values which make up the supply and demand in the market of natural values. On the side of the supply, these consist in all the natural values offered for sale. On the part of the demand we find the sums of money which are available for price payments. It is a matter of indifference in what particular monetary form these amounts exist. Sums which are available in bank notes or checks as well as in commercial paper are all to be counted. No less are those amounts which are credited and carried to an open account. These all influence the formation of price. Of all the prices paid in the market, those payments made for consumption goods are decisive for the exchange value of money; it is from these that the prices of productive means are derived. In a static economy, with neither progress nor retrogression, the money income is all used for the purchase of the consumption values necessary for the households. Thus we arrive at the brief expression that in a static economy, the general level of prices is determined by the newly produced natural consumption values on the one side and the monetary income on the other.

Payments by assignment do not influence the exchange value of money. They have no other effect than that they bring about a change in the individuals who are entitled to dispose of the money. The national income is neither immediately increased nor diminished by them. Indirectly, however, more remote effects may arise and may result in appreciable modifications of the national income because of the influence of these payments upon the distribution of the social income. The number of units of money to be used to express a unit of utility cannot be predetermined. They may be many or few. As a matter of fact, the value of money has been quite diverse both at various times and in different localities. It is invariably a matter that is historically determined. At any given time every economy finds the value of money determined by prior development. During a new period the development proceeds continuously from this condition with historical precision. No matter what factors operate on the side of natural values or of money to influence the general price level, they always operate from the basis of a preëxisting level of prices. The existing price structure is never changed simultaneously in all its parts. New facts affect only individual prices. Momentous influences on the price level accumulate little by little with the ceaseless occurrence of new events which affect ever new sections of the market. In a particular case the parties to a transaction compute a new price from the one with which they are familiar. "If such and such things cost so and so much, then I shall have to ask this or that price for my wares"; or, "I can only pay such and such a price":

thus any formation of prices is popularly worked out. When the conditions of the market are more disturbed, the new prices will depart more rapidly and in larger numbers from the old ones; but no matter how great the disturbances of the price level, even at times when they lead to a violent upheaval of the value of money, the leap to the new value always proceeds from the basis of the old value, historical continuity is maintained.

The theory of the value of money must start from the service of money, just as that of the value of wares starts from their serviceability. The prevailing doctrine has failed to do so; it fell into the error of drawing the exchange-value of money too closely to the pattern of that of wares. It has sought to construct the closest possible parallel between the two. Just as the exchange-value of goods was founded in their money-price, so the exchange-value of money was to be found in the "goods-price" of money. By this phrase they meant the quantity of goods which are to be obtained for money or rather for a unit of money. Properly speaking, however, money has no price. We pay prices in money. It is only in the primitive exchange of the natural economy that each of the two commodities transferred is the price of the other. Furthermore it was held that for both goods and money supply and demand are determining. This is also mistaken; as far as money is concerned neither the concept of stock nor of need applies to it in the same sense in which it applies to wares. The theorists were therefore compelled to resort to all manner of modifications of the two concepts, changes which were more or less forced. It was recognized that the credit substitutes also influence the "stock of money." Obviously the extent to which specie and credit substitutes are used is also important, and the idea took root of appealing to a third factor of the supply as well, the rapidity of the circulation of the monetary symbols. But specie, credit media and rapidity of circulation are only the elements for the auxiliary movement of money; the prevailing theory never succeeded in assembling the elements in the one concept of money income. In connection with interest on capital we shall have to discuss the particular sense in which the money market speaks of the value of money.

§ 51. The Monetary Material and the Bullion Value of Money

Coins, standard of coinage, price of coinage—The material unity of international monetary systems—Bullionist theory, money made of valueless materials.

Among all civilized peoples and for a long period a mass habit of use has attached to the precious metals. These metals do not satisfy all the requirements of a perfect money. As we shall show later money is subject to a variability of value because the quantity of money in circulation depends on the fluctuating productivity of the mines. This detracts from its usefulness as money. Aside from this consideration coined money is excessively bulky for large payments. Credit instruments are particularly convenient media of payment in these cases; they perform the service with scarcely any difficulty and almost without expense. On the other hand the precious metals do possess in high degree the quality of divisibility which is important in minting. They have greater durability than most other monetary materials. Moreover they have purity, lustre and a high bullion value due to their scarcity: all qualities that were particularly important in the beginning of the monetary economy and that are not to be overlooked today. Ultimately the historical force which was invoked by the use of precious metals among the most advanced peoples determined the dominance of these metals over all other monetary materials. Unity of the monetary systems is essential to an unchallenged functioning. Thus the backward economies were forced to adopt the material used for money by the nations controlling world commerce unless they wished to be isolated from the money economy of the world. The ousting of silver and the transition to the gold standard, which most advanced nations have accomplished with the last decades, is to be traced back to this cause. However, it is not part of our task to describe these events which are not adapted to purely theoretical exposition but demand extensive materials that may only be collected by empirical methods of investigation.

In the following analysis we shall take advantage of the right to adopt the method of theoretical simplification. We shall assume a condition in which the money of a country consists exclusively of gold and requires no supplementary coins or small change. As before, we shall disregard all international relations and assume a closed social economy entirely dependent upon its own resources.

While a certain amount of the gold which is held in reserve to secure the payment of notes may be uncoined, the gold destined for circulation is coined. Only for large transactions is gold in bars used. Our next problem is to explain the significance of the coined form of money.

The standard of coinage determines the number of units of money: i. e., pieces of money, to be coined from a unit weight of bullion. Thus 1395 Marks are made from one German pound [1] of fine gold in ten and twenty mark pieces, or 139.5 ten mark pieces or 69.75 twenty mark pieces. Applying the standard of coinage of the Austrian crown to the German pound (the law expresses it in the kilogram of fine gold), 164 ten crown pieces or 82 twenty crown pieces are ob-

[1] Trans. note: *Zollpfund.* The customs union adopted a unit equalling a half kilogram.

tained. Accordingly the bullion content prescribed by the coinage law is 1/69.75 of a German pound for a twenty mark piece and 1/82 for a twenty crown piece. The technical process of coining is so accurately controlled that this content can actually be adhered to except for altogether insignificant variations. Since the coinage law provides that every coin must be accepted at full value, whose departure from the standard does not exceed certain narrowly defined limits of error, the twenty mark piece and the twenty crown piece are to be held equivalent to 1/69.75 and 1/82 German pound of fine gold respectively. To this extent, then, the well known definition of Goldschmidt for a standard coin applies to the gold coin: i. e., "a bar or ingot of precious metal legitimized or approved by the state as regards purity and fineness." The stamp of the unit on a twenty mark or twenty crown piece, not too greatly worn, is evidence that it contains the quantity of gold prescribed by law.

From this point of view the form of the coin is a mere matter of authorization whereas the true worth of the coin, the bullion value, is determined by the metal content. The latter would also seem to give its essential nature to the coin. However, all of this fails to enlighten us fully as to the significance of the coin as the standard money. Certain controlling provisions of the coinage law have not yet been considered.

The state reserves the exclusive right of coinage. No one other than the state may impress upon the material the mark which makes it money. No other evidence of the money content than the impress of the state is permitted. To what other authority could a function so important to the regular course of affairs be entrusted without incurring the risk of grave abuses? It is true that in earlier days even the government did not always prove deserving of the confidence to which they pretended. Only too frequently they shamefully abused the right of coinage by debasing currency and later by issuing worthless paper money in order to increase revenues. However, for a considerable time now in all modern countries the function of coinage has been recognized as an important duty which every government has faithfully discharged. Wherever this stage of development has been reached the restriction of the right of coinage to governmental authority has been upheld in the recognized interest of the public.

Similarly all people have a common interest in the legal enforcement of the validity of the currency created by the state. Once the state creates money that shall serve as legal tender, in which all payments shall be made except those for which a contract stipulates payment in a different kind of money, the monetary system has reached a stage of the greatest possible simplicity. The state then protects all individuals against the chicane of those who would refuse to receive the universal means of payment in settlement of their demands. The power of the state to give currency to its coins gives the legal basis for the mass habit of acceptance which always forms about every well administered domestic currency. Whenever foreign coins or bars of gold are to be used in particular cases, special agreements to this effect are required; the universal means of payment is to be found exclusively in the form of the familiar domestic coin which it becomes almost impossible to dissociate from the idea of money.

Every people who recognize a specialized monetary system come to regard the precious metal itself merely as merchandize. They look upon it as nothing more than the material of which money is made, and respect it as money only when it is coined. The public at large and even the great majority of business men have become so thoroughly accustomed to the coined form of money and repose such confidence in the official coinage, that they take little thought of the material content of the coins. This is true more especially as few who use them know accurately the precise quantity of gold each coin should contain. However if the currency should again be debased as in former times, it would soon come to pass again that the fineness of the material would be tested and the weight verified on the jeweler's balance. With the present historical background, the magic of the coin form nowhere goes to the length of making the material of the money a matter of indifference.

That the coin has never attained this position despite the governmental privilege is explained by a section that is incorporated in every system of coinage regulations. This section supplements the restriction by virtue of which the right of coinage inheres in the state alone. Every private individual has the right to have coined for his account gold which he delivers to the government mints. For the monetary material which he surrenders, he receives the amount of money determined by the standard of coinage. In most countries a brassage charge is made for this service; but there are coinage laws which meet the public need to the extent of coining gold free of all charges.

It might be held that this transaction between the state and a private individual consists in an exchange of wares for money. In fact it is customary to speak of the "coin-price" received by the individual from the state, but in truth there is no exchange, and there is no price in this transaction. The two parties do not meet as supply and demand and no trace may be found of the determinations of value which accompany an exchange. All that happens is that the mechanical process of minting, which as a rule the state performs for itself, according to the monetary standard, is now performed at the request of a private individual. A bar of gold is turned in, weighing one German pound and is divided into 69.75 or 82 pieces which the state fashions into the form prescribed by the coinage regulations and designates as 20 Marks or 20 Crowns. These names are simply statements of the amount of the fine metal content. They do not express an exchange value, and, as we shall see later on, do not in the proper sense establish a nominal value. The concept of the value coins, which we all automatically associate with their names, arises exclusively from their value in exchange which is formed socially in the market. Even where the name of the coin is a direct derivative of its weight, as, for example, the Pound which occurs in so many languages, the exchange-value concept is immediately associated with the weight name. The former so impresses everybody that it inevitably transforms the weight name into a value name. This term of value remains current even after the coin has long since relinquished the mere semblance of its original weight.

The governmental prerogative of minting is largely compensated for by free coinage for private account, and by the effect which the exercise of this right has on the value of the coin. If this right did not exist and the state were negligent in the process of coining for its own account, so that it supplied less than the number of coins required for trade, then the value of money would necessarily rise, perhaps to a marked degree above the value of the bullion. The reverse condition, that with over-abundant coinage, the value of money would fall below the value of the bullion content, can never become a practical fact. It will be seen at once that as soon as the depreciation of the money became noticeable, people would withdraw money from circulation and melt it up in order to take advantage of the higher value of the metal. By the right of free coinage the determination of the quantity of money is left to private individuals. Dealers in precious metals and speculators will recognize opportunities to realize a profit from differences which may arise between the price of the coin and the price of the metal. The expenses which arise in these manipulations irrespective of brassage, such as transportation, loss of interest and the like, are small. The coin price will probably always be the most important component of the market price. Though the fluctuations of supply and demand exert their influence in the money market and the metal market, the market price of gold is never able to depart widely from its coin price. On the other hand, the disparity which may arise between the two prices when the right of free coinage is abolished may be seen in the fall of the price of silver since the cessation of its free coinage.

The result of our investigation of the significance of the coin form, may be summarized in the conclusion that in principle money and the monetary material are to be distinguished, but that in practice the values of money and bullion coincide wholly, or almost wholly.

The right of free coinage has important effects in the international money economy. International monetary systems are kept apart by the jealously guarded independence of the state coinage laws and by the historically transmitted diversities of the standards of coinage. On the other hand they are united by the homogeneity of the monetary material in all countries which are on a gold standard. The value of money by virtue of the right of free coinage is held in agreement with the value of gold in the world market save for trifling fluctuations and departures. Thus a condition is brought about internationally by the material identity of gold which after all closely approaches complete monetary unity in the essential effect of constancy of values.

The more accurate and detailed exposition of these relations properly belongs in the theory of world economy. In the closed social economy, another problem demands our consideration. If the relationship between bullion and money is such as we have represented it to be, the question must be raised in what manner the value which is transferred to money from its material is related to the exchange value which it derives from its service of the payment of prices.

The relationship of bullion and money being such as we have shown, it would seem that money derives its value from the value of the monetary material. But we have deduced the exchange value of money from another source, namely from its service in the payment of prices. Does this not involve a contradiction?

There is in fact no contradiction; the two ideas may be shown to be entirely consistent. The resultant force of two streams from different sources establishes the value of money. It is a compound of the value in use which the bullion acquires from its manifold industrial employments—its use for purposes of ornament, for utensils and technical services of every description—and of the exchange value which it derives from functioning as a means of paying prices. Each of these two streams, the use service of the material and the service in payment of the money, flows independently. It is the same condition that one encounters so often of a commodity receiving a direct use-value from its consumptive employment in the household and acquisitive- or yield-value from its assignment to production. For instance when a landowner himself consumes a part of his crops and sells another, his valuation will be determined by both uses. The decisive marginal utility is ascertained by balancing the services against each other. The same conditions hold in the case of money; its value is the resultant of the joint force of the effect produced by the service of the coin as a medium of exchange and by the industrial uses of the gold.

This joint resultant is noticeable in the value of gold as well as in the value of money. The value of gold is increased because of the fact that it satisfies not only industrial but also monetary demands. The value of money stays in close accord with the value of gold which is thus ascertained. Under present conditions the monetary use is the more important of the joint forces, since far more gold is coined than is used industrially.

We may go still farther and insist that each of the two uses is sufficiently independent so that it would continue even though the other should disappear. The practical use of gold would not cease, should the minting of gold be discontinued. No more would its use as money end, if the state were to prohibit its industrial use and were to seize all gold for coinage. In both cases an enormous disturbance of values would follow, as occurs whenever the conditions of demand are fundamentally displaced. The disturbance would be greater if its use as money were to cease, because this employs the larger quantity of the metal; but in either case after some time a regular series of values would be re-established on the new basis.

The prevailing bullionist theory follows a different reasoning. According to this theory the bullion value of money is equivalent to the use-value of the monetary material. When the exchange-value of money coincides with the bullion value, it shows simply the use-value of the bullion. The current bullionist theory could not conceive of money made of valueless material; it holds that money could surely never measure the value of commodities if in its own material it did not possess value.

However, this constantly repeated argument is not conclusive. It is true that worthless money could never be a standard of value in commodities; it would therefore be useless as a standard of value. But it does not follow that money is worthless merely because it is made of worthless material. The material of paper money is as nearly worthless as can be imagined. Paper money is useless in foreign countries and does not serve as money in international transactions. Yet, despite the worthlessness of its material, the history of almost every country shows that it is fitted to perform the function of money in the markets of natural values and therefore to measure the value of commodities. As soon as a circulating medium has gained general acceptability, it also acquires exchange-value whether the material of which it is made has exchange-value or not. Paper money for which the mass habit of acceptance has been historically formed is given and received not merely as a symbol of value, as a mere order to deliver natural values, but exactly like metallic money itself it becomes a vehicle of individual value. As soon as the general public is assured of the universal acceptability of paper money, each of the individual economies participating in the general traffic attaches its personal exchange-value to the money by the same rules that determine the exchange-value of metallic money; on the basis of the generally adopted appraisal of its exchange-value, paper money will acquire a social economic exchange-value exactly as does metallic money.

It may possibly also be objected that every exchange-value presupposes use-value and that therefore money must also have use-value if it is to have exchange-value. This argument also is inconclusive. A means of transportation does not need to have any other use than the carriage of goods in order to possess exchange-value. No more does money, the means of transportation in the traffic of value as it might be called, have to convey use by virtue of its material composition in order to have exchange-value. It is sufficient, if the money facilitates the circulation of other things which have use-value.

As we have shown in an earlier connection, the prevailing doctrine denies its own principles if it develops a theory of its own of the exchange-value of money. If money-value were always riveted to the use-value of the monetary material, what influence could the facts of the demand for money, rapidity of circulation and quantity of credit substitutes still exert?

The kernel of truth in the bullionist theory is this: the use-value of the precious metals was significant during the period of the adoption of money. Had silver and gold not been esteemed as materials for ornament, for use in utensils and the like, these metals would never have been selected to serve as media of exchange in trade. Metallic money had to plead its cause to traffic by its material value, in order that the mass-habit of use could attach to it. By virtue of its material value it inaugurated its service as money. But once the mass habit was formed, the historical aid which was indispensable to its introduction could drop out without endangering its further use as money and its fitness for use as an exchange value. Once this money-value is acquired, in historical continuity it becomes the basis on which the money-value of the future will further assert itself and will continue its course.

§ 52. The Nominal Value of Money

The nominal value of small change and silver-coin—The nominal value of the banknote and the check—The nominal value in changes of standard—Debasements of coin—Paper money—Knapp's "state theory of money," and nominalism.

The monetary unit, the declared standard money, is insufficient to fulfil the requirements of trade. Over and above the means of payment by credit, it is everywhere supplemented by other sorts of coins. We find as such the commercial coins, small change and the current silver money. We shall not have to discuss here the commercial coin, which is intended for foreign trade. Small change and current silver are used exclusively in internal dealings; they are constituents of the monetary system of the country.

The small change, made of base metal or of silver, is intended for small payments which cannot be made in the larger coin. Small change is composed of fractional coins. As such it must be in determinate proportions to the unit of the standard money. The regularity of payments throughout the country would be seriously impaired, should this token money be subject to fluctuations of value in terms of the standard coin. For the purpose of regulating this value, the state issues a denominational value-order, declaring how many fractional coins are to be computed to the standard coin; the order directs that the fractional coins have to be accepted in smaller payments, up to a certain amount, in this proportion.

To enforce the denominational value-order, it is necessary to issue small change below value, i. e., with a bullion content or value, lower than the denominational value specified in the coinage law. If small change were brought out at full value, there would be danger of the coins becoming excessive in value with the smallest rise of the market-price of their metal. This, then, might tempt the public to withdraw them from circulation and melt them down. The issue below value has the further advantage that the coins are of more convenient form, while the state realizes a profit, which can be conveniently used in covering the considerable expense of coining.

The right of free coinage cannot be granted in the case of small change. The decision to coin these must be left exclusively to the state, otherwise the denominational value could not be maintained. If private persons might give orders to coin, the value of the coins would always be reduced to costs, i. e., metal value plus expenses of coining.

Silver currency is an intermediate form between small change and standard-money. As the best known illustrations, the thaler in Germany and the silver gulden in Austria may serve. We have here an historical result of the peculiar circumstances under which the countries on a silver standard and double standard accomplished during the last decades the transition to the gold-standard. This transition was accomplished by a severe drop in the price of silver, which made the rejection of the old stores of silver standard-coins the source of such amazing losses, that it was decided to retain such remaining bullion as could not be immediately transformed into small change. This was done by the express retention of the traditional, compulsory acceptance law of historical origin. By a different method, the United States of America have obtained their silver currency; but it is not part of our task, and cannot serve our purpose, to enter into details of this sort. All that we can wish to accomplish, is to determine the concept of this silver currency. Now, as heretofore, payment of even the largest sums of money may be lawfully offered in this money as well as in the standard. The seller or the creditor is bound to accept this payment. As a matter of fact, to be sure, it is never used for really large payments, but only for such as rise only slightly above the level of those in which small change is used. For the rest, these coins are legally, too, placed on a level with small change; their coinage for private account is barred—and the state goes even further, renouncing for itself as well all further coinage. The coinage-law accords to them the nominal value of a fractional coin. Although issued in its day as of full value, this current silver has become depreciated by the drop in the price of the metal. Its nominal value has been taken over from the old relation existing between gold and silver before the silver crisis, and stands high above the money-value.

The nominal value of small change and of silver currency is to be defined as the value established by the state for the fractional coin in terms of the money-unit. But the command of the state does not by itself accomplish the end. Should the state issue more fractional coin than the traffic can absorb, the state's edict would never be able to uphold the denominational value. The ultimate source for increased denominational value of the fractional coins is to be found in the socially established exchange-value of the standard-money to which they are allied by the universal practice, regulated by government. In their increased denominational value, they participate in the value-producing effect of monetary service, which has created the exchange-value of the standard-money. This is the same effect which maintains the exchange-value of the gold money high above the level at which the gold price could maintain itself, were gold to derive its value solely from its industrial uses. It is also the same effect as that to which paper-money, similarly prepared from worthless material, owes its value in the last instance.

The nominal value of bank-notes and checks signifies something very different from that of the fractional coin. Banknotes and checks are not worth less than face value; their nominal value is placed at par, the amount at which they are to be taken up. Every well administered bank of issue or clearing-bank maintains the nominal value, without being directed to do so by some supporting governmental command. There are many countries where banknotes, unaided by obligations which have been legally imposed, remain in circulation at full face value; certainly in the case of checks a compulsory rate of exchange has never been considered.

The monetary standard has no nominal value. It does not even admit of such a concept; for there is no higher money to which it might be subordinated, like a fractional coin, by a law to that effect. Nor is that notion of a nominal value, which is peculiar to the payment by credit instruments, presently to be redeemed, to be applied to the metallic standard. The currency legislation, which establishes compulsory acceptance of the standard money, does not set its nominal value. Even such an edict would fail to operate in the case of price-payments, where parties are always at liberty to agree upon the sort of money in which the price is to be paid and, in case they decide to pay the price in standard money, are free to agree upon the price. The state has no power to control the exchange-value of money; the only way to bind it to a constant norm would be by market-legislation. The state would have to make the hopeless attempt to fetter by law the prices of all things or the general price-level. In the case of assignment-payments the parties also are at liberty to determine the species of money, as well as the amount to be paid. This is not true in the payments of debts which do not call for especial kinds of money. The creditor is bound to accept payment in standard money. But even here the compulsory acceptance of the gold standard coins does not in point of fact carry a command regarding value; the law declares nothing further than that the Mark or Crown pieces, issued by the state, are the coins in which the debt of Marks or the debt of Crowns may be legally discharged. A broader intention thus to enhance the value of either Mark or Crown is wholly foreign to the law.

In countries with a double standard it is necessary in the interest of unity and the stability of the monetary system to bring the standard gold and silver coins into a firm relation of nominal value to each other. It would never do to permit their relative value to depend on the fluctuations of the market prices of gold and silver. As to the value of the standard money as a whole, nothing is determined by this edict of nominal value either.

Just as regard to the certainty of transactions demands that the monetary system should possess homogeneity in itself, so it renders imperative the preservation of unbroken unity in the transition from standard to standard. With every change of the standard, whether it be in the metal employed or the standard adopted, it is indispensable that the value be regulated by laws, which the unit of the new standard money is to possess in comparison with the old. There must, especially, be provisions as to the manner in which obligations, demanding the old standard, are to be fulfilled in the new standard. The relation of the two standards to each other should be so regulated, that neither the party making nor the party receiving payment is detrimentally affected. The law fixing the nominal value in the case of change of standard, should never have the effect of increasing the value of coins, as it does in case of fractional currency. With a mere change of the coinage standard, the relation is to be computed accurately according to the ratio of the weights of the old and the new coin; in case of change of the standard metal—and similarly in case of change from paper money to metallic standard—the proportion will be taken to aid the computation, which exists between the old standard and the foreign standards employing the newly selected standard metal. The test of the correct computation of the relation is that the market prices in the new money remain in exactly the same relation as the old market-prices.

Debasement of coinage in former times introduced changes in monetary standards with the intention of obtaining a pecuniary gain for the state. A coin of less weight was issued under the same name as the old coin, subject to a law fixing the nominal value so as to place it on a par with the old and heavier coin. The power of the state is equal to the task of enforcing a law of nominal value for those payments which the state itself makes to dependent officials and military men; it is equal to the task of enforcing it in the case of the payment of debts to its own creditors, as well as in case of the payment of debts in private intercourse; the judge, called upon to decide the question in litigations, is bound by the state coinage law. But as against the market, the state proves powerless; price-payments are beyond the jurisdiction of the state, they are exclusively controlled by the agreements of the parties of interest.

When a sovereign state finds itself without the means of defraying expenses and issues irredeemable paper-money, it adopts the outward form of banknotes; but the nominal value attached to its symbols of money is not secured by cash reserves or approved evidences of indebtedness as in the case of banknotes. The nominal value of paper-money is the value which the state decrees for its notes in terms of the standard metallic money; it designates the number of units of metallic money for which the state's note is to be accepted in payment. What has just been said in regard to the debasement of coins applies to the effect of this law fixing nominal value. The state can enforce it in payments to its employees, and it can also enforce it in payments of debts. But it can never maintain an order of this sort in the market of natural values.

Let us confine ourselves to the exchange-traffic of a closed economy. We disregard all speculative influences to which the rate of exchange of paper-money in the international markets is subject. This is influenced by the probability of ultimate redemption, a condition which we do not feel called upon to discuss at present. It is quite clear that in such an economy the formation of the exchange-value of paper money in the market is controlled by exactly the same law as the exchange-value of money generally, and that the effect of an excessive issue of paper-money must be essentially the same as that of an excessively augmented production of the precious metals. When the state increases its emissions of paper money in rapid succession to enormous sums—as happens in times of great financial stress—the depreciation of paper-money must result even more rapidly and in a higher degree than has ever occurred through the depreciation of metallic money. The effect on the national economy will, therefore, be much more ruinous. At short intervals of time the exchange-value of money will be lowered again and again, just as the individual economies have barely adjusted their plans of acquisition and expenditure to its limits. Those who have just been confidently named among the wealthy, will perhaps be wealthy no longer; those who to-day were able to meet their obligations, will perhaps not be able to meet them to-morrow. Numerous and momentous displacements in acquisitions and possessions will take place. They necessarily lead to disastrous disturbances of the entire national economic process.

The evil results of experiments which have so far been made with paper-money, issued as a sovereign state's signal of distress, prove absolutely nothing against paper-money in itself. In its own nature, paper-money is by no means of uncertain or fluctuating value; it becomes so only by the circumstances under which it is ordinarily issued. If once the state should issue it, no longer in its own immediate and selfish interest, but solely in order to substitute a well regulated monetary symbol for the costly, inconvenient hard money, which depends so much on the results of the production of the precious metals, the effect will be an entirely different one. If the owners of the notes but feel assured that in seeking to purchase commodities they will not be exposed to loss from the face-value of their paper, the old prices will still be asked in every sale. The reappraisal of all market-values to fit a new standard, on the part of all buyers and sellers without exception, is an exceedingly complicated and laborious process which the market is not overready to undertake. Experience has shown in many places that the mass-habit of acceptance for emergency money of the state is easily enough formed—in this direction the power of the state proves exceedingly effective—and that at first, so long as the state's emergency money is issued only in moderate amounts, no higher domestic prices will be contracted for in paper than those in metal had been up to that time. Nor would the market be revolutionized even later by a well regulated body of paper-money. The notes would take over the exchange-value of the coin, in the place of which they would appear. They would retain this value without being exposed to the disturbances which, to-day, have their origin in the production of the precious metals.

That state-controlled paper-money has not already successfully occupied its position in the economic and financial world, may be explained from the fact that money must serve its purpose as a means of payment not only in domestic but also in foreign commerce. So far in the commerce of the world, only gold has historically acquired this mass-habit of acceptance. It is this fact which secures to gold, for the present, the controlling position also as domestic money. Gold money, as a free, social institution, has prevailed beyond the boundaries and the oppositions of states. These have so far made a common regulation of paper-money impossible, and will possibly prevent it for a long time, if not forever. All the states which have been forced to issue emergency money and whose citizens become accustomed to the use of paper-money, would surely have preferred, when they proceeded to the stabilization of the disordered monetary system, to regulate paper-money as such, rather than assume the enormous burdens incidental to the resumption of the metallic standard. But the losses, threatening the national economy from the isolation of its monetary system, are the greater of the two evils. The costly, inconvenient coin, affected by the fluctuations of the production of precious metals, is the less objectionable evil because it best secures an international constancy of values; it is thus preferable to the best regulated paper-money, confined to a single state.

Knapp's "State Theory of Money" starts from the fact that the original "pensatorical" payment by weighing the metal has been abolished in every country, and that men pay everywhere by surrendering imprinted pieces, invested by the authority of government with authoritatively definite validity in units of value. He calls this "chartal" payment, by the side of which prevails "giral" payment or transfer of a credit on some central office. Money involves "chartal" payment. In order that legal regulation should be able to confer on money a definite validity in units of value, the idea of value-units (Mark, Franc, Rubel, Pound Sterling) must have been formed during the period of pensatorical payment; the legal regulations must have set out from this concept. At the present stage of development, the Mark can no longer be defined as the $\frac{1}{1395}$ part of a pound of fine gold. It has to be defined in the sense of the German coinage legislation, as the third part of the earlier unit of value, the German Thaler. The manner in which the state settles the value of money is by determining the basis on which units may be used in the payment of debts, especially in payments made to the state itself.

Knapp's nominalistic theory, contrasted with the bullionist theory, is an important advance. He finds that fundamentally the historical value-unit of a developed money has become independent of the metallic basis; and he succeeds in setting up a broader concept of money, surpassing that of bullion or cash.

For monetary policy, too, this theory is of importance. Knapp declares the state bound to regulate the system of payments; bound, especially, to steady the rate of exchange of the state's domestic currency, in its intercourse with important adjoining countries. He decides, that, for this purpose, the state has means at its disposal which, according to the strictly bullionist theory, must be barred.

The advance of Knapp's nominalistic theory is, however, counter-balanced by the narrowness to which it restricts the problem of the theory of money. Knapp is satisfied when he has discovered that the historical value-units of money have been formed; he makes no attempt whatever to explain how they could have been formed. As far as he is concerned, at any rate, the fact that money possesses value deserves no further consideration; all he knows is, that there are prices and levels of prices. But how—it must be asked—can the concept of a value-unit be understood by anyone who cannot explain how money becomes valuable? And what do we learn by a price-level, symbolized by money, if we are unable to evaluate the sums of money which are paid out as prices? As little as Knapp is able to explain how money has historically attained the standard of its value-unit, is he able to explain how the value-units, which have arisen historically, continue to change; neither can he explain in any way whatever the meaning of the changes which have occurred. To this extent, his theory, with its self-imposed limitations of enquiry, is indeed anything but an advance on the old bullionist theory, which stated the problem of the value of money with its fluctuations of value. Despite inadequate theoretical foundations of the latter theory, it nevertheless made important contributions to the solution of his problem. A satisfactory theory of money will have to unite both points of view; it will have to recognize the way in which the value of money is historically conditioned, detach it from its metallic basis, and disclose the final law of its social formation and change.

The theoretical shortcoming of Knapp's theory shows itself also in the practical application, made by himself to monetary policy. He overestimates the power of the state's determination of the nominal value, originating in the legal system of the state. The state can never succeed in finally settling, as regards other countries, the rate of exchange of its money; the state cannot maintain the nominal value of an excessive issue of paper-money. At this day there exists no full-fledged security for the money-system of any country, other than its being made to rest on the gold-basis, which alone has hitherto historically won the mass-habit of acceptance throughout the world. The power which the state exercises over money by virtue of the determination of the nominal value proves, as regards the effect in world-economy, too feeble. By its value in the commerce of the world, money shows itself to be not an institution of the state but of society, which the state must be held to regulate on the basis society affords.

§ 53. The Law of Change In the Value of Gold

The change of the general price level—The depreciation of money—Money-value and credit-crises—"Appreciation of money" and "general overproduction."

The changes in the value of money which we shall now have to discuss are exclusively those of its exchange-value. Changes in the use-value of the monetary material and in the rate of interest, "the price of the use of money," "as it is generally called, only indirectly influence the value of money. The direct effect of the value of the material is so insignificant that we need not further discuss it; that of the rate of interest we shall consider in its appropriate connection. We need not speak at all of nominal value. Under normal conditions the state is not called upon to label the standard money with a nominal value which is intended to fix its value and to affect the exchange value of money.

Every change in the value of money presupposes a change in the general price level, but not every general shift in prices points to a change in the value of money. A progressive rise of the general price level—a similar distinction would have to be made for the process of a progressive reduction of prices—may be accompanied by such a marked reduction in the supply of goods that the public has to curtail its consumption of the daily necessities as well as its total consumption. But a progressive rise of the general price level may also occur while the margin of supply for the mass of the people remain unchanged; more than this, the margin may possibly be extended at this time.

There is an essential difference between these two conditions of rising prices. In the final analysis the first affects the natural values. The second affects only money. The first arouses a deeper and more general anxiety; the second affects only individual groups of people and excites a theoretical rather than a personal interest. The rising prices which are at present to be observed in all directions, may possibly be a resultant of the two causes.

Scientific explanations are agreed as to the practical aspect of the two conditions. They are at variance as to the terminology to be used in presenting the problem. A large number, probably the majority of economists speak in both cases of a change in the value of money, distinguishing the change of money-value itself from that of the supply of commodities. However, as we shall immediately see, the distinction does not wholly coincide with the opposition of the two conditions. Before defining our attitude in the matter, we shall enter upon a more accurate investigation of the actual course of events.

The most frequently discussed and the most obvious case of change in the value of money is the shrinkage of value or depreciation of money, as it occurs in consequence of an increase of the available amount of standard money. Excessive production of the precious metals or excessive issue of paper money will both alike lead to depreciation. The equation of supply and demand is disturbed by the increase in the quantity of money. The demand, which originates with the money form, increases, but the supply of natural values remains the same. Neither the gold miner who has struck an exceedingly rich deposit or the state which issues paper money in huge quantities are under any compulsion to introduce beforehand into the economic organism natural values in equal amounts which would prepare the ground for their demand. They appear as purchases in a market which they have never entered as sellers. Therefore they do not meet ready sellers without disturbing the market. Their demand may possibly contribute to an enlargement in production and to an increase in the supply. However this possibility is another matter which we shall presently consider in another connection. For the present let us simplify our investigation by assuming that production is incapable of development or is capable of only slow growth. Under such conditions the newly added demand can only be satisfied as it secures a part of the supply by out-bidding the earlier demand. The prices of those articles to which the new purchasing power is directed will rise. In further sequence the prices of all those goods will rise which are demanded by the sellers who have been thus enriched. If the quantity of new money which is thrown into the market is sufficiently large, the entire general level of prices must ultimately rise. Within the restricted area of a mining district which is scantily supplied with commodities the increase of the demand in times of abundant yields will be strongly felt and will rapidly exert marked effects in increasing prices. In the broad world markets during short periods of time, the effects are less perceptible, for the significance of the annual increment of gold, however great, is small when contrasted with the enormous monetary income of the entire world. However, when the metallic supplies remain large during a longer period of time, their effects will be felt by virtue of a summation of the annual increments even in the world market.

The multiplication of commercial paper of banknotes and checks does not act to depreciate the money market, for all these means of payment by credit are the outgrowth of the monetary requirements of increased commercial intercourse; their appearance does not affect the equation of supply and demand. The well managed bank does not force its credits upon commerce. It extends its discounts only so far as the business would offer acceptable commercial drafts. The amount of the new means of payment which it issues on discounting a draft is limited by the quantities of products which have been freshly introduced into trade. Credit media come and go with the movement of commodities in business; they sublimate the natural values and are their companion values in monetary form. They afford one of those surprising examples of free, individualistic, yet social institutions which are more perfectly adjusted to the general interest than would be possible through the most thoroughly considered, purposeful contrivances of the state. The voluntary organization of credit has achieved what no regulation of state-contrived monetary systems has heretofore been able to attain: a standard which receives its quantitative norm from the service of money itself. Banks and the large business houses whose commercial paper the banks discount are the guardians of this standard. The volume of minted gold money which is valid in all modern states is determined by the manifestation of the spirit of enterprise in mining operations. Nowhere has this been subjected to the monetary system; it is not even being attempted. Great as the disturbances in the economy of the world may be as a result of the decreasing value of gold, entrepreneurs will continue to mine gold as long as in so doing they realize personal profit. In contradistinction, credit-money fulfills the spirit of the institution of money as enlightened statesmanship would determine it. The latter would provide for impounding the gold obtained from the mines in order to hand it over to trade and to reappropriate it as the needs of commerce may demand.

It must be admitted that the voluntary reorganization of credit is not always equal to the magnitude of its task. It has often happened that the possibilities of credit have been abused. Although men have learned much in the school of experience, such abuse is likely to recur frequently. The great profits derived from rapid and extensive improvements in production tempt new enterprises which too rapidly exceed the limits fixed by commercial opportunity. Credit is then extended to the products of over-production which lack the fundamental inner qualifications by which credit is merited. The ease with which means of payment are magically procreated by an incautious administration of the credit system seduces the spirit of enterprise, especially when accompanied by declining rates of interest and carries enterprise farther and farther into the labyrinth of overproduction. Once credit is thus misapplied, the equation of demand and supply is interfered with. The frantic demand of entrepreneurs, operating with unsecured means of credit, enhances the price of productive means. These increased cost-prices raise the price of products as well. Then, when overproduction ends in crises of liquidation, the balance of supply and demand is disturbed in the opposite direction; there remains a supply of goods for which there are no buyers and the edifice of high prices collapses. The fabulous rise of prices is succeeded by a precipitate drop, with economic after-effects which may be devastating and of long duration, until finally the equilibrium of supply and demand is re-established.

The process of depreciation through an increase of metallic currency or paper money runs a different course from start to finish. Its progress is without ebb. It moves slowly, sometimes exceedingly so, without the strain of violent disturbances; but its effect on the monetary system is more lasting and more deeply rooted. There is no section of the nation's economy which does not suffer change, for money is the instrument which binds together all individual economies. The abuse of credit and overproduction after all affect only certain groups directly, and even mediately are not likely to make themselves felt in all directions. By the depreciation of money all prices are affected. The prices are permanently increased; the value of money is permanently changed. Because its value becomes unstable, money functions with constant friction. The plan of all private and public economies is adjusted to the presupposition of the constancy of the value of money; money is given and received by those who assume that in the future it will have the same purchasing power as it has here and now. When this assumption proves incorrect many expectations remain unfulfilled, numerous economies are disorganized and more than one is ruined. The groups who suffer most severely under such conditions are those drawing fixed incomes: officials, wage-earners, pensioners and annuitants who are unable to increase their capital. These men can no longer meet their accustomed expenses; they must reduce their demand, and this in turn reacts on the incomes of those whose customers they were.

Depreciation of money may result not merely from an inflation of the currency but also from changes with respect to goods. In the theory of changes of value and price we have already had occasion to discuss the effects which may result from the operation of the law of diminishing returns with regard to the value and price of products of the soil. Our explanation must now be amplified. In our earlier discussion we pointed out that the market follows one course when the effect of the law which increases costs is compensated or even overbalanced by advances of industrial technique or accumulations of capital and another when this is not the case. We shall now have to distinguish these two cases.

The development is more favorable under the first set of conditions. To be sure the historical continuity of price-formation will lead from increased costs of production to increased prices for the products of the soil. The latter are important constituents of the general price level, which will therefore rise. The prices of raw materials which the soil supplies, enter as elements of cost into their finished products. Similarly the cost of subsistence enters into the prices of products, in so far as it influences the rate of wages. Everything will be more expensive, but the marginal utility of food and expenses generally will not be raised. Despite the increased expenditure of money, men will be able on the average to provide for themselves as abundantly or more so than they did before; the per capita budget of goods will not have decreased. If we assume that a hundred weight of wheat was formerly sold for 10 units of the standard money, its price will now be higher, perhaps 12 units. However, since the personal margin of use has remained the same or has even been lowered, the larger price is the expression of the same or a lower marginal utility: i. e., the value of money must have fallen, since the same unit of utility is expressed in more units of money. On "the side of commodities" the value of money has changed.

In the second case the price for products of the soil will rise but the per capita volume of the means of sustenance is also changed. It will fall and the margin of use will be higher. If the price of a hundredweight of wheat rises to twelve units as in the first case, although the relationship of price and quantity is the same, conditions will have changed radically in that the hundredweight of wheat represents a different number of units of utility. In all households the unit quantity of food is represented by a higher marginal sum in the scale of needs and thus an exact foundation for arithmetical comparison is lacking; the increased degree of intensity of the new marginal use cannot be arithmetically compared with the older and lower one. Only one thing is clear: the average personal appraisal of a hundredweight of wheat, i. e., its general subjective economic evaluation is higher. Because this is so the conclusion will be reached that the increased price level is an adequate expression of the changed value of goods. Change has occurred, not in the value of money but in that of wares. Indeed it is not proper to say that the value of money has declined when the price of wheat rises in a transition from a period of ample supply to another with a restricted supply and a higher rate of marginal expenditure. On the contrary, precisely because money indicates the changed value of goods and the alteration of the general price level, it has shown itself to be an accurate and stable measure of price. Money under these conditions is analogous to the column of mercury in the thermometer which shows itself to be a reliable gauge by registering a higher index with a rise in temperature.

But if the ratio of agricultural products to population becomes permanently and to an increasing extent unfavorable, the entire structure of the national economy must be shaken. Under these conditions, an increasing proportion of the productive means must be devoted to raising the fruits of the soil which are indispensable to the maintainance of life. Industrial technique will not be able to effect further advances. It will even become impossible to maintain the established technological procedure because productive means will have to be withdrawn in greater and greater quantities from industry and turned over to agriculture. Large numbers of individuals will be deprived of their means of earning a livelihood. The total national income will be lowered in both its monetary and its natural forms. Gradually the entire economy of the nation will collapse; its capital will be consumed, yields reduced and industries will be forced to resort to a less intensive use of capital. All this will be accompanied by progressive thinning out of the population and subsequent upheavals of the price-level and the value of money. The course of these latter events, however we shall not trace in our present investigation.

It has become customary to contrast depreciation with the appreciation of money. As the former is the result of an increase of money, so the latter is popularly held to be the result of glutting the market with commodities, until the need of money exceeds the available amount of this medium. Under these conditions it is thought the prices of all commodities and the general price level must fall and the value of money must rise. One may well imagine conditions in which there would be no demand, supported by an adequate supply of money, for the abundant and newly manufactured products and natural values. Even the resort to credit, and payment by means of credit media might not be sufficient to raise the demand to the extent of the supply. Hence producers would have to cut their selling prices in order to dispose of their stocks.

This doctrine of the appreciation of money originates in the fact that its authors have misunderstood, or, at any rate, not altogether properly interpreted the idea of the "need for money." It goes without saying that we cannot impute to the discoverers of the quantitative theory the gross blunder of deducing the demand for money[1] from a "need"[2] for money in daily life. But we are

1 Geldbedarf.

2 "Geldbedürfnis.

safe in maintaining that their doctrine of the appreciation of money was largely dictated by their leaning in the theory of the value of money excessively to the pattern of the theory of the value of goods. Especially they draw too close an analogy between the concepts of the need of money and that of goods.

The appreciation of money of which they treat is the exact counterpart of the law of demand applicable to natural values just as depreciation is the counterpart of the law of supply. As a matter of fact the need of money is nearly akin to the need of commodities. In the monetary economy, everyone meets his personal need of goods by first covering the need of money. The latter, like the former, is also influenced in the final analysis by the magnitude of the needs and the law of satiety. On the other hand it must not be forgotten that the monetary need is also determined by the historical value of money. Those who speak of the appreciation of money misjudge the power of this historical value for which every business man makes allowance in calculating his costs and prices. The appreciation of money would thwart the anticipations of every business man, would depress all sales prices and would decrease or wipe out all expected profits. Should it go still further, it would become impossible to recover costs incurred and would bring in its train a universal crisis which would be more ruinous than any crisis engendered by over-production in particular industries. Is it possible to believe that such a crisis will break upon the commercial world just as a general progress in all phases of production and of the preparation of values is being effected?

An old doctrine asserts correctly that a condition of "general overproduction" cannot arise. Partial overproduction is possible inasmuch as a particular type of production may be excessive, passing the general limit and reaching a point at which sales cannot be affected for the surplus product. "General overproduction" is inconceivable. A condition which would seem to warrant the use of this term would not be overproduction at all but would be a general production of surplus. The increased volume of products would bring with them increased sales, "wares being paid for by wares," natural values exchanging for other natural values. Where natural values increase in adjusted proportions there will be no difficulty in arranging for payments without provoking crises. Money will circulate more rapidly as sales are more numerous than before. Means of credit payments will be better organized as all improvements in their organization have been made under the increasing pressure of the need of money. The least favorable case will merely involve the retardation of production, perhaps its premature curtailment; it is possible that not all the natural values which may technically be produced will actually be; but those whose production has been determined upon will surely be sold without engendering a crisis, and therefore also without an appreciation of money.

During such periods of general progress whenever it is possible to stimulate the mining of precious metals, the bullion thus accruing is readily absorbed by commerce without producing the depreciation which at other times would necessarily follow. These mineral resources in their turn are the means of preventing a retardation of progress which it might not otherwise be possible to overcome. During such periods, the increase of money which permits all producible values to be actually turned out, results in the beneficial effect which some authors mistakenly ascribe to it under all circumstances.

The multiplication of the means of payment by credit alone will not overcome the obstacles to general progress. As they are at present developed, credit media do not enter all channels of payment. They cater to commerce and to the payments of the wealthy classes. Under present conditions ready money is absolutely indispensable to enable the payment of the new groups of workers which flow into industry during periods of industrial advance and to make possible the increased exchanges in rural districts which receive an impetus from the industrial advances. The sums of ready money which were sufficient during the mercantilistic period to carry on the households of wage-earners and the country population, would not even approximately meet the requirements of any industrial country today. Moreover increased amounts of ready money are necessary as a guarantee in developed credit transactions. Despite the admirable improvements in the use of bullion which have been worked out by the inventive genius of the English business communities the amount of actual cash carried by the Bank of England when it first entered business would be much too small to meet the present payments required under the English organization of credit. It is possible that a shortage in the mining of precious metals might give to nations who were unwilling to be hampered in their economic development, the impulse to use for the benefit of their industrial and financial progress the auxiliary paper money which so far has only been resorted to for the exigencies of war.

So far at any rate the most important periods of productive progress have always coincided with those of the most extensive gains in the mining of precious metals. The century of geographical discovery which disclosed new routes to the American sources of gold and silver supply was also the century of the evolution of the national economies of Central and Western Europe from the town and local economies of the Middle Ages. The modern growth of industrialism and capitalism has been accompanied by the discovery of new deposits of gold and silver in numerous newly settled districts. This is not an historical accident. The same spirit of progress, the same inventive intelligence, the same technical imagination, the same practical knowledge and organizing ability produce the two effects. Without the marine compass America would never have been discovered; without modern machinery the mines of South Africa would never have been exploited. The conclusion cannot be drawn from the historical parallelism that all future technical advances must equally increase man's hoards of the precious metals. We are satisfied to say that the trend of a process of appreciation in the value of money, as taught, cannot be reasonably maintained and that a cursory survey of past development shows not even the actual conditions which must be presupposed in a theory of appreciation. It must be left to the economic historian to furnish proof to the contrary by a careful examination of historical data.

While we deny the contention that increased commercial intercourse may lead to an appreciation in the value of money, we admit as a matter of course that an increase of goods, which extends to the margin of the provisioning of the mass of people and lowers the margin of use, must in historical continuity lead to a gradual decrease of the general price level. This is true under the supposition that a counter-effect induced by the law of diminishing returns does not manifest itself. This decrease of prices can no more be traced back to the value of money than can the general increase discussed above. It should properly be interpreted as an expression of the decreased value of goods.

§ 54. Historical Changes in the Value of Money and the Disappearance of Natural Economy

The development of the monetary economy since the century of geographical discovery—Concerning the causes of the present increase in prices.

The instruments of theory will never enable us to ascertain the extent to which the increased production of precious metals after the discovery of America had a share in the depreciation of money which has since taken place. To answer this question economic history should again examine the evidence and determine whether the quantitative theory offers sufficient explanation. There are inconsistencies between the dates of the beginning and end of this process and those which measure the period of the influx of the precious metals. Since Bodin, the quantitative theory has been used exclusively in the dominant explanation of this great phenomenon. It is not particularly in the convincing power of the proofs offered that the reason for the prevalence of this theory is to be sought. The reason lies rather in the fact that much as the quantitative theory has been disputed, it has never yet been supplemented, much less displaced by any other theory which admits of a wholly satisfactory explanation. Nevertheless, a consideration of the economic development of Europe which has taken place since the beginning of the discoveries, leads up to an idea of this kind. There is a temporal parallelism which suggests some sort of causal connection between the two processes of the depreciation of money and the disappearance of the rural natural economy as it was absorbed into the monetary economy.

Theory must at least examine by means of its typifying assumptions the manner in which the gradual absorption of the natural economy was bound to affect the price level and the value of money. At first glance it seems clear that prices which originate in the market are bound to grow with it. Nevertheless such an examination as this has been hitherto omitted. Until now all investigations of the change in the value of money have been undertaken with the tacit assumption that a complete monetary economy had already been established. As a matter of fact, this was anything but true at any time during the century of the great geographical discoveries; even today in Europe it is not wholly so.

The essentials at this point may be explained in a few words. Where the natural economy obtains, the producer in disposing of his wares includes in the money cost of his products only a fractional part of the total costs of production. Therefore the price which he demands and recovers is lower than it would be with an accurate calculation. That is to say, the producer allows only for the cost of materials. As a general rule, he sets down correctly only the most obvious even of these and neglects altogether the general costs of equipment or plant. Moreover he appraises the cost of his own labor at a very low figure, firmly believing that this is already covered by natural economic yields. In the first instance his sales are always sales by special opportunity; one might say by accident. Even if a producer should occasionally arrange for the production of certain industrial wares under the division of labor, he still continues to live in his own house, and to a large extent to provide all necessaries for himself from his own soil. Even when the further stage has been gradually reached at which the urban tradesman satisfies most of his household needs from the market, the prices of foodstuffs on the basis of which he calculates his costs, are still extremely low. The farmer who is selling his goods in the market does not figure his full expenses, for his own sustenance is still obtained in a natural economic way; he sells only such of his produce as is in excess of his personal wants. Even today in modern European countries, agriculture is not as completely adjusted to the money economy as are urban trade and industrial enterprise. In countries with an economic development such as that now existing in Austria Hungary or even in Germany, the natural economic process is still very prevalent and ties up a large aggregate of economic values which therefore do not attain their full significance in the computation of prices.

Only because of the intensified economic development of the last decades, has the absorption of peasant production by the money economy gone so far. The high money wages of industry have advanced the rates which the farmer is compelled to pay for labor. The towns have ceased to be the only great markets for the produce of the soil; industry has spread over the countryside, creating large markets even there. The mass of products purchased by the farmer have increased relatively as well as absolutely. Side by side with the sale of food-stuffs there has been an increase in the sale of raw materials. The peasant also begins to make pecuniary investments on a larger scale. Domestic agriculture comes more and more under the division of labor and is imbued with the spirit of the money economy. All these facts contribute to increase the outlay of money which the farmer should seek to recover in the price of his goods. Hence there is an increase in the selling prices which he must ask in order to meet his reckoning. Through the interrelationship of all production this process spreads; the enhanced cost of all necessaries of life raises the cost of industrial wages and, as a result, the price level of industrial products.

The increasing tendency to industry may increase the productivity of the national economy and the general prosperity of the country. It may more abundantly provide all classes of the people with natural values and may lower the margin of use for households throughout the land. None the less, the monetary expression of natural values in the general price level must rise so long as the absorption of natural economic elements persists, for during this period monetary computation penetrates more and more deeply into effective sources of goods which it had hitherto not reached. This expression includes more completely than before, the elements of price formation. Therefore, the continuity of the process must bring it about that to the price which had formerly prevailed and had covered only certain of the elements an addition must be made for the newly included ones. An identical degree of utility is compensated by an increased price; the value of money has been lowered.

The increasing burden of taxation contributes largely to the present increase in the general price level and to the depreciation of money. Taxes on production, being both direct and indirect, as well as those imposed on transfers, increase costs and must be recovered in the sales price. In so far as these payments are used to defray costs of government which directly increase the economic productivity of the country, it is true enough that the increased taxes will fall at a lower rate on the unit of resulting product and that the price level will not be increased by the amount of the tax; on the contrary, it will be reduced. But taxes paid to defray military expenses, interest on loans for mobilization, war debts and the like, increase the rate of cost and the price level. The same is also true of taxes to be applied to school expenses and other similar charges which look to distant improvements that can stimulate productivity only after a long lapse of time. The enormous increase of modern military expenditures has been caused by the system of military preparedness, increasing expenditures in times of peace in order—it is fondly hoped—thus to prevent wars or more speedily to end wars which cannot be prevented and to end them with smaller destruction of values. The proportion of the national wealth which has been destroyed by the last European wars is small in comparison to that caused by the devastations of the Thirty Years War.[1] Admitting that these hopes are justified and

[1] Trans. note: It should be recalled that this was written before the World War. The statement may possibly be true of it. It is less surprising when we recall that it refers to such events as the Balkan War and the Franco-Prussian

that the general prosperity of the country is increased in spite of the enormous expenses of preparations for war, these non-pacific expenditures will necessitate an increase in the prices of natural values. In fact the process which goes on here is the same which we found to occur in the disintegrating natural economy. The increasing preparedness of the government extends the process of the monetary economy to a safeguarding of the provision of commodities which had not hitherto been undertaken. The payment for this service must increase costs, while the war losses against which we seek to insure ourselves do not enter into the costs. The process of the formation of value is thus more comprehensively controlled by the money economy, than it was before. The continuity of price-formation must increase the price and the value of money must fall below its former level.

The striking rise of the general price level which is to be observed in all modern countries, in so far as it cannot be traced to the absorption of the rural natural economy, may be due to three different causes: a depreciation of money owing to increased production of the precious metals; growing burdens of taxation; and the influence of the diminishing returns of the soil. We shall not inquire here whether the decreasing productivity of metal and coal mines is another factor. Neither can the theorist be expected to decide how much of the general effect is to be attributed to any of the three main causes, nor to answer the question whether the increase of the general price level is accompanied by a lowering of the average standard of living.

§ 55. Measuring the Value of Money

Measuring the price level by means of index numbers—The problem of measuring the value of money.

Index numbers are resorted to in order to measure the value of money and the variations of this value. Reduced to its essential elements this method of measurement consists in selecting a number of goods whose market prices are regarded as characteristic of the general price level, in aggregating the prices of all selected articles in the years which are being compared and in accepting the relationship of these sums as the expressions of the variations of the value of money from year to year. The value of money is considered to have fallen or risen by as great a per cent as the sum has increased or decreased. The earliest series of index numbers, that of 1850, contained the wholesale price of 23 articles, one of which was subsequently omitted. The series was confined to the most important food-stuffs and industrial

War, which in the light of the experience of 1914-1918 may hardly be considered as modern warfare.

raw materials. In later series, the number of articles was greatly increased; 34, 114, even 223 prices were noted. In place of average prices, effective prices were observed; retail prices replaced those of the wholesale trade. Wages were inserted by the side of prices of merchandise. One point should be especially observed: consideration was given to the quantities of the selected goods which entered the market.

In all its multifarious forms, the method of index numbers has a fundamental defect. The method is a useful expedient by which to appraise the general price level and its variations through the selection of characteristic prices. However, it by no means measures variations in the value of money. No matter how precisely the method may be elaborated there will always remain a difference of opinion as to whether the ascertained variations are to be traced to the value of money, or whether they have originated independently of that value. For instance after the general crisis of 1873, the index numbers dropped for a number of years. One group, the bimetalists, who expected to derive an argument in favor of their proposals, claimed that this was an expression of the appreciation of money which was bound to occur because silver had been ousted and gold made the exclusive standard. On the other hand, the advocates of the gold standard contended that the phenomenon was the result of the conditions of production in the world-markets. They held that the crisis depressed prices by excessive competition on the part of the supply, whereupon producers had lowered their costs as much as possible in order to adjust their production to the reduced receptivity of the market. Similarly in nearly all such cases two points of view can be maintained for the changed expression of price: the change starts "from the wares" or "from money," or, as it should be more properly stated, it is the outgrowth of changed conditions of the supply of goods or else occurs without such change.

The simple proposition already put forward by Adam Smith is much more to the point than this modern and over-subtle method. He suggests the use of grain which is man's principal food as a standard for the value of money, and for the variations of this value over periods of time or in different localities. He says that the value of precious metals changes but little during short periods of time, but in the long run is subject to great variations. In contrast to this he maintains that the value of grain varies greatly from year to year with the condition of the harvest, but that the average over longer periods shows only trifling fluctuations. It is true that this proposition cannot be accepted to the full extent of Adam Smith's statement. But we are in accord with it with the limitations that in all observed cases the same type of nationality is presupposed; that the conditions of production are not too diverse; and, most important of all, that the mass-energy of labor is the same. With these limitations it appears to be true that, while man does not control the production of grain quite so completely as regularly to secure an annual harvest that bears a fixed relationship to his needs, in the long run he none the less does steadily maintain the desired proportion. For these longer periods, despite all fluctuations, the average value of grain is held at approximately the same marginal utility. Subject to the limitations mentioned, we may therefore safely conclude that the value of money has been lowered in the same proportion as the average price of grain rises, and vice versa.

Daily experience points the way to a more accurate scientific method of measuring the value of money which might be elaborated. Every traveller visiting a foreign country in which the market prices are different from those to which he has been accustomed at home soon notices the departure from his calculations in the new standard. Also he will have little difficulty in finding an expression for the difference of value in the foreign market and at home. He is likely to determine the general price level of the new market in so far as it affects him personally; but he will not stop there as the method of index numbers erroneously does. He will probably compare the observed price level with the amount of his income and he will reach the conclusion that the value of money is higher if he can purchase more natural values for his household with the prevailing income, and that it is lower if he has to content himself with a smaller quantity of natural values. The scientific method of ascertaining the value of money should start from precisely this basis; it must compare the sums of money that are necessary for a certain provision of natural values with the money income. It should do this for all strata of the people and for all local differences of the price level, thus relating a series of index numbers of prices with one of income.

§ 56. The Money-Form of Capital

The concept of capital in daily speech—Money capital, loan capital, entrepreneur's capital—Private and social capital—The ultimate scientific concept of capital.

In the exchange-economy the natural form of values generally finds expression in a monetary form. This is even more true of capital. By the side of capital in its natural form we find its monetary counterpart. Money has won for itself a most comprehensive place in the thought of people because of its uniformity, its unmistakable characteristics and its adapatibility to numerical expression. This broad understanding of money has generated the ordinary concept of capital. When men speak of capital in daily intercourse, they invariably refer to the monetary form. We have already seen in the theory of the simple economy that there is no uniform scientific concept of capital but rather a number of conflicting ones. However, they are almost without exception in agreement in one respect: with a complete disregard of the current phrase, they are seemingly formed in opposition to it. The same theorists who could not break free from the fetters of daily speech in their ideas of value and other fundamental concepts, fell into the opposite error in defining capital and broke loose from the common usage with bold indifference. It is only recently that a few authors have sought to come in touch with the common meaning.

We ourselves shall conform to the principles of our general methodology. We take it for granted that the wealth of economic experience has shaped the connotation of words dealing not only with other fundamental economic concepts but with capital as well. We are entitled to expect that from this source will flow intimations which coalesce to render invaluable assistance in shaping the scientific principles which we seek. However, it cannot be expected that our progress should end on the threshold of common experience; science, to be true to its calling, must on occasion go far beyond the interests of daily life. Therefore we may need to supplement popular verdicts in one direction or other. But first of all it is incumbent upon us to interpret as carefully as possible the popular ideas that are here significant.

Such concepts, taken from the lips of laymen, are not readily definable. Their application is uncertain; towards the borderland of their associations they are indistinct. This is the case with the concept of capital as we get it from every-day speech. It includes a series of images of capital of which only the central one is clearly outlined and vivid; all the others merge into the twilight of inadequate definition. We are most likely to succeed if we direct our inquiry to the first of these figures, the central one, which is also the one most clearly defined.

The solid nucleus of the popular concept is the idea of monetary capital in the narrowest sense. Every sum of money that has been brought together to be expended in the process of acquisition is called money capital. This includes not only cash reserves but also those much larger sums which are held in other liquid form, especially those already invested at interest during the process of accumulation, provided that they may be cashed or transferred on short notice. Externally there is no difference between monetary capital and those sums of money designated for household expenditure. The two forms are usually held apart but not infrequently they are one mass. They are distinguishable solely by the use intended for them by the owner. Money capital is to yield acquisitive profits; the ready money of the household is to be used directly to cover domestic needs.

The most closely related type of capital to this first kind is the loan form. There is a liquid flow binding it to money capital invested at interest. All capital lent, that is not money capital, is loan capital, from short term business credits to long term or perpetual mortgage loans and annuities which are usually spoken of as capital investments.

There is a double connection between these two forms of capital. In the first place money capital is offered in the loan market and is transformed by the contracts there made into loan capital. Subsequently the repayment of the loan restores the funds as money capital. In the case of commercial and other short term credits the transactions are executed in rapid succession. The repayment of investment loans may be distributed by instalments over a long span of years. There is generally no repayment of government rentes. But in a well regulated market the creditor has opportunities to dispose of his capital demands and to sell especially those securities listed on the exchange at comparatively stable prices. Thus there is a way for him to turn even long term or irredeemable loan capital into liquid monetary capital. In an unfavorable market he must assume the loss involved in conversion. The entire safety of short term demands is taken for granted and the holder may count on recovering the full nominal value.

The capital assets of an enterprise are another form of capital that is distinguished in ordinary speech. This does not mean the accumulated reserve of money destined to establish or enlarge a business, for this is monetary capital. It means the entire capital which has been invested and is actively used in the enterprise. This includes the liquid cash items which are to cover payments of wages and other current operating expenses, that part outstanding as loan capital and also the remainder which has been transformed into natural capital and furthers the enterprise as such. An entrepreneur receives a yield in natural form as a result of the productive use of capital goods, but he also finds a monetary expression for this yield. He appraises the circulating capital goods in money to determine his working capital; the fixed capital goods in terms of money are his plant investment. Together these two sums are his capital assets which he regards as a numerical expression of a demand on the business. In the same manner he credits accounts receivable which, while not strictly a part of his possessions, must be productive in that they return the customary rate of interest. As each item of his natural capital is consumed in the productive turn-over, he meets the demand for its replacement from the gross monetary yield. The monetary nature of capital is particularly apparent in the rapid turn-over of the components of working capital; at short intervals it is transformed over and over again into monetary or natural form. These periods are longer in the case of capital equipment, but in principle the same relationship holds. Because of the monetary yield all the component parts of the capital of a business are constantly becoming monetary capital, the form in which they were brought into the business. Thus they tend to form a homogeneous mass with money- and loan-capital, a unity which shows itself in the tendency to an equalization of the yield of capital.

It must be admitted that the outlines of the concept become indefinite when the capital of an enterprise approximates a condition of immobility, as with investments of specific capital. In certain situations, when specific equipment goods have become "immobilized," they are denied to have the character of capital. For example when a business man has tied up his wealth in fixed improvements so as to have no working funds, it is usually said that he lacks capital. But by the side of this concept the popular mind harbors the conviction that the whole investment in a business partakes of the characteristics of capital. Along this line the boundaries of the general concept are overstepped, for the realty, which is part of the possessions of the enterprise, is considered as part of the capital on which it trades.

On the other hand money-capital, as it is usually referred to, loses the characteristics of capital whenever it is used by anyone who is not an entrepreneur: when an individual uses it to buy a dwelling, tenement house or the like or when a farmer buys land. In the hands of a builder or contractor a house is capital; in the hands of one who purchases it as an investment, without keeping strict account of its monetary expression as an entrepreneur would do, it is no longer capital. The house has become property, although even in this case the owner would have to consider that, precisely as in the case of capital, the value of the building is little by little being consumed and must be allowed for by a reserve fund created out of the interest received. When an estate is not purchased with the object of resale, it is not regarded as capital. Stocks, held by a banker or speculator, are capital; the nature of those held by an individual for investment is doubtful. Usually they are listed as property, but it is easy to understand how the usages of ordinary speech may vary here because they are so nearly akin to bonds and other market securities that are allied to loan-capital.

The connotations of speech are therefore uncertain. But at the core of all these interpretations is a nucleus that clearly shows the form of capital, a form that is fundamental to all variations. In the habitual meaning capital includes monetary capital and also all other acquisitive property in which monetary capital is invested and which reverts to the monetary type. Capital in this sense I shall designate as the monetary form of capital.

The results of scientific analysis, especially as promoted by the classical school, have been to increase largely our knowledge of capital, as for example, when its natural form was discovered. This we have described in the theory of the simple economy where it was defined as the sum of all capital goods and was recognized as the necessary instrument of all production. In the face of the socialistic criticism of capital, taking its rise in the monetary form, a scientific justification of capital would have been impossible, had not the homogeneous monetary form first been analyzed and the natural form set off as a phenomenon by itself.

These great advances, however, were not achieved without serious mistakes. Thus it was an almost fatal error to transfer to the new concept the traditional name of the old one, and to do so without supplementary explanation. Science has neither the right nor the power to deprive a name that is deeply rooted in popular usage of its traditional meaning, and to force a new connotation upon it. The error, however, was corrected in the further elaboration of terminology, and the natural form of capital was distinguished by the name of productive or natural capital. It is also called social, or socio-economic capital; we prefer to use this term. Although under the existing legal order this economic capital has also been respected as private property, the name is justified by its socio-economic effect as a coöperating factor in production, increasing the national income.

A second grave mistake has been committed and must here be discussed. At first only one form, productive capital, was recognized. It was not until some time later that a second type was recognized which was characterized as acquisitive capital. The natural "enterprise capital" of commerce and its auxiliaries, especially transportation, of service trades, rented dwellings and finally the entire loan- and money-capital are classified as acquisitive capital. We distinguish acquisitive capital from productive capital in so far as the former produces interest for the capitalist without increasing the social economic income. It is held that productive capital is social capital, while acquisitive capital is purely private.

The concept of acquisitive capital represents an important advance of the scientific approach but it requires analysis. It groups together types of capital which differ radically in their application. The "enterprise capital" of commerce and its auxiliary trades coöperates in producing a yield. Therefore, by the definition of production to which we have adhered from the beginning, it is to be treated as socio-economic capital. That of the service trades, together with rented dwellings and other possessions that are enjoyed directly form a group by themselves. They consist of material goods of the first order, the greater number of which are durable.

In the case of loan-capital or monetary capital—these include most banking and insurance capital—we must distinguish the use to which they are put. Their effect and classification are dependent on whether the loan is used to further production, for other acquisitive enterprise or for consumption. Capital lent for production increases the productive yield. It is secured by the natural form of capital goods into which it is transformed. For the creditor, who counts the demand among his possessions, it is private capital. But in securing the natural form of which the debtor has possession it performs the service of social capital. This effect is reflected back upon the private capital of the creditor of which, therefore, it cannot be said that it is private capital pure and simple. Capital loans for other acquisitive activities, among which we should mention mortgages on rented houses, are secured by goods which remain in permanent use. Capital lent for consumption is covered by the household goods into which it is transformed. Such a loan does not increase the socially available income; the interest which the debtor pays must be met either at the expense of his household or from yields coming from some other source than the use of the loan. The use of these household goods can result in no return for this capital which is the most pronounced form of private capital.

Beside the socially productive capital, with which we class the natural capital of commerce and its auxiliaries, we must distinguish the following forms of private capital: productive loan-capital, most closely resembling social capital and not to be considered by us a purely private capital; acquisitive capital in the narrower sense, consisting of the material possessions of service trades and goods rented for use and including loan-capital destined for lending on these goods; and finally consumptive loan-capital which is pure private capital.

The special definitions of natural social capital and the various types of acquisitive capital are fruitful. Without them the different effects of capital could not be understood. Nevertheless, science cannot stop with these distinctions. It must return under the guidance of ordinary speech to a unifying concept which science need only deepen for purposes of professional employment. The concept delivered by language is held together by the monetary form. In a similar manner science must formulate an ultimate homogeneous concept, comprehending by means of the monetary form all the observed types of capital.

In the money economy, if natural capital in the hands of entrepreneurs is properly to perform its social function of increasing the yield, it requires the supplement of money-capital and constant reference to the monetary form. It is only thus that the natural capital forms a unit and may be united with other forms of capital. This homogeneity has always been tacitly assumed by theory, for in asserting the equalizing tendency of interest it presupposes the monetary form of capital in which alone the individual kinds of capital may be compared. If we were to ask the questions, by what means has our era become capitalistic and in what does the nature of capitalism consist, it would be wholly inadequate to point out merely the occurrence of capital goods. The entire importance of capitalistic power is never appraised in the natural form alone, great as is the productive wealth of the goods involved. The ultimate support of this power is to be found in the unifying monetary form and especially in the primary type, money-capital. The latter is the nucleus not only of the practical concept but of the actual power of capital as well. The ruling power of large aggregates of capital is acquired by transforming it into those particular forms which at the time promise the largest rewards.

In the scientific concept of capital the monetary form must not be absent. We shall therefore have to add to the narrower concepts of social capital and acquisitive capital one which will embrace all forms: the natural, the monetary, and even the consumptive loan types. In this sense we shall define the extended ultimate concept of capital as the total mass of the monetary and natural forms treated as a unit.[1] The effect of all individual aggregates is derived from their use as parts of this unit.

§ 57. The Process of Capital-Formation in the Money-Economy

The participating groups of individuals—The money capitalists—The parallelism in the formation of the money-form and the natural form.

The process of the formation of capital in the monetary economy is essentially the same as in the simple economy, but only very rarely does it follow a course so conspicuously transparent and self-contained. Thus, for example, a large land-owner may discover that conditions on

[1] In diesem Sinne definieren wir den erweiterten Schluszbegriff des Kapitals als die *Einheit* der Geldform und Naturalform des Kapitals.

his lands favor the establishment of a factory, through which he could turn to account his agricultural products, without incurring further expenditures in the way of purchasing materials or supplies beyond the unavoidable ones required in paying the wages of the laborers employed in erecting his buildings. Then, if he compensates his laborers largely in natural wages, he would require but little cash or money-capital for the payment of the wages also. In every other respect, he would control the natural conditions for the formation of the productive capital as completely as he would have to in a simple economy. Only rarely, however, is there such an opportune coincidence of conditions; the formation of capital in the money economy would be an exceedingly slow process and would be confined within narrow boundaries, if a conjunction of circumstances so rare and well adapted had to be relied on. In most cases, the requirements for this formation are distributed over a large number of individuals; at least two, and sometimes three groups of persons are usually needed, each group containing a large number of interested individual economies. The manufacturer of machinery usually does not himself make use of the machines which he constructs, as he is forming natural capital. He sells them to other entrepreneurs who use them in their operations. A spinner who is getting ready for his industry will not only purchase the spinning-machine of the manufacturer of such machines, but he will also buy of capital-producing entrepreneurs all the other constituents of the natural capital which he needs for equipment and manufacture. Under the division of labor of the exchange-economy the process of the formation of natural capital is completed only by the joint work of the capital-producing and capital-employing entrepreneur. The machine is not a capital good merely by the fact that it has been built by the former; for, if no one should appear who could make use of it, although technically unobjectionable in its construction, it would not be a part of the national capital; it might not even be a good. It would have to be regarded as an economic blunder of the capital-producing entrepreneur, when he sacrificed money-outlay in its construction. We must add here that even in case an entrepreneur should be found who might wish to use the machine, it would not, for this reason alone, be certified as a part of the natural capital. In order that this can take place, the second entrepreneur must realize an economic gain with the machine. Only when he reaches the stage where he succeeds in realizing the usual net-earnings from his enterprise, has the process of the formation of natural capital been finally terminated.

In order that this may be accomplished for the money-form of capital, the formation of natural capital, which is initiated by the two groups of entrepreneurs here mentioned, must be supplemented by a companion-process. To the same extent to which capital goods are formed, money-capital will also have to be formed. This is true not only for the increase of capital, but also for its mere preservation which, as we have seen in the theory of the simple economy, makes part of the formation of capital. The formation of money-capital is accomplished by saving or by laying aside money. The saving of capital is accomplished among people of small means by serious self-denial and by the imposition of severe deprivations in their consumption in order to obtain from their limited incomes an excess over and above the expenditures for the preservation of life. What is laid aside in well-to-do and wealthy families is not savings. No "saving" is required in their circumstances. Here it is possible to "lay aside" while living comfortably and luxuriously, for the incomes are so large that they can no longer be exhausted by personal expenses but only by dedications to foreign uses, unless they are squandered in senseless prodigality.

The formation of money-capital is often accomplished by the same individuals who take part in the formation of natural capital. Whenever the business enterprises of the capital-employing entrepreneur prosper, he will be able to make his investments from the surplus over his current expenses. But numerous enterprises are started or enlarged, in which the entrepreneurs do not derive the money-capital required from their own means. Under these circumstances it may be the capital-producing entrepreneur who opens credits to the employers —a proceeding which, however, he will only be able to adopt, when surplus revenues of his own enable him to do so. In cases where neither the one nor the other group of entrepreneurs are able to contribute the capital required, these must turn to a third group of persons, the owners of money-capital who have saved or laid aside money, and whom, in this broader sense, we shall call money-capitalists. These persons may themselves be producers or other traders, who cannot find employment for their reserve-funds in their own businesses; or they may be money-capitalists in the narrower sense, living on money-interest and on annuities, and still able to spare money-capital by way of making loans. Finally they may also be men of small means with small savings. When the money of such men has, by an efficient organization of credit, been scraped into one heap from all parts of the country, it forms enormous aggregates, figuring largely in the capital supply of the largest money-capitalists of the country, the banks.

Where the money-capitalists, as a third group, take an active part in the process of capital-formation, the process becomes more than ordinarily complicated, and the view of its working is greatly obscured. To this state of facts, then, we will devote our closest attention. The fundamental idea which is to guide us in the labyrinth of tangled relations, is the law of the equation between supply and demand, which we have already demonstrated for the market of natural values and which is valid for the capital-market as well.

In our exposition we shall first make the simplifying assumption that the money-capitalists, to whom the capital-supply is to be ascribed, are themselves producers and have, as such, introduced natural values into the economy. In order that they may thus be able to come forward with offers as money-capitalists, it is necessary that through sale they should have introduced more natural values into the economy, than they withdraw as buyers. From the money-yield which they obtain for the surplus of natural values sold, they form the money-capital, by the loan of which—as we know from our investigations of the national-economic community of payment—they transfer the claim for a corresponding quantity of natural values to the debtors who, in their place, as assignees, exercise the demand. That the spinner, who works with borrowed capital, was able to obtain the spinning machine which he needed from the manufacturer of machines, was only made possible by the fact that the national economy had the disposal of a surplus of natural values. This was brought in by the money-capitalist himself or his predecessor,[1] without, so far, having been conclusively withdrawn by a successor; the spinner finds this surplus, now in the shape of the spinning-machine, ready for his demand.

All complications of the market, no matter how intricate, may be reduced to this type. If the money-capitalist, granting the loan, was not a producer himself, but formed his capital from derived income, from the interest of loan-capital which he already owned, then the debtor who pays the interest in money must on his part have brought in that surplus of natural values, or some predecessor of the debtor must have done so. If the money-capitalist has obtained his money-capital from the sale of realty or other property-possessions, then either the persons to whom he sold or some of their predecessors, must have brought in that surplus. The interconnections become especially complicated by the fact that by no means the entire annual formation of money-capital can be placed to the door of the formation of productive capital. A large proportion of loans is granted for non-productive acquisition and for urban mortgages; an-

[1] Trans. note: For the use of predecessor and successor see § 30. Wieser pictures sales as forming a chain in which a pair of buyers and sellers form the links. Each individual appears once as vendee, once as vendor. In the first capacity he is the successor of the earlier members of the chain; in the latter capacity he is the predecessor of later buyers.

other all too large quota for consumption. Especially the public economies, above all the state, come in for an exceedingly large share of funds for consumptive purposes.

It is not permissible to invert the proposition that, without new money-capital, there can be no new productive capital. It is not correct to say that, with all new money-capital, new productive capital is also being formed. The consumptive-debtor utilizes the right to demand goods, which he has obtained as assignee, so as to withdraw consumptive values from the national economy. Thus his demand furnishes an incentive to prepare that surplus of natural values in consumption goods. While the formation of the productively lent money-capital runs parallel with the augmentation of the national-economic natural capital, this effect does not follow the formation of the consumptively lent money-capital. It is thus that, farther on, the payments of interest and the repayments of the producer-debtor are covered by natural yield-values, which this debtor has been able to form and bring into the national economy, owing to his use of the borrowed capital, while he was not compelled to consume the yield himself. The interest payment and repayment of the consumer-debtor, on the other hand, are not covered in this way. In his hands the borrowed capital does not create a natural fund, securing the debt. Unless he gains other income in addition to what is here indicated—as a rule he does not—the debtor will have to obtain the surplus in natural values, which he is bound to bring in to cover the money-form, by a retrenchment of his own consumption. In case of the public credits, the interest service of which is met by taxation, the relation is still somewhat more complicated. The debtor-state, itself, is not the party to retrench the consumption of natural values. The citizens, paying the taxes, will have to do this in the state's place; their purchasing ability is lessened by the additional taxes, which cover the interest service. The natural values, the purchase of which the citizens will have to abandon, form in the first place the ultimate security required, in order that the chain of payment-community may be closed. The creditors of the state or their assignees dispose in any form of payment determined by the community, of the surplus of natural values, which has to be brought into the economy by the tax-paying citizens.

In the course of the formation of capital as here described, the pure, private form of the consumptive loan-capital also has its place. As regards the saver of capital, it merges indistinguishably with the other forms of money-capital. It forms part of the great unit of the broader capital-concept.

The parallelism, existing between the money-form of capital and its natural security-cover, likewise becomes apparent when the economy of the debtor breaks down. The creditor must wipe from the inventory of his possessions, the money-demand which is no longer recoverable. If the economy of the producer-debtor breaks down because the capital was injudiciously invested, then coincidently with the natural form, the money-form of the capital is also destroyed. In every national economic crisis this process is repeated on a large scale. Extensive aggregates of capital-goods have been unsuitably invested. Their productive employment produces yields far inferior to those expected by the vivid imagination of the speculative impulse. To some extent, perhaps, they have turned out to be wholly unproductive. The losses which consequently result and cut down the estimated figures of the national-economic natural capital, fall to an equal extent upon the capitalists who have advanced the money-capital to the speculating entrepreneurs. The creditors must charge off large amounts with far-reaching economic results, in order to re-establish the disastrously disturbed equation between money-values and natural values.

§ 58. The Capital Market

Money market—Investment market.

We have already treated quite completely most of the details of the capital market which interest us in the course of our explanation of credit transactions, the advantages of exchange by means of credit, the community of payment and money- and loan-capital. On the whole there is little left for us to do now but to summarize these details.

The capital market may be subdivided into the money and investment markets.

In the money market, transactions are concluded in the most liquid forms of loan capital, that is such as are acceptable for banking security and the discount business which we have described, especially the so-called Lombard transactions, whose details we need not go into. By means of foreign drafts or bills of exchange, the transactions in varieties of foreign money which they represent are also brought within the scope of the money market. In this market the supply comes from banks or individual bankers; the demand from such business men as enjoy credit with the former. The quasi-commercial market for drafts and other liquid loans is only loosely connected with the official money market; on the side both of the demand and of the supply it is differently constituted. The market of the usury business is wholly detached, if, indeed, this may be referred to as a market.

In the investment market, loans for long terms are granted for permanent investment. The German name *Anlage* is probably to be traced to the fact that the capitalist permits the money to "lie" (*liegen*) without being obliged to incur further labor than is involved in selecting the investment and, if need be, taking the necessary steps to insure its safety. These are two functions, however, in regard to which mediating banks may relieve him to a great extent. Closely akin to the investment market for stocks and bonds is that branch of the realty market where real estate is acquired for purposes of investment: rented urban houses and also such country estates as the owner does not wish to farm himself, or cultivates only for pleasure. Real estate, purchased as an investment, is looked upon by the buyer precisely as are securities. Both are sources of a money income which is derived without appreciable effort. The only distinction is that one investment may be considered safer or more convenient than the other, or that one may offer greater chances of a rise in value at some future date. In the case of real estate, purchased for the purpose of somehow making it productive, still another consideration governs its appraisal. It is looked upon as a means of turning individual effort to better account and frequently a considerable portion of the purchase money is paid with this in view.

All branches of the money and investment market are mutually connected. Equalizing movements may constantly be observed in which funds are transferred from those uses of lower returns to those of higher ones. To this extent theory has the right to assume in idealization a single market striving to realize a single rate of interest. As a matter of fact the movements of capitals are never able to bring about a complete equalization. Even with complete security of the loans, the interests of the different groups composing the supply and the demand are too diverse as regards the period of the loan and a number of other conditions for a central market to form in which the law of the unity of price might prevail. The contrast between the market for commercial paper and the investment market is particularly striking. The more mobile commercial interest rate may always be plainly distinguished from the steadier investment rate or the customary current rate.

For us, the composition of the money and investment markets is primarily of interest in so far as it bears on the problem of the interest on capital with which we must concern ourselves under the theory of income. The explanation of interest which we have attempted in the theory of the simple economy is applicable only to that on productive business capital and, in connection with this, to the interest on productive loans. It is not an adequate explanation to cover interest on natural acquisitive capital or on commodities rented for direct use or on loans secured by these. Nor does the explanation cover interest on capital used for consumptive loans. Each of these capital groups shows in somewhat different form variations of the problem of the interest on capital and thus attains theoretical importance.

In another connection we shall make brief mention of the significance of speculation in the capital market.

§ 59. The Computation in Money

The monetary computation in the process of private and national economy—The arithmetic expression of power.

In every household, constituting a unit of the economic whole, incomes and expenditures are computed in money. In every well managed household, the expenditures should be confined within the limits of the receipts. Even a trifling overstepping of the margin indicated by the relation of expenses to income, is considered improper. But the mere observation of the balance of the figures on either side of the account does not exhaust the import of the record which is being kept, for this should always include a due regard to the purposes of the expenditures incurred. The account is to furnish the guarantee, that the receipts are never expended for uses whose personal use-value is less than the exchange-value of the sums of money given up and that, therefore, only such uses are permitted as correspond to the personal marginal utility of the money. The money-computation in the household is a computation of utility, precisely like the one as to which the theory of the simple economy has already enlightened us. Like the latter, therefore, it is largely a matter of common sense. It is not merely an approximate numerical expression which is aimed at, when the sums of items on either side of the account are compared. Rather, when by their means arithmetical operations are performed, when they are added, subtracted or subjected to any manner of calculation required by circumstances, the number of units of mass is computed, which are available within the margin of use. The ends of the household are best served when the margin of use is respected for all the units of mass included in the computation.

The natural values, employed in the domestic economy, are appraised directly by their marginal utility. Only those of their number, for the repeated purchase of which sufficient means are available, are, for the sake of simplification, appraised by their purchase-value in money. By the instrument of the marginal utility, this internal natural household-account is combined into one unit with the account of moneys received and expended. The personal acquisition-account is also adjusted to the same unity in every private economy; and similarly the investment-account, containing such possessions as are expected to yield money-returns, and as are appraised according to the exchange-value of their yield.

For the comparison of individual economies of different degrees of wealth, valuation in money is inappropriate. The greater this difference, the less appropriate is such an appraisal. Doubling the amount of the income does not mean doubling the attainable enjoyments of the household; much less does it mean that the enjoyments are a hundredfold increased, if the income is increased a hundredfold. The accounts kept in case of an income of 100 and those kept for an income of 10,000 money-units are not commensurable. They are founded in different personal units, different personal appraisals of the money-unit, of which it is well enough known that the one is larger, the other smaller. However, it is not known to what extent these appraisals are multiples one of the other, or are in other ways arithmetically related.

In order to reach, also, an understanding of the economic money-computation, we will start from the assumption of complete equality of the related individual economies. We assume that for all the incomes, needs and values are the same. The assumption is contrary to all experience; such a condition has never yet existed, perhaps it never will; but we require this idealizing simplification, in order to obtain a preliminary survey.

With an assumption such as this, the economic exchange-value equals the unitary personal exchange-value of all connected individual economies. The money-computation in the national-economic process has, therefore, precisely the significance it would have in the simple economy of a people. We refer to our exposition in the theory of the simple economy; in this connection we confine our remarks to a few points of especial importance, which it is desirable to bring out emphatically. In the first place, it will be observed that in the national-economic process it is not only on the occasion of exchange-transactions, that the computation is made in money; the exchange-value of products and of other natural values, becomes also the arithmetical basis for carrying through operations in the private economies, connected by the division of labor. Planning and final accounting of the operations are, throughout, effected in money. Here all divisible stocks of material and personal values are computed as multiples of marginal value and quantity; by such an accounting the economic success of the acquisitional process is most accurately verified. It should furthermore be observed that also for dealings in capital the computation in money makes it possible to identify the greatest economic success. The accounting of interest and compound interest between creditors and debtors, and in internal management the discounting and capitalization in money have the same economic import which we have demonstrated for the appraisal of capital in the simple economy. Throughout, the money-form coincides with the natural form; throughout,, the units of the money-computation are units of the economic utility.

Owing to the stratification of economic society, especially when it has been intensified to power, money-computation in the economic process loses this simple significance. The superior, the more powerful, the dominating strata are able with the given prices to extend their margin of use far beyond the margin of the mass of all other strata. The unit of the national economic value, under the influence of the variously graded personal states of needs, incomes and wealth, breaks up into the most multiformly differentiated units of personal exchange-values, running from the marginal utility of abject misery, with its maximum tension, to the condition of extreme luxury with its scarcely perceptible strain. Nevertheless, money-computation does not altogether lose its arithmetic significance.

The competitive struggle, in its effect on prices, constantly provides the key for the computation, stratum by stratum, of utility-units in money. Instead of operating with simple social utility-units, units of the stratified marginal utility are employed; but these, too, lead to strictly arithmetical sums. In the case of mass-values as well as in the case of medium and luxury values, the business-man ascertains the arithmetical foundations, in order to keep exact track of the mutual relation of costs and of gains. Enormous as are the variations in the margins of use thus brought about between strata, the calculation as such preserves its full significance at all times in the valuation of partial stocks and their most proximate uses. The exchange value, thus calculated, furnishes an expression as accurate for the estimate of power, as is practically demanded, and this power prevails in most exact adjustment to the existing conditions. The stratification of prices evidences the intention of the wealthy buyers precisely to the extent to which they desire precedence; they receive their desired share of the cheaper products, as regards which they compete with the less wealthy buyers, while they themselves secure the exclusive delivery of the more costly wares, to the acquisition of which they do not wish to admit competitors. In the further stages of the process, the stratified price of the products furnishes the standard for the extent of productive investments which, in the course of economic development, are to be devoted to each of them. Here, too, then, the desire of the wealthy buyers ensures that, in procuring the highest priced products, the greatest productive efforts are to be made. Precisely in this manner the price enforced by the more powerful producer in the market, is accurately adapted to restrain weaker competitors; and that enforced by the supplying monopolist is exactly adapted to wring from purchasers the highest profits which can be realized with the prevailing condition of technical art and the market-situation. From the basis of the price-level of consumption-values, the large entrepreneur or the monopolist extends his calculations with strictly logical continuity; the attribution, the computation of costs and the capital-computation, which he makes, preserve their full significance in that they verify arithmetically, with the utmost exactitude, the attainment of the greatest gain possible, at least as regards the most immediately recognizable partial stocks and yields.

The problem of power has not been disposed of by this formal statement. In order to attack it from the standpoint of actuality, we shall first have to acquaint ourselves with the economic process of acquisition. In that connection we shall see the economic sources of the formation of power in action, so as to enable us to form an opinion as to the meaning of the formation of power itself.

By its services as the instrument of money-computation, money becomes the means of computation in the economic process. It is not simply the "standard of price"; the economic exchange-value is also computed in money, and similarly the parallel forms of the exchange-yield-value and the use-value;[1] just as it is generally used as the arithmetical expression, where a uniform, comparative expression is required for the values which are active in the economic process.

[1] Anschaffungswert.

PART III

THE CREATION OF THE COMMUNITY OF ACQUISITION AND THE FORMATION OF INCOME

A. Weber, *Ueber den Standort der Industrien*, 2nd ed., 1922; Sombart, *Das moderne Kapitalismus*, 1902; Schumpeter, *Das Grundprinzip der Verteilungslehre*, 1923; Wicksteed, *The Coördination of the Laws of Distribution*, 1894; Sax, *Die Verkehrsmittel in Volks- und Staatswirtschaft*, 1918–22; Davenport, *Economics of Enterprise*, 1913; Marshall, *Industry and Trade*, 2nd ed., 1919; Mitchell, *Business Cycles*, 1913; Pigou, *Economics of Welfare*, 1920; Veblen, *Theory of the Leisure Class*, 1918; Diehl, *Die Lehre von der Production*, 1924; Mayer, *Wesen des Einkommens*, 1887; Schäffle, *Theorie der ausschlieszenden Absatzverhältnisse*, 1867; Schumpeter, *Das Rentenprinzip in der Verteilungslehre*, J. F. G. V., 1907; Naumann, *Städtische Grundrente*, Z. F. V., 1909; Wieser, *Theorie des städt. Grundrente*, 1909; Oppenheimer, *Wert und Kapitalprofit*, 2nd ed., 1922; Budge, *Der Kapitalprofit*, 1920; Mataja, *Unternehmergewinn*, 1884; Brentano, *Das. Arbeitsverhältnis gemäsz dem heutigen Recht*, 1877; and, *Die Lehre von dem Lohnsteigerungen*, J. f. N., 1871; Taussig, *Wages and Capital*, 1896; Herkner, *Arbeiterfrage*, 7th ed., 1921; Zwiedineck, *Lohntheorie und Lohnpolitik*, 1900; Bernhard, *Arbeit*, E. d. V.; Schüller, *Die Nachfrage nach Arbeitskräften*, Archiv, 1911; Pesl, *Mindestlohn*, 1914; Verrijn Stuart, *Die Grundlagen der Lohnbestimmung*, Z. F. Volksw., 1922.

§ 60. The Division of Labor

Horizontal and vertical division of labor—The articulation of labor—Fundamentals and laws of the articulation of labor.

The most striking feature of the entire structure of the economic community of acquisition is the division of labor which is more conspicuous than the community of acquisition itself and was therefore observed at an earlier date. Only subsequently was it realized that the observed division of labor is the expression of an extensive community which unites all those who take part in labor. The division of labor was peculiarly in accord with the ideals of the classical masters; it harmonizes with their theory of labor and with their individualism, both of which place the individual workers in the foreground of theoretical inquiry. From his point of view, Adam Smith could not have found a more suitable introduction to his work on the Wealth of Nations than his remarks concerning the extraordinary effects of the division of labor, which, he says, has contributed more than anything else to increase its productivity.[1]

He explains these effects from the example of a small Scotch pin factory which he had visited. We shall briefly reproduce this illustration which has become famous in the history of our literature. We call attention to it not merely because of the clearness and pregnancy with which it presents the problem to the reader but even more because it shows unmistakably the limits that confine the classical view of the subject. In this pin factory ten workers were employed; there were approximately eighteen operations required to get the pins ready for packing and shipping. These started with the drawing out and smoothing of the wire. The eighteen processes were divided among the men. Owing to the ingenious distribution of their labors they were able to turn out 48,000 pins daily, an average of 4800 pins per man. Adam Smith believes that if one of the men had been working alone he could not have turned out more than twenty pins at best, and perhaps only a single pin. He thus calculcates that the division of labor in this case has increased productivity at least 240 fold, possibly even 4800 fold.

The illustration is too narrow in that it does not show the large share in augmenting the yield that is attributable to a division of capital goods and the soil; and in that it shows only the favorable effects of the increase of the yield without even alluding to the numerous and grave disadvantages which may appear as a consequence of the division of labor. In both these respects the development of the classical doctrine has supplemented the statement of its founder. But as regards a third consideration, it has never advanced beyond the limits set in this illustration. The ten workmen to whom Adam Smith refers perform coördinate operations and his example illustrates that type of differentiation which in our "theory of economic society" we designated as horizontal articulation.

Actually there is also a vertical stratification in the division of labor. It gives rise to relations of superiority and subordination such as we witness in the case of the entrepreneur and the body of wage earners. It is quite clear that the classical doctrine did not fail to observe this important relationship; it fully appreciated the heavy pressure with which this condition bore down upon the mass of laborers. Adam Smith was particularly aware of it and pursued the concept of freedom not only theoretically but with a fully sympathetic penetration. Still he and his school neglected to refer their observations on the

[1] Inquiry into *The Wealth of Nations*, vol. I, chap. 1.

wage relationship back to the division of labor. From the very beginning the two dimensions of the division of labor should have been distinguished in order to show how it divides the acquisitive community not only into a lateral framework of trades, enterprises and operations but also into a vertical relationship of power and dependency. The structure of the economic whole is seen first from a deceptive angle if the two functions of articulation and stratification in the division of labor are confused.

For the present we shall refer exclusively to the articulation of labor. Of its stratification we shall speak later when we come to discuss the stratification of wealth.

We may pass over the details of the manifold forms of the organization of labor. They are of little importance in the erection of the acquisitive community. It will answer every purpose if we describe the phenomenon as a whole; this can be done in a few words. The domestic production of a closed economy is so organized as to provide for the total needs of the household. But in so far as the division of labor extends, every individual confines himself to the preparation of a narrow group or single variety of products or other natural values. He may even confine himself to the performance of a restricted group of functions that are required along with others for the preparation of a product. In a well organized national economy the labors of individuals supplement one another so that, according to the standard of existing means, the entire needs of the people are provided for. How does this enormous process of the organization of work develop? Why is it that men, workers generally, divide and apportion labor among themselves? To what extent does this division proceed? Who directs the process? These are the questions which we must answer.

Adam Smith explains the division of labor or, as we shall call it, the articulation of labor from its effect of increasing yield. This he explains, for one thing, by the saving of time achieved by the individual worker who confines himself to a certain number of repetitive performances, with a resulting increase in skill acquired by persistent practice. However he has shown that at any one time definite limits to the articulation of labor are set by the extent of the market. In a limited market with a moderate demand such as occurs even today in the more remote sections of a country, the producer will not find a sufficient number of purchasers for articles of any one kind. In order to prosper he must therefore turn out a larger variety of articles. On the other hand, in the much frequented market of a large city, or in an industry which supplies a nation or the world, it will be possible to carry the articulation of labor to much greater lengths, provided the increased quantities may be remuneratively sold.

The propelling force in this social process is the expectation of obtaining yields and an increased income by more advanced methods in the articulation of labor. This furnishes to the individuals united in commerce both the motive and standard for the movement.

The explanation offered by Adam Smith has been most carefully supplemented by his disciples until everything that may be stated regarding the articulation of labor from the standpoint of the individual has been gathered into their records. The entire doctrine has long been the common property of science. It may be indorsed without reserve provided the process is confined to the forceful and leading personalities who succeed in aptly adjusting their actions to the requirements of their well-considered advantage. This limitation is assumed by the individualist doctrine to be implicit in the process. We may be sure that the great mass of humanity actually decides here as elsewhere according to the coöperative economic principle; in the articulation of labor the average man will go just so far as others went before him or as his fellows do every day.

All that can be said from the point of view of the individual is by no means equivalent to the last word of science on the articulation of labor: its foundations, its effects, its limits.

The individual is invariably dropped into the midst of the historically formed process of the division of labor. His observation and reflection are turned to but one problem: whether, and to what extent, it is advisable to advance beyond the degree of division hitherto practiced. It is neither his intention nor within his power to look back upon the whole process and survey the sum of its effects. This must be done by theoretical inquiry. It has not been done by the individualistic school. The latter, clinging to considerations of the market, attends merely to the monetary form of the process; but back of the money form hovers the natural form whose description is one of the missions of theory.

The articulation of labor is not merely a phenomenon of the money economy. Smith's ten Scotch workers would have apportioned their performances among themselves in exactly the same manner had they worked, not for the market, but as coöperators in a socialist state. In every economy bent upon a larger yield, no matter what the juridical organization, the articulation of labor is indispensable. Even a Crusoe in his individual economy would provide for an ample articulation as soon as his means allowed him to supply his needs more abundantly. For his various activities he would make a definite division of time, an adjustment of the hours which he would devote to each type of performance. Assuming that he reached a stage where he could make pins, he also would be able to divide his labors in this process. Like the Scotch craftsmen, he would draw the wire of a length to produce a number of pins and he would lump the individual manipulations to be performed in succession. With some little practice he might be able to turn out not one pin daily but possibly more than the twenty pins which Adam Smith expected of the single isolated worker who had no idea of the advantage to be derived from the articulation of labor.

In order to gain a view of those conditions of the articulation of labor which are apt to elude individual observation, we must first recognize that the prerequisite to this partitioning of labor is its variety. Wholly simple labor cannot be apportioned among persons because technically it is not divisible. So long as mankind knew no other method of acquiring goods than hunting, men had to be hunters in order to live. In order that the articulation of labor might be initiated and continued, it was necessary that the diverse methods of productive work afforded by agriculture and the trades be discovered and that sufficient quantities of the various types of agricultural and industrial capital goods be produced.

The forces which here guided mankind are not only personal but social impulses. A small tribe of hunters might well confine itself to the simple indivisible labor of hunting whereby to provide, precariously and scantily, the needs of its members. But by their natures men are fitted to respond to an increasing number of needs. These they presently discover as civilization progresses. More still, the ever increasing numbers of the population to be provided for urge an improvement in the arts and an increase in the instruments of labor. But how is this goal to be attained other than by penetrating deeper and deeper into the more remote orders of the economic elements, harboring in their hidden recesses the most bountiful treasures of life? If we would bring these to light, we must apply the enormous forces of united effort by the masses before which the power of the individual, in the apt comparison of Karl Marx (*Capital,* vol. I, sec. 1, ch. II), is as the offensive or defensive power of the single warrior against a host. To be brief, we must apply the community of production of mankind. The articulation of labor is the personal expression of this social community, formed long ago, carried along through the ages by historical powers and progressively developed. Into this existant whole the individual is set as a coordinate unit. In so far as he is bound to rely upon his labor for self-preservation, he must somehow form a link in the chain of the general community of labor. Positive law may guarantee to the worker a certain limited freedom of choice in directing his demands and supply; but it can never liberate him from the necessity of demanding and of offering a supply, if he would live. Thus he must submit to the general conditions of the market. We do not mean to deny that personal advantage is the main incentive leading men to an articulation of labor, but it must be added that they no more have complete freedom of choice in this respect than they do in their economy generally. Though they feel personally free, their freedom here as elsewhere is under the ægis of social powers. The methods by which individuals seek their personal advantage are socially indicated; workers turn from old over-crowded trades where adequate inducements are no longer offered to newcomers, to lines indicated by the tendencies of the time. Developing past experiences, zealously testing every new opening, the leaders advance step by step. The masses follow as the success or failure of their teachers encourages or disheartens the crowd. The entire development rests upon the basis of tradition and forms a continuous development.

The scope of the activities of the average worker is the personal exponent of the degree of energy attained by the social community of acquisition. The greater this energy, the narrower is his field. If it were possible to imagine that the infinite field of the world's activity were served by as homogeneously organized a group of all workers as is a close net-work of railroads by its employees, and that this group were aided by the uniformly organized apparatus of the world's capital, then the average breadth of the field might possibly be as narrow, compared with that of today, as the latter is in comparison with that of the Middle Ages.

The dependence on the market establishes in monetary form the limits to the articulation of labor. This can be traced back to the dependence of the natural field of an individual's labor on the social community of acquisition. The ultimate basis for the articulation of labor is in the superior energy of this social community. The limit of its extension is always indicated by the point where this superiority ends.

§ 61. The Localization of Industry

Town and Country—The natural historical form of economic acquisition.

The division of town and country is an historical result of the articulation of labor. Although in periods of insecurity the peasantry may jointly set up their abodes behind protective walls, agricultural labor is, in the nature of things, spread over the soil. But nascent trades and industries early located the seats of their activities in the towns. Here, too, the leading motive may have been protection against hostile powers which was needed in turbulent times even more urgently by industrial wealth than by the humble farmer. The requirements of the great men of the church and state may have offered another reason. But in the last instance the scales were turned by considerations of remuneration. A highly articulated trade seeking correspondingly large yields breaks through the framework of domestic and village economy. Less dependent on the soil, it endeavors to secure the utmost concentration. One craftsman needs another in order to obtain the wherewithal to practice his trade; one and all they need the merchant and trader who facilitates their intercourse with foreign places. Then the fact that they are thus brought together in one place creates for the artisan as well as for the merchant a local market of mutual exchange. The proverbial "golden soil" tilled by the craftsman of the Middle Ages made these men mutually receptive customers for each other's handiwork. But in the cities they also found the demand of the great men of the state and of the liberal professions. These conditions would have held even had the urban centers not been naturally the most convenient and cheapest market for the surrounding country. Finally, the concentration of nascent industries in definite localities led to the organization of guilds, which opened the way to a far-seeing and comprehensive policy for the protection of mutual interests, while the various governments were induced in their economic administration to take an active interest in these matters.

The segregation of town and country is the fundamental manifestation of the economic localization of industry. It marks on the economic map the more densely populated points of urban acquisition. Succeeding stages of development have brought out more clearly the images of town and country.

Agriculture extends from the earliest settlements step by step over the entire area of a country which is fitted for cultivation, and little by little there arise about the urban centers those zones of agricultural activity which Thünen in the *Isolated State* has described in so masterly a fashion. Thünen sought to ascertain arithmetically the dependence of industries on the costs of transportation which must be incurred to bring agricultural products to the town. To do this, he applies the instrument of idealization in a most far-reaching manner. He assumes a single urban market about which the natural conditions of cultivation and transportation are identical in all directions. Thus he obtains an entirely regular configuration of zones of dairying, farming, forestry and other branches of agriculture. These are distributed in rings around the town. We know that the actual outline of this distribution is irregular because of the varying distribution of the natural factors of soil and routes of transportation. What we find are not rings, but variously designed zones in which the forms of cultivation are adapted to the urban market. Interspersed with these are zones whose produce is destined for the foreign market, with here and there others which are to provide for the domestic wants of the farmer.

The extraordinary technical development of the last century has also largely affected the growth of cities. So marked has this been, that in many cities the population has increased even more than in the rural districts. Only such cities as offer no opportunities for modern business life drop behind. On the other hand, the surplus rural population congregates in those cities whose industrial progress offers new opportunities to the leaders and the masses in their struggle for existence. The advantages of local concentration are no less attractive under modern conditions for the trades and industries than they were earlier. To be sure, the security of life and liberty and the protection of his property are now guaranteed to every man anywhere in the country. But over and above these immunities, the more important cities have become the centers of modern transportation; they have gained importance as the seats of numerous public offices; the organization of credit is there represented; and there, the most reliable information of the business world may be most quickly obtained. The exchanges have long been established in the largest cities. The cities are the principal destinations towards which flock travelling foreigners. Hence they also supply the market for these visitors. Moreover, every large city is of itself an important local consuming center and labor market which attracts new dwellers from the country. As a rule all other cities are eclipsed in size and importance by the political capital of the country, which unless special conditions prevent, is also the intellectual, social and commercial center of the land as well as the pivotal point of all traffic facilities. Plainly in the case of the capital, the formative influence of historical power is to be seen; the supremacy is not so much an economic and geographical one, as it is one dictated by historical traditions. The capital has received a preëminence through state institutions of every description and through the habits of life inculcated in the mass of the people. These assure it a further and continued distinction so long as new developments do not overcome it by elsewhere giving rise to the growth of superior historical forces.

Modern industry has also made its way far out into the open country wherever the resources of the soil in raw materials or of auxiliary materials, or willing and cheap labor offer inducements to its location. The routes of transportation, railroads or rivers and other waterways, also frequently determine the choice of industrial location. Especially those districts are much sought after where large deposits of coal or great water power are at hand for the liberation of the enormous energies which must be harnessed for modern industry.

These remarks show only in the most general outline the picture of the distribution of productive enterprise. Yet they are sufficiently precise to permit the theoretically significant conclusion that in localizing the centers of production and acquisition the community of exchange is guided by those economico-geographic conditions which are given by natural position and historical development. The aims of private interest, seeking the greatest remuneration, and social interest, desiring the highest natural yield, converge here, in so far as the demands of the wealthier strata do not deflect private interest to an undue extension of the local zones devoted to the production of comforts and luxuries.

Historical power is conservative and favors the older industrial centers. It shows its preference for these, while other conditions are equal; but it is not sufficiently strong to prevent the rise of new historical institutions when new technical processes utilize new natural conditions. The historically acquired power of the old centers of acquisition in a unified natural economy gives an effective aid to the general development. As a result the natural sources of national wealth in their local distribution will always be exploited in a degree corresponding to the stage of development generally attained.

§ 62. The Economic Stratification of Society

Stratification in antiquity and the Middle Ages—In modern times and the capitalistic age—Downward stratification in the trades—The modern proletariat of the workers—Dangers of proletarization in the country.

The structure of the acquisitive community and the formation of income are always determined by the stratification of the people. At every stage of civilization and in any given period, despite individual diversities, there is a certain typical social stratification to which the general order is adjusted. The classical theory has taken the typical condition, as it existed for the civilized nations of their own period, as the foundation for its investigations of acquisition and income. Without establishing theoretically the concept of stratification the theorists of the period were none the less too strongly under the influence of the conditions which surrounded them, not to give theoretical expression to the facts of stratification. For instance, they could never have described the formation of income without recognizing the existence of a class of laborers wholly without wealth and obtaining its income solely in the form of wages. Similarly the theoretical investigations of today reflect the important displacements which social stratification has undergone since the period of the classical masters. We shall take a step in advance; we shall expressly distinguish the vertical and horizontal articulations of labor, as set forth in our precis of social theory, in order to discriminate accurately between the effects of the two types of social order. As in the case of all other assumptions, we must be clearly aware of those we make in regard to stratification. Thus we are compelled to give a description of the prevailing typical stratification, which we shall work out in such detail as our investigation requires.

In the world of antiquity and of the Middle Ages the governing strata of priests and warriors, great men of the church and state, were raised to their eminence by the power of leadership. This they had won in the process of the formation of states and in the cultural evolution which invariably accompanied this process. The cultural growth, starting from the religious, created sciences and arts and, with these, the industrial or practical arts. The governing strata profited by their spiritual and secular power in order to secure for themselves the greatest economic power as well. Thus they became the great owners of land, holding multitudes of slaves and servitors in subjection.

The effects of the positions of power, which were seized by the great lords of the Middle Ages in Europe, may be felt to this very day. To be sure, serfdom and vassalage have been done away with everywhere, but in many of the old countries the intellectual standard of the peasantry is perceptibly a survival of earlier conditions. National economic legislation cannot but take into consideration these shadows of the past. The after-effects are still more important in those districts in which the lords succeeded by forcible ejection or by enforced surrender in seizing the peasant property completely. In such districts we now find a proletariat of possessors or of tenants with inferior titles and of agricultural day laborers.

We may be quite sure that in antiquity as well as during the Middle Ages the economic process played its part in the social stratification. For example, during the period of the Roman world economy the power of economic leadership was sufficiently great to elevate its possessors to the highest strata. At the height of its prosperity the peasantry was sustained by its economic efficiency. It dropped behind only when it had to seek the protection of the great men of the church and state because its own forces were no longer able to resist aggression in the never-ending turmoil and the perils of war-like depredations. At the same time in such a period its cultural development was not yet such as to enable it to take an active part in matters of civil administration and judicial procedure. On the other hand a new social class, the hitherto unknown industrial bourgeoisie, was rising in importance in the towns of the Middle Ages. It owed its importance to its economic achievements. Beside it, the liberal professions were coming forward soon to become the leaders of a modern intellectual trend among laymen. They were advanced to more exalted positions in the social scale. Then appeared individuals, first singly but presently in increasing numbers, who as the economic leaders of huge enterprises amassed large capital wealth, especially in the form of money capital. In their industries the journeyman system of the Middle Ages was transformed into an amalgamation of proletarian wage-laborers. From this class but few distinguished by their talents or favored by fortune ever rose to economic independence. The greater number of them, losing the opportunity of ever becoming masters in their trade, were doomed for all time to content themselves with the position of dependent laborers.

Thus a process of transition grew irresistibly. It was pregnant with the development of the modern era. It was not complete until the close of the eighteenth century or the first half of the nineteenth. In middle and eastern Europe, it was not until the second half of the nineteenth century that the transition had progressed sufficiently to exhibit the full type of the modern capitalistic stratification of society.

The modern social stratification has by no means wholly eliminated the earlier historical institutions but it has thoroughly displaced them. Under modern conditions one fact is of the utmost theoretical importance: the present economic stratification is controlled almost exclusively by forces that take their rise in the heart of the economy itself. The conditions of acquisition have developed in such a way that a class of capitalistic entrepreneurs and moneyed capitalists can now form. This class, with others, rises to the highest stratum, while the middle class of the industrial bourgeoisie is broken up to no small degree. In the competitive conflict with larger enterprises many of moderate or small size succumb; their small owners lose economic independence and are forced down into the proletarian strata of which they form the upper layer as skilled workmen. This movement is in some ways akin to the ejection or removal of the peasantry. But it is essentially different in that it has not been effected forcibly by the abuse of power but by legal means, by decisions obtained in the market in harmony with the law of prices with the assent and active participation of the social demand. We shall, unless the term be deemed too bold, speak of this displacement as the downward shift of the industrial middle classes.

Another downward displacement of this sort with an even more decisive effect took place among the workers in the large industries. This was once more accomplished by legal means and in harmony with the law of prices. The large industries, owing to the enormous sales of their products, were in a position to increase the division of labor to a degree which had before been unknown in the trades. They could reduce the labor to the simplest performances for whose execution the worker no longer required previous training in an established trade. Then, since these simple operations had to be performed on an exceedingly large scale, multitudes of workers could be engaged whose service was confined to these simplest of manipulations and in extreme cases exhausted itself in the continued mechanical repetition of these few excessively simple acts. Thus the composition of the body of industrial workers has become a different one. The skilled workers have been supplemented by large numbers of untrained operators taken from the lowest strata of the population; and side by side with the male workers, large numbers of women, girls and children have been employed. Wherever a rural proletariat was within easy access, it served to recruit the ranks of unskilled industrial workers. Moreover the surplus population which increased enormously under the influence of the industrial development was absorbed to a large extent by the industrial demand for labor. As a consequence of all these circumstances, the number of workers without pecuniary resources has increased greatly both absolutely and relatively. Within this class, again, the numbers of unskilled workers of the lowest strata have increased. Undeniably, the body of trained workers, especially after it had become organized, was in a position to increase its income materially and improve its social position. For it a general upward trend was possible so that the upper groups frequently rose even above the lower strata of the middle class. But this did not equalize the effects on the composition of the population which were brought about by the continued downward shift of the strata of unskilled laborers.

In view of these facts our problem is a twofold one. In the first place the assumptions of our investigation must be sufficiently broad. In the second place we must inquire how the development of acquisition and the formation of income is influenced by the fact that there is a capitalistic upper class and a lower stratum, itself subdivided, composed of multitudes of workers deprived of all pecuniary means. In carrying out this investigation we shall have to take into consideration the relations of power and lack of power in these lower and higher strata. Moreover we shall have to show how the continued increase of acquisition and income further influences the stratification; how power and powerlessness are additionally increased.

Large industries have by no means entirely crushed the industrial middle classes. There are still numerous industrial enterprises for which wholesale production is not remunerative and to which neither the technique nor the organization of the large industries are as yet suited. But the position of even such of these trades as have been preserved is frequently unsatisfactory. Among them are many establishments which are unremunerative. Some which are exposed to the competition of large manufacturers are severely handicapped. Still others suffer from an internal competition which they themselves set up and which is intensified by the disturbance of the smaller industries by capitalistic development. It can be readily seen that along with the master craftsmen their assistants are as severely if not more severely injured.

In agriculture so far, large scale production has not demonstrated its practical superiority. Where the peasantry has maintained itself against the ejections of landlords, it is today scarcely subject to any downward shift because of the competition of the large landowner. In other respects, too, the conditions of European agriculture are uninviting to the capitalistic spirit of enterprise. Opportunities are lacking for the realization of large capitalistic profits while generally agricultural methods as such are only to the slightest extent formative of capital.

In other ways, capitalistic development endangers the ownership of land and especially the middle classes and the peasantry. These classes are frequently still in a state of transition from the natural to the monetary economy. As a consequence they have a large need of capital in order to equip themselves on a money-economic basis. Moreover as their need of capital is increased by the growing intensity of methods, these peasants are apt to be financially distressed even where the difficult task of organizing peasant credit has been accomplished. In coincidence with a failure of harvest and unfavorable market conditions these credit obligations may become a matter of grave peril to them. In such times the peasant holdings are apt to fall into the hands of the moneyed capitalist. It is under conditions like these that money usury in rural districts is a serious menace.[1]

A further consequence of the capitalistic development is to be found in the fact that the increased industrial wages raise the wages which must be paid in rural districts and thus promote the scarcity of hired help which so greatly embarrasses the farmers. Less conspicuous, but in its lasting effect more serious, is another danger which constantly shows itself where the natural economy is gradually being eliminated. So long as the peasant's natural economy still strongly reinforces his position, the prices which he recovers from his products do not make allowance for his own costs of subsistence; in other words, the full costs of production are not covered. In order, on passing to the complete monetary economy, to remain on a remunerative basis, he must sell at greatly increased prices. But even when he obtains payment at higher prices for the foodstuffs that are urgently demanded by the recently added urban population he is not sure of recovering his cost without loss. He may be the loser by finding himself compelled to resort for his personal consumption to foodstuffs of inferior nutritive qualities. In many localities the generation now growing up is no longer being fed so as to keep its members in fit condition for the exhausting work to which they are bred.

Relieved of the strain of local feuds and the devastation of wars, of the visitations of famines and plagues, the peasantry in the capitalistic era finds itself threatened by evils far more disastrous on the whole, though less harassing to the individual, than all past tribulations. When thousands upon thousands were swept away by sword and pestilence, the natural fecundity of the survivors brought new life again into the desolated homesteads. The succeeding generations stood as before with the sturdy characteristics of a rural race. In the capitalistic age, the life of the peasant is more secure in many respects, but in large districts the permanent condition of peasant husbandry, the vigor and health of the peasant, are exposed to grave risk and to the serious menace that in his habits of life and his natural aptitudes, the peasant will be carried down into proletarian degradation.

§ 63. The Enterprise

The entrepreneur—The owner's enterprise—Capitalistic enterprise—Collective (officials') enterprise, stock companies, associations for enterprise—The modern concept of the entrepreneur—The development of the large enterprise.

The social acquisitive community, technically articulated, geographically localized and under the influence of tradition, has been organized into numerous individual establishments for concrete economic problems. These individual plants are the cells out of which has

[1] Trans. note: It is of interest to note that if the farmers' condition is sufficiently bad, the lender has no chance to resort to usury. In the drastic post-war readjustment in the United States, more than 50 per cent of the interest due on mortgages held by insurance companies on Montana farms was overdue. Foreclosure was of no avail for no insurance company wanted to hold a plow and surely no one else did.

grown the acquisitive community. The organization of the latter determines the character of the entire structure.

The most simple organization conceivable is that of the individual establishment which in the beginnings of trade was widely disseminated. But no sooner are men confronted by tasks of somewhat greater magnitude, than communities of operation have to be organized where a number of persons provided with the necessary tools are set to work under single direction. The family, governed by its head, is the most obvious and natural form of organization. Increasing acquisitions lead to ever more widely ramified communities of operation.

According to that general law of society by which the multitude becomes capable of action only through leadership, every large community of operation demands a leader who binds it into an active unit. In the course of historical development many forms of qualification for leadership have existed in the communities of acquisition. In times when personal slavery exists, the most oppressive type of economic leadership is found; the leader of a slave-gang is its master in the most rigorous sense of the term. Under a milder law the owner or proprietor takes the place of the overlord. These terms suggest rights in material productive goods. The name of master [1] as used in the gilds implies a mastery of the trade by means of which the proprietor of a shop became the teacher of his fellow workers. The modern development has given rise to the entrepreneur of the money economy, who invests capital in order to realize a monetary profit.

Theory is concerned almost exclusively with the enterprise [2] as the free form of organization of the community of acquisition in the money economy. It habitually looks upon the older types of individual establishments [3] that are still functioning in both city and country, as less developed forms of undertaking which it can well afford to neglect in its investigations. We too shall neglect all forms but the enterprise; but we shall do so fully conscious of the fact that this is merely a resort to idealization and simplification and that the conclusions which we reach are applicable to the other forms only when our assumptions have been revamped to fit the particular condition of facts.

The institution of enterprise is the organ of the modern economic stratification of which we have just spoken. In its simple forms it in-

[1] Trans. note: In the German the distinction of names is clearer than in English. The master of slaves is *der Herr;* the master craftsman is *der Meister.*

[2] Unternehmung.

[3] Sonderbetriebe.

vests the entrepreneur merely with personal superiority; later, when large enterprises develop, it gives him a degree of power that finally swells to capitalistic supremacy.

The purest type of his class is the individual entrepreneur, or as we may briefly call him, the entrepreneur. He is the director by legal right and at the same time by virtue of his active participation in the economic management of his enterprise. He is a leader in his own right. He is the legal representative of the operation, the owner of the material productive goods, creditor for all accounts receivable and debtor for all accounts payable. As a lessor or lessee he is obligated or privileged. He is the employer under all contracts for work and labor. He is the owner of all products and disposes of them. For his account the products are disposed of and the proceeds collected; on the other hand, all payments are a charge on his personal account. But he is not merely the legal head; he is also at all times the economic leader. His legal power of disposition reaches its full significance in securing to him complete freedom of economic management. His economic leadership commences with the establishment of the enterprise; he supplies not only the necessary capital but originates the idea, elaborates and puts into operation the plan, and engages collaborators. When the enterprise is established, he becomes its manager technically as well as commercially.

Among the numerous qualities which he requires in order to do justice to his task, there is one which is most important. It is the one which provides his very name; he must be enterprising; he must possess the quick perception that seizes new turns in current transactions as his affairs develop; he must possess the independent forcefulness to regulate his business according to his views. There is also the requirement that he must have the courage to accept the risks which are connected with every capital investment. This is especially true with one who enters a new and untried field. But not mere boldness of action, much less the fascination of gambling prompts his enterprising spirit; the impulse which drives him forward is the joyful power to create.

The uncertainty of future events must be accepted by every economy not excepting the simplest natural one. It must be assumed from the moment that the worker begins to provide conscientiously for needs beyond those of the moment. At this point every human enterprise must stake material goods or personal efforts. For those undertakings which are articulated with the money economy, the risk is increased; all chances are staked on the one card of the selected specialty of production, the adopted calling of a life-time. But the risk of the entrepreneur is even greater than any of these; the success of an entire community of operation is in his charge. Still the element of possible disaster should not be too strongly insisted upon in the case of the entrepreneur. By far the larger number of business ventures which are entered upon offers fair prospects of success; the number of those which miscarry is, after all, smaller. Moreover it should not be overlooked that there are always other persons who are also subject to the hazards of the enterprise. Thus there are the creditors and, above all, the workers, Under some circumstances the latter are the first to be affected by failure. Even before the entrepreneur feels the effects of disaster they are injured by the dismissals to which the entrepreneur resorts when unfavorable business conditions force curtailment upon him.

The individual enterprise is adapted to a certain degree of expansion. It may develop until a point is reached at which a directing[1] entrepreneur is needed to achieve successful results. On the other hand, the extent may not be greater than permits the entrepreneur still to imbue the entire operation with the spirit and will of his ownership.

Most nearly akin to the individual enterprise is that conducted by a partnership or some other small association of persons where several men share the task of the entrepreneur. Whenever full confidence and a friendly understanding exist between these parties and their abilities mutually supplement each other, the alliance is advantageous in that they are better able to do justice to the exigencies of a large business than can a single individual unless he be possessed of peculiar personal powers and material resources. Such an association of persons is able to exercise leadership with the perfect efficiency of the owner. Together with the individual enterprise, we shall speak of it as the owner's enterprise, wishing to indicate that in these cases the entrepreneurs fulfill the tasks of their station as their own agents. The owner's enterprise is indissolubly bound to the persons of the entrepreneurs; regular vicarious action of any kind whatever for long periods of time, by guardians, officials or the like, is excluded.

The owner's enterprise on a large scale is the original form of capitalistic enterprise. The large capital which it amasses enriches the one owner or possibly the small group, and makes them large owners of capital or capitalists.

Numerous other forms of large enterprise have sprung up by the

[1] Trans. note: ein führender Unternehmer: i.e., an entrepreneur with large qualities of leadership.

side of the large owner's undertaking. They are intended to compete with it and are calculated to turn to account the advantage of large scale operation for wider circles. As undertakings of large capital they are capital enterprises but they are not capitalistic. Among them are state enterprises and those of self administrative bodies, whose gains are for the people generally. Again, we find among them coöperative organizations with an open membership which enables the middle and laboring classes to become interested. These carry out either the purely coöperative idea or combine it with that of the stock company. Among them should be mentioned mutual companies and savings banks conducted by philanthropic societies. All these forms may be designated by general name, collective enterprises, for they unite a large number of persons who share responsibilities and interests. In its legal form, the stock company is also to be classed with these organizations as it unites a large number of associates. The collective enterprise is managed by installed leaders, i. e., elected or appointed officials. It may therefore also be called an officials' enterprise in clear distinction from the owner's enterprise.

We thus find on the one side the leader by individual proprietary right who therefore has unrestricted power of disposition. On the other hand is the appointed responsible leader bound by the terms of his mandate and answerable to his principal. These are the two great types of leadership. They are the result of historical development in the state as well as society. Both are designed to provide for the masses the faculty of action which they can never attain for themselves.

Looking not at the legal form but at actual conditions, we shall recognize in the stock company the transition from owner's to officials' enterprise. It combines the two types of leadership; the large stockholders are installed in their leading positions by election and are in part entrepreneur-owners, in part officials. We find similar conditions in the kartel and trust where forceful leaders find the opportunity to act as representatives of the modern economy without becoming such by any full-fledged personal right. Through these agents the large enterprise associations become main organs of capitalism in the same manner as do stock companies through their founders and the large stockholders.

The capitalistic owner's enterprise, the collective enterprise pure and simple, the stock company which is a mixed form half way between the two, as well as the great enterprise-association, has each its peculiar function in the complete structure of enterprise. The owner's undertaking possesses the initiative. It ferrets out new possibilities and forms of acquisition; it brings new men into prominence by competitive selection. The capitalistic owner's enterprise is in every instance the primary form out of which investment banks fashion stock companies. Only certain establishments are so large that the resources of an owner's enterprise would be inadequate for them from the very beginning and are therefore destined in the first instance to take the form of stock companies. The great associations of enterprises gather up owner's enterprises and stock companies so as to produce the most powerful effect. The pure form of collective enterprise is the last to appear. It does not begin to spread until by means of the experience of other organizations the rules of business management have been settled and ample security for the public funds or the investments of the masses has been obtained. It is possible that in the near future a new alinement will be brought about, that the increasing capitalistic domination of private enterprises will induce the state and the public, even more than it has so far, to meet them in competition by collective enterprises. For the supremacy of capitalistic power has induced the counter-movement of socialism, which plans to profit by the concentration of the capitalistic enterprises in order to establish the entire acquisitive economy of the people for all time on a collectivist basis.

In capitalistic enterprise the great personalities of entrepreneurs have risen to their full stature: bold technical innovators, organizers with a keen knowledge of human nature, far-sighted bankers, reckless speculators, the world-conquering directors of the trusts. However, considering all the effects of mammoth enterprise, it is safe to say that it has encroached upon the influence of the entrepreneur and that it is destined to do so still further as the field of such enterprise is extended. Even in the capitalistic owner's enterprise the entrepreneur can no longer do full justice to the tasks of an owner; he must entrust important functions to subordinates. While he may direct and supervise them, he can never infuse them with his own initiative. In the collective or officials' enterprises the entrepreneur is in no sense a fully empowered manager; the legal ownership and the duly appointed management are wholly distinct. Again, the legal ownership is vested in so many persons, such a trifling and indirect responsibility is apportioned to any one of them, that they can scarcely feel themselves to be real workers in the undertaking. The small stockholders and even those with larger holdings look upon their enterprise almost as strangers expecting to collect an annuity. Their attitude is somewhat like that of creditors. An even wider gap separates the interest of the citizen from state or city enterprises, which still are matters of public interest. When it comes to the duly appointed managers, officials of all degrees of importance, they are so restricted by their responsibility to others and their own binding norms of action, their powers of leadership are divided among so many underlings that they lose a large part of their directing forcefulness. The ostensible leaders are fundamentally dependent upon the manner in which subordinates execute their orders. The orders are thus shaped in the inception by the expectations raised by previous experience of the manner of execution. Frequently in enterprises that have assumed large dimensions there is no entrepreneur proper; there may be not one man actively employed who possesses and demonstrates a spirit of enterprise. The exceptions to this statement are only those stock companies and associations in whose struggles and achievements the personal force of great leaders has maintained itself.

In beginning this discussion we pictured the entrepreneur of the normal owner's enterprise. This figure is no longer a replica of the present dominant type. A definition that covers all modern concepts of the entrepreneur must be the result of the mere probing of the legal concept. The requirement of economic management is no longer fulfilled in all cases. Today the enterprise is a voluntary community of commercial operation in the money economy subject to one entrepreneur. It may be a unified group of such operations. The entrepreneur is any legal owner of an enterprise. He may be an individual person or "he" may be the large group who comprise the artificial person and public coöperation whose organization is so complicated that the forces of personal efficacy are largely dissolved in the deadening formalities required to obtain a valid resolution.

At all times there have been isolated commercial enterprises of large size, but modern development has vastly multiplied their number and extent. The impetus has been supplied by the growth of the markets. This in turn is a consequence of increasing domestic population and colonial expansion. That this impetus should so markedly have affected industrial conditions while those of agriculture were little changed is explained by the original contrast of the two types of activity. The extent of agriculture is limited by the soil and fully as much by the succession of the seasons. On the other hand the trades may be quartered in more restricted areas, where the process of industrial production may be better controlled by human art and thus rendered susceptible to both temporal and local concentration. The technical possibility of concentration was invoked as soon as the expanded markets offered an opportunity to dispose of large quantities of products. Technical concepts that had no practical application in the era of narrow markets but were only idle playthings, now suddenly took on an immediate usefulness and loomed large with undreamt of values. The increased sales yielded interest on the investment in large plants and promised large profits in addition. Thus large-scale enterprise won over the entire field where power-driven and labor-saving [1] machinery and other extensive plants could be used. Factories, mines, railroads and steamships came under its dominion.

Large-scale operation forced its way also into many branches of industry that were not open to the machine and vast fixed capital but had to depend as before on human skill and diligence as the essential factors of production. The ready-made clothing trade is a most apt illustration. Under the influence of enlarged markets it became possible to split up the traditional process, which had been adapted to the local custom-trade, into a number of the simplest operations. Thus an articulation of work was achieved by which particular training became unnecessary and almost primitive manipulations might be performed by girls or other cheap help. The remainder of workman-like operations which could not be further divided were then put in the hands of well paid, or better paid, operators. Only a few of these were now required. The conduct of the business, especially the salesmanship, remained in the hands of the entrepreneur. A well organized enterprise of this sort easily expelled the old-style tailoring trade. It lowered the cost of production and controlled the market which was immediately satisfied by an abundant supply of ready-made garments of every description. It was not even necessary for the success of the business to provide a common working place for all its workers. Many of the operations did not need to be done on the premises; a single shelter was only required for the final operations and for the business offices.

Large-scale operation reached its fullest development in the associated undertakings comprising the kartels and trusts, which we discussed at length in an earlier connection. Kartels aim in the first place at a monopoly of the market. In addition trusts turn to account in a most promising manner wide fields of activity that modern technical and organizing invention have laid open to large-scale operation. Their final goal is the enjoyment of the extraordinary productional and marketing advantages of the self-contained enterprise.

The modern giant-enterprise stands unique not only in the tremendous extent of its operations but also in the multiplicity of related branches which it integrates under one management. In discussing trusts we went into sufficient detail on this point. It is customary to speak of these comprehensive organizations, through whose activities is sought control of all phases of the productive and commercial process, as unit industries; [2] it might be more appropriate to refer to them as unit enterprises. Their tendency is in marked contrast to the specialization of enterprise, which was still the order of the day a generation ago. The explanation of the change is probably to be found in the rise of the enormous power of modern money-capital which has been amassed and is held in fabulous amounts by the large banks. This power gives a guarantee, such as never existed before, of an unprecedented control of the productive and marketing processes. It enables one industrial group to attempt the unparalleled task of absorbing every opportunity for profit that the gigantic markets of our age offer. The technical articulation of labor is by no means neglected in the vast unit industries; in them it can be pushed further than it has been heretofore.

The colossal bank is not to be separated from the modern development of large-scale industry. The great growth of the natural form of capital demands and caters to an equally large growth of the monetary form. Never has money

[1] Kraftmaschinen, Arbeitsmaschinen.

[2] Gesamtbetrieben.

capital been so enabled to thrive upon its rapid transmutability as in our time with the incessantly repeated new accumulations of capital goods. It is offered especially enticing opportunities in the underwriting of new enterprises and in speculation on the stock exchange. A common feature of both is the continuous turn-over. The professional promoter seeks his profit in the disposal of enterprises which he has organized; they interest him only until he has turned their management over into other hands. The speculator seeks his profit in the purchase and sale of securities and commodities originating in some outside enterprise in whose existence he is not otherwise interested. In their worst degeneration, promotion and speculation on the Exchange drift into the character of parasitic enterprise which clings to other branches of acquisition in order to exhaust their substance.

§ 64. Social Economy and Social Income

The unity of the social economy—Yield and income—Distribution of income—Wealth, social wealth.

The appraisals of all enterprises are in terms of economic exchange value. They are all members of the community of exchange, which is an institution of exchange and expands with the full development of the monetary and credit systems into the community of payment. Owing to the fact that all enterprises are adjusted for exchange, they actually enter into a close community while still preserving legal independence. They thus form a productive and acquisitive body in which labor is divided and articulated. The organization of this body is also determined by the social stratification. The localization of its activities is fixed by the existing economic conditions. Thus arises the economic community of production and acquisition, the highest institution of the intercourse of exchange.

The economic community, as established in the full breadth of its operations by exchange, is spoken of in economic theory as the economy. From a legal point of view the social economy is the sum of the private economies bound together by trade; from the economic point of view it forms a unit through its ubiquitous relationships. We admit it is not the ultimate community of effort that is the dream of socialism. Neither is it the unified social institution that we assumed at the beginning of our analysis of the theory of the simple economy. Far more important, it is the economy of the people as handed down by historical tradition. History does not warrant the assumption that a people for economic purposes will subordinate itself to the management of a single organization. Such an assumption may not be admitted by empirical theory in which only actual typical conditions should be described. It may only be resorted to in the manner in which we used it in our theory of the simple economy: as an idealizing assumption that should lay the foundations for an investigation of actual conditions.

No sooner are the people organized as the state, than the latter becomes part of the historical setting of the people. The state has had an exceedingly important part in shaping the historical institution of the economy, both in earlier times and at present through its protective and promotional activity. But there is a wide difference of opinion as to the manner in which this share is to be correctly appraised. We shall not be able to form an adequate judgment of this until after we have analyzed the process of the formation of income when it is not affected by the intervention of the state. Therefore it seems best for the present to eliminate the agency of the state entirely, and to look upon the economy as we have defined it, solely as a voluntary, social institution arising in exchange. In so doing we must not regard the participating individuals as actuated solely by personal egoism; they are also prompted by a social egoism and are generally subject to social powers. This we have already explicitly demonstrated in an earlier connection.

In the regular course of affairs the net yield of natural material and personal values gained in the economic process of acquisition supplies the means to cover the needs of the people. This yield is subject to fluctuations and economies may therefore be compelled at times to fall back upon their reserves in order to satisfy requirements. None the less, in so far as the sources operate permanently from which this flow springs, it may be regarded as regular. Thus this net yield is to be distinguished from the irregular receipts arising from a direct increase of possessions or from their appreciation in value. By this regularity it meets the periodical recurrence of needs, for which every economy must provide. In every systematic economy the primary duty of securing an adequate yield to meet the regular needs is recognized. Moreover, an economy that would advance in prosperity must see to it that the yield is sufficient, over and above the requirements of its households, to permit the setting aside of savings that may be turned to the formation of capital.

In so far as this net yield is referred to the personal economies among which it is distributed, it is spoken of as the social income. Legally it is to be defined as the sum of the individual incomes gained in the social economy. However, economically it is a unit because it is formed in the unified process of the social economy. Thus its name is appropriate, as is that of the social economy to the system whence the social income arose. But to properly estimate the effects of this income we must be informed how it is distributed to the broad strata of the private economies. Its sum total does not instruct us intelligibly on this point; as a whole the social income may increase and yet the effect of its employment may diminish, when the distribution becomes unfavorable and the large mass of smaller incomes is curtailed for the benefit of higher strata.

Looking at the economy as a whole, it is evident in the nature of things that yield and income coincide. In this respect the social economy is in exactly the same position as the economy of a Crusoe or any other simple economy. However, this relation does not necessarily hold for the individual household within the social economy. It is conceivable that an income might be allowed to persons who are in no way productive fellow-workers in the social economic process of acquisition. Again, the participating parties might be allotted an income by a standard different from that of their participation. Such would be the case, for example, under a legal code like the one demanded by the socialist party who would distribute the national income according to a standard of "rational requirements." Quite in the spirit of the simple economy the established legal order links together yield and income. Except in instances of gift or charitable donation, persons to acquire incomes must somehow take part in the acquisitive process, in the formation of yield, by means of labor performed or the possession of personal wealth. The personal income is the sum of the yields which flow into an individual economy. Its amount is measured by the yields or part of a yield that is attributed to anyone on account of his participation.

The grave significance of the established legal order is that it gives juridical recognition to the traditional stratification of property. Acquired property confers a well-founded right in acquisition. Those who possess large wealth are in a position to gain large incomes without labor. The man without means, with only his labor to fall back upon, is unfavorably situated from the start. His position is still more difficult when he is not a member of the educated classes and therefore is able to offer only his physical labor.

At this point in the investigation we must content ourselves merely to indicate these conditions, for the present refraining from any interpretation of their significance. The immediate problem before us is simply to examine the formation of income according to the course of events under the existing legal order.

We already have within reach for this investigation a series of fundamental theoretical considerations. As the income is derived from yields, the rules of the attribution of yields with which we became familiar in the theory of the simple economy are controlling upon the formation of income. Furthermore as income is gained in a price form in the money economy, the general laws of the formation of prices, as set forth in our general theory of prices, are also decisive. On the one hand the theory of income is a continuation of the doctrine of attribution when this has been adjusted to the monetary formation of yields; on the other hand it is the sequel of the doctrine of prices when the latter has been adjusted to the special market indices obtaining in the existing acquisitive process and under the prevailing stratification of the large yield-producing factors.

The principal distribution of income, to which our investigations must conform, coincides with the division of the sources of yields. Wealth and labor, or rather the union of the two, being the sources of yields, we shall distinguish pure income from possessions, pure labor income that in the widest sense is called wage-income, and the mixed entrepreneur-income that is obtained from the union of possessions and labor. Pure income derived from ownership, income without labor as it is also called, may be either ground-rent or interest on capital. The income from wealth and entrepreneur-income are known as funded income since both rest upon a basis of possession. Wage income is not funded. In our analysis we shall still further subdivide these principal divisions of income in order to regard also the typical stratifications of income distribution. In the case of entrepreneur's income we shall consider more especially the capitalistic formation of income. In wage-income the broad strata of the liberal professions, skilled and unskilled labor must be distinguished. Whenever it is necessary for theoretical purposes, we shall also accord a place in our assumptions to conditions of power and weakness which are typical of modern stratification.

In this analysis we have followed the universal practice in our use of the term, possessions. Its meaning has been transferred from the relations of the simple economy. Under the conditions of developed exchange-economy it loses part of its original connotation, for, as we showed in its proper connection, property is distinguished from possessions owing to the appearance of credit transactions. Possessions embrace the entire holdings of material goods to the extent to which these are considered permanent in opposition to yield or income. They therefore embrace not merely industrial real estate and capital possessions, but also permanent household possessions. Beside these possessions of material goods, legal demands on other persons also figure as property. These are known as credits, while obligations of indebtedness must be deducted as debits. The property or net worth is determined as the remaining monetary sum when credits and debits are balanced against each other according to their exchange value. It only remains to be added that not only rights of demand but other rights as well, for example a copyright or under certain circumstances actual relations, say "good will," may be reckoned as property as long as they promise future yields or money returns and may be controlled to some extent or transferred by their owner.

The national wealth is the aggregate of the individual properties of any people. Demands and obligations within the national jurisdiction cancel each other. Thus the social wealth of an economy, conceived as isolated from others, coincides with the possessions of material goods. Its statistical inventory is most simply taken by listing its existing material goods. When it comes to a national economy as related to the commerce of the world, the demands against foreign countries or their nationals must be added to the inventory; obligations toward them must be deducted.

§ 65. Agricultural Rent

Natural and contractual rent of lands—The general occurrence of differential rent—Ricardo's theory of rent and the "monopoly of the soil."

The agricultural rent of land is that portion of the agricultural yield which is attributed to the soil as such. Those qualities which are exhausted by cultivation are not part of the land as such. Its permanent cultivation involves replenishing this transitory constituency, and the share of the yield which is attributed to the latter is interest on capital. Only the inexhaustible elements of the soil may be credited with ground rent.

Ground rent is drawn either as natural or contractual rent. The owner of land who cultivates it himself obtains a natural rent in the excess of the net money yield over the interest on his invested capital. In this case we assume the customary methods of cultivation and disregard the increased entrepreneur-income which may be realized from superior husbandry. The lessor of agricultural land draws a contractual rent as the excess of the rental over the interest on the capital goods leased at the same time. Of these two forms of rent, the natural one is the original. From this form the contractual variety has been derived. When it comes to theory, the explanation of the natural rent of land is the first and most important problem.

In the theory of land and also in that of attribution we have so far prepared the explanation of the natural rent of land that we may confine ourselves here to a few summarizing statements.

In the theory of land the existence of various classes of land was noted: i. e., classes of land that vary in fertility, in proximity to the market and in qualities of the soil. The better grades yield the larger net gain from the given market prices of the crops, for the reason that their costs of cultivation are less. The theory of land has further shown that the better grades of land are taken under cultivation before the poorer ones, also that in the expansion the classes last taken into use have not entered the economic quantitative relation and that besides these there remain unused reserves still to be disposed of. Assuming these conditions to be the general rule, we recall that it was seen in the theory of attribution that the class last brought under cultivation, the marginal land as we may call it, being free, cannot pay rent. Following the law of highest costs, the price of the crops is determined by the costs of cultivation on the marginal grade. The excess that remains in the case of the better classes of land is attributed, according to the law of specific attribution, to the factor of the soil. This excess yield is the rent of land.

Finally, the theory of attribution has demonstrated that as the intensity of culivation increases, the rent rises which tenants may expect to pay for land. Cultivation is most intensive on those parcels of land with the highest fertility and lowest costs of transportation. In these cases the ground rent rises to the height of an "intensity rent."[1]

Under such conditions rent is a differential which does not enter into the price of products; the marginal classes of land and soil qualities are worked free without paying rent. However, as soon as the demand increases and forces the marginal grades into the economic quantitative relation, a price must be allowed which leaves an excess, a rent, for those classes as well. Nevertheless, so long as there still remain reserves of uncultivated land, the increasing demand resulting in an extension of cultivation and its greater intensity will always bring it about that hitherto unused grades are taken under cultivation. These once more are free and used without paying rent. The prices of products are therefore stabilized at the costs of cultivating these lands.

Ground-rents are lowered by improvements in agricultural methods or in the means of transportation as also by the settlement of new tracts of high grade land. This result is explained by the fact that it becomes feasible to discontinue the cultivation of the poorest lands. The margin of cultivation is then formed by better classes which produce their yield with a smaller outlay of money. Lower prices for the crops will result and the differential in costs that formerly benefited the higher grades of land will be reduced.

So far this retarding effect of improvements in methods has always been overtaken in the long run by increase in population. Historically, therefore, the general tendency has been toward an increase in ground-rent.

[1] Intensitätsrente.

Contractual rent oscillates about the norm of the natural rent. The fluctions are dependent upon the proportions existing between the supply and the demand for farm properties. When the supply preponderates, the owners of estates will have to make concessions to prospective tenants; the rents will not reach the full amount ascertained by adding natural rent and interest on the capital. Conversely, rents will rise when the demand exceeds the supply. It frequently happens that small tenants anxious to turn their abilities to account, and impelled by competition, agree to excessive rents which curtail the yield of their labor. In countries where large landed properties prevail, the condition of the small tenant-farmers lacking capital and exploited by oppressive rents, may become a very wretched one.

The ground rent which we have hitherto described may be called quantity-rent. From this is to be distinguished the quality-rent that attaches to such parcels of land as offer the advantage of yielding for an equivalent expenditure, crops of better quality or those for which a higher price may be obtained.

In the case of mines and all kindred industries in which accumulations of natural wealth are being removed or exhausted, the annual amortization of the existing stores of ore, coal and so forth is part of the costs of operation. In so far as such an establishment is worked under more favorable conditions and therefore at less expense than the marginal operations of its type it is entitled to a differential rent, which, precisely like the rent of land, follows the laws of highest cost and specific attribution. Similarly, for all enterprises of whatever description which operate under more advantageous conditions than the marginal plant [1] with a consequent saving of cost, there is a differential rent, the so-called industrial rent. It is also proper to speak in the case of personal services of a rent of efficiency and talent, a preferential rent due to individuals whose performance exceeds the marginal one.

Our exposition agrees in its main results with the prevailing doctrine established by Ricardo and elaborated by Thünen. Of all the doctrines of Ricardo, only the theory of ground-rent has survived to our day. Here there was a task to be performed which offered Ricardo a signal opportunity of displaying his truest scientific vision. Though obviously his acumen is much broader, it is fundamentally that of a man of business who has received his training in the broadly instructive school of practical affairs. Ricardo does not attempt to simplify in the manner of scientific isolation and idealization. He simplifies like

[1] Trans. note: The phrase "than the marginal plant" does not occur in the German which is written with an undefined comparative.

a man of affairs who eliminates whatever effects are small enough to remain concealed in his general results. Without paying any attention whatever to the significance of the intimate association of ideas, this business-like manner of observation has disqualified him for working out his serviceable theory of value and of price; for the explanation of agriculture rent, it was precisely what he needed. It may easily be explained how the most favorably located and conditioned parcels of land resulting in a saving of costs, yield to the owner a surplus from the price of the products. This explanation may be made even though in giving it we are unable to say what the costs are which are saved, or what the components of the price are which is obtained for the crops. To do this, however, requires a broad outlook which grasps in its survey the vast stratifications of the masses. In this sense Ricardo explained the rent of land; he showed that the highest values of the produce from the best situated grades of land exceed the general average although he was unable to explain conclusively how this general average is determined.

The peculiar short-comings of Ricardo's method of scientific thought may also be explained in his theory of rent. While he plainly recognizes the gradations of rent as conditioned by the variations in the saving of costs, he finds no explanation for the manner in which the movement takes place from the stabilized condition of one gradation to that of the next. The most serious defect of his theory of rent is to be found in the fact that he does not grasp the nature of the economic quantitative relation. Therefore he fails to see this relationship in the case of capital and labor and exaggerates it in the case of the best lands, declaring them to be a "monopoly." He has permitted his opinions to be too greatly shaped by conditions in England, where land is in the hands of comparatively few owners and where the owners of the great estates collect their rents most frequently in the form of a contractual rent on leaseholds. In the economic and social organization of England the rent of land is the most odious part of the national income. It is an income obtained without labor by a privileged minority at the expense of all other classes of society. If the full amount of it is not unearned, at least those increments are which arise without the slightest contributing effort on the part of the owner merely from the increased demand of a constantly growing population. That income is wholly unearned which is obtained through the exploitation of the contractual renter by encroaching upon the yields of his labor. But even in these cases, a monopoly in the true sense of the word does not exist in land; absolutely and relatively the number of farms is exceedingly large in proportion to the needs. So far as free grades of land are still available as is the general rule, the economic quantitative relation is even less pronounced than in the case of capital goods or of labor; only the parcels of land in the best locations occupy a highly favored specific position in the market.

In all countries where ownership of the land is more equally distributed, and the greater portion of the land is held by peasant owners, no question of an exploiting monopoly arises. The ground-rent obtained by the owner farming his own land is the result of labor and is well earned. Even when it is attributed to the land as such, the full yield of the soil can only be gained if the owner uses his best efforts. The owner would be greatly disappointed in his well-founded expectations if he failed to obtain the usual rent from his land, the rent which he anticipated and which is an important constituent of his income. Even the "intensity-rent" which may arise when the demand increases must be gained by serious effort. The estimation of the proper degree of intensity of cultivation is one of the most intricate problems; its correct solution has every claim on the undivided interest of the owner. As the yield increases, as the agricultural population grows and as the average acreage of the farms decreases, the most reasonable method of socially meting out the ground-rent which could be conceived within the constitution of private economies may be said to have been reached.

§ 66. Rent of Urban Lands

Urban rents and the Ricardian theory—Advantageous locations for dwellings and business premises—Urban intensity-rent—The tenement house—Urban rents as unearned income.

The rent of urban land is obtained as a contractual rent where dwellings or business premises are leased. It is the remainder of the net yield realized by renting real property after deducting interest on the capital employed. It is the amount attributable to the land as such. The rent of urban land or, as we may call it more briefly, urban rent, is analogous to the rent of agricultural land. Like the latter it is locally confined, a differential rent based upon the permanent advantages of favored parcels of land, a specific yield or surplus over and above costs obeying the law of specific attribution.

None the less, urban rent demands an explanation of its own. In the case of agricultural rent the prices obtained for the products are uniform but the costs vary on different grades of land. In the case of urban rent, on the other hand, the prices which are paid for rent vary while the building costs are the same everywhere. The advantages which certain sites offer are not economies in building costs. To some extent they do result in savings of time and money costs to the tenant which he would otherwise have to incur in traversing the distance to the center of the town. But this does not account for the origin of urban rent. Such savings are too trifling to establish the standard of urban rents. The fares on urban rapid transit facilities which would in the main be the determining cost in the presupposition involved in the above statement show but few and minor gradations while the variations in urban rents are both numerous and exceedingly disparate. In the heart of the city itself, where differences in the cost of transportation disappear altogether, extraordinary variations in rent may be observed between the locations having the heaviest traffic and those which are less frequented though in the immediate neighborhood of the former.

Ricardo and the older theorists generally have neglected the theory of urban rent. Such a theory seemed less important in their day than one of agricultural rent. Moreover the classical theory of prices lacked the key for an explanation of this sort. As a matter of principle it looked to the costs and these, as regards urban rent, decide nothing. On the other hand, the function of demand in establishing prices was neglected by Ricardo and his disciples, and it is the demand above all else which determines urban rents. Owing to the enormous growth of cities since Ricardo's time, urban rent has outstripped agricultural rent in importance. Modern theory may not neglect their explanation.

In order to explain urban rents, their formation must first be explained. The market of urban land may be broken down into a large number of local markets in which advantages of location are the distinguishing characteristic. We shall arrange these partial markets in an order that allows us to consider the poorest locations first, then to proceed to the better ones and to those of unsurpassable advantages.

In the least desirable districts, if we assume a free market, the rentals are known to leave no remainder of urban rent; they are just high enough to repay the costs of maintenance. Should an increasing demand make higher prices possible, then the supply will always bring about an equalization. The costs of maintenance are composed of current expenses for taxes, management, repairs, amortization of the building capital, as well as the provision for customary interest on the capital still outstanding from the costs of construction. The so-called building capital is composed of the sums necessary to cover the costs of construction. These include carrying charges until the house is occupied, payment in full to the entrepreneur and the purchase price for the building lot. Speculative influences left aside, this purchase price in the least desirable districts which we are now considering will exceed but little the agricultural land values to be computed by the capitalization of the agricultural rent of the land. To this extent agricultural rent forms an element in the determination of urban rent. This is one of the rare cases where real estate loses its specific character and operates as a cost means.

In the more favorably located sections, rentals are paid which exceed costs. The classes of tenants who wish to be admitted to the preferable locations must, in the spirit of the fundamental law of price-formation outbid correspondingly the competing strata less able to pay. They do so by allowing an excess over and above the maximum offer of the latter. The amount of this allowance is determined by the marginal bid within the paying ability of the marginal tenants. These tenants are those within this class of the lowest standing and financial power; but who are admitted of necessity in order that the entire supply of the particular market may be absorbed by the demand. The higher we mount in the series of partial markets, the higher will be the excess charge to be added to the regular rental. The group desiring to secure the very best locations must allow something more than the excess already paid by the lower strata in their locations.

Urban rent is that part of the rental which is paid as a premium for the advantages of the better location. The concept is simple, as simple as that agricultural rent has its origin in the saving of costs due to superior grades of soil. Just as this latter conclusion is ample to support the entire theory of agricultural rent, so the former is all that is needed as a foundation for the entire theory of urban rent. In order to complete our theory of urban rents, we have now only to show the actual development of advantages of location in regard to city real estate.

This development will be most apparent if, by means of idealizing simplification, we picture the city as laid out in strictly concentric areas with its most desirable locations for occupancy at the center, let us say around the principal square. All other settlements will then be arranged in circular form about this primary ring down to the poorest quarters in the outskirts of the town adjoining the fields of its suburbs. The cities of the Middle Ages often closely approached this idealized plan. In each of the rings surrounding the heart of the city, the different parties compete with one another grade by grade. The poorest group of tenants, the one paying the lowest prices, will be forced to the extreme periphery. The second group, but little better situated than the former, will cling to the next area, being unable to satisfy the prices demanded in the third ring, which are slightly in excess of those in the second. Through continued conflict or price competition, step by step and grade by grade, with a continued out-bidding by competing groups, as many different levels of rent are established as advantages of location are distinguished by the tenants. Urban rent is the most significant concrete expression of the law of the stratification of prices that could be adduced.

If we pass from this ideal view to the diverse relations of real life we shall have to distinguish residential and business districts.

In the large, modern cities the location of dwellings has broken through the older concentric arrangement that may frequently still be traced. Not only the most indigent groups, but large numbers of the well-to-do and wealthy seek homes on the borders or even beyond the borders of the closely packed masses of houses and at a distance from the large cities. Here one finds distinct communities, some large and some small; some which themselves have a town-like development. These areas we may speak of as zones of the "ultra-periphery." The configuration of the modern city has become highly irregular. Central location is still counted as an advantage but beside it others are finding recognition such as healthfulness, beauty and restful quiet. In part these are even more highly prized than the first. Especial stress is laid on the restriction of a neighborhood to members of one's own stratum. A fashionable section should not be contaminated by proletarian intrusion. Owing to the fact that the concentric form of cities has been broken down, their further growth has been promoted in a manner that seeks to reduce expenses. New buildings are erected where open space invites settlements and there is no need of clearing the land by demolishing older structures. The space for superior residential purposes, however, having been greatly extended, the increase of rentals and of urban rent is moderate. Nevertheless, the system of gradual out-bidding among tenants is by no means obliterated. Now, as heretofore, residential districts are classified by the advantages which they offer. The wealthy invariably show an inclination to occupy the best locations which are always more limited than the less advantageous ones. The sections where "one may decently live" will always be available in smaller amounts if for no other reason than that "one" would always make his home where others of the "best families" are already known to live.

The market of business rentals is much more restricted than the residential one. As far as is possible, the wholesale trade concentrates at a center in a conveniently situated spot. Important public offices, popular institutions and points of interest [1] are also centrally located where the means of communication converge from all directions. As far as local trade is concerned, those locations and streets must be considered which are the most populous thoroughfares: the heart of the city into which all radial means of access pour their traffic and finally the great radial avenues themselves. The increased rentals paid for central locations by business tenants crush the residential demand. But aside from this fact, there is a sharp conflict of competitive demands for the most advantageous locations that arises within the business demand itself.

Theoretically it is of special importance that the increased business profits which may be realized in the favored locations increase the funds from which the excess rents are paid; while in residential districts these amounts are fixed by the incomes of the tenants. We have

[1] Sehenswürdigkeiten.

here the characteristic in which urban rents are most nearly akin to agricultural rent. Like the cultivation of fertile land, business conducted on the best located premises offers the advantage of large sales at the established market price. The profitableness of the enterprise therefore increases. Assuming an industry is bound to a particular spot to effect its sales, the entire surplus there realized would, like the surplus yield of the fertile field, be attributed to the land as such. It would then lie within the power of the owner of the building to appropriate to his own use the entire profits of the business by demands of increasing rentals. The enterprise would then, as the saying goes, "work for the landlord." As a rule this is not the case. The tenants have a choice of more than one parcel out of a number that are available in a definite local market. The rents in this partial market are determined by the marginal offer that is permissible for the least remunerative establishments which must still be admitted to rent all of the premises in this particular market. For all other establishments earning larger profits the business man retains out of the increased earnings, a surplus that is not consumed by rent. This surplus accrues to the entrepreneurs whose business, owing to its specific character, succeeds most thoroughly in profiting by the advantageous location. In these cases, the landlord must content himself with the marginal profit of the specific partial market.

As the city grows, the simple rent of the location becomes an intensity rent. The buildings are erected closer together, of greater height and of more costly materials in order to benefit to the full from the advantage of location. There is a horizontal, vertical and qualitative intensity. The last meets the desires of the strata best able to pay, and is indulged in to attract them as tenants because they are expected to make the highest excess offers. The horizontal intensity represents a striving by the addition of buildings to utilize the largest possible percentage of space in any given area. The vertical intensity piles floor upon floor in its sky-scraping efforts. In so far as the most wealthy stratum cannot be depended upon to fill the closely built and tall rear houses, thus shut off from light and air, these are fitted for tenants of smaller means who are brought in to maximize the gross rents collected. In order to increase the total yield through these strata, it is important that building operations proceed with a reduced qualitative intensity with the utmost possible saving of expense. In the vertical utilization of space it is especially note-worthy that within certain limits every additional floor is built at less expense, as the divisor is increased by which is apportioned the cost of construction for foundations and roof. Notwithstanding all economies, a limit must finally be reached at which building more compactly and at greater height ceases to be profitable. Up to this limit a law of diminishing returns operates for accommodations added laterally and vertically, which is in some ways akin to the law of diminishing returns for agricultural land. The elevator has raised the limit for the upward construction of buildings, as may be plainly seen in the American skyscraper. Ultimately the building codes may, from considerations of public health, place more rigorous restrictions upon the congestion and height of building operations than does the personal interest of the speculative builder.

The growth of a city increases rents in residential as well as business sections, because for both classes of property the stratification increases, and with it the appraisal of differential advantages of location becomes sharper. The number of locations that are distinguished increases and with it grows not only the number of those offering premiums but also the amount of the premium that may be obtained in the most advantageous locations. The most effective means of depressing rents is the multiplication and improvement of urban transportation facilities, for these greatly enlarge the available sections. Our present theoretical inquiry cannot consider to what extent it would be possible favorably to affect building operations and rentals by administrative measures, by an adjustment of building codes and by an organization of credit facilities.

It is charged with even greater insistence that a monopoly exists in the case of urban land than in that of agricultural land. But even the most pronounced specific market position, conferred by locations of unsurpassed advantages, does not convey a monopolistic position. In those markets with less evident advantages, parcels of land, dwellings and business properties are available in large number both absolutely and relatively. Unless obstructions are purposely introduced, such properties are capable of considerable multiplication at the expense of arable land. To what extent an artificial monopoly may be created, possibly by the agency of speculators buying up building lots, must be decided by an investigation of individual cases. The great increase of prices to which such lots have been subject in every rapidly growing city, offers welcome opportunity to speculation; but enormous capital would be required to gather in under the monopolistic control of an individual or pool the total plottage in the circumference of any large city. Even this would not cope with the situation, for to be fully effective, the monopoly would also have to control all older buildings permitting of reconstruction. Wherever speculators step in without reaching some agreement, such as is the case with pools or trusts, they invariably create competition among themselves.

To explain the quick increase of urban rents in rapidly growing cities, an increase which is extremely burdensome to the population, it is not at all necessary to assume a monopoly. The determining factors are found in the inrush of tenants who outbid each other in their desire to live in close proximity to each other because they wish to trade together, make gains together and enjoy city comforts. The supply of the building entrepreneur responds to the demand. It carries out the exactions of these tenants or would-be tenants in furnishing available space. According to these dictates, it builds more luxuriously, more compactly and higher. The tenement house need not, as has often been contended, represent the result of a "prohibition of building," a rule imposed by those with a monopolistic power over free building lands. It may also be explained as the structural form of the intensity rent towards which the demand moves in densely populated areas in the premiums which it offers for the privilege of living close together. Just so the sky-scraper is the structural form of intensity rents in the business world.

In a similar manner, one may explain the surprising phenomenon of the tenement house in the outskirts of the rapidly growing city without jumping to violent conclusions like those of a capitalistic injunction against building. In a city of slow growth, the intensive structure of a tenement house in the outskirts would not be remunerative. Builders have to be satisfied to utilize the land by erecting scattered and low buildings. It is otherwise in a quickly growing city. There, men will reason, extensive construction in the outskirts of densely populated sections will not be profitable, because in a short time the smaller buildings erected at so late a day, will have to be torn down. These will go to make room for tenement houses as soon as the demand of the largely increased population makes the latter profitable. The anticipated urgent demand of the future exerts its influence in advance, making it appear profitable, notwithstanding the immediate loss of interest, to reserve building lots for the huge tenement house that is coming. A broadly conceived urban housing policy might possibly discover different means of satisfying the requirements of the population. But for private enterprise, where freedom of movement is not lacking, the method here indicated may be the shortest and easiest way that could be suggested by business calculations.

To explain this matter fully, a further short remark might be of service. We have spoken of urban rent as a differential rent. We have explained it by the excess payments or premiums which are paid for the better locations. Consistently with this explanation, the poorest location would be rent-free. Truly enough, the rentals would cover its agricultural rent, but they would leave no surplus for urban rent. In the face of this statement it is no contradiction if we find in the outskirts the tenement house, the structural embodiment of intensity rent. These outskirts are the extreme border of the compact nucleus of the city, but before we reach them we must traverse a fairly wide zone of urban settlement in the "ultra-periphery." If the tenement house on the rim of the city yields to its owner an intensity rent, this is altogether in keeping with its location. It already possesses the one great advantage of location, direct connection with the heart of the city.

The influence of speculation would never have been so greatly over-rated as it is, had the nature of the outlay incurred by the speculator in purchasing plottage been fully understood. This expenditure is not one of the initial costs of acquisition which determine ultimate prices. It can figure only in the entrepreneur's own costs which, as we know, cannot settle the final price. Merely because the speculator has paid a relatively high price for his land, he is not enabled to force higher bids from the demand. It is precisely the reverse that is true: the ultimate offer by the demand is the standard for the price which the speculator would have been justified in paying for the lots. The land is the specific factor in the building enterprise. The share of the yield attributable to it and its capital value are ascertained by specific attribution. This yield is the balance remaining after the costs, properly speaking, have been deducted. On the books of the speculator, where the enterprise results unfavorably, the loss must first be charged against the acquisition-value of the lots.

The assault on urban rent as the creature of monopoly and speculation is for the purpose of making it appear as a gain not earned by labor. No such exaggerated assumptions are necessary to reach this conclusion. Our premises are far more convincing if we start with the recognition of the fact that urban rent is the result of progressive outbidding on the side of the demand. The share of labor, especially that of the entrepreneur, in bringing about urban rent is indeed slight. Only once during the life of a building is the labor of an entrepreneur required. That is during its erection, which term includes any major reconstruction or alteration. The task of the entrepreneur in building operations, however, is very important. It is above all especially important to decide correctly upon the degree of intensity to be observed in construction. For the many decades which follow, a simple routine of administration is all that is required. This a paid official can attend to as well as, perhaps better than the owner himself. For this additional span of the life of the buildings, urban rent is gained without labor. All increments which accrue during this period are unexpected and unearned. This is the significant difference between urban and agricultural rent. The latter in the majority of cases is a rent earned by the owner's personal labor. There can be no objection from the point of view of the economic theory of urban rent to those proposals of taxation which purpose to appropriate the increments of urban rent for public use. No more can objection be raised to the seizure of the land itself by the cities. However, methods must be formed of protecting the architectural development of cities against bureaucratic regimentation.

The many and serious evils of urban housing: extortion in building operations and for dwellings, the wretchedness of housing facilities in proletarian sections, cannot be entered into in this theoretical inquiry.

§ 67. Productive Interest

Natural productive interest—Productive loan interest—Loan interest and money capital—The "abstinence" of the capitalist.

In the money economy productive interest may be drawn as natural or as contractual interest. As in the case of agricultural rent, so here the natural form is the original one. From it the contractual one is derived. This natural interest is that share of the yield which the producer attributes to the capital employed. We have explained the law of its formation in detail in the theory of the simple economy. It is unnecessary to add to our earlier remarks. Unless additions to the productive capital are accompanied by advances in the technical arts, they reduce the productive interest since they decrease the marginal contribution of capital. Improvements in technique at first increase this interest; but at the same time they foreshadow its reduction at a later day since, by increasing the yield, they enlarge the fund from which capital savings can be made.

Contractual productive interest, productive loan-interest, is drawn from money capital lent out for productive use. In deriving the law of its formation, we shall assume that no loans for other than productive purposes are made: i. e., that this is the only form of loan-interest. For brevity's sake we shall call it simply loan-interest while we adhere to this assumption. As a further simplification we shall disregard the mediation of banks which bring together the supply of and demand for capital and whose compensation is stipulated to be a share of the interest. We shall assume that the entire supply and demand are able to meet directly and that the interest agreed to by the demand reaches the supply without deductions. We shall also assume the participation of all three groups whom we distinguished in our exposition of the formation of capital in the money economy: the moneyed capitalists, entrepreneurs producing capital goods and those using them. Finally, we shall assume an undisturbed course of events.

Under these conditions the supply of loan capital comes from the moneyed capitalists. For every sum of money which they advance, the natural guarantee is deposited with the entrepreneurs who are forming capital goods and who have produced more than they themselves can use. They must therefore sell this surplus product. The demand comes from entrepreneurs using capital goods in their operations in larger quantities than are met by their own capital reserves. The basis of the interest which these men offer to pay is the marginal contribution of the capital or the productive interest which they anticipate. In an orderly market competition will bring about a rate of interest which reaches, but does not exceed, this marginal contribution. Moreover, the entrepreneurs always enjoy the advantage from the use of the capital of extending their operations and of increasing their entrepreneur-incomes from other sources. When because of improvements the marginal yield of capital rises, the loan-interest rate will also rise. Those entrepreneurs, who under these conditions cannot obtain a correspondingly higher yield from their capital, will not be successful in their applications to the loan market. They will be outbid and excluded by others. To make possible the provision of loan capital for uses with smaller marginal yields, new savings must first be made from the increased yields.

In the business world these relations frequently are subject to a different interpretation. Men claim that the quantity of money available in the national economy is of itself the determining factor. Surely, they say, the "price of money" depends on the "abundance" or "scarcity" of money. Moreover they contend that every financial stringency arises from the fact that they "are short of money" and they can think of no better relief than that more money should circulate in the country. This line of reasoning arises from a misconception that is current in speech, the interpretation of the money form of capital baldly as capital. In truth, like any other partial capital, money capital is only capital when functioning as part of the total capital of the country. In order thus to function, it must be backed by the natural form, its constant concomitant. The mere increase of the physical supply of money carries advantage only to the individual entrepreneur by adding to his share of the natural wealth of the country. For the national economy as a whole, it is of no advantage; the increase of the volume of money is off-set by the decrease of its value when the national wealth of the country remains the same.

The business-man's point of view has a certain justification only in times of crisis in the money market. During financial crises, the supply of money capital is suddenly and sharply reduced while the demand increases. Liquid capital is held back as much as possible by its owners; many payments which would have been made in the market cannot be effected because sales cease. On the other hand, the demand is extensive, as many obligations fall due from the period of intense business activity which preceded the crisis. This demand is most urgent; capital is needed in order that obligations may be promptly met and solvency maintained. Under such difficulties a much higher value is placed on the right to dispose of capital than at other times when it is demanded for investment in new enterprises. In such a period money capital is looked upon as a prerequisite to the preservation of business standing and even to the existence of the business itself; there is a willingness to pay a rate of interest that exceeds the contribution of the capital and to curtail entrepreneur-incomes or the substance of the capital itself. It will, indeed, scarcely be possible to relieve the tension except by multiplying the media of payment. Those entrepreneurs whose accounts show them to be solvent but who lack the means of immediate payment, must have credits extended to them. The credits must continue until the condition of the market has become sufficiently stabilized to allow the values prepared by these men to be disposed of, or until their debtors, from whom collections are expected, have themselves succeeded in making sales and effecting a collection. During periods of extreme tension, the substitutional service of the means of credit payment may be somewhat extended. Ordinarily, they are only issued after natural values, which are to provide the customary security, have been sold to solvent buyers. Now they may be issued against values not yet sold, although naturally there may be some risk of default in the security if the market should not be receptive for the values actually prepared.

So far we have assumed a capital market which is an ideal unit. The assumption, however, is never realized. The market is split up into a number of separate markets between which an equalizing process operates through more or less obstructed channels. We shall have to keep in touch with actual conditions, at least so far as to distinguish with decreasing abstraction, the two partial markets for commercial loans and investment. In the commercial section of the money market, short term transactions involving liquid working capital are considered by both the supply and the demand. In the investment market, longer periods, even permanent investments, are expected. In the money market a period of intense business activity and correspondingly active demand alternates in the course of a year with a period of quiescent business and less active demand. Allied to this, there is a corresponding movement on the part of the supply. During the first period, the business community holds back its own means; during the second, unemployed capital is held in readiness for short loans. Thus within the year the commercial rate of interest is subject to relatively wide fluctuations. These variations would be even broader if it were not possible to resort to the elasticity of payment by means of credit.

During the entire course of economic development the trend of the rate of productive interest is downward. Despite all technical progress, the increase of capital reduces its marginal yield.

Just as agricultural rent is gained by laboring and is therefore earned, so natural productive interest is earned by active effort. It is a problem apart from our present study whether an economic order apart from the existing one would or would not make possible an increase of the earned yield of capital and its more appropriate distribution. This question arises especially in the case of the socialistic economy.

Precisely as urban rent accrues to the lessor, so loan-interest does to the moneyed capitalist irrespective of any exertion on his part. Is loan-interest for this reason unmerited? The question leads us to the doctrine of the "abstinence" of the capitalist. This theory attempts to prove that although the capitalist does not earn the interest by his labor, he obtains it for sound economic reasons.

When he collects funds it is always altogether within his choice to consume these in the satisfaction of his personal needs. When he does not do so, he receives in the interest on his money a fit reward for his abstinence from personal consumption.

The name of this doctrine must in the first place be regarded with disfavor. The term "abstinence" applies properly only to the saving of capital by those persons of small and moderate incomes. These individuals actually do have to curtail their enjoyments in order to save. When applied to the conditions of the upper and highest strata, abstinence is a misnomer. These classes of society are abundantly provided with means to meet all current expenses. In their circumstances saving is facilitated and assures an increased income for the future as well, but it may hardly be regarded as a sacrifice. We much prefer to have recourse to a different name and to speak of a willingness to dedicate capital which the capitalist is bound to practice. He must maintain this willingness not only for his own desires but equally because of a wish to cater to the immediate needs of other persons. This willingness must extend not only over the period of the actual formation of the capital but must continue throughout the entire period during which the existing capital is to be preserved.

Furthermore it should be clearly understood that "abstinence" alone is insufficient to explain productive interest. The "abstinence" of the moneyed capitalist would be wholly unproductive, were not the natural capital, which is the source of loan-interest, created by the effective activity of the producer. "Abstinence" or, to use the term we prefer, the willingness to dedicate capital which the moneyed capitalist must exhibit has a more restricted effect. It aids in forming and preserving the money form which supplements the natural form in a monetary economic order.

Against the doctrine of abstinence, Lasalle has directed the entire acumen of his criticism. However, his sarcasm is justified only in so far as the theory is applied to the wealthy classes who make no sacrifice of personal consumption, and to the natural form of capital goods which cannot be personally consumed. While the willingness to dedicate capital cannot be ascribed to the great moneyed capitalists as their especial merit, it cannot be dispensed with in the given economic order. It is true that should they all by common assent at the same time proceed to call in their outstanding loans in order to squander their wealth in lavish and increased outlay, they would be unable to carry out their intentions to the letter. Their holdings could not be turned into cash on short notice nor could the demanded consumption goods be made ready at once. But such action would precipitate an economic crisis that would shake the whole productive edifice of the country. In the long run it would also endanger the existence of more durable natural investment-goods for whose care the indispensable working capital could no longer be secured. Productive loan-interest and the yield of productive capital are so intimately connected in our economic organization that the one can never be obtained without the other.

The willingness to set aside capital arises from a desire to equalize as far as possible the means which provide for the present and the future, or else to better the future provisioning as circumstances allow. Even in the case of persons of small incomes this tendency is emphatically induced in order to protect oneself and family from hazards of unusual needs or of disturbances in the conditions of acquisition. It may be observed that the inclination to save is stronger among that part of the working population that is above the subsistence level than it is in the lower reaches and even the higher strata of the middle classes, whose income is exhausted by the expenses that are indispensable to their manner of living and who may also be protected to a greater extent against fortuitous events by the institutions of their social station. The readiness to dedicate capital is especially marked when the current income is increased but the external conditions of life are not raised to higher standards and subjected to the demands of a more exalted social position. Individuals, raised to frugal habits and with little imagination to kindle their desires, are more favorably inclined to saving than others. But the one most predisposed is the miser, inured to the lure of extravagance and inclined to gloat over the charms of swelling revenues.

As needs increase or the accustomed incomes dwindle the willingness to capital dedication is impaired. Under the worst conditions the withdrawal of savings effected in more prosperous times has to be determined upon. In the case of individuals who plan to invest capital savings in their own enterprises the resolve to save is reinforced by the prospect of entrepreneur's profits and wages in addition to interest.

When the rate of interest is lowered owing to the continuous increase of capital, the willingness to practice savings is weakened. Some of the intensity of the desire, which a higher rate could have aroused, is lost. This is true, however, only in the case of individuals whose income has been increased and who are participating in the increase of capital. Those for whom the lower rate has brought about a loss are more inclined to save to make up the shortage in their revenues.

§ 68. Consumptive Interest

Interest on urban mortgage loans.

Consumptive interest is only drawn as a result of contract. The use of the credited sum of money does not enable the debtor to obtain a yield from which to pay interest, much less to repay the principal. Both of these must be met from other income of the debtor. The principal itself is consumed in the current expenses of the household.

When an economy is properly managed, the motive to incur consumptive indebtedness is found in a desire to equalize present and future satisfactions. When increased receipts may be expected in the future, when immediately larger expenses must be met or when both contingencies occur simultaneously, consumptive indebtedness is permitted, nay, even called for. It would be uneconomic to disallow important satisfactions which might be enjoyed by anticipating receipts through a recourse to credit. This statement assumes that the receipts would otherwise be later dedicated to less important satisfactions. Thus consumptive indebtedness may be justifiable for personal education or training, the raising of children and similar expenditures of providing in advance for the future, none of which properly fall within the province of the acquisitive economy.

But in numerous economies consumptive indebtedness proceeds from that undervaluation of future desires which is characteristic of weak management. Here we should explain that by weak economies we mean generally those of small incomes. However, the term also includes those that are not managed with strong forethought and are slavishly subject to the passion of the moment. Such consumptive indebtedness adds to the gratifications of the present at the expense of those of the future. In the case of distress loans such a course of action on the part of the debtor is excusable, possibly justifiable and unavoidable. He may have no other choice than to provide momentarily for the preservation of his existence and the immediate pressing need, leaving all else to the future. On the other hand the debtor who owes his position to recklessness or lack of thrift acts uneconomically; most uneconomically, of course, if he drifts thus to complete economic ruin. He places the desire of the moment above the needs of the future for no better reason than its present appeal. He atones for thoughtless gratifications and passing allurements by enduring privations and social ostracism.

The debts of the state and the debts of other public bodies are, for the greater part, incurred for consumptive purposes or, to speak more accurately, for purposes of public administration. They are incurred to cover current expenses which the public bodies have to defray for purposes of the protection or education of the people: for carrying on wars, for preparing and maintaining military outfits, for maintaining schools and the like. As in the private economy, so in that of the community, consumptive indebtedness may be justified by the circumstances, nay, even demanded; but it must be burdensome and perilous, whére it is decided upon as a result of short-sighted undervaluation of the demands of the future, as the outgrowth of an insatiate desire for power, of unbounded ambition or party passion.

In all cases of consumptive indebtedness, justified or unjustified, the debtor finds in his divergent appraisal of the present and future effects of commodities, the inducement for the payment of an interest which he agrees to discharge over and above the principal sum of money borrowed. As regards the private as well as the public emergency-loan, the disposal of an immediate pressing need is justly more highly estimated than the care for a less urgent need to be experienced later. From expenditures devoted to the advancement of personal or social position, increased future effects are expected, which induce parties to look upon the payment of a premium as justified. The reckless or unthrifty debtor places present desires, considered less important by the dispassionate observer, above future ones, which should be more highly appraised. Passion clouds the understanding; but in so far as men yield, it is an impelling motive for the payment of a penalty in the way of interest.

In all these cases, the difference of present and future appraisals offers an exact standard for the amount of the premium, or excess payment, which the debtor is willing to offer when the need is greatest. In the market, where supply and demand come together, the offer of the marginal debtor determines the rate, i. e., the lowest bid of those applicants for credit who must still be admitted in order that the entire capital in the market may be absorbed.

The coincidence of productive and consumptive demand offers no difficulty to the theoretical solution of the problem. If we regard the market as a closed unit, the marginal offer at the time is always decisive. As far as the moneyed capitalist is concerned, it is a matter of indifference to him what use is made of the sum lent, provided only that the payment of interest and principal are assured. It may often be that he knows absolutely nothing of the use to which the money is to be put. Private capital forms a unit; its unity binds together the supply and creates a tendency to a single rate of interest.

This fact does not do away with the contrast in the natural forms of guarantee for the two types of loan. The social effects of purely private capital that is consumptively lent and is secured exclusively by natural consumption goods, are radically different from those of productively loaned money-capital, whose increase is accompanied by a growth of the possessions of natural productive goods in the national economy. Loans for consumption must always unduly hamper the formation of national capital when they extend present consumption beyond the margin that an equalizing foresight would allow. As regards the debtors there arises the added burden of an increase in the rate of interest.

It is not our purpose to inquire in this connection whether a homogeneous capital market actually forms or whether in its place separate markets arise between which the rate of interest is not wholly equalized. We have already explained in its proper place the fact that the cases of the weakest debtors, exposed to usurious exploitation, detach themselves from the well regulated capital market and give rise to the prices of usury.

The interest on capital to be obtained by renting or leasing urban dwellings is a natural interest to be explained from the cost-law. As for any other use, private capital can be obtained for building purposes only when the customary interest on the principal is added to the costs and is repaid from the yield. If it were not paid, the demand for dwellings would be met by an insufficient supply. Presently the tenants would be forced to pay permanently higher rentals that would yield the appropriate interest to the entrepreneur or the owner of the house. In the long run the extent to which capital is set aside for urban building tends to balance with the dedications of productive capital and consumptive loans.

The loan-interest on urban mortgages rests on the basis of this natural interest.

Our discussion of the "abstinence" of the capitalist in connection with productive interest applies also to consumptive interest and to the interest which is drawn from urban building capital and mortgages.

§ 69. Entrepreneur Income and Profits

The specific form of entrepreneur income—The specific nature of entrepreneur profits—Capitalistic entrepreneur profits.

Entrepreneur income is that part of the yield of an enterprise that falls to the share of the entrepreneur. In order to determine its amount, there must be deducted from the gross yield of the enterprise all costs of materials for production, all shares that are paid out in any form to other parties to the operation including wages of employees and the costs of their insurance, rentals and the expenses of hiring the use of outsiders' material values, and interest on borrowed capital. The entrepreneur frequently keeps his account of net yield so as to allow by previous deduction for all these shares. In this event, if we disregard taxes and other public dues, we may say that entrepreneur income and net yield are coincident.

The entrepreneur's income is composed of a series of items of varying origin: entrepreneur's wages, interest and profits. The wages of management are that part of the net yield against which is charged his labor performed as entrepreneur. If in addition he performs other executive work, such as an employee might at times discharge, the amount that is due for such service should be deducted before determining the net yield. Entrepreneur's interest is the interest on that part of the entire invested plant capital of which the entrepreneur is the owner, or more briefly on the entrepreneur capital. Customarily the rent on personally owned land is included in this interest. Entrepreneur's profits is the balance of the entrepreneur income after deducting the first two items.

The theoretical problem on which our attention is centered is the entrepreneur's profit. This is the particular part of the entrepreneur's income against which the objections are most forcible. It is the part which he claims as entrepreneur even when wage, interest and rent are drawn by other parties. Even a socialist would hardly object to wages of management, though he might depart from current views by drawing the lines more narrowly as to the work of conducting operations and appraising its value at a lower figure. For accurate calculation entrepreneur's wage and interest are part of his operating costs. He should constantly see to it that his own labors are as remuneratively employed in the enterprise as though employed in the service of another for the same purpose, or, in the case of his capital, as though it were lent to others in consideration of the payment of interest.

There is little in substance that must be added to these remarks on wages of management and entrepreneur's interest. However, we still must give attention to the form in which they are drawn. In all other cases wages and interest are a matter of agreement in exchange. Only the entrepreneur draws these not by way of exchange but in their "natural" form. Hence through this form the entrepreneur's wage and interest are combined with profits to constitute the whole of the entrepreneur's income, which is the only income drawn in the money economy without exchange.

This does not mean that his income is cut loose from the market and its laws. Quite the reverse is true, for it is set in the midst of the net-work of economic relationships. While it is never directly agreed upon as a price to be paid, it is the final result of the entire computation of price in these transactions. It is from the entrepreneurs that the entire supply of products and other prepared natural values arises. They also constitute the entire demand for means of acquisition. Their income is the excess that remains when the total proceeds realized by the supply are determined and the gross costs to which this acquisitive demand has agreed are deducted. In the final analysis the formation of the entrepreneur income is dependent on the relationship between this total supply and acquisitive demand. The more persons who seize the opportunities for enterprise at any one time, the more meager will be the entrepreneur's income. The fewer their number, the more advantageous will be the position of the entrepreneur, for there will be a better selection of the more favorable openings promising the largest profits with the lowest costs of acquisition.

Entrepreneur income is drawn in the form of a specific attribution. It is the amount left over after deducting the shares of the yield attributable to other participating factors. But in this respect also our conclusions must not be too far-reaching. This specific attribution follows in the first place from the legal position of the entrepreneur; it is an expression of the fact that every enterprise is undertaken for the account of its legal owner. From an economic point of view by no means the entire entrepreneur income, that is computed as a remainder, is of a strictly specific nature. Entrepreneur interest like any other has a cost character. So in the majority of cases have wages of management. In principle, only entrepreneur profits have a specific character. We may thus call these profits the specific yield of the position of entrepreneur. All too often, however, this is no such profit.

The attempt has been made to base the entrepreneur's profit on the particular risk to which he is exposed by virtue of the fact that the enterprise is carried on for his account. It is claimed that he would never expose himself to the possibility of loss had he not reason to expect profits from the venture. If this is true, should not enterprises involving the greatest risks entitle the men who pursue them to the largest profits? Would we not have to expect that in the sum of all cases, profits and losses would balance?

The position of the entrepreneur derives its specific character from the fact that it demands the combination of a service of management in the nature of labor with the possession of a certain amount of capital. The latter may be either property, or, owing to the ability to obtain credit, a power over the disposition of capital. Selection is considerably restricted; many individuals who may be qualified to direct work, refrain from seeking entrepreneur employment because they lack capital; many who have capital refrain because they lack personal qualifications. Nevertheless, there remains an abundant number of candidates for the enterprises to be undertaken, persons able to comply with both conditions, except in a comparatively limited number of cases. For these the selection is still further narrowed either because especially rare services are imperative or a specific command of capital is needed, specific in its unique character or else in its magnitude. Only in these cases does an enterprise acquire a specific nature that establishes the basis for the entrepreneur's profit.

For the larger number of small and medium-sized trades, the favorable market position which they formerly enjoyed has long since passed away. They are today, with scarcely an exception, all in a sorry plight. They yield not only no profit, but often no more than a scanty wage. The skill which they require has become the common property of great numbers. They no longer offer a problem of economic leadership. Their relationships have become altogether typical, while essentially new methods of prosecuting them can no longer be introduced. Agricultural pursuits in the majority of cases have never, either under peasant management or on the large scale of modern methods, offered prospects of entrepreneur's profits. The large scale industrial enterprise has always been the source of enormous entrepreneur's profits. During our capitalistic period it has become so to an even greater extent.

When we look back upon the road which industrial development has travelled from its beginnings down to the present powerful forms, we can well understand why what we have witnessed has happened. In its journey hitherto, the extraordinary advances in the technical arts and in methods of organization have opened to modern industry wider and wider fields of production and trade and have unlocked the gateways of constantly expanding markets. Thus there have been created numerous new opportunities for labor. These have imparted an impetus to the increase of population and thus have contributed not a little to the enlargement of the markets. Despite the reverses which, here as elsewhere, were bound to occur, increasing opportunity was assured through the broadening markets. Larger quantities of commodities could be disposed of at prices which had originally been computed in anticipation of much smaller sales. The advances in technique and organization at the same time secured diminishing costs over a long period of years, even though in the end the larger demand for materials necessarily resulted in a rise of cost prices. The condition of the labor market was especially favorable to these industries for a long time. To this market they attracted the new and at first seemingly inexhaustible supply of untrained men, women and children. These people who hitherto had not been industrially employed could be secured for very low pay. At the same time extensive discharges of old trained workers assisted in depressing wages.

The striking successes achieved by large-scale capitalistic enterprise in its rise have not been due to its large capital alone. Indeed the capital was not primarily responsible for the development; rather the capital was built up from profits. Originally the main force, which secured a preferred market position of specific character for capitalistic enterprise, was the impulse of its superior leadership. The pioneers who opened the new paths had to be men of unusual ability and training, combining technical knowledge and capacity with market experience and organizing power. In addition they required the audacity of the innovator, a quality that often coarsened in the severity of the fight. In all industrial countries many of the great industrial magnates rose from small beginnings, a fact which demonstrates above all else the importance of personality in the position of the capitalistic entrepreneur.

This statement holds good only for the initial rise. In later periods when the opportunities for capitalistic enterprise have been discovered and seized upon to a great extent, the established enterprise provided with a large capital obtains a supremacy against which the gifts of the new-comer cannot easily prevail. Then too the problems of leadership are simpler. Actions are taken according to rules which experience has already established with tolerable definiteness. There has also arisen a new class, a well-trained personnel; schooled in the new methods, they are ready to aid the entrepreneur in his problems of leadership at a wage-rate by no means exorbitant. In the end the prospects of profit for even the older established enterprises will become less favorable. The organization of the workers and their compulsory insurance has even now increased the costs of operation in many localities. The abundance of accumulated capital will ultimately assert itself by crowding all opportunities for business enterprise; the increased competition will force upward the prices of cost-goods.

For the present at any rate this has not yet become the general condition of large-scale capitalistic enterprise. The giant enterprise and the great combines of businesses have introduced a new type which is only now developing. In its turn it lends new significance to the genius of leadership. In the present generation also there are industrialists whose names are known the world over and who started as workingmen to end as multimillionaires. The enormous capital invested in the American trusts and the property of large numbers of individual owners, is confided to the superior management of a small group. The talent of economic leadership has never before had the opportunity of displaying itself on so broad a base of capital. Never before has the general yield been so great on which to reckon the share attributable to leadership. As these leaders are also in a position to draw revenues as promoters, their profits are realized not only in the yields but in the capital itself. Only for the coming generations of trust leaders will the chances of profit be less favorable, owing to the vast wealth now accumulating.

Enterprises, operating under particularly favorable conditions, add to the entrepreneur's profit an industrial rent that follows the same law as the agricultural rent of better grades of land.

With the exception of the remarks in the last paragraphs regarding combines of enterprises, this exposition has presupposed the owner's enterprise. When it comes to the collective enterprise, conditions are in many respects different. The wages of management are apportioned among officials; in the case of the mixed forms of the stock-company and combine these wages are very large for the highest managers. They are lower in the pure form of officials' enterprise, because the most forceful leaders naturally prefer to connect themselves with the former class. Nothing inures to the legal owners in these cases except entrepreneur's interest and profit. The prospects of profit are, however, materially diminished. In the case of stock-companies and combines this is because of the intervention of the promoters which we shall presently discuss in more detail. In the case of the officials' enterprise the main factor is that, as the most recent form of enterprise, it made its appearance only in a period of waning entrepreneur's profits and must cling to the narrower and safer ground of approved technical and commercial experience, which is taken for granted under the management of officials. When such concerns take over existing owner's enterprises or stock-companies, they are charged from the start with interest on the purchase price, in which the full specific entrepreneur's profit of the preceding owner has been capitalized. Especially the state and city, because of their governmental trusteeship, are bound to exercise greater leniency as employers; they are also more inclined to yield to expressions of public opinion. In general they are likely to be less vigorous in defending the interests of the entrepreneur.

§ 70. Promoter's Enterprise and Profits

Management and the masses in the stock-company and in the officials' enterprise.

A partnership is formed by the same individuals who will carry on the business. In the case of the stock-company, as a general rule, the promoters promptly retire from the enterprise and make room for the stockholders who come in subsequently. For this very reason they are called promoters, their participation being confined to the act of promoting the business. Only in the case of smaller, local stock-companies is a form of organization adhered to, the so-called successive founding, in which promoters do not take any active part. In these cases conferences and action leading to incorporation are taken by the individuals who are themselves to be permanently connected with the company. Of course among these men there will be some who are prominent as leaders, who make the first proposal and who lead the discussion in conferences. But these "leaders," proponents as they are called, differ from promoters, properly speaking, in that they wish to remain active members of the companies they form. In the case of all large stock-companies the so-called "simultaneous promotion" has become customary which takes its name from the fact that the founders come before the public with the enterprise completely constituted in one act by the publication of the charter [1] to give it its legal basis and by paying the capital into the treasury [2] to establish it economically. The term, "simultaneous promotion," does not accurately portray the nature of the formalities observed. Under this procedure, as is also the case in successive foundation, lengthy conferences and consultations between promoters have occurred. Moreover, although the association is truly formed when announced, the business of promotion is not yet completed. The first act, the foundation, has to be followed in due course by a second, the sale of securities. The stock is placed on the market in order for the promoters to realize their profits. Even on this flotation the stock does not always reach its ultimate destination, the investing public. It is frequently first taken up by speculators on the Exchange who hope at an opportune moment to turn it over to the ultimate purchasers at a profit. But with the emission of securities the promoters have completed their work; the profits which may later be realized by speculators are speculative profits which, though akin to the promoters' profit, are to be distinguished from the latter in kind.

The promoters' profit is computed as the remainder after all costs

[1] Veröffentlichung des Statuts.

[2] Trans. note: It must be borne in mind that the corporation is a legal as well as an economic creature. Under the more advanced European laws the process of formation differs from American practice. The *Grunder*, founder, is not identical with the American promoter although the more familiar term is generally used in the translation. One of the striking differences is in the clause noted.

of promotion are deducted from the proceeds of the sale. In the many instances where the founders have created an enterprise whose net yield exceeded the return which the public expected for its capital subscription, this promoters' profit has been realized without injury to the public. As a rule the return will exceed somewhat that of good securities paying at a fixed rate of interest; since the number of individuals who invest in industrial stocks is somewhat smaller than that of those seeking fixed investments, a special inducement is required to secure the necessary number of subscriptions. It is difficult to understand why the promoters, if indeed they have succeeded in obtaining a still higher rate of return, should not retain for themselves the added value thus created. They fulfill the justifiable expectations of the subscribers if they quote a rate of emission that is based on a capital value derived from the rate of interest at which the subscribers perform their calculations. Whenever this capital value leaves a surplus over and above the costs of promotion, this surplus is due to the promoters according to the rules of specific attribution of yield.

Promoter's profits are a particular kind of entrepreneur's profit. They are the reward for "undertaking the enterprise."[1] These profits collect in advance on a capitalization of the profits of the enterprise.

The rare opportunity that inheres in the promoter's position to realize entrepreneur's profits from increases of property value is sedulously sought. It is easy to understand how at times it is shamelessly abused, calculated as it is to give to those who would employ their economic superiority unfairly a ready means of robbing others on a large scale and, as one might say, at a single stroke. The malfeasance of exploiting promoters deserves the most severe criticism because of the pernicious effects which accompany it.

So long as there are stock-companies the system, as such, of founding industrial enterprises is scarcely to be dispensed with. While the form of association with which it deals cannot be spared, it must be tolerated. The widely scattered multitude of those who wish to subscribe at the time of emission are individuals of the most diverse callings and stations in life. Not infrequently they live in countries thousands of miles apart. Many of them are wholly unqualified for the conduct of acquisitive enterprise generally and the majority have no call whatever for the management of the particular enterprise involved. Counsel and resolution among them cannot be thought of.

[1] Für die "Unternehmung der Unternehmungen."

In order to make their decisions they must be faced with an enterprise which is ready for action. Yet the enormous sums of capital absorbed by stock-companies cannot be raised except by the coöperation of the public at large. The process of promotion systematizes the act of foundation by the best informed experts of the market. At this time it appears to be indispensable to the enlistment of public subscription for any definite enterprise.

The social theorist sees in the process of founding stock-companies a special case of that leadership in general which is a prerequisite whenever large masses of human beings are to be enabled to act. The initiative of the promoter and the subsequent subscription of the stockholders are a typical example of the relations of the leader and multitude. The success that is achieved in bringing about an acquisitive increase of invested capital is attributed to the promoters. Malignant, unearned promoter's profits are evidence of the power of leadership pitched against the weakness of a public, devoid of judgment, that blindly allows itself to be led.

In the days of liberalism this relationship had not been understood in the legislation regarding stock companies. Their formation was regarded as little different from the establishment of partnerships. The one like the other is executed as a private contract of association. But the same legal form of contract covers two essentially different phenomena. In a partnership only a few individuals associate themselves. They actually meet as free agents. Each one is brought in for a well known purpose, is perfectly aware of his individual interests and is able to protect these. In a stock-company a large number of persons have to become associated. By virtue of their very number they are unfitted for unrestricted deliberation and the adoption of resolutions. In the same manner they are unqualified to execute of their own initiative the introductory steps in the formation of the association. They are wholly dependent on the enterprise of the promoters and must thus be satisfied if the latter convert to their own use the increment of the entrepreneur's profits that has been created by their initiative. The stockholders, who without the aid of the leaders would never have been stockholders, must content themselves from the beginning with a modest entrepreneur's profit that still gives them somewhat more than the customary rate of interest with which they would otherwise have had to content themselves in another investment. The improvement that modern legislation has worked in stock-companies arises from the recognition of the superior power of the promoter. The contract of association is no longer treated as a mere contract but as a mass phenomenon producing, in the form of a private contract, social powers of leadership and creating opportunities of the gravest abuse. This recognition results in placing this mass phenomenon under legal control.

The business of promotion has passed in the present day mainly into the hands of large banks. These alone have at their disposal the abundance of money capital that is indispensable to form stock-companies on the large scale required at present. The administration of this business by the large banks is an important element of added security. On the other hand it involves a monopolistic or monopoloid relation as soon as the large banks by express or tacit agreement come to an understanding of their market territories. When the opportunities of promotion are so extensive that even the enormous capital of the large banks is fully employed, such an understanding may be easily reached. Carried on with proper caution, the business of promoting enterprises is a source of generous profits to the promoting bank if it is in a position by further promotion to compound the entrepreneur's profit which it realizes from the property-gains in the founded enterprises. Even under such conditions, however, mammoth capital is not the single decisive factor. The genius of the leader will always have its share. The conduct of the business of promotion demands a high degree of intelligence and business ability which are paid for in the exceedingly liberal compensations appropriated by the large banks for the services of their managers. But another fact is still more important. We have already explained that the promotions of stock-companies under present conditions for the most part are not the foundations of new enterprises. They rest upon a substratum of successfully conducted owners' enterprises which the promoting bank acquires and enlarges. The successful entrepreneur-owners who sell their establishments to the promoting bank are fundamentally the founders of the stock company. To the business ability of these men is due the most important achievement in the whole development and the share of the promoter's profits justly inures to them.

The incongruity that exists from the start between the legal position of the stockholders and their task as entrepreneur makes itself felt throughout the life of the corporation. The mass of the stockholders remains at all times unfitted for the management of the business. It never performs the services of entrepreneur and must perforce, therefore, be content when it is barred from drawing the higher entrepreneur's profits. Even the restricted entrepreneur function delegated by the established corporation law to the general meeting is scarcely exercised by the mass of stockholders. If they are to be induced to assert their rights in opposition to the directors, a special agitation among the stockholders is always required. This in itself must be set on foot by the leaders of the opposition. At the general meeting the large stockholders are in power. Above all else they control the elections and set up the board of directors and other organs of the company. They are the leaders of the corporation and through them the mass of the stockholders becomes capable of action. As a natural consequence their services must be rewarded at a correspondingly high rate. The stock of companies which promise especially large profits are little by little bought up by capitalists qualified to estimate correctly the economic situation. Stocks which are most attractive to speculation are accordingly eagerly purchased. They may at times become the objects of fierce struggles between the great market controlling capital powers who acquire them in the pursuit of far-reaching schemes, possibly for purposes of reorganization. Stocks which offer possibilities of rising quotations rarely remain in the hands of small capitalists. Men must become entrepreneurs either in a good sense or a bad one if they would draw the higher entrepreneur profits.

In the case of purely collective enterprises, the great undertakings backed by the capital of cities, states and nations, legal status and economic position are more nearly in harmony. The capitalists from whose wealth the funds are derived lend their capital as creditors in consideration of the payment of a fixed rate of interest and without assuming any of the duties of the entrepreneur. The economic management of the enterprise as well as its establishment is entrusted to trained officials held to strict performance of their duties and receiving a fixed though not an excessive compensation. The entrepreneur's profits become a public revenue. Nevertheless it remains true, as has previously been explained, that the purely officials' enterprise loses much of the freedom of action found in the stock-company and is thus confined to a narrower field of usefulness and smaller prospects of profit.

§ 71. Speculation on the Exchange and the Profits of Speculation

Creative speculation and price-speculation—Pools.

Speculation in the narrower sense, on the exchanges or in prices, takes advantage of the constant fluctuations of the price of commodities dealt in on the exchanges or in the great real-estate markets. The speculator endeavors to foresee the future price. He buys whenever he anticipates a rise in order later to sell at a profit. He sells whenever he expects a decline in order to buy later and thus realize a gain. For his operations he selects large markets because in those he is confident of always being able to effect his purchases and sales. On the stock- and produce-exchanges he finds the conditions that make possible his operations. Also the real-estate markets of a large city offer opportunities of price-speculation.

The productive trades are enemies of the speculator. They accuse him of seeking to enrich himself without labor from the values which they have created by hard work. By them his occupation is regarded as that of a man playing a game or laying a wager and as unproductive as either. They mean by this that the gains of a speculator can never be effected except at the expense of someone else who is bound to lose whatever the speculator gains, and who, but for the intervention of the speculator, would have lost nothing. They are opposed to those features of the exchanges which facilitate speculation by the settlement of operations in the most convenient manner, i. e., by doing away with the actual transfer of goods or stocks and substituting a balancing of demands and counter-demands which requires actual payments only for the differences in the account. These charges are by no means invalidated when the producers are told that they too are only attracted to their calling by the desire for gain, and that their profits as well are only functions of the differences existing between sales-prices and the prices of acquisition.

In a moral appraisal of the two activities, account must necessarily be taken of the differences which exist. The energies of the speculator are focussed exclusively on the final act of the acquisitive process through which the profit is realized. In his case the passion for profits is continually aroused without being tempered by any reaction. In the case of the producer, the entire prolonged labor of the acquisitive process must first be performed in order to mature the fruits of his efforts. This process calls forth the highest powers of men and strengthens their better natures. Superficially the merchant is approximately in a class with the speculator but he also realizes his gains from purchase and sale only by laborious efforts. He must discover the goods which he presently purchases at the source of production. He must take possession of them, provide for their transportation, their storage and safe-keeping, sort them, find purchasers and deliver the merchandise. All this he must do with the utmost attention to an economical use of capital and labor. In a similar manner, the merchant dealing in securities and capital mediates between the supply and the demand. In contrast to these men, the speculator builds his nest in a completed market. It is never his intention to contribute anything by way of improving relations between the supply and the demand. His highest goal is reached when he can gather in his profit. He triumphs without taking pains to find goods, assume their possession or deliver them to others. His entire effort is directed to the simple goal of the most proximate gain. Although as a matter of legal interpretation, his actions cannot be construed as gambling, none the less the one passion which prompts them is that of the gambler.

The activity of the promoters of industrial enterprises is also frequently spoken of as speculation but it is far more nearly akin to that of the productive trades. His efforts are creative. Indeed he selects as his field of action, precisely that section of the acquisitive process in which creative power is most needed. The interests of the ideal founder turn to new ideas: to the plan, the organization, the first experiments. Once these have been accomplished, the work started upon its course and its progress assured, the attention of the promoter turns to other problems. His speculation is a creative speculation, or as might possibly be said with better propriety, it is speculative creation. It is concerned with those first stages in which creative effort is still shot through with speculation, and is only preparing to enter upon its course of regular execution.

The speculation of promoters and that on the exchanges nevertheless have many features in common. In the first place, there is an external contact. The promoters by virtue of their issuance of securities, turn straightway to the Exchange. Here speculators are frequently the first purchasers of newly emitted papers. More often than not the promoter counts upon their coöperation, through which he gains financial support. But the two types of speculation are intimately connected in the development of their business. It is the peculiar trait of both classes, that they specialize in the smallest possible portion of the entire acquisitive process. The promoter takes for his part the introductory act of the establishment of the enterprise. The speculator on the Exchange selects the final act, the sales which are to be effected. A further characteristic that is peculiar to both is that they pursue their businesses under a constant change of objective. They seek to isolate the precise situation in which the value-forming idea may materialize or where values that have been economically created may be realized. Thus they are not permanently attached to one repetitive process of enterprise but take hold now here, now there, as opportunities offer and promise the largest apparent profit. Both groups of men fully utilize the mobility of money-capital. Their commitments in the form of natural values are for the shortest possible period; from these they return again and again to the liquid monetary form. Speculation on the exchanges makes the more advantageous use of the monetary form. The period of enterprise, during which the transfers yielding value are completed, is shorter. This sort of speculation may pile up its business transactions in more rapid succession. When fortune smiles, its profits may be reaped in a few days. The speculations of the promoter as a rule must be adjusted to a period of years.

Because of the short enterprise-period covered by price-speculation the impression is created that this type of speculation lies wholly outside the acquisitive process. However, this is not the case and therefore the denunciations of the productive trades are not altogether well founded. The defendants of speculation quite correctly insist that by its agency one of the most important services to enterprise is achieved. The speculator devotes his entire acumen and often extraordinary effort to the calculation of the prices of goods sold on the exchanges. In many instances he corrects and refines the calculations of the producer and the merchant. At the same time he aids commerce by his own capital and that which is placed at his disposal by credit transactions. These funds he employs to absorb the values flowing towards the exchanges. The accurate determination of prices is a matter of great economic interest. It cannot be denied, therefore, that the speculator, when he contributes to this accurate determination, renders a distinct economic service. He devotes his talents to a specialized entrepreneur's activity; the gains of legitimate speculation are true entrepreneur's profits.

The opponents of speculation do not admit the truth of the assertion that speculation aids in making the formation of prices more precise. On the contrary they contend that it falsifies prices because in its supply and demand it does not set out from the actual figures of supply and demand but from fictitious quantities. Its protagonists reply that in the long run no speculative position can prevail against the actual condition of the market, that speculation can only be successful when the conditions of the market are precisely foreseen that will obtain under the future supply and demand.

The theorist should persist less in this case than in any other in clinging to idealizing assumptions. These he cannot dispense with in pursuing his initial and most general inquiries, but speculation should be grasped as it truly appears. It should be appraised in accordance with the manifested natures of the persons participating and with the actual distribution of power.

The passionate craving for quick riches lies at the root of speculation. This is dangerous even for the professional speculator who after all succeeds in controlling it more or less by his market experience. It may be ruinous to the many from the general public who follow in the wake of trained speculators, impelled by the irresistible fascination of participation in the tremendous fluctuations of values which do occur in the economies of nations and the world and by which so many large fortunes have been started.

Promotional activity has its origin in the same root. But in so far as it has been passed on to the custody of large banks it has been held to safer limits. Their permanent interests call for guarantees to preserve their business reputation and to retain a favorable attitude of the market towards new foundations of industrial companies.

Price-speculation as such is bound by no such enduring interests. It is true that the professional speculator feels the necessity of maintaining his reputation on the Exchange, but he and the speculating public have no permanent interest in the objects of speculation. His interest is confined to one problem: did he or did he not, for the brief period to which his speculation is adjusted, appraise correctly the condition of prices that was about to prevail according to the circumstances of the individual case and also to the general tenor of the market. From this manner of thought arise during periods of generally increasing business prosperity and persistent increases of values the speculative errors that end in disastrous crises. Prices are forced to higher and higher levels so long as there is the chance of finding further buyers. It makes no difference that experienced speculators themselves realize that the pyramided structure of high prices cannot possibly be much longer maintained. In due time—and in saying this the defenders of speculation are correct—every such artificial structure must collapse. The facts of supply and demand finally assert themselves. But in the meantime the periods of universal frenzy are sufficiently prolonged to inflict enormous damage.

The distribution of power between speculators on the one side and producers and the public proper on the other, is on the whole more favorable to the first group. The professional speculator is superior to the public in his market experience. More frequently than not he has the advantage over the producer in that the weapon which he wields, money-capital, may be made more rapidly to serve his speculative intentions than the fixed, natural capital of the producer. Again it is sufficient if the speculator can make his superiority felt during a brief period that enables him to influence the formation of prices by an adroit use of the speculative forms of business.

When professional speculators of equal power confront each other, speculation will perform its economic service more effectively. But even in these circles the power of large capital makes itself felt. Under certain circumstances an individual speculator or an allied group may subject the market in certain articles and for a definite time to their power. On all the large exchanges from time to time such combinations of speculators, the so-called pools, are formed with the intention of creating such a power over one or other business territory. They are akin to the kartels in that they strive to gain a monopolistic power. They differ from the latter in that they have no other purpose than the control of prices. Pools are especially made use of to control the market when production is too extensive to allow of any but indirect means of influencing the market, as, for example, is the case with agricultural staples. Pools are among the most reprehensible abuses of speculation. Their profits have nothing of the character of entrepreneur's profits. They are unearned, call for no services of leadership and are extorted merely by the application of superior external means of force.

§ 72. The Theory of Wages

The subsistence wage—The productivity wage—Wage-tendency to equilibrium; the isohypses of the labor-market—The wages-fund.

The wage of labor is the price paid for free, independent labor, for the labor of the worker, legally free but employed in the service of another. Entrepreneur's wages are not wages, properly speaking; the term is derived from the fact that the entrepreneur computes the amount due to his own labor by the standard of the wage paid for the similar services of another.

We shall examine the theory of the wages of labor primarily under the assumption of a well-regulated, ideal market, permitting all parties to protect fully their economic advantage, while all disturbing influences are eliminated. The existence of stratification we shall allow to influence our assumption only in so far as it may be the objective basis of the labor relation. We thus assume the existence of a class of society without financial resources, that offers its labor in order to gain an income. We also assume a demand from a class so situated as to employ workers and pay them a wage; but we shall disregard for the present altogether the attendant, subjective influences of power and weakness.

We shall examine the theory of the wages of labor subject to the assumptions of the theory of utility which, as we know, is valid for the developed national economy. By way of introduction we shall only briefly sketch the theory of wages that may be deduced for those primitive conditions, as to which the theory of labor correctly assumes that labor does not yet occupy the quantitative relation. But, even so, labor under primitive conditions is always too imperfectly developed to be pronouncedly stratified; common labor is the whole of labor. We shall disregard the fact that the freedom of the laborer, which we have assumed, is scarcely to be reconciled with the actual conditions of primitive society. The mass of the indigent population, depending solely upon their active forces for subsistence, is likely to be too weak for the safeguarding of their individual freedom; a market of free labor is not likely to exist. Free laborers, wishing to enter the service of others, will be extremely oppressed by the competition of slave-labor—if it may be called competition. But even disregarding this last condition, the fact that labor has not yet entered the economic quantitative relation, that the supply is therefore greater than the demand, will lead to the deplorable consequence that the wage does not find its standard in utility, for, where the assumption applies, the marginal utility is zero. Neither can the supply expect to be rewarded in accordance with the risks and efforts of its performance. This is the standard, as we have seen in the theory of the simple economy, by which the laborer himself appraises his performance, while an abundance of strength remains to him. The employer does not feel called upon to accept the personal appraisal of the worker and to attempt computations based upon such factors as efforts and risks. He is in a position to dictate his terms, and the supply has no choice but to agree with these terms. Competition will compel the workers to accept efforts and risks as they come, merely to gain their subsistence. The wage will be simply preservative. It will amount to the minimum which the employer must allow in order to maintain the laborer in the condition of strength and well-being that is required for his task. Quite often the lowest minimum of existence will not be exceeded. In more highly developed social conditions, the number of domestic servants is reduced. This is a symptom of the increased demand for acquisitive workers. In a similar manner a characteristic of primitive and barbarous times is the great number of subordinate servants who find placement at the courts of the powerful, often for a mere preservative wage. The excess supply of workers has to fall back on the callings of war or make new settlements within the borders of the state or in foreign countries. Where these employments also fail them, there is nothing left but robbery, begging and unparalleled misery.

The theory of wages, applicable to the developed national economy in which all kinds of labor have entered the economic quantitative relation, may be briefly explained on the basis of the general theory of prices.

The relation is plain as regards personal services, beginning with menial domestic services and ascending to the highest services of the liberal professions in the state and society. All these directly serve the needs of the private or public economy just like consumption goods; like these, they are of the first "order." They are economic means of the nearest order, and like consumption-goods are therefore subject to the fundamental law of price-formation. However, services are part of the personal life. As such, they are not subject to the cost-law as are consumption goods. Hence the fundamental law of price-formation applies to them, without being more definitely determined by the cost-law. The offer of the marginal demand, determined by marginal utility and ability to pay, decides the rate of wage. This wage is also subject to the law of stratification.

The general law of price has been sufficiently explained to allow us also to deduce the law of wages for acquisitive labor. Acquisitive labor renders its services in conjunction with material productive means to produce goods that it does not consume directly. The demand for it does not come directly from the consumer but from entrepreneurs who prepare values for consumption. Its wages are based on the productive marginal contribution of labor as measured by the laws of attribution. It is then a yield-wage determined by that share of the yield which is attributed to labor. Inasmuch as the mass of workers, unskilled, skilled and even educated labor, possesses a cost-character, the law of common attribution is applicable to most cases. The advantage of a specific attribution accrues only for a comparatively few services that require the highest qualifications.

The marginal contribution as computed for the lowest strata of workers, even in those national economies that have reached the highest present development, is meagre. It barely covers or only slightly exceeds a minimum of subsistence wage. In certain respects these groups are worse off than in earlier periods. Their situation has improved in so far as their supply finds a regular demand, owing to which they enter the economic quantitative relation. But the demands made upon them are greater than ever. In order to obtain a subsistence wage they must assume larger burdens of service under the most objectionable conditions. The entrepreneur tries to make the labor fit his calculations and to raise the hours of labor. If owing to any sort of change the marginal productivity drops below the subsistence wage, the labor-conditions of the workers involved will be disturbed; their supply no longer meets an effective demand. Unless they can find employment in other enterprises, they will be thrown into the same channels to which the superfluous labor in primitive times was directed.

The law of population always exerts its most oppressive influence on the lowest strata of the workers. The entire excess of the population that is ejected from the lower groups of the moneyed class and from the higher groups of workers because it can no longer find customary employment, increases the supply at the bottom. This is in addition to the increase that takes place by the direct growth of population in the lowest classes.

In the development of the law of wages we have not approached the problem of the relationship of the numerous partial markets which exist for the individual types and strata of labor. In this connection are we concerned with independent markets or only with one large market whose subdivisions are in the last analysis subject to the law of the unity of price? It is customary to speak of an equalizing tendency in wages which, if it were fully effective, would have to be considered an expression of the law of the single price. On the other hand we hear of obstructions to this tendency which counteract the law when they are sufficiently broad in their operation. To clearly understand the answer to the question it is necessary to distinguish between the horizontal articulation of the branches and the vertical stratification of labor. An enumeration of the details of this articulation and stratification would serve no useful theoretical purpose. It will answer every purpose to maintain the distinctions already enumerated: between personal service and acquisitive labor; the strata of educated professional work, skilled labor and common labor; and finally between the work of men, women and children.

There is an effective tendency to equalization only between groups of the same level, between the isohypsemetric [1] districts in stratified labor as we might call them. The mass of common laborers is unable to turn at short notice to the market of skilled labor. It cannot even overcome the obstacles of the required apprenticeship and the attendant cost of learning a trade. The same remark applies to the skilled worker seeking higher levels. Indeed, as we ascend in the economic scale, this condition applies to all individuals who may aspire to still higher callings in which personal qualification is indispensable.

Also along the isohypses there are effective obstructions. To apply himself to a different trade of the same level the skilled worker must again incur

[1] Trans. note: At the risk of being ridiculous, the translator ventures to insert an English definition. Isohypsemetric districts are areas at an equal height above sea-level. An isohyps is the line connecting such districts. In several standard dictionaries the translator found no clue to the word. It is used so frequently in Wieser that a synonym seems out of place.

the expense of an apprenticeship. This is a difficult barrier to pass; only the rising generation has the possibility of overcoming the obstacle. Unless other obstructions interpose themselves, children will be deterred from entering the overcrowded branches of labor and will train for the best-paid ones. Thus they initiate an equalization of wages between isohypsemetric markets.

From the lower levels to the higher ones, even in the rising generation, no such equalization takes place; or, if it does, it is only in a restricted degree. Generally only highly gifted individuals under especially favoring circumstances find their way to higher levels. If an extensive upward movement is to be achieved, there must needs be taking place propitious economic and social changes on a large scale.

The theoretical expression for these facts is that there is not a single labor market; there are a large number of distinct, stratified, partial markets of labor between which the tendency to equalization is almost inoperative. For the higher strata there are a number of only loosely connected markets for various branches of labor between which it operates with reduced force and speed. The amount of the wages is accordingly variously articulated and stratified.

The supply of workers is attracted not merely by the amount of the wage. The conditions of work and living always exert their influence as well. Those positions that are regarded as preëminently distinctive or as more promising than others, are preferred even at a lower wage than could be obtained elsewhere. Conversely it is said that jobs involving unusual exertion and danger or those looked upon as degrading, are much less sought after, and that higher wages have to be offered for these in order to attract a sufficiently large supply. This last contention, however, is not confirmed by experience, as Mill ascertained when he laid down the proposition that the most onerous, dangerous and repulsive operations are the lowest paid. Such employment is shunned by all who have the choice of other opportunities. It is left to those who have no other chance of employment and must therefore consent to the lower wage as well. The multitude of those who are forced down to the lowest strata and must accept the most crushing conditions, is everywhere and at all times too large.

The costs of the worker's subsistence do not exert the equalizing effect on wages that we have observed between the cost of production of commodities and their prices. One of the most serious errors of the labor-theory was to transfer the law of costs from products to human labor. It is an entirely different relationship when higher wages and abundant subsistence attract a supply of labor and, encouraging marriage, lead to a higher birth-rate.

This stratification of wages that has just been described, is a consequence of the stratification of the labor markets. It has nothing in common with the stratification of prices set forth in the general theory of prices. The latter follows from gradations in the consumers' ability to pay. This is not a factor that generally makes itself felt as regard the wages of labor. High priced luxuries, for example, do not indicate that all workers employed in their production have been paid high wages. Only those few groups of workers who possess the advantage of a specific position in industries of this sort, will be able by virtue of specific attribution to command a higher wage. The others, whose work is clothed with a cost-character, are paid the marginal wage of their partial markets. Thus, for example, common laborers in diamond mines receive the common-wage rate of all other industries.

A certain proportion of the entrepreneur's capital, the so-called wages-fund, is directly assigned to the payment of wages. However, it would be a mistake to believe that this fund of itself determines the rate of wages. Its amount is always determined in accord with the total amount of the entrepreneur's capital, the conditions of labor and the state of the technical arts. When wages are low because of a large labor supply, entrepreneurs will find it to their advantage to increase the amount of the wages-fund. They will use a relatively large amount of cheap human labor. In this case a relatively small amount of capital will be used per man. With a smaller supply and higher rates of wages, they will be induced to use larger amounts of capital to save labor-costs. A growth of capital wealth would increase the marginal productivity of labor as it offers the opportunity for a more intensive use of capital; but this conclusion presupposes that the quality of labor is not reduced. As a matter of fact the quality is much reduced as the growth of capital wealth facilitates the development of large industries, although these require higher qualifications of some of their workers.

The capital of an enterprise and the wages-fund are variable quantities. They grow with the expansion of production. In the active economic movement that has heretofore characterized rising capitalism, they grew rapidly. Nevertheless for short periods of time they both show a certain inflexibility. There is some delay before entrepreneurs can follow up the contingencies of the period and of the labor market by technical changes of their large fixed plants. Because of the magnitude of their technical plants, entrepreneurs can only determine their demands for labor on a large scale. Thus the erection of a smelting furnace leads to the immediate employment of a large number of new workers. On the other hand the restricted operation characteristic of periods of depression often affects a large number of men at once.

§ 73. The Formation of Wages in the Modern Labor-Market

The wage of unorganized workers—Subsistence income—Maintenance and income suitable to social position—The wage of organized workers—Class consciousness of labor organizations—Law of combinations.

The idealizing assumptions, with the aid of which we deduce the theory of wages, have never been realized in the past, nor are they in the present labor market. They are the instruments of investigation which serve as a starting point for an empirical theory. With decreasing abstraction such a theory will replace them in due course by assumptions adjusted to the typical indices of supply and demand in the modern labor market. The latter has reached its large dimensions by the spread of large scale capitalistic industries, but it is not confined to the workers in these enterprises. It embraces all the remaining industrial and agricultural laborers in a further series of partial markets.

The market conditions are essentially different for organized and unorganized labor and the resulting formation of wages differs accordingly.

In the unorganized labor market, the individual worker is left wholly to his own resources. He is left without other support than that derived from his immediate surroundings. Custom is the decisive influence. Among the lower strata of the working-class, families live from hand to mouth. The wage income is used up as soon as it is received. Frequently, also, it is consumed in advance by means of consumptive credit. These families have no reserves, no savings. They possess scarcely more than the most wretched household goods, and these are often sacrificed in a final attempt to meet dire needs. Because the penniless worker cannot make use of his labor power by himself his need for employment is all the more urgent. Lacking, as he is, in the complementary means, his forces have no utility value for him. He is thus wholly dependent on the appraisal of the demand. Moreover, the supply is under the pressure of strong competition because of its great numbers. The markets themselves extend over wide areas. Conditions and prospects are such that it is far beyond the ability of an individual worker to view and appraise them correctly. Under these conditions, competition is readily transformed into over-competition. When it comes to the worst, the weakest group is willing to agree to a subsistence wage that covers the most immediate needs of the day. After the fashion of weak economics, they appraise these with the recognized underestimation of future needs.

The provident worker, in estimating his minimum of subsistence, should always add to his immediate needs the minimum requirements to make provision for periods of illness, convalescence after accidents in the course of employment, invalidity, old age and the care of widow and orphans. He should also make further allowance for periods of unemployment and loss of wages by strikes. These provisions should be effected by insurance premiums or by direct reservations from income. Such a minimum income may be designated as a maintenance income. The subsistence wage, computed to the needs of the day, which the poorest strata agree to accept under the pressure of over-competition, does not by any means yield a maintenance income. At best it is computed only with an allowance to cover those portions of the year during which seasonal workers cannot find useful employment. With this exception it yields to the workers a meagre living only for the time that they are usefully employed in their full strength and willingness. At the end of this period they are thrown back into privations of the worst kind with no recourse except to public charity or the poor law.

The higher the worker's position in the social scale, the more favorable are his chances in the unorganized labor market as well. The smaller number of applicants, their better knowledge of the market and their stronger economic backing assert themselves. Inasmuch as all these circumstances have been effective for some time, often for long periods, the market is governed by a tradition that is favorable to the worker. The supply is habituated to a customary wage which offers the usual maintenance considered suitable to the worker's station. He will therefore not be readily persuaded to accept a lower wage. The higher a man's position in the social scale, the more effective will be his inclination so to compute the maintenance wage as to secure an income wholly suited to his station. He will attempt to make this wage large enough to maintain his position when he is no longer able to work and to allow a tolerable provision for the satisfaction of the demands of his widow and the bringing up of his children, both of these in ways suited to their station in life.

Whether the supply will be able to uphold the traditional standard in the long run naturally depends upon the condition of the market. The customary maintenance suited to a particular station in life indicates at all times only the proximate starting point of the supply price. It does not indicate either the obtainable maximum or an inviolable minimum. Like anyone else, workers also endeavor to profit by the opportunities to improve their position. They raise their demands when the prospects seem favorable. On the other hand, they must submit to the exigencies of the market situation whenever their market yield drops below the customary standard. At all times marginal productivity conclusively determines the maximum of an acquisitive age. The after-effects which make themselves in regard to marriages and birth-rates, whenever the wage rises above the customary maintainance or drops below it, become effective only for the supply of the next generation of wages. Through the latter, these effects modify the future productive. For the given market they are of no importance whatever.

In the demand index of the entrepreneurs, the described indications of economic weakness are absent. But beside this exception there is another decisive consideration: the entrepreneurs are either regularly organized as were the guilds in the Middle Ages, or they are so closely allied by actual conditions that they may be considered to constitute a sort of natural organization. It is obvious how great an advantage the manufacturers in a given district, because of their small number and their close personal relations, have over the multitudes of the workers. A mutual understanding among the former may easily be brought about so that they will not "spoil prices" for each other nor "make men fastidious by raising wages." Each one of them sees at once the disadvantage to himself that lies in an attempt to increase his own force by attracting workers from other establishments by an increase of wages. Such an increase could never be withheld long from his regular employees.

When the entrepreneurs in a locality are in agreement with each other, their situation is nearly equivalent to a demand monopoly. They are able to apply considerable pressure to unorganized workers who are too weak economically to take advantage of conditions which may possibly be more favorable in some other market. Under such circumstances wages may be maintained which do not reach the standard which would be established theoretically. These wages may either still be adjusted to subsistence under conditions in which higher acquisitive wages might be allowed, or it may be merely that the wage does not reach the marginal productivity which the entrepreneurs have determined by attribution.

In order to break up the understanding between entrepreneurs, and to create in the labor market that actual competition on the part of the demand which we found in the deduction of the general law of prices to be the effective force of price formation, an active expansion of business will be required. Just as the rival demand of consumers runs up the prices for goods which may be of no value to the producers themselves, so the rival demands of entrepreneurs will increase the scale of wages although the services which are being offered may be of no value to the workers themselves, and although their economic weakness may prevent the workers from determining an appropriate wage. An entrepreneur who faces the risk of losing his trained workers to another paying higher wages, must decide to increase the wages which he offers as much as the attributed marginal production may allow. Such competition may become effective even for unskilled workers. This is plainly shown in the case of increased wages by which industry is attracting agricultural laborers. Once such competition has been effectively aroused, the fundamental law of price formation obtains even in the unorganized labor market; a conflict necessarily ensues which calls for a decision as to who is to be admitted to the process of acquisition, and who excluded. The wage will be fixed at a point determined by the appraisal of the marginal demand.

What influence does the organization of the workers have on the formation of wages? In answering this question let us assume that the entrepreneurs also are organized. Let us neglect for the time being all the effects produced by the organization in the regulation of other working conditions. It is beyond the scope of our present inquiry to seek an answer to the further question whether organization may not possibly enable the workers to employ the influence of their mass so as to acquire increased social power or even to gain social supremacy.

In the wage conflict, only such organizations are influential as combine all or nearly all the supply of labor in a definite partial market, i. e., such as result in the combination of all or nearly all the workers in a particular industry. The combination must not be threatened by competition on the part of workers who have not joined it. If this is not the case the union is unable to employ successfully its most important weapon, the strike. A strike on the part of a smaller group would be ineffective beyond depriving the strikers of their incomes without materially affecting the entrepreneurs. Only a cessation of work by all the workers, or at any rate by far the larger number of them in a partial market—the strike, properly speaking—results in forcing the entrepreneurs to discontinue operations in their plants.

In its external appearance the union is a monopoly by the elimination of competition that differs in no way from a kartel or trust that unites in an artificial body all the entrepreneurs of the branch affected. But in their effects there are radical differences between an organization of workers and a supply-combine that faces the consumers monopolistically. The kartel is opposed to unorganized consumers; the union is pitted against entrepreneurs who are themselves monopolistically organized as regards the demand for labor. The workers' organization cannot expand production; it cannot divide the market and classify consumers. It must adjust itself to the conditions of production, and these conditions are created by the entrepreneurs. Finally, whereas the kartel controls the whole of production, the union controls only a single one of the contributing productive factors. By withholding its coöperation, labor may of course render production impossible, as it throws the complementary factors out of action. It thus seriously injures consumers and entrepreneurs. But the weapon which strikes this blow is two-edged; it descends upon the workers themselves at the same time. It is not merely that the strike suspends the workers' pay and cannot therefore be maintained for any length of time. The entrepreneurs may succeed in forcing up the marginal utility by a restrictive monopoly policy. But this tool is denied to the workers; they are subject to the constant necessity of placing the entire supply in the union. They may be able to shift small parts of the supply from over-crowded positions to others less congested, but they cannot reduce the aggregate of the supply. Neither can they successfully carry through a policy of reducing the hours of labor below the standard of the most efficient working-period; if they attempted to do so, the only effect would be to reduce the marginal productivity, which forms the basis for the computation of wages.

The hope of the workers is that the injury which they inflict on the entrepreneurs by the cessation of work, may be seriously felt. Therefore, so far as the determination of the period for action lies within their voluntary control, they select times when the entrepreneurs are heavily involved by the conditions of the market or by contractual engagements, and when they themselves are as well supplied through the collection of strike-funds as is possible.

The entrepreneurs, on their part, have to allow not only for the immediate injury inflicted by a shut-down; they must also consider the permanent loss occasioned by granting increased wages. Considerable as the transient injury may be to their interests, the permanent injury is far more serious if they agree to wages which cannot be recovered from the marginal productivity of labor. In the long run they would have to retire from enterprises that did not yield the entrepreneur's wage and interest on capital that might be obtained elsewhere.

Thus the most a well organized body of workers can obtain by the strike is that the full marginal productivity of labor be paid out in the wage. This is the productivity of the marginal workers, the last men whom the entrepreneurs have to employ to absorb the entire supply in the organization. In the rare cases where a particular branch of industry is so favorably situated that even the enterprises working at least advantage yield an entrepreneur's profit, a body of men, working exclusively for this industry and thus enjoying a specific position in the market, may even succeed by a successful strike in obtaining a portion of the entrepreneur's profit itself. This is due to the body of workers by virtue of specific attribution.

This conclusion coincides with the proposition set out in the theory of the simple economy, that value and attribution receive their standard, not from the injury that follows the loss of an economic good or complementary factor, but from the increase of utility that is established in the economy. It is also confirmed by experience. Generally strikes are successful when they coincide with periods of rising business activity in which the capacities of entrepreneurs are increased. They fail most frequently when they are begun in periods of business depression with a view to protecting the established wage-rates against reduction.

When a union enforces a wage-rate that allows the full marginal productivity, it has won a considerable success for its members. It counteracts the unhealthy consequences of the over-competition of unorganized workers on wages, as well as defeating agreements between entrepreneurs to control wages. The union compels the entrepreneurs to agree to the price that would be established by an effective competition of demand. It forces an agreement to this price without delay as soon as the changed market conditions allow it. It does this, although even an effective demand-competition acts slowly when it relies solely on the mechanism of the unsatisfied demand. When the general price-level rises and the established money-wage or nominal wage may be exchanged for a smaller quantity of goods, i. e., when the real wages fall, when at the same time the entrepreneurs sell their goods for more money, even without an agreement between entrepreneurs it will require a long period before the monetary wage is raised to cover the full marginal productivity of labor.

The unions, originally designed for conflict and strife, would render their members the highest possible service, if by a judicious use of their power they should become the agents for an amicable determination of the wages that are economically demanded. It must be admitted that such a goal can be attained only when the marginal productivity of labor yields an income adequate to maintenance. The collective agreements and wage-contracts concluded by labor organizations with associations of entrepreneurs for all their members, i. e., for all workers and employers in the particular market, still breathe the animus of the conflict that gave them birth.

The union offers no prospect of higher wages for those strata of workers whose marginal productivity covers merely a subsistence-income or a wage that maintains life from day to day. For such men the advantages of organization lie in directions which we have not yet made the subject of inquiry.

Many wage-workers are not effectively organized, nor do they possess even the capacity for effective organization. To be effective a union must first have able leaders who stand out from the masses. Then, too, the multitude must be conscious of a common interest and must be endowed with the faculty of subordination. Groups of workers whose pay falls below certain limits cannot establish reserves. Those widely scattered have no communication. Agricultural laborers, women and unskilled industrial laborers, not to mention working children, do not readily form effective organizations. Skilled industrial workers, especially those in the best paid groups who, by virtue of their position, are protected against equalization movements from below, form the core of organized labor. They have achieved unparalleled successes. They are able to wring wage increases even from the monopoly profits of kartels and trusts although they themselves are not clothed with monopolistic power.

Labor unions are institutions of class consciousness. They further individual interest as these are interpreted by the majority of the members of a class; the personal interest of the more enlightened, better situated minority may not infrequently suffer under the rule of the mass. The more capable, intelligent, better trained workers do not find the organizations to their advantage when the standard of average performance falls much short of their individual achievements. In the long run this may injure the interest even of the class, as men may find that the ambition to accomplish more than their fellows is paralyzed and as the educational force of the outstanding example ceases to impress them. The men best qualified for their technical tasks by natural talents, who would under different conditions have become anonymous leaders, by their example teaching a higher workmanship, are forced into obscurity by other leaders. The latter possess the talent of organization, of public speaking, of handling men, and of appearing before the crowd, and are able to carry the masses along no matter how grave the misgivings of their followers as the firm ground seems to crumble beneath their feet.

The liberal school regards coalitions as restraints upon personal liberty, operating on the side of the workers through the strike, and on that of the entrepreneurs through the lockout. It looks upon the collective agreement and wage-contract in the same light. During the liberal period, the legislation on combinations did away with ancient prohibitions that could no longer be sustained; but, following the point of view outlined above, it restrained the freedom of combination by not making such contracts legally binding. In other words legal proceedings cannot be instituted to enforce the performance of such a contract. But whoever heard of a resolution to strike being defeated by the reflection that its contravention is not an actionable wrong? Or when did such a consideration ever make the conduct of a strike less forceful? The resolution of a combination of the masses is not a contract in the sense of private law. Even more than the agreement between the stockholders of a corporation, it is a crowd phenomenon. Fundamentally its power lies in the social forces inherent in an organization of the masses, that seeks the recognition of neither judge nor jury. To this extent, then, legislation dealing with combinations has failed.

The freedom of personal contract, however, is not that supreme blessing that the liberal school sought to portray. With the existing weak position of the laboring class, class consciousness resting upon coöperative solidarity is to be appraised at a higher value than individual liberty based on personal egoism. Only the former is strong enough to present to good effect the egoism of the masses. Thrown upon their own resources, the individual interests of the masses are nearly powerless. In view of the helplessness of the weak individual, the slogan of the liberal school, "Laissez-faire, laissez-passer," becomes almost a mockery. Those who truly wish freedom must not begrudge it to the class, though they may be fully aware that in its class egoism it is inclined to encroach on the individual interests of some of its members too freely. This recognition of the class must also be accorded even though it is further recognized that the spirit of the class is that of the conflict which it must wage and that it has not yet learned to fit itself into the general interests of society.

Despite all these considerations, the current law of combinations is appropriate to present conditions. The union has come to be a weapon of social conflict.

It arose in response to a need to bring order to the market. Too often it brings chaos out of order and plunges the market into danger. While these conditions prevail the labor organization must stand or fall by its own social power; the vindication of the general law cannot as yet be called to its aid.

§ 74. Yield-Wage and the Value of Labor

The exchange value of labor and the errors in its computation—The life-values of the worker—The will to work.

The source of power enjoyed by large-scale capitalistic enterprise is found in the supremacy which it possesses in the formation of exchange values. In the open conflict it ousts weaker competitors because it is able to turn out more and perhaps better products at less expense and to bring them into the market at lower prices. It creates itself a large part of the demand which will be required to withdraw from the market the increased supply which it produces. In so far as the capitalistic entrepreneur spends more from his large income for household expenses, it has the effect of "making money change hands." These men induce a correspondingly large supply of high-priced goods. In turning these out many workers gain a living. To the extent to which entrepreneurs make capital savings from their income, as they must do on a large scale in order to remain on top and to preserve their competitive power, they add places for workers in their own enterprises. The increase in the demand for workers which has been opened up by large-scale industries is so extensive that it is scarcely satisfied by the entire growth of population and by the women and children and the reserves of unskilled workers from the country whom they call to their benches. The reserves from the masses in eastern Europe have to be drawn upon. The mass-values which the great industries turn out and the multitudes of human beings whom they employ, are to a large extent mutually conditioned. A large proportion of their products are mass-values, goods produced in quantities for the masses. The purchasers for such consumption goods are largely the employees. To the extent that this is the case this production is itself the basis for the higher exchange-value of the labor employed.

One can understand the feeling of pride that so many an entrepreneur experiences, in that he has become the organizer of labor and has given to thousands a means of providing for their families. Not only the entrepreneurs but society as a whole indulged throughout the first period of the industrial age in the illusion that they were on the way to such all-embracing and astounding progress as had never before been witnessed in the history of human achievement. Science itself agreed; it also was deceived by constantly advancing exchange-values and populations.

At last the truth had to be realized. The contrasts of capitalistic affluence and proletarian misery became too glaring. Observers could no longer conceal from themselves the fact that an error lay hidden in the constantly growing figures by which exchange-values were computed. Let us assume that existing conditions become ever more acute until ultimately society is split into two groups: a very small number of individuals of unmeasured wealth and a multitude in abject poverty. It would then be obvious, despite all the enticing demonstrations of calculations of exchange value, that social economy had wholly lost its significance. This most extreme condition has not yet been even approximated in any part of the world. Everywhere there may still be found strong middle classes fundamentally sound and striving to raise themselves to higher levels. At the same time, their marginal members must struggle to avoid defeat and still others vanish out of sight into lower strata. On all sides one may also see the upper groups of workers tending higher and coalescing with the lower levels of the middle class; everywhere large masses of the lower strata of the working population still preserve their social power. In all places there are high lights in the picture of the social economy. But despite these assurances, no one may deny a discrepancy between the actual social conditions and the ever ascending mathematical expression of exchange-values.

An accurate examination will show that in the capitalistic computation of exchange-value a number of sources of error are operative. Most of all they concern wage-labor.

The most obvious of these is one that relates to a different problem. Whenever inequalities in the distribution of income become excessive, disparities in the stratification of prices likewise become much too great and the prices can no longer be socially justified. A computation of exchange-value based on these prices is not equitably defensible. The excess of enjoyments that is accessible to the rich man destroys not only his capacity for pleasure but also his ability to work. There is a limit beyond which an increase of yield no longer encounters a healthful need, and beyond which, therefore, an increase in goods[1] ceases to be an increment in value. The capitalistic upper class of today reaches this limit much more quickly than did the nobility of earlier

[1] Werten.

war-like periods. To maintain their dominant position in the state, the latter had to preserve the virtues of heroic manhood above all else.

The computation of exchange value is again misleading in several respects for that group of workers whose yield-wage furnishes only a scanty subsistence wage. The same indifference to the future which induces the masses of laborers of the lower strata to content themselves with a wage that covers only immediate needs, tempts them also to assume obligations which, in the long run, they are not able to fulfill. They are dazzled by the numerical expression of the money-wage offered them; it is above anything to which they have been accustomed. The laborers attracted from agriculture to industry, received their previous wage largely in the natural form; only a trifling percentage was paid in money. Therefore when they are promised a wage, not only computed entirely in money but also above their former rates, they lack the experience to recognize into what sums of practical values they can actually transform it. Children and young workers who are drawn to the factories, receive wages at an age at which they had formerly never dreamed of being able to earn anything more than a nominal one. Similarly the services of women, whom the factory now attracts, were hitherto ill-paid if they were remunerated at all.

These individuals now make no allowance for the fact that their new employments impose duties upon them to an extent and under conditions which make incomparably greater demands upon their forces than their earlier occupations. These were occasional, varied and perhaps only now and then really exacting services which they had been called upon to perform at home or upon the farm. Their environment, though it may have been primitive, was simple and healthful. At first such people are probably comparatively immune to the inroads which the unaccustomed work makes upon their health. In the freshness of their youthful power they know little of the dangers and suffering in store for them. They are lavish of their excess vitality. Possibly the first generation, still embued with the strength of the soil from which it has sprung, may withstand in comparative ruggedness the debased conditions of life to which it is physically and morally chained by the narrow confines of the city and of the industry. This is not true of the children growing up in this environment and without the protection of the moral powers which even among simple and crude associations are active, wherever fixed relations of life have evolved historically. Side by side with the children, the remaining groups with the least power of resistance are exposed to the gravest danger. Of these groups, the women are most important. The effects upon them radiate to the family which is estranged from mother and daughter because of their acquisitive labor.

In this connection we need not conceive of the worst possible case in which the power of labor is completely mechanized because the worker harnessed to the machinery of the establishment is restricted to the narrowest possible motions and is doomed to an eternal stultifying repetition of an identical performance. Also in the majority of the other cases as well, the sum of the pure life-values accruing to the lower strata of workers, is curtailed in a most revolting manner. Only too often, unless there is timely help, the danger of over-fatigue threatens the victims. When the process of degeneration has lasted too long, its damage can never be repaired. All sources of personal power are then forever exhausted among the down-trodden groups. Never again will they give forth services of higher exchange value. The moral values that economic labor requires for its guidance are deadened. So, too, social groups that have been made completely proletarian can never contribute to the cultural values of society. Culturally, they become destructive. All through the Middle Ages and down to the beginnings of modern times, our ancestors were threatened with barbarian aggression. Modern civilization has grown so strong that it no longer fears this invasion, but the people tremble with fear lest there spring from its midst a new barbarism which may some day overpower them.

The stratum of workers of whom we have just spoken, includes for the most part unskilled laborers. But even the lower groups of trained operators are not wholly secure from the dangers of over-exertion and inner degradation. More important still for the skilled workers, and especially for their higher levels, is another effect which, as an incident of the capitalistic relation of employment, detracts value. The will to work is impaired. This also is one of the moral values which are decisive in the success of labor. For unskilled workers it is of less importance if there be no real inner impulse to labor. To master the monotonous performances which these workers have to carry on in industry, sufficient incentive proceeds from the will to live and the pangs of hunger. The land owner comes to feel the evil effects of drudgery more quickly than such men, as he strives to direct the manifold operations of agriculture. The effect is most striking in the case of the highest groups of skilled industrial wage workers. The labor to be performed by these men is of a similar character to that of the artisan; not infrequently it demands a skill and mental agility that exceeds the latter. For operations of this sort, the worker's delight in his task is not a matter of indifference.

The large industrialist, unlike the master craftsman, no longer takes a personal part in the details of execution. This is by no means because the manner of their execution is no longer of equal importance, due to the great size of the enterprise. It is because the number of activities combined in these large industries, has increased so enormously that the entrepreneur must confine his personal attention to the most vital tasks of superintendence. All other duties he must delegate to other men, necessarily assuming that they will apply all the interest of an owner. The wage contract into which he enters with these men is, in point of fact if not of law, always a partnership agreement. They are subordinate partners. Their functions, however, are of such vast importance that the unstinted devotion of a partner should never be lacking in their services. When the entrepreneur speaks of them as his fellow workers, as he is apt to do on occasions when exalted sentiment suggests the right word at the right moment, he gives suitable expression to the relation of these men to himself and his plans. The materials and tools that the entrepreneur uses allow their full useful content to be extracted. They need not offer living coöperation; they are material aids to production. But those human beings who are called on for any higher service must give more. If they are to surrender that which is best and which is demanded of them by the fundamental social relationship, they must give their good will.

The will to work arises in part from motor-stimuli inciting to action. Men are pleasurably conscious of this stimulus in the joy of work. In part the will arises from anticipation of the success which it is hoped will attend the effort, i. e., from the desire of achievement. The joy of labor may continue even when the effort is wage-labor, only care must be exercised that the motor stimulation is not exhausted by fatigue. The joy of achievement cannot be maintained except when the relation of employment is so regulated that the worker secures the full reward of his labor. The classical doctrine fully recognized this in the case of the services of independent business-men. Its decisive argument for the freedom of acquisition was that freedom induces the utmost tension of the will to work, since it is liberty that promises the maximum reward.

Does not this argument apply to any service for a wage that requires a true will to work? The contracts into which the large entrepreneur enters with his higher employees are drawn in this spirit. They are binding for considerable periods of time. As a rule the relationship of employment is even assumed to be a permanent one. Articles are inserted to provide for the future of these employees and, in a measure, for that of their families. Now and then shares in the net earnings are expressly granted to them; or they may feel reasonably certain that such shares will in some measure be credited to them. In any event their compensations are settled at such substantial figures that their interest is felt to harmonize with that of their employer.

In the case of wage-labor proper, different methods have been resorted to. Wage systems have been devised such as piece-work, contract-work and bonuses, which are intended to adjust the wage as accurately as may be practicable to the individual's effort. Employment itself may be terminated by notice. In the interest of both parties such notices are limited by law to the shortest periods. To strengthen their position in conflict, the workers have wholly renounced the privilege of notice to be free at all times to order strikes.

The actual order does not, as a rule, agree with the legal order. As a matter of fact, more often than not employments last through long periods, frequently for a life-time. The tradition of cordial relations between the entrepreneur and his workers has by no means disappeared everywhere. Through all conflicts the actual interrelation of interests has sustained a tolerable harmony between the two parties, a harmony which is solidified also by the respect which the worker cannot but entertain for the power of the entrepreneur, and the latter for the strength of the labor unions. Among well-intentioned entrepreneurs, there exists a patriarchal spirit that extends beyond the bounds of legal obligation.

Can a condition of law be accepted as satisfactory which is endurable only because the actual condition is, as a rule, more favorable than that which the law has decreed? If no other considerations led to the conclusion, the continuance of strikes and lock-outs, which so frequently disturb the course of events with heavy losses to both sides, show that the final equilibrium of the legal order has not yet been reached. In fairness, we should not draw the worst inference by suggesting that the entrepreneurs, wishing to evade conflict with the organized skilled workmen, laid their plans consciously to degrade labor progressively by unfitting it for anything but mechanical operations in order that there should be only unorganized workers of the lowest power of resistance with whom to deal. But it surely is obvious that the constantly repeated interruptions and costs of labor wars with their forcible suspension of operations are making inroads upon the yield and value of labor. This applies not only to services rendered by the wage-laborers but also by the entrepreneurs themselves. It is equally apparent that under the present law the full latent power of even the well-paid, well-nourished worker is not called into play in the performance of his task. The entire potential yield of his efforts does not materialize nor is the full value released from his labor for the good of society because the whole-hearted, faithful will to work has not been called into action. Faithfulness and devotion are not for sale in the market at a fortnight's notice. The number of those who are called upon to perform an owner's duties in the large-scale industrial enterprises of our day, without possessing the interests of ownership, has become too large.

When we ask what it is that labor does to man, the answer is simple enough: labor makes man what he is. The man who does not work finds that his power and his capacity for enjoyment decay. The greatest wealth will no longer profit him. However simple the conditions of his fellow-men, he has cause to enjoy them so long as they may delight in the unrivalled happiness of useful exertion. The continuous exercise of power, according to the dictates of reason, is among the noblest aims of the economy. All increased satisfactions of needs fulfill the intentions of economy only for him who has been purged by labor. Wage labor, as it is found at present in the large-scale industries, does not make of the laborer that which he might be were the meaning of the word, economy, wholly realized for him. The yield-wage of today obstructs the unfolding of the full values of labor and with it of the full values of life. This is not an indictment of the capitalistic entrepreneurs. They are not alone responsible for this state of affairs. It is only a description of existing conditions, a strict performance of the duties of theory.

The will to work has been greatly increased by the refinement of contracts of piece-work, special agreements and bonuses, in so far as the workers are called upon by these to make increased efforts in order to raise their productivity and with it the yield-wage. However, no matter how far such refinements may be carried, they will not overcome the incongruity of the trained worker's position in large-scale industry, which lies concealed in the fact that an owner's duties are delegated to them while yet their position is not such as would call out an owner's interest. Even should they so improve their position that the full yield-wage which may be attributed to them in these forms is actually paid to them, they will still not be paid according to the full productivity that would be achieved by a body of workers heart and soul with the entrepreneur, such as we assumed in the theory of the simple economy. The basis of the attribution of yield is always too narrow when the body of workers stands apart from the entrepreneur and is not attuned to the willingness and zest of contributing every effort, its full vigor and force, its full economic sympathy.

The advanced forms of profit-sharing yield very different results from these forms of wages. The former not only improve the conditions of the workers as such, but confer on an élite group of the workers a share of the entrepreneur's position. For some of them this may be dignified into a promotion to the entrepreneur's office proper, without in the least impairing the authority of the entrepreneur's leadership. It is possible that in this direction, methods may be found that will reconstruct the organization of the great industries in a manner satisfactory to all concerned. For the present, theory as such must renounce the pursuit of this suggestion; so far the facts are only nascent and there are no completed results to which one may appeal as to the common property of experience.

As a rule labor organizations are inimical to refinements of the wage system which aim at bettering the yield-wage by enhancing the individual productivity of workers. The personal enhancement of the yield of labor affords an immediate advantage only to a small select minority of workers. For the large mass it is disadvantageous, at least in its proximate effect, because it tends to depress wages as the direct result of raising the total of services supplied. Even the profit-sharing system conflicts with the class-consciousness of the labor unions. The former gives separate interests to the élite and the mass of labor. Furthermore it isolates the workers in each plant, for those employed in the most profitable plants are given an opportunity to share in the industrial rent of the establishment and their interest is thus estranged from the common one of their class. So long as the class as such has to be adjusted to struggle, an agitated class consciousness will tolerate no wage system that threatens the fighting power of the class. However, in their own productive associations workers begin to look favorably on profit sharing. This may well be a sign that their goal will change when their attention is no longer centered on conflict.

The labor organizations have been as much concerned with the problem of the adequate determination of the conditions of labor as with that of the wage-rate. The struggle for a reduction of the hours of labor has furnished not less frequent incentive to strike than has that for the increase or maintenance of wages. Even those groups whose marginal productivity is too slight to promise any success in the adjustment of the rates of wages, find a wide field for effective effort in regard to the conditions of labor.

The protective legislation of the state has hitherto been almost exclusively confined to safeguarding men against oppressive services. It has accordingly limited the hours of labor. It has also required suitable provisions to protect the life and health of the workers. In social insurance there has been recognition of the task of securing immunity for future cases of working-time lost by sickness or accident. Such legislation has prescribed the formation of reserve-funds for this purpose and has granted corresponding subventions.

Historical judgment may be passed on the current capitalistic relations of labor only when their future evolution sheds light on the results to which they lead. If our era should turn out to be the necessary transition to a safe and humane provision for the excess population that could not be cared for in earlier times, then the eulogies bestowed today on its technical achievement would be finally due. However, if society should be torn asunder so that only a small class of enormous wealth remained in contrast with a proletarian mass while the middle class had disappeared, or even if the present status should merely congeal, then the much lauded age of capitalistic technique and organization would be condemned as the end of human culture. For the present let the words of Wilhelm Foerster in *Jugendlehre* be borne in mind as a warning: "intellectually and morally modern society is unequally matched against the enormous material forces which it has unchained through its science and technical arts."

PART IV

THE CONSTITUTION OF THE PRIVATE ECONOMY

Beside those works mentioned in "I. Theory of Economic Society" by Wagner, Schmoller, Philippovich, Doria, Oppenheimer, Stammler, Böhm-Bawerk and M. Weber, the following are to be added: Sombart, *Moderne Kapitalismus*, 1902, 4th ed. 1922; Mann, *Wirtschaftliche Organisationsideen der Gegenwart*, Weltwirtsch. Archiv, vol. XIX; Dalton, *Some Aspects of the Inequality of Income in Modern Communities*, 1920; Bücher, *Die Sozialisierung*, 2nd ed. 1919; Passow, *Kapitalismus*, 1918; Liefmann, *Kartelle, Trusts und Weiterbildung der volkswirtsch. Organisation*, 4th ed. 1920; A. Weber, *Der Kampf zwischen Kapital und Arbeit*, 4th ed. 1921; Pigou, *Economics of Welfare*, 1920.

§ 75. The Constitution of the Private Economy at the Dawn of the Capitalistic Era

Private property and the meaning of economy—The struggle for wealth—The historical development of the constitution of the private economy—The social character of the private economy—The inequality of distribution—Law and its supplement: charity—The private law of inheritance—The disciples of the classicists.

We have so far treated the private economic order merely as an assumption, a given fact, from which we proceeded to follow the course of the national economic process. We inquired by what rules the private legal subjects, who meet in exchange, determine the natural performances and the price; and how, from the basis of exchange, they construct their acquisitive economy, whenever they mean to comply with economic requirements in their personal economies. With the results at which we arrived, however, our task of explaining the spirit of social economy is not as yet fully accomplished. To this end, the problem will have to be considered, whether or not the institution of private property is consistent with the idea of a social economy. Is private property an institution of economic endeavor or is it not, much more properly, to be called an institution of superior power? Or, to be more precise, is private property an institution subservient to the economic requirements of society, or is it merely the creature and tool of those who wield socio-economic power? We shall not be entitled to look upon our theoretical exposition of the national economic process in its entire course as formally complete, until we shall have discovered the final answer to this last important question.

That the institution of private property is most intimately interwoven with all the implications of the individual economy, may be demonstrated with the utmost brevity. Only such goods are made private property, as have entered into the economic quantitative relation. Who would ever dream of asserting rights of private property in goods abundantly free to everyone; goods from the enjoyment of which he could exclude no one, which no one could dispute to him? The rationale of private property is the rationale of all economy. Being forced to husband the utility of economic goods, we feel compelled to vindicate their possession in the face of all other claimants; the question of Mine and Thine becomes vital; the right of property which we set up, is to confer legal security with respect to economic use. By this chain of reasoning, the theory of utility explains not only the actual progress of the economy, but leads moreover to the demonstration of its legal basis.

It must be admitted, that these facts do not fully explain the obvious outcome. It must be admitted that, just as I endeavor to maintain and extend my ownership-interests, every other member of society will endeavor to do the same for his. The universal interest will not, *ipso facto,* create a universally valid legal condition, but only a universal conflict. Thus a struggle for possession is kindled, and the stronger will triumph. Since the prostrate enemy, who, as a slave, was forced to work for his conqueror, became, during centuries and centuries one of the most valuable constituents of economic wealth, the struggle for the possession of material economic goods was extended to the person of the individual, and became the struggle for personal liberty. Ever since the liberty of the person has been guaranteed by law, the struggle for personal freedom has become a struggle for the proceeds of labor. In this form, it has survived down to our own day. The struggle for wealth, with these rank accompaniments, was in the earliest times a struggle of force against force, violence against violence. Later on, it lurked under legal forms. To the observer it is plainly discernible in the escheats, forfeitures and sequestrations of later periods, in the economic wrongdoings of the powerful, the predatory expeditions of robber-tribes, the innumerable feuds of every type and description which, down to the colonial wars of our own times, have been and are being carried on for the sake of economic interests. Less transparently obvious is the struggle for wealth, for possessions, when carried on by conqueror-nations who have won dominion by sheer force, and who, as they proceed, feign formal observation of a law which they have shaped to suit their own interests, and which they uphold by their superior arms. In every exploiting legal system, power is one of the concommitants of private property, and possibly a system of law has never existed, which succeeded in maintaining altogether its independence from the pressure of power. Perhaps there never will exist a legal system of this sort.

Just before the beginning of the capitalistic era, too, private property was by no means free from the encroachments of power; nevertheless all in all, it was at that time, beyond any doubt, sanctioned by public opinion as just and proper. When the constitutions of that period safeguarded the sanctity of private property, they gave expression to the sense of justice of the people. Tradespeople and peasantry, as well-to-do classes, were satisfied to see their interests protected in private property; the proletarian workers were still a small minority, and this group had not yet, in its views of economic matters, signalled its dissent from the mass of the people; the socialistic doubt as to private property had not yet raised its head; the system of private economy was the living law of the land.

To this condition, as it existed at the threshold of the capitalistic era, we will for the present confine our investigation. This enquiry can prove nothing directly, concerning the state of things, as it exists to-day. Before such an application of the past to the present may be made, we shall first have to ascertain whether or not the momentous actual changes which have since taken place in the economy, have essentially modified the significance of private property.

The center of gravity for the system of private economy is acquisition. That the means of enjoyment, which have been produced, are finally surrendered for private disposition, is of minor importance; even in socialistic circles the coming order of things is generally so conceived that only the means of acquisition are placed at social disposal, while the means of enjoyment produced, are to be turned over to individuals as private property. We shall, therefore, confine ourselves to the exposition of the private system of acquisition.

The essential factors of this system as it existed prior to the spread of the capitalistic large-scale industries, may be briefly summed up as follows: The entire national-economic process of acquisition may be resolved into an incalculably large number of private economic partial-processes, mostly small, some of medium size, working jointly under the division of labor. Similarly, the wealth of the nation splits up into innumerable nuclei of individual wealth. Economic goods, personalty as well as realty, are held by private owners; money-demands and all other economically important rights are distributed among private legal subjects. The private individuals participating in the national-economic process, when not more closely related by family-ties, are related by contract, especially the contract of exchange in all its modifications. Incomes can be acquired only by the individual taking part one way or the other, by his labor, by his property or his other possessions, in the acquisitive process or elsewhere creating values. The personal income is composed of the prices realized in the commerce of exchange, and falling to the share of each participant according to the laws of attribution. Disregarding enhancements of value, we may say that wealth is increased or new wealth is created by successfully effecting savings from values received. The law of private inheritance adds to private wealth, when in case of death the estate of a decedent passes to surviving members of his family or to legatees, who become the private successors to his rights. Estates of those dying intestate and without heirs, pass to the state by escheat; but, with the wide circle of relatives and the next of kin entitled to lawful succession, cases of this sort are extremely rare. The state, municipalities and also the church, as artificial persons, may also be private juridical subjects, and as such take part in the national economic process; but their private participation, when contrasted to that of natural persons, is much less conspicuous. What influence they possess over the economy as dispensers of public powers, is not to be discussed in this place.

A large part of the current, private economic system is written law. The civil law, commercial law and the law of commercial paper regulate the material law of property and acquisition. The criminal law offers protection from offences against property and acquisition. The law of criminal and civil procedure and proceedings out of court regulate the forms of remedial protection offered to the economy by the state. An exceedingly large number of relations of the economic system are regulated by the administrative law. Constitutional law, finally, extends increased protection to the established order, by bestowing on private property, as a fundamental legal institution, the sanction of the state. But the essential part of the prevailing, private, economic system is unwritten law, and survives by its inherent power. Neither the fact that the social acquisitive process is the sum of countless private partial processes; that the national wealth is the aggregate of any number of private, individual units of wealth, together with the proportion, according to which the units are allotted to the participants; nor the fact that the state and all other public corporations as incumbents of private economic rights, give way to private, natural persons, has been guaranteed by written law. Yet these facts are the controlling foundations of the existing economic system. They supply to the written economic law the wide field of its validity. In the form of these traditional quasi-laws, the constitution of the state, which orders the public legal relations of the people, is confronted by a private economic constitution, its equal in importance as regards the public welfare, and possibly its superior in prestige.

That this salient component of the social constitution should have remained unwritten law, can be explained only from the fact that it possesses the incisive power of sound historical evolution. The private economic constitution has attained the unchallenged authority, which was its own even before the beginning of the capitalistic era, because of its historical success.

The historical growth of the private economic constitution runs through thousands of years. For our theoretical purposes we need not follow its course into all those details which only scientific specialization can ascertain. They are not subject-matter for the theorist's inclinations or qualifications. For our part, let us survey the development in its most general features, the features which are familiar to every educated man. Even of these, we need not trace the record to its earliest beginnings. If we go back to the period of the closed domestic economy, entered upon as soon as mankind succeeded in cultivating the soil with sufficient results to maintain fixed dwellings, it will be all we require. During this period, the Germanic people were already politically organized into distinct tribes; but there was not yet a social economy. The combinations of popular strength had become imperative by the exigencies of war, for whose successful conduct the means of common power had to be collected under a unifying command. On the other hand, the economic calling had not yet become so extensive as to present a social issue and to excite a social economic process. For the daily demands of the economy, taking all in all, the single unit of power comprised by the household was entirely adequate. The assembly of the entire social force and a single-voiced command would have offered no advantage for this pursuit; endless confusion would have been the outcome of such interference. No sooner had the social army under its princely commander fought its battles against the enemy, than it became a matter of course for it to disperse, leaving every man to attend to his economic duties in the household. The well-known tale of the Roman dictator, who, after his military feats, retires from his high office with its power of life and death over all his fellow-citizens to the seclusion of his country-seat and there follows the plow like any other Roman, illustrates vividly, how differently the law under which men live adjusts itself to the aims of war and the aims of economy. War, from the beginning, was the concern of the multitude; it affected common interests. The economy of early periods was a matter of individual interest to small, localized groups; its organization and management were disjointed.

To this extent, even in the days of the natural economy, there existed a private constitution of economy. However, the private economic constitution of early days by no means coincides with that of to-day. The individual economic processes were in those days not, as they are to-day, partial processes of a great national economic aggregate. They were small, locally isolated and independent processes. In our investigation it is of especial significance, and should be emphasized, that nevertheless their private character was not nearly as sharply developed as it came to be after they had coalesced to become partial processes of a large social whole.

In any event it is improper to speak of private property in a strict sense in those early times. In like manner the relations of person to person were but little regulated by private contract. The greater part of the soil, the arable land, the pasture and the woodland, were common property of the village or march; the individual fellow-townsmen were confined to a right of personal use. When, later on, private property in the soil was recognized, the owner was essentially restricted by the rights of his family in the disposition of his property during his life or in the event of his death. The peasant owners, moreover, were hemmed in by the rights of the lord of the manor. The peasant was not even free to choose the methods of cultivating his land; he was bound by rights of vicinage, which were frequently strengthened into compulsory rules regarding manner and times of planting and harvesting. The relation of service, for those who were not free men, was regulated by a compulsory code. Later on, the greater number of the peasants fell into villenage, which only very gradually was relaxed into milder forms. The urban trades, to be sure, strove from the very beginning to obtain personal freedom together with recognition of private property, but even in their business-dealings personal freedom of action was greatly restricted. The guilds compelled all to join and prescribed to individual members the rules of technical procedure. They dictated, down to the very prices which were to prevail, the terms of the contracts which masters were to enter into with their apprentices, journeymen and customers.

The power of the state, as it gained strength and made its influence felt after the beginning of modern times in order to energize the economic process, did much to protect the peasants from the ill-treatment of their lords and the public from the abuses of the guilds, and to clear the way for the nascent large industries. But after all the greater part of its benefits it conferred by means which again fluctuated from beneficent tutelage to rigorous legal compulsion.

Not until the economic process had finally gained impetus, were the shackles of locally restricted economy, endured for centuries, and the oppression of paternal government-interference felt as intolerable clogs. Liberation of the peasants, popularization of the land, trade and commercial freedom were demanded and obtained. Now, at last, the private character of economy achieved complete recognition. Under the pressure of free competition nearly all of the industries established by the state during the earlier period were repressed and dissolved. Since the greater part of the landed estates, which had also been held by the state ever since its inception, were surrendered to private owners whose management of agricultural property showed their superiority to the state, the private constitution of economy had won a complete victory. The victory was all the more significant in that it had been won against the old-established powers of the lords of the soil, against equally strong local influences, against the state itself and all its prerogatives and means of coercion. It was won by the burghers, long politically debased, and the peasants, but recently a political nonentity. No external power, only the inner power of success, the true spirit of economy, made these conquests.

As the social economy grew larger, private disposition became much more prominent and unrestrained than in the beginnings of the locally scattered economy. This is conclusive proof that, under the historically presented conditions of the pre-capitalistic era, the private constitution was consonant with the inner nature of the economy. Under the earliest conditions, the isolated economy was the result of a compelling external circumstance, altogether distinct from the nature of economy; it was the consequence of local separation, forced upon mankind while inadequate manual skill, as well as scant capital wealth, permitted neither larger concentrated populations to find means of subsistence, nor enabled them to overcome the difficulties opposed to joint economic action by greater separation. But that men adhered to the private isolation of economy, even after they had combined to a social economy, had commenced to live close together and had learned to overcome the impediments of distance, can only be explained by the greater success which attended the private system of the social economy; greater, for example, than was possible in the narrowly secluded monastic communities or the unitary community of the state. The fact that the private isolation was not only adhered to but that private disposition, overcoming all early restrictions, gained strength and constantly increasing freedom, admits of only one interpretation. The private economic system gained constantly increasing security by the progressing social education of the individuals in technical art, morals and organizing capacity. Ultimately men were trained for freedom of action and the educative powers of coercion, long indispensable to evolution where personal interests had to be coördinated to considerations of general welfare, could at last be spared.

As its success became greater, the economy naturally also increased in social importance. In the success of the closed domestic economy, only the individual family is interested; but all at once the general interest of the state was connected with the circumstance, that the peasant provided food for the burgher and that the burgher was to enrich the state. While, formerly, economy had to be subordinate to war, to statesmanship and to cultural efforts; while the "constitution" of economy was subordinate to genealogy and the constitution of armies, to the constitution of churches and states, every one of which was more important to the preservation of society, it now unfolded in their midst and was able to display the essence of its nature.

The private economic system is the only historically tried form of a large social economic combination. The experience of thousands of years furnishes proof that, by this very system, a more successful social joint action is being secured, than by universal submission to one single command. The one will and command which, in war and for legal unity, is essential and indispensable as the connecting tie of the common forces, detracts in economic joint action from the efficacy of the agency. In the economy, though it have become social, work is always to be performed fractionally. Some part of the total labor is always to be applied to some particular goods, in order that the greatest possible utility may be realized in this segment and that the margin of use may be extended as far as possible. Part-performances of this sort will be executed far more effectively by thousands and millions of human beings, seeing with thousands and millions of eyes, exerting as many wills: they will be balanced, one against the other, far more accurately than if all these actions, like some complex mechanism, had to be guided and directed by some superior control. A central prompter of this sort could never be informed of countless possibilities, to be met with in every individual case, as regards the utmost utility to be derived from given circumstances or the best steps to be taken for future advancement and progress. In such situations, therefore, subordinate officials would have to be left to follow typical rules, rules which, naturally, obstruct ready efficiency and demand costly reconsideration, here and there. Even were greater freedom of action conferred on the individual official, he would lack sufficient interest in the matter to assume the increased responsibility incurred in departing from the beaten path and attempting new methods. The case of the private producer is different. His income depends on the yield of the venture. His vitally felt interest calls all his energies into action. The private constitution of economy is what is needed to enlist the stupendous force of egoism in the service of economy—the force which, in case of impending war, submits without demur to the command of one leader.

This egoism, which from scattered, personal beginnings has erected the structure of the national economy, is a social egoism in the true meaning of the term, which we explained in our brief outlines of social theory. It has stood the test socially, adding section after section to the labor-dividing edifice of national economy, and proving in the market for group after group of commodities its faculty to fulfil the sense of social economy more fittingly than it had been fulfilled theretofore. It was fit that society should free it legally; the individuals under its influence are sufficiently bound to social coordination of their egoism by their actual dependence, in regard to their partial processes, on the national economic process. The liberated private economy remains one with the national-economic whole. It is not the individual economy of a Crusoe but a section of the national-economic process in which the right of personal disposition is legally reserved. The egoism which guides it never ceases to be socially controlled; it remains under the ægis of law after, as it was before its recognition. Socially approved, recognized and controlled, it is appreciated by man as a social power of his freedom, fit to receive its supreme sanction in the approval of the law of the land.

Taking into consideration the great inequality between the rich and the poor, which has prevailed in the distribution of wealth at all times and even at the threshold of the capitalistic era, one can scarcely overcome a doubt whether an egoism is to be called social, which leads to a condition so unsocial. Economic principle demands that, at all times, the highest attainable satisfaction of needs should be the aim of economic efforts. Goods should never be applied to lower needs, while higher needs call for satisfaction and could be covered accordingly. But the private constitution of economy permits the rich to satisfy their luxurious needs, while the poor are scarcely able to satisfy the needs of this existence. Is this not, after all, the grossest egoism which we here find tolerated? Does not the economic constitution become the handmaid of the egoism of power in a manner to offend shamelessly the spirit of social economy?

The answer to this question cannot be deduced from the psychology of the model man, from which we deduced our assumptions in the theory of the simple economy. Law is of historical growth. It has been formed under the influence of success, as it had to be in order that living men might perform, in the most successful manner, the tasks of the economy. Were the task of economy to consist merely in distributing stores of goods, given without human coöperation, to the most needy, then indeed no other distribution could be tolerated but one guided by "the rational needs," as the well known socialistic formula prescribes. But the most important task of economy consists in acquisition. The stores of commodities are not turned over to man by nature, ready for immediate use; they have to be procured painstakingly before they can be enjoyed. And to this principal problem of acquisition the economic law, now become a fact of history, is fittingly adjusted. It is not a simple law of enjoyments to be obtained; it is a rigorous law of acquisitions to be made; it is a law shaped, as it should be, for men as they are, disposed to do their best only for themselves and their flesh and blood. When, in a scheme like this, the shares of individuals are unequally cut and allotted—very unequally, it may be—no indictment of the wisdom of the legal system can be based on that fact. It may well be that a system of rules, which distributes very unequally the enormous gains to which it is instrumental, is after all more beneficial to the mass of the citizens than another, doling out its much smaller proceeds according to "principles of right and reason."

The unequal distribution of income is to no small degree caused by inequalities of personal talent, skill and will-power. When the man who is not willing to work, is sent home empty-handed, no one will take umbrage. He is able to work; so let him work, then, if he would live. He certainly shall not be permitted to live on the efforts of others. So, too, that the less gifted, less skilful worker should gain less than the more gifted or the more skilful one, is too well founded in the laws of economic and social attribution generally to be seriously denied. Society dares not withhold the higher wage from the competent worker. To do so, is to risk losing the most valuable services. But when the strict rule declares against him also, who, without fault of his own, lost what he had and perhaps even his working-ability as well, sympathy prevails and we cannot quite approve of the rigorous discipline. So, too, the excessive incomes and riches which go far beyond moderate wealth, can no longer be sanctioned by the general conscience, when they lead to idleness and dissipation or when, more iniquitous still, they have been handed down to the present owner as wholly unearned wealth, an inheritance from earlier generations who, perhaps, themselves acquired them by wrong-doing and abuse of power. In the distribution of property and income, as it existed at the threshold of the capitalistic era, inequalities against which a sentiment of fairness revolted were to be observed in plenty. Still, taking all in all, the private constitution of the economy at that time might well have satisfied a general sense of justice. On the whole, a satisfactory state of affairs had been reached. An attempt to replace the historically settled rule by a different one, and to obtain for it the ratification of popular approval, would have proved a failure. There was no cause for an individual to feel uneasy in enjoying that which was his, where the mass of others were also satisfactorily fixed. Where sentiment was pained at the rigors of the law, he might surely extend a helping hand and mollify its severities.

At all times the private legal order has been supplemented by an extensive charitable system of philanthropy, beneficence and altruistic care for others, supported by the force of morality, religious sentiment and the dictates of the church. These charitable provisions are designed to bridge over the hiatus, felt by human sympathy to occur here and there, in the strict application of positive law, and resented as harsh and cruel, in the absence of some sort of mitigation. The system of poor-relief has, in progressive development, even been cast into legal form, though it naturally was restricted to the necessities of existence. The extreme individualists have energetically opposed the organization of charity, as tending to impair the energy of economic forces and increasing the dangers of overpopulation. Still, it is quite clear, that, whoever, out of his affluence or plenty, aids the needy, cannot be said to proceed, like the spendthrift, uneconomically. Although not demanded by the immediate interest of his own economy, his action is justified by the spirit of the social economy, from which his private economy can never be detached. In these cases, an undefined consciousness of the insufficiency of legal rules guides human conduct, the social egoism is felt to be inadequate to the occasion, too egoistical in individual instances, too little social, to prevail without supplementation from other springs of action. The legal system is not disturbed by measures of this sort; it is, if anything, supported and strengthened, whenever the gaps are properly closed, which interrupted its continuity.

The private right of the inheritance will stand or fall with the institution of private property. While private economy is held to be socially demanded, the private law of inheritance cannot be repudiated. Should all property of decedents be seized by the state, as it is for want of heirs, the state would very promptly be the owner of all the means of acquisition. This the state cannot be permitted to become, so long as its administration of the means of acquisition cannot be as efficient as that of private owners. A man's economic forethought, moreover, is greatly stimulated by the desire to leave an inheritance to his children on his demise. The economic equilibrium obtaining between the present and the future, would be greatly disturbed, should this desire be repressed by legislation. The seizure of decedents' estates in behalf of the state would sensibly diminish all savings out of income. Condemnations of the law of inheritance are an indication that the distribution of wealth does not impress the public as taking place according to principles of equity and reason. Where the distribution of wealth meets with the approval of common sense, the private law of inheritance is accepted as a matter of course.

The classical masters have clearly recognized the social significance of the private constitution of economy. It was one of their greatest achievements, when they discovered and described the interconnections between personal and social interest. They were never individualists in the sense of exalting the individual interest of the powerful above the universal interest of the people. The doctrine, that the individual interest coincides with the universal interest of society, they derived from the more simple economic conditions of their own time, idealized as these had been under their contemplation, and they had hemmed in their theory with all sorts of provisos. That their successors adhered to the doctrine, even after capitalism had become powerful, this alone, in fact, constitutes the serious error into which these writers had fallen. The doctrines of the founders of the school left to the disciples an abundance of starting-points, whence to develop and elaborate their teachings after the conditions of life had materially changed; but preoccupied with dogma, the epigones remained blind before the new facts which developed rapidly as capitalism waxed larger and larger. When the revolution had already come to the pass, when Lassalle could describe as hopeless the future of the men who had fallen victims to the brazen law of wages and could liken their fate to that of the lost souls in Dante's inferno, a man like Schultze-Delitzsch, himself full of good will, still held to the view that, even in the capitalistic era, "every man's fortune was of his own making."

§ 76. The Domination of Capitalism in Modern National Economy

Sense and non-sense of economic power—Freedom in law and freedom in fact—Proudhon's antinomy of exchange-value—Karl Marx and the doctrine of surplus value.

At the threshold of the capitalistic era the conditions, prerequisite to the private constitution of economy, had matured to an extent never known before. It seemed as though all the historically transmitted methods of tutelage and restraint on economic freedom had been needlessly imposed. The traditional education of the burghers, which was to fit them for economic coöperation, seemed completed. The problem of unity in the social economy seemed to have found its solution for all civilized nations in the gradually unfolding germs of the powers of freedom. This was the soil from which presently sprang the classical theory of freedom. It was called forth in large part by the spread of large industries for whose success complete freedom of action was required in order that they might blaze new paths by which to carry to society the fruits of the latest conquests of the technical arts. But the superiority of the large industries turned into autocracy and despotism in their uncontrolled development. In a short time the equilibrium of the private constitution of economy was so disturbed that, in wide fields of the national economy, the doctrine of freedom ceased to apply.

In our exposition of the modern economy of acquisition we have discussed the particular conditions which favor the rise of capitalistic power. Our former discussion must now be concluded; we must view as a whole the stages of formation of the capitalistic power, and follow through the problem it presents and at which we stopped in the précis of social theory.

The process of development, which immediately attracts our attention, is the same process that is met with in all fields of joint social action where the common work is sufficiently important to demand forceful leadership and the subordination of the masses, if effort is to be crowned with success. The superiority of the leadership, securing success to the masses, results in power to the leaders. This power ultimately becomes autocracy, despotism. The lament that the people are oppressed by powers whose efficacy is the gift of those who become its victims, is as old as the history of the human race. Where the masses degenerate, lasting oppression is the outcome of the process. However if the people preserve the vigor of their manhood, they will eventually throw off the yoke of their oppressors under new leadership. They will recover their liberty at the stage of development which they had attained. Then in the process of evolution the same cycle is repeated with new actors. Not a few of the undulations observed by the historian, find their explanation in the rise and fall of the supremacy of leaders and the liberation of multitudes.

The historical process of the rise of modern empires, now almost complete, exhibits in its earliest division, reaching its apex in dynastic ascendency, a process closely analogous to the growth of capitalistic supremacy and furnishes instructive insights into its relationships. We cannot more fitly usher in our examination of the capitalistic supremacy in industry and commerce, than by heralding it concisely in an exposition showing the rise of the great empires which have stood foremost among the family of nations. The second division, showing absolutism ousted by more liberal institutions, is of interest as an illustration of the collapse of a power which, so long as it was unassailed, seemed invincible. This is of interest, although the capitalistic development has not yet come near enough to the end of its career to enable either the historian or the theorist to draw comparisons as to the closing stages of the phenomenon.

The establishment of the great states was a boon. The peace which it promised met a profoundly felt need of peoples who had suffered unspeakable distress through the endless feuds of the petty kingdoms and principalities of Europe. These great empires extended the peaceful enjoyment of civil rights and a unified administration over far greater territory. And when the great states strove to introduce between themselves as well a condition of equilibrium, a balance of rights and powers less and less frequently broken in upon by wars and dissensions, there resulted increased security to person and property even beyond the borders of states. Towns and provinces submitted cheerfully to the authority of the vigorous dynasty whose leadership promised exemption from untold horrors and perils. After the first and most hazardous victories had been won and the rising dynasty had gained an ascendency over neighboring rivals, it might well rely upon the allegiance of its faithful subjects and master the more easily all remaining opponents, until the empire had been consolidated within its natural boundaries.

These advantages secured, the historical tendency toward absolutism was manifested. Thereafter, the contrast of ruler and ruled becomes prominent. Their interests diverge; but the historical power, once acquired, outlasts its justification. In the absolute ruler is united the power to dispose of the entire forces of the people. No one, however influential he may be, dares to oppose him. Whatever large schemes may be set on foot, are carried out by him, and therefore for him. Sense becomes nonsense. The absurdity comes to pass, that he may use and abuse the forces of the people to his own single advantage. He uses them, if he will, to the undoing of the people. At all times, he is able to defeat the resistance of individual groups and individual persons by the superior instruments of his power. The resistance of the entire people he need not fear, so long as the main-springs of the public mechanism are united in his hands. He may justly say of himself, "I am the state." The great states of antiquity, one and all, finally perished under the crushing power of their despots. Certain states of modern Europe seemed doomed to share their fate. But much was still sound of their active inner forces. When the occasion arose, they responded to the call and established under new leaderships the unvanquished capacity of their masses for renewed progress, so that at last the detested yoke was thrown aside and liberal constitutions were wrung from the oppressors.

As the transition to the modern empires was accomplished under dynastic leadership, so the transition to the modern mammoth industries was brought about under capitalistic leadership. It never could have been brought about in any other way. Just as conquerors by nature, like Cortez and Pizarro, were needed to establish Spanish dominion in Mexico and Peru, so economic conquistadores were needed to create the organizations of the trusts. The overnumerous majority of small and less important businessmen could not free themselves from the traditional narrow confines of their trade and industrial handicaps, however much they were threatened by the competition of their mammoth rivals. As little as their masters, did the equally endangered workmen evidence ability to call into existence large industries of coöperative unions. At first it was not the possession of capital but personal strength, which was the decisive element. Frequently the new leaders rose from small beginnings or from the strata of the laboring-classes themselves. Those men of keen insight were destined to be leaders, who discerned the superior efficacy of the large establishment and who, in conjunction with this vision, possessed the unswerving fortitude to discover the avenues to the new methods.

In its own territory, the modern large industry showed itself as much superior to the old petty workshop, as the great, modern empire was showing itself to be in comparison to the petty principalities of bygone days. For numerous problems of commercial and industrial enterprise, victory was assured to these mammoth undertakings in the competitive conflict. The ease with which economic relations may be arithmetically expressed, the distinguishing characteristic of economic activity above all other human pursuits, is the factor which allows an unmistakable numerical expression of the elements which control this success. In numerous branches of acquisition computation shows reduced costs of production for the large plant, which enable the entrepreneur on the larger scale to undersell smaller competitors and secure the demand for his own output. He can well afford to attract fellow-workers by higher wages, if they are not to be otherwise obtained; and he is also in a position to employ much cheap help, which the old trade was unable to employ for want of sufficient training.

The victims of his conquests, the competitors driven from their employments, the workingmen turned into proletarians, are at first as little taken account of as the victims on the battle-fields where the great empires offered sacrifices to their ambitions. Public opinion becomes subservient to the new master, in whose train come progress and improvement as he carries into practical execution the economic inventions of the technical arts. He is the man of the day; he himself has been instrumental in calling into being the new methods of the mammoth-industries. He may well say, "I am large-scale industry!" When workmen become rebellious, he can break down all rebellion by discharging the discontented. The market never fails to supply him new forces to replace the old ones. The number of men fit to be entrepreneurs is too small, the number of mammoth establishments is at first too limited, to think of effective competition.

Just as the success of an army is ascribed, in the first place, to its commander who revels in glory and booty, so to the successful economic leader falls the lion's share. Once more the ready accessibility of economic interconnection of affairs admits here of numerical expression of the law of distribution. The personal ascription of the success becomes specific attribution; by this method the entire newly acquired surplus yield is turned over to the entrepreneur who leads the way. And still, at this stage of the development, his extraordinarily large profits are not looked upon as prejudicial to the public; in the eyes of public opinion, they are deemed justified by the social advantage, the social significance of his leadership.

The social conditions of economic power offer to capital, in its money form, still other opportunities for growth and the acquisition of additional influence. With the abrupt leaps of modern developments and the enormous extension of the markets, money-capital is in a position to profit most effectively by its prompt mobility. The speculations of the promoters and on the Exchanges are constantly discovering new opportunities for an activity, wide in its scope and promising munificent gains in the event of success. As we have shown on an earlier page, the founder and the speculator, too, are called to perform social services of economic leadership in pursuits in which the multitudes need leadership; but we have also shown, how promoters' speculation and speculation on the Exchanges may degenerate and realize gains by deception and exploitation. Urban building-speculation is more nearly akin to the operations of founders, urban land-speculation to that on the Exchanges, where the intent is, more pronouncedly, to operate by force of capital than by achievements of leadership.

The most comprehensive opportunities for the exertion of power fall to the share of the large money-capital, when it succeeds in obtaining monopolistic control of a market. The profits which may be realized in this way are so temptingly high, that the endeavor is constantly renewed, difficult as it may be, to gain exclusive control of the extensive markets of national and world economy. Kartels and trusts, in their final development, are monopoloid institutions establishing control of the market on a foundation of the control of production. Pools and corners endeavor to operate merely by control of the market; they resemble somewhat the old-time money-usury which, today, by a superior organization of credit has been largely suppressed in the open market. They work greater mischief than usury in so far as their aim is to levy their extortions upon the entire demand; usury seeks its victims among individuals and occupations of the least power of resistance. On the other hand, it must be admitted that pools and corners do not imperil economic existence, grievously as their effects may sometimes be felt, while usury, if left ample scope, seldom fails to ruin its victims.

All gains which mammoth-capital realizes merely by control of the market without rendering services of social leadership, are justly condemned, as unearned, by public opinion. They are offences against the social spirit of economy; they displace, at the expense of the public and in favor of the capitalistic despots, the distribution of incomes and property. They do not only this, but, as soon as the newly rich capitalists come to the market with their increased purchasing power, such gains displace the distribution of natural values in favor of these latter purchasers.

Burdensome as these effects may be to society, they do not mark the climax of capitalistic supremacy. Ascendency in its fullest significance, a despotism which crushes, accrues to entrepreneur's capital, once it has become strong enough to turn the power of its historical growth against weaker competitors and the body of workers. This supremacy becomes a social evil as soon as large-scale industry has reached a point where it operates as a mass-phenomenon. Next will occur a general lowering of industrial strata, a concentration of many in a proletariat of working-people. When it comes to the worst, there is a mechanization of labor and a lasting, physical and moral degradation of the proletarian strata. At this point, we have arrived in national economy at the same social absurdity which we have met with in the despotism of dynastic usurpers; we have arrived at a national economy that destroys the economy of the people or, to say the least, of multitudes of the people, who labor as a part of the system but are none the less crushed by it.

Throughout its sphere of action, capitalistic supremacy has cut the ground from under the classical doctrine of freedom. The laborer, despoiled of his best possessions by superior forces, is no longer able to enjoy his legal rights, to exercise his legal privileges in actual life. Rodbertus spoke truly when he asserted that for these men hunger is what the scourge was to the slave. Only the strongest individuals will be able to escape unharmed; they may rise to strata of greater liberty. The vast majority, of average or inferior powers, will cease to be able to make rational use of liberty; they will be driven to appraise their needs and to effect their exchanges with the weak. In order to satisfy the gross demands of the moment, they will have to sacrifice vitality, physical health and the dignity of their manhood. Every power, even the merely personal superiority of the more gifted or the more active individual, restrains the freedom of choice for the less gifted, the less active; the stronger individual, preëmpting the more favorable opportunities, leaves the less desirable ones to his less fortunate brother. Domination, however, even though economic, abolishes once for all the freedom of the oppressed. It turns freedom into slavery and compels its victim to work his own destruction. Personal supremacy has this effect in individual cases; with the social supremacy of the capitalistic class it is a mass-effect, enforced by the compulsion which the compliance of companions exerts on crowd-instincts. Even in itself the capitalistic class experiences a certain social compulsion to despotism; the individual entrepreneur feels himself bound by the example of his companions, forced to proceed farther, perhaps, than he had meant in the path he once chose to travel. Competition compels him, if he would save himself, to squeeze more tightly the men whom he employs. In the organizations of the capitalistic entrepreneurs, the social compulsion to which this class also is subject, finds its most pronounced expression. On the part of the laboring population, competition is intensified to over-competition. Not until the workers have been taught to organize themselves, do they gain increased powers of resistance; then the feeling of solidarity unites them in organizations, exerting social powers of their own and thus enforcing universal membership and common action under unified leadership. It may possibly be that a beginning has been made here to break down the domination of the entrepreneur strata which, surely, must be vulnerable when even the absolute power of hereditary rulers can be overcome by new social movements. Initial efforts, though largely latent, are surely indicated towards a new legal constitution of the large industries, efforts starting from displacements of the actual constitution, i. e., displacements in the conditions of supply and demand; but the movement in this behalf is only preparatory. The unions have so far been successful only among groups of more highly trained and better informed workers. Capitalistic despotism still dominates wide fields of enterprise. If its effects do not seem too outrageous, society is indebted to the protective legislation of the state for this result. In the absence of such legislation the abuses would be even greater, the misery more unbearable and the restraints on freedom more oppressive than now.

The extreme partizans of the prevailing order decline to recognize the evils of the existing disproportion of economic power. They deem it sufficient to maintain that the capitalistic mammoth-industry is victorious by its superior efficiency, which assures it control of the market demand. They contend that the capitalistic power, having in this way sprung from the spirit of the economy, cannot but continue to be of permanent service to the economy.

The opponents of the existing order look upon it as nothing more than a contrivance to serve the egoistic interest of those in power. Without any enquiry whatever into the origin of the capitalistic power, they pronounce it, more often than not, an example of brute force, breaking into the fold from outer regions and foreign in every sense to the spirit of economy.

Of more deeply rooted theoretical significance are the arraignments which endeavor to deduce capitalistic exploitation from the laws of exchange-value. For men of these convictions, economic exchange-value presents an essentially irreconcilable antinomy; it is a value directed against the spirit of the social economy, and society will never be able to restore this spirit, except by replacing the private community of exchange by a superior social order.

Proudhon has shown himself a disciple of this school. He speaks, point blank, of an antinomy of the exchange-value. He reasons from the well-known experience that, certain premises assumed, the price-yield may be increased by diminishing the quantities carried to the market. We have already shown in the theory of value that from this circumstance the conclusion of a paradox of value is not logically permissible, that profit is always the controlling consideration of economy. When the seller diminishes the stock, he does so simply, because from the higher yield thus expected, he promises himself higher profit, and because the power is his to further his individual advantage at the expense of the demand. Concerning the origin of this power, which is the important thing, the doctrine of the antinomy of exchange-value makes no disclosures whatever.

Another representative of these objectors is Karl Marx in his theory of excess-value. The theory contends that the exchange-value takes its measure from the working-time devoted to and socially required for the production of an article; that, therefore, the wage must receive its measure also from the working-time which is socially necessary for producing the means of subsistence for the commodity, labor. The theory further contends that to the entrepreneur, who finds it in his power to keep the laborers at work beyond this length of time, accrues the product of their excess-labor. As we know, this argument is not conclusive, if for no other reason than simply because it takes the ground of the labor-theory which cannot be maintained for the developed conditions of national economy. But even if Marx's reasoning were conclusive in other respects, it would never explain the origin of capitalistic power. This power is alone decisive, because through it the entrepreneur controls the working-hours. Karl Marx fails to grasp the spirit of economy, not merely in his attempt to deduce it from labor only, but also in losing sight of the connection which the power of capital, admitting its origin, possesses over the spirit of economy. He chooses to veil the interconnections of the exchange-traffic in ghostly obscurity; determination of value is to him, "a social process, shunning the eye of the producers"; the law of value, a self-regulating law of nature, prevails by sheer force, "like the law of gravity, bringing the house down, on occasion, over its owner's head." He quotes Engels who harangues about a law of nature, "supported by the unconsciousness of those consciously concerned."[1] But laws of nature never guide human economy. What is attempted to be accomplished by economy, is attempted in the spirit of economy. Even the opponent of the prevailing order will have to admit that every power, growing contemporaneously with the economy, can thus grow, simply because it fulfills the intent of the economy; just as the champion of the prevailing order will have to admit that every power at the apex of its growth will be transformed into social unreason, unless opposed by forces sufficient to keep it in check.

The manner in which we have found sense and nonsense combined in economic power contains no antinomy whatever. We maintain that economic power obeys the same law as political and any other power. Society never controls its ends unconditionally; it is, itself, controlled by historical powers which arose in the process of giving birth to the social force. The process of the dissolution of traditional historical powers always requires time, until new leaders guide the masses into new paths. No one is entitled to assert that such new paths may not be discovered in the community of exchange. There is sufficient scope for new developments within the borders of the community of exchange. The community of exchange does not, of inner necessity, force upon society exploitations inimical to itself; nor will, on the other hand, the dissolution of the community of exchange relieve society from the possibilities of economic despotism. Even the socialistic state of the future will need leadership; will, by leadership, create power; and, as the outgrowth of power, there will again be despotism, under the pressure of circumstances, whenever the masses are not sufficiently strong to offer resistance to the prevailing leaders.

§ 77. The Theoretical Foundations for the Domestic Policy of the National-Economy of the Present Day

Modern policy, classical theory and modern theory—The egoism of the State—The State and the economic conformity to law.

For the inner policy of the social economy as represented by the classical theory, the foundation was presented in the proposition that a free economy of individuals, observing the limits of law and morality, would secure the maximum social utility that could be attained. If this statement is accepted as valid on principle, it becomes the momentous duty of the state to establish order and see to the protection of legal rights. Aside from these requirements, however, it can

[1] Kapital, Vol. 1., Sect. 1., Chap. 1, D. 4.

only be expected to provide those general foundations of national economy, the establishment of which surpasses the capacity of individual forces. The state should not interfere in the executive economy, especially not in acquisition, either by regulating through command or prohibition or other intervention the economic decisions of the citizens, or by engaging on its own account in acquisitive trades. In this way the demand for non-intervention of the state is deduced, altogether conclusively, from the major proposition which was the starting point of the school.

The classical theorists thought the doctrine of non-intervention applied for all succeeding periods. In the rapid development of capitalism, however, social policy found itself once more confronted by problems concerning the "general foundations of social economy," whose solution passed the "strength of individuals." The measures to be adopted against capitalistic despotism, which have become necessary by this development, give its essential character to the modern, domestic economic policy. The conflict of opinion arises primarily in connection with these measures. Only for the problem thus presented shall we endeavor to ascertain the theoretical foundations in the succeeding investigations. The theoretical foundations of the foreign policy of national economy will not occupy our attention until we reach the theory of the economy of the world. All other problems of national economic policy we refrain from considering at all.

The modern policy of national economy has decisively repudiated the doctrine of non-intervention. When it came to the great reforms in favor of the workers, which at last became imperative, it took, after considerable hesitation, its final leave from the doctrine of absolute freedom. At first the English legislation was molded on the opinion that its protection should be confined to women and children, as to whom the idealizing assumptions of the doctrine of freedom surely did not apply. But the last step was finally taken, and social protection was extended to adult males as well. The most important work, and the one which has been carried farthest in this direction, is the protective legislation for the worker, which restricts of the liberty of the labor-contract in the interest of the worker's welfare. This legislation was further supplemented by the compulsory insurance of laboring-men. Still later there even developed a policy for the protection of the middle-classes which were threatened by the capitalistic development. Of other measures, we will mention, besides the new rules of the usury-legislation, especially the standardizing regulation of stock company matters; the exchange-regulations, directed against the abuses of speculation; the beginnings of a national housing policy and urban land-reform. Where the regulation of feudal conditions of ownership has been neglected, there is also the necessity of reforming the conditions of land-ownership in rural districts. In a large number of states the modern policy has led to a state-control of the railroads, similar to the town-control of a large number of centralized monopolistic enterprises, adopted almost everywhere in the larger cities.

With the trend towards the new policy of national economy, the theoretical foundations handed down by the classicists were by no means altogether abandoned. Now as heretofore, true to the spirit of the classical doctrine and acquiescent to its arguments, the private constitution of economy is adhered to. But the theorem that private freedom guarantees the attainable maximum of social utility, is no longer regarded as sacred. In this respect, a compromise with the classical doctrine is aimed at, by declaring that its teachings are valid only under conditions of a general equality of forces. Where this equality does not prevail, complete freedom can only result in disadvantages to the weak. The state alone has a call to protect the weak. In these two sentences the state is recognized as an indispensable factor of the national-economic process.

The recognition of the state's protective duty is the most important theoretical result of modern national-economic policy. German scientific enquiry may take pride in having established it and broken the spell of the classical dogma. But much is still wanting before we may say that the theoretical foundations of the modern national-economic policy have been completely set right. If the classical theory of freedom miscarries wherever economic inequality exists, it would logically follow that the state is bound to interfere until complete equality has been established. On the other hand, the formula of the protection of the weak does not cover the entire content of modern national-economic policy. The motive leading to state-control of the railroads is not the same motive of protection and philanthropy, which prompted factory-legislation. As yet, modern economic science has not endeavored to lay down for modern policy full theoretical foundations, nor to replace the rigidly delimited classical principle of non-intervention by a new principle, as rigidly delimited. Science has confined itself to offering to social policy advice as to particulars of its tasks. Thus policy has been left to itself when it came to justifying its attitude on principle; the evil consequences of this circumstance are noticeable in the tentative irresolution as to the boundaries and instruments permitted to state policy.

This reticence on the part of science may be explained from the theoretical skepticism which seized economic thinkers when, placed before the problems of modern national-economic policy, they found themselves reminded of the classical theory. A notable performance of scientific acumen, the classical theory accomplished what was required for its period. Accomplishing this, it performed a most important mission, for the problems which were there presented were of the highest importance. But modern problems are of a different sort, and the theory of the classicists will no longer dispose of them. The classical labor-theory does not go to the root of the economic interconnections sufficiently to explain the meaning of a developed national economy. It does not enable us to refute the socialistic criticism of the prevailing order; it has, on the contrary, supplied the most important arguments of that criticism. The classical theory of freedom, above all, results in a vindication of capitalistic domination. Anticipating somewhat our investigation, we will add that the classical doctrine of international free trade is equally little consonant with the interests which a modern foreign economic policy of the continental states is bound to protect.

The new theoretical endeavors which, in contrast with the classical labor-theory, seek to find an exact scientific expression for the old conception of the utility-theory have, so far, not been bent on establishing relations to practical policy. It is therefore not to be wondered at, if the latter does not expect much encouragement from that quarter. The modern theory of utility in common with the classical theory holds to the method of idealizing simplification and, precisely like the classical labor-theory, it sets out with the most abstract assumptions. Like the latter, it refers its first, most general enquiries to the individual, without mentioning the social interconnections and the state. Throughout, it appears as though this theory, in common with the classical theory, must have its absolute principle of freedom as well. In fact, however, this is by no means the case. On the contrary, there is an essential distinction, not only between the economic motives from which the two theories start, but between the scientific ends which they pursue, as well. Using the same forms of abstraction, they follow in their journey entirely different paths.

It was a proximate, practical application to the particular problems of their day, which the classicists were anxious to establish. They were in quest of liberty, freedom; and the most stringent, theoretical proofs were to support their theory of freedom. Thus they stopped at the motive of labor, as the simplest economic motive offered to the thinker, when he contrasts man and nature in the most primitive relations of economy. From these simplest assumptions, as starting-points, they demanded freedom for their ideal householder, as the condition of a signal success.

The modern theory of utility, on the other hand, arose aside from the problems of national-economic policy, as the outgrowth of the mere need, the urgency of scientific quest. It aspires to be an empirical theory, pure and simple, not aiming at any definite, practical application. It employs the method of idealizing simplification, because it considers this method the indispensable instrument for deducing from the varied wealth of phenomena the most general, typical nature of economy. If, in the first place, it assumes an isolated individual, the intention is not by any means to stop short at this assumption; there is always a readiness to expand the assumptions by decreasing abstraction to any state of facts, however complicated, presented in history or existing in actuality. If it has really succeeded in formulating its earliest simple assumptions so as to disclose by their means the approaches to the nucleus of the spirit of the economy, it should succeed in tracing from this foundation all the actual forms. By correspondingly expanding its assumptions, it should supply for every condition the theoretical expression. With this intention, we have tried, after first describing the conditions at the dawn of the capitalistic era and leading to its free economic constitution, to explain the rise of capitalistic despotism by introducing into our assumptions the facts of the large industries and supplementing it by a theory of economic society which, in place of the idealized individual of highest efficacy thrown entirely upon his own resources, sets up the reality of leaders and the masses. Even if we ourselves should not have succeeded in finding the precise theoretical expression for the conditions of the capitalistic domination, there can be no doubt that this aim may be attained from the basis of the utility-theory. Nor can there be any doubt that, once this expression has been found, a sound modern economic policy will find in such a completed utility theory the fundamental substructure which it requires. For a sound modern economic policy, the safeguarding of the highest possible social benefit in the face of the capitalistic despotism must be the paramount law. A completed theory of utility will be able to demonstrate to that policy under what conditions the law will meet with compliance, under what conditions it will miscarry.

We will conclude our investigation by summing up, with the utmost brevity, the theoretical axioms which may be deduced from it as fundamental for the tasks of a modern policy of national economy. Possibly we may be entitled to hope that we have made some things clearer than they were before. Certain problems, however, it must be admitted, still call for solution in our statements, and unfortunately, they are the very problems to which the keenest theoretical interest attaches, whence the tensions are the most severe, the movements most energetic.

First: The national economy, freed by the state, is not yet, by virtue of this fact alone, free. Not only is it guided by forces to which it submits voluntarily, but it is susceptible also to the formation of those compelling powers which arise, in joint social action, from the relation of leader and led. In the capitalistic era, the economy is controlled by capitalistic compelling forces which disfigure the social spirit of the economy from which they arose. If the state succeeds in protecting the economy from capitalistic interferences, the state's action is in harmony with the social spirit of economy.

Second: In the entire field of national economy, except for the large industries, the private constitution of the economy maintains, everything considered, the success which it has historically achieved. In this field its position has not been shaken by the capitalistic power; here the latter has not become a crushing despotism. A change of the common, economic, legal order is therefore not in the spirit of the social economy, no matter how much it may offend universal ideas of right and wrong. In so far as, at any one point of this field, capitalistic influence, by its control of the large capital, may unsocially displace the distribution of property, of income and the satisfaction of needs, the state, by opposing this influence, places itself among the defenders of social economy. What means may be instrumental to the state's efforts in this respect, can only be ascertained by accurate investigation of the relevant facts, an undertaking in which the theoretical description of typical conditions and processes is to be supplemented by painstaking observation of the peculiarities of each individual case. In no small measure, the profits of the mammoth capital are unearned winnings, obtained without efforts of leadership. Where this assumption is found to be realized in fact, the state may, without fear of harmful results, take energetic measures against the capitalists. We have identified, as cases of this sort, the formation of rural ground-rents for the large landed estates, urban rents raised by the increase of the population, as well as abuses in founding stock-companies and in speculating on the exchanges.

Third: In large-scale industry, capitalistic power is greatly augmented, and not infrequently it verges on a crushing despotism. The labor organizations, however much they accomplish, do not by any means form a complete instrument of defense. On the other hand personal leadership is indispensable just in these enterprises, and thus under any circumstances, the private constitution is to be maintained here too. Only under quite definite circumstances, to be met with in comparatively few enterprises, will the state or municipality be able, in place of private enterprise, to institute management by officials successfully. A mere charitable system caring in its way for the victims of capitalistic despotism, will be inadequate; the constitution of the large industries will have to be transformed by law. What, so far, has been accomplished in this direction, consists in the main in the reform-work of the workers' protective legislation and the social insurance, which restrict the private constitution as regards the contract of labor by certain prohibitions and by compulsory insurance. This reform-legislation, in its present status, probably does not exhaust the possibilities of social reform. Indications are not lacking, which suggest the methods according to which a new constitution of the large industries might be formulated, a constitution following the middle course between the despotism of the all-powerful entrepreneur and socialistic demands, in a manner resembling the attitude observed in a constitutional monarchy between absolutism and republicanism. It cannot, however, be expected of a theoretical exposition, resting solely upon data of the known, to go in quest of further possibilities.

Fourth: Of the existing organizations, some serve the purpose to intensify the capitalistic despotic powers by increased social influence. The organizations of the laboring-men are, according to the present state of affairs, for the greater part destined to resist capitalistic power. They are, to this extent, active as powers of freedom, although naturally not without some sort of restraint on conflicting interests of larger groups of workers. The organizations of the capitalistic leadership serve partly the more adequate, social regulation of acquisition. In so far, they are also effective as powers of freedom. In other respects, it must be admitted, they are often subservient at the same time to the organization of despotic powers. The individualistic view is bound to condemn all organizations which do not present themselves as organizations purely of freedom. Modern policy is more discriminating. Subject to certain safe-guards, it permits coalitions and peaceful organizations to proceed, while yet it is inimical to capitalistic monopoly-organizations and already, here and there, interferes by more energetic means. The distinction observed by policy agrees with the view hitherto taken by theory. But practical observance and theoretical insight are, so far, still equally undecided in their attitude; and naturally so, for the growth and development of organizations has only commenced, and our experience as to their activity is still narrowly bounded. Similarly, experience is still exceedingly limited as to the means at our disposal to effectively combat the organizations and the powers which stand behind them.

Fifth: Despite the need of many restrictions and much supplementary activity, the private organization of the economy is in the main also recognized as socially active in the capitalistic era. Similarly the private exchange-value appraisal is, now as heretofore, recognized as the appropriate valuation in the national economic process. The valuations departing from this rule, which the state adopts in its restricting and supplementing measures, call for particular, theoretical investigation. This we shall enter upon in connection with our description of the process of public economy.

That the state, as the historically evolved organ of the common power, is bound to take whatever measures may be at its disposal for the protection of the common interest against the despotic powers of capitalism, requires no further proof. It need only be emphasized, that besides the impulses which the spirit of justice supplies in this direction, strong impulses proceed from state's egoism as well, i. e., from the impulse of self-preservation and the development of power, which are active in every sound body politic and are experienced, as by the people themselves, especially by those persons and strata who, as the wielders of the power of the state, are most strongly interested. Just as personal egoism, through the conflict of competition, is exalted into social egoism, and enlisted in the service of public interest, thus the egoism of the ruling political parties is, by the conflicts constantly waged between states, exalted into public spirited egoism, and made to serve the general interest of the people. In the struggle for freeing the peasants, the dynastic interest was an essential, active agent. For the sake of strengthening the power of the state, a sound peasantry had to be preserved, able to provide soldiers and pay taxes. As in the feudal state the public egoism turned against the power of the feudal lords in favor of the suppressed peasants, so to-day, in the modern state of social classes, it turns against capitalistic power, in order to accomplish the undertaking of the liberation of the workers.

Among the considerations which the liberal school advances in opposition to state-intervention, a leading argument has been that the state, after all, can achieve nothing in opposition to the largest private interest by whom its ordinances would always be eluded. It has become a favorite diversion to declaim about natural economic laws, which operate by an inner necessity and in the consummation of which the state cannot interfere. In our day, this argument is scarcely to be taken seriously. Of the many examples which we now possess concerning the success of state-intervention, we will mention only the one, confirmed by the testimony of Karl Marx,[1] who assures us that the English factory-legislation has led to the physical and moral regeneration of the factory-operatives. As there are forces of nature, unconquerably stronger than any hu-

[1] Kapital, Buch. I, vol. 8, chap. 6.

man efforts and technical means to subdue them, so, surely there are also social economic powers of uncontrollable vigor. But, for the rest, it is precisely the uniformity of events which, in the economic universe as in external nature, establishes the opportunity for successful interference not only of the producer, who pursues his individual interest, but more especially of the state, bound to safeguard the general interest. Practical experience, aided by theoretical enquiry in regard to the broad interconnections, impenetrable to practical insight, will always disclose the suitable points of application and appropriate means, at which, and by which, the state should take its measures, whenever it becomes desirable to modify the free, unimpeded course of the economic process by proper means in the spirit of the tenets of social economy.

BOOK III

THEORY OF THE STATE-ECONOMY

Meyer, Prinzipien der gerechten Besteuerung, 1884; Sax, *Grundelgung der theor. Staatswirtschaft*, 1887; and, *Die Progressivsteuer*, Z. f. V., vol. I; Pierson. *Grond beginselen der Staatshuishoudkunde*, 2nd ed., 1886; and, *Leerbock der Staatshuishoudkunde*, 1890; Cohen Stuart, *Bijdrage tot de theorie der progressieve inkomsten belasting*, 1889; Wieser, *Der natürliche Wert*, 1889; Edgeworth, *The Pure Theory of Taxation*, Econ. Journal, vol. VII; Mannstädt, *Finanzbedarf und Wirtschaftsleben*, 1922; Pigou, *Economics of Welfare*, 1920; Lindahl, *Der Gerechtigkeit der Besteuerung*, 1918; see in this connection, *Lehrbuch der Finanzwissenschaft* by Lotz (1917), Földes (1920), and Eheberg (19th ed. 1922).

In the "Theory of the State Economy" it will not be necessary for us to concern ourselves with the duties devolving upon the state within the limits of the social economy. So far as these problems are susceptible to theoretical exposition, we have discussed them in the preceding part of this book. Here we shall describe exclusively those characteristics by which the economy of the state is to be distinguished from private economy. To some extent the classicists neglected these problems. Their object was to eliminate the state as much as possible from the social economy. Nevertheless, the theory of the revenues and expenditures of the state necessarily affords an opportunity to explain the special forms of public economy in the narrow field here indicated. But even in this respect, their investigations were not searching. The advocates of protective tariffs later found it necessary to turn in the pursuit of other inquiries to an examination of the theory of state economy. Friederich List actually did so. Even stronger inducements have existed for the modern economists who turn over to the state tasks of much enlarged scope. But little has been accomplished so far to advance the theory of state economy. Most that is brought forward develops in the exposition of public finance. Finally, a more modern theoretical tendency has sprung from the theory of taxation. The bibliography, which precedes this section, mentions only the foremost treatises of the latter group. Beyond these, we confine ourselves merely to mentioning the systematic presentation of the science of public finance, laying particular stress on the name of A. Wagner. [See also his *Grundlegung*, and his article *Staat* in the *Handwörterbuch der Staatswissenschaft*.]

§ 78. The Public Economic Process

Collective expenditures and their classification—Public economy, an economy of expenditures—The nature of the receipts in the public economy.

The economy of the state is often popularly characterized as the "state's housekeeping." By this term we apply to the whole of the public economy a manner of thought derived from a single part of the private economy. In the same way, nearly all scientific attempts to explain the nature of the public economy start from a method of observation which reduces the phenomena to the familiar ideas of private economy. In the classical theory, the economic relation of the state to its citizens was regarded as that of an exchange in which taxes are paid as a remuneration for administrative services. Modern theories look upon the activities of the state as a special sort of production, an immaterial kind, which is aided by impalpable capital funds to call into being the intangible products of peace and legal security.

Such views only serve to obscure the nature of the public economy. Essentially it is not to be distinguished in concept from the private economy. Both have an identical basis and pursue the same end; both serve the purpose of turning to the greatest possible usefulness the commodities that are found in the economic quantitative relation. But the state in its economy has unique means of power placed at its disposal. It is therefore faced with unique tasks and travels its own peculiar course. The types of public economic income of which the science of finance treats are entirely unknown to private economy and are in no way related either to exchange or to production. The supposition that a tax is in the nature of a payment for immaterial products is in no way suited to become the basis of a theory of taxation, for the principles observed in levying taxes have nothing in common with the law of price.

There are different economic processes for the state, for communities and for other self-administrative bodies. The municipalities in their management are more nearly akin to private economy but they are too dependent on the particular forms which self-administration takes in the various states to be adequately described in a general theoretical exposition. However, we may not evade the duty of describing the typical state economy. If this is not done, no theory of social economy is complete nor could it supply the necessary theoretical bases for the science of finance and the administrative policy [1] toward the social economy.

The most instructive view of the structure of the public economy is obtained by starting with the expenditures of the state. Every activity of the state, whatever its kind, is accompanied by expenditure. In these disbursements, the entire system of state activity receives its economic expression. In surveying the expenditures of the state, economic theory will bear in mind its special object, and will not follow a division by administrative branches but rather an economic

[1] Volkswirtschaftspolitik.

principle of classification. We propose to classify state expenses under two principal heads. In the first group we bring together the outlays most nearly akin to the private economy. These are the costs incurred for services which the state performs separately for individual people, in the same or nearly the same manner as characterizes private exchange. These are therefore services for which the state is entitled to demand a price, or, at any rate an individual counter-performance. We shall refer to these expenditures as those which are personally distinguishable or, briefly, as personal outlays. They are to be distinguished from the other groups of inseparable, collectively incurred expenses.

The state incurs personal outlays in its purely private economic enterprises. They arise in the same manner in the conduct of the postal service, the railroads and all other public undertakings maintained as a matter of administrative policy. In all these cases the state enters into an exchange with the parties receiving the service. They pay a price covering the state's expenses just as they would to a private entrepreneur. It makes no difference to our present purpose that the state may at times adjust the payments required for such public services by methods that are at variance with those which a private entrepreneur would follow in seeking a price-advantage. Even when this happens, the process initiated by the state does not differ essentially from the private economic process. Therefore we do not need to go into its details.

The state also incurs personal outlays for numerous administrative functions, including those of the law, when the costs are incurred for performances that the state undertakes at the instance of an individual and in his particular interest, or that are called for by the culpable conduct of an individual. Such expenditures the state properly charges directly to the interested or culpable party by fees that are intended to cover official expenses wholly or in part. A ready illustration is found in a civil process the court costs of which must be borne by the unsuccessful party. The litigants and judge do not meet as "parties to a market"; they do not effect an exchange. The fees therefore are not a price. They have only one characteristic in common with prices: they are for a performance rendered to an individual and necessitating individual chargeable costs. Although fees well merit explicit discussion in a systematic presentation of the science of finance, they are of no importance to our general theoretical problem. We shall not consider them further. All other administrative expenditures induced by individuals but not recovered in fees, we include under collective expenditures.

In the following remarks we confine our attention exclusively to collective expenditures. These alone prepare us for the public economic process on which our theoretical interest centers. They may themselves be divided in three subgroups according to the degree in which they approximate the nature of private economic expenditures. The first is comprised of the expenses of economic administration. These are costs incurred for the protection and the advancement of the private economy, more particularly the economy of acquisition. In the broadest sense they would include the costs of colonial or other wars entered upon for the sake of the national economy. They are made with the same aim as private acquisitive outlays and their effect is to be observed in the amount of the private yields which they are intended to assure or increase. The method followed in the private and public outlays does differ somewhat. The state itself does not in this case produce goods. It merely renders assistance to their production by preparing the foundation through its administrative activity. The state leaves it to private effort to make a proper use of the institutions or conditions which it establishes. Those national economic administrative expenditures particularly benefit the moneyed class which draws the largest gains.

The second subgroup of collective expenditures are for domestic administration. Here again the administration of the law is to be included. Into this category fall the costs for the care of the poor and for the public welfare in general. Equally to be included are the expenses for social reforms that are not intended primarily to increase the social income but to improve the conditions of life for the masses.

Finally the third subdivision embraces expenditures for the needs of the state in the narrowest sense: for its preservation, the maintenance of domestic and foreign power and authority, the protection of prestige, the expenses of the representatives of public power and of the military establishment. In general this class includes expenses for "state necessities" that are often contrasted with the interests of the people in that the power and splendor of the state becomes an end in itself whereas in truth it may be justified only as it is indispensable to and serves the welfare of the people.

Collective expenditures are collective in that they employ common means under unified direction for services that accrue to individuals indiscriminately. They are not so much collective in the sense that they serve collective needs, properly speaking. In the main the economy of the state caters to general or wide-spread individual needs, the same ones it should be noted to which private economies cater, starting with the need of food and other physical means of subsistence up to the highest cultured needs, intellectual, æsthetic or moral. These needs are served by the private economies in that the latter make possible their direct economic satisfaction or by means of production or acquisition provide the economic agencies of their satisfaction. Public economy serves these needs by such accompanying and controlling activity on the part of the state as is required to protect social and economic life from dangers and to advance its well-being by acts that are beyond the power of individuals. The individual protects himself against minor dangers; several persons may jointly agree to stand together. For example, by insurance the harmful after-effects of loss may be neutralized. In the same way that insuring a dwelling does not satisfy a special "need of insurance" but arises from the same personal need that originally demanded the possession of a house, the activity of the great protective association of the state is directed, not to a special collective need of protection, but to the same needs of life that are met by economic goods in the possession of individuals.

Even the expenditures for the narrower needs of the state do not meets the needs of the state, as such, but the personal needs of its citizens. When one speaks of the requirements to the existence of the state, it is in the more general sense of the word need, a meaning from which at the beginning of our study we distinguished the narrower economic concept of need. The so-called subsistence needs of the state are not like those of the individual directed to the consumption of means of satisfaction. They do not strive for satiety and are therefore not subject to Gossen's law. They are such as the "need" to possess and wield power or to possess and enjoy liberty. Their goal is the independence of the citizens in every one of the acts which the state performs for the satisfaction of physical or intellectual needs.

From this exposition it follows that the character of the economy of the state differs from that of the private household or of private acquisition. It differs from that of the household in that in all essentials it is directed not to the immediate satisfaction of needs, but to the protection and advancement of these satisfactions. From acquisitive economy, especially production, it is distinguished by the fact that of itself it does not bring forth productive yields. It is true that in the economic administration of the state there are created certain material values, such as streets and highways, whose technical preparation and control of use are similar to those of products turned out in private production. But it must not be overlooked that also with these values, because they are dedicated to a public use, it is not intended that they shall bring forth direct gains for the state but that they shall manifest their virtue in furthering yields in the private economics. The products that are thus turned out by private agencies are not in any technical sense also products of the governmental administration. There is a marked cesura between national economic administration and production that is indicated by distinct methods of valuation that are followed in the two.

The remaining activity of the state, directed to the establishment or protection of moral values, is even more sharply and significantly separated from private economic production. It is only metaphorically that one may speak of it as immaterial production. Only figuratively can one refer to peace, legal security and other valuable conditions of life, in whose shaping and protection the state is instrumental, as immaterial products. Strictly this is no more allowable than to speak of a statesman or military leader as a producer. The means placed at their disposal, the corps of officials and the armies, are not controllable material values like the material goods of which the producer disposes, nor is it possible technically to separate effective value and inherent value as in productive labor. The conduct of war, the dispensation of justice and the administration of law are just as much preparatory to future national life as they are part of the present.

The closest analogy to the process of state economy in the forms of private economy is to be found in that of an association in the interest of whose members a common enterprise is undertaken and common expenses are incurred. Like such an association the state economy is essentially an economy of common expenditures. As such the state economy is closely akin to the private household and to this extent the designation of the state's housekeeping which is popularly used, is well chosen. Neither the state nor the association provides from its own economy an income to meet expenses; both are expenditure-economies and are confined to the collection of dues or contributions from their members who meet the assessments from their private incomes.

The state does not have an independent income. The contributions of its citizens constitute a special form of derived income. Owing to its sovereign power, the state can provide for the compulsory collection of the contributions for which it calls; but it cannot make arbitrary use of these sovereign rights any more than in any other field. In the model economic state that we presuppose in theoretical enquiry, there is an economic apportionment among its citizens of the compulsory contributions. Their assessment is an important function in the state's economic process. We shall have to discuss it in some detail and show how it should be done in order to conform to the economic principle.

§ 79. Value in the Economy of the State

The state's computation of exchange-value—Use-value in the state economy—The state's appraisal of social interests—Partial value and total value—List's theory of productive forces.

The state is guided like any other entrepreneur in its purely private economic undertakings entirely by value in exchange. It would be an error to make calculations on any other basis than that adopted by any private owner governed by rational economic principle. If the conditions of the worker are bad, the state should surely be the first to set an example of reform by improving conditions in its industries, just as the enlightened absolutist governments set the first example in improving conditions of life for the peasantry on the state domain. In acting as a private entrepreneur the state should also bear in mind its duties as state and avoid increasing its revenues by means which as the state it must condemn and oppose. Thus the exchange-value computation of the state is illumined by a ray of purer social valuation.

Public enterprises like the postal service and railroads are acquisitive undertakings conducted by the state for administrative considerations. Therefore they may suitably be referred to as administrative enterprises. They have become administrative institutions without losing their character as enterprises. In these undertakings too the accounts are kept on a basis of exchange-value but they must be interpreted in the light of administrative interest. The immediate purpose of retaining public control is to prevent monopolistic exploitation by private capital. Unless other considerations arise, the state is not called upon to depart from the exchange-value computation; the service and prices should be such as would result from a well regulated competition.

Frequently these administrative enterprises are operated with other than the directly obvious aims. For example, the postal service carries the mail of the state gratuitously. It frequently happens that even the public is not charged a price that returns the customary net earnings; the charges may actually result in an undisguised loss. In such cases the intention is to increase production and trade. Such an adjustment of rates may be made even when the desired increase of the social income will not result for many years. Finally it is observed a rate of this sort is maintained for certain groups or localities even when it becomes obvious that the districts affected can never be stimulated to an increased remunerative traffic. The first of these conditions is of no theoretical importance. The last two are treated in the succeeding exposition of national economic administration.

At this point we shall consider only services rendered at a permanent loss. Examples are found in a city railway that establishes reduced rates, that leave no profit to the railway, for workers who travel in the early morning hours; in an additional service above that following from the general postal rate, that is established for a remote district with stagnating traffic and results in loss. In these cases the exchange-value computation is affected by a social valuation that is foreign to the market place. The price in the market is a compound of need and ability to pay. The private entrepreneur who supplies the market never provides for the need as such; he caters exclusively to the effective demand. But the administrative enterprises under consideration undertake to serve a need which may lack adequate power to pay. They do so because the need to be served is sufficiently important to be cared for under any circumstances. They do not calculate by exchange-value but by the use-value which a unified economic society would follow according to the laws of the simple economy.

In contrast with the administrative undertaking,[1] the national economic administration [1] does not calculate by exchange-value. It is not adjusted to gains. Excepting fees and other income from interested parties, it offers its services gratuitously. A street that produces no yield has no exchange-yield value. Not being intended for sale, it has no exchange-value either. It possesses public economic use-value by virtue of its service in the national economic process. To be sure this public economic use-value is supported by the private value that inheres in the road for those who use it. Roads and all other instruments of the national administration would be without value to the public economy if they were not suited for use and were devoid of personal value for everybody. In the main the national economic administration must be adjusted to result in the highest possible net monetary earnings for the private economics. It would

[1] Trans. note: The contrast is between *Unternehmung* and *Verwaltung*, between the conduct of a business by government and the determination of the framework in which all business functions.

be entirely inconsistent for a state that accepts the private constitution of the economy as sound to reject the valuations that its citizens set by the standard of market prices.

It is only exceptionally that the state in the common interest, in order to support its judgments of value, takes active measures to supplement or rectify private economic exchange-values. As is the case with the state enterprise, the state in its economic administration seeks especially to serve those needs that are deserving of consideration but are not supported by an adequate purchasing power. When a state places an embargo on the export of grain after a crop failure, its decision is not governed by considerations of exchange-value but wholly by those of the use-value in the simple economy. This use-value is determined by the principles of the public economy on the basis of the need as such without regard to recompense. The state in such a case sets the needs of the poorer citizens, who cannot compete with greater buying power of foreigners, above the profits that might be realized in exchange by the producers, exporters and transportation companies.

This use-value of the state economy in its administration makes in common with private economic exchange-value the presupposition to which we referred in the theory of the simple economy as the universal hypothesis of economy, i. e., that the economy is carried on by separable quantities of goods and labor. The use-value of the public economy is a partial value whose standard is derived from the partial utility of the last available unit.

In numerous fields outside of economic administration, however, this partial utility does not serve the purposes of the state. This is true whenever the public economic process is of a sort to forbid the assumption of partial disposition. Such is the case when the forces of the community are to be enlisted as a whole and the total effects appraised. This cannot be done, as it is for a yield of commodities, by a summation of partial values. Even in the national economic administration, although on the whole it is adjusted to partial-value computation, there are exceptions. Thus in determining whether a state shall become industrial or agricultural it is not sufficient to estimate the yields that may be expected from greater industrial or agricultural effort. It is also necessary to consider the effect of each system on the composition of the population, its health, the military resources of the state and other like interests of great importance. The marginal law is not respected in these cases; valuations are established beside which the derived partial value measured from the marginal use is small. The primary interests of society dictate the point of view; the sum total of the public interests is evaluated, in whose behalf the common force is to be exerted.

For the individual goods and labors that are used in the interest of the public the computation by partial value is not discarded by following this rule. The weapons and all other munitions, stores of foodstuffs collected for the eventuality of war, buildings and ships are paid for individually at the marginal value. Similarly army officers and state officials are paid at a rate following in the main the marginal law of the market. The almost parsimonious care to which the war office is held because of its enormous aggregate expenditures, restrains it in individual cases strictly to the law of marginal value. But by the side of the appraisals and extending beyond them is one of the military interests of the state as a whole. This is imperative. It starts with the effect which a display of military power may have on the sovereignty of the state. The pecuniary sacrifices that its citizens are supposed to bear for purposes of public defense derive their standard from this total valuation. In view of this, compulsory military service is imposed on all citizens capable of bearing arms, while the people are burdened with other oppressive obligations that must be assumed in the event of war. If universal military service were wrongfully taken advantage of for dynastic wars, it would be an intolerable drain upon the forces of a people, far more iniquitous than the worst exploitation by entrepreneurs. Confined to national defense, it rests upon a social valuation of the state's interest that attaches such importance to military service, that the state imposes it on all its citizens. This is done despite the fact that the men are thus barred from peaceful occupations. It is the latter which are most highly appraised on the market basis of exchange-value.

The greatest divergence of social valuation by the state and private exchange-value is in regard to the personal appraisal of workers. The entrepreneur looks upon wage-labor as nothing more nor less than an instrument of realizing expected profits. Economically he regards the worker as merely a party supplying wage labor. The entrepreneur pays him nothing more than the marginal value of his labor. However, the state would not be justified to content itself with a valuation which actually implies that the worker is nothing more than a tool to the realization of pecuniary gains. The state cannot consent to any interpretation by which a fellow worker in social production is at an unsocial disadvantage when the yields are distributed. The state must bear in mind the dignity which clothes the laborer as a man and as a member of human society with all the claims of man upon this life. It does not follow from these premises that the state will wish to subvert society and the civil code and to make war upon a distribution of yield which follows the valuations of the market. Nevertheless the state will feel it a duty to provide as far as may lie in its power the public means of protecting the life values of the laboring class. It will couple with this the further aim of seeing that the workers are qualified to bring into action forces that promise appropriate rewards for their labors.

There has been but little inquiry into the theory of public economic value. The most important effort along this line was probably made by Friederich List in his "Theory of Productive Forces" which he opposes to the "Theory of Value" of the English school.[1] In this theory List intended merely to present the theoretical foundations of his national protective policy. But the form in which he states it is general; it is a universal theory of public economic value which he develops to suit his particular purpose. According to List the state does not calculate by private exchange values like an entrepreneur. Its sole aim is the development of national protective forces. The sacrifices which the state incurs primarily in exchange value will later bring bountiful rewards. The state should proceed precisely as does a father who ensures the welfare of his sons to better purpose by defraying costs of education to prepare them as well as may be for their tasks rather than by setting them to practical work at the earliest possible moment and turning their work to account in the market. The very illustration which List uses in an attempt to show the contrast between exchange value and productive forces furnishes the proof that there is no contrast. The father who has his sons educated in the most approved manner in order that they may later earn higher incomes calculates on the basis of an exchange value deduced from the productive forces expected at a later day. Every entrepreneur calculates in precisely this manner when he makes up his mind to operate at a loss for a longer or a shorter period. In this respect there is no essential difference between the computation of the entrepreneur and that of the state. There is only this difference: the state can hold out for a longer period than even the richest entrepreneur would be willing or able to do. List's terminology is justified only in so far as the periods of time covered by the entrepreneur are of such short duration that the exchange values which are expected later may be ascertained with considerable certainty in advance. In this respect the position of the state is quite different. A policy of protective tariffs must be made for extended periods. In this interval a thorough-going development of productive forces is expected. These changes are so large and the period so long that there is no way to make an accurate determination of the future values involved. For the present there is no other feasible procedure than to appraise the productive forces as such. It is a form of public economic use-value which List describes. It is a use-value of productive forces that evolve over long periods and for which the complimentary agents that are necessary to their fruition are lacking. Those points at which the contrast between exchange value and public economic use-value really lie concealed. List has not touched upon at all.

[1] The National System Of Political Economy, 7th ed., 1883, chap. XII.

§ 80. The Economic Principle in State Economy

The inaccessibility of computations of public economic use-value and of the valuations of state interests—The economic plan of the State and the marginal law—Economic theory and the theory of taxation.

To the extent to which the state computes by exchange value in its private and administrative enterprises, it is obviously guided strictly by the economic principle like any other entrepreneur. The highest net yield is sought. This may be ascertained by a numerical comparison of the costs incurred and the utility secured. However, it is perfectly evident that there is no violation of economic principle if the state in these enterprises, rather than reckon by exchange value, in exceptional cases considers the simple social use-value. In every such instance the state would arrive at its decision with a view to that result which under the given conditions it regards as the highest possible.

From this reasoning it follows that the state in its national economic administration obeys the economic principle even when it does not calculate directly by exchange value but by public economic use-value. The latter also leads to the maximum utility. However, the indirect productivity of administrative institutions does not lend itself so readily or exactly to verification as does the direct productivity of a private enterprise after the regular working routine of the latter has once been entered upon. A manufactured article is the fully controlled resultant of productive means. It is quite feasible to calculate the precise gains to be expected from products for which certain costs have been incurred. The indirect advancement of industry which is anticipated from an administrative institution can never be foreseen with equal certainty; the private initiative of free entrepreneurs is an imponderable, though it may be the decisive factor in the problem. When the opportunities offered by the administration are taken advantage of on a long and broad scale the results may be great. But it is quite within the range of possibilities that though the administration has done its best, the results lag behind and are meagre because private initiative fails to take advantage of the opportunities offered.

If one follows this train of thought from the national economic administration into the broader fields of the state's activity that is animated by its estimation of the general social interest, it is evident that here also the economic principle as such maintains its validity. But its obedience to mathematical rule and expression is wholly lost. The state determines the numerical expression only for the partial values which it acquires at market prices: costs for the services of employees and purchases of supplies. These may be entered item by item in official budgets and final accountings; but against these costs, no figure can ever be set for the total value of the effects of the state's administration, no figure which shall serve as a spur to its efforts and set the ultimate limit for the amount of its disbursements. Who would seek to give arithmetical expression to the "benefits" of a victorious war and to equate these numerically against its costs and other sacrifices! And yet when the existence of the state is endangered, national consciousness will sound a call to war. The intensity-values of the interests to be protected are carefully appraised. Definite decisions are arrived at as soon as public opinion had agreed upon its verdict in the appraisal or sentiments. But throughout this process, numerical expressions for those things which are intensely felt cannot be found, are not sought and are considered of minor importance. Under other conditions to be sure the conflict of opinion regarding political decisions arises largely from an uncertainty as to their consequences when numerical data are lacking.

In any event the state's economic plan should be in harmony with the economic principle; less important interests should be kept in the background while the most vital ones allowed by the available means are assured. The more abundant these means are, the larger will be the amounts brought forward from the common force and the greater the effects anticipated. The richer state can offer its citizens greater military protection; the poorer one must be content with a more modest military display. To this extent the plan of state economy even where it is determined by aggregate valuations is controlled precisely like the economy which computes according to partial value and desires to extend the margin of use as far as possible.

When scheduling the plan for the state's expenditures, it is of particular importance that the state is bound to act as a protective association. The amount of its expenditures to meet this duty must therefore always depend upon the nature, degree and imminence of the danger against which it is to protect the people. A rushing torrent requires more extensive precautionary measures than a quiet pool. During a period in which the great nations are pushing their armaments to the extreme and national passions and jealousies are inflamed it is not safe for any state unduly to curtail its military outlays. The poorer state will not set a standard of its military preparation only to accord with its economic power. It must also consider the general state of preparedness. Even a state whose wealth is declining may feel compelled in times of danger to increase its military budget.

Such conditions give rise to the much invoked rule that whereas in private economies expenditures have to be adjusted to the available income, in the case of the state income must be adjusted to expenses. As it is formulated, however, the rule has too broad a meaning. In its expenditures as well the state must be guided by the revenues which a dutiful observance of economic margins permits it to secure from the incomes of its citizens. These problems we shall presently discuss more fully. However, it is true that the state more frequently than the private citizens is under the necessity of suddenly and substantially increasing its necessary expenditures. The reason for doing so is to be found in the uniqueness of the economic task that faces the state. The principal problem of the private economy is the economic approval or disapproval of the needs to be satisfied and the acquisition of the required means. By its partial satisfactions and labors it is possible for this economy to adjust itself with a certain fluidity to the point indicated by Gossen's Law of Satiety through the marginal utility. But, as has just been shown, in so far as the public economy is serving the ends of a protective association, it is bound to accept the measure of its expenditures for the greater part from facts which are beyond its control. The increasing imminence of war may suddenly endanger national life and all its values for which, under the quiet conditions of peace, no consideration or foresight was necessary.

Among other limitations that always bind the state in its tax policy is the condition of the private economies on which the state levies its compulsory contributions. Were all the citizens equally well to do, theory might be satisfied after it had established the simple rule that the rate of taxation is to be so determined as to create a single margin of use for the economy of the state and of the citizens. It would not be permissible for the state to lay claim for public purposes to means which might be used by private individuals to greater advantage, and vice versa. However, the inequalities of wealth are so great that this rule is inadequate to obtain an economic standard for the apportionment of the burdens of taxation among individuals. It is not part of the task of a general economic theory to seek the complete solution of this principal problem of the theory of taxation. On the other hand our treatment of economic theory would not be exhaustive if it failed to set forth at least the general theoretical foundations required by the theory of taxation in the solution of the problem.

The two foremost principles of the equitable assessment of taxes, universality and uniformity, follow directly from the social value of the state. Its character would be destroyed if the state departed from the rule that all its members are to be held to contribute for common purposes. Similarly it would be abolished were they to be so held according to an unequal standard. The problem of the theory of taxation consists in showing how the principle of uniformity is to be carried into effect in individual cases. In the development of the subject, the views of thinkers have undergone changes. The classical doctrine held that contributions should be graded according to the amount of the income. They should, as Adam Smith [1] says, be proportionate to the income which the citizens enjoy under the protection of the state. It is assumed that the performances of the administration will manifest themselves for all citizens in an increase of their personal income. This assumption may possibly conform to fact as regards the national economic administration, but it does not by any means do so for all remaining state activities.

Modern doctrine has departed from this early rule. It demands an incidence of taxation based on personal ability, a capacity which is measured either in the ability to pay or in the magnitude of the sacrifice which the individual suffers in paying the tax. The present advanced point of view regards the payment of a tax levied upon a subsistence income as so oppressive that it should not be demanded under any circumstances. Assessments are considered unjust that make no allowance for the number of children in a family and other like circumstances that condition needs. Higher taxation for funded and for unfunded income is insisted upon as well as progressive taxation of higher incomes. It is possible that these doctrines go too far in what they advocate, that at least the expenditure for economic administration should be covered as the earlier theory held strictly according to the amount of the income. However, it is not within our province at this time to enter into detailed inquiries of this sort. From the point of view of general economic theory we must offer a different kind of objection. We fail to discover among the criteria to which the modern doctrine appeals the firm foundations of economic theory. Neither the ability to render services,[2] tax-paying ability nor the sacrifice involved are well settled concepts of economic theory. Therefore, so long as the theory of taxation supports its demands by invoking these criteria only, it lacks connection with the general body of economic theory.

The concept of subjective value, personal value as we called it, supplies the missing link for which we search. Each of the qualities which are here grouped together, ability to serve, to pay and sacrifice are fundamentally instances of the personal determination of value. The number of children and all other factors that determine needs are clearly to be recognized as moments of needs in the same way that the amount and the funding of income are moments of the distribution of income and property in the money economy. In the case of subsistence incomes the condition is measured by the standards of the needs of existence. Where progressive taxation is demanded the higher level of the income is compared with the decreasing intensity of the needs as shown by Gossen's Law of Satiety and the marginal law. The ultimate basis for any progressive rate of taxation is to be found in the general scale of desires. According to this basis the personal value of the money unit is appreciably higher for the first thousand than for the second and is hardly to be compared with the appraisal in the case of the 99th or 100th thousand. Furthermore, the difference between the first and second thousand is appreciably greater than that between the 99th and 100th. Thus, all tendencies of the modern policy of taxation find a firm theoretical basis in the concept and laws of economic value.

[1] Wealth of Nations, Book V., Chap. II., 2 part 1.

[2] Leistungsfähigkeit.

It is not the function of the state in any of its administrative branches to interfere with the private constitution of the economy. This is an historically tested social institution which the state is bound to accept. This holds also in the administration of taxes. The state should never so use its prerogative of taxation as to eliminate existing inequalities of income and property; but in determining the contributions to be demanded of its citizens it should take into consideration the gradations of personal value that are the expression of inequalities of income and property. The plan of the state's management would offend economic principle were the private economies which are being assessed to be treated as units of equal wealth.

A consideration of personal valuation in the assessment of taxes and progressive taxation in particular has its prototype in a phenomenon of commercial exchange that was discussed in the case of a monopoly of supply in connection with the doctrine of joint costs. It was seen that a monopolistic classification of the demand, popularly felt as exploitation, may at times be the only available method of sufficiently increasing the yield of a socially required enterprise to ensure its continued operation. Special reference was made to experiences in connection with the operation of railroads and canals. Had it not been for the rule to charge what the traffic will bear, many extensive enterprises could not have been carried through. A progressive tax is the application of the principle to the whole administration of the state. Precisely as the railroad tariff classifies both travellers and merchandise in order to realize the large revenues that are required for the financial obligations of the road, just so a progressive rate classifies tax payers in order to assess each according to his tax-paying ability. It has become recognized that each must pay taxes according to the margin allowed by his circumstances, if the public economic process is to be maintained. A progressive tax-rate and a consideration of personal wealth in a system of taxation are therefore logical applications to public economy of experiences practically tested in private economies. The heavy burdens falling upon financially weaker households, owing to the increased demands of modern public economy, can only be relieved by a policy that continuously undertakes so to assess the compulsory contributions of citizens that the more wealthy are taxed correspondingly higher. By such a distribution of taxes a public economy may obtain the widest possible extension of its boundaries without violating in any particular the limits drawn for private economy.

Up to a certain point the modern state thus approaches the socially equalizing use-value computation of the simple economy. But it does this without offence to the spirit of the private constitution of the economy itself, for it refrains from interfering with private property as such and the historically transmitted inequality of its distribution. Modern policies of taxation do not seek to rectify the existing distribution of wealth. They are intended to do no more than adjust the incidence of the burden of taxation in accord with the distribution of wealth, so that the margin of use by the state economy may be extended through the larger contributions of those citizens whose incomes allow them a broader margin of use in their private economies.

BOOK IV

THEORY OF THE WORLD-ECONOMY

§ 81. The World Economy

The unity of national economy—Obstacles to equalization in world economy.

Wagner, *Grundlegung.*—Dietzel, *Theoretische Sozialökonomik*, 1895.—Calwer, *Einführung in die Weltwirtschaft*, 1906.—Harms, *Volkswirtschaft und Weltwirtschaft*, 1912.—Lexis, Art. *Handel*, Schönberg Handbuch II.—Sartorius von Waltershausen, *Das volkswirtschaftliche System der Kapitalanlage im Auslande*, 1907.—Helfferich, *Geld*, 2. ed. 1910.—Knapp, *Staatliche Theorie des Geldes*, 1905.—Wieser, *Der Geldwert und seine Veränderungen*, Sch. d. V. f. Soz., vol. 132.—Hertzka, *Wesen des Geldes*, 1887.—Bastable, *Theory of International Trade*, 4. ed., 1903.—Hobson, *International Trade*, 1904.—Schüller, *Schutzzoll und Freihandel*, 1905.—Fellmeth, *Zur Lehre von der internationalen Zahlungsbilanz*, 1877.—Petritsch, *Die Theorie von der sog. günstigen und ungünstigen Zahlungsbilanz*, 1902.—A. Weber, *Standortslehre und Handelspolitik*, Archiv, vol. 32.—Furlan, *Die Standortsprobleme in der Volks- und Weltwirtschaftslehre*, Weltwirtsch. Archiv, 1913.—Harms, *Wesen und Begriff der Weltwirtschaft*, Weltwirtsch. Archiv, Bd. 13.—Wiedenfeld, Art. *Weltwirtschaft*, W. d. V. Dietzel, *Weltwirtschaft und Volkswirtschaft*, 1900.—A. Weber, *Ueber den Standort der Industrien*, 2. ed. 1922.—v. Mayr, *Volkswirtschaft, Weltwirtschaft und Kriegswirtschaft*, 1915.—Schultze, *Die Zerrüttung der Weltwirtschaft*, 2. ed. 1923.—Oppenheimer, *Weltwirtschaft und Nationalwirtschaft*, 1915.—Földes, *Zur Theorie vom intern. Handel*, Jahrb. f. N., Bd. 49.—Zollinger, *Die Bilanz der intern. Wertübertragungen*, 1914.—Goschen, *Theorie der auswärtigen Wechselkurse*, 1915—Herzfelder, *Die volkswirtschaftliche Bilanz und eine neue Theorie der Wechselkurse*, 1919.—Cassel, *Das Geldproblem der Welt*, I 1921, II 1922.—Pesl, *Das Dumping*, 1921.—Marshall, *Money, Credit and Commerce*, 1923.

The highest unifying agency in the national economy is the state. It guards the social legal order, protects common interests against conflicting private interests and manages public finances. The unity of the state's economic leadership and administration rests in a feeling of community or kinship, a sentiment which is more powerful than the contrast of personal interests, strongly as the latter may make itself felt. This unity is supported by an apprehension of political homogeneity, uniting the entire people by the strong bonds of an historical force to which they submit without knowing that they are bound. In states of homogeneous nationality, it is fortified by a national consciousness. But at the same time it is sustained by the experience of the people that leads to a recognition of the value of economic unity and the solidarity of interests, factors that have contributed in calling forth an economic feeling of statehood which becomes imbued with the power of an historical force.

The fact of unity finds its clearest expression, in the image of the social economy as already presented, at the heart of the capital city. A more thorough-going examination shows the marks of unity in all the numerous zones into which this image may be resolved. Their arrangement obeys a historico-geographical law of localization. In all the zones, notwithstanding the great diversities occasioned by the nature of the soil, changes of occupation, and the rich articulation and stratification of the people, there are the same types of men. In all places the same types of large entrepreneur, burgher, peasant and worker are found. Anyone changing the location of his acquisitive activity feels at home in the new place. It is not merely that he is still a citizen of the state. Economically he feels himself among his fellows; he finds the same types of companions, the same composition of upper and lower classes. Thus it happens that a tendency to equalization operates almost unimpeded throughout the entire national economy. Economic concepts, products, capital and human beings of all strata pass between all points. As they move, they disseminate uniformly the effect of progress or of retrogression.

In world economy there is no supreme political agency. Political power influences world economy only through treaties in which the contracting parties unify their sovereign wills. Even as between small groups of sovereign states few matters have been thus regulated by treaty. In this regard the respective governments follow the prevailing currents of popular sentiment. As between nations a harmony of interests is too little felt, while antagonistic contrasts of motives separate groups all the more sharply. To prepare a state administration of world economy by a system of treaties is historically not timely; indeed it is as little so as would be an attempt at a political unification of the world by all-embracing treaties of alliance.

The configuration of world economy shows the lack of unity in the fact that there is no capital city of world economy. Similarly there is no thorough-going localization of acquisitive centers from the point of view of world economy. The international division of labor has lagged behind the national one. For a long time after a national community of acquisition had been developed in the more advanced states, the exchanges between countries were confined to "parting with the superfluous in order to gain the indispensable." Whatever domestic products existed in excess of an effective domestic demand were surrendered for foreign products that could be used but were of a variety that could not be turned out at home.

The international division of labor has now passed far beyond these beginnings. All countries have adjusted themselves extensively to foreign needs and foreign products. A country like England has long been able to feed that large part of its population, whose incomes are derived by industrial production for export, only by importations of food-stuffs from distant lands and widely scattered parts of the globe. The collapse of foreign intercourse would inflict on such countries a catastrophe unparalleled in history. Even on less developed nations a crisis in the economic relations of the world would lead to serious disturbances. But taking all in all the domestic economic relations are far the more important; the aggregate incomes derived from domestic commerce are much the greater.

The difference between the two economies is not merely a matter of the amount of the commerce. There exists a difference in their essential nature. Each national economy is a unit bound together by the powers of historical growth. The world economy is not a unit. Within it the most diverse types of national economy confront each other. They are widely separated by race, talents and historical background. Even civilized nations of the same race feel their historical and national diversity as such. Within one nation there are great classes that stand in opposition to one another. But there is yet room to hope for an amicable adjustment of their relations and that the tragedy of an economic civil war may be spared to humanity. It is only infrequently that mankind witnesses what may be called an economic civil war. On the other hand the economic wars between nations have crowded many of the last centuries and are still present as striking examples of the incomparably more violent contrasts which cleave asunder the economics of different nations.

If we follow further into the details of the picture of the world economy, we shall look in vain for uniform social types. The typical entrepreneur, burgher, peasant and worker are different in the different countries. Just as hostility arises from national sentiment, so international conciliation is obstructed by the diversity of the typical nature of the individuals. These differences least affect the flow of products. They restrict the flow of capital somewhat more. The greatest barrier is to the migration of men and the passage of ideas.

The national economy is not tied into the world economy in the same manner as are the economic zones into the national economy. Every national economy is a unit composed of coördinate zones. In the world economy, however, the national economies are the most important; they are the great units of social economy and are themselves but slightly connected by international trade and an international community of acquisition. The economic condition of the world is to be described as a juxtaposition of unified national economies, interconnected by trade relations only to a certain extent. The national economy on the other hand, even if it is not a single economy of the entire people, has uniformity and cohesion for all individual economies that are connected in trade. This is so quite irrespective of the homogeneity induced by a single state economy and by the single representation of the common interests by the state, as well as by the unity of the dominating historical powers. This cohesion rests upon the unity of the market, of price-formation and exchange-value which offers a single base for the establishment of a social acquisition whose divisions are connected and whose localization has unity. Even in this restricted sense world economy is not a unit. And because it is not, many things happen differently from the way they occur in the national economy, starting with the formation of prices and running into the structure of international acquisition.

We have drawn an ideal picture of an extensive, unified, national economy that is actually not realized anywhere in its pure form. Owing to the historical conditions of its rise, there are irregularities of development in every national economy. Many have foreign sprinklings in the body of the people. A nationally mixed state of such comparatively late rise as Austria-Hungary, entirely disregarding the newly acquired district of Bosnia-Herzegovina,[1] is far removed from the ideal type of the unified national economy. Austria-Hungary even lacks complete state unification in economic management as each of the two halves of the state follows its own course. But the various parts are further separated by contrasts of education and wealth, thus greatly impeding economic freedom of movement within the country.

There is an intermediate type of relationship between the colonies and the mother country. They are not fused into one national economy with the mother-country. Still the relationship is greater than that which arises from the continuity of world economy alone. Moreover, it is necessary to distinguish two types: plantation colonies and white colonies. The plantation colonies are subordinate to the mother-country which combines, along with military and political superiority, advantages of race, civilization and wealth. The greater power of the mother-country may easily lead to abuse and economic exploitation; but under equitable adjustments the relation is of advantage to either side. The migrations of men are confined to members of the leading classes of the mother-country. Climatic conditions bar mass migrations outward; a counter-migration from the colonies faces a series of obstacles. The passage of ideas is limited by contrasts of racial characteristics. These exist despite the unity of the central government because both state and colony are controlled by widely disparate historical influences and face each other like strange worlds. The white colonies are less dependent politically on the mother-country as soon as they have somewhat gathered strength and self-reliance. There is also less

[1] Trans. note: It will of course be realized that this was written before the war. The change of tense would not affect the theory. Austria-Hungary doesn't exist and Bosnia-Herzegovina has been taken away!

economic dependence, though the colony may lag behind for a long time in its development. Such colonies are frequently the objectives of mass migration from the mother-country. The common nationality binds together the economic interests of state and colony; but it is possible for a conflict of economic interest to develop to the point of hostility.

Today the United States of America and a number of other colonial settlements on virgin soil are the termini of the great migratory highways by which the surplus population of Europe seeks new homes. These goals of emigration are subject to special conditions so that the general rule is suspended and the migration to them meets less obstruction than do changes of domicile within the national economy itself.

In commercial speech the unity of the national economy is too strongly emphasized. The customary statement that "England" or "Germany" buys or sells is misleading. England or Germany, as a whole, does not buy or sell. It is the individuals of the English or German national economy who buy or sell. At all times their personal motives, their personal appraisals are as important to international trade as they are in domestic trade, although it must not be forgotten that one of the factors controlling their actions is the historical power of economic national consciousness. This force like all others the classical doctrine has wholly neglected in its individualistic striving. This theory looks beyond the boundaries of the national economy. In the theory of free-trade it fuses the national economies into a cosmopolitan world economy. The historical conditioning of national economies, the task of national economy and the individualistic bias of the classical doctrine were not fully understood until Friedrich List demonstrated them in his principal work already cited.

§ 82. The International Formation of Prices

Price-formation between localities in the national economy—Obstacles to the equalization of costs in world economy.

There are a number of local partial markets in every national economy. Prices are by no means the same in all of them. The localization of industry under the division of labor always exerts its influence. The prices of wares differ between points of origin and the market by an amount that in the long run equals the costs of transportation and commercial handling. Generally the price of food is highest in the capital. Because of the large demand there, the provisioning of the city requires the maximum transportation with resulting high price, unless the international imports that seek this secure and capacious market tend to keep prices lower. The lowest prices for food-stuffs are found in the most remote areas supplying the capital and exposed to the largest transportation and handling costs. In the intermediate zones the prices advance by the differences of these costs. The smaller urban markets that are within the sphere of the central district suffer from the influence of the great demand of the center which enhances prices, while their own demand contributes to maintain the price. Neither in the prices of products nor of cost-productive-means can greater differences be maintained for any length of time than those justified by costs of transportation and commercial handling. Wages are adjusted to the local prices of the means of subsistence of the masses. All large departures from the normal are adjusted in every instance by shipments and migrations.

In each individual case the actual conditions will depart more or less from these idealized conditions. We have outlined our illustrations with this extreme precision in order that the contrast to conditions of world economy may be seen.

In international trade the distances to be covered are greater and the costs of transportation are usually higher, despite the lower rates on water-borne freight. Here and there prices are artificially increased by the imposition of duties. More important, though, than these facts that lead to a quantitative difference in prices, is a qualitative difference in the relations of national and world economy. The local zones of national economy are partial markets of the great national economic market. But the national districts are not partial markets of a world market; they are principal markets, independent of each other for the most part and only connected with world commerce at certain points. There are particular goods for which a true world market exists and for which world-market prices, properly speaking, may be said to exist. There are a variety of wares that have conquered a limited international market and whose price is internationally determined. But there is no all-embracing world market; there are not even market districts that unite limited groups of national economies. Therefore, in world economy as a whole and also in the international trade of narrower districts, there are lacking strong tendencies to equalization.

Even before a national community of markets and production had been evolved, the economy of men of the same nationality had always possessed a certain pervading type. In the districts inhabited by fellow nationals men of the same type could be found, experiencing the same needs, and exhibiting the same vital and practical energy in similar social organizations. These people, despite the fact that mutual exchange may have been restricted, assimilated the ideas of the period and developed them further in identical ways. In these cases the seeds of new growth fell upon similar soils. The same manner of life and labor resulted in approximately the same basic prices for the most important material and personal values.

The relations of one nation to another are essentially different from those just described. It is not necessary that the homes of the people differ by contrasts of geographical position and climate nor that their historical development be separated by long periods of time. They themselves may not be separated by racial disparity. And yet by other habits of domestic economy the consumer's demand operates from different bases; different composition of the population or varying levels of civilization differently condition acquisition. Even the external aspect of the markets may be distinct; the natural values dealt in may not be the same and the fundamental prices from which historical evolution progresses may lie widely apart.

When in the course of time diminished costs of transportation permit an expansion of exports, the majority of the products as they have been shaped for consumption are too closely adapted to domestic requirements to be readily accepted in foreign countries. A large proportion of the productive materials are permanently barred from shipment by low specific values that do not cover costs of transportation. Aside from agricultural staples there remain for export mainly the more valuable capital goods demanded everywhere, as for example, metallic productive materials, used in manufactures throughout the world. Not until production is highly developed does it adapt itself to the manufacture of foreign forms of goods for export. Even today the sum of the material values made available for export, which cannot be transformed in domestic use, is only a rather trifling part of the entire production. Even the shipment of money capital and the migration of wage laborers meet so many obstructions that wages and the rates of interest on capital are by no means internationally equalized. This fact itself has the further result that there is no decisive equalization of rates of cost.

In the lending of money capital through mercantile credits or for permanent investment costs of transportation do not enter as a practical consideration. But since capitalists must be careful of the security of their loans, it may be readily understood that the supply is conservative whenever the business practices of foreign countries are unfamiliar or the means of legal aid are not conveniently accessible. The rates of interest for investment capital vary strikingly as between nations of different wealth; they are by no means equalized even between the richest European nations between which there is an active commerce.

When even the supply of liquid money capital so haltingly follows the tendency to international equalization, the hesitancy of the body of workers to follow this tendency is all the more easily understood. The emigrant laborer is compelled to change not only his habits of life and his home associations; he must also adapt himself to foreign methods of working that are not those to which he has been accustomed. Therefore, neglecting those countries in which migration plays an important part and also certain customary seasonal migrations and some particular branches of trade, the international exchange of workers is exceedingly limited. Every national economy possesses its own nationally characteristic labor which in the process of its evolution it develops further. The character of the English and the Russian worker differs radically in the racial predispositions of the two nationalities. Their diversity is still further accentuated by the unlike tendencies of the national economic education inherent in the conditions of production and the general political and social environment. All those factors which influence the rate of wages: the minimum of existence, the standard of living, the productivity of labor and organization vary from nation to nation. It is inconceivable, therefore, that wages of labor should not be differently adjusted in various countries. Even the stream of emigration to the United States could never reduce to one level European and American wages.

Not even the entrepreneurs are sufficiently mobile as a group to spread themselves out uniformly over the world. The majority of entrepreneurs prefer—neglecting the relations of the mother country to her colonies—to send their products to foreign countries rather than to settle there themselves.

§ 83. Exchange-Value and Current Values of Money in International Trade

Local variations of the value of money—National exchange-value of money and the quantity theory.

The facts which have just led us to our conclusion as to the formation of prices in different localities find their expression in variations in the value of money in these places. In the financial centers price determinations converge for all values found in the market and the exchange value of money reflects their aggregate position. When the exchange value of money is high, the general price level is low and vice versa. Zones of low price level in the national economy are zones of high money value. The same is true of national economies when considered as units in the world economy. The local variations of money value within the national boundaries are measured approximately by the costs of transportation and the commercial handling of wares. But the international gradations of money value are even more numerous because the international differences of the price levels exceed even the costs of transportation and handling. The local variations within the national economy have a regular structure. In similar zones the money value is approximately the same; it is highest in the agricultural areas, and decreases towards the denser industrial populations in the urban centers. It drops in proportion as the prices of principal necessities of life are increased by the expenses of carriage. The international gradations of the value of money are not equally regular. It may safely be contended that the national money value recedes as the national wealth advances. As the natural economies are progressively absorbed and the influence of the law of diminishing returns from the soil sets in, the general price level rises. Besides these factors, however, the national exchange value of money is everywhere historically conditioned. It may be influenced primarily by the evolution of the institution of money, by conditions in the production of precious metals, or by the after-effects of more or less frequent and lasting manipulations of paper money.

The differences in the value of money between the zones of the national economy cannot be equalized. They decrease as the costs of transportation diminish but they never disappear altogether unless we assent to the utopian assumption that some day commerce and traffic will be carried on free of costs to the beneficiaries. It must be admitted that the lower rural prices from time to time invite equalizing movements. Certain industrial establishments are transferred from the city to the country in order to profit by the lower wages of labor. The large cities seek to relieve the increasing pressure of population by transferring hospitals, schools and other similar institutions to the country where their domestic economy is more cheaply managed. For like reasons even various individuals living on fixed incomes and not tied to definite places of acquisition make their homes in rural sections unless they are restrained by the social attractions of large cities. But under present conditions these movements are not sufficient to lead to a complete equalization in the density of settlement and wholly to disintegrate the urban centres. On the contrary, the movement toward the cities is becoming more pronounced and their increasing population necessitates ever-increasing supplies for their provisioning, with increased costs of transportation and larger variations of the price level and the value of money. To the extent to which there is a movement back to the country that increases the density of population, even there the price level rises and the value of money falls. The basis for the computation of the urban price level is thereby raised without doing away with the gradations as such.

It is no more possible to equalize international differences in the value of money, in so far as these are due to the costs of transportation and handling. But over and above this fact, these gradations are supported by the historical powers that impede international movements of equalization. While these obstacles continue, the corresponding variations of national money values must continue. Only when the hindrances are no longer felt that today bar an international equalization of the rates of interest and wages and when all other barriers to the tendencies toward equalization of prices disappear, will the deviations of national exchange-values be reduced to the standard given in the costs of transportation and handling. However, this is a condition that one cannot expect to find realized until the national economies shall dissolve and become zones in a unified world economy. This condition will not be realized until a world citizenship has effaced all national contrasts of race and culture and political rivalry is lost in a unified republic of the world.

The classical quantity theory, in contrast with this view, holds that the value of money is automatically equalized between nations. Like any other commodity, money is said to tend constantly towards the centers of highest value, flowing thither from the sections of lower value.

Two serious errors invalidate this doctrine. Both arise from the fact that the method of idealizing simplification has been carried to an extreme. For one thing the contrast between wares and money has been obliterated. In every instance wares are the objects of exchange, money its medium. The movement of the latter is ancillary to that of the former. When the principal movement is limited because there are not sufficient quantities of wares, the auxiliary flow is correspondingly small. It is obviously on this account that the higher money value of rural sections does not induce an equalizing movement of money from the cities: there are not enough goods in such regions for which the money may be exchanged.

The second error of the doctrine is that it neglects the historical obstacles to which individuals are constantly subjected in the national economy. When it is said that money and wares tend towards the centers of highest value, the assumption is made that men are free of any kind of hindrance and execute all productive and commercial transactions that conditions allow. But all people are under the spell of social historical powers. When these influences work as "free" powers, they intensify personal forces. But they also act as coercive powers and tend to narrow the field of personal activity. In even the most favorable case long periods are necessary before the mass of the population overcomes the obstacles to the movement of products and money. It is even more difficult to break down the barriers to the migration of men and to a qualitative and quantitative equalization of culture.

The quantity theory, moreover, requires important supplementation. It treats exclusively of the exchange-value of money. But in international payments still another form of the value of money makes its appearance, i. e., the rate of exchange. Fluctuations in the rate of exchange furthermore give rise to speculative transactions that entail considerable international movements of money and are quite similar to speculation induced by fluctuating quotations on the Exchanges. Similarly extensive movements arise to profit by differences in the rates of interest on commercial paper in the great money markets. For both purposes considerable sums of money are held in readiness by brokers, speculators and dealers in precious metals, sums which are available much more promptly for international transfer than would be possible by the round-about method of producing and shipping wares. These capital movements have attained particular importance in the settlement of international balances; to them the leading banks of issue refer their discount policy. We shall confine ourselves to the most general remarks concerning rates of exchange and the theory of rates on commercial paper. The details cannot be explained by mere theoretical instruments and are not considered here. Our primary interest attaches to the fundamental conditions under which the settlement of international balances takes place. Here is a problem deserving the most serious consideration and soluble only by the aid of theory.

Domestic money is money only in the country of issue. In foreign countries it is merchandise and cannot be used to make money payments. Those who must make such payments abroad must first turn their domestic money into foreign money. On the money exchanges the various national currencies are traded one against the other. There we also find that other means of payment are exchanged especially foreign bills of exchange or drafts which have the advantage that they are more cheaply transported than cash. The international exchange value of money is expressed in its current price on the Exchange or in the rate of exchange of the foreign drafts. It is a special variety of exchange value; it is the value in terms of the rate of exchange which domestic money bears to foreign. The rates of exchange of commercial paper and of foreign values generally obey the general law of prices. They follow the conditions of supply and demand as indicated at the time being by the international balance. In the case of dealings in bills and drafts, we have to conceive of the supply and demand as graduated according to the urgency of the need of the foreign means of payment. As for any other price the marginal series is decisive. For countries on a paper standard or under present conditions for countries on a silver standard with restricted coinage, the fluctuations of the rates of exchange according to the balance of payments may be wide, more especially when speculation enters into the transactions and evaluates the expectations of a future adjustment of the standard. For countries on a gold standard the regular fluctuations are narrowly limited, due to the influence of coinage for private account. The currencies of these countries are related. They are connected by the homogeneity of the monetary material. The coins of each of these countries can be transformed into those of any other by incurring the moderate costs of shipment and recoinage. Like any other price in a free market the rate for drafts and acceptances is subject to the law of costs. Fluctuations of these rates, therefore, can never appreciably exceed the standard indicated by these costs so long as the private right of coinage may be practically exercised.

Fluctuations in the rate of international exchange are strongly felt in the national economies affected. As in the case of domestic payments, so here the community should, at least for short periods of time, feel reasonably certain of the effect which may be anticipated on later paying out a sum of money that is received. Governments evaluate the stability of international money value so highly that they occasionally accept considerable sacrifices in order to steady the rates of currencies which are not, like those of the gold standard, more firmly secured by their material homogeneity. Even the less marked fluctuations which are unavoidable in the case of currencies related by the gold standard become a source of annoyance to persons who are held to payments in foreign money which they must purchase above par.

The fluctuations of the money market become more distressing than usual whenever the demand for foreign means of payment grows so large that domestic gold reserves have to be resorted to in order to cover the demand. The most accessible means of covering the shortage is recourse to the gold reserves of the banks of issue which are open to universal demand in pursuance of their duty of redeeming notes. But according to the banking law these reserves are the basis for the emission of notes, and consequently for the entire credit structure of the country. These banks, therefore, are under the necessity of most careful guarding their gold reserves. To accomplish this they raise the rate of discount whenever the withdrawal of gold becomes excessive. They thus not only restrain all demands for credit, but invite back to the domestic market all those capital funds of which we have previously spoken that are ready for international loans. The Austro-Hungarian Bank holds ready for call a large amount of foreign gold-drafts to meet the demand for foreign means of payment without reducing its gold reserve. Both expedients have been shown in practice to be suited to their end, but it is obvious that either way, even with the support which the government can lend for the protection of the domestic money market, the measures of relief are rather limited. Neither bank nor central government can provide means sufficiently large to satisfy a persistent demand for foreign payments. These expedients can bring relief only on the assumption that the funds are demanded for only a comparatively short period, and that even under this condition the amounts are not excessively large. Reliance must be placed on the belief that after some reasonable time a counter movement will set in which will restore the equilibrium of supply and demand in the international money market. Furthermore, one must trust that even during the period of disturbance the equilibrium will not be too severely upset.

Are such equalizing counter-flows actually effective and how are they induced? This problem must now occupy our attention.

§ 84. The Equalization of the International Balance of Payments and the Movements of the Trade Balance

The starting point of the doctrine of free-trade, credit and debit balance of trade—International balance of payments; favorable and unfavorable balance of payments—Creditor-countries, debtor-countries.

The classical school has taken its position on the problem just stated in its theory of free-trade. The large interests of foreign trade aroused economic thought at an early date. The economic policy of the great rulers and statesmen of the mercantilistic era and the mercantilist doctrine accompanying this policy were what the classicists first considered. In their polemics directed under the leadership of

Adam Smith against the mercantilists, the theory of international trade ranks foremost. Economic science is indebted for a number of its most important discoveries to the keen investigations carried on by the classical school, in an attempt to establish their theory of freedom also for international trade. The mercantilists had contended that commercial policy should strive to increase the money wealth of the country. To this end it was necessary to bring about a surplus in the value of its exports when contrasted with imports. The arguments by which the classicists met this view were chiefly instrumental in broadening the scientific structure of economic theory. But by this very exposition, it may be shown that the classical doctrine did not penetrate to the roots of economic theory. As has already been pointed out in an earlier connection, so here, it is undeniable that the classical masters failed to carry their individualism to its final consequences, and that they did not lay bare the ultimate individual bases for economic theory.

They contend that a permanent excess of exports over imports is impossible. In international trade "goods must finally be paid for in goods"; no country can continually pay for its imports in money excepting only those countries which mine gold and silver and in which, therefore, gold and silver are practically wares. Even for short periods of time, no country can entirely divest itself of its money wealth. Where too much money has passed out to other countries, a rise in the value of money would necessarily induce a return flow. This would establish the equilibrium of the international distribution of money as the export of goods from the country with lower prices to those with higher ones would be increased until the equilibration resulted.

These deductions assume that the major portion of international payment takes its rise in the exchange of goods. If we speak of the sum of imported and exported values of wares as the commercial balance, and of the sum of payments received and made as the international balance of payments, the condition assumed is such that the international balance of payments is primarily composed of those payments which are made for the values of the commercial balance. Such an assumption, however, does not do justice to the present facts. In international trade large sums of money are now paid to meet obligations of an entirely different nature. In the traffic in goods, not only are the price payments for the values of the wares themselves to be considered, but allowance must also be made for those which arise from their transportation between countries. The related movements also in the commercial credit transactions are important items of the international balance of payments. Moreover, capital is loaned internationally for investment; from this there is a return flow of interest and sums repaid. International travel and the homeward transportation of emigrants bring large sums into circulation. As between the mother country and her colonies there is to be added the pension of officials who performed their services in the colonies but retired to the mother country. Occasionally the international balance of payments is increased by extraordinary payments: war-subsidies, tributes, and reparations. Especially the last items may set enormous sums in motion. It may well be that a "country"—meaning by country all the inhabitants who take an active part in foreign trade—covers a large proportion of its imports not by exports but from other sources of the balance of payments without being obliged to send out money. The affluent countries, England, France and Germany, have for some time shown a large debit balance of trade with excesses of imports which have been liquidated by these countries from other surpluses. As things are, we can have no doubt that if England, France, and Germany permanently maintain their position as wealthy nations they will constantly show a debit balance of trade. The classical argument no longer applies in the original form of its statement. In the more comprehensive balance of payments today, "goods are no longer paid for exclusively in goods."

This is by no means the only objection to the classical doctrine of international equalization. It is far more unsatisfactory in that it fails to throw light on the manner in which the credit and debit items of the international balance of payments are connected and adjusted. Even though the movements of wares in foreign trade were wholly to be interpreted in the exchange value of money, all appeal to this value would be of no use in supplying the motives for the transfers of capital, the payments of interest, the homeward transportation of emigrants, or the movements of money in connection with international travel. How is one to explain the mutual balance of all these multifarious payments, coming from thousands and thousands of individuals between whom there is no personal contact? We can understand how international receipts and expenditures of money may balance each other, when a relatively poor state places orders for its military requirements with foreign industrialists, and provides the means of doing so by contracting a foreign loan; or when bankers lend capital for foreign enterprises on condition that correspondingly large industrial orders be placed with their domestic clients. But how are we to imagine a balancing of accounts where items appear which have as little connection as the savings that Austro-Hungarian miners send home from America and the interest that the Austro-Hungarian government pays to its creditors in France and Germany? There is surely no superior jurisdiction here, through which the equilibrium might be restored. In what way is there a mediation between the determinations of such large numbers of independent individuals so as to insure beyond any reasonable doubt the preservation of an equilibrium? Or is it conceivable that the international balance of payments is in constant danger of collapse; is it merely accidental that an equilibrium is maintained?

In the face of doubts of this sort the classical exposition leaves us hopelessly adrift. More than this, it is misleading. It proves to be one of these half-truths of genius which established the fame of the classicists and at the same time are their weakness. These semi-verities offer insights that are seductive in their unparalleled simplicity but are subversive of penetration and truth. It is possible that the classical masters were the victims of that manner of speech which personifies native and foreign countries, and all too easily refers to them as units neglecting the individuals who really count. In any event they have made too far-reaching a use of idealizing simplification, the instrument of theory and exposition. They have described the conditions of the money economy as though they were simple, like those of the natural economy, where wares truly pay for wares, and where each trader surrenders his natural performance to the same person from whom he receives a counter-service. But it is the essence of the money economy that the natural values are surrendered to other persons than those from whom equivalent natural values are received. This essential condition must not be overlooked in theoretical inquiry. Owing to this circumstance all personal relations are of broader scope; the theoretical problem presented is more comprehensive, including, as it does, the entire series of relationships between individual determinations. Thus a theory that is expected satisfactorily to interpret the process must look correspondingly far afield. It must show how the unity of the economic resultant is finally realized despite the number of actively participating individuals. To this end the broad general exposition of the classicists, offering a primary survey of the movements of the balance of trade is inadequate.

The problem of an international balancing of accounts offers no fundamental difficulties for a theory that has reduced the national economic community of payment to the participating individuals. A solution is prepared by the results already arrived at in our investigation of the national economic equation of supply and demand. The individual is guided by the same personal motives in his trade with foreign countries as he is in his domestic trade. The international balance of payments is nothing more than the sum of the personal balances of payment for all the people; the commercial balance is only a similar sum of the personal balances of wares. As soon as we have recognized the motives that lead to an equilibrium in the individual economy, there can no longer be a riddle in world economic relations, for these are the aggregates of the personal relations. In the latter case, these are more numerous, extensive, and complex; but the same constructive individual force moves through them all, even though the individual may receive his reinforcement from historical powers, and these forces may interpose more effective obstacles.

We may thus readily understand that a people may permanently maintain a credit as well as a debit commercial balance. In any individual economy the personal balance of wares, or for any group of such economies, the sum of the balances may be permanently a credit or a debit. In a national economy whenever the debtor-owners preponderate, who have to surrender more products than they may retain for themselves, this excess production must be turned over to foreign nationals, and the commercial balance will close with a repeated excess of exports. In other words the balance will show a constant credit. The reverse relationship holds for economies in which moneyed individuals preponderate, who draw more products than they surrender.

It is also possible to understand that the international balance of payments of a nation constantly strives towards an equilibrium since this same desire may be assumed to activate each of the related individual economies, however numerous they may be. Only those economies are excepted that are conducted negligently or unskillfully or which suffer unmerited catastrophe—all exceptional cases that are not decisive. Even in these cases the equilibrium of incomes and expenditures can be only temporarily disturbed; for although no funds will be forthcoming to cover the expenditures incurred by means of credit and the creditors will lose all or part of their demands, in the long run even for the ruined debtor-economies and the injured creditor-economies, a new equilibrium must be established. However, if we assume ideal national economies, consisting of none other than well regulated individual economies, the equilibrium of all personal balances of payments, and consequently also the equilibrium of their net foreign payments, i. e., the international balance of payments, must prevail undisturbed.

Just as the balance of personal payments may at times be favorable and at times unfavorable, so may the international balance; but it can never be permanently a credit or a debit. At all times the equation of supply and demand must enforce itself in the markets; the excessive supply encounters an unsatisfied demand, the chain of exchanging pairs is closed, and a state of rest is reëstablished in the market, though there may be certain permanent changes of quantity and price. This statement holds for the market of all products as well as for money. It obtains in domestic as well as foreign trade. In either case, there need be no radical changes of the general price level or the value of money to achieve this result. The only difference between domestic and foreign trade is that in the latter case the intentions leading to exchange are formed and carried out against the stronger resistances offered by historical powers which impede the international movement of products, capital funds, and human beings. To overcome such resistance there must be comparatively large discrepancies in the selling prices of goods and in the rates of interest on money. When the domestic market slumps and persons must turn to the foreign market for the excessive supply or unsatisfied demand, serious disturbances must occur; the balance of payments will become unfavorable in a relatively large number of individual economies until equilibrium is at last restored.

The opposition of favorable and unfavorable balances of payment does not coincide strictly with the opposition of poorer and richer national economies. A poor nation may enjoy a favorable international balance of payments if it has always adequately anticipated payments due to foreign countries. The balance may be temporarily or even permanently unfavorable for the richer nation, if its individual economies have not been sufficiently conservative in making loans to foreign countries and in foreign purchases. The strain on the international balance of payments will be all the more severe, the smaller are the reserves of ready money retained for the credit payments of the country. Even a wealthy nation is seriously inconvenienced by an unfavorable fluctuation of the balance, when its system of payments rests upon a meagre foundation of ready money.

We have observed that the international market for negotiable paper recovers its equilibrium in a comparatively short time and that it is the policy of the banks of issue to govern the adjustment with comparatively small means. We have now discovered the final explanation of these facts. Whenever the international balance of payments is unfavorable in a country, personal forces exert themselves in the individual economies affected and strive to reëstablish the equilibrium. Business men seek to make sales in foreign countries for goods which they could not sell at home, or an attempt is made to obtain from abroad capital funds for which credit could not be secured in the domestic market. The counter-movements that are thus called forth reëstablish the international equilibrium coincidentally with the equilibrium of the personal balances of payment. The discount policy of the banks of issue need only be invoked to control the situation for comparatively short periods of time until the individual efforts of the separate economies have consummated these counter-movements. The banks of issue are further supported by the fact that, in the money markets, large sums are always kept in readiness for international distribution. These funds follow the law of the largest gains; their flow is obstructed only by a possible lack of security in granting loans.

National economies are ordinarily classified as creditor and debtor countries. In the former, a surplus of loan capital is available and is placed abroad. Consequently among the individual economies, the creditors outweigh the debtors. In the debtor countries, the debtor individual economies preponderate; the demand for capital not being satisfied at home must turn to foreign countries. Preponderancy, in these cases, is determined not by the number of economies but by the magnitude of the capital sums involved; the single debtor economy of the state itself may outweigh large numbers of private creditor economies.

The balance of payments of debtor countries is somewhat more liable to tend to a narrowly confined unfavorable condition. But under certain conditions it may be favorable: at the time when large sums of borrowed capital are paid in; or when the country develops favorably, fulfilling its obligations as they fall due, and actually places capital in reserve. The obligations of indebtedness form only a single item in the total balance of payments, an item whose effects may be offset by other items; it would be as improper to argue from these obligations alone to an unfavorable balance of payments as to argue, let us say, from a credit commercial balance alone to a favorable balance of payments. The latter balance of creditor countries is more likely to be favorable, but under some conditions, it may superficially appear unfavorable; for example, when large money capital has just been loaned to foreign countries.

In debtor as well as creditor countries, the balance of trade may be formally credit or debit. A country whose economic development is in its infancy is unable to use in the home markets the purchasing power which it acquires through loans; it is compelled to buy the wares desired in foreign countries. Frequently, the necessity of purchasing foreign goods results in the contraction of debts. On the other hand a debtor country developing its production favorably tends toward a credit commercial balance. The domestic market still fails to provide purchasers for the increasing quantities of manufactured goods. The domestic purchasing power is impaired by the interest and the repayments of principal which the debtor citizens are required to pay to foreign countries. It may possibly be further reduced by taxes which the state, also indebted to foreign countries, is obliged to levy in order to meet its obligations. From the side of the supply, therefore, as well as from that of the demand, everything points to foreign countries, if the chain of exchanges is to be closed. In proportion to the payments sent out in money form, natural values must be shipped abroad to cover the transactions.

A rich country developing still further to become a creditor country and increasing its production tends thereafter to a credit commercial balance. Its nationals having gained increased purchasing power by their larger production do not employ this to absorb, themselves, the entire domestic product. Therefore, for the surplus of their production, they must seek purchasers abroad, just as it will be necessary for them to look to foreign countries to absorb loans of the money capital they save, because at home the supply of capital begins to exceed the demand. Thus, again, exports made in money form run parallel with the covering natural values.

With a further development of production and wealth, the body of industrial workers and the urban population increase to such an extent that they can no longer be fed from domestic food stuffs. Food must be imported in large quantities, just as industrial raw materials must be brought in from foreign countries. Whereas, the importation of wares is thus increased, exports are not correspondingly enlarged. Cover for the former may be provided without necessitating the shipment of natural covering values to foreign countries. The payments which become due for interest on money capital invested abroad are so large as to be ample to effect a balance. They may even be large enough to allow additional foreign investment. The natural values, covering these transactions and running parallel with the payment of interest, are shipped by the debtor countries either in the form of increased export of goods to the creditor country or to countries where the latter may make new investments.

These typical and fundamental forms that arise from the elements of the commercial balance and the credit relationships are constantly being crossed or intensified by other elements of the balance of payments. For example, the workmen of a debtor country may cross the sea because the opportunities of employment at home are ill-paid and the demand of American entrepreneurs promises high wages. These workers may then make remittances from their savings to the home country. In the balance of payments of the latter these remittances appear as considerable additions to receipts. The increased domestic purchasing power will bring in its train an increased demand for wares or an increased supply of capital. Both of these must ultimately turn to foreign countries if they cannot be satisfied in the domestic market where the chain of exchanging pairs has already been closed. In a national economy of an ill-balanced composition, such as that of Austro-Hungary, the tendencies of one district may occasionally be offset by opposite ones in another. While the Austrian half of the empire has become a creditor country, Hungary still remains a debtor. Again, in Austria the German portions with the rich metropolis are in strong contrast to the poorer Slavic districts. While Hungary and the poorer districts of the Austrian half of the Empire must still pass through the earlier stages in the formation of the commercial balance, the richer districts have already reached a high level. The interaction of such different developments may at times lead to far greater fluctuations than any shown by a well-balanced national economy.

The payment of a war-indemnity always disturbs the international balance of payments. It is imposed on the national economy by external compulsion; there has been no preparation by internal movements of natural values. But even the payment of so large a sum as that demanded by Germany from France after the war of 1870–71[1] was accomplished without impairing the parallelism between the money-form of payment and its covering natural form. Even by this method of extreme compulsion a country cannot be stripped of its bullion resources. France raised its war-indemnity mainly by a loan which was largely subscribed by French citizens who secured the necessary means by the sale of securities abroad. The French had to pay the interest on this loan by additional taxes whose payment reduced their purchasing-power and the natural values left for their disposition. As their successors, the German states, enriched by the indemnity, then came forward.

§ 85. The Development of National and World Economies

The international stratification and localization of industries—Theoretical foundations for a foreign trade policy—Tariff for industrial education and the preservation of agriculture—National economic solidarity.

The main problem of national economic policy relating to foreign trade is reflected in the controversy between free-trade and protective tariffs. As was to be expected, the classical school resolved this problem in favor of its controlling principle,—freedom. Its most important argument is derived from the epoch-making concept of the division of labor whose success causes its development from the free community of exchange. The classical school argues that if the division of labor be in any case economically advantageous, it should also be so in world economy. Just as within the nation it creates opportunities to use their forces to the best advantage of all, thus in the world at large it should give each people the opportunity to employ its peculiar advantages for the greatest general welfare. Here is a truth of the broadest significance broadly stated; but again the classicists did not wholly grasp the full import of their theoretical discovery. They did not properly observe the shadow of economic stratification which occasionally obscures the light of the international division of labor. Just as the social stratification within the national economy may become one of the gravest evils, so internationally stratification may subordinate the weaker people to its own injury as well as to that of all other nations.

In his acute observation Ricardo certainly did not miss the fact of international stratification. He considers it and endeavors to harmonize it theoretically with his views. In his investigation, he has expressly dealt with the case of two countries who enter the community of exchange and invoke the division of labor, one of which countries is incontestably superior in every branch of production. But he in-

[1] Trans. note: *"Nach dem letzten Kriege"* should obviously be changed as it has been in the text.

clines to the opinion that even in this case an international division of labor must further the interests of both countries. He finds an exact analogy in the case of two men, of whom one is superior to the other in every type of acquisitive labor. They will both find it to their advantage to unite in a community of exchange under a division of labor in which the better workman confines himself to the production of those specialties in which he most excels and the less capable one undertakes the remaining productive labors that are beyond the available time and effort of his fellow. So also the two countries should derive advantage from a division of labor; the total product that may be distributed between would be enlarged. As Ricardo formulates his assumption, an international division of labor would necessarily be of advantage to both parties. It remains incontestably true that the free community of exchange between primitive peoples and those more civilized is best for all concerned.

Ricardo did not fully probe the effects of international stratification. He stopped with the simplest assumption of a static condition without development. He does not investigate the effects of economic evolution. The theorist must always start from the static assumption. It yields most readily to his idealizing method. Dynamic relationships cannot be clearly defined in his thinking until after the static condition has been fully apprehended. But the investigator falls into a serious error as soon as he applies conclusions deduced from a state of rest to a condition of evolution unless he remodels his conclusions by a process of decreasing abstraction. This error Ricardo and the classical school, generally, have made. They did not perfect a theory of world economic development. Nor as spokesmen of the economically strongest nation, England, did they have any practical interest in the formulation of such a theory; for without further ado free trade offered to England the desired opportunities for evolution, despite the fact that the free-trade theory rested on the static assumption. It was reserved to the economists of the economically weaker continental countries to guard the interest of their national economies, at that time surpassed by England, and to show that these countries needed protective tariffs if their development were not to be permanently arrested by the despotism of England. This could never be accomplished by the economists unless they elaborated the static English theory and developed a dynamic theory.

The protest against free trade was first made in the interest of industrial development. Friedrich List demanded adequate "duties for industrial education." These should run for periods of one or two generations in all national economies which possess the natural and social prerequisites for the development of a large industry but are retarded in this development by the historical headway gained by England. Under free competition they could never overcome this lead, but must inevitably succumb to the more powerful, older, financially stronger industry working at considerably lower costs. List has here discovered a great truth. He has shown that we must distinguish between the natural conditions of production and those which are historical. The free-trade school failed to recognize this. It deals with the case in which one country is superior to another by virtue of its soil or climate, and the other case where its superiority consists in the head-start of its industry, as if the two were in the same category. These theorists assert that governments endeavoring to develop their historically backward industries by protective tariff act as foolishly as those who strive by this means to raise their production to competitive levels when production is burdened by naturally disadvantageous conditions. In both cases it is said that costs of production are needlessly thrown away, and grievously increased prices forced upon consumers. This chain of reasoning disregards the fact that natural disadvantages of production are permanent, whereas the historical handicap of industrial backwardness may be removed by further development.

When with this end in view, industrial educational duties are imposed, increased costs of production are exacted from the national economy for the immediate future. To begin with this is simply loss. But it is a loss which will be repaid by later increased yields. Free trade which meets the immediate interest of the consumers checks the aggregate development. Nascent domestic industry cannot cope with the competition of foreign countries. The individual efforts of ambitious entrepreneurs are in vain. Try as they may, they cannot pass the barriers of the national economic environment that hopelessly hems them in. An individual enterprise is at all times merely a link in the great community of acquisition where labor is divided. In its development it can never exceed the general condition of the national economy. In order to raise the general level, and overtake the head start of foreign countries, there must be long continued and combined efforts. Helplessly exposed to overpowering competition, an infant industry cannot accomplish this. It will be unable to find foreign markets for its products and will even be unable to keep foreign products out of the domestic market. Thus domestic industry, in such a country, is tied down to locally restricted products or at best to the cultivation of certain specialties. In such a country awaiting industrial awakening, mineral wealth and arable land will continue untouched; the industrial genius of workers and entrepreneurs will remain dormant. In this general stagnation the agricultural population suffers with the rest; the great remunerative market never opens that would accompany the growth of domestic industry.

All these ideas have been clearly set forth by List. He lacks only the ultimate explanation that clearly shows the opposition in the development of the national and international division of labor. The national economy and the world economy are differently composed. Within the national economy, because of its uniform composition, every advance spreads in all directions. It is imitated everywhere because the new accomplishments and newly acquired information spread without hindrance, unless it happens that the new development is affiliated by natural conditions to certain localities. In so far as this is the case, men and capital funds will assemble from all parts of the country at the localities thus naturally assigned, for there are no hindrances to migration. Consequently, industrial centres are always relocated in accord with progress so that at their locations the most favorable conditions may be found. Those historical powers which contribute within the national economy to the localization of industry do not counteract natural conditions but act with them.

This is not so in world economy. Knowledge and experience, men and money capital do not move freely. The progress of more advanced people does not flow in equal measure to the others. Internationally, there is an uneconomic localization of industry. Industries are massed in the more advanced country even when it does not possess the most favorable natural conditions. Other countries must neglect opportunities although the germs for exploitation are naturally provided. The total production of the world falls short of existing possibilities, and countries with a retarded development are the primary sufferers. That country which is the more fully developed accordingly gains a position of superior power in international stratification, a position that exceeds that to which it is entitled by virtue of its natural advantages. It assembles within its borders the peculiarly lucrative industries using much capital. It has an advantageous position that enables it to lessen or balance the evils which accompany capitalistic development, for it may raise many individuals from among its workers to the well-paid higher levels. Conversely, the more disastrous results accrue to those countries which are satisfied to cling to the less remunerative industries that are forced to expose their laboring population to the most extreme efforts at minimum wages. These are the countries which, in the long run, must bear the brunt of all the evils of capitalistic operation.

List opposed protective duties for agricultural products. He feared that they would unfavorably influence industrial development by increasing the prices to be paid by workers for the means of subsistence, and would furthermore increase the cost of labor itself through an increase of wages. Then, too, agriculture as the oldest domestic branch of production should not require educational duties. But when List wrote, it was not necessary to make allowance for conditions that later arose when improved means of transportation and reduced freights opened the markets of western and central Europe to the products of virgin trans-oceanic countries as well as of Russia. Preservative duties are necessary, in the face of the overwhelming competition which these countries wage against domestic agriculture raising its produce at greater expense.

It may also be shown that the national and international conditions of labor are differently conditioned. In the home-country when virgin soil is brought under cultivation, or increased quantities of food stuffs are obtained at lower costs, because of improvements in cultivation or in the breeding of cattle, the prices of agricultural products will be reduced so as to injure a number of farmers. But this disadvantage is offset by other benefits that accrue to agriculture. Moreover, it is neutralized by counter effects that make their appearance with comparative rapidity. Cheap food encourages domestic industry which finds new purchasers in the enlarged agricultural areas. As industry grows stronger, it sends back new purchasers to agriculture. In old settlements, changes in the cultivation of land and prices are not abrupt; they work themselves out gradually and without shock. But the blows dealt by trans-oceanic and Russian competition have been great and prolonged. They have brought about severe disturbances and have threatened the greater part of European domestic agriculture in its very existence. Such a loss threatens domestic industry as well, because it removes from the market the most accessible and safest purchasers. It is impossible with sufficient promptness to accomplish an agricultural transition to the cultivation of special crops that may compete with foreign agriculture. Neither is it possible to transfer to industry the bankrupt owners, the laborers thrown out of employment, and the capital made to lie idle. Industry, on its part, is unable to find adequate compensation abroad for the loss of domestic purchasers. In domestic disturbances, some relief may be found in equalization brought about by migrations and the relocation of industry. Internationally such equalization meets with greater obstructions. Fundamentally, every national economy must rely upon its own resources. For all their importance, world economic relations are secondary. Once the internal structure of the world economy has been shaken, it is not possible so readily to prop it by a newly established world trade. Such considerations make preservative duties for agriculture appear fully justified. This is so true that even for an industry that is well developed such duties may be called for at times.

Educational and preservative duties rest on a common basis. They are intended to protect the interests of the national economy against over-powerful forces exerted from foreign economies that either possess a traditional supremacy or acquire it in later development. The first demand for these duties arises from a mysterious feeling of national economic solidarity. This origin may lead to their occasional misdirection, but they are also demanded by a logically correct fundamental idea. This feeling of economic solidarity is an indication of the peculiarly close connections that exist within the national community of acquisition because of its great density and the unifying free powers that guide its development. All external interference with this closely woven pattern must make itself widely felt. The experience becomes all the more disastrous when the equalizing movements towards the edges that are meant to remedy the distress can only be accomplished against powerful obstruction.

The state in its interests is bound to sympathize with such conditions. Earlier than in other respects, the state felt called upon to use its power to protect domestic interests against the dangers of foreign economic domination. In this case also the classical individualism was indisposed properly to appraise the importance of the state's intervention. Here as elsewhere it espoused the cause of personal liberty; nay here more than elsewhere, since step by step it was here advocating the cause of the English national economy. In international relations, the classical individualism recognized only one aspect of the relationships of power. It recognized only the constructive aspects of economic power that gained its superiority in social service. It failed to see that in this case also reason is reduced to absurdity when firmly rooted economic domination retards or prohibits foreign development. A well-considered system of protective duties secures to the domestic national economy threatened by foreign domination the widest possible economic margins of use. In so far as this system leads to the greatest possible equalization of development, it has a similar ultimate effect for the entire world economy.

This presentation gives the theoretical foundation of a foreign policy for the national economy. The detailed form that this policy will take depends too largely upon the circumstances involved to be opened to theoretical exposition. At this point, theory has accomplished its task; it now makes room for other forms of inquiry which are able to elaborate concretely its universally valid assumptions.

THE END

ABBREVIATIONS

1. Hermann, *Untersuchungen*—v. Hermann, *Staatswirtschaftliche Untersuchungen*, 2. ed. 1870.
2. Knies, Pol. Oek.—K. Knies, *Die politische Oekonomie vom Standpunkt der geschichtlichen Methode*, 2. ed. 1882 (1. ed. 1853).
3. Mill, *Pol. Oek.*—J. St. Mill, *Grundsätze der politischen Oekonomie*, translated by Soetbeer.
4. Philippovich, *Grundriss*—E. von Philippovich, *Grundriss der politischen Oekonomie:* vol. I., *Allgemeine Volkswirtschaftlehre.* 10th revised edition, 21–23 Tausend), 1913; Vol. II. *Volkswirtschaftspolitik.* I Part 7 revised edition 1914; Vol II. *Volkswirtschaftspolitik.* 2 Part 5th revised edition 1915.
5. Roscher, *System* I (bzw. II, III, IV)—W. Roscher, *System der Volkswirtschaft;* I. *Grundlagen der Nationalökonomie*, 24th ed. 1906, published by Pohlmann; II *Nationalökonomik des Ackerbaues*, 14th ed. 1912, published by Dode; III *Nationalökonomik des Gewerbefleisses und Handels*, 8th edition, published by Stieda; IV *System der Finanzwissenschaft*, 5th ed. 1901, revised by Gerlach; V *System der Armenpflege und Armenpolitik*, 3rd ed. 1906, enlarged by Klumker.
6. Schaffle, *Bau und Leben*—A. E. Schaffle, *Bau und Leben des sozialen Körpers.* 2 ed, 2 vols., 1896. (1st ed., 4 vols. 1874–1878).
7. Schmoller, *Grundriss* I, II—G. Schmoller, *Grundriss d. allgemeinen Volkswirtschaftsehre*, First Part 1900, 1901 (7–10 Tausend 1908), Second Part 1904.
8. Schmoller, F.—G. Schmoller, *Staats- und sozialwissenschaftliche Forschungen.*
9. Schönberg, Hdb. I (bzw. II, sind III, III, —*Handbuch der Politischen Oekonomie*, published by G. Schönberg; I und II, II, *Volkswirtschaftslehre;* III, und III, *Finanzwissenschaft und Verwaltungslehre*, 4th ed. 1896–1898.
10. E. d. Vl.—*Die Entwicklung der deutschen Volkswirtschaftslehre im neunzehnten Jahrhundert*, 2 Parts, 1908. (40 Abhandlungen zur Literaturgeschichte der Nationalökonomie.)
11. G. d. S.—*Grundriss der Sozialökonomik.*
12. Hdw. d. Stw.—*Handwörterbuch der Staatswissenschaften*, published by J. Conrad, L. Elster, W. Lexis und Edgar Loening, 3. ed. 1909–11.
13. Schr. d. d. G. f. S.—*Schriften der deutschen Gesellschaft für Soziologie.*
14. Schr. d. V. f. S.—*Schriften des Vereins für Sozialpolitik.*
15. W. d. d. St.—u. V. R.—*Wörterbuch des deutschen Staats- und Verwaltungsrechts*, published by Fleishmann, (2. ed. d. v. Stengel herausgeg Wtb.)
16. W. d. V.—*Wörterbuch der Volkswirtschaft*, published by L. Elster. 3 ed. 1910–11.
17. Archiv—*Archiv für Sozialwissenschaft und Sozialpolitik.* Neue Folge des Archivs fur Soziale Gesetzgebung und Statistik.

18. Jahrb. f. N.—*Jahrbücher für Nationalökonomie und Statistik.*
19. T. f. G. V.—*Jahrbuch für Gesetzgebung, Verwaltung und Volkswirtschaft im Deutschen Reich.*
20. Z. f. S.—*Zeitschrift für Sozialwissenschaft.*
21. Z. f. Stw.—*Zeitschrift für die gesamte Staatswissenschaft.*
22. Z. f. Volksw.—*Zeitschrift f. Volkswirtschaft, Sozialpolitik und Verwaltung*
23. V. d. V. D. I.—*Zeitschrift des Vereins Deutscher Ingenieure.*

INDEX

For Product Safety Concerns and Information please contact our EU representative GPSR@taylorandfrancis.com
Taylor & Francis Verlag GmbH, Kaufingerstraße 24, 80331 München, Germany

www.ingramcontent.com/pod-product-compliance
Lightning Source LLC
LaVergne TN
LVHW011102300926
849160LV00008B/260

9780415607322